World Scientific Proceedings Series on
Computer Engineering and Information Science 8

Decision Making Systems in Business Administration

Proceedings of the MS'12 International Conference

The MS'12 Rio de Janeiro International Conference is supported by:

A.M.S.E.
Association for the advancement of Modelling & Simulation techniques in Entreprises

Real Academia de Ciencias Económicas y Financieras

UNIVERSITAT DE BARCELONA

UNIVERSIDADE DO ESTADO DO RIO DE JANEIRO
UERJ

CÁMARA OFICIAL ESPAÑOLA DE COMERCIO EN BRASIL

unesp

IS CONSULTORIA
MAIS QUE SOLUÇÕES ACESSÍVEIS.
RESULTADOS SUSTENTÁVEIS.

World Scientific Proceedings Series on
Computer Engineering and Information Science 8

Decision Making Systems in Business Administration

Proceedings of the MS'12 International Conference

Rio de Janeiro, Brazil 10 – 13 December 2012

editors

Anna M Gil-Lafuente
University of Barcelona, Spain

Luciano Barcellos-Paula
IS Consultoria, Brazil

José M Merigó-Lindahl
University of Barcelona, Spain

Fernando Augusto Silva-Marins
State University of Sao Paulo, Brazil

Antonio Carlos de Azevedo-Ritto
State University of Rio de Janeiro, Brazil

World Scientific

NEW JERSEY • LONDON • SINGAPORE • BEIJING • SHANGHAI • HONG KONG • TAIPEI • CHENNAI

Published by

World Scientific Publishing Co. Pte. Ltd.
5 Toh Tuck Link, Singapore 596224
USA office: 27 Warren Street, Suite 401-402, Hackensack, NJ 07601
UK office: 57 Shelton Street, Covent Garden, London WC2H 9HE

British Library Cataloguing-in-Publication Data
A catalogue record for this book is available from the British Library.

World Scientific Proceedings Series on Computer Engineering and Information Science — Vol. 8
DECISION MAKING SYSTEMS IN BUSINESS ADMINISTRATION
Proceedings of the MS'12 International Conference

ISBN 978-981-4452-04-5

Printed in Singapore by World Scientific Printers.

Preface

The Association for the Advancement of Modeling & Simulation Techniques in Enterprises (AMSE), IS Consulting, the Rio de Janeiro State University (UERJ) and the State University of Sao Paulo (UNESP) are pleased to present the main results of the International Conference on Modeling and Simulation in Engineering, Economics and Management for Sustainable Development, held in Rio de Janeiro, Brazil, 10 – 13 December, 2012, through this Book of Proceedings published in the Book Series "*World Scientific Proceedings Series in Computer Engineering and Information Science*".

MS'12 Rio de Janeiro is co-organized by the AMSE Association and IS Consulting, with the institutional support of the Department of Business Administration of the University of Barcelona (UB), the Spanish Royal Academy of Financial and Economic Sciences (RACEF), the Spanish Chanber of Commerce in Brazil, the Production Department of the Faculty Engineering Guaratinguetá (FEG) of the Paulista State University "Júlio de Mesquita Filho" (UNESP) and the Rio de Janeiro State University (UERJ). It offers a unique opportunity for researchers, professionals and students to present and exchange ideas concerning modelling and simulation and related topics and see how they can be implemented in the real world.

We would also like to mention that Da Ruan, the founder of this Book Series, passed away in July 31, 2011. We are very sad for this loss and would like to express our condolences to his family. He was an incredibly active researcher and was one of the main leaders in fuzzy logic and soft computing of our generation. Moreover, we would also like to express our condolences to the family of Pablo Sebastián García, a very good friend from the AMSE Association and a member of the governing body of the International Association for Fuzzy Logic Management and Economy (SIGEF) that passed away in July 2012. We hope their spirit and legacy will remind with us forever.

In this edition of the MS International Conference, we want to focus on to the emerging area of Sustainable Development. In particular, we want to give special attention on the implementation of Modeling and Simulation methods in this field. This includes a wide range of topics including fuzzy logic, soft computing, intelligent systems and decision support systems. Since the main background of most participants is in the economic sciences area, we want to draw special attention in the analysis of decision making processes. Thus, the title of this book is "*Decision Making Systems in Business Administration*". Decision Making Systems are used in a wide range of areas including management, economics, sustainable development, engineering and medicine. Its growing importance is motivated by the importance of reaching efficient decisions that maximize the benefits or minimize the costs. This is particularly important in business problems due to the high amounts of money involved. Every year new ideas and changes are appearing in the markets making them very flexible. Thus, in order to correctly assess these problems, we need decision making systems that are ready to deal with this environment and maximize the potential benefits of a decision maker as much as possible.

MS'12 Proceedings is constituted by 39 papers selected from 60 submissions from 19 countries, making an acceptance rate of 65%. We have also included the presentation given by the plenary speakers: Beat Grüninger, Federico Gonzalez-Santoyo and Gorkhmaz Imanov. The book is divided in 4 parts: (1) Sustainable Development, (2) Management, (3) Finance and Economics and (4) Other Applications.

We would like to thank all the contributors, referees and the scientific and honorary committees for their kind co-operation with MS'12 Rio de Janeiro; to Jaime Gil Aluja for his role as the President of AMSE; to the whole team of the organizing committee, including Christer Berger-Vachon, Messias Borges Silva, Antonio Fernando Branco Costa, Aline de Castro Rezende, Jaime Gil Lafuente, Wendy Haddad Carraro, Anna Klimova, Salvador Linares Mustarós, Carles Mulet Forteza, Heechang Shin and Emili Vizuete; and to Chelsea Chin (Editor, World Scientific) for her kind advise and help to publish this volume. Finally, we would like to express our gratitude to World Scientific and in particular to Jie Lu (Editor-in-Chief of the book series "*WS Proceedings Series in Computer Engineering and Information Science*") for his support in the preparation of this book.

Anna M. Gil Lafuente, MS'12 Rio de Janeiro, Chair.
Luciano Barcellos de Paula, MS'12 Rio de Janeiro, Chair.
José M. Merigó, MS'12 Rio de Janeiro, Co-Chair.
Fernando Augusto Silva Marins, MS'12 Rio de Janeiro, Co-Chair.
Antonio Carlos de Azevedo Ritto, MS'12 Rio de Janeiro, Co-Chair.

Rio de Janeiro, September 2012.

Honorary Committee

Special thanks to all the members of the Honorary Committee for their support in the organization of the MS'12 Rio de Janeiro International Conference.

Honorary Committeee

Jaime Gil-Aluja	President of *AMSE* and President of the *Spanish Royal Academy of Financial and Economic Sciences*
Lotfi A. Zadeh	*University of California at Berkeley*

Scientific Committee

Special thanks to all the members of the Scientific Committee for their support in the organization of the MS'12 Rio de Janeiro International Conference.

Christian Berger-Vachon
(Co-President)

Anna M. Gil-Lafuente
(Co-President)

Said Allaki, Morocco
Noura Al-Khaabi, UAE
Mercedes Ayuso, Spain
Luciano Barcellos de Paula, Brazil
Houcine Chafouk, France
Bernard de Baets, Belgium
Nashaat El-Khameesy, Egypt
Kurt Engemann, USA
Joan Carles Ferrer, Spain
Fares Fraij, Jordan
Hamido Fujita, Japan
Lorenzo Gascón, Spain
Jaime Gil Lafuente, Spain
Robert Golan, USA
Marta Gómez Puig, Spain
Federico González Santoyo, Mexico
Montserrat Guillén, Spain
Rainer Hampel, Germany
Kedi Huang, P.R. China
Korkmaz Imanov, Azerbaijan
Janusz Kacprzyk, Poland
Uzay Kaymak, Netherlands
Yuriy Kondratenko, Ukraine
Gang Kou, China
Viktor Krasnoproshin, Belarus
Prabhat Kumar Mahanti, India
Francisco J. Maqueda, Spain
José M. Merigó Lindahl, Spain
Onofre Martorell Cunill, Spain
Radko Mesiar, Slovakia
Ramir Mirsalinov, Azerbaijan
Vladimir S. Neronov, Kazakhstan
Ahmad Nuseirat, Jordan
Ahmed Oulad Said, Morocco
Witold Pedrycz, Canada
Emmanuel Perrin, France
José J. Pintó Ruiz, Spain
Ramón Poch Torres, Spain
Alfredo Rocafort, Spain
Mohamed Saighi, Algeria
Heechang Shin, USA
Wilfred I. Ukpere, South Africa
Emili Vizuete, Spain
Iskander Yaacob, Malaysia
Ronald R. Yager, USA
Constantin Zopounidis, Greece

Organizing Committee

Special thanks to all the members of the Organizing Committee for their support during the organization of the MS'12 Rio de Janeiro International Conference.

Chair of the Organizing Committee

Anna M. Gil Lafuente, Spain

Luciano Barcellos de Paula, Brazil

Co-Chair of the Organizing Committee

José M. Merigó Lindahl, Spain

Fernando Augusto Silva Marins, Brazil

Antonio Carlos de Azevedo Ritto, Brazil

Organizing Committee

Christian Berger Vachon, France

Messias Borges Silva, Brazil

Antonio Fernando Branco Costa, Brazil

Aline de Castro Rezende, Brazil

Jaime Gil Lafuente, Spain

Wendy Haddad Carraro, Brazil

Anna Klimova, Russia

Salvador Linares Mustarós, Spain

Carles Mulet Forteza, Spain

Emili Vizuete, Spain

Contents

PLENARY SPEAKERS

GOING GREEN IN EMERGING ECONOMIES: BUILDING A BRIDGE BETWEEN MARKET DEVELOPMENT AND SUSTAINABILITY

BEAT GRÜNINGER

Professor at FGV Sao Paulo, Director of BSD Consulting and Partner of BSD Group, Rio de Janeiro, Brazil

Abstract

The important advancement which has taken place during the last decade in the process of the creation of a society with progress without precedent throughout history, has led to a quasi generalized economic and financial crisis that has ended by stirring up the very foundations of our life in society.

These achievements that have been attained are the result of a whole conglomerate of effort carried out by the most diverse classes, with the common denominator of freedom in stability. The development of research in the different spheres of knowledge, in our opinion constitutes one of the fundamental axes around which the progress attained has revolved. This progress can be seen today as menaced by the ghost of the crisis, which is hitting, particularly all the under privileged, so hard.

Brazil is the place to be for companies that try to increase their market share and leave the classic markets in Europe and USA behind where stagnation and decrease reign. Brazil is now the sixth largest economy in the world. Even showing stronger growth rates, countries like China and India are surpassing rapidly the former dominant western economies, overtaking their rank of consumer paradises.

But unlike China and India, Brazil is at the forefront of a new era: The search for sustainable development driven by the private sector. Brazilian companies are very pro-active in reporting their sustainability, with 123 reports published against the Global Reporting Initiative (GRI) standard and 253 reporting progress as signatories of Global Compact in 2012. Brazilian companies are under the leaders in the use of social and environmental certifications such as SA8000, ISO14000 and labels such as FSC. Bovespa, the local stock market, has created its own Sustainability Index, with an each year growing portfolio. Furthermore, Brazil has 7 companies in the Dow Jones Sustainability Index, against only 1 from China and 1 from India, their emerging market competitors.

But, unfortunately, there is an opposite side of the medal, which is common to all emerging economies.

There is still a large social gap: While having managed to reduce the poverty rate (people that live with less than 2 USD a day) by 10% from 21% in 2003 to 11% in 2009, the income inequality has only decreased 2,1% in the last ten years. There are also huge environmental challenges: While the GDP increased in the past 18 years by 36%, the natural capital of Brazil has declined 46%. If emissions from the deforestation were considered, Brazil is number 5 on the world´s polluter ranking.

All in all, there is a large spread between growing market and sustainable development and Brazil as well as other emerging countries are forced to bridge the poverty and degradation gap and re-invent their development strategies.

Therefore, sustainability practices developed by the companies cannot stay only within their doors, they have to trickle down along the value chain, achieving also millions of all small and medium entrepreneurs in their harsh daily reality. Many issues need cross-collaboration of governmental, society and business sectors to be solved. Companies and NGOs in the emerging world have already started partnerships, but the government must jump on the train and share the vision of a green economy in order to realize really breaking changes. Rio+20 was an exciting event with innumerous ideas that brought the necessary food for thought and exciting new ideas. But now the bridge between the market growth scenario and sustainability has to be put in place so that next generations can safely enjoy their lives without being afraid to lose ground under their own feet.

OPTIMAL INVESTMENT IN PORTFOLIO SELECTION USING THE KNAPSACK MODEL

FEDERICO GONZÁLEZ-SANTOYO, BEATRIZ FLORES-ROMERO, JUAN J. FLORES, ANNA M. GIL-LAFUENTE

Universidad Michoacana de San Nicolás de Hidalgo, Mexico

ANNA M. GIL-LAFUENTE

Department of Business Administration, University of Barcelona, Av. Diagonal 690, 08034 Barcelona, Spain

Nowadays, it is of fundamental importance to use optimization methods and techniques in financial decision making. These methods provide (in real time) effective and efficient information to take the investor to success with a lesser amount of uncertainty, as to maximize the benefit levels under high-risk scenarios. In this work we use the knapsack model as an optimal investment portfolio selection strategy. This is accomplished through the analysis of diverse scenarios obtained in real time. These scenarios provide the decision maker with information to make rational and efficient decisions.

1. Introduction

Since the beginning of mankind, the human being started financial and commercial transactions. The responsibility in making the right investment decisions relies mainly on experience and a good criterion by the investor. There are investors whose experience and ability make him so efficient, and take him to the right choices most of the time. Nevertheless, an experience-based decision is still a qualitative and not quantitative circumstance. This does not entail the inexistence of an experience-based decision that yields excellent outcome; excellent is not necessarily optimal, though.

Optimization techniques present an option to evaluate quantitatively all those systems amenable to be modeled mathematically. Through computer implementations we can obtain in a systematic way the exact magnitudes of the variables that yield optimal levels of the variables subject to optimization.

The problems in finance, specifically investment options problems, are of course feasible to model through mathematical equations. Therefore, we can apply optimization techniques to find the exact mixture of investments to yield maximum benefits. This fact transforms decision making from a problem whose solution depends on experience and criteria of the decision maker to a problem that can be solved systematically by a computer. Such a computer program can take as input the changing conditions of investment options and return the optimal misture of the investment options that maximize the benefits for the investor; this software will act as an assistant in the decision making or even an autonomous decision making tool.

Through the years, many optimization techniques have been developed, each with its own characteristics. Some of the most know techniques are lineal programming, integer programming, dynamic programming, etc. (González S.F. 1995, 2005, 2011). Other optimization methods or techniques studies in the last few years solve problems of different complexity. An outstanding problem, which has been extensively studied, is the knapsack problem. The study of this problem has produced a diverse range of solution techniques applicable not only to it, but to other problems as well. These techniques are the object of study of the work presented in this paper.

2. Knapsack Models

You wish to invest all or part of $\boldsymbol{c}$ investment units, considering $\boldsymbol{n}$ possible investment options; each investment options yields p_j and requires w_j as minimum investment amount. The solution to the optimal investment is the set of selected investment options x_j such that the total benefit z be the maximum possible. This kind of optimization problem is known as the knapsack problem.

Mathematical Models

The knapsack problem can be stated mathematically, numbering variables from 1 to n and introducing a vector of binary variables x_j ($j=1, \ldots ,n$), where:
During the last decades, the knapsack problem (KP) has been studied from different approaches. The first algorithms were produced in the 1950's through Bellman's dynamic programming. Dynamic programming solves exactly the binary knapsack problem. In 1957 Dantzing generates an efficient method to determine the solution to the continuous relaxation problem, obtaining an upper bound for z, which was used the following 2o years in almost every KP study [Martello y Toth, 1990].

En the 1950's Gilmore and Gomory investigated the approximation of dynamic programming to the solution of KP problems. In 1967 Kolestar presents the algorithm *Branch and Bound.* In the 1970's the approximation method of Branch and Bound is completely developed; this is the only method capable of solving problems with a large number of variables. Among the most known algorithms in that period are those developed by Horowitz and Sahni, with contributions by Ingargiola and Korsh with the first reduction procedure, Johnson the firs polynomial approximation scheme. Shany extends this result to the binary knapsack problem. Martello and Toth proposed the first upper bound dominating the continuous relaxation value.

In the 1980's the main results in this area aimed to solve large-scale problems. For this kind of problems sorting time take most of the execution time. In 1980 Balas and Zemel present a new approximation to solve the problem sorting (in many cases) only a small subset of variables, which represent the main part of the problem.

Mathematical Models

The knapsack problem can be stated mathematically, numbering variables from 1 to *n* and introducing a vector of binary variables x_j (*j=1, ... ,n*), where:

$$x_j = \begin{cases} 1 if\ object\ j is selected \\ 0 otherwise \end{cases} \tag{1}$$

p_j represents the expected yield for investment option j, w_j represents the minimum amount required by that investment option, and c is the available capital in monetary units (knapsack size). The problem is to select from the binary vector all variables x that satisfy the constraint:

$$\sum_{j=1}^{n} w_j x_j \leq c \tag{2}$$

and maximize the objective function:

$$z = \sum_{j=1}^{n} p_j x_j \tag{3}$$

Equation (2) indicates that the sum of investments cannot be greater than the available capital. Equation (3) states that from all possible options we will choose the assignment that maximizes the total benefit.

One way to solve this problem is to analyze all possible combinations and choose the one that satisfies Equations (2) and (3). Nonetheless, this procedure would be inefficient and intractable for large-size problems. In the last decades several exact and approximate algorithms have been developed to solve the knapsack problem.

Types of Knapsack Problems

Depending on the generality or specificity of the solution to the knapsack problem, several types of problems are derived. In general, we assume that the benefits (p_j), the required amounts per investment option (w_j), and the available capital (c), are general integers. Nevertheless, the results can be extended to the real-valued case, and in most cases to non-positive values.

The different types of problems that can be generated are:

Binary Knapsack Problem (KP 0-1)
Multiple choice Knapsack Problem
Restricted Knapsack Problem
Unrestricted Knapsack Problem
Subset Addition Problem
Change Machine Problem
Binary Multiple Knapsack Problem
Generalized assignment Problem

This paper addresses the Binary Knapsack Problem KP 0-1 problem, which will be defined in the next section.

Bynary Knapsack Problem

The Binary Knapsack Problem is the most important knapsack problem and one of the most studied in discrete optimization. Mathematically, it can be described by Equations (1) TO (3). The reasons of its importance are the following:

It can be seen as the simplest integer-programming problem.
It appears as a sub-problem in many more complex problems.
It can represent a large number of practical situations.

The solution to the Binary Knapsack Problem can be obtained using several exact and approximate algorithms, such as: Horowitz-Sahni's greedy algorithm, Martello-Toth's dinamyc programming, dynamic programming and polynomial approximation developed by Balas-Zemel, and Fayard-Plateau, among others. This type of problems is NP-Complete.

In this paper we use the greedy algorithm to solve the study case for the investment portfolios optimal selection.

Greedy Algorithm

The most immediate way to determine an approximate solution to the binary knapsack problem exploits the fact that the solution vector of selected investment options x has only one non-integer variable x_s (critical element: investment option that will not fit whole in the investment portfolio or knapsack; i.e., it would make the solution more expensive than the available capital). Unselecting this option ($x_s = 0$) we can obtain an acceptable z' very close to the optimal solution z.

$$z' = \sum_{j=1}^{s-1} p_j \tag{4}$$

One would normally expect the approximate solution z' to be very close to the exact solution z. Nevertheless if the benefit the critical p_s yields, is relatively large one can obtain an improved heuristic solution z^h considering:

$$z^h = \max(z', p_s) \tag{5}$$

We assume the investment options to be sorted by yield value per monetary unit per investment option. That is,

$$\frac{p_1}{w_1} \geq \frac{p_2}{w_2} \geq \cdots \geq \frac{p_n}{w_n} \tag{6}$$

3. Developed Program

This section presents Matlab® code of the implementation of the greedy algorithm to solve the binary knapsack problem.

```
Clear all
close all
% Program that implements the greedy algorithm
```

```
% to solve the Binary Knapsack Problem
%

% Reading data from keyboard
%

disp('Program that implements the greedy algorithm');
disp(' ');

n=input('Number of investment options n: ');
c=input('Total available investment capital c: ');
p=input('Benefit vector for each investment option {p}: ');
w=input('Vector of required amounts for each investment option {w}: ');

% The program produces zg (Optimal total benefit) and {x} (vector of selected
options)

ct=c;
zh=0;
ja=1;

for j=1:n,
   if w(j)>ct
      x(j)=0;
   else
      x(j)=1;
      ct=ct-w(j);
      zh=zh+p(j);
   end
   if p(j)>p(ja)
      ja=j;
   end
end

if p(ja)>zh
   zh=p(ja);
   for j=1:n,
      x(j)=0;
   end
```

```
  x(ja)=1;
end

disp('Optimal total yield:')
zh
disp('Selected options vector:')
x
```

4. Case Study

The IGOWAWAD operator can be further generalized by using quasi-arithmetic means in a similar way as it was done in [1,5,7]. We will call it the quasi-arithmetic IOWAWAD (Quasi-IOWAWAD) operator. It is defined as follows.

Case 1.

As a study case we will take a hypothetical example. Let "W" be the investor, with a financial resource of $25,000,000.00 mexican pesos, who whishes to obtain an optimal financial yield, given the investment options in the financial market. As a result of an investigation at the time of the investment decision, the weighing or importance levels for investment options 1, 2, 3, 4, 5, 6, and 7 in a per unit basis: (w_j/c) = (0.5, 0.02, 0.3, 0.431, 0.25, 0.49, 0.41) and the yield levels per unit are (p_j/w_j) = (1.5, 2, 5, 0.5, 3, 0.1, 1.1). The investor would like (a priori) to invest in all options. Nevertheless, to make the final investment decision he would like to know the optimal solution. The greedy algorithm determines quantitatively what are the most convenient options.

To solve this case using the greedy algorithm for the knapsack method, we need to sort the investment options according to Equation (6). After sorting, the investment options are shown in Table 1.

Table 1. Data for study case 1

OPTION	**WEIGHT** w_i	**YIELD** p_i	p_i/w_i
3	$ 7,500,000.00	$ 37,500,000.00	5.0
5	6,250,000.00	18,750,000.00	3.0
2	500,000.00	1,000,000.00	2.0
1	12,500,000.00	18,750,000.00	1.5
7	10,250,000.00	11,275,000.00	1.1
4	10,775,000.00	5,387,500.00	0.5
6	12,250,000.00	1,225,000.00	0.1

Once sorted, data is fed to the program shown in Section 3. The output results are the following:

Total optimal benefit $z =$ **$ 68, 525, 000**
Selected Options: 2, 3, 5, and 7

Table 2. Investment Portfolio for case 1

INVESTMENT OPTION	AMOUNT
2	500 000
3	7 500 000
5	6 250 000
7	10 250 000
TOTAL	**24 500 000**

Case 2.

As a second case let us assume the yield amounts per unit of investment are modified due to changes in the investment options. The investment options for this case are the following: (p_j / w_j) = (2, 1.1, 1.5, 0.7, 1, 2.5, 2.5). After sorting the investment options are shown in Table 3.

Table 3. Data for case 2.

OPTION	**WEIGHT** w_i	**YIELD** p_i	p_i / w_i
7	$ 17,250,000.00	$ 43,125,000.00	2.5
6	12,250,000.00	30,625,000.00	2.5
1	12,500,000.00	25,000,000.00	2.0
3	7,500,000.00	11,250,000.00	1.5
2	500,000.00	550,000.00	1.1
5	6,250,000.00	6,250,000.00	1.0
4	10,775,000.00	7,542,500.00	0.7

The application of the greedy algorithm to data in Table 2 yields the following results:

Total optimal benefit $z =$ **$ 54, 375, 000**
Selected options: 3 and 7

Table 4. Investment Portfolio for case 2

INVESTMENT OPTION	AMOUNT
3	7 500 000
7	17 250 000
TOTAL	**24 750 000**

Changing the yield values of the investment options, the selected options in the optimal investment portfolio change as well. The total optimal benefit also changes, but it is still optimal.

5. Conclusions

This paper uses an optimization technique known as the knapsack problem. This technique is applied to the optimal selection of investment portfolios as an exact quantitative technique.

The use of mathematical algorithms amenable to implementation to solve the optimal investment portfolio selection allows automation of decision-making. This implementation works in real time, taking into consideration the changing conditions of the investment options at every time.

When the problem is too big, i.e., when the number of investment options is big, the experience of a financial adviser may not be enough to produce the best selection of investment options. This problem gets worse in dynamic scenarios, where investment options change continuously. In these conditions a computer implementation of a greedy algorithm is of great help in the solution of the problem of optimal selection of investment options.

The application of these kind of modes is indispensable for real time decision-making, when the basic information of references of the investor is known.

References

Gil Aluja J., González Santoyo F., Flores R B., Flores R. J. (2005). *Techniques and Metodologies for Modelling and Simulation of Systems.* AMSE,UMSNH. México.

González S.F., Flores R. B., Gil Lafuente A.M. (2010). *Modelos y teorías para evaluación de inversiones empresariales.* UMSNH. México.

González Santoyo F., Flores Romero B., Gil Lafuente A.M. (2011). *Procesos para la toma de decisiones en un entorno globalizado.* Editorial Universitaria Ramón Areces. Madrid España.

González Santoyo F, Alfaro Calderón G., Flores Romero B. (1997): *Modelos clásicos para la selección de Carteras de Inversión.* Ciencia Nicolaita No. 15. Agosto 1997. Pp.102-118. Morelia México. UMSNH.

González S.F., Alfaro C.G. (1996). *Las carteras de inversión en las decisiones financieras.* 1er Foro Nacional de Inv. En Disciplinas Administrativas. FCA-UNAM. México. D.F.

González Santoyo F. (1995). *Planeación de la producción usando técnicas de descomposición Jerárquica.* Tesis Doctoral (Doctor en Ingeniería-Investigación de Operaciones). Facultad de Ingeniería- División de Estudios de Posgrado UNAM, México.

González S.F. (1995). *Optimización en el Diseño de Carteras de Inversión y su aplicación en la Industria.* Reporte interno de Inv. Coordinación de la Investigación Científica – UMSNH. Morelia, México.

Markowitz H (1959). *Portfolio selection: efficient diversification of investments.* Jhon Wiley sons, New Cork.

Martínez Cárdenas F., González Santoyo F., Flores Romero V., Vargas Uribe G. (2005). *Selección óptima de carteras de inversión usando el problema Knapsack.* XIV International Conference AEDEM. Morelia México.

Silvano Martello; Paolo Toth (1990). *Knapsack Problems Algorithms and Computer Implementations.* John Wiley & Sons.

Flores, Juan J.; Avila, Javier; Gonzalez, Federico; Flores, Beatriz; Gil Lafuente, Anna M. Fuzzy Near-Optimal Algorithm for the Determination of Investment Options. International Journal of Financial Decision Making. Vol.3. No.1. pp 1-12. Greece. 2007.

Flores, Juan J.; Avila, Javier; Gonzalez, Federico; Flores, Beatriz. Heuristic Analysis of Near-Optimal Algorithm for the Determination of Investment Options. Revista Matemática: Teoría y Aplicaciones (ISSN 1409-2433). Editorial de la Universidad de Costa Rica. Vol.13. No.2. pp 125-138. Costa Rica. 2006. http://revista.emate.ucr.ac.cr/index.php/revista/issue/view/27

FUZZY MODELS IN SOCIAL AND ECONOMICAL SYSTEMS AND QUALITY INDICES

GORKHMAZ.C. IMANOV

Fuzzy Economic Department, Cybernetic Institute, National Academy Science of Azerbaijan, Baku Az 1141, Azerbaijan

In this paper investigated social system with subsystems – economical, social, political, spiritual, natural environments and economical system. On the construction process of the fuzzy models of these systems information of the International Organizations, Azerbaijan Republic and expert opinions were used. For assessment social and economical system quality indices were solved problems by weighted rules algorithms.

1. Introduction

The economic, social and political events occurring in the world, demand revision model of evolution of the problems of social and economic system. As it is known at an estimation of parameters of social and economic system basically theories of J.M.Keynes and M.Friedman are used. At the same time, such approach not always corresponds today's requirements and there was a necessity of revision of existing approaches to modeling of social and economic system.

The Socioeconomic system is a basis of each society, which consists of economic and social systems. Concept of social system is wider economic so as its basis are the human. The economic system basically describes processes of production, distribution, an exchange and consumption of products and services. Basic indicator of the economic system is Gross Domestic Product, which components characterize market processes acts. Functioning of economic system is very narrowly connected with the processes occurring in social system.

There is a set of approaches to investigation of the theory of social systems, however in the fullest and finished kind it has been presented in T.Parson's [1,2] and N.Luhmann's works [3,4], which has made an attempt to create the logic-deductive theoretical model of a society, covering a human reality in all its integrity and variety. In opinion, it is accepted to understand the ordered, hierarchical set of individuals, social groups as social system, community of the organizations united by stable connections and relations, interact with environment as a unit. Each social system should satisfy certain material, social and spiritual needs of the members of the society.

Macrolevel of the social system is societal system, which include economic, social, political, cultural, etc. subsystems. The social system constantly reproduces social quality of the structures and, accordingly, social quality of individuals and groups.

The theory of social quality has been offered by U.Beck, V.Maesen, L.Thomese and A.Walker [5,6,7]. Social quality represents degree of participation of citizens in social and economic life of a society at which their well-being and individual potential raises.

In offered article doing attempt of construction fuzzy models of definition of indices qualities social SSQI) and economic system (ESQI).

2. Problem statement

Today for define the level of development of society (country) various indices, such as human development index (HDI), life quality index (LQI), sustainable development index (SDI) etc. are widely used. At the same time, a number of lacks is inherent in each of them, they cannot be regarded as comprehensive, universal indexes as the data obtained with their help needs deeper detailed elaboration on the basis of the additional statistical information on the country, its features and problems. Besides, use of these indices leans against a number of assumptions which, certainly, not always represent the facts.

For modeling societal systems we are investigated economical (EE), social (SE), political (PE), spiritual (SPE), and natural environments (NE) of dwelling of the person. These environments are interconnected and their functioning result defines quality of social development of a society (SSQ). As components of social system act:

I. Economic environment characterized by rates of increase of gross national product (ΔGDP), gross national product per capita (GDP/P), a rate of inflation (CPI), a share of import products in consumption (FIM), a share of hi-tech production in export (TEX), financial stability (FIS), business environment index (BEN). Output parameter of this subsystem is the economic environment quality index (EEQI).

II. Social environment includes such indicators, as life expectancy of the population (LEP), decile (a parity between the income of 10 % of the richest population and the income of 10 % of the poorest population) (DEC), a rate of unemployment (UNE), the relation of number died to number born (RDB), expenditures for education (EXE), public health services (EXH), culture (EXC), science (EXS)and a monthly average salary (WAG), the state pension expenses (PEN). Output of this subsystem is social environment quality index (SEQI).

III. Components of the political environment are the risk of the military conflict (RAC), risk of social explosion (RSE), the constitutional mechanisms of delegation of power (CMP), the relation between the state and opposition (GSO), threat of politically motivated violence (TPV), the international disputes and tensions (IDT), a government policy towards business (GPB), effectiveness of political system in policy formulation and executing (EPS), quality of the bureaucracy (QUB), a transparency and fairness of legal system (TLS), efficiency of legal system (ELS), corruption (COR), impact of crime (CRI). Output of this subsystem – political environment quality index (PEQI).

IV. Spiritual environment includes level of religiousness of a society (LOR), tolerance level (LOT), level of impact religious to society development (LOI), quality of cultural of the society (QCS), level of information support (LIS), quality of a science (QIS), and quality of health care (QHC). Output of this subsystem – spiritual environment quality index (S_pEQI).

Natural environment is characterized by quality of air (AQI), water (WQI) and land (LQI), biodiversity (EBI), environmental protection investments (EPI), environmental damage (NED). Output of this subsystem – natural environment quality index (NEQI).

The system of indicators of various environments are heterogeneous, i.e. the majority of its indicators have not only quantitative measurement but also qualitative.

At an initial stage gathering of the necessary information on subsystem indicators societal systems for what reports of the United Nations Organization, the World bank [8], the International Monetary Fund [9] and other international organizations [10], and also expert opinions of various profiles were used is carried out. Indicators of political environment are completely borrowed from [11]. The collected information has given the chance to define linguistic variables and their corresponding intervals.

At the problem decision the algorithm of the weighted rules has been used. Application of this algorithm is caused by that at the solution of problem with linguistic variables definition of scales of input and output characteristics is required. It allows to reduce number of possible rules, which gives the chance to improve accuracy of results. On the base of the following indices – EEQI, SERI, PEQI, S_pEQI, NEQI we must calculate composite social system quality index – SSQI.

3. Algorithm of the weighted rules

At formation of algorithm of the weighted rules were used ideas Mamdani's fuzzy inference method and algorithm of the batch least square of groups [12]. For demonstration steps of algorithm were use information of the economical environment model (table 1).

Table 1. Parameters of the economical environment model.

İndicators Azerbaijan	Terms and supports					
1). GDP/P	Very low 0.320- 17	Low 16.5 – 33	Moderate 32.5 – 50	High 49.5 – 67	Very high 66.5 – 84	Very low 4.0
2). Δ GDP	Very low -∞ - 1	Low 0.8 – 3	Moderate 2.8 – 5	High 4.5 – 8	Very high 7.5 - ∞	Moderate 5
3). CPI	Very low 0.1 – 3	Low 2.5 – 5.0	Moderate 4.5 – 8	High 7.5 – 10	Very high 9 - ∞	Moderate 5.8
4). FIM	Very high 0 – 4	High 6 – 12	Moderate 10 – 20	Low 18 – 30	Very low 25 – 100	Low 30
5). TEX	Very high 10 – 7.5	High 8 – 5.5	Moderate 6 – 3.5	Low 4 – 1.5	Very low 2 – 0	Very low 2
6). FIS	Crises 100 – 79	Nearly crises 80 – 59	Weak stability 60 – 39	Stability 40 – 19	Very stability 20 – 1	Stability 40
7). BEN	Very bad 0 – 2	Bad 1.9 – 4	Moderate 3.9 – 6	Good 5.9 – 8	Very good 7.9 – 10	Moderate 5.3
8). EEQI	Very bad 0 – 2	Bad 1.5 – 4	Moderate 3.5 – 6	Good 5.5 – 8	Very good 7.5 – 10	Moderate 4.7

On the table 1 indicators: GDP/P – GDP per capita in thousand USD, Δ GDP – GDP rate of gross in percent, CPI – level of inflation, FIM – portion of imported food in consumption, TEX – portion of advanced technology products in export, FIS – financial stability index, BEN – business environment score are input and EEQI – economical environment quality index is output variables. On the first step it is carried out fuzzification at which were used Gaussian functions. Further on the basis of quantity of terms are defined initial fuzzy rules (in our case terms 5, quantity of initial rules to equally five). By using n-factorial base on inputs and output, considering terms, all possible rules generated in the program.

Further the peak point - c_j^i of each corresponding to support of the fuzzy number of the terms were defined. On the basis c_j^i matrix $C = (c_j^i)$ were constructed. Initial rules are expressed on the basis c_j^i. For our example matrix C may be the following:

$$C = \begin{pmatrix} C1 & C2 & C3 & C4 & C5 & C6 & C_y \\ 8.66 & -1.50 & 1.55 & 2.00 & 8.75 & 89.50 & 1.00 \\ 24.75 & 1.90 & 3.75 & 9.00 & 6.75 & 69.50 & 2.75 \\ 41.25 & 3.90 & 6.25 & 15.00 & 4.75 & 49.50 & 4.75 \\ 58.25 & 6.25 & 8.75 & 24.00 & 2.75 & 29.50 & 6.75 \\ 75.25 & 10.25 & 14.50 & 62.50 & 1.00 & 10.50 & 8.75 \end{pmatrix}$$

After that by means of the below-mentioned formula degree of membership every points of support part fuzzy number corresponding to linguistic variables were define:

$$\mu_i(x) = \prod_{j=1}^{n} \exp\left[-\frac{1}{2}\left(\frac{x_j^i - c_j^i}{\sigma_j^i}\right)^2\right] \tag{1}$$

Where n – number of input variables; x_j^i – meaning of support points of the fuzzy number of the terms; i – an index of term; c_j^i - a peak point of corresponding terms i; σ_j^i - average square deviation of an interval of the corresponding term.

For our example meaning of σ_j^i calculated as following:

	VERY LOW	LOW	MODERATE	HIGH	VERY HIGH
GDP/P	4.8208	4.8499	5.0517	5.0517	5.0808
ΔGDR	0.3317	0.6364	0.6708	1.0400	0.7517
CPI	0.8367	0.7517	1.0400	0.7517	0.9000
FIM	2.3402	1.7635	2.8870	3.4643	21.6797
TEX	0.7517	0.7517	0.7517	0.7211	0.5788
FIS	6.0918	6.0918	6.0623	6.0623	5.4850
BEN	0.5788	0.6055	0.6364	0.6364	0.6519

By using meaning of σ_j^i were defined meaning of $\mu_i(x)$ for every terms:

	VERY LOW	LOW	MODERATE	HIGH	VERY HIGH
GDP/P	0.000000000	0.0000000000	0.000000000	0.000000000	0.000000000
ΔGDP	0.004086771	0.0000167017	0.000010130	0.000000015	0.000002260
CPI	0.000000504	0.0000022603	0.000000015	0.000002260	0.000000185
FIM	0.000000000	0.0000000000	0.000000000	0.000000000	0.000000000
TEX	0.000002260	0.0000022603	0.000002260	0.000003726	0.000045399
FIS	0.000000000	0.0000000000	0.000000000	0.000000000	0.000000000
BEN	0.000045399	0.0000275364	0.000016701	0.000016701	0.000016701

After that define weights antecedent of initial rules:

$$w_i^a = \frac{\mu_i(x)}{\sum_{i=1}^{R} \mu_i(x)} \tag{2}$$

$$\sum_{i=1}^{n} w_i = 1$$

Where w_i - weight antecedent of initialed rules, $\mu_i(x)$ - degree of fuzzy variables entered in the antecedent a part of rules.

Substituting value of the formula (1) in the formula (2), we receive:

$$w_i^a = \frac{\prod_{j=1}^{n} \exp\left[-\frac{1}{2}\left(\frac{x_j^i - c_j^i}{\sigma_j^i}\right)^2\right]}{\sum_{i=1}^{R}\prod_{j=1}^{n} \exp\left[-\frac{1}{2}\left(\frac{x_j^i - c_j^i}{\sigma_j^i}\right)^2\right]} \tag{3}$$

w_i^a - weights of terms of the antecedent part looks as :

	VERY LOW	LOW	MODERATE	HIGH	VERY HIGH
GDP/P	0.0000	0.0000	0.0000	0.0000	0.0000
ΔGDP	0.9884	0.3425	0.3480	0.0007	0.0350
CPI	0.0001	0.0464	0.0005	0.0996	0.0029
FIM	0.0000	0.0000	0.0000	0.0000	0.0000
TEX	0.0005	0.0464	0.0777	0.1641	0.7034
FIS	0.0000	0.0000	0.0000	0.0000	0.0000
BEN	0.0110	0.5647	0.5738	0.7356	0.2588
$\sum_{i=1}^{n} w_i$	1.00	1.00	1.00	1.00	1.00

The following step by means of the mentioned below formula w_i^c - defines weighted values consequence part of rules:

$$w_i^c = \frac{\sum_{i=1}^{R} b_i \prod_{j=1}^{n} \exp[-\frac{1}{2}(\frac{x_j^i - c_j^i}{\sigma_j^i})^2]}{\sum_{i=1}^{R} \prod_{j=1}^{n} \exp[-\frac{1}{2}(\frac{x_j^i - c_j^i}{\sigma_j^i})^2]} \quad (4)$$

b_i - - a peak point of corresponding terms of the consequence part of the rules,.

Further, using the maximum values w_i^c, w_i^a we define new system of rules:

R1: If GDP/P=Moderate – 41.3 (w_1^a =0.000) and ΔGDP= Very Low – 0.5 (w_2^a=0.9884) and CPI=High – 8.8 (w_3^a=0.0996) and FIM=Very Low – 4 (w_4^a=0.000) and TEX=Very High – 1 (w_5^a=0.7034) and FIS=Very High – 10.5 (w_6^a=0.000) and BEN=Moderate 5 (w_7^a=0.5738) then EEQI =Moderate – 4.8

R2: If GDP/P = Very Low -4.0 (w_1^a=0.000) and ΔGDP = Moderate -5 (w_2^a=0.9884) and CPI= Moderate -5.8 (w_3^a=0.0001) and FIM= Low-30 (w_4^a=0.0005) and TEX=Very Low-2.0 (w_5^a=0.7034) and FIS=Stable-40 (w_6^a=0.000) and BEN= Moderate -5.3 (w_7^a=0.0110) then EEQI=?

In new system of rules R1-are rule, which we find and R2- rule, which correspond to fixed meaning of input variables (last column table 1). By using composition operation were defined corresponding fuzzy number.

At last stage, using Centroid methods defuzzification of fuzzy numbers were carry out.

As result, we find crisp meaning of EEQI =Moderate-4.763.

By using this algorithm were define – SEQI = (moderate – 0.5); PEQI = (moderate – 2.95); S_pEQI = (moderate – 4.75); NEQI = (bad – 2.95).

4. Results of the solution problems of assessment of social system quality index

On the base defined indices – EEQI, SEQI, PEQI, S_pEQI and NEQI were define social system quality index (SSQI), which were equal to moderate 4.25. On the meaning Azerbaijan SSQI basically was affected moderate qualities of economical, political, social, spiritual environments and bad level of natural environment.

The average percent of inflation (5,8 %), high share of import products (30) in consumption and a low share of high technological products (2) in export has affected quality of the economic environment; quality of the social environment was characterized by very low level of the monthly average salary (401 USD), low level of expenses on public health services (3,7), low level of pension expenses (3,7), expenses for education (1,9) and very low level on development of a science (0,241); quality of the political environment was affected, mainly, bad mutual relations between the government and opposition, low degree of a transparency and justice of political system, efficiency of legal system and high level of corruption; quality of the spiritual environment was defined by very low level of influence of the religious organizations on increase of a standard of living of the population, a low degree of quality of public health services and education; on quality natural environment very bad quality of air, bad quality of water, a bad index of a natural biodiversity and very low level of capital investments for environmental protection has affected.

5. Fuzzy macromodel of economic system

Quality of social system mainly depends on quality of functioning of economic system. For fuzzy revisio were used following indicators of a financial and monetary policy:

1. Rate of increase of gross national product - ΔGDP;
2. The rate of refinancing of the Central Bank – RCB;
3. Consumer price index – CPI;
4. External government debts – EGD;
5. Budget deficit – BD;
6. Tax revenue – TR;
7. Parity of purchasing capacity of national currency – PPP;
8. Currency reserves – CR.

For solution this problem were used the algorithm of the weighed rules, too. The economic system quality index equal – average – 0,5. To value of economic system quality index was affected, mainly, low level of taxation. It is necessary to notice that in Azerbaijan besides currency reserves exist as well reserves of oil fund which could be used as social investments that, undoubtedly, would improve quality of social system.

Table 2. Indicators of economic system model

Variables \ Terms	Very low	Low	Moderate	High	Very high	Azerbajjan
1. Δ GDP	Very low <1	Low 0.8 – 3	Moderate 2.8 – 5	High 4.5 – 8	Very high > 7.5	Moderate 5
2. RCB - %	<1	0.75 – 2	1.75 – 3	2.75 – 5	> 4.75	High 5
3. CPI - %	<4.5	5 – 9	8-10	9.5 – 12	> 11.5	Low 5.8
4. EGD - % GDP	0 – 19	18 – 26	25-30	28 – 35	> 34	Very low 6
5. BD - % GDP	0 – 0.6	0.7-1.5	1.4-3	2.8 – 6	> 5.5	Low 0.9
6. TR - % GDP	1 – 10	9 – 20	19 – 30	29 – 40	> 39 – 70	Low 17.8
7. PPP	<2	2.85 – 1.85	2.2 – 1.9	2 – 1	> 0.94	Very low 2
8. CR – in days	<30	29 – 60	59 – 370	360 – 730	> 720	Moderate 219
Economic system quality index – ESQI	Very bad 0 – 0.2	Very bad 0.15 – 0.4	Moderate 0.35 – 0.6	Good 0.55 – 0.8	Very good 0.75 – 1	Moderate 0,5

6. Conclusion

The constructed approach to define of social and economic systems quality indices allows decision makers at macrolevel, to controlling and regulate development parameters socioeconomical systems. At a following stage decomposition of social system quality index by social mobility quality and criteria of the European Union, such as quality of socioeconomic security, social inclusion, cohesion and empowerment must be developed.

References

1. Parsons T. Societies evolutionary and comparative perspectives.Prentice Hall, (1966).
2. Parsons T. System of modern societies. Prentice Hall, (1971).
3. Luhmann, Niklas. (1995). *Social Systems, Writing Science*, Stanford, Calif.; Stanford University Press.
4. Luhmann, Niklas. (1990). The Autopoiesis of Social Systems. In *Essays on Self-Reference*, edited by N. Luhmann. New York; Columbia University Press.

Social Quality of Europe. The Hague, Netherlands: Kluwar Law International.
3. Beck, W., van der Maesen, L., Thomese, G. And Walker, A. (2001). "Introduction: who and what is the European Union for?" in Beck, W., van der Maesen, L.
4. Thomese, G. and Walker, A. (eds) *Social Quality: a Vision for Europe*. The Hague, Netherlands: Kluwer Law.
5. World Bank, World Development Report 2010: Development and Climate Change, November (2009), 300 pp.
6. International financial statistics, International Monetary Fund, June, 2008.
7. Transparency International the global coalition against corruption. Annual Report (2009), 68 p.
8. World investment prospects to 2011. Foreign direct investment and the challenge of political risk. Written with the Columbia Program on International Investment, 250 p.
9. Ross T. Fuzzy Logic with Engineering Application, second edition, WILEY, England, (2004), 629 pp.

PART 1:
SUSTAINABLE DEVELOPMENT

APPROACHES TO MANAGING SUSTAINABILITY AMONG ENTERPRISES

GIL LAFUENTE, ANNA MARÍA
Faculty of Economics and Business, University of Barcelona, Av. Diagonal 690 Barcelona, Catalonia 08034, Spain

BARCELLOS PAULA, LUCIANO
IS Consulting, Lúcio Bittencourt Street, nº 109/509, Vila Santa Cecília, Volta Redonda, Rio de Janeiro 27260-110, Brazil

The stakeholder theory posits that a firm's ability to generate sustainable wealth over time, and thus its long-term value, is determined by its relations with its stakeholders. The challenge for the companies is to decide what actions and initiatives to continuing and the best way of handling them. Because of the complexity to managing sustainability is essential to address the analysis with an approach based on complex systems and models that help entrepreneurs in making decisions, especially in an uncertain environment. For these reasons, it is justified to analyze the sustainability using fuzzy logic algorithms. To complete the study, we present the contributions and conclusions of our investigation.

1. Introduction

In recent decades various changes have occurred in the context of business, such as technological innovations and regulatory policy changes, social trends and market development. These changes have altered the nature of relationships between companies and its stakeholders. The companies have turned from traditional business interactions with employees, customers, suppliers, investors and regulators to interact with larger groups, with local communities, workers in the purchasing chain, relatives of employees, civil society organizations, medium environment, among others. Another change relates to the topics discussed with interest groups, legal and contractual issues, such as marketing, industrial relations, choice of locations for plants, business planning and shopping, to emerging issues and new responsibilities, such as corruption, social exclusion, human rights, health risks, economic development, working conditions in the purchasing chain, environmental impact. Ultimately the way to make communication with stakeholders has also changed such as market research, corporate communications, advertising and broadcast media, to dialogue and cooperation, consultations, advisory panels, feedback online, call networks, forums and partnerships of multiple stakeholders. As changes have occurred in the business environment and nature in the relations with stakeholders, therefore the relationship of companies with interest groups have evolved. Initial experiences of relationships with interest groups responded to external pressures, limited to certain issues that generated conflict with stakeholders. Subsequently, the companies have demonstrated their potential to increase mutual understanding, manage risks and resolve conflicts more effectively. Currently, the relations with stakeholders enable companies to align their social, environmental and economic with its main strategy. This new context in the business underscores the complexity of acquiring the management of stakeholders in the companies with the expansion of emerging groups and emerging issues and new responsibilities. Together the company's relationships with stakeholders get greater importance through dialogue and collaboration. Certainly this new reality allows us to consider how it can be the management of interest groups so as to enable a comprehensive strategic relationship for achieving sustainable competitiveness.

In this paper, we will focus our research on sustainability management among enterprises. Because of this complexity, it is essential to address the analysis with an approach based on complex systems and models that help entrepreneurs in making decisions, especially in an uncertain environment. For these reasons, it is justified to analyze the sustainability using fuzzy logic algorithms.

The fuzzy sets theory [27] is a mathematical theory in the field of multivalent logics. Its origin is in the work done by Professor Lotfi A. Zadeh and is the starting point for a mathematical theory currently expanding in all scientific disciplines and built with the entire rigor that enables the treatment of subjectivity and/or uncertainty [9]. At first, the fuzzy sets theory has been applied in the field of formal science, but in the last 45 years, researchers around the world have published many papers and studies with applications in various fields. It should be noted, the pioneering and important contribution to science of the teachers Kaufmann and Gil Aluja who published the first book in the world dedicated exclusively to the processing of financial and management problems with the mathematics of uncertainty [2]. It included very diverse studies (investments, renewal of equipment, inventory management and product distribution). Currently, the use of fuzzy logic takes place in practically every field of science studies. It is in the business management, engineering, biology, medicine, geology, sociology, phonetics, and even in music, among others. Every problem is located in the area of uncertainty is likely to be treated by the theory of fuzzy subsets and that as time passes it is becoming increasingly feasible to introduce in formal schemes, mechanisms of thinking, such as sensations and numeric views.

To complete the study, we present the contributions and conclusions of our investigation. We believe that our contribution will serve to support future research on the application of algorithms to business sustainability, a field that has been only scarcely investigated.

2. The challenges in relations with stakeholders

According to Freeman [32], the stakeholders of a company are by definition any group or individual who can affect or is affected by the achievement of the objectives of the revision 1 . Since Freeman's research, other authors have revision the concept of stakeholders [8, 7, 16, 30, 18, 10, 12, 39, 33, 17, 29, 35, and 37] with the publication of several books and articles on the subject.

There is a generic list of stakeholders from business, even for a single company, because they change over time [33]. The groups and individuals affected and affecting businesses rely on the industry, business, geographic location and subject matter. The new business strategies and contextual changes often determine a new set of stakeholders. For Elkington [14] through the constructive engagement of stakeholders, companies can increase external confidence in its intentions and activities, helping to improve corporate reputation and catalyze the diffusion of more sustainable practices in the enterprise system in general.

According to Post *et al.* [17], stakeholders of a firm are individuals and groups who contribute, voluntarily or involuntarily, to its capacity and wealth-creation activities, and therefore they are potential beneficiaries and/or risk bearers. Interest groups cover a wide variety of stakeholders, including shareholders, employees, customers, local communities, government, NGOs, suppliers. For Freeman and Evan [31], stakeholder theory predicts that sustainability should have a positive impact on financial results because companies benefit from 'addressing and balancing the claims' of the many key stakeholders. Moreover, "the continuing failure to address the concerns and expectations of the groups, ultimately, reduces the confidence of investors in company shares, which affect their cost of funds (weighted average cost of capital) and therefore, opportunities for profit" [38].

To do sustainable business, companies must have good knowledge of all actors with influence in its sphere of activity. This identification of stakeholders is the first step. Once organisations have become aware of the various publics that interact with them, it is important to categorize in terms of expectations, problems, geographical areas, its impact on business activity and vice versa. The result of the identification and segmentation is called mapping stakeholders. To do a map involves identifying stakeholder expectations and influence of each. This helps establish priorities that meet, while allowing an overall view of other possible interactions between groups. Subsequently, companies must establish a hierarchy among them, in order to determine the relevance of their modes of interaction.

According to the stakeholder engagement manual [40], engaging with all stakeholders or on all issues is neither possible nor desirable. This would go beyond any available resources, and at the same time make it very difficult to adequately respond to stakeholders, leading to frustration. Therefore, the enterprise should try and prioritise its stakeholders and issues to ensure that time, resources and expectations are well managed. Another item relevant to the topic relates to compliance with the Guidelines for Sustainability Reporting [13]. According to the GRI in subsection 4.15, the revision 1 must submit the procedure for defining its stakeholder groups and for the determination of the groups involved and those not.

3. Approaches to managing sustainability among enterprises

The main aim of sustainability is to reconcile economic growth with social care environment and environmental protection. However, in an uncertain environment, enterprises need tools that help both decision making and the definition of their strategies. Therefore, with this new reality is necessary to raise the use of models to rediscover new ways to manage not only businesses but also their objectives, strategies and policies to simultaneously support the prosperity of enterprise and promote a sustainable quality of life at the planetary level. To do this, we must rely on flexible models that enable the hybrid treatment of objective and subjective estimates and allow estimates of the future conduct of companies, institutions and social actors, thereby offering a redesign of economic relations that affect all entities involved. In figure 1, we propose an approach to managing sustainability among enterprises.

General Objective	Particular objectives	Action Lines	Techniques
To propose the model utilization that there allow to rediscover new ways of managing the sustainability in enterprises.	To develop new applications and management models for decision making.	Risk management: social, economic and environmental.	Hamming's distance (Hamming, 1950), Expertons Method (Kaufmann, 1987), Coefficient of Qualification (Gil Lafuente, A.M., 2001), Hungarian Algorithm (König, 1916).
		Business decision processes.	Theory of the Forgotten Effects (Kaufmann y Gil Aluja, 1988).
	To show the utility of these models in sustainable development in companies by the Stakeholders Theory.	Supplier management	Clans Theory (Courtillot, 1973), Theory of Affinities (Gil Aluja y Kaufmann, 1991), Model of Subjective Preferences (Kaufmann y Gil Aluja, 1987).
		Human resources management	Hamming's distance (Hamming, 1950), Coefficient of Adequacy (Gil Aluja,1996), OWA Operators (Yager, 1988).
	To implement new contributions to the methodological knowledge in decision theory	Customer management	Teoría de Afinidades (Gil Aluja y Kaufmann, 1991).
		Identification, prioritisation and dialogue with stakeholders.	Clans Theory (Courtillot, 1973), P-Latin Composition (Kaufmann, A.; Gil Aluja, J., 1991).

Figure 1. Approaches to managing sustainability among enterprises

The application of Hamming distance [36] to sustainability in business is an innovation to be used in the selection process for proposals and sustainable management of human resources and enables decision-making considering the subjective weighting priority on the criteria of sustainability in business [21]. In the case of Experton Method [6], this algorithm can facilitate decision making by obtaining qualitative data from the dialogue with different stakeholders. This is a useful tool to be used in the processes of aggregation and unification of views or differing expectations among its stakeholders [24]. The model also allows knowing the distribution function levels characteristic of belonging to the aggregate values. The Model of Subjective Preferences [5] can be applied in the ordering process by facilitating decision making in various contexts in companies, such as the revision 1 of stakeholders [26]. On the other hand, OWA operators [34] can facilitate decision making in the field of corporate sustainability in general and particular aspects of it such as environmental management, economic, social and human resources, among many other approaches [26].

Another contribution concerns Hungarian Algorithm [11] that can be used in decision-making processes in implementing eco-efficiency practices. It is also a model for the resolution, among others, the important problem of mapping tools that help the scope of eco-efficiency in business [19]. The Clans Theory [28] as a grouping algorithm can facilitate decision making by obtaining qualitative data from a dialogue with managers or specialists on a certain subject and used in the process of identifying stakeholders [20]. The results with the application of the Theory of the Forgotten Effects [3] provides a model that allows sequential nature of causality introduced to the study of sustainability in the company, be a useful tool for use in processes targeting [23]. In the case of P-Latin Composition [4], this technique can be applied in ordering processes and provides a useful model in making decisions, for example, the revision 1 of stakeholders considering criteria for sustainability in business.

On the other hand, the Theory of Affinities [1] can facilitate decision making by obtaining qualitative data from a dialogue with managers or specialists on a particular topic. The model can be used in the process of identifying stakeholders and serves to establish the level of relationship between different stakeholders and obtain affinities [22, 25]. Using the Adequacy Ratio [15] can facilitate decision making by obtaining qualitative data from the dialogue with different stakeholders and can be used in the selection process for proposals and sustainable management human resources in enterprises [26] and institutions, among others. And the Qualification Ratio [9] can be used in the stakeholders management and facilitate decision making in different areas of the company as human resources, finance and purchasing.

4. Conclusions

The study about the stakeholder shows that compared with the changes we are living is essential to find models that will help employers in making decisions, especially in an uncertain environment. Because of the importance and complexity that is the sustainability management for companies in our research we try to analyse these complex systems using fuzzy logic.

First we look at how changes in the business environment and nature in relations with stakeholders also have influenced and changed the relationship between companies and their stakeholders. Secondly, we briefly review the literature on the concepts of the Theory of Stakeholders and the challenges in relations with them. And finally, we propose the use of flexible tools that assist it in making decisions and help improve management with stakeholders and thus to contribute to the treatment of problems in the future.

The article's main contribution is to managing sustainability in enterprises, and providing a useful model in making decisions. We believe that our contribution will serve to support future research in the field of application of algorithms to business sustainability in general and particular aspects of it such as environmental management, economic and social, among many other approaches.

References

A. Kaufmann and J. Gil Aluja. "Seletion of affinities by means of fuzzy relations and Galois lattices". *Actas del Euro XI Congress O.R. Aachen*, 16–19 July. (1991b).

A. Kaufmann and J. Gil Aluja. *Introducción de la teoría de los subconjuntos borrosos a la gestión de las empresas*. Editorial Milladoiro. Santiago de

Compostela, Spain. (1986).
A. Kaufmann and J. Gil Aluja. *Modelos para la investigación de efectos olvidados*. Editorial Milladoiro, Vigo. (1988).
A. Kaufmann and J. Gil Aluja. *Nuevas técnicas para la dirección estratégica*. Ed. Universidad de Barcelona. Barcelona, (6). (1991a)[a]
A. Kaufmann and J. Gil Aluja. *Técnicas operativas de gestión para el tratamiento de la incertidumbre*, Barcelona, Hispano Europea, 219–234. (1987).
A. Kaufmann. *Les expertones*. Ed. Hermés. París. (1987).
A.B. Carroll and A.K. Buchholtz. *Business and Society: Ethics and Stakeholder Management*. Southwestern Publishing Co., Cincinnati. (1989).
A.F. Alkhafaji. *A stakeholder approach to corporate governance: Managing in a dynamic environment*. New York: Quorum Books. (1989).
A.M. Gil Lafuente. *Nuevas Estrategias para el análisis financiero en la empresa*, Ariel Economía, p. 390–393. (2001).
C.W.L. Hill and T.M. Jones. "Stakeholder-Agency Theory". *Journal of Management Studies*, **29**, 131–154. (1992).
D. König. *Théorie der endlichen und unendlichen graphen*, 1916. Chelsea Publ. C.º.Nueva York. (1950).
D.J. Wood. "Social issues in management: Theory and research in corporate social performance". *Journal of Management*, 17, 383–405. (1991).
Global Reporting Iniciative. *Guía para elaboración de Memorias de Sostenibilidad, versión G3*. (2006).
J. Elkington. Cannibals with forks: the triple bottom line of 21st Century Business. Oxford, U.K. Capstone Publishing Limited. (1998).
J. Gil Aluja. *La gestión interactiva de los recursos humanos en la incertidumbre*. Madrid: Ed. Centro de Estudios Ramón Areces. (1996).
J. James Brummer. *Corporate responsibility and legitimacy: An interdisciplinary analysis*. New York: Greenwood Press. (1991).
J.E. Post, L.E. Preston and S. Sachs. "Managing the Extended Enterprise: The New Stakeholder View". *California Management Review*, **45(1)**, 5–28. (2002).
K.E. Goodpaster. Business ethics and stakeholder analysis. Business Ethics Quarterly, **1(1)**, 53–73. (2006).
L. Barcellos Paula and A.M. Gil Lafuente. "Algorithm applied in the implantation of practices of eco-efficiency in the companies". *Current Development in Theory and Applications of Computer Science, Engineering and Technology*. Volume 1, Number 1, 31–48, ISSN: 0976-1438. (2010b).
L. Barcellos Paula and A.M. Gil Lafuente. "Algorithm applied in the identification of stakeholders". In: *Proceeding of International Conference on Modeling and Simulation in Engineering, Economics and Management* (AMSE), Barcelona, Spain, 15-17 July, 2010, Vol.3, 257-264. ISBN: 978-981-4324-43-4 / 981-4324-43-4. World Scientific Publishing Co. Inc. New York. (2010f).
L. Barcellos Paula and A.M. Gil Lafuente. "Algorithms applied in the

sustainable management of human resources". *Fuzzy Economic Review*. Volume XV, Number 1, May. (2010c).
L. Barcellos Paula and A.M. Gil Lafuente. "Fuzzy logic algorithm applied in the corporate sustainability: analysis of an empirical study in the management of suppliers". *International Review on Computers and Software (IRECOS)*. Special Issue dedicated to the Advanced Artificial Neural Network Approaches with Applications to System Management, Vol. 5, number 4, 460–463. Print ISSN: 1828-6003, Cd-Rom ISSN: 1828-601. (2010e).
L. Barcellos Paula and A.M. Gil Lafuente. "Proceso de selección de elementos que contribuyen al crecimiento sostenible de la empresa". In: *Proceeding of International Conference and Doctoral Consortium for ISEOR and Academy of Management*, held at Lyon, France, **(1)**, 773–788. (2009a).
L. Barcellos Paula and A.M. Gil Lafuente. "The expertons method applied in the dialog with stakeholders". In: *Proceeding of the 2th International Conference on Computer Supported Education* (CSEDU), held at Valencia, Spain, 7-10 April, 2010. Vol. I, 402–406. ISBN: 978-989-674-023-8. (2010a).
L. Barcellos Paula and A.M. Gil Lafuente. "The theory of affinities applied to the suppliers' sustainable management". In: *Proceeding of the 10th International Conference Artificial Intelligence and Soft Computing*, Zakopane, Poland, June 13-17, 2010, 461–467, Part II. ISSN 0302-9743; ISBN-10 3-642-13231-6 Springer Berlin Heidelberg New York. (2010d).
L. Barcellos Paula and A.M. Gil Lafuente. Algoritmos aplicados en la gestión sostenible de los recursos humanos. Economic and Financial Crisis: "New challenges and Perspectives". *In: Proceeding of XV Congress of International Association for Fuzzy-Set Management and Economy* (SIGEF), Lugo, Spain. (2009b).
L.A. Zadeh. "Fuzzy sets". *Information and Control*, **8 (3)**, 338-353. (1965).
M. Courtillot. "Structure cononique des fichiers". *A.I.E.R.-A.F.G.E.T.* Vol. 7. January, 2–15. (1973).
M.A, Rodríguez, J.E. Ricart and P. Sánchez. "Sustainable Development and the Sustainability of Competitive Advantage: A Dynamic and Sustainable View of the firm". *Creativity and Innovation Management*, 11. (2002).
M.B.E. Clarkson. "Defining, evaluating, and managing corporate social performance: A stakeholder management model". In *J. E. Post (Ed.), Research in corporate social performance and policy*, pp. 331–358, Greenwich, CT: JAI Press. (1991).
R.E. Freeman and W. Evan. "Corporate Governance: A Stakeholder Interpretation". *Journal of Behavioral Economics*, **19 (4)**, p. 337–359. (1990).
R.E. Freeman. *Strategic Management: A Stakeholder Approach*. Pitman Series in Business and Public Policy. (1984).
R.K. Mitchell, B.R. Agle and D.J. Wood. "Toward a Theory of Stakeholder Identification and Salience: Defining the Principle of who and what really Counts". *The Academy of Management Review*, **22(4)**, 853–886. (1997).

R.R. Yager. "On Ordered Weighted Averaging Aggregation Operators in Multi-Criteria Decision Making". *IEEE Transactions on Systems, Man and Cybernetics*, Vol. 18, p. 183–190. (1988).

R.V. Aguilera and G. Jackson. "The Cross-National Diversity of Corporate Governance: Dimensions and Determinants". *The Academy of Management Review*, **28(3)**, 447–465. (2003).

R.W. Hamming. "Error detecting and error correcting codes". *Bell System Technical Journal*, **26 (2):** 147–160. (1950).

S.L. Hart and S. Sharma. "Engaging Fringe Stakeholders for Competitive Imagination". *Academy of Management Executive*, **18(1)**. (2004).

Sustainability Asset Management and PricewaterhouseCoopers. *The Sustainability Yearbook 2009*. Zurich, p. 13. (2009).

T. Donaldson and L.E. Preston. "The Stakeholder Theory of the Corporation: Concepts, Evidence and Implications". *Academy Management Review*, **20(1)**, 65–91. (1995).

T. Krick, M. Forstater, P. Monaghan, M. Sillanpää, C. Van der Lugt, K. Partridge, C. Jackson and A. Zohar. *From words to action. The Stakeholder engagement Manual. Vol. 2: The practitioner's handbook on stakeholder engagement*. London. Accountability, United Nations Environment Programme, Stakeholder Research Associates Canada Inc. (2005).

ESTIMATION OF THE EFFECTIVENESS OF REGIONAL INVESTMENT PROJECTS BY FUZZY CONCLUSION METHOD

RAMIN RZAEV

Signal Analysis and Information Systems, Institute of Cybernetics of National Academy of Science, 9 B. Vahabzade str.
Baku, AZ1141, Azerbaijan

ELCHIN ALIEV

Innovation Systems and Networks, Institute of Cybernetics of National Academy of Science, 9 B. Vahabzade str.
Baku, AZ1141, Azerbaijan

ROVSHAN AKBAROV

International Economic Relations, National Academy of Aviation, Bina 25 km.
Baku, AZ1045, Azerbaijan

NIJAT ASKEROV

Signal Analysis and Information Systems, Institute of Cybernetics of National Academy of Science, 9 B. Vahabzade str.
Baku, AZ1141, Azerbaijan

Methodology for estimation the effectiveness of regional investment projects aspire to receive budgetary appropriations of the National Investment Fund for Support of Entrepreneurship in Azerbaijan is proposed. This Methodology is based on verbal estimation models that are realized by the fuzzy inference method on a limited number of real alternative investment projects.

1. Introduction

Analysis and evaluation of the economic efficiency of investment projects is one of the difficult problems in the economy, production and management. Its complexity is specified, on the one hand, the presence of uncertainty, because when problem solving on investments always it is necessary to anticipate the future, and the other – the presence of set of knowingly conflicting criteria that are both quantitative and qualitative nature.

Quantitative criteria are usually expressed in money equivalent and/or in arbitrary units in a scale of unit segment, if there are criteria, which are reflected in monetary terms is difficult or undesirable. In particular, units of measure of any quantitative criteria can be unified and reduced to a unit segment by a simple functional mapping $x = a + t(b - a)$.

Qualitative criteria can not be described by monetary or some other quantifiable expression and can not be aggregated with of monetary estimates by traditional methods. Though they need to be taken into account in investment calculations to analyze the social effectiveness of the proposed regional investment projects. This comprehensive approach will allow more accurate to consider and estimate all aspects of economic efficiency, and hence identify the most important and priority projects for the development of the state subject.

For the involvement of qualitative categories to the computational process it is proposed to use verbal model for the estimation of investment projects. By their nature, qualitative categories are semistructured or unstructured, i.e. such, which is known only by their belonging to a particular type. For example, qualitative data can be specified as interval $x \in [x^{\min}, x^{\max}]$ or in the form of statements such as "x is close to 7", i.e. in the form of fuzzy sets. Therefore, to conduct a comprehensive analysis of the project including and its socio-economic component it is proposed to use the Soft Computing technology, where criteria are adequate described by representation in the form of fuzzy sets.

Moreover, analysis of investment projects under uncertainty is based on the verbal (fuzzy), sometimes conflicting expert information, i.e. under fuzzy informative environment. The results of analysis of solutions obtained by any methods lose their value as the accuracy and validity of the results of calculations can never exceed the accuracy and validity of input data [1].

2. Problem definition

Estimating the effectiveness of regional projects allows the regional authorities to judge at what cost goals are achieved [2]. Therefore, the regional authorities should estimate the cost-effectiveness of submitted regional investment projects and carry out selection of the best of them. A more specific formulation of this problem may have different interpretations – depending on the scheduled goals for regional socio-economic development, the amount of finance, the propensity of regional authorities to risk, the environment and possible predictions for the future.

The task of the managers of regional authorities in Azerbaijan is to choose the most rational investment project under limited amount of public investment, and they must be guided by a system of estimation criteria approved by the

Decision of the Supervisory Board of the National Fund of Entrepreneurship Support (hereinafter Fund) in the Azerbaijan Republic [3]. Added to this is that the personally managers of regional authorities as public officials are not prone to high risk and have a sober judgment about possible future trends in the regional socio-economic development. In this case, the rational choice is associated with a desire to obtain a solution which is characterized by reasonable estimates for all of the criteria, although their relevance to individual managers of regional authorities may be different.

3. Performance criteria of investment projects and the traditional system of numerical score

There are many traditional methods for determining the efficiency of investment projects based on the use of different systems of estimation criteria [4], which, though adapted to the specific territorial conditions, but on a large scale do not differ from each other. In particular, for estimating the effectiveness of investment projects realized in Azerbaijan, the Fund recommends the authorized credit institutions to use the following specification of estimate criteria [3]:

1. Adequacy of investment project to the current state economic policy and the priorities established by the Fund.
2. Adequacy to minimum requirements for the preparation of the project.
3. Planned manufacturing technique of products (or services).
4. The regional relevance of investment project.
5. Innovation, manufacturing of import-substituting goods and export-oriented goods.
6. Economic performance of the investment project.
7. Influence on increasing the competitive environment of planned output of products (or services).
8. The business history (entrepreneurial activity) of enterprise subject.
9. Influence of the investment project on the social, cultural, and ecological environments.
10. Creating new jobs provided the investment project.

Each of these criteria has its own components – sub-criteria based on which, in fact, estimates the project. On the score for each sub-criteria it is estimated the general score for correspondent criterion. In Table 1 shows a fragment of such scoring projects on the first criterion.

Specified criteria of the commercial and fiscal performance reflects the economic interests of the regional authorities about the correlation of cost and results, and are expressed in money equivalent, while the estimation criteria of general, normative-legal, and, in particular, the indicators of social effectiveness reflect the qualitative aspects of the investment project, including rise of income, improving of working conditions and ecology, increasing the number of jobs in the region and other social outcomes that, ultimately, improve the quality of life or, in other words, human capital [5].

Table 1. Estimation of investment projects by first criterion

Estimation criteria of investment projects						
Adequacy of investment project to the current state economic policy and the priorities established by the Fund						
Sub-criteria	Score and estimate terms					
	0 – inadequacy fully	**1** – inadequacy	**2** – adequacy partly	**3** – adequacy	**4** – adequacy fully	Σ
Adequacy to Executive Order and Directions of the President of AR, as well as Goal-Oriented State Programs of Development						
Adequacy to the priority areas of economic sectors						
Adequacy to the priority areas of economic regions						
Role in the implementation of state economic policy and achieving regional stability						
Adequacy to the traditional professional skills						
Total:						

However, it should be noted that in order to make the final decision on the choice of the investment project methodologically very difficult to carry out a comprehensive assessment of financial, economic and social (socially important) solutions, as traditional mathematical methods it is difficult to aggregate estimates for all indicators. Recommended in [3] system of numerical score of estimation is subjective and depends entirely on the level of competence of the appraiser – the manager of regional authorities. Therefore, it is proposed to use fuzzy models realized by mechanism of fuzzy inference, which can significantly increase the objectivity of the assessments and make the process of alternative choosing of investment project more substantiated.

4. Point estimate of fuzzy alternative inferences

Consider the problem of a point estimate of alternatives under information environment of the fuzzy reasoning on the base of preferences of responsible person of decision-making. To solve it we use the following methods of fuzzy inference [6].

Let U be a set of alternatives, and $\tilde{A}$ be its fuzzy subset. Belonging of the elements of U to $\tilde{A}$ is defined by the values from [0;1] of corresponding membership function. Assume that the fuzzy set $\widetilde{A}_{ji}^{k}$ describes the j-th value (term) of linguistic variable x_i^k – i-th sub-criteria k-th criterion (k = 1 ÷ 10). Then, for example, for a first criterion the set of solutions (alternatives) can be characterized by the set of values of linguistic variables (sub-criteria) x_i^1 (i=1÷5), in particular, by term "ADEQUACY PARTLY" of linguistic variable x_2^1=*Adequacy to the priority areas of economic sectors*, or by term "ADEQUACY FULLY" of linguistic variable x_5^1=*Adequacy to the traditional professional skills.*

The bounded aggregate of linguistic variables (criteria) taking similar values can characterize the representations of decision maker about the degree of satisfactory of considered alternatives for the selected criteria. Then, assuming S=*satisfactory* (of project) as a linguistic variable, the typical implicative rule can be introduced, such as:

"If x_2=ADEQUACY PARTLY and x_5=ADEQUACY, then S=SATISFACTORY".

In general, the p-th (p=1÷q) implicative reasoning of decision maker on the selected k-th criterion can be summarized as follows:

$$e_p^k : \text{"If } x_1^k = \widetilde{A}_{j1}^k \text{ and } x_2^k = \widetilde{A}_{j2}^k \text{ and ... and } x_5^k = \widetilde{A}_{j5}^k \text{, then } S = \widetilde{B}_t^k \text{"}. \quad (1)$$

The next step is finding the intersection of fuzzy sets in the left-hand sides of rules: $(x^k = \widetilde{A}^k) = (x_1^k = \widetilde{A}_{j1}^k) \cap (x_2^k = \widetilde{A}_{j2}^k) \cap ... \cap (x_5^k = \widetilde{A}_{j5}^k)$. As is known, in the discrete case the operation of intersection of fuzzy sets is determined by finding the minimum of the corresponding values of its membership functions, i.e.

$$\mu_{\widetilde{A}^k}(v) = \min_{v \in V}(\mu_{\widetilde{A}_{j1}^k}(u_1), \mu_{\widetilde{A}_{j2}^k}(u_2), ..., \mu_{\widetilde{A}_{j5}^k}(u_5)), \quad (2)$$

where $V=U_1 \times U_2 \times \ldots \times U_5$; $v=(u_1,u_2,\ldots,u_5)$; $\mu_{\widetilde{A}_{jr}^k}(u_r)$ is degree of membership of element u_r (r=1÷5) to fuzzy set $\widetilde{A}_{ir}^k$. Then the expression (1) can be represented in more compact form:

$$e_p^k : \text{"If } x^k = \widetilde{A}^k \text{, then } S = \widetilde{B}_t^k \text{"}. \quad (3)$$

In order to generalize the designated expressions denote basis sets U and V in the form of W. Then respectively $\tilde{A}^k$ will be fuzzy subset of the basis set W, and $\widetilde{B}_t^k$ – fuzzy subset of the unit interval I=[0,1]. These rules are realized by the operation of implication. In our notation, we choose the Lukasiewicz's implication as follows:

$$\mu_{\widetilde{H}}(w,i) = \min_{w\in W}(1, 1-\mu_{\widetilde{A}^k}(w) + \mu_{\widetilde{B}_t^k}(i)), \tag{4}$$

where $\widetilde{H}$ is a fuzzy subset on the $W\times I$; $w\in W$ and $i\in I$.

Similarly, the reasoning (rules) $e_1, e_2, \ldots, e_q$ are transposed into the corresponding fuzzy sets: $\widetilde{H}_1, \widetilde{H}_2, \ldots, \widetilde{H}_q$. In this case, denoting them product as $\widetilde{D} = \widetilde{H}_1 \cap \widetilde{H}_2 \cap \ldots \cap \widetilde{H}_q$ for each pair $(w,i)\in W\times I$ we obtain:

$$\mu_{\widetilde{D}}(w,i) = \min_{w\in W}(\mu_{\widetilde{H}_j}(w,i)),\ (j=1\div q). \tag{5}$$

Then, the conclusion about satisfactory of alternative described by fuzzy set $\tilde{A}$ in W one can define by compositional rule:

$$\widetilde{G} = \widetilde{A} \circ \widetilde{D}, \tag{6}$$

where $\hat{G}$ is fuzzy subset of unit interval I. Finally, we have:

$$\mu_{\widetilde{G}}(i) = \max_{w\in W}(\min \mu_{\widetilde{A}}(w), \mu_{\widetilde{D}}(w,i)). \tag{7}$$

A comparison of alternatives is carried out on the base their point estimates. With this purpose in the beginning for the fuzzy subsets $\hat{C}\subset I$ is defined α-level sets ($\alpha\in[0;1]$) in the form of $C_\alpha = \{i | \mu_{\widetilde{C}}(i) \geq \alpha, i \in I\}$. Then, for each of them it is defined the mean values of the corresponding elements $M(C_\alpha)$. In general, for the set consisting of n elements,

$$M(C_\alpha) = \sum_{j=1}^{n} i_j / n;\ i\in C_\alpha. \tag{8}$$

As a result, point estimate of a fuzzy set (alternatives) $\widetilde{C}$ can be obtained from:

$$F(\widetilde{C}) = \frac{1}{\alpha_{\max}} \int_0^{\alpha_{\max}} M(C_\alpha) d\alpha, \tag{9}$$

where $\alpha_{\max}$ is maximum value on the $\widetilde{C}$.

5. An example of a typical verbal model for the estimation of investment projects

To criterion estimate of investment projects effectiveness are proposed to use appropriate verbal model, which assumes that the sub-criteria are ranked according to the degree of their importance (according to their numbering), and the degree of importance decreases with increasing the order number. In particular, the first criterion (adequacy of investment project to the current state economic policy and the priorities established by the Fund), corresponding verbal model is as follow:

R1: If the investment project adequacies to Executive Order and Directions of the President of AR, as well as Goal-Oriented State Programs of Development, priority directions in the economic sectors and economic regions, then it is satisfactory;

R2: If in addition to the above requirements the project means in the realization of state economic policy and achieving regional stability, then it is more than satisfactory;

R3: If in addition to the conditions of R2 the investment project adequacies to the traditional professional skills, then it is perfect;

R4: If the investment project adequacies to Executive Order and Directions of the President of AR, as well as Goal-Oriented State Programs of Development, priority directions in the economic sectors and economic regions and adequacies to the traditional professional skills, then it is very satisfactory;

R5: If the investment project adequacies to Executive Order and Directions of the President of AR, as well as Goal-Oriented State Programs of Development, priority directions in the economic regions and adequacies to the traditional professional skills, but inadequacies to priority directions in the economic sectors, then it is just the same satisfactory;

R6: If the investment project inadequacies to Executive Order and Directions of the President of AR, as well as Goal-Oriented State Programs of Development, and inadequacies to priority directions in the economic regions, then it is unsatisfactory.

As examples, we chose six investment projects with different profiles including in volume of required investment resources: 2 small (up to $100,000.00); 2 middle (from $100,000.00 to $1,000,000.00), and 2 large (over $1,000,000.00). Concise description of these projects is given in [7].

Thus, taking into account the above data on the criteria and the alternative projects, as well as on the basis of formulated for each case verbal models solve the assigned tasks.

6. Estimation of investment projects by first criterion (adequacy of investment project to the current state economic policy and the priorities established by the Fund)

Appropriate typical verbal model provides a multicriteria estimation of alternatives, where the criteria are linguistic variables: X_1 – *adequacy* (to decrees); X_2 – *adequacy* (to direction by sector); X_3 – *adequacy* (to direction by economical region); X_4 – a role (in the implementation of state economic policy and achieving regional stability); X_5 – *adequacy* (to the traditional professional skills); Y – satisfactory. To adapt this verbal model define the possible values (terms) of these linguistic variables, which will be used to estimate the projects by following scenario:

R1: If X_1=REQUIRED and X_2=APPROPRIATE and X_3=SUFFICIENT, then Y=SATISFACTORY;

R2: If X_1=REQUIRED and X_2=APPROPRIATE and X_3=SUFFICIENT and X_4=APPRECIABLE, then Y=MORE THAN SATISFACTORY;

R3: If X_1=REQUIRED and X_2=APPROPRIATE and X_3=SUFFICIENT and X_4=APPRECIABLE и X_5=ОРГАНИЧНОЕ, then Y=PERFECT;

R4: If X_1=REQUIRED and X_2=APPROPRIATE and X_3=SUFFICIENT and X_5=DOMINATING, then Y=VERY SATISFACTORY;

R5: If X_1=REQUIRED and X_2=INAPPROPRIATE and X_3=SUFFICIENT and X_5=DOMINATING, then Y=SATISFACTORY;

R6: If X_1=INADEQUASY and X_3=INSUFFICIENT, then Y=UNSATISFACTORY.

We define a variable Y on a discrete set $J=\{0;0.1;0.2;\ldots;1\}$, and its terms, describe by fuzzy sets with corresponding membership functions:

- $\widetilde{S}$ =SATISFACTORY: $\mu_{\widetilde{S}}(x) = x,\ x \in J$;
- $M\widetilde{S}$ =MORE THAN SATISFACTORY: $\mu_{M\widetilde{S}}(x) = \sqrt{x},\ x \in J$;
- $\widetilde{P}$ =PERFECT: $\mu_{\widetilde{P}}(x) = 1$ with $x=1$ and $\mu_{\widetilde{P}}(x) = 0$ with $x<1$ ($x \in J$);
- $V\widetilde{S}$ =VERY SATISFACTORY: $\mu_{V\widetilde{S}}(x) = x^2,\ x \in J$;
- $U\widetilde{S}$ =UNSATISFACTORY: $\mu_{U\widetilde{S}}(x) = 1 - x,\ x \in J$.

In view of the fact that the chosen example considers six investment projects the estimation will be carried out on a finite set of alternatives $U=\{u_1,u_2,u_3,u_4,u_5,u_6\}$. In this case, U is the support vector on the base of which there are described the terms of input characteristics by correspondent fuzzy sets. Obviously, the number of its components is determined by number of the estimated alternative projects. Such approach allows to adapt the semantic content of terms and estimation to the relevant information.

Assume that on the base sub-criteria of the first criterion the corresponding indicators of investment projects are estimated by five experts in the subject area thought the instrumentality of a numerical score system. Their average values are ordered in the Table 3.

Table 3. Average estimations of projects indicators relative to sub-criteria of the 1st criterion

Symbolic notation	Adequacy to Executive Order and Directions of the President of AR, as well as Goal-Oriented State Programs of Development	Adequacy to the priority areas of economic sectors	Adequacy to the priority areas of economic regions	Role in the implementation of state economic policy and achieving regional stability	Adequacy to the traditional professional skills
	$\tilde{A}_1$ (REQUIRED)	$\tilde{A}_2$ (APPROPRIATE)	$\tilde{A}_3$ (SUFFICIENT)	$\tilde{A}_4$ (APPRECIABLE)	$\tilde{A}_5$ (DOMINATING)
u_1	3.60	3.40	3.40	2.80	1.00
u_2	2.80	3.00	3.20	3.40	3.80
u_3	3.40	3.80	3.60	3.60	4.00
u_4	3.00	3.40	3.80	3.80	4.00
u_5	2.00	2.80	2.40	3.20	3.80
u_6	3.20	3.20	3.60	3.20	3.80

Then, based on these values one can construct the fuzzy sets $\tilde{A}_k$ (k=1÷5) of considered six criteria on the support vector $U=\{u_1,u_2,u_3,u_4,u_5,u_6\}$ with the corresponding Gaussian membership functions $\mu_{\tilde{X}_k}(t)=\exp\left(-(t-4)^2/\sigma_k^2\right)$, where σ_k is the density of scattering which select subject to the priority of the corresponding sub-criteria. It should be noted that the configuration of the Gaussian membership functions, as, properly, a set of rules can be adapted by experts to various conditions. If it was necessary to find the absolute (optimal) estimations of the investment projects, then it should be used, for example, Neural Network based Fuzzy Inference System [8]. In our case, estimation of the project for each sub-criteria is calculated in accordance with the value of corresponding Gaussian function from [0;1]. For example, estimate u_1 by first sub-criteria will be $\mu_{\tilde{X}_1}(3.6)=0.9314$.

Thus, with σ_1=1.5, σ_2=1.75, σ_3=2, σ_4=2.25 and σ_5=2.5 adopted sub-criteria will be as follows:

- REQUIRE (adequacy to Executive Order and Directions of the President of AR ...):

$$\tilde{A}_1=\frac{0.9314}{u_1}+\frac{0.5273}{u_2}+\frac{0.8521}{u_3}+\frac{0.6412}{u_4}+\frac{0.1690}{u_5}+\frac{0.7524}{u_6};$$

- APPROPRIATE (adequacy to the priority areas of economic sectors):

$$\widetilde{A}_2 = \frac{0.8891}{u_1} + \frac{0.7214}{u_2} + \frac{0.9870}{u_3} + \frac{0.8891}{u_4} + \frac{0.6249}{u_5} + \frac{0.8114}{u_6};$$

- SUFFICIENT (adequacy to the priority areas of economic regions):

$$\widetilde{A}_3 = \frac{0.9139}{u_1} + \frac{0.8521}{u_2} + \frac{0.9608}{u_3} + \frac{0.9900}{u_4} + \frac{0.5273}{u_5} + \frac{0.9608}{u_6};$$

- APPRECIABLE (role in the implementation of state economic policy and …):

$$\widetilde{A}_4 = \frac{0.7524}{u_1} + \frac{0.9314}{u_2} + \frac{0.9689}{u_3} + \frac{0.9921}{u_4} + \frac{0.8812}{u_5} + \frac{0.8812}{u_6};$$

- DOMINATING (adequacy to the traditional professional skills):

$$\widetilde{A}_5 = \frac{0.2369}{u_1} + \frac{0.9936}{u_2} + \frac{1}{u_3} + \frac{1}{u_4} + \frac{0.9936}{u_5} + \frac{0.9936}{u_6}.$$

Based on these fuzzy formalisms fuzzy rules are formulated as:

R1: If $X_1=\tilde{A}_1$ and $X_2=\tilde{A}_2$ and $X_3=\tilde{A}_3$, then $Y=\widetilde{S}$;
R2: If $X_1=\tilde{A}_1$ and $X_2=\tilde{A}_2$ and $X_3=\tilde{A}_3$ and $X_4=\tilde{A}_4$, then $Y=\widetilde{MS}$;
R3: If $X_1=\tilde{A}_1$ and $X_2=\tilde{A}_2$ and $X_3=\tilde{A}_3$ and $X_4=\tilde{A}_4$ and $X_5=\tilde{A}_5$, then $Y=\widetilde{P}$;
R4: If $X_1=\tilde{A}_1$ and $X_2=\tilde{A}_2$ and $X_3=\tilde{A}_3$ and $X_5=\tilde{A}_5$, then $Y=\widetilde{VS}$;
R5: If $X_1=\tilde{A}_1$ and $X_2=\neg\tilde{A}_2$ and $X_3=\tilde{A}_3$ and $X_5=\tilde{A}_5$, then $Y=\widetilde{S}$;
R6: If $X_1=\neg\tilde{A}_1$ and $X_3=\neg\tilde{A}_3$, then $Y=\widetilde{US}$.

Next, for the left sides of these rules on the basis of Eq. (2) we compute grades of membership: $\mu_{\widetilde{M}_i}(a)$ (i=1÷6), and represent the rules in the more compact form:

R1: If $X=\widetilde{M}_1$, then $Y=\widetilde{S}$,

$$\widetilde{M}_1 = \frac{0.8891}{u_1} + \frac{0.5273}{u_2} + \frac{0.8521}{u_3} + \frac{0.6412}{u_4} + \frac{0.1690}{u_5} + \frac{0.7524}{u_6};$$

R2 If $X=\widetilde{M}_2$, then $Y=\widetilde{MS}$,

$$\widetilde{M}_2 = \frac{0.7524}{u_1} + \frac{0.5273}{u_2} + \frac{0.8521}{u_3} + \frac{0.6412}{u_4} + \frac{0.1690}{u_5} + \frac{0.7524}{u_6};$$

R3 If $X=\widetilde{M}_3$, then $Y=\widetilde{P}$,

$$\widetilde{M}_3 = \frac{0.2369}{u_1} + \frac{0.5273}{u_2} + \frac{0.8521}{u_3} + \frac{0.6412}{u_4} + \frac{0.1690}{u_5} + \frac{0.7524}{u_6};$$

R4 If $X=\widetilde{M}_4$, then $Y=\widetilde{VS}$,

$$\widetilde{M}_4 = \frac{0.2369}{u_1} + \frac{0.5273}{u_2} + \frac{0.8521}{u_3} + \frac{0.6412}{u_4} + \frac{0.1690}{u_5} + \frac{0.7524}{u_6};$$

R5 If $X=\widetilde{M}_5$, then $Y=\widetilde{S}$,

$$\widetilde{M}_5 = \frac{0.1109}{u_1} + \frac{0.2786}{u_2} + \frac{0.0130}{u_3} + \frac{0.1109}{u_4} + \frac{0.1690}{u_5} + \frac{0.1886}{u_6};$$

R6 If $X = \widetilde{M}_6$, then $Y = U\widetilde{S}$,

$$\widetilde{M}_6 = \frac{0.0686}{u_1} + \frac{0.1479}{u_2} + \frac{0.0392}{u_3} + \frac{0.01}{u_4} + \frac{0.4727}{u_5} + \frac{0.0392}{u_6}.$$

To convert these rules we use Lukasiewicz's implication (4). Then, for each pair $(u,j) \in U \times Y$ on $U \times Y$ we obtain the following fuzzy relation:

$R_1=$

	0	0.1	0.2	0.3	0.4	0.5	0.6	0.7	0.8	0.9	1
u_1	0,1109	0,2109	0,3109	0,4109	0,5109	0,6109	0,7109	0,8109	0,9109	1	1
u_2	0,4727	0,5727	0,6727	0,7727	0,8727	0,9727	1	1	1	1	1
u_3	0,1479	0,2479	0,3479	0,4479	0,5479	0,6479	0,7479	0,8479	0,9479	1	1
u_4	0,3588	0,4588	0,5588	0,6588	0,7588	0,8588	0,9588	1	1	1	1
u_5	0,8310	0,9310	1	1	1	1	1	1	1	1	1
u_6	0,2476	0,3476	0,4476	0,5476	0,6476	0,7476	0,8476	0,9476	1,0000	1	1

$R_2=$

	0	0.1	0.2	0.3	0.4	0.5	0.6	0.7	0.8	0.9	1
u_1	0,2476	0,5638	0,6948	0,7953	0,8800	0,9547	1	1	1	1	1
u_2	0,4727	0,7889	0,9199	1	1	1	1	1	1	1	1
u_3	0,1479	0,4641	0,5951	0,6956	0,7803	0,8550	0,9225	0,9845	1	1	1
u_4	0,3588	0,6750	0,8060	0,9065	0,9913	1	1	1	1	1	1
u_5	0,8310	1	1	1	1	1	1	1	1	1	1
u_6	0,2476	0,5638	0,6948	0,7953	0,8800	0,9547	1	1	1	1	1

$R_3=$

	0	0.1	0.2	0.3	0.4	0.5	0.6	0.7	0.8	0.9	1
u_1	0,7631	0,7631	0,7631	0,7631	0,7631	0,7631	0,7631	0,7631	0,7631	0,7631	1
u_2	0,4727	0,4727	0,4727	0,4727	0,4727	0,4727	0,4727	0,4727	0,4727	0,4727	1
u_3	0,1479	0,1479	0,1479	0,1479	0,1479	0,1479	0,1479	0,1479	0,1479	0,1479	1
u_4	0,3588	0,3588	0,3588	0,3588	0,3588	0,3588	0,3588	0,3588	0,3588	0,3588	1
u_5	0,8310	0,8310	0,8310	0,8310	0,8310	0,8310	0,8310	0,8310	0,8310	0,8310	1
u_6	0,2476	0,2476	0,2476	0,2476	0,2476	0,2476	0,2476	0,2476	0,2476	0,2476	1

$R_4=$

	0	0.1	0.2	0.3	0.4	0.5	0.6	0.7	0.8	0.9	1
u_1	0,7631	0,7731	0,8031	0,8531	0,9231	1	1	1	1	1	1
u_2	0,4727	0,4827	0,5127	0,5627	0,6327	0,7227	0,8327	0,9627	1	1	1
u_3	0,1479	0,1579	0,1879	0,2379	0,3079	0,3979	0,5079	0,6379	0,7879	0,9579	1
u_4	0,3588	0,3688	0,3988	0,4488	0,5188	0,6088	0,7188	0,8488	0,9988	1	1
u_5	0,8310	0,8410	0,8710	0,9210	0,9910	1	1	1	1	1	1
u_6	0,2476	0,2576	0,2876	0,3376	0,4076	0,4976	0,6076	0,7376	0,8876	1	1

$R_5=$

	0	0.1	0.2	0.3	0.4	0.5	0.6	0.7	0.8	0.9	1
u_1	0,8891	0,9891	1	1	1	1	1	1	1	1	1
u_2	0,7214	0,8214	0,9214	1	1	1	1	1	1	1	1
u_3	0,9870	1	1	1	1	1	1	1	1	1	1
u_4	0,8891	0,9891	1	1	1	1	1	1	1	1	1
u_5	0,8310	0,9310	1	1	1	1	1	1	1	1	1
u_6	0,8114	0,9114	1	1	1	1	1	1	1	1	1

$R_6=$

	0	0.1	0.2	0.3	0.4	0.5	0.6	0.7	0.8	0.9	1
u_1	1	1	1	1	1	1	1	1	1	1	0,9314
u_2	1	1	1	1	1	1	1	1	1	0,9521	0,8521
u_3	1	1	1	1	1	1	1	1	1	1	0,9608
u_4	1	1	1	1	1	1	1	1	1	1	0,9900
u_5	1	1	1	1	1	1	0,9273	0,8273	0,7273	0,6273	0,5273
u_6	1	1	1	1	1	1	1	1	1	1	0,9608

As a result of the intersection of the relations $R_1, R_2, \ldots, R_6$ finally obtain the general functional solution:

R =

	0	0.1	0.2	0.3	0.4	0.5	0.6	0.7	0.8	0.9	1
u_1	0,1109	0,2109	0,3109	0,4109	0,5109	0,6109	0,7109	0,7631	0,7631	0,7631	0,9314
u_2	0,4727	0,4727	0,4727	0,4727	0,4727	0,4727	0,4727	0,4727	0,4727	0,4727	0,8521
u_3	0,1479	0,1479	0,1479	0,1479	0,1479	0,1479	0,1479	0,1479	0,1479	0,1479	0,9608
u_4	0,3588	0,3588	0,3588	0,3588	0,3588	0,3588	0,3588	0,3588	0,3588	0,3588	0,9900
u_5	0,8310	0,8310	0,8310	0,8310	0,8310	0,8310	0,8310	0,8273	0,7273	0,6273	0,5273
u_6	0,2476	0,2476	0,2476	0,2476	0,2476	0,2476	0,2476	0,2476	0,2476	0,2476	0,9608

Apply described in Sec. 4 procedure for obtaining numerical estimates for each of the considered investment projects. So, for the first project u_1 we have the estimate in the form of fuzzy sets (1st row of the output matrix):

$$\widetilde{\mathbf{E}}_1 = \frac{0.1109}{0} + \frac{0.2109}{0.1} + \frac{0.3109}{0.2} + \frac{0.4109}{0.3} + \frac{0.5109}{0.4} + \frac{0.6109}{0.5} + \frac{0.7109}{0.6} + \frac{0.7631}{0.7} + \frac{0.7631}{0.8} + \frac{0.7631}{0.9} + \frac{0.9314}{1.0}.$$

In the beginning we compute its α-level sets and correspondent cardinal number $M(E_{j\alpha})$ by Eq. (8):

- for $0<\alpha<0.1109$: $\Delta\alpha=0.1109$, $E_{1\alpha}=\{0;0.1;0.2;0.3;0.4;0.5;0.6;0.7;0.8;0.9;1\}$, $M(E_{1\alpha})=0.50$;
- for $0.1109<\alpha<0.2109$: $\Delta\alpha=0.1$, $E_{1\alpha}=\{0.1;0.2;0.3;0.4;0.5;0.6;0.7;0.8;0.9;1\}$, $M(E_{1\alpha})=0.55$;
- for $0.2109<\alpha<0.3109$: $\Delta\alpha=0.1$, $E_{1\alpha}=\{0.2;0.3;0.4;0.5;0.6;0.7;0.8;0.9;1\}$, $M(E_{1\alpha})=0.60$;
- for $0.3109<\alpha<0.4109$: $\Delta\alpha=0.1$, $E_{1\alpha}=\{0.3;0.4;0.5;0.6;0.7;0.8;0.9;1\}$, $M(E_{1\alpha})=0.65$;
- for $0.4109<\alpha<0.5109$: $\Delta\alpha=0.1$, $E_{1\alpha}=\{0.4;0.5;0.6;0.7;0.8;0.9;1\}$, $M(E_{1\alpha})=0.70$;
- for $0.5109<\alpha<0.6109$: $\Delta\alpha=0.1$, $E_{1\alpha}=\{0.5;0.6;0.7;0.8;0.9;1\}$, $M(E_{1\alpha})=0.75$;
- for $0.6109<\alpha<0.7109$: $\Delta\alpha=0.1$, $E_{1\alpha}=\{0.6;0.7;0.8;0.9;1\}$, $M(E_{1\alpha})=0.80$;
- for $0.7109<\alpha<0.7631$: $\Delta\alpha=0.0522$, $E_{1\alpha}=\{0.7;0.8;0.9;1\}$, $M(E_{1\alpha})=0.85$;
- for $0.7631<\alpha<0.9314$: $\Delta\alpha=0.2205$, $E_{1\alpha}=\{1\}$, $M(E_{1\alpha})=1$.

Further, by Eq. (9) one can find numerical estimate of satisfactory of the first project:

$$F(\widetilde{\mathbf{E}}_1) = \frac{1}{0.9314}\int_0^{0.9314} M(E_{1\alpha})d\alpha = \frac{1}{0.9314}(0.5\cdot 0.1109 + 0.55\cdot 0.1 + 0.6\cdot 0.1 + 0.65\cdot 0.1 + 0.7\cdot 0.1 + 0.75\cdot 0.1 + 0.8\cdot 0.1 + 0.85\cdot 0.0522 + 1\cdot 0.2205) = 0.7311.$$

Similarly define numerical estimate for the remaining projects: for u_2 – 0.7226; for u_3 – 0.9231; for u_4 – 0.8188; for u_5 – 0.4630; for u_6 – 0.8712. The most satisfactory investment project is one that has the highest numerical estimate. In this example, such is the project u_3. In second place is the u_6, the third – u_4, the fourth – u_1, the fifth – u_2 and the sixth – u_5.

Applying this procedure to the realization of verbal models for the estimation of investment projects by other criteria, in the issue one can calculate the numerical estimates for the given set of alternative projects (Table 4).

Table 4. Numerical estimation of investment projects for each criterion separately

Project	Criteria of estimation									
	X_1	X_2	X_3	X_4	X_5	X_6	X_7	X_8	X_9	X_9
u_1	0.7311	0.8750	0.8811	0.4903	0.3464	0.8556	0.7290	0.3317	0.7540	0.7223
u_2	0.7226	0.9253	0.9800	0.4009	0.4957	0.9231	0.9741	0.9019	0.6569	0.5176
u_3	0.9231	0.6307	0.6013	0.5548	0.4996	0.6612	0.6773	0.8284	0.4559	0.5061
u_4	0.8188	0.7414	0.5254	0.5467	0.5200	0.4955	0.6859	0.8681	0.4850	0.5016
u_5	0.4630	0.7489	0.7601	0.4919	0.3912	0.8605	0.4826	0.7981	0.4851	0.5112
u_6	0.8712	0.6118	0.8128	0.6746	0.6341	0.7540	0.6859	0.6743	0.6974	0.6528

7. Comprehensive assessment of investment projects

Now, after we obtained the numerical estimation of projects for each criterion separately, resolve the problem of integrated assessment. For this purpose, as a basic verbal model we choose the following set of typical implication rules that can be easily adapted to different regional conditions, as well as the preferences of the region authorities – responsible for decision making on project selection.

So, as a basis for future model we choose the following reasoning:

R1: "If the project adequacies the current state economic policy and the priorities established by the Fund, and adequacies the minimum requirements for its preparation, and has regional relevance, and also has good performance of economic efficiency, then it is satisfactory";

R2: "If the project is in addition to above requirements provides for using of modern technologies of production (or service), and also influences the strengthening of competitive environment, the development of social, cultural and ecological environments, and provides for the creation of new jobs, then it is more than satisfactory";

R3: "If the project is in addition to the conditions specified in the R2 provides for innovation, manufacturing of import-substituting goods and export-oriented goods, and the business entity has sufficient business experience and is characterized as a partner for its reliability, then it is perfect";

R4: "If the project has everything specified in the R3, except the ability to influence the development of social, cultural and ecological environments, then it is very satisfactory";

R5: "If the project adequacies the minimum requirements for its preparation, and has regional relevance, influences the development of social, cultural and ecological environments, and provides for the creation of new jobs, and also has good performance of economic efficiency, but, meanwhile, do not adequacies the current state economic policy and the priorities established by the Fund, then for all that it is satisfactory";

R6: "If the project do not adequacies the current state economic policy and the priorities established by the Fund, and do not adequacies the minimum requirements for its preparation, and also has no good performance of economic efficiency, then it is unsatisfactory".

To formulate the fuzzy implicative rules it is necessary to adjust the input and output characteristics of the model – the possible values of the corresponding linguistic variables X_k and the degrees of satisfactory project Y. In our case, the rules are as follows:

R1: «If X_1=ADEQUACIES and X_2=ADEQUACIES and X_4=ESSENTIAL and X_6=HIGH, then Y=SATISFACTORY»;

R2: «If X_1=ADEQUACIES and X_2=ADEQUACIES and X_3=MODERN and X_4=ESSENTIAL and X_6=HIGH and X_7=APPRECIABLE and X_9=VISIBLE and X_{10}=SUFFICIENT, then Y=MORE THAN SATISFACTORY»;

R3: «If X_1=ADEQUACIES and X_2=ADEQUACIES and X_3=MODERN and X_4=ESSENTIAL and X_5=PROVIDES и X_6=HIGH and X_7=APPRECIABLE and X_8=HAS and X_9=VISIBLE and X_{10}=SUFFICIENT, then Y=PERFECT»;

R4: «If X_1=ADEQUACIES and X_2=ADEQUACIES and X_3=MODERN and X_4=ESSENTIAL and X_5=PROVIDES and X_6=HIGH and X_7=APPRECIABLE and X_8=HAS and X_{10}=SUFFICIENT, then Y=VERY SATISFACTORY»;

R5: «If X_1=INADEQUATE and X_2=ADEQUACIES and X_4=ESSENTIAL and X_6=HIGH and X_9=VISIBLE, then Y=SATISFACTORY»;

R6: «If X_1=INADEQUATE and X_2=INADEQUATE and X_6=LOW, THEN Y=UNSATISFACTORY».

Terms (values) of the linguistic variable Y are described in Sec. 4, and for fuzzy interpretations of terms of linguistic variables X_k used in the rules take an advantage of numerical estimates of the projects (Table 4) and membership functions: $\mu_{\tilde{X}_k}(t) = \exp\left(-(t-1)^2 / \sigma_k^2\right)(k = \overline{1,10})$, where σ_1=0.35; σ_2=0.4; σ_3=0.45; σ_4=0.5; σ_5=0.55; σ_6=0.35; σ_7=0.6; σ_8=0.65; σ_9=0.7; σ_{10}=0.75. Then, on a bounded set of alternatives $U=\{u_1,u_2,u_3,u_4,u_5,u_6\}$ we have following fuzzy sets:

ADEQUACIES (to the current state economic policy and ...)

$$\tilde{A}_1 = \frac{0.5542}{u_1} + \frac{0.5336}{u_2} + \frac{0.9529}{u_3} + \frac{0.7649}{u_4} + \frac{0.0950}{u_5} + \frac{0.8733}{u_6};$$

ADEQUACIES (to minimum requirements for the preparation ...)

$$\tilde{A}_2 = \frac{0.9070}{u_1} + \frac{0.9657}{u_2} + \frac{0.4264}{u_3} + \frac{0.6584}{u_4} + \frac{0.6743}{u_5} + \frac{0.3899}{u_6};$$

MODERN (manufacturing technique ...)

$$\tilde{A}_3 = \frac{0.9326}{u_1} + \frac{0.9980}{u_2} + \frac{0.4561}{u_3} + \frac{0.3288}{u_4} + \frac{0.7526}{u_5} + \frac{0.8411}{u_6};$$

ESSENTIAL (regional relevance)

$$\tilde{A}_4 = \frac{0.3537}{u_1} + \frac{0.2380}{u_2} + \frac{0.4526}{u_3} + \frac{0.4396}{u_4} + \frac{0.3561}{u_5} + \frac{0.6547}{u_6};$$

PROVIDES (innovation, manufacturing of ...)

$$\tilde{A}_5 = \frac{0.2436}{u_1} + \frac{0.4314}{u_2} + \frac{0.4370}{u_3} + \frac{0.4669}{u_4} + \frac{0.2937}{u_5} + \frac{0.6424}{u_6};$$

HIGH (indicators of economic performance)

$$\tilde{A}_6 = \frac{0.8435}{u_1} + \frac{0.9529}{u_2} + \frac{0.3918}{u_3} + \frac{0.1252}{u_4} + \frac{0.8531}{u_5} + \frac{0.6102}{u_6};$$

APPRECIABLE (influence on increasing the competitive environment)

$$\tilde{A}_7 = \frac{0.8155}{u_1} + \frac{0.9981}{u_2} + \frac{0.7488}{u_3} + \frac{0.7603}{u_4} + \frac{0.4754}{u_5} + \frac{0.7603}{u_6};$$

HAS (business history ...)

$$\tilde{A}_8 = \frac{0.3475}{u_1} + \frac{0.9775}{u_2} + \frac{0.9327}{u_3} + \frac{0.9597}{u_4} + \frac{0.9080}{u_5} + \frac{0.7780}{u_6};$$

VISIBLE (influence on the social, cultural and ...)

$$\tilde{A}_9 = \frac{0.8838}{u_1} + \frac{0.7864}{u_2} + \frac{0.5465}{u_3} + \frac{0.5820}{u_4} + \frac{0.5821}{u_5} + \frac{0.8296}{u_6};$$

SUFFICIENT (new jobs)

$$\tilde{A}_{10} = \frac{0.8719}{u_1} + \frac{0.6612}{u_2} + \frac{0.6481}{u_3} + \frac{0.6430}{u_4} + \frac{0.6539}{u_5} + \frac{0.8071}{u_6}.$$

By described in Sec. 4 transformations it is obtained the general functional solution of the complex problem of projects estimation as following output matrix:

R =

	0	0.1	0.2	0.3	0.4	0.5	0.6	0.7	0.8	0.9	1
u_1	0,6463	0,7463	0,7564	0,7564	0,7564	0,7564	0,7564	0,7564	0,7564	0,7564	0,9070
u_2	0,7620	0,7620	0,7620	0,7620	0,7620	0,7620	0,7620	0,7620	0,7620	0,7620	0,9657
u_3	0,6082	0,6082	0,6082	0,6082	0,6082	0,6082	0,6082	0,6082	0,6082	0,6082	0,9529
u_4	0,8748	0,8748	0,8748	0,8748	0,8748	0,8748	0,8748	0,8748	0,8748	0,8649	0,7649
u_5	0,6439	0,7439	0,8439	0,9050	0,9050	0,9050	0,9050	0,9050	0,9050	0,9050	0,8531
u_6	0,6101	0,6101	0,6101	0,6101	0,6101	0,6101	0,6101	0,6101	0,6101	0,6101	0,8733

Thus, taking into account the described input and output characteristics of the fuzzy model finally one can obtain comprehensive estimation of alternative investment projects by application of the numerical estimation of fuzzy conclusions (defuzzyfication). Table 5 also shows the cumulative expert estimation by numerical score system (see Table 1).

Table 5. Comprehensive assessment of investment projects

Symbolic notation	Numerical estimation method of fuzzy conclusions	Order	Cumulative expert estimation	Order
u_1	0.5896	4	144.00	3
u_2	0.6055	3	158.60	1
u_3	0.6809	1	140.00	4
u_4	0.4932	6	137.60	5
u_5	0.5238	5	132.00	6
u_6	0.6507	2	150.80	2

As follows from the table 5, the results of eastimation or, more precisely, the ranking of investment projects are the same only for the 2nd project. In other cases the results differ. It is because there is in the multi-criteria estimation of regional investment projects used fuzzy implicative rules take into account the dominance of one over the other criteria.

8. Conclusion

The proposed Methodology is intended to estimate the effectiveness of regional investment projects aspired to budgetary appropriations of the National Investment Fund for Support of Entrepreneurship in Azerbaijan in accordance with established criteria. In other words, this Methodology can be used for the preparation of decisions on assignment the Fund's budgetary appropriations for realization the investment projects.

The most important advantage of the proposed Methodology is its ability to quickly and relatively easily adapted to specific conditions and the requirements and preferences of persons responsible for decision-making about the choice. More specifically – is that the criteria for estimation of investment projects (especially those that are largely subjective) are formulated on the basis of all alternatives, which ultimately increases the objectivity of the choice.

The decision the problem of choice the best investment project by the fuzzy inference method on the selected limited number of alternatives has shown that this method is compared with the numerical score system provides more objective and balanced estimation of the projects. The main reason for the differences of final results of the comprehensive estimation of projects is that the fuzzy conclusion mechanism takes into account the dominance of one over the other criteria, i.e. construction of rules provides to obtain the more balanced profile of the project.

The resulting aggregated numerical estimates of six selected investment projects are not absolute, since used set of linguistic rules and parameters of Gauss membership functions are not optimized. It is not the purpose of this study. On the basis of the proposed Methodology can be efficiently and more objectively rank the investment projects. However, it should be mind that these rules are not purely arbitrary, since their construction assumes dominance the more essential criteria. Eventually, management of each region has the right to select a set of linguistic rules, based on the specifics its region and own preferences.

References

1. http://ecosyn.ru/index.html
2. Мухетдинова Н. Проблемы инвестиционного роста российских регионов // Финансы, Деньги, Инвестиции. 2008. № 1. С. 15.
3. http://www.anfes.gov.az/saffman/show.img.php?id=81
4. Пчелинцев О.С. Региональная экономика в системе устойчивого развития. М.: Наука, 2004. С. 117.
5. Бобылев Г., Кузнецов А., Горбачева Н. Условия и факторы реализации инновационного потенциала региона//Регион: экономика и социология. 2008. № 1. С. 117.
6. Рзаев Р.Р. Нейро-нечёткое моделирование экономического поведения. Verlag: LAP Lambert Academic Publishing GmbH & Co. KG, 2012, 104 с.
7. http://www.anfes.gov.az
8. Lin C.T., George Lee C.S. Supervised and Unsupervised Learning with Fuzzy Similarity for Neural Network – Based Fuzzy Logic Control Systems. Fuzzy Sets, Neural Networks, and Soft Computing/Edited by Yager R.R., L.A. Zadeh. New York: Van Nostrand Reinhold, 1994, pp. 85-125.

SUSTAINABILITY: A CONTRADICTORY CONCEPT

JOSE DANIEL BARQUERO CABRERO
Professor Researcher of the European Superior Council of Doctors & D.H.C., Girona, 24
Barcelona, 08010, Spain

MANUEL MEDINA ELIOZONDO
Research and Post Grade Coordinator, Universidad Autónoma de Cohauila
25280 Cohauila, México

JOSE LUÍS SOLÍS GONZÁLEZ
Professor Researcher, Universidad Autónoma de Cohauila
25280 Cohauila, México

CARMEN FATIMA BARQUERO
Professor Researcher, ESERP University Foundation (F.U.E.)
07004 Palma de Mallorca, Spain

Abstract

Contemporary human societies face with perplexity and lack of fundamental solutions challenges represented by current sustainability crisis, in the context of increasing economic and social inequalities in despite of the expansion and deepening of market logic on a global scale, unprecedented in humankind history. That has challenged not only our perceptions about the benefits of economic growth and capitalism, but also about the capacity of planet to absorb damage inflicted by humankind "ecological footprint". Over recent decades, various debates about *sustainability* and *sustainable development* have developed, but they finally failed to address the problem of sustainability from an organic and holistic perspective. An alternative approach allows the characterization of the (lack of) sustainability as an historical and structural phenomenon that opposes society as a whole to a system based on an unbridled pursuit of profit.

1. Introduction

In the economic, social and political contemporary context, the issue of sustainability has become in vogue and at the center of debate.[*] Conspicuous representatives of the *status quo*, as well as detractors, seem to be deeply concerned not only about the problems of ecological deterioration, but also about aspects related to the lack of economic and social sustainability prevalent in modern societies.[†] Regardless of the sign of their ideologies and their belonging to different economic systems and political regimes, the various contemporary human societies face with perplexity and lack of fundamental solutions challenges represented by resources depletion, air, soil and water pollution, destruction of ecosystems and global warming phenomenon. All this happening in the context of increasing economic and social inequalities, despite of expansion and deepening of market logic on a global scale, unprecedented in humanity history.

Thus, the sustainability discourse has been appropriated not only by the 'green' parties or environmental organizations like *Greenpeace*, but also by national governments and global agencies guarantors of international establishment. Apparently, there seems to be a common concern for saving the planet from self-destruction, after decades of rampant ecological degradation as a result of the quest for finding a social welfare allegedly deriving from economic growth.[‡]

2. Growth, Industrialization and Global Capitalism Crisis

Particularly in the postwar period, industrialization at all costs became the *leitmotif* of governments on a global scale, regardless of their different political ideologies. The phase of capitalist expansion sustained on the emergency of "Fordist" mode of regulation[§] in main central economies, radiated its effects not only economic but also political and ideological to the peripheral economies of underdeveloped capitalism, leading to the flowering of "developmentalist" ideology[**] and to the setting up of a series of public policies based on the state

---

[*] See the work of Foladori and Tomassino (2000).

[†] Leff, E. (1998). *Saber Ambiental: Sustentabilidad, racionalidad, complejidad, poder*, Mexico: Siglo XXI Ed. and PNUMA.

[‡] On the appropriation of sustainable development discourse by international agencies and individual governments, see Riechmann, Naredo et al (1995).

[§] See in this respect Aglietta (1976) and Boyer (1979).

[**] For a critique of "developmentalist" ideology, see Rodriguez (1980).

intervention in the economy.[*] All this made with the purpose of promoting and, in some cases, of creating the conditions for the widespread of trade and monetary relations by means of a deliberated industrialization under the state protection.[†] In the Latin American case, this gave rise to a form of peripheral capitalism based on what some authors call a "late and subordinated" industrialization model (Orive y Cordera, 1970), conducted under the tutelary presence of state and under the ECLAC's political and ideological orientation,[‡] as a way to bring Latin American economies with lower relative backwardness to economic progress and modernization of its societies according to the Western model.

However, after the wave of optimism raised by the "Keynesian spring" in the Western world and by the so-called "real socialism" in Eastern Europe, the world capitalism crisis in the seventies and the collapse of Soviet bloc in the eighties opened an era of pessimism and puzzlement. That has challenged not only our perceptions about the benefits of economic growth and capitalism, but also about the capacity of planet to absorb the damage inflicted by humankind "ecological footprint".[§] Both in the center and in the periphery of global capitalist system, the crisis widespread because of decline in industrial productivity (and consequent general rate of profit slow down), the bankruptcy of the international financial system created at Breton Woods and the external debt crisis of main Latin American economies such as Mexico. The advent of neoliberal policies in the eighties and the dictates of Washington Consensus in the nineties, with its claim for the creation of a single global market and realization of total capitalism utopia,[**] have aggravated the ecological, social and economic sustainability crisis that is living the contemporary world.

3. The Terms of Debate on Sustainability

However, for several decades there has been a wide range of perceptions and proposals around sustainable development or, if you prefer at this very moment, about *sustainability*, which makes us wonder about the intimate nature

[*] For a deliberate policy of the State in favor of industrialization at all costs, see Pinto (1975).

[†] See in this respect the work of Salama (1976).

[‡] See the pioneering work of Prebisch (1962) and the Tavares and Serra's work (1971), to mention only the most representative authors on this matter.

[§] See Leff (2007), op. cit.

[**] For a critique of Neoliberalism and the "Decalogue" of public policies advocated by the Washington Consensus, see Bustelo (2003).

and the theoretical status of this phenomenon in order to place it in a proper analytical and praxiological perspective. Therefore, we will try to identify the various schools of thought on sustainability in order to analyze critically the viability of their proposals and its relationship with the social interests that represent and advocate. Later, we will move on the elements of an alternative interpretation based on the theory of social forms,* which keeps all its force in light of current transformations of global capitalism, which is experiencing the deepest crisis in its history.

Debate on sustainability has developed following in general the argument lines that define the different paradigms of thinking about the nature of modern societies. Therefore, encompasses a wide range of positions and shades ranging from the most obtuse conservatism to necessary transformation of society as the only path to reach an effective sustainability of collective existence. The debate includes various reformist proposals that approach one or other extreme positions. This seems to obey, of course, to the fact that the sustainability crisis has become a privileged dimension for expressing social antagonisms (Foladori, 1999), which reflects the varied perceptions and ideological representations of social groups according to their particular interests, depending on their place in the existing economic and political power structures.

This ideological prism has been conditioned (though not necessarily in all cases) by the concrete material interests of countries, corporations, international agencies and individuals. This fact largely explains the difficulty to reach a praxiological convergence and a minimum of common goals in the search for sustainability. That happens in despite of the concerns on this matter and the collective belief (at least on the rhetorical plane) on the severity of disaster that looms over the planet due to the lack of sustainability of the current collective modes of life.

The very term *sustainable development* has generated a variety of interpretations that hinder the achievement of a shared understanding and unity of action in the field of collective work and public policy. As rightly pointed out Hopwood, Mellor and O'Brien (2005: 38-52), sustainable development represents a major effort to understand man's relationship with nature and relationships between men themselves, beyond the dominant Western dichotomous thinking based on a clear separation between the environment and

---

* See in this respect the work of Girard (1983).

economic and social problems. However, the lack of a defined and rigorously constructed theoretical statute for this concept has led to abuse and ineffectiveness in the sphere of social practices and even to see it as a logical contradiction: the terms of *sustainable* and *development* would be, by definition, mutually exclusive.*

Thus, over recent decades various debates about *sustainability* and *sustainable development* have developed, which we believe are false or at least insufficient; not so much because its particular content be false, but because they finally have failed to address the problem of sustainability from an organic and holistic perspective. Such is the case of the opposition between "weak" sustainability and "strong" sustainability, centered on the degree of substitution/complementarily between capital and technology vis-à-vis natural resources, as if the problem of lack of sustainability be purely technological (Moran, 1999). This has led to treat environmental issues as mere productive variables, with varying degrees of technical interchangeability among themselves, thereby neglecting the factors related to the lack of economic and social sustainability.

A similar situation exists in the divergent character (and even contradictory one) of the approaches in which predominate environmental concerns and those with a strong emphasis on issues related to equity and economic and social welfare (O ' Riordan, 1989: 77-102). This has led to discuss the different approaches and contributions about sustainability in terms of a double dichotomy. On the one hand, the opposition between the degree of "ecocentrism" or "technocentrism" existing on them and, on the other hand, the opposition between approaches with a complete lack of concern for social and welfare issues and those with such concerns as the core of its argument.

However, despite the many combinations that can be made from these coordinates, the truth is that this type of analysis, even with an undeniable taxonomic value, is insufficient to adequately understand the sustainability crisis that face the modern world. Even the effort for locating the various contributions on sustainable development according to its degree of defense of the *status quo*, and its character reformist or revolutionary, hides at heart a moralist and ahistorical approach that rather than help the understanding of the phenomenon mystifies it, obscuring its understanding.

* See the recent contributions of non-growth theorists, including that of Kempf (2007).

Such is the case of the Brundtland Report,* which gives rise to ambiguity that leads to private companies, governments and global organizations to stand up for sustainable development, without questioning the changes that are necessary to achieve it, especially those that might call into question the current *status quo* and the dominant tangle of vested interests. However, it also is the case with approaches that combine a strong concern for equity and welfare with an equally urgent concern about the increasing environmental degradation, as the currents of social ecology (ecosocialism, ecofeminism), radical ecology, anti-capitalist movement of environmental justice and the group ATTAC.†

4. Towards an Alternative Interpretation of the Sustainability Crisis

Despite its large and obvious ideological and programmatic differences, these "leftist" or "rightist" currents have a common denominator in its approach to sustainability crisis in terms of more or less undesirable and/or avoidable consequences derived of the functioning of market economies. They fail to perceive that this crisis exists *in embryo*, so hidden, in the elementary social form in which modern capitalist society originates, that is to say the merchandise-form. Therefore, it is in the deployment of the antagonism that defines the intimate nature of the merchandise (the contradiction between its *use value* and its *exchange value*), that we can understand the genesis and historical evolution of the contemporary sustainability crisis. This crisis is inseparable from the very genesis and historical evolution of capitalism as the dominant social and economic system on a global scale.

Phenomena such as depletion of natural resources and the increasing deterioration and contamination of soils, forests, air, and waters (including oceans) have certainly rooted in consumerism inherent to a regime of growth based on mass production and the insatiable search for profit. Therefore, in spite of the existing regulations of governments and global organizations on the environment and ecosystems, all collective effort not leading to limit the private use of social richness and its effects on income concentration is doomed to

* See the *Brundtland Report*, United Nations World Commission on Environment and Development, 1987.

† The Association pour la taxation des transactions financières et pour l'action citoyenne (*Association for the Taxation of Financial Transactions and for Citizens' Action*, ATTAC) is an activist organization originally created in France in 1998 for promoting the establishment of a tax on foreign exchange transactions.

failure from the standpoint of the (lack of) sustainability. As it has already been mentioned above, the market economy incessantly reproduces the antagonism that opposes, on the one hand, human activity in capitalist conditions of social production and reproduction and, on the other, nature; that is to say between capitalist economic growth and sustainability. For this very reason, the term "sustainable development" is self-contradictory: by definition, all capitalist development breeds unsustainability, which in some cases mitigates through state interventions carried out under the pressure of social agents involved. Consequently, it is peremptory to promote the organization of society as a collective team in defense of sustainability projects. This alternative approach, of which there are already some elements in several notable contributions,* allows the characterization of the (lack of) sustainability as an historical and structural phenomenon, that does not depend on the goodwill of companies, governments and citizens or on partial actions, whether at global or local level. It opposes society as a whole to a system based on an unbridled pursuit of profit. In this sense, sustainability crisis is located in a privileged dimension of social conflicts. In this approach, *nature* is no longer conceived as opposed to society and subject to be exploited for the enjoyment of a minority of the latter, but as an integral (embedded) part of nature, whose irrational use has catastrophic implications for human life and viability of the planet Earth.†

5. Conclusion

The generalization of the merchandise form associated to the development of contemporary global capitalism has led to sustainability crisis to a situation that many authors define as a non-return point, and that compels us to contemplate it, on a global scale, as a task and an inescapable dimension of social transformation. This forces us to wonder seriously about the very relevance of the concepts of development and social transformation: if we are not able to build new social forms based on equity and social justice, and to restore the original unity between man and nature, perhaps we deserve as a species to disappear from the planet like modern dinosaurs.

---

* See for instance the works of Foladori already cited.

† On the threat of global catastrophe, caused by a lack of sustainability, which looms over the planet, see Kempf (2007), op. cit.

References

Aglietta, M. (1976). *Régulation et crise du capitalisme. L'expérience des Etats-Unis*, Paris : Calmann-Lévy.

Boyer, R. (1979). "La crise actuelle : une mise au point en perspective historique. Quelques réflexions à partir d'une analyse du capitalisme français en longue période", *Critiques de l'économie politique (nouvelle série),* no. 7-8, april-september, Paris : Maspero, pp. 5-113.

Bustelo, P. (2003). "Desarrollo económico: del Consenso al Post-Consenso de Washington y más allá", in *Estudios en homenaje al profesor Francisco Bustelo*, Madrid: Editorial Complutense.

Foladori, G., and H. Tomassino (2000). "El concepto de desarrollo sustentable treinta años después", in *Desenvolvimento e Meio Ambiente*, no. 1, january/june. Curitiba: UFPR, p. 41-56.

Foladori, G. (1999). "Sustentabilidad ambiental y contradicciones sociales", in *Ambiente & Sociedade*, Ano II, no 5, 2nd semester, Sao Paulo.

Girard, R. (1983). *La violencia y lo sagrado*, Barcelona: Anagrama.

Hopwood, B., M. Mellor and G. O'Brien (2005), "Sustainable Development: Mapping Different Approaches", in *Sustainable Development*, vol. 13, no. 1.

Kempf, H. (2007). *Comment les riches détruisent la planète*, Paris : Ed. du Seuil.

Morán Seminario, H. (1999). "Presupuestos filosóficos del desarrollo sustentable, in *Revista de la Facultad de Ciencias Económicas*, Año V, nº 17, Lima: UNMSM.

O'Riordan, T. (1989), "The Challenge for Environmentalism", in R. Peet and N. Thrift, (ed.). *New Models in Geography*, London: Unwin Hyman.

Pinto, A. (1975), "Política de industrialización", en *América Latina: dependencia y subdesarrollo*, San José: EDUCA.

Prebisch, Raúl (1962), "El desarrollo económico de América Latina y algunos de sus principales problemas", in *Boletín Económico de América Latina*, vol. VII, no. 1, february, Santiago de Chile: CEPAL.

Riechmann, J., J.M. Naredo et al (1995). *De la economía a la ecología*, Madrid: Trotta Ed.

Rodríguez, O. (1980), *La teoría del subdesarrollo de la CEPAL*, México: Siglo XXI.

Salama, Pierre (1976), "Au-delà d'un faux débat : Quelques réflexions sur l'articulation des États-Nations en Amérique Latine", in *Revue Tiers-Monde*, no. 68, Paris.

Tavares, M. C. and J. Serra (1971), "Más allá del estancamiento: una discusión sobre el estilo de desarrollo reciente en Brasil", in *El Trimestre Económico*, núm. 152, México: Fondo de Cultura Económica

THE IMPORTANCE OF SUSTAINABLE MANAGEMENT: A STUDY OF STRATEGIC PLANNING AND RISK MANAGEMENT AS FACTORS OF ENVIRONMENTAL PLANNING

BRUNA BARELA DE SOUZA

Departamento de Ciências Contábeis e Atuariais, Universidade Federal do Rio Grande do Sul (UFRGS), Av. João Pessoa, 52, Porto Alegre, Rio Grande do Sul, 90040-000 – Brasil.

WENDY BEATRIZ HADDAD CARRARO

Departamento de Ciências Contábeis e Atuariais, Universidade Federal do Rio Grande do Sul (UFRGS), Av. João Pessoa, 52, Porto Alegre, Rio Grande do Sul, 90040-000 – Brasil.

This study is aimed at demonstrating the importance of a sustainable management, since non-renewable resources over-exploitation and the occurrence of major environmental disasters from waste generated by companies are placing a change of scene and a deeper awareness of society. The deductive method of approach was used when thinking about the descriptive and bibliographical research. Particular emphasis was placed on strategic planning and risk management, managing tools capable of making it easy for the companies to an environmental politics, addressed to the preservation, the risks reduction and environmental impacts, as fines, legal actions and accidents, entailing damages for companies and for the society. Likewise, the benefits acquired by the companies while acting with sustainability were specified as: to improve the organizational procedures, to reduce waste removal costs and to establish a socially responsible image toward customers and stakeholders, with products that combine design and sustainable marketing. The society expectations regarding socio-environmental responsibility have increased at a greater speed than organization's ability to improve their standards, which does not exempt them from criticism.

1. Introduction

Due to the changing in the world the organizations are prioritizing the environmental issues and on adapting themselves to the socio-environmental liability standards, since they are aware that acting in the environment preservation and recuperation and interacting with the society, beyond what the legislation stipulates, can bring profitable benefits.

Tinoco apud Kraemer [10] emphasizes that many barriers and difficulties must be overcome in order to enable the spread of a business culture for a proper treatment of effectives or potentials environment harms that are arising from economic activities. However, prior observing the managerial mechanisms that assist in environmental issues, it is important to understand the concepts of Sustainability and Environment Accounting, which have a significant influence over the planning and the environment management.

Strategic planning is suitable as an alternative to better align the environmental practices to the organizational structure; and the management of risks is indicated as an option to help risks control and reduction; and the environmental impacts caused by the thoughtless use of natural resources.

2. Sustainable Development and Social Responsibility

For Medeiros, Nogueira and Arruda [12] the definition of sustainable development and its dissemination in the globalized world produced a new understanding of the organizations that, linked to the legal restrictions, began to prepare new strategy. Thus, the concern with the environment has created whole new scenery: the style of managing has been markedly changed and the modern executive must develop analysis and interpretation capacity for social-environment dynamics of the changing with a systemic vision.

Albuquerque [1] emphasizes that the environmental protection turned to be a necessity and at the same time the business source of profit. Donaire [5] completes saying that “the pollution problem has been doing the enterprises re-value their productive process, in order to get cleaned technologies and the re-use of the waste”.

3. The Organizational Changes Imposed by the Environment

According to Albuquerque [1], the advantages of environmental management are the result from rules and pre-determined administrative practices that are working for further reduce the environmental risks of the activity quoted by Dias [4], increasing motivation and satisfaction of its employees. According to Chiavenato [2], “the Management is the primary key solution for most serious problems that beset the modern world”. For him, the difference between developed and undeveloped countries is knowing or not how to administrate the technology and the potential resources that are available.

The environmental management provides new business opportunities, that is to say that windows of opportunities are beginning to open up for those who are already thinking and acting on the environmental issue. Aside from generating new business opportunities, the environmental management may promote the emergence of major technological innovations. To innovate in order to match the regulations can bring compensation: to improve the use of inputs; to create better products and to improve the products results [16].

The time we are living is filled with complexities, transformations, changes and uncertainties and because Oliveira and Silva [14] believe that "the management task for the next decades will be uncertain and challenging and will face multifaceted problems increasingly complexes". In other words, the role of the organizations has been expanded for political and social issues, turning the manager task even more complicated. So, the internal policies are entirely depending on the power of the organization and the decision making and strategic choices processes present an important relationship with the organizational structure.

The strategic decisions, according to Hall [6], are high risk and can lead the enterprise into new markets, and to develop new services, products or to begin with new programs or to end the existent programs and they can also result in installation shut down. Finally, they involve great changes of the organizations.

The ecological theory covers also the further transformations that occur among those organizations that survive the changes. These organizations are able to adapt themselves to environment modifications, allowing them to beat their competitors or, at least to coexist with them. Such adaptations constitute an organizational reassignment [6].

Donaire [5] states that this change in the business environment and the result of its impact in the management has been altering the way the directors manage their business, moreover they lead to change in the definition of the role which society expects them to play. For this author, "the profitability and the company returns are strongly influenced by their capacity of anticipate and react to social and political changes occurring in their business environment. Many companies have been losing a lot of money because they had ignored these trends, which also generate barriers to the institutional image".

4. The Sustainability in the Organizational Environment and the Competitive Advantages Offered by an Environmental Management

Dias [4] notes that, from the last decade of the 20th century XX the human being life quality became the condition for the progress and, for this reason, the sustainable development proposals are based on the perspective of natural resources current use as long as they are preserved for the future generations.

Albuquerque [1] believes that the concept that enables a better understanding of the environmental discussions is the one about sustainable consumption or sustainability, which is connected to the idea of:

The rational use of nature resources;

Respect to the (regenerative) capacity of ecosystem support;

5. Commitment to Future Generations

The awareness of sustainable development, “a guideline for processes that are able to announce a transition of that society to a new one” [1], “is the current debate on the environmental issue in every sector of human activity” [4]. This author presents three dimensions for this development: economical (growth), social (equity) and environmental (preservation). The dynamic balance between the three is necessary and continuous.

Given the rising competition coming from globalization, society is more and more informed and willing to buy and to use products that respect the environment and, according to Albuquerque [1], “the organizations are more and more aware that eco-friendly product sells more and holds the consumer preference”.

Several concepts on sustainable products development approaches has arisen, however all have evinced the identification, reduction and elimination of environmental impacts of a product throughout its life cycle [11]. The cleaner production is, in essence, a sustainable production [7] that can be defined as a production that efficiently uses the resources.

For Dias [4] over the past years the environmental management has secured a prominent position, in terms of competitiveness and according to the benefits that productive process can bring. The concept of environmental excellence is being firming due to these competitive advantages, and it evaluates the industry not only for its productive and economical performance, but also for its performance regarding the environment.

6. The Environment Accounting and the Strategic Planning in the Environment Management

The company needs to establish planning forms in order to use the environmental preservation and the non-renewable natural resource to its advantages. According to Paiva [15], it is the Environmental Accounting that identifies the data and records the environmental events, process and generate information \that subsidize the user and it works as a parameter for the taking decision.

Ribeiro [17] mentions that the Environmental Accounting development results from the need to provide suitable information to the environmental management. Kosztrzepa [8] believes that it will be a management tool, qualified to assess the company environmental performance, because it will provide information related to activities that could damage the environment and also reflect economically and financially in it patrimony. Ferreira apud Tinoco and Kraemer [22] complete that "the accounting will not solve environmental problems, but, against its capacity of providing information, it can forestall several social actors of the severity of the problem, helping in looking for solutions and in taking decision inside the companies".

7. The Advantages of Aligning the Strategic Planning to the Environmental management

The strategic planning projection is "a technique or a methodology that, when applied or submitted by the organization, contributes so that it defines its own purposes, reduces its risks and increases its success opportunities" [14].

The insertion of values, beliefs or tenets associated with environment preservation and sustainable development is important because it functions as standard in the orientation for decisions, guiding the people behavior and avoiding that sense of purpose meets environmental objectives. When the values contained in a culture can not only help the company to adapt the environmental changes, but also being appropriate and strategies supporters, there is great potential to provide superior performance over time [9].

Establishing Strategies to Reach Goals

Every company adapts internal strategies to deal with the pressures coming from its environment [6]. "For environmental management, the administration must establish which politics to adopt, regarding environmental issues and defining strategies to reach those predetermined goals" [5]. One of the most critical strategies to deal with its environments, according to Hall [6], is the attempt of shape its own environment.

Benefits of Adjustment to Environment

Donaire [5] defines which Projection area, together with the environment area, will have to determine the steps that will have to be given regarding the changes in the immediate environment, which will demand adaptation of the organization concerning the future changes on the environment. Oliveira and Silva [14] affirm that the strategic planning revisio the role in adjusting and correcting routes, besides defining necessary resources to reach goals.

The Role of Strategic Planning and Improving Organizational Performance

The strategic planning [5] will have to evaluate the external environment to identify its ecological issues, the opportunities and the existing risks in the environmental legislation, at consumers and society level, as well as possible amendments in the competition behavior and in the technology advancement in this field. For Stephen Robbins apud Oliveira and Silva [14] those organizations which have strategic planning manage to have both income and the growth on its profits 50 % higher than those that do not have it.

Donaire [5] adds that "the organization, while implementing a strategic planning must look into its internal factors, in order to analyze its strengths and weaknesses to adapt them to the established goals". So, it will be possible to formalize a solid environmental strategy that has support from the board and gets all the necessary resources required for its implementation and propagation in all the hierarchical levels.

The Evolution of Environmental Planning and the Impact of Ecological Variable on the Organizations Strategy

Albuquerque [1] emphasizes that in the past years besides the sustainable attitudes of the organizations to remain competitive and to be accepted in the market, the principle of paying-pollutant is being strengthened, it establishes that industries also have taxes responsibilities for causing pollution, even if it is controlled. This could be a threat for the enterprises, but several examples show the opposite. Donaire [5] claims that "in the countries where environmental restrictions are more severe like Japan, Germany, Sweden, etc., its organizations developed excellent new business opportunities related to the environmental matter, and now-a-days they export know-how to other countries".

The level of the enterprise´s commitment with the environmental matter will vary, according to Dias [4], "by virtue of the importance that the organization gives for the ecological variable and its decision depends on the external environment near the plant, the natural resources that the company needs and the extent of environmental contamination caused by its production process". Other factors that affect the enterprise involvement with a most effective environmental management, according to Dias [4], are: the difficulty of getting the investment required for adapting its production process; the lack of scientific-technical knowledge on the environmental issue; and the level of commitment of its staff with the environmental ethics.

Dias [4] found that "the companies that adopt proactive strategies present three possibilities for competitive entry: the adoption of procedures besides the ones required by legislation; the search for the environmental excellence as a component of quality prime focus; and turn to be a leader in its sector of environmental terms, for a better positioning on the market".

For this author the emerging strategic necessity while preparing the planning is to take into account the ecological motivations that are rising due to the increase of the ecological awareness, caused by the growth of population access to the information, and to the unceasing work undertaken by several nongovernmental organizations and governments in all its levels. If the company does not consider these motivations they can significantly affect the companies and the industry sector competitive position, because they influence several markets behavior.

Roome [18] displays the commercial and environmental excellence as a strategy option of companies in terms of environmental legislation. For this author strategy based on the premise that the "environmental management is a good administration" is the one adopted by companies that are searching for environmental excellence, on a quality as a driver, seeking to design and develop clean products and processes. From this point of view, these companies consider that the accounting is equivalent to inefficiency.

So, Donaire [5] shows that "the impact of the ecological variable in the organization strategy is directly connected to its potential of pollution; if it is high, its importance is vital in the strategy and its correct evaluation is a matter of survival, in both short and long term. If it is reduced, the ecological variable can be considered, but its impact will have minor importance in the organizational strategy formulation".

8. The Advantages of Risk Management to Minimize the Environment Impacts

In business environment, according to Oliveira et al. [13], "the risk is contextualized in the events that cannot be controlled or that do not depend on managers actions". Oliveira et al. [13] mention that to avoid losses from situations without the control of the managers, there is the need to used tools of identification, management and risks protection of operational processes losses.

In risks management, according to Santos, Almeida and Leite [19] is necessary to maximize the probability of positive events and to minimize the probability of negative events, thus providing advantages for the strategic planning and helping with the taking decision process.

The Correlation between Risk Managing and Strategic Planning

The risk and impacts management appears as a worthy ally for the strategic planning implementation, it must be aligned with the changes the company needs to reach its goals. Aware of risk factor, the managers must introduce methodologies for proper identification of the main events which may cause finance losses and any harm for the company´s image. In these terms, Oliveira et al. [13] sustain that "the vision of the risk forces all to be concern with the main events and activities which may endanger the persons, the information, the environment and, therefore, the profit of the company".

The Awareness in Regard to the Environmental Risks

The increase of the socio-environmental awareness in the society has been pressing the organizations to embody these values in their administrative and operational procedures. The main goals of the environmental and develop mentalist policies quoted by Seiffert [20] are:

1. to restore growth;
2. to changer the quality of development;
3. to meet the main needs for employment, food, energy, water and sanitation;
4. to maintain a sustainable population level;
5. to preserve and to improve the resource base;
6. to redirect the technology and to manage the risk; and
7. to add the natural environment and the ecology in the decision making process.

According to Thomas and Callan [21], the risks management, with emphasis in the environmental issue, is characterized as "the process whereby the person in charge for the decisions evaluates and selects alternatives for the environmental risk". Thus, the manager to rum the risk management must follow some few steps to facilitate this process. Among them we can quote:

1. to identify and to understand the risks;
2. plan to deal with these risks;
3. to embed the risk management to the planning;
4. to continuously evaluate the risks; and
5. to act, if possible preventively, on the impacts caused by the events [19].

When a risk is identified, the directors assess the significance and the way this risk can be managed. On the basis of these information, the managers have started a plan or several actions to specifically guide the risk and possibly to accept it due to its cost and benefits.

The Environment Risks Assessment before their Management

Thomas and Callan [21] expose that "one of the most important concern of the managers about the environmental issues is to determine the environmental risk and the involuntary risk of exposure to threats, such as emissions of pollutants and toxic substances". To evaluate several policies options, these authors suggest that the manager in charge must take into account not only all the information he got from the risk characterization, but also factors as technologic feasibility, implementation costs and other economical implications. Costa [3] emphasizes that "if changing is necessary', it is also needed to control and to manage the changing process, its risks and the impacts on all person involved and on the whole organization".

9. Final Consideration

This essay aimed to analyze the importance of sustainable practices for the companies and for the society. It started observing that a new scenery is arising in which the concern with the environment is changing the style of management, with the aim of ensure the competitive advantages in the market. And, for this reason, the society requires more from the companies which must act with environmental practices, to gain more and more space in the market.

The Environmental Accounting is an important managing tool, since it favors the integration of the environmental aspects in the strategy of the company. When used efficiently it can supply data which allow identifying methods and proceedings for operations control that reduce the emission of residues; it can recognize the sustainable practices impact on the profitability; and provide information for the decision making, in addition to help on the elaboration of the strategic planning and on the management of the target activities. The companies are looking for management tools which assist in the implementation of environmental practices, such as strategic planning and risks management.

Companies that adopt proactive strategies are rare, just a few adopt procedures other than those demanded by the legislation, because there is still no conscience of the managers concerning to a more sustainable economical development. And, to incorporate these tools in the company strategy, it is mandatory that all its physical and financial resources are involved and maintained by the environmental involvement of the staff and the directors. The society expectations concerning what it considers socio environmental responsibility increased faster than the capacity of the organizations on improving their standards. For the future, meantime, it is aimed that companies act with the harmony predicted in the concept of "sustainable development", that is to stay, in the socially fair manner, economically viable and environmentally correct.

References

1. J. L. Albuquerque. Gestão ambiental e responsabilidade social: conceitos, ferramentas e aplicações. 2009.
2. I. Chiavenato. Teoria geral da administração. 2001.
3. G.M. Costa. Change Management: uma abordagem prática e sistêmica. 2008.
4. R. Dias. Gestão ambiental: responsabilidade social e sustentabilidade. 2011.
5. D. Donaire. Gestão Ambiental na Empresa. 2010.
6. R.H. Hall. Organizations: structures, processes and outcomes. 1987.
7. M.M. Hamed; Y. El Mahgary. Outline of a national strategy for cleaner production: The case of Egypt. 2004.
8. R.O. Kosztrzepa. A evidenciação dos eventos relacionados com o meio ambiente: um estudo em indústrias químicas. 2004.
9. J.P. Kotter; J. L. Heskett. Corporate Culture and Performance. 1992.
10. M.E.P. Kraemer. Contabilidade ambiental como sistema de informações. 2005.
11. D. Maxwell; R.V. Vorst. Developing sustainable products and services. 2003.
12. M.A.A. Medeiros; J.M. Nogueira; F.S.T. Arruda. Valoração econômica do meio ambiente: ciência ou empirismo? 2000.
13. A.M.S. Oliveira et al. Contabilidade internacional: gestão de riscos, governança corporativa e contabilização de derivativos. 2008.
14. J.F. Oliveira; E.A. Silva. Gestão organizacional: descobrindo uma chave de sucesso para os negócios. 2006.
15. P.R. Paiva. Contabilidade ambiental. 2003.
16. M.E. Porter; C.V. Linde. Green and Competitive: Ending the Stalemate. 1995.

17. M.S. Ribeiro. Contabilidade ambiental. 2005.
18. N. Roome. Developing environmental management strategies. Business 1992.
19. L.C.M. Santos; V.C. Almeida; V.F. Leite. Aplicação de gerenciamento de risco como forma de suporte a iniciativas de empreendedorismo social. 2009.
20. M.E.B. Seiffert. Gestão Ambiental: instrumentos, esferas de ação e educação ambiental. 2009.
21. J.M. Thomas; S.J. Callan. Environmental economics: applications, policy and theory. 2010.
22. J.E.P. Tinoco; M.E.P. Kraemer. Contabilidade e gestão ambiental. 2004.

AGENDA FOR RESEARCH AND TECHNOLOGICAL DEVELOPMENT: EGG AGROINDUSTRIAL CHAIN

CLAUDIA MILENA ACOSTA GUERRERO
Universidad Libre Colombia, Avenue Caracas # 3-53 apto 4-21
Bogotá D.C, Cundinamarca

ALEXANDER LUAN NARANJO LADINO
Semillero of investigation SAIOP, Street 32ª Sur # 68ª 59
Bogotá D.C,Cundinamarca

EVER ÁNGEL FUENTES ROJAS
Universidad Libre Colombia, Director, Avenue. 70 No. 53-40
Bogotá D.C,Cundinamarca

In Colombia, the Ministry of Agriculture and Rural Development has promoted policies to strengthen the competitiveness of the productive sectors through the creation of research agendas and technological development of agro-industrial production chains and the poultry union is no stranger to these processes. He has presented a steady growth in egg production especially in the last year had an increase of 9%. The area selected is the department of Cundinamarca and has proven to be the largest producer but with higher costs in the industry. This research has worked on performance analysis, such as the establishment of links in the chain and the determination of the constituent segments, analyzing the institutional and organizational environment of the same, and the identification of opportunities and limitations through technological and market surveillance. In this way for more competition on egg production in Colombia and a lower production cost in the department of Cundinamarca, managed to position the product at both the national and international high quality standards.

1. Introduction

In Colombia, the Ministry of Agriculture and Rural Development has promoted policies to strengthen the competitiveness of the productive sectors through the creation of research agendas and technological development of agro-industrial production chains and the poultry union is no stranger to these processes.

He has presented a steady growth in egg production especially in the last year had an increase of 9%. The area selected is the department of Cundinamarca and has proven to be the largest producer but with higher costs in the industry. This research has worked on performance analysis, such as the establishment of links in the chain and the determination of the constituent segments, analyzing the institutional and organizational environment of the same, and the identification of opportunities and limitations through technological and market surveillance.

In this way for more competition on egg production in Colombia and a lower production cost in the department of Cundinamarca, managed to position the product at both the national and international high quality standards.

2. Description of the problem

Colombia is ranked 22 in the world's egg, has a marginal equivalent to 0.6%. The main producers are China and the United States account for 51% of world production. The Egg production in Colombia is dispersed among large number of producers, with scales ranging from 500 to more than 500,000 hens. The Chain in Colombia is not organized in clusters, and conversely, every stage of it is independent and are scattered throughout the Department. The production costs are higher in Cundinamarca to the rest of the following problems identified in the following diagram:

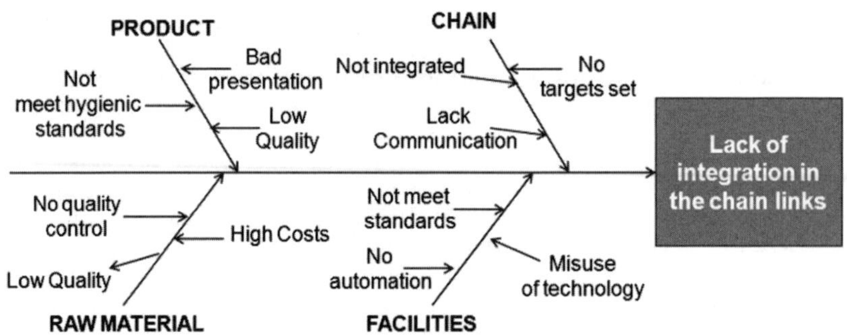

Source: 2012 Authors

3. General Objective

Determine the agenda for research and technological development in the agribusiness productive chain of the egg in the department of Cundinamarca.

Specific Objectives

To characterize the egg production chain and its links into segments to identify problems related.

Conduct an analysis of supply chain performance through benchmarking.

Identifying technological and non-technological chains for the generation of development strategies in the long term by agreement with the actors.

Perform commercial surveillance to identify new market trends related to global market.

Identify technology gaps and opportunities in the chain according to national capacities and global trends by technology and business vision.

Develop a prospective vision that conditions the performance of the chain on the opportunities and constraints arising from the agribusiness productive chain.

4. Methodology

Prospective agenda for research and technological development of the egg production chain relies on technological surveillance, commercial surveillance, benchmarking, performance analysis, forecasting and other tools for generating knowledge and strategies, which seek to identify markets products and services, and technology platforms as shown in the graphic.

Equations should be centered and numbered consecutively, as in Eq. (1). An alternative method is given in Eq. (2) for long sets of equations where only one referencing equation number is wanted.

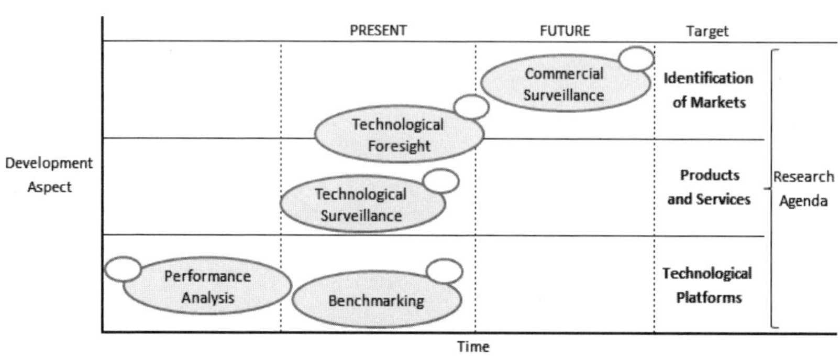

5. Results

Diagnosis of agribusiness: It is noted that in Colombia the demand for eggs is greater than domestic production because there is an optimal use of resources on producers. Thus there is an opportunity because there are markets for attending and can give an increase in production to prevent the importation of eggs because domestic products are quality.

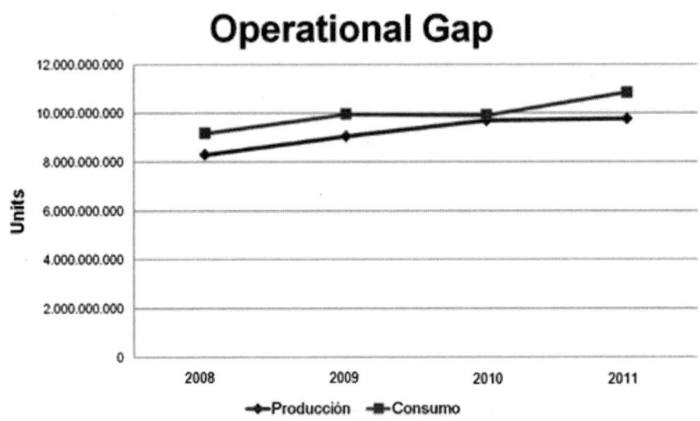

Egg production in Colombia has an increasing trend over the past five years, turn shows that most egg production is red, which is why the study focuses on this class of eggs. It was determined that such production is dispersed among a large number of producers, with scales ranging from 500 to more than 500,000 layers and is distributed as follows: Central Region (Cundinamarca, Tolima, Huila and Meta) 35.8% Santander, 24.7%, Valle, 21.5%, Atlantic Coast, 5.1%, Antioquia, 9.3%, Coffee, 4.3% and 1.9% Oriental. In recent years there has been the move towards the red egg production (67%) based on consumer preference for this product.

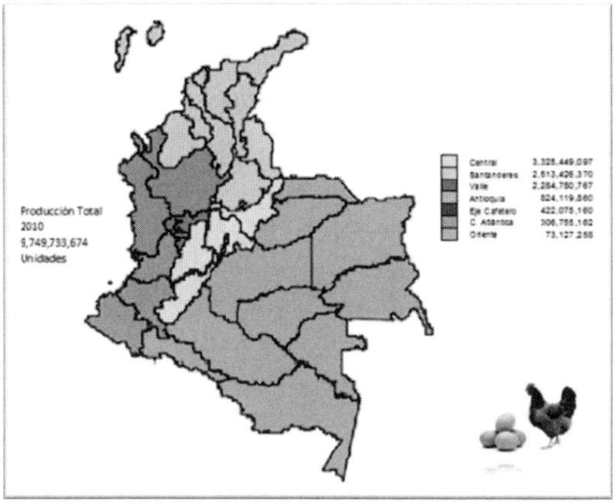

There is great fluctuation in sales prices of eggs, the changes are presented daily, in the graph shows the monthly behavior and comparison between prices in Bogota and Bucaramanga.

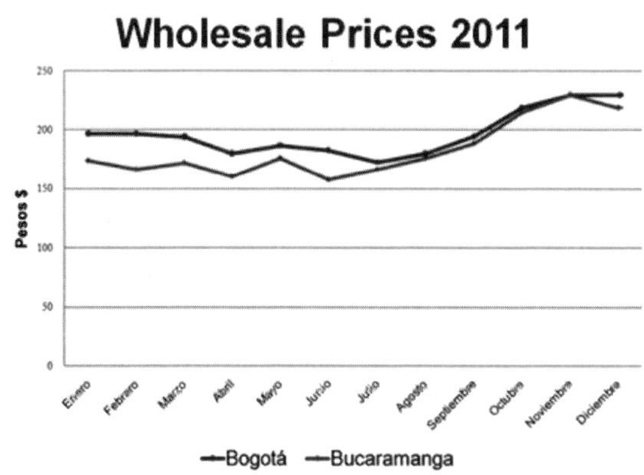

Characterization of the chain

The model took as reference the results of field visits in which established the reality of integration of chain actors in the regions of the department of Cundinamarca, performed and validated with input from experts in the chain. In such models are presented fluxes of material and consists of six links referring to the main actors in the chain such as end customers, retail marketers, retailers wholesalers, suppliers of chicks, poultry man and input suppliers.

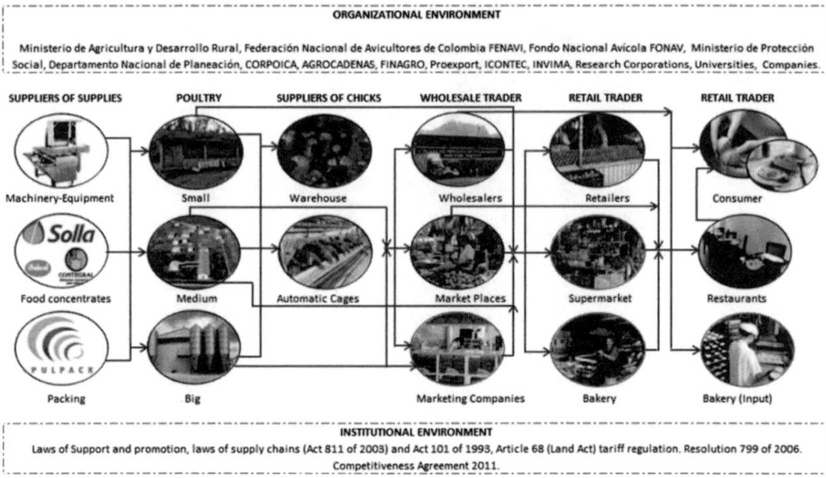

6. Conclusions

Large Poultry are now at the forefront of technology as these new technologies offer greater efficiency in collecting eggs, feeding chickens, maintenance leases, and the move from conventional sheds automatic cages a greater number of birds in the same area which generates an increase in daily egg production on farms and therefore generates a reduction in production costs.

The challenge facing Colombia is to ensure that small and medium producers automate their processes to ensure quality and biosafety requirements that are required, so you will have the opportunity to become more competent and effective so that the chain has sustained growth. In addition to creating a social fabric in the production chain makes all actors benefit and the sector more productive and competitive.

References

Castellanos D. Oscar Fernando, Torres P. Luz Marina, Flórez M. Diego Hernando. Agenda prospectiva de investigación y desarrollo tecnológico para la cadena productiva de la panela y su agroindustria en Colombia. Bogotá D.C, Giro editores Ltda. 2010.

Castellanos D. Oscar Fernando, Torres P. Luz Marina, Domínguez M. Karen Patricia. Manual metodológico para la definición de agendas de investigación y desarrollo tecnológico en cadenas productivas agroindustriales. Bogotá D.C, Giro editores Ltda. 2009.

Observatorio agrocadena, La competitividad de las cadenas agroproductivas en Colombia: Análisis de su estructura y dinámica (1991 – 2004)

Arias A. Plinio Antonio, Rojas Moreno Alexandra, Cuesta Claudia Esperanza, Castañeda Alexis Morales. Agenda prospectiva de investigación y desarrollo tecnológico para la cadena productiva forestal madera muebles en Bogotá y Cundinamarca. Bogotá D.C. Giro Editores Ltda. 2010.

Parra Morera Marisol, Aguilera Alvear Alexis, Escobar Torres William, Rubiano Zambrano Víctor, Rodríguez Carlosama. Agenda prospectiva de investigación y desarrollo tecnológico para la cadena productiva de granadilla en el departamento del Huila. Bogotá D.C. Giro Editores Ltda. 2010.

Bonilla C. María Hersilia, Toro Julio César, Mejía M. Andrés Daniel, Landìnez Lina Marcela, Castellanos Julio César, Cardozo Puentes Fernando. Agenda prospectiva de investigación y desarrollo tecnológico para la cadena productiva de mango criollo procesado para exportación en Colombia. Bogotá D.C. Giro Editores Ltda. 2010

Fenavi http://www.fenavi.org/fenavi/precios-sipsa.php?idm=81

Fenavi, http://www.fenavi.org/fenavi/estadisticas-produccion-avicola-pub.php?idm=113

http://www.agronet.gov.co/agronetweb1/Estad%C3%Adsticas/ReportesEstad%C3%Adsticos.aspx

http://www.ica.gov.co/Importacion-y-Exportacion/Estadisticas.aspx

CORPORATE SOCIAL RESPONSIBILITY AND SUSTAINABILITY: TOWARDS CAPITALISM SELF-REGULATION?

JOSE DANIEL BARQUERO CABRERO

Professor Researcher of the European Superior Council of Doctors & D.H.C., Girona, 24, Barcelona, 08010, Spain

MANUEL MEDINA ELIOZONDO

Research and Post Grade Coordinator, Universidad Autónoma de Cohauila 25280 Cohauila, México

VÍCTOR MANUEL MOLINA MOREJÓN

Professor Researcher, Universidad Autónoma de Coahuila 25280 Cohauila, México

MARIO BARQUERO CABRERO

Professor Researcher, Universidad Rey Juan Carlos & ESERP University Foundation (F.U.E.), 28016 Madrid, Spain

Abstract

Diffusion of corporate social responsibility practices in the capitalist countries seems to set a new phenomenon of capitalism self-regulation, which in the presence of obvious and irreversible damage to society and natural environment resulting from pursuit of profit, would finally willing to rationalize the use of productive resources with the more or less explicit goal of limiting its destructive effects and thereby to preserve the material and social foundations of market economy. Corporate social responsibility would then appear to be a component of the new paradigm of economic, social, and ecological sustainability. However, the current crisis of global capitalism conditions the progress and consolidation of this phenomenon, particularly in underdeveloped capitalist countries and in the so-called "emerging economies".

1. Introduction

The phenomenon of *Corporate Social Responsibility* (CSR)* has become one of the most discussed issues of economic governance. The biggest concern for environment, human rights (particularly those related to labor and gender) and community life, shown by a number of companies in industrialized countries, has experienced some international diffusion in which underdeveloped countries have not been entirely exempt.† It seems that, after all, globalization would have as one of its few positive results the emergence of a "human-faced capitalism" which, unlike the Welfare State age, its principle of regulation does not lie in state intervention or, as today neoliberal ideology intends to, in the abstract and impersonal market mechanism, but in the same cell of the economic tissue, that is to say in the modern capitalist enterprise.

It would thus face a phenomenon of capitalism self-regulation that, given the obvious and irreversible damage to society and natural environment derived from the pursuit of profit, would at last willing to rationalize the use of productive resources with the more or less explicit goal of limiting its destructive effects and thereby to preserve the material and social foundations of market economy.‡ CSR practices would therefore be in process of becoming a fundamental component of modern business management, as part of a strategic conception of it that would transform both the organizational structure of firms and their links with the social and natural environment, bringing important changes not only in their production and marketing processes but also in the relations between companies and their stakeholders (employees, customers and suppliers) and its stockholders (shareholders).

The growing importance of this phenomenon and its presence in the contemporary debate makes it necessary to contribute to theoretical reflection on this matter. To this end, a first section analyzes the causes of CSR emergence, its general characteristics and development trends in major industrialized

---

* The Dow Jones' Sustainability Index defines Corporate Social Responsibility as "a business practice that increases long-term value shares of a company, by taking advantage of opportunities and proper management of risks derived from economic, environmental and social development". See Crawford and Scaletta (2005).

† See the report of Webb and Hohnen (2006) on the CSR practices around the world.

‡ See in this respect the work of Roegen (1971) and that of Pearce and Warford (1994) on the destructive effects of capitalism, the entropic nature of economic processes and the need to review economic theory in the light of cumulative and irreversible phenomena such as environmental pollution and massive destruction of natural resources.

economies. A second section reflects in a general way on the current connotations of CSR in underdeveloped countries and emerging economies, with particular emphasis on those of Latin America region. Finally, a third section examines the CSR phenomenon in relation to sustainability new paradigm.

2. CSR: Emergence and development

The impressive growth experienced by industrialized capitalist economies after World War II ushered in a new way of regulating the market economy, which incorporated as one of its key components increasing state intervention. Welfare State, as a central element of monopolist regulation mode*, favored the emergence of a "virtuous circle" where industrial productivity increases, resulting from the Fordist production standard, allowed an extension of consumption standard based on both a sustained increase of real wage rate as in a state socialization process involving part of labor cost of production and reproduction (the so called "social wage" or indirect salary) in the form of state social spending. This resulted in an unprecedented boom in the development of capitalism, which brought to it a material support apparently unmoved in order to assure harmony and social peace; picture slightly marred by the West confrontation with the Soviet bloc and the reality of underdevelopment in the Third World. However, Western opinion leaders lost no opportunity to express their conviction that, sooner or later, Third World countries would reach the stage of development, to the extent that they improved their market structures and advanced in their industrialization processes, in accordance with Rostow's (1967) optimistic view, in vogue in political and academic circles of the time.

In this context of abundance (the well known JK Galbraith's affluent society expression) began to appear a number of business practices associated with caring for the environment, labor rights, respect for human rights and community settings. Increasingly, in both sides of the Atlantic European and American companies began to incorporate into their management scheme factors related to *social impact* of business activity. Many of these companies set up specific areas in their organizational structure in order to make operative this new approach. They also created audit instances to verify the compliance with these new standards and with socially responsible management practices,

* See Boyer (1979), op. cit.

including in their reports to shareholders specific chapters on this matter (Crowther and Rayman-Bacchus, 2004).

This trend, which emerged initially as a response to the need for companies to improve their external image before their customers and suppliers, thereby strengthening its market position against its competitors, also had the virtue of becoming in a more functional relationship with the social and community environment. A major concern for the rights of its workers, the adoption of preventive security measures to avoid or at least reduce workplace accidents and the application of non-discriminatory criteria for gender, race or religion, began to have a relatively significant impact in the working environment, which led to the conclusion that CSR practices, by raising labor productivity, should have a positive effect on corporate profits. Consequently, their relationship with stakeholders and society in general has become one of the key components of intangible assets of organizations, which has been argued that CSR practices are a form of intellectual capital accumulation for companies (Donaldson and Preston, 1995 and Freeman, 1984)[*]. Compliance with labor and environmental standards has thus become a very powerful marketing argument (Coors and Winegarden, 2005) in many advanced countries: the public does not want to contribute with companies that prey on the environment or violate workers' human rights. Thus, what began as a voluntary adoption by some companies of this type of practices in a context of prosperity and abundance, to some extent is tending to become enforcement and compulsory non-discretionary rules in most developed economies.

Unions and business groups affected by competition from emerging countries in global markets (based on low labor costs and where it is common to use child labor and underpaid female labor), which violate working women's basic rights and predate environment in order to reduce production costs, have organized to lobby the legislatures of their countries to transform into law labor and environmental standards of global reach. Thus, what began as a mixture of altruism and convenience by some private corporations has resulted in an increasingly important component of modern business management strategy. Additionally, pressure from social organizations in developed countries and the growing scientific evidence of environmental degradation, has led to CSR practices also become matters of public interest and, therefore, capable of being

[*] "The stakeholder theory" Donaldson and Preston 1995

incorporated to the sphere of public policy and legislative task in the form of laws and labor and environmental standards (Mander, 1992).

3. CSR and underdeveloped capitalist economies

Moreover, to the extent that multinational companies of developed countries have been the sector of industrial structure more inclined to adoption of CSR practices (Murray, 2004), these corporations have become the most important vehicle for dissemination of these practices in developing economies through its subsidiaries and its network of international suppliers (Peinado-Vara, 2004: 4). Currently, the adoption of these standards is spreading to the multinational providers anywhere in the world which they operate, which in the case of underdeveloped economies has become an additional barrier to the integration of domestic suppliers to production and marketing processes under foreign control. Thus the pressure to comply with CSR standards has come from developed countries to the rest of the world. Trade unions and industries adversely affected by globalization have demanded of their legislative bodies and their governments negotiate the adoption and enforcement by its trading partners in the Third World of CSR standards to limit unfair competition from emerging countries, mainly the Asian ones. Thus, it was the pressure exerted by the losing sectors in developed countries which largely explains the increased interest in dissemination of socially responsible management practices (Freeman and Medoff, 1983). In other words, it was the defense of self-interest of the industrialized world rather than altruism, the germ of global dissemination of CSR, regardless of the fact that defense of social and environmental rights globally constitutes a value in itself.

However, such practices are perceived primarily as an additional and unnecessary cost for local firms in emerging economies and, in an immediate optic, as a loss of competitiveness (Peinado-Vara, 2004: 3). Moreover, governments of these countries, particularly in Latin America, have shown less interest in this type of approach to corporate governance than those of developed world. Apparently, competition between emerging markets to attract foreign direct investment (FDI) has tended to limit the adoption of CSR practices in developing countries where low labor costs and tax incentives are perceived as the true factors for attracting foreign investments.

In the case of Mexico, the government and workers themselves seem to have convergent interests to promote the adoption of CSR practices at a international level,* since they have lost markets and revenues in favor to countries (like the Asians) who base their competitiveness on an exploitation of its workers even greater than that prevailing in the Mexican economy itself, as well as in the predatory use of natural resources. However, there is a perception that indifference prevailing in Latin American countries in relation to CSR has its point of departure in a poor understanding of it (Webb and Hohnen, 2006). On the one hand, it is thought that the CSR increases operating costs of businesses, making them less competitive against its internal and external competitors. On the other, one fails to appreciate the contribution that the CSR can make to company profitability and, much less, the effect of "protection" that CSR may have against unfair competition in global markets. This explains the low or no participation of Latin American countries in adopting socially responsible codes of conduct, such as the Social Accountability 8000 Standard,† which highlights the presence of Brazil and the total absence of Mexico (see Table 1).

Table 1
Industrial Facilities Certified with SA8000 by Country
September 30, 2006

Country	No. Of Facilities	% of Total
Italy	395	38.05%
India	141	15.80%
China	129	12.43%
Brazil	99	9.54%
Pakistan	53	2.89%
Vietnam	30	2.02%
Thailand	21	1.45%
Spain	15	0.77%
Sri Lanka	8	0.77%
Taiwan	8	0.67%
Indonesia	7	0.67%
Poland	7	0.67%

* See the work of Salazar (2004) on the incipient spread of CSR practices in Mexico.

† The SA8000 is a certification subject to external audit based on international standards of ILO, the Universal Declaration of Human Rights and the United Nations Convention on the Rights of Children.

Switzerland	7	0.58%
Israel	6	0.58%
Filipino	6	0.58%
Turkey	6	0.48%
Argentina	5	0.48%
Greece	5	0.48%
Korea	5	0.39%
Belgium	4	0.39%
Bolivia	4	0.39%
France	4	0.39%
Hong Kong	4	0.39%
Romania	4	0.39%
United Kingdom	4	0.29%
Portugal	3	0.19%
Bangladesh	2	0.19%
Costa Rica	2	0.19%
Czech Republic	2	0.19%
Japan	2	0.19%
Malaysia	2	0.19%
Mauritius	2	0.19%
Other	77	5.11%

Source : http ://www.sa-intl.org/

4. The CSR and sustainability paradigm

According to the precedent discussion, socially responsible corporate governance can be characterized as the beginning or the embryonic form of a new component of advanced capitalism, with an element of self-regulation linked to the concept of sustainable development or, more precisely, to the concept of sustainability,* where the dynamic adjustment mechanisms would rest not only in the market or in state intervention, but in the crystallization of commitments made by individual centers of capital accumulation themselves, i.e. companies, according to sustainability imperatives. Although it is a fact that the CSR has become a compelling theme in the contemporary debate on corporate

* For some authors, the concept of sustainable development in capitalism constitutes a sort of antinomy or logical contradiction, given that any type of capitalist development, oriented by definition to obtain economic profits, necessarily leaves an "ecological footprint" and thus generates *unsustainability*. Therefore, we must turn rather to the concept of sustainability and not to that of sustainable development. See the Preface of Solis Gonzalez to the book of Gonzalez Gaudiano (2009).

management, the concrete and effective dissemination of such practices, both in the developed world and in the emerging economies depends on a number of factors, variables in each particular case. It is undeniable that the context of prosperity of the postwar years has been replaced by another very different, marked by the crisis of monopolist regulation mode (Mazier, Basle and Vidal, 1984). Sustained increases in labor productivity that characterized the performance of the advanced economies until the early seventies have given way to a marked deterioration in the conditions of capital valorization and consequently in an erosion of corporate profitability. The advent of the new wave of globalization that is currently living the capitalist world, focusing on the growing internationalization of financial capital and on the quest for a "free management" of labor force based on the so-called "labor flexibility", as well as the full entry in the *Information Age*, have so far been unable to configure the foundations of a new era of prosperity for the world capitalist system.

Moreover, the impressive development of global interconnection through new technologies of information and communications, which some authors characterize as a "third" industrial, scientific and technological revolution, was not yet sufficient to set a new "locomotive" of economic growth overall, with "backward" and "forward" dynamic effects as it was in the era of Fordism with the automotive industry. The extensive consumption norm that characterized the central Fordist regime has also been severely eroded by the new management of the workforce, underpinned by the dismantling of Welfare State institutions and the neoliberal policies that have characterized the governance of capitalist countries during the recent decades. In fact, globalization has generated its own opposite in the fragmentation and differentiation of the world economic space through the formation of regional and sub-regional economic blocs that obey increasingly to a geopolitical multi-polarity (Altvater and Mahnkopf, 2002). In this game of forces, a desperate search for competitiveness at all cost has emerged as the standard operation of global economy, largely replacing the mechanisms of international cooperation conceived in the boom years.

In this context of uncertainty that has characterized the global capitalism crisis, it can hardly be verified, at least in the short term, a significant spread of CSR practices in developing countries, also starting to appear in the advanced countries themselves unmistakable signs of this trend weakening. According to a study made by Porter and Kramer (2002) for the U.S. economy, corporate social investment, after a relatively long period of growth, experienced a 50% drop between 1986 and 2001, particularly those related to charities. Apparently, the CSR is tending to move towards "philanthropic strategic" investments where the company does not just look for the public good but also, crucially, the own benefit (Milchen, 2002). The truth is that in the current crisis and recession in the U.S. economy, investments in CSR practices are increasingly difficult to justify in the eyes of shareholders, given the increasing difficulty to show the direct benefits of contribution to social causes. Presumably, the incorporation of socially responsible management practices in strategic management models in the future will involve a more careful selection of those social causes in which firms are willing to participate, as well as a more accurate determination of the levels of such involvement, all in a perspective of tangible economic benefits for the company itself not only in the short term but also in the long run (Siegel and Vitaliano, 2005).

Therefore, solution to the current crisis (and thus the emergence of a new mode of regulation of capitalism) is still far from being found. Globalization of economic processes has not completely defined, at least in the central economies, a new standard of production, despite the undeniable advances in robotics, advanced technologies (biotechnology, nanotechnology, new materials, etc.) and information and communications new technologies. Moreover, current consumption norm, eroded by the previous dismantling of the Welfare State institutions, has also been negatively affected by the new models of production processes automation (which expel labor), exacerbation of competition in global markets (where it seeks to reduce at all costs the wage bill) and new forms of work management, based on a high degree of labor exploitation and precarious employment. Finally, the autonomy of finance in relation to production processes in the real economy, has led to a bigger concentration of globalization gains by speculative capital, with consequent damage to growth of productive investment and jobs. So, global financial crisis it has been installed as the sign of our times. In turn, emerging economies are torn between productive stagnation (such as Latin America, particularly Mexico) and successful accumulation models with high growth rates achieved however at the expense of a ruthless exploitation of labor force and marginalization of large groups of population, as in the case of China and most Southeast Asian economies. This set of phenomena imposes limits on the processes of diffusion and adoption of the CSR practices, both in the center and the periphery of world system, so that its future is surrounded by a high degree of uncertainty and by the constant threat of decline.

In short, the emergence of new paradigm of sustainability, that incorporates in a comprehensive way socially responsible business management will depend, most likely, on social action and collective participation, and on civil society organizations that subscribe the sustainability demands and, therefore, the exigency for a style of economic and social development more harmonious and balanced, with substantially lower levels of inequality that the current ones and that place at the center of their concerns and their political action the problem of environment and biodiversity preservation before it is too late. In fact, only achieving at least a minimum of sustainability society would be able to ensure in the medium and long term historical viability of capitalism *or of any other form of economic and social organization* and thus, the permanence of human being on the planet. In this respect, issues outlined here are aimed at opening new avenues of research on CSR, which attempt to go beyond limitations of conventional approaches in order to provide a new basis for the study of this phenomenon.

5. Conclusion

The phenomenon of CSR has transcended the sphere of management and business to position itself as the embryo of one of the constituent features of a new mode of regulation of market economies, in which the core of its organization and operation seems to point toward the sustainability paradigm. Although it is too early to draw definitive conclusions about the validity of this hypothesis, there is evidence that socially responsible management practices tend to become institutionalized and translated into rules that must be observed as a result of social pressure and mobilization of civil society organizations in defense of environment, human rights (labor, gender, children, etc.) and a community life with greater social equity and citizens participation. On the other hand, as a result of this social pressure, CSR practices have become part of the field of public policy and therefore, of the community's general interests represented in the State. This means that, predictably, companies will be forced to adopt CSR practices increasingly advanced. So, in the context of an economic crisis like the current one, it is expected that CSR practices represent additional elements of tension on economic and social structures. Therefore, the moving towards a form of capitalism self-regulation, at least in developed countries, depends on a set of structural and conjunctural factors whose specific outcome can only be discerned in the long term.

References

Altvater, E. and B. Mahnkopf (2002): *Las limitaciones de la globalización. Economía, ecología y política de la globalización,* Mexico, Siglo XXI Ed.

Boyer, R. (1979), « La crise actuelle : une mise au point en perspective historique. Quelques réflexions à partir d'une analyse du capitalisme français en longue période », in *Critiques de l'économie politique* No. 7-8, nouvelle série, avril-septembre, Paris, Ed Maspero.

Coors, A. and W. Winegarden (2005): "Corporate Social Responsibility-Or Good Advertising?", in *Regulation*, spring issue.

Crawford, D. and T. Scaletta (2005): "The Balanced Scorecard and Corporate Social Responsibility: Aligning Values for Profit", in *CMA Management*, October.

Crowther, D. and L. Rayman-Bacchus (2004): *Perspectives on Corporate Social Responsibility*, Aldershot, Hants, England, Ashgate Publishing, Ltd.

Freeman, R. (1984): *Strategic Management: A Stakeholder Perspective.* Englewood Cliffs, NJ: Prentice-Hall.

Freeman, R. B. and J. L. Medoff (1983): *What Do Unions Do?* New York, Basic Books.

Mander, J. (1992): *In the Absence of the Sacred,* San Francisco, Sierra Club Books.

Mazier, J., M. Basle and J.-F. Vidal (1984) : *Quand les crises durent ...*, Paris, Economica.

Milchen, J. (2002): *Inherent Rules of Corporate Behavior*, Bozeman, MT, ReclaimDemocracy.org.

Murray, J. (2004): *Corporate Social Responsibility: An Overview of Principles and Practices*, Working Paper No. 34, World Commission on the Social Dimension of Globalization, Geneva, ILO.

Pearce, D. W. and J. Warford (1994): *World without End: Economics, Environment and Sustainable Development*, Oxford, Oxford University Press.

Peinado-Vara, E. (2004): *Corporate Social Responsibility in Latin America and the Caribbean*, Washington DC, IDB.

Porter, M. and M. Kramer (2002): "The Competitive Advantage of Corporate Philanthropy". *Harvard Business Review*, 80, (12), pp. 57-68.

Roegen, N. G. (1971): *The Entropy Law and the Economic Process*, Cambridge, Mass., Harvard University Press.

Rostow, W. W. (1967): *Las etapas del crecimiento económico*, Mexico, FCE.

Salazar, S. (2004): *La responsabilidad social corporativa en México como una herramienta estratégica para la competitividad: Un enfoque econométrico y prospectivo*, Master Thesis, Monterrey, ITESM.

Siegel, D.S. and D. F. Vitaliano (2005): *An Empirical Analysis of the Strategic Use of Corporate Social Responsibility*, New York, Rensselaer Polytechnic Institute.

Solis Gonzalez, J. L. (2009): "Foreword", in E. Gaudiano Gonzalez (ed.), *Trends and opportunities of sustainability in Mexico*, Mexico, Plaza y Valdes, p. 11-15.

Webb, T. and P. Hohnen (2006): "Corporate Responsibility – The Connected World in 2006", in *Ethical Corporation*, January.

WELFARE LINGUISTIC SUBJECTIVE INDICATOR

LUISA L. LAZZARI
CIMBAGE, Facultad de Ciencias Económicas, Universidad de Buenos Aires,
Av. Córdoba 2122, Ciudad de Buenos Aires, C1120AAQ, Argentina

MARIA JOSE FERNANDEZ
CIMBAGE, Facultad de Ciencias Económicas, Universidad de Buenos Aires,
Av. Córdoba 2122, Ciudad de Buenos Aires, C1120AAQ, Argentina

PATRICIA MOULIÁ
CIMBAGE, IADCOM, Facultad de Ciencias Económicas,Universidad de Buenos Aires
Av. Córdoba 2122, Ciudad de Buenos Aires, C1120AAQ, Argentina

Poverty is an unacceptable reality in any society. It violates the constituent bases of human life and represents the potential loss of people's being and acting. Although there may be universal requirements for not being poor, it is possible that these required standards may vary from one society to another, from one household to another and even from one individual to another. People's perceptions constitute an indispensable point of analysis, and subjective indicators could be a good guide to these objectives. In this paper we present the subjective poverty approach; we develop a linguistic subjective indicator of economic welfare and we show an example of its application.

1. Introduction

Poverty is an important issue for most of the countries, not only for developing countries but also for the developed ones, since the efforts to fight against it generally have high priority among the objectives of economic and social policy [1].

Poverty is an unacceptable reality for any society. It breaks the constitutive foundations of human life and represents the potential loss of being and acting of people [2].

The poverty concept does not arise outside the context of a social philosophy that theorizes about the nature of human needs and the importance of certain short comings. Since the philosophical and theoretical contexts are different, the implications for measuring poverty are diverse. Understanding poverty as a lack of food does not necessarily define the importance of assets that provide nutrition, or what constitutes sufficiency of food, potential food or worthy of being considered as basic [3].

Although universal requirements may arise for not being poor, it is possible that what can meet this standard varies from one society to another, from one household another and even from one individual to another [2].

In welfare and living standard literature, the term poverty is not clear and universal because, in the analysis of this phenomenon, we tend to relate to many aspects of human condition. As these issues are related not only to goods' and services deprivation but also to issues of values and moral, which weighs each individual differently at any given time, could hardly be a single criterion for defining and measuring poverty.

Is that while some associate poverty with the ability of people to meet their basic needs for food, others use criteria related to health, housing, education, income, expenses, or broader issues such as identity, human rights participation, among others, arriving to different magnitudes of poverty. That is, you can have many definitions and quantifications of it, as aspects or criteria exist to measure it.

The expectations of the population and well received by each individual member of a society are a reflection of the kind of country that is being built. Perceptions of people are an essential analysis and subjective indicators could be a good guide to the objectives.

This paper analyzes the subjective poverty approach. We develop a linguistic subjective indicator of economic welfare and is an example of its application. It is structured as follows. The second section deals with the subjective poverty approach; the third one shows the linguistic approach to be used in the design of the indicator. The fourth part presents the linguistic subjective indicator of economic welfare. The fifth section develops an example and finally some conclusions are presented.

2. Subjective poverty indicators

The study of welfare has been one of the central topics of Economics from its origins as a science. Utilitarianism raised by Bentham [4] and Mill [5] laid the foundation from which modern Economics began a study of welfare. Amartya Sen [6, 7] departs from the utilitarian and introduces the concept of welfare from focusing on the abilities of agents.

Economic Welfare assessment can be made from two types of indicators-quantitative objective indicators (poverty lines, unmet basic needs, human development index, anthropometric indicators) and subjective-qualitative indicators (calculated from surveys that reveal perceptions of individuals or households) [8]. Poverty can be understood as subjective perception of poverty that has a sector of the population that feels and defines himself as poor by not having access to a range of goods and services considered of great importance. The success or failure of any public policy should be reflected in the evolution of perceived well-being of society that is the ultimate objective is pointing towards any economic measure is implemented [9].

The welfare measure is a task that is performed frequently, and there is a high consensus on the need to quantify, but there are certain differences as to which indicators to use in reflecting the state of being of a society and little information on how to evaluate people what happens to their own welfare. In recent decades there have been some studies of subjective well show great diversity in the type of approach they perform. Some have focused on finding the variables that determine the welfare of households. Others stress the importance of how to quantify the welfare and finally a group investigates the determinants that make some people declare high levels of welfare and not others. Nowadays, studies on welfare are concentrated in two main planes, one related to defining what are the aspects that determine the welfare and the other about how to measure it. Anyway, whatever the concept of poverty measurement to which one adheres, a successful implementation is a prerequisite for their proper use in social policy [10]. While there is a worldwide trend to make more and more studies on poverty and subjective well-being in Argentina, public statistics have not yet made such measurements.

3. Linguistic approach

The existence of qualitative variables inherent in human behavior, or material in the external environment are difficult to quantify objectively, makes individuals have difficulty in representing a numerical value assessment of the various aspects related to their welfare that want to evaluate. Under such circumstances it is more appropriate to express your answers using linguistic values rather than exact numerical values.

This approach a decision problem is based on the theory of fuzzy sets and is called the linguistic approach. It applies when the variables involved are qualitative [11, 12]. Thus, it is possible to model more adequately many real situations, since it allows to represent information of individuals, which is almost always inaccurate, more appropriately.

A linguistic variable is a numerical difference in their values are not numbers but words or sentences in natural language or artificial language [11].

In this paper, we use the approach of the operators developed by Xu that compute with words directly, so there is less loss of information [13,14].

We consider a finite and totally ordered label set $S=\{s_\alpha / \alpha=0,\ldots t\}$, which cardinality value is odd, and t is a positive integer. Each term s_α represents a possible value for a linguistic variable [15] and it must have the following characteristics:

$s_\alpha > s_\beta$ iff $\alpha > \beta$.

There is the negation operator: neg $(s_\alpha) = s_\beta$ such that $\beta = t - \alpha$.

The mid linguistic label s_0 represents an assessment of "indifference" and the rest of labels are defined around it symmetrically.

To preserve all the given information, Xu [15] extended the discrete linguistic label set S to a continuous linguistic label set $\overline{S} = \{s_\alpha / \alpha \in [-q, q]\}$, where q $(q > t)$ is a sufficiently large positive integer.

If $s_\alpha \in S$, then s_α is called an original linguistic label, otherwise, s_α is called a virtual linguistic label. Generally, the decision maker uses the original linguistic terms to evaluate attributes and alternatives, and the virtual linguistic labels can only appear in calculations [14].

Considering any of the two linguistic terms $s_\alpha, s_\beta \in \overline{S}$, and $\lambda \in [0,1]$, Xu [30] introduces operational laws of linguistic variables as follows:

$$s_\alpha \oplus s_\beta = s_\beta \oplus s_\alpha = s_{\alpha+\beta}. \quad (1)$$

$$\lambda . s_\alpha = s_{\lambda\alpha}. \quad (2)$$

Xu [13,14] defines many linguistic aggregation operators based on (1), (2), as functions $\overline{S}^n \to \overline{S}$, that compute with words directly. Among others, the *extended arithmetic mean* (EAA) and the *weighted arithmetic mean* (EWAA).

Definition 1 [27]: Let *EAA*: $\overline{S}^n \to \overline{S}$. If

$$EAA(s_{\alpha_1}, s_{\alpha_2}, \ldots, s_{\alpha_n}) = \frac{1}{n}(s_{\alpha_1} \oplus s_{\alpha_2} \oplus \ldots \oplus s_{\alpha_n}) = s_{\overline{\alpha}} \quad (3)$$

where $\overline{\alpha} = \frac{1}{n}\sum_{j=1}^{n} \alpha_j$, then *EAA* is called *extended arithmetic mean operation.*

Definition 2 [27]: Let $EWAA: \overline{S}^n \to \overline{S}$. If

$$EWAA(s_{\alpha_1}, s_{\alpha_2}, \ldots, s_{\alpha_n}) = w_1\, s_{\alpha_1} \oplus w_2\, s_{\alpha_2} \oplus \ldots \oplus w_n\, s_{\alpha_n} = s_{\overline{\beta}} \quad (4)$$

where $\overline{\beta} = \sum_{j=1}^{n} w_j.\alpha_j$, $w = (w_1, w_2, ..., w_n)$ is the weighting vector of the linguistic labels s_{α_j}, $j = 1,..., n$, $w_j \in [0,1]$ y $\sum_{j=1}^{n} w_j = 1$, then *EWAA* is called *extended weighted arithmetic mean operator.*

The fundamental aspect of the *EWAA* operator is that it computes the linguistic labels taking into account the importance of the information [14]. In this study we use sets of seven labels totally ordered according to the theoretical framework defined by Xu [14].

4. Welfare Linguistic Subjective Indicator

Since subjective well-being indicators are built through surveys that reveal the individual's perception that each individual with respect to certain areas considered and used qualitative scales, is very relevant the use of linguistic variables in their formulation.

To define the Welfare Linguistic Subjective Indicator (ILBE) disaggregates the concept of economic welfare in five areas: 1. Health, 2. Education, 3. Housing, 4. Income and 5.employment. It is considered that the economic welfare of an individual is determined by their perception address these aspects that characterize the quality of life, evaluating the level of public satisfaction regarding the valuation of each type of access to these goods.

The measurement is taken from direct surveys of heads of households. The questionnaire induces households to assess their access to the five areas considered, using linguistic labels. The assessment of each area will provide a component of ILBE and aggregation enable an indicator for each household.

The survey will inquire about the perception of individuals on the following aspects to analyze the welfare of a household: 1. Access to health system, 2. Access to medicines and vaccination, 3. Compliance with the education level of the head of the house, 4. Access to the education system, 5. Housing conditions, 6. General conditions of the neighborhood where they live, 7. Compliance with their income level, 8. Amount of additional income that the househols would need not to feel poor, 9. Compliance with working conditions, 10. Poverty feeling, 11. Level of economic welfare.

According to the domain of the variables involved, it is assumed the use of one of the following sets of linguistic terms for heads of households express their views on the items to evaluate:

$S_1 = \{s_0 = \text{dreadful},\ s_1 = \text{very bad},\ s_2 = \text{bad},\ s_3 = \text{mean},\ s_4 = \text{good},\ s_5 = \text{very good},$
$s_6 = \text{excellent}\}$

$S_2 = \{s_0 = \text{absolutely poor},\ s_1 = \text{very poor},\ s_2 = \text{rather poor},\ s_3 = \text{nor poor}$
$\text{or not poor},\ s_4 = \text{somewhat poor},\ s_5 = \text{almost non poor},\ s_6 = \text{non poor}\}$

$S_3 = \{s_0 = \text{unimportant},\ s_1 = \text{rather uninportant},\ s_2 = \text{little important},\ s_3 = \text{careless},$
$s_4 = \text{pretty important},\ s_5 = \text{very important},\ s_6 = \text{absolutely important}\}$

Household Economic Welfare Linguistic Subjective Indicator

The indicator id disaggregated in the 5 items mentioned, that will be indicated as $j / j = 1, 2, \ldots, 5$. In turn each comprises one or more components denoted $t / t = 1, \ldots, m$.

Step 1. Components for each household

Let h the surveyed household $(h = 1, \ldots, n)$.

The assessment of the degree of satisfaction of each home for each area that integrates the $ILBE_h$ is obtained by using the aggregation operator of linguistic information EAA defined in (3), with the information gathered from surveys (a sample form is contained in the Appendix).

Assuming that the survey *m* questions correspond to *j* area, then the value of the component for this item to *h* household is given by:

$$I_{jh} = EAA_j\left(s_{\alpha_1}, s_{\alpha_2}, \ldots, s_{\alpha_m}\right) = s_{\overline{\alpha}_{jh}} \tag{5}$$

where m is the amount of question from area, $s_{\alpha_t} \in S_1$ $(t = 1, \ldots, m)$ is the linguistic label that indicates the given answer by the household *h* to the question *t* for the area j ($j = 1, \ldots, 5$).

Step 2. Weighting of components

Since not all areas that compose the indicator are equally important for all households, the survey includes a question which asks the degree of importance assigned to each family to each of them (Question 13, appendix) corresponding to a linguistic label in the set S_3.

If $s_{\alpha_{jh}} \in S_3$ is the linguistic label that shows the importance allocated by the household h the area j ($j = 1, \ldots, 5$); the weighting, w_{j_h}, correspondent must verify that $w_{jh} \in [0,1]$ and $\sum_{j=1}^{5} w_{jh} = 1$, and is obtained by applying (6).

$$w_{jh} = \alpha_{j_h} \Big/ \sum_{j=1}^{5} \alpha_{j_h} \quad (h = 1, \ldots, n) \tag{6}$$

Step 3. Calculation of the indicator for each household.

Having assessed the components of the index and obtained their respective weights, the $\mathrm{ILBE_h}$ is obtained by the use of aggregation operator of linguistic information EWAA defined in (4).

$$ILBE_h = EWAA_h\left(s_{\overline{\alpha}_{1h}}, s_{\overline{\alpha}_{2h}}, s_{\overline{\alpha}_{3h}}, s_{\overline{\alpha}_{4h}}, s_{\overline{\alpha}_{5h}}\right) = s_{\overline{\beta}_h} \tag{7}$$

where $\overline{\beta}_h = \sum_{j=1}^{5} w_{jh}\, \overline{\alpha}_{jh}$, $h = 1,...,n$, w_{jh} is the weighting of household h to the area j, $w_{j_h} \in [0,1]$ y $\sum_{j=1}^{n} w_{j_h} = 1$, obtained on *Step* 2, and $s_{\overline{\alpha}_{jh}} \in \overline{S}_1$ is the linguistic label correspondent to the valuation of household h of the component j of the indicator obtained on *Step* 1.

If you want to express the degree of aggregate welfare of each household by a term of the set S_1, the sub index of the virtual label $S_{\overline{\beta}h}$ is approximated to an integer value through the usual rounding operation (*round* $(\overline{\beta}_h)$) and it is got a linguistic original label.

Global Linguistic subjective economic welfare indicator

After surveying the n households that comprise the studied population we calculate for each the corresponding ILBE_h and then the information obtained is aggregated through the application of EAA operator defined in (3).

$$ILBE = EAA\left(s_{\overline{\beta}_1}, s_{\overline{\beta}_2}, ..., s_{\overline{\beta}n}\right) = s_{\overline{\gamma}} \tag{8}$$

where $s_{\overline{\beta}_h} \in \overline{S}_1$ indicates the value ILBE_h for household h and $\overline{\gamma} = \frac{1}{n}\sum_{h=1}^{n} \overline{\beta}_h$.

If you want to express the degree of aggregate welfare of the population by a term of the set S_1, the sub index of the virtual label is approximated $s_{\overline{\gamma}}$ to an integer value, through the usual rounding operation (*round* $(\overline{\gamma})$) and an original linguistic label is obtained.

5. $\mathrm{ILBE_h}$ calculation for a household

Step 1. $\mathrm{ILBE_h}$ Components

With the information obtained in fieldwork the indicator value for a family is obtained. This value is calculated for each area of satisfaction for the selected household.

- Health Area: Evaluation will be based on household responses to questions 1 (access to health care) and 2 (access to medicines and vaccination). The respondent household (household 1) considers that access to health care is bad (s2) and access to medicines and vaccination is mean (s3), then the assessment is: $I_{11} = EAA_1(s_2, s_3) = s_{2.5}$.

- Education Area: Evaluation will be based on household responses to questions 3 (conformity to the educational level of the head) and 4 (access to the education system). The head of household 1 found that both their level of education and their access to the education system is *good* (s_4), then the assessment is: $I_{21} = EAA_2(s_4, s_4) = s_4$.

- Housing Area: Evaluation will be based on household responses to questions 5 (housing conditions) and 6 (neighborhood general conditions).

The head of the household believes that their housing conditions are *bad* (s_2) and their neighborhood is *good* (s_4), then the assessment is: $I_{31} = EAA_3(s_2, s_4) = s_3$.

- Income Area: Evaluation will be based on household responses to questions 7 (income) and 8 (household income need not to feel poor). The head of the household think their income is *very bad* (s_1) and they need twice their income needed to not feel poor (s_1), then the assessment is: $I_{41} = EAA_4(s_1, s_1) = s_1$.

- Employment Area: Evaluation will be based on household responses to questions 9 (number of hours worked) and 10 (working conditions). If the head of household 1 assessed with the label *mean* (s_3) both the number of hours worked and the conditions of employment, then the assessment of the employment area: $I_{51} = EAA_5(s_3, s_3) = s_3$.

Step 2. ILBE's components weighting

The degree of importance of each area is shown by means of filling Table 1. If the importance of the household respondent assigned to each area is:

$P_1 = s_4$, $P_2 = s_5$, $P_3 = s_2$, $P_4 = s_6$ and $P_5 = s_5$, with $s_j \in S_3$

The weightings are obtained by the application of (10).

$w_1 = 0.18$; $w_2 = 0.23$; $w_3 = 0.09$; $w_4 = 0.27$; $w_5 = 0.23$

It is verified that $w_j \in [0,1]$ and $\sum_{j=1}^{5} w_j = 1$.

Step 3. $ILBE_h$ calculation for household 1

With the information from the evaluations of the components and their respective weights, the $ILBE_1$ is given by (7):

$$ILBE_1 = EWAA_I\left(s_{2.5},\ s_4,\ s_3\ ,\ s_1\ ,\ s_3\right) = s_{2.6}$$

If the degree of aggregate welfare is desired to be expressed in a linguistic way, the rounding operation is performed round (2.6) =3 and is got the label $s_3 \in S$. Then the household 1 perceived *mean* economic welfare when considering the five areas surveyed.

Questions 11 and 12 of the questionnaire will be used to compare the consistency of the households' responses.

Question 14, will allow classifying the household as poor or not poor according to their income, because it is important to analyze how poor households perceive their welfare as how they do the non-poor ones. Moreover, by this way it is possible to can combine a subjective measure of poverty with the poverty or indigence fuzzy lines, which is an objective measure.

6. Conclusions

Subjective welfare measures should be seen as a complementary tool of objective indicators to assess the correspondence between objective and subjective improvements and evaluations performed by the people on them. This type of indicators allows differentiating between income ranges priorities and knowing the impact on them.

Since the type of questions used to define an index of subjective welfare are qualitative, the use of a linguistic model that operates with words directly allows aggregating individual's opinions in a accurately and less loss of information.

The proposed approach allows to capture the nuances and degrees of being present in human perceptions, while the classical models only allow binary contrasts between positive and negative perceptions, not including the variations of intensity between them.

In this type of linguistic model it can be introduced quantitative variables and combining them to operate for another diagnosis, depending on the problem to be analyzed. Likewise, you may introduce welfare assessments in addition to other areas considered in this paper.

Acknowledgements

The authors thanks to the Secretaría de Ciencia y Técnica of the Universidad de Buenos Aires (UBACyT Project 20020100100025), to the Facultad de Ciencias Económicas of that University where the Project belongs to and to the Consejo Nacional de Investigaciones Científicas y Técnicas (CONICET).

Appendix. Survey form

You consider that your access to health care is:
Dreadful – very bad – bad – mean – good- very good – excellent.
You consider that your access to medication and vaccination, if needed, is:
Dreadful – very bad – bad – mean – good- very good – excellent.
You consider your education level is:
Dreadful – very bad – bad – mean – good- very good – excellent.
4. You consider that access to the education system is:
Dreadful – very bad – bad – mean – good- very good – excellent.

1. You consider that your housing conditions are:

Dreadful – very bad – bad – mean – good- very good – excellent

2. You think that the general conditions of their neighborhood (asphalt, lighting, sewers, etc..) are:

Dreadful – very bad – bad – mean – good- very good – excellent

3. You think your income is:

Dreadful – very bad – bad – mean – good- very good – excellent

4. How much extra home income you need not to feel poor?

Income amount	*Linguistic label*	*Income amount*	*Linguistic label*
More than double	Dreadful	40 – 50% more	Good
double	Very bad	10 -30 % more	Very good
80 – 90% more	Bad	nothing	excellent
60 – 70% more	Mean		

9. Considering the number of working hours, you find it:
Dreadful – very bad – bad – mean – good- very good – excellent
10. You think that your working conditions are:
Dreadful – very bad – bad – mean – good- very good – excellent
11. Do you feel poor?
Absolutely poor – very poor – rather poor – nor poor or not poor – somewhat poor – almost non poor – non poor.
12. How do you evaluate your level of economic welfare?
Dreadful – very bad – bad – mean – good- very good – excellent
13. Indicate the importance of each area for your welfare.

Area	Absolut. Important	Very important	Pretty important	Careless	Little important	Rather unimportant	Unimportant
1. health							
2. Education							
3. Housin							
4. Income							
5. Employment							

14. What is the amount of household income?

Household income	*Linguistic label*	*Household income*	*Linguistic label*
more than $10000	excellent	$2000 - $2999	bad
$8000 - $10000	very good	$1000 - $ 1999	very bad
$5000 - $7999	good	Less tan $1000	dreadful
$3000 - $4999	mean		

References

L. Beccaría, J.C. Ferres and P. Sáinz, "Medición de la pobreza. Situación actual de los conceptos y métodos". Informe del Seminario de Santiago (1997).

J. L. Ávila Martínez, F. Cortés García, R. De la Torre, D. Hernández, E. Hernández Laos, G. Leyva Parra and L. F. López Calva, "Medición de la pobreza. Variantes metodológicas y estimación preliminar". *Serie Documentos de Investigación* (2002).

J. Domínguez and A. M. Martín Caraballo, *Revista de Métodos Cuantitativos para la Economía y la Empresa*, **2**, 27 (2006).

J. Bentham, *An Introduction to the principles of morals and Legislation* (Oxford Blackwell, Oxford, 1948).

J. S. Mill, *El Utilitarismo* (Ediciones Aguilar, Madrid, 1971).

A. Sen, *Oxford Economic Papers*, **35**, 153 (1983).

A. Sen, *Choice, welfare and Measurement* (Oxford, Basil Blackwell, 1993).

L. F. Aguado Quintero and A. M. Osorio Mejía, *Reflexión Política*, **8,** N° **15**, 26 (2006).

B. M. S. Van Praag, *Cesifo Economic* Studies, **53** (**1**), 42 (2007).

A. Kapteyn, P. Kooreman and R. Willemse, *Journal of Human Resources*, **23**, 222 (1988).

L. A. Zadeh, *Information Sciences*, **8**, 199, *Information Sciences*, **8**, 301, *Information Sciences*, **9**, 43 (1975).

L. Lazzari, *El comportamiento del consumidor desde una perspectiva fuzzy una aplicación a turismo.* (EDICON, Buenos Aires, 2010).

Z. Xu, *International Journal of Uncertainty Fuzziness and Knowledge-Based-Systems*, **12**, 791 (2004).

Z. Xu, in: H. Bustince and J. Montero (eds.), *Fuzzy Sets and Their Extensions: Representation, Aggregation and Models*, 163 (Springer-Verlag, Berlin, 2008).

Z. Xu, *International Journal of Information Technology & Decision Making*, **4**, 153 (2005).

ENVIRONMENTAL IMPACT AND PROFITABILITY OF ORGANIZATIONS

JOSE DANIEL BARQUERO CABRERO
European Superior Council of Doctors & D.H.C., Girona, 24 Barcelona, 08010, Spain

MANUEL MEDINA ELIOZONDO
Universidad Autónoma de Cohauila 25280 Cohauila, México

VÍCTOR MANUEL MOLINA MOREJÓN
Universidad Autónoma de Coahuila 25280 Cohauila, México

MARIO BARQUERO CABRERO
Universidad Rey Juan Carlos & ESERP University Foundation (F.U.E.) 28016 Madrid, Spain

The central idea of this article is to show some aspects related to issues of environment and sustainability which are discussed by two Mexican institutes: the Mexican Institute for competitiveness A.C. (IMCO) and the Institute for the promotion of Total quality A.C. (IFCT), as well as the international standard ISO 14000. Also it wants to encourage the awareness that protecting the environment is not a waste of money, but in fact it is a perspective of business that contributes to achieve the profitability of organizations, it shows some stages of the GRECO initiative applied in the Mediterranean area, which facilitates the incorporation of SMEs to a better environmental management which is translated into an increase of profitability.

1. Introduction

First of all, let us introduce some basic concepts. The urban competitiveness of IMCO General Index measures the ability of a city to attract and retain investment and talent. In general, this is achieved when the countries, regions, entities or cities offer conditions integral to maximize the socio-economic potential of companies and people. One of the indicators that measure relates to the environment. The IFCT is responsible for the design and evaluation of the national model for the 2009 competitiveness which measures Corporate Social responsibility, which includes the environment within one of its proponents. The ISO 14000 standards focuses on the organization by providing a set of standards based on procedures and guidelines from which a company can build and maintain an environmental management system.

Various sources from the above-mentioned institutes and the ISO 14000 standard, a part from the other United Nations program for the environment (UNEP) have been consulted in this article. In the first part we commented how this general information is handled by the IMCO here, as you probably know, deals with the competitiveness at the level of country and region. Then, we analyze the participation of enterprises in this own theme but from a purely business environment, how this issues are handled by the national model for competitiveness in its 2009 version, the final part is related to the ISO 14000 standard that was designed to deal with environmental issues. It is completed with the results of a survey to a group of thirty businessmen of the Comarca of La Laguna where they commented their perception about a group of questions made in models of competitiveness in Mexico.

From their answers it is possible to form a panorama on the aspects on which it is necessary to have greater impact to improve the effectiveness and efficiency and to reduce the environmental impact.

Development: The IMCO report of Urban Competitiveness 2010 studied 86 cities through the analysis of 10 factors of competitiveness based on 111 variables. This allows them to establish a rate that becomes a useful tool for the recommendation, implementation and improvement of public policies relating to the cities of the country, that these should steadily increase their welfare level, beyond the inherent possibilities that offer their own resources, technological and innovation capacity; All the above mentioned, is irrespective of the normal economic fluctuations that the country may suffer. The ten indicators underlying this report to measure the competitiveness of the nation and of the regions is shown in table 1.

Table 1. Indicators to measure the competitiveness of the Nation and Regions.

1.	Reliable and objective law system
2.	Sustainable management of the environment
3.	Inclusive, prepared and healthy society
4.	Stable Macro Economy
5.	Stable and functional political system
6.	Efficient factors market
7.	Precursor sectors of world class
8.	Efficient and effective Government
9.	Benign International Relations
10.	Economic sectors in vigorous competitions

The second of these indicators relates with the sustainable environment management (SME). This subscript describes both the state of environmental conservation and the rate of degradation of the main environmental assets and its interaction with the productive activities and consumption. This factor considers the environment as an essential condition to generate sustainable long-term growth and development.

When in 2008 the IMCO processes the results of this variables in homogeneous groups of competitiveness, the La Laguna territory –our influence area- is situated in a middle-low group, position which shares with other 28 cities o metropolitan zones that together accounts the 19,4% of the country population and at the same time they generate the 17,51% of the Mexican GDP. This is not a good position because before this middle-low group, there are others qualified as High, Adequate, and Middle High.

Table 2 shows the ten indicators which measured this index, referred only to the variable environmental management; the second column includes the results of our territory and the third a similar value but at Mexico. The call to attention is referred to aspects such as protected natural areas or treated sewage volume or the aspect of green areas in which we have values well below those of the country.

Table 2: Environmental management indicators for the year 2009 at the Level of La Laguna, Mexico

INDICATOR	Value of La Laguna Indicator 2008	Value of Country Indicator 2008
Protected natural areas Indicator: % protected surface / total area	1,83	6,2
Indicator annual reforestation rate: % reforested surface / total area	0,22	0,22
Companies certified as "Clean" Indicator: # comp. with PROFEPA certify by millions of PEA	53,21	33,8
Environmental emergencies Indicator: # of average emergency	3,29	2,4
Extreme climatic conditions Indicator: standard deviation of daily temperature	3,10	3,7
Green areas Indicator: % of the territory with forests, jungles and vegetation	6,0	11,3
Controlled disposal of solid waste Indicator: % of waste that are deposited in controlled sites	46,05	57,3
Water stress Indicator: average annual precipitation	75,93	53,1
Overexploitation of aquifers Indicator: % surface over-farmed / total area	20,32	25,3
Volume treated sewage Indicator: liters per second for every million inhabitants	619,43	1108,2
Soils with chemical degradation Indicator: % degradation surface chemistry/sup. Total	66,17	57,6

The IMCO/2008 report raises that at country level –comparing 2006-2008 – the variable which improved further in this subscript was the rate of urban reforestation, which rose from 0.15% of the territory of the cities to the 0.22%, on average. In the same way, it achieved a positive change in the territory corresponding to natural protected areas. The worst was the water stress which fell by 42%.

The table also set out the positive situation on this moment of the cities of Aguascalientes and Monterrey which are at the forefront, not only of the final disposal of solid waste in controlled sites (100% and 97%, respectively), but also of its final use. Since 2007 in Aguascalientes operate two captivating of biogas factories, in the landfills of San Nicolás and Las Cumbres. Since this year there has been an annual burning of biogas from 16.2 million m3, receiving in 2008 more than 600,000 dollars for royalties from the sale of carbon credits. In addition, in April 2009 he began the construction of a factory generating electricity from biogas.

In the same way, the first plant of electrical generation from biogas in the metropolitan area of Monterrey, operates since 2003. The functioning of this plant, has avoided the emission of more than 46 thousand tons of gas methane, which leads almost 836 thousand tons of carbon dioxide. With biogas they produce the electrical energy equivalent to consumption per hour of seven thousand houses with ten spotlights of 100 watts each. This energy supplies the 80% of the energy used in lighting, the operation of the subway and pumping of potable water in the metropolitan area of Monterrey. In 2009 they began the third phase of expansion of the plant that seeks to increase energy production equivalent to the consumption of twenty-five thousand houses and a biogas destruction equivalent to three million tones of CO^2.

The Mexican Institute for Total quality promotes the national competitiveness 2009 model, characterized by its emphasis on cause the strategic thinking for a better understanding of the environment in which the Organization operates and the basis of resources that are available to respond to this; It promotes also the development of an external vision to provide a flexible an agile adaptation, to an environment which in a continual evolution, and in which industries, markets, technological changes and the stakeholders of the organizations, are continually posing new challenges.

The model comprises seven drivers of value that contribute to raise the competitiveness of the Organization: leadership, customers, planning, processes, personnel, information and knowledge and Corporate Social Responsibility, in which the environment is included. These drivers allow evaluating the competitiveness and sustainability of the Organization through a group of questions.

Seven are the questions which are subject enterprises to evaluate them in order to assure the lowest environmental impacts:

1) What indicators are used to measure: emissions into the atmosphere, water consumption, consumption of energy and waste generation?
2) What actions have been generated to reduce the impact on climate change?
3) How is decreased energy intensity in the processes of operation?

4) What actions are undertaken to reduce the environmental footprint of products?
5) How are integrated the indicators which apply the concept of eco-efficiency to assess the environmental performance of the organization?
6) What commitments exist with the community to promote education and environmental awareness?
7) With what initiatives it responds to the requirements of recovery of ecosystems?

Two concepts we want to point out, the first referred to the environmental footprints as cargo measures imposed on the natural environment by a population given, expressed in the surface area required to sustain their levels of consumption and waste production; they consider the effects of the technological and commercial development in the carrying capacity of the planet. Its objective is to assess needs in natural capital, derived from consumption. And within the environmental footprint MNC 2009 promotes the study of the environmental footprint of the product when it comes to assess how green is a green product?, i.e., what amount of greenhouse gases were generated during the manufacture of this product?, for what would have to take into consideration a number of factors, such as of what is done the product and where are the elements that make up it –in many occasions, even the manufacturers – and much less consumers – have this information. The other concept is eco-efficiency, understood as the possibility of creating more goods and services using fewer resources and creating less waste and pollution.

In short: any company that is aspiring to the national quality award will be evaluated on the theme of environment through these questions, same that in a brief synthesis manages to grab the most important aspects that must be satisfied.

The ISO 14000 standard is a set of documents of environmental management which, once implemented, will affect all aspects of the management of an organization in their environmental responsibilities and help organizations to systematically address environmental issues, in order to improve the environmental performance and profit opportunities. The standards are voluntary, have no legal obligation and do not establish a set of quantitative goals regarding levels of emissions or specific methods of measuring these emissions. On the other hand, ISO 14000 focuses on the organization by providing a set of standards based on procedure and guidelines from which a company can build and maintain an environmental management system. The system of environmental management according to ISO 14001: 2004 and ISO 14004: 2004 is the tool that allows organizations to formulate policies and objectives, taking into account the legal requirements and information relating to its aspects and environmental impacts. It is defined as that part of the system of overall management of the organization that includes organizational structure, planning activities, procedures, processes and resources to develop, establish, achieve, reviewing and maintaining the environmental policy.

ISO 14001 is an internationally accepted standard that expresses how to establish a system of management of the environment (EMS) effective. The standard is designed to strike a balance between maintaining profitability and reducing impacts on the environment and, with the support of the organizations, it is possible to achieve both goals.

ISO 14001 is focused to any organization of any size or sector, which are looking for an improvement of the environmental impacts and complying with legislation in the field of environment.

An EMS is a mechanism for regulation of business management in the following aspects:

- Identify and control the environmental impact of its activities, products or services.
- Continuously improve their environmental performance.
- To apply a systematic approach to establish environmental objectives and goals to achieving these and to demonstrate that they have achieved.

What is sought is to minimize the generation of waste in the various productive activities and services, through the adequacy of facilities and processes.

CAR-PL cleaner production Regional Activity Centre strengthened during the 2008 and 2009 their actions aimed at the promotion of the consumption and production patterns, creating alliances with the Marrakech process, the global initiative on consumption and sustainable production driven by UNEP and the Department of economic and Social Affairs of the United Nations. The CP/RAC, in the implementation of its mission to promote the production and sustainable consumption, and the sound management of chemicals, puts a special emphasis on three specific areas, in which the Centre has a remarkable experience and a great potential: the diffusion of cleaner production and green competitiveness, through the GRECO initiative, sustainable consumption and finally, the rational management of chemicals substances. The Greco initiative, which has tried for a decade in different companies in the Mediterranean region, seeks to involve and engage small and medium-sized enterprises in the integration of the environment as a strategic element of profitability. The project aims to "educate the companies that protecting the environment is not a waste of money, but it is actually a business perspective". The initiative aims to provide SMEs with assistance and financial resources to discover what the best pollution prevention techniques appropriate for each case, calculating the profitability of projects implementation and evaluating the environmental benefit obtained. It is, ultimately, the bet value creation based on the improvement of the environmental performance of organizations, understood as a whole.

The GRECO initiative is based on:

- Disclosure of information related to available PL techniques in enterprises of the Mediterranean (it will be important to the exchange of experiences including MedClean files). Through the publication of the GRECO report (based on one hundred cases MedCleans analysis) and wide dissemination, conferences, activities in network, website and annual report.
- Provide technical assistance to SMEs, through training on ways and means to introduce solutions PL more adapted to these companies, and to evaluate the growth of profitability and the environmental benefits of the adaptation of these solutions. This activity will take place primarily through technical workshops.
- Provide financial aid to SMEs which wish to adopt techniques, through international relevant financial institutions (IFC).
- Involve all public institutions and relevant agencies in all actions relating to el GRECO.
- Promote public-private partnership for green competitiveness.
- Promote the role of the social responsibility of enterprises (CSR) on green competitiveness and sustainable consumption.

The strategy is based on the disclosure of the implementation of environmental techniques (PN) in the Mediterranean region, which have been implemented successfully in more than one hundred SMEs (MedCleans chips) and that it has become a genuine strategy of green competitiveness with which everybody gains, for the Mediterranean partners.

To demonstrate that the Greco initiative is not a utopia, the CAR-PL has one hundred examples of companies that have successfully implemented the use of alternative raw materials, the energy savings and the recovery and recycling of gas, heat and organic matter derived from the production process, among other measures.

Results:

Topic: Perception held by entrepreneurs of the Comarca of La Laguna on the status of the environmental management following a guide contained in the national model for competitiveness.

I. The questions are based on a set of selected issues and responses are encoded in either; Regular or bad according to the perception of respondents that are themselves leaders in their companies.

To ensure the lowest environmental impacts:

• Which indicators are used to measure: emissions into the atmosphere, water consumption, consumption of energy and waste generation?

• How are the indicators to assess the environmental performance of the organization integrated to implement the concept of eco-efficiency?

• What commitments exist with the community to promote education and environmental awareness?

• What initiatives have to respond to the requirements of recovery of ecosystems?

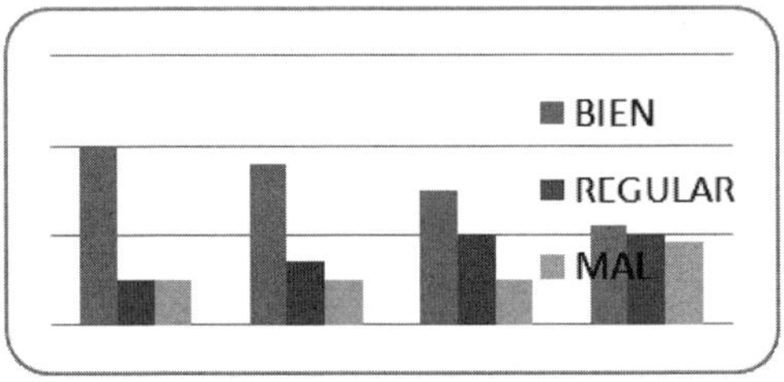

II. To respond to the requirements of the sustainable development strategy as regards personnel:

• How does make sure of the development of competencies of the staff?

• Which is the process followed to manage learning and organizational knowledge?

• How does make sure about the satisfaction and quality of life of the staff?

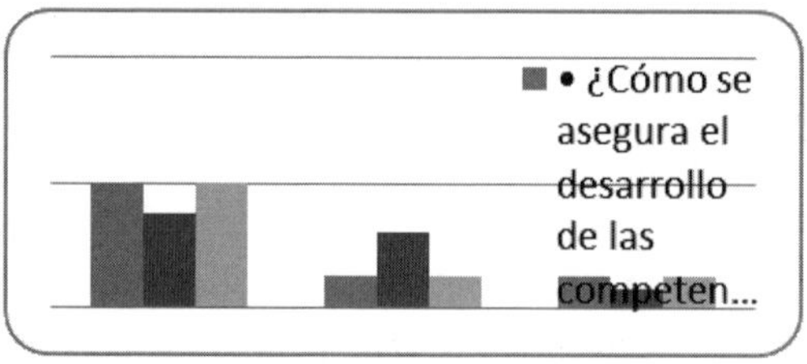

III. To respond to the requirements of the strategy of sustainable development in the community and consumers:

• How is supported the capital resource in the communities where it operates?

• Which are the practices and systems that supports the generation of confidence in consumers and communities where it operates?

• How are encouraged in the business partners: suppliers and subcontractors to have good practices of organizational behavior?

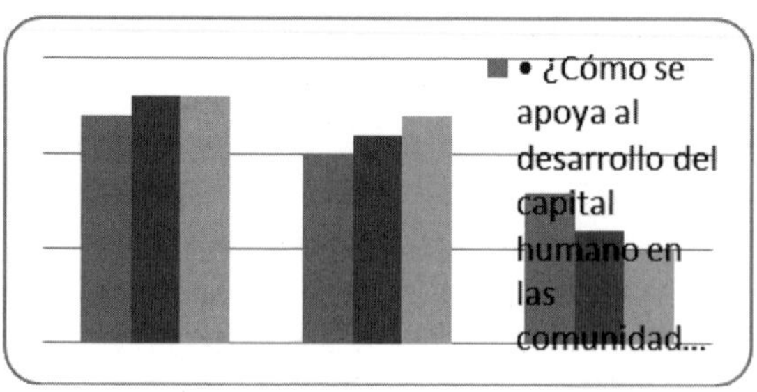

IV.For accountability to society:

• What means are used to report the results of performance of the initiatives generated by the organization with regard to a sustainable development to society?

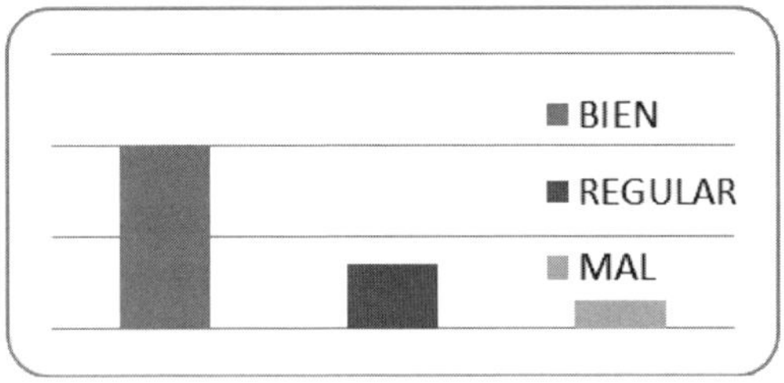

V. To respond to the needs of the sustainable development. Strategy for staff

How to make sure that the development of competencies of the staff to respond to the requirements of the sustainable development strategy in?

- Knowledge
- Abilities
- Capacities
- Values

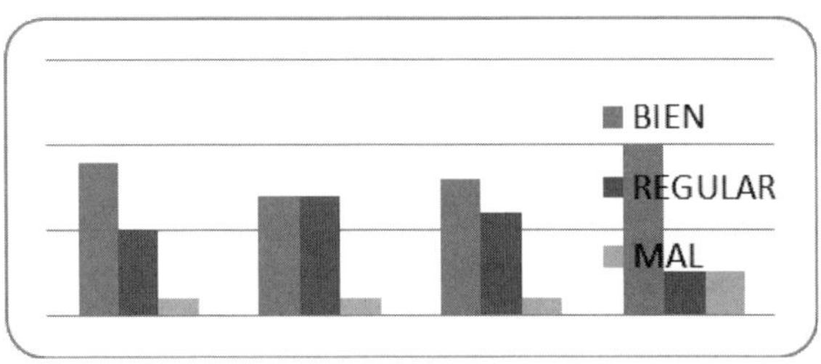

Conclusions

The process of negotiation regarding the Climate Change goes through a critical stage which accredited the consideration of different options for its reorientation to the effective achieving of agreements.

- The Conference of the Parts (COP), which took place in Copenhagen, Denmark, reached progresses in the negotiation group work without reach the adoption of any result multilaterally agreed.

- The results pursuing by the COP16 held in Mexico are hierarchical by order of ambition, and range from the adoption of a new legally binding instrument, to a simple reconstruction of the mutual trust enabling a breakthrough with regard to the inherited elements of Copenhagen

- The result of the COP 16 was a balanced package of decisions called Cancun Agreements so, as per the United Nations, will promote the commitment of the nations to improve the actions related to the Climate Change and not to compromise its development.

The Universidad Autónoma de Coahuila, Mexico in its mission of being an entrepreneurial University, works and is making progress in activities that facilitate:

- Apply the profitability of a good environmental management in their classes and researches:

  - Study of methodologies of costs of emissions into the atmosphere, consumption of water, energy consumption and waste generation in particular in SMEs.
  - Handling of the concept of eco-efficiency.
  - Study and management of issues related to “Carbon bonds” and payments for “environmental services”.

- Incorporating in their studies competencies enabling graduates to acquire the knowledge, skills, abilities and values to design, establish, improve and measure aspects that help to mitigate climate change.

- It is necessary to design the work of environmental management in the territory related rather than environmental technology companies:
  - Training in skills of the staff to respond to the requirements of the sustainable development strategy.
  - Design and implementation of sustainable development strategies customized in the community and consumers.
  - Commitments to the community to promote education and environmental awareness.

References

International standard ISO 14000, consulted in September 2010. http://www.iso.org/iso/iso_14000_essentials
History and Foundation of the center of Regional activity for the clean production CAR PL. Consulted in October 2010 in http://www.cprac.org/es/car-pl/historia
GRECO initiative work plan. Consulted in October 2010 http://www.cprac.org/es/ revi/plan-de-trabajo.
Mexican Institute for competitiveness. IMCO. http://imco.org.mx
Institute for the promotion of Total quality. IFCT. http://www.ifct.org
The United Nations Environment Programme. PNUMA
COP 16, http://www.cc2010.mx/.

THE OIL & GAS INDUSTRY ANALYSIS WITH THE ELECTRE III METHOD

CARLOS EDUARDO DURANGE DE CARVALHO INFANTE
Industrial Engineering, Federal University of Rio de Janeiro, Cidade Universitária – CGTEC/CT2
Rio de Janeiro, Brazil

ALINE MUNIZ DE SOUZA
Industrial Engineering, Advanced System and Production Management Laboratory, Cidade Universitária – CGTEC/CT2
Rio de Janeiro, Brazil

ROGERIO DE ARAGÃO BASTOS DO VALLE
Industrial Engineering, Advanced System and Production Management Laboratory, Cidade Universitária – CGTEC/CT2
Rio de Janeiro, Brazil

The aim of this study was to develop an integrated of economic, environmental and social issues about the impact of major oil and gas companies in the world, featuring its activities through sustainability indicators. The ELECTRE III method was used to verify the ranking of companies according to sustainable direct reports. It was concluded that strategic sustainable, combined with the Triple Bottom Line is a corporate and operational differential. Thus, it is expected to contribute to the deepening of enterprise policy across all strategic decisions, with a sustainability focus.

1. Introduction

In the context of globalization, new technological trends, cycles of innovation increasingly accelerated and intensified competition, the discussion on sustainable development grows and intensifies.

The relationship between development and environment is now considered a central point in understanding the ecological problems. The concept of sustainable development is specifically about a new way for society to relate to their environment to ensure its own continuity and its external environment. However, the formulation of a definition for the concept of sustainable development still generates different interpretations. Exist, according to some authors, a degree of consensus on the need to reduce environmental pollution, eliminate waste and reduce the poverty rate (Baroni, 1992).

From an economic standpoint, sustainability provides that companies must be economically viable. Their role in society should be completed taking into consideration the aspect of profitability, i.e., provide feedback to the investment made by private capital.

In social terms, the company must meet the requirements to provide the best working conditions for their employees, seeking to address the cultural diversity of society in which it operates, and provide opportunities in general.

From an environmental standpoint, the company should be guided by eco-efficiency in their production processes, providing conditions for the development of an organizational culture of environmental as well as adopting an attitude of environmental responsibility. However, it is necessary that a dialogue for which the three dimensions are contemplated to maintain the sustainability of the system.

The multicriteria decision aid is called by the French School, Multicriteria Analysis, and the American School, Methods of Multicriteria Decision Aid (MCDA – Multiple Criteria Decision-Aid) or Multicriteria Decision Making (MCDM – Multiple Criteria Decision Making) (Vincke, 1992).

Roy (1985) shows that the current European differs from current U.S. regarding the use and definitions of multicriteria methods. The current U.S. concentrates its efforts in the discovery and description of the decision maker, and to build on theorems, corollaries, concepts and axioms in the search for "optimal solution". Already the EU side seeks to find the "best compromise solution," which means that in the case of multiple criteria, it is impossible to think of the optimal solution.

Outranking methods are not adapted to the uncertainty with uncertain and imprecise data, as explained below:

• Inaccurate Criteria, the difficulty in determining them: Projects can fit in many ways and goals. Project A with an environmental focus and Project B with social focus. This vagueness of the criterion choice impacts the final outcome (Bowden, 2000);

• Criteria indeterminate, since the method of evaluation criteria is arbitrarily selected among several possible definitions;

• Criteria uncertain, because the measured values refer only to a point in time and some values vary in the long run. For example: "employability" of projects depends on the economic situation. "Investments in facilities" cannot be evenly distributed over time.

2. Methodology

The various versions of the ELECTRE family are based on one fundamental concept, but differ in their operationalization (Buchanan et al., 2004).

In applying the ELECTRE method family, there are two concepts of great importance to be consider: the threshold concept and the hierarchy concept. Assuming the existence of a set of criteria and actions The g_j, where j = 1,2, …, n, which are to maximize the traditional model of preference can be found two possible relations to a pair of shares (a, b) where (Buchanan et al., 2004):

APB: a is preferable to b, if gj (a) > g, (b)
AIB: indifferent to the b, g, is (a) = g_j (b)

The method ELECTRE III model described above introduces a threshold value preferably pj and a threshold value indifference qj, for each criterion gj. Thus the decision maker can establish a range of values in which an action is strictly preferable to the other and an interval in which an action is indifferent to the other. With the introduction of these limits, the preference relations are as follows (Buchanan et al., 2004):

APB: a is preferable to b, if gj (a) > g, (b) + p_j
AIB, is immaterial to ab, where g_j (a) – g, (b) ≤ q_j

These indifference and preference thresholds are set by the decision maker, and they show how sensitive the decision maker wants to compare two actions. Thus, the above-mentioned relationships were as follows (Buchanan et al., 2004):

APB: a is preferable to strictly b, if g_j is (a) > g, (b) + p_j
AQB: the poor have a preference to b, if g, (b) + q_j <g_j (a) ≤ g, (b) + p_j
AIB: a is indifferent to b, g_j(b) – q_j, q_j ≤ (a) ≤ g, (b) + qj

Through these limits, the ELECTRE methods establish a relationship of hierarchy denoted by S, where an action ASB, i.e., the action "is at least as good as b" or "not worse than b".

It is at this point to comment that the introduction of preference thresholds (p) and indifference (q) redefines the criteria in pseudo-criteria, since the difference between gj (a) and gj (b) ceases to be judged solely by the value for the that criterion, and begins to establish a zone of indifference, through these limits (q).

In Multicriteria analysis performed by the ELECTRE method, beyond the level of agreement, it has an index mismatch, d (a, b), which measures how much disagrees aSb.

At this point, there is one of the innovations of the ELECTRE III, with the introduction of a new threshold called threshold of veto (v). The veto threshold v is the one at which, from him, the claim is rejected, i.e. there is no possibility of being at least as good as b, in this case is that g_j (b) ≥ g, (a) + v_j.

Now, with the two indices calculated (agreement and disagreement), it is possible to determine the credibility of the ranking matrix, which measures how strong is the claim ASB.

After analysis, it is necessary to analyze the robustness of the results presented. This analysis is performed by varying parameters, weight and preferably limits, indifference, veto originally established in order to determine the scope of variation of certain parameters within which a recommendation remains stable. It serves to provide a recommendation to the decision maker and robust synthetic, to report on the proposed solution's ability to withstand the variations between reality and the model assumed to represent it (MAYSTRE et al 1994).

This paper is based on the study of the likely improvement of sustainable performance for a set of five oil companies, by analyzing the performance of fifteen sustainability indicators, reported in their sustainability reports, in the period 2005 to 2009.

The five companies selected were defined according to their market value. In Table 1 we can see the five largest companies in the oil and gas, respectively, with their ratings.

Table 1 – Selected companies

Companies	**Rating**
Petrobras S.A	E1
British Petroleum	E2
Royal Dutch Shell	E3
Exxon Mobil Corporation	E4
Chevron Corporation	E5

To analyze the likely improvement in sustainable performance, indicators of environmental performance reports, economic and social development of all companieses were collected and analyzed. An important contribution can also be seen in (Lang et al., 2007). It is noteworthy that as signatories of the Global Reporting Initiative (GRI), apply the GRI G3 Guidelines for the preparation of sustainability reports.

We sought to compare the evolution of the activities of these firms over five years, i.e. 2005 to 2009.

The indicators were selected from the following criteria:

Relevance to the sector of study;

Contribution to the Triple Bottom Line analysis; and

Reporting and full disclosure by all companies selected.

The criteria for ranking of the companies studied were the total production (EC1), development and impact of investments in infrastructure and services (EC8), Direct energy consumption by primary energy source (EN3), total withdrawal of water source (EN8), total direct emissions of greenhouse gases, by weight (EN16), total indirect emissions of greenhouse gases, by weight (EN50), Sox, by type and weight (EM20), Nox by type and weight (EN60), total water discharge by quality and destination (EN21), total weight of waste (EN22), total volume of significant spills (EN23), total investment and environmental protection expenditures by type (EN30), total workforce by employment type, employment contract and region (LA1), rates of deaths related to work (LA7) and rates of occupational illnesses related to work, by region (LA70).

3. Results

By applying the ELECTRE III method may be obtained the following results.

Destilations

Each alternative is connected with another alternative by two arrows, one in each direction, indicating the reliability index. For many alternatives, the graph is highly complex. An automated procedure, with the name of distillation should be used to rank the alternative. The name "distillation" was chosen because the analogy with alchemists who distill mixtures of liquid to extract a magic ingredient. The algorithm to classify all alternatives can be divided into two pre-classifications.

The first pre-classification is achieved with a descending distillation, selecting the highest ranked alternative first and ending with the worst. The best alternative is extracted from the whole by applying very strict rules. In this subset, the best alternatives are selected by application of less restrictive rules (not previously used the same rules would bring a different result). The procedure continues with less restrictive rules and a smaller number, subsets of

alternatives. The procedure ends when it remains only one alternative or a group of alternatives that cannot be separated. The second distillation using the same procedure, but in the original set of alternatives removed, first, the best results from the distillation. Thus, a new subset is obtained in each distillation, which contains the best alternative. In each distillation, the alternative extracted is placed in an inferior position. As an alternative is connected with each other by two arrows, one in each direction, but not necessarily with symmetrical credibility index, a second pre-sorting is constructed with an upward distillation. In this case, the worst alternatives are selected first and distillation ends with the award of the best alternative. To the distillation, the necessary condition is that an alternative a is the preferred tob is defined as follows: the alternative a is preferred to b when the degree of reliability that "A exceeds B" exceeds the threshold $\lambda 2$ and significantly higher than the degree credibility "B beats A".
Applying this procedure for all 2005 to 2009, gets the distillation shown in Figure 1 and Figure 2.

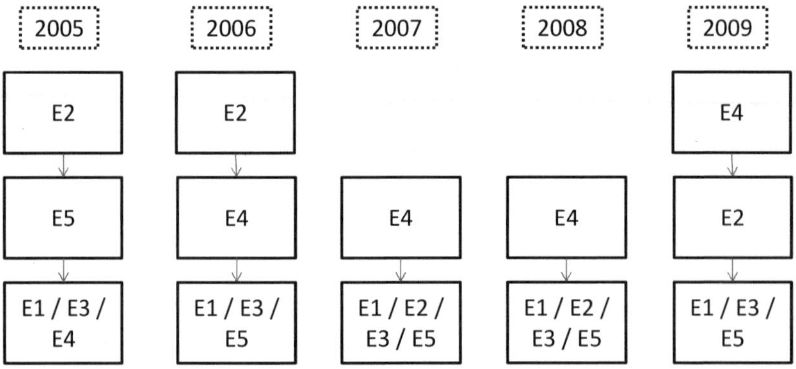

Figure 1- Results of descending distillation – pre-classification of five companies (E1-E5)

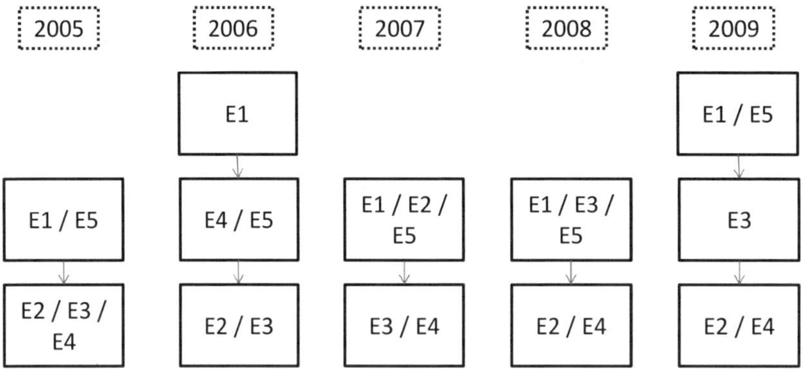

Figure 2 – Results of ascending distillation – pre-classification of five companies (E1-E5)

It can be seen that for the years 2006 distillation ascending E1 showed that the company got preference over the others, followed by companies E4 and E5. The others did not receive preferences related, resulting in an indifference between them.

In the year 2007 and 2008, we find that the results were similar in ascending distillation. For the former, firms E1, E2 and E5 were ranked as the best and second best placed companies were E1, E3 and E5. It is noticed that only E2 is not indifferent to the others in the second year under review. For other companies, there was no preference between them.

Ending with the year 2009, it was observed that the result of ascending distillation showed the preference for companies E1 and E5, followed by company E3. There was no preference between companies E2 and E4 (Figure 2).

4. Ranking

The spatial period (Figure 3) is obtained by combining two pre-classifications. Partial results of pre-rankings are aggregated in the classification matrix. We have four possible cases:

The alternative A is better than B or in both the distillation is better than B in one distillation and has the same position in other distillation, then A is better than B: $\mathbf{A\ P^{+}\ B}$;

A is greater than B in a distillation, but B is better than another distillation, then A is unique to B: **A R B**;

A has the same position in both distillations B, so A is indifferent to B:**A I B**;

A is smaller than B or in both the distillation is less than B in one distillation and has the same rank in other distillation, then A is worse than B: $\mathbf{A\ P^{-}\ B}$.

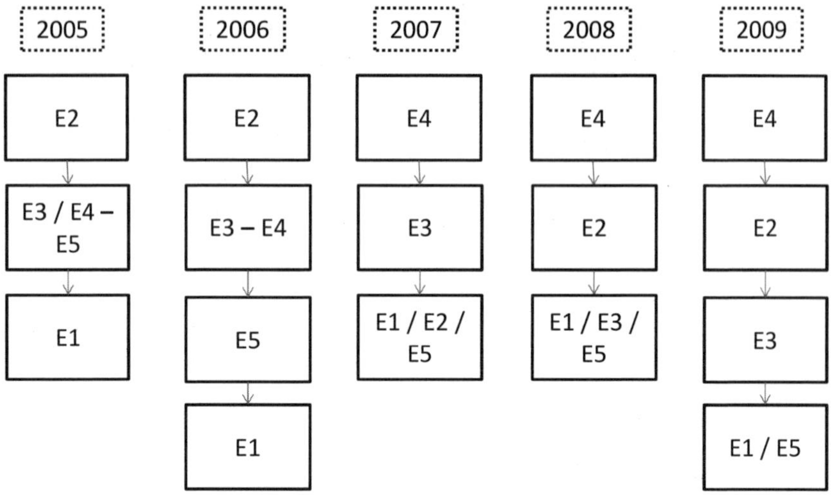

Figure 3 – Final ranking

Company E4 had the best performance, considering its evolution. This company, in 2005, was indifferent to E3 (E4 I E3) and incomparable to E5 (E4 R E5), respectively. Futhermore, it won the second place in the ranking, however, in the following years its performance was considered more relevant, providing a prominent position before the others.

The company E2 obtained the second best performance, considering its evolution. This company ranked first in the ranking, in 2005 and 2006, only falling to the second place in the other years. This favorable performance in five years provided a guarantee of effective implementation of the criteria analyzed.

The company E3 has remained virtually constant in all years. In the years 2005 to 2007 it took the second place in the ranking, dropping to third in the years 2008 and 2009, which earned him third place overall. This company, in 2008, was considered indifferent to enterprises E1 and E5 (E1 I E3) and (E3 I E5), which does not happen again in 2009.

Company E5 began 2005 in the second place. It is indifferent to company E3(E4 I E3) and incomparable to E4 (E5 I E44). In the years 2006 to 2008, it remained in third place, being indifferent to enterprises E1 (E1 I E5), E2 (E5 I E2) and E3 (E3 I E5). In the year 2009, E5 got the last place, being indifferent to the company E1 only. This little improvement of this company performance, allowed his fourth overall in the final ordering.

Company E1 got the worst outcome, according to analyzed criteria. This one got the last place every year, being indifferent to companies E2 (E1 I E2) and E5 (E5 I E1), in 2007, E3 (E1 I E3) and E5 (E5 I E1), in the year 2008 and E5, in

2009. In short, we can summarize the results of the evolution, as shown in Figure 4.

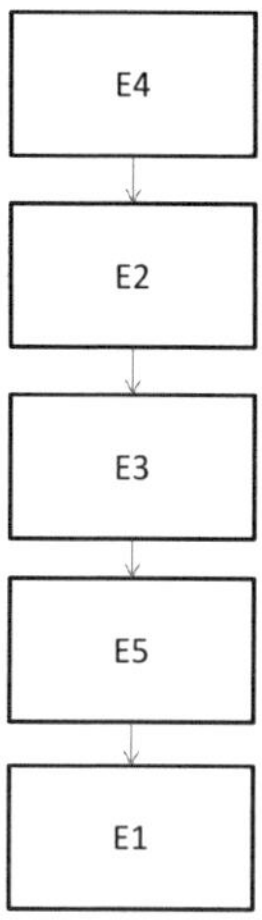

Figure 4 – Summarize Ranking

5. Conclusions

The method application provided a ranking of companies, which proved to be susceptible in some variation of the weights of the criteria, as well as in changing the arrangement of some other criteria.
The criteria presented and discussed were adequate for the evaluation of companies in the oil & gas industry, as they encompassed economic, environmental and social reasons for this study. It should be noted that, regarding the risk of environmental criteria, there is a need for more accurate survey in the field, in order to evaluate all parameters that influence such criterion, but for the present study, the evaluation had to be satisfactory.
ELECTRE III method works with objective variables (criteria values) and subjective variables (weights and thresholds of the criteria), a characteristic that directs a process hierarchy understood as more sensitive to the complexity of decisions.

References

Vincke, P. *Multicriteria decision-aid.* 1 ed. John Wiley & Sons Ltd. England. (1992).
ROY, B. — *Methodologie multicritè red'aide à la decision*. Paris: Economica, (1985).

Bowden, R. *Fantasy Higher Education: university and college league tables.* Quality in Higher Education 6 (1). Pg. 41-60. (2000).
Maystre, L. Y.; Pictet, J. & Simos, J. — Méthodes multicritères ELECTRE. 1. Ed. Lausanne: Presses polytechniques et universitaires romandes, (1994).
Lang, D. J., Binder, C. R., Scholz, R. W., Wiek, A., Stäubli, B., Sieber, C. *Sustainability Potential Analysis (SPA) of landfills—a systemic approach: initial application towards a legal landfill assessment.* Journal of Cleaner Production 15, 1654-1661. (2007).
Baroni, M. *Ambiguidades e deficiências do conceito de desenvolvimento sustentado.* In Revista de Administração de Empresas. São Paulo, 32(2), abril/jun., (1992).

THE TRANSPARENCY OF THE LAWS OF INFORMATION AS A TOOL TO THE IMPLEMENTATION OF POLICIES FOR MODELS OF SUSTAINABILITY

MANUEL MEDINA ELIZONDO
Research and Post Grade Coordinator, Universidad Autónoma de Cohauila Cohauila, 25280 México

JOSE DANIEL BARQUERO CABRERO
Professor Researcher of the European Superior Council of Doctors & Professor Researcher of the ESERP University Foundation (F.U.E.) Barcelona, 08010 – Spain

CARMEN FÁTIMA BARQUERO CABRERO
Professor Researcher, ESERP University Foundation (F.U.E.) Palma de Mallorca, 07004 – Spain

In this article that we are presenting, we want to put the emphasis on a study made by the European Superior Council of Doctors and Honoris Causa Doctors in Spain, to show the direct relationship between the implementation of policies of sustainability, environmental improvements and coexistence of the ecosystem with the need of people to have existing laws allowing full transparency of information by private and public institutions to implement the effectively of this type of policies.

That is why when we talk about models of sustainability that we develop in order to improve the environment and the living conditions of persons, we should first examine whether countries have a law of transparency that allows the development of these models.

Transparency is a key element to remove the opacity of information, and thus corruption. The more transparent we are in the access to information, a better health, environment, justice, security, and education services, members of the community will have.

Why are we speaking of transparency of information? Because to improve sustainability and environmental models that benefit society, we must have full assurance of knowing public administrations in general, and information concerning their actions that allow us to improve every day for the benefit of the citizens on political decisions taken and which affect these models.

If we focus in the case of Spain we realize that is one of the few countries in Europe that does not have a transparency law together with Luxemburg, Malta y Cyprus*. The adoption of a law on transparency from the political parties will allow knowing themes as simple as the number of cars that have been stolen in a population, people who have died in traffic accidents, people who have died in surgery rooms, money received by the political parties, trade unions and employers organizations, Spanish soldiers who have died or who have been wounded in a line of duty, the reclassification of land in protected areas, and other more.

The knowledge of this information would make possible to create models of sustainability and the improvement through their analysis and thereof they could be compared with those of other countries which are implementing these policies and models. Similarly, the information between the different provinces and Spanish corporations could be compared with the aim to allow us to reduce the negative impact of these actions.

Those countries that have decided to introduce a law on transparency (Open Government)[†] have mostly social policies that reach to the majority of the population, in special in the Nordic Countries. This does not imply that in the United States, in some countries of Latin America and in other countries that are part of the Open Government still exist social injustices.

In the United Kingdom My Society[‡] project was applied in 2003. Through its web page www.theyworkforyou.com[§] citizens act as supervising of politicians and officials so that any person can ask about any topic of interest and it will be answered by the administration. Similarly they can make suggestions for

[*] Diario El País, 10-11-2011 Ley de transparencia, ya Autor: JESÚS CEBERIO http://elpais.com/diario/2011/11/10/espana/1320879608_850215.html15134

[†] Lathrop, Daniel; Ruma, Laurel, eds. (February 2010). Open Government: Transparency, Collaboration and Participation in Practice. O'Reilly Media. ISBN 978-0-596-80435-0.

[‡] http://www.mysociety.org/about/ mySociety is a project of UK Citizens Online Democracy (UKCOD). UKCOD is a registered charity in England and Wales, no. 1076346. Its company number is 03277032, and mySociety Ltd's is 05798215

[§] http://www.theyworkforyou.com/about/

improvements such as e.g. the arrangement of the streets to help disabled people and be more sustainable with the environment.

After the analysis of the developed questions both open as closed and the study shows that access to information through a law of transparency would allow:

On environmental issues accessing public reports on possible toxic contamination with minerals such as mercury or discharges into rivers and swamps which would allow to require companies and municipalities greater compliance with environmental laws. Citizens could apply for and denounce actions not lawful if they had information about it.

Regarding Health system, it will be possible to know which is the index of mortality caused by possible hospital infections, by the King of surgery operation, in which hospitals this deceases have occurred, the Doctors infringements, between others in order to revisi the causes and if they are recurrence. To know at any time the number of patients who are on waiting lists, which is the King of surgery that they needs to really know the needs of these patients and unfortunately the number on deaths while they are waiting to be operated.

Concerning justice, to know the resolutions that punish the misconduct of judges and in this way the citizen creates justice in his own right and not in terms of who is going to judge him.

Politically more confidence in our representatives to know the details of the income perceived by the State trade unions, political parties, employers business, foundations and NGO's, and where are they investing or spending these economic resources. In the same way to know the number of freed trade unionists and political advisers and what are their salaries, for a greater confidence in these institutions. Remember that part of the money earmarked for the payment of these expenses come from the payment of taxes of citizens.

To know the number of public companies and semi-public of the Central, Autonomous Community and local governments, the salaries of people working in them and what is the recruitment procedures for the employees and managers of these companies [*]

Citizen Security. To know the number of polices who are punished for actions exceeding their legitimacy and the reason that has generated them, to improve in the future. Information about the number of robberies, rapes, gender-

---

[*] http://www.farodevigo.es/economia/2012/03/15/gobierno-suprimira-hoy-27-empresas-publicas/632750.html

based violence, in which areas took place, and if there is recurrence therein to implement policies in society to prevent future incidents.

Greater transparency by the Ministry of Defense of the number of soldiers who have died or have been injured in humanitarian actions or on their day to day work and find out how to avoid similar situations in the future.

Access for all the citizens to the data of the budgets of public, regional administrations and local and to have the possibility of knowing allocations of projects and works, who have been adjudicated and the process that has been followed, meet suppliers and the services that they offer*. This will ensure that any citizen may require greater control and rigor in public accounts and a better use of the incomes used by these administrations and which come from the taxes paid by the citizens.

The need to adopt in Spain a transparency of the information Law is evident not by the conclusions of the study butt in addition the past December first 2011 was presented to media, the index of perception of corruption in the year 2011 that developed the international agency "Transparency International – the global coalition against corruption" of one hundred and eighty-three countries concerning the public sector. (The 2011 corruption perceptions index measures perceived levels of public sector corruption in the one hundred and eighty-three countries and territories around the world)†

This index assesses one hundred and eighty three countries with a score ranging between zero (the nearest is to zero the index obtained by a country indicates a high degree of corruption) and ten (the nearest is ten the index obtained by a country indicates very low levels of corruption.

To be able to develop this index, have been used seventeen survey data that analyzes various factors such as access to information by individuals, laws which have been adopted against corruption, conflicts of interest generated in the country itself and others.

If we look at this report we will see that the countries who head the tail in this ranking, at negative levels, are Somalia, Korea of the North and Myanmar (Burma).

---

* http://www.minhap.gob.es/es-ES/Estadistica%20e%20Informes/Presupuesto%20y%20cuentas%20publicas/Paginas/presupuesto.aspx

† Transparency International – the global coalition against corruption. Report Corruption Perceptions Index 2011
http://cpi.transparency.org/cpi2011/results/

Table with the ranking of the ten worst countries for index of perception of corruption of the year 2011*

Ranking	Country	Score out of 10
172	Venezuela	1,9
175	Iraq	1,8
175	Haiti	1,8
177	Uzbekistan	1,6
177	Turkmenistan	1,6
177	Sudan	1,6
180	Afghanistan	1,5
180	Myanmar	1,5
182	North Korea	1,0
182	Somalia	1,0

Similarly we can see how the countries that led the rankings with a low corruption are New Zealand, followed by Scandinavia such as Finland, Denmark and Sweden.

Table with the ranking of the ten worst countries for index of perception of corruption of the year[8]

Ranking	Country	Score out of 10
1	New Zeeland	9,5
2	Finland	9,4
3	Denmark	9,4
4	Sweden	9,3
5	Singapore	9,2
6	Norwegian	9,0
7	Holland	8,9
8	Australia	8,8
9	Sweden	8,8
10	Canada	8,7

* Transparency International – the global coalition against corruption. Counttry results Report http://cpi.transparency.org/cpi2011/results/#CountryResults

It should also be noted that two thirds of the countries that appear in this ranking have a score less than five.

The report itself shown as Spain declined a post, 30 to 31, in the 2011 corruption perception index. Analyzing our country in the past three years, corruption has stalled and is maintained with a grade point average of six points.

If we ask ourselves which are the causes of the stagnation of corruption in Spain, we will come to the conclusion that has been caused by the real estate crisis[*]. In Spain real estate boom has led to keep the levels of corruption in both, central, regional or local government administrations and they must be largely the responsible of enabling the recovery of the crisis if we are able to give an image of transparency in all sectors public and private.

Curiously the five countries of the zone euro that are in a situation of debt crisis, we can observe that only approve three, Ireland (7.4 points), Spain (6.2 points) and Portugal (6.1 points), while suspended Italy (3.9 points) and Greece (3.4 points).

Table with the ranking of the ten worst countries for index of perception of corruption of the year[8]

Ranking	Country	Score out of 10
24	United Estates	7,1
25	Uruguay	7,0
25	Santa Lucia	7,0
25	France	7,0
25	United Arab Emirates	6,8
28	Estonia	6,4
29	Cyprus	6,3
30	Spain	6,2
31	Botswana	6,1
32	Portugal	6,1

In the table we appreciate which countries are above Spain and have a better rate of reputation and we can also get an idea of the weight of their economies

[*] Parlamento Europeo. Informe sobre el impacto de la urbanización extensiva en España en los derechos individuales de los ciudadanos europeos, el medio ambiente y la aplicación del Derecho comunitario, con fundamento en determinadas peticiones recibidas - A6-0082/2009 http://www.europarl.europa.eu/sides/getDoc.do?pubRef=-//EP//TEXT+REPORT+A6-2009-0082+0+DOC+XML+V0//ES

MAP OF THE 2011 INDEX OF PERCEPTION OF CORRUPTION

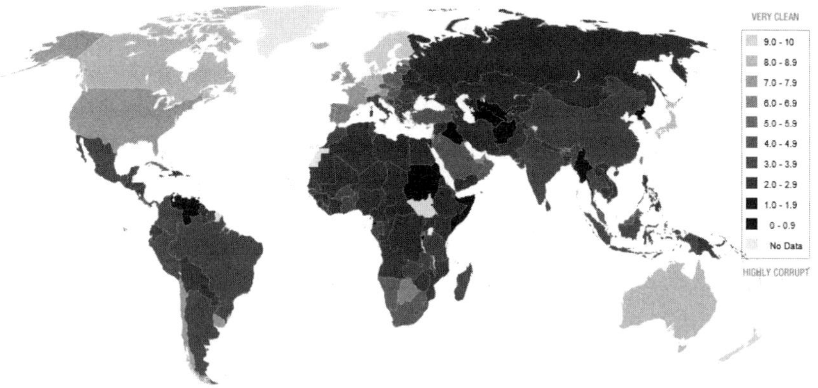

The unification of the laws of transparency between different countries would allow that any citizen Spanish for instance could know the reports that prepare economic advisers to the Presidency of the Government Spanish as such is the case with the Council of economic advisers of the President of the United States*, or for example to know the reports developed by the members of the Executive Committee of the Bank of Spain as well with the members of the United States Federal Reserve.

If we follow the Nordic model we will see that this kind of legislation allows that any kind of organism financed with public money and public administrations can be controlled through their budgets by citizens. So you can know social programs if the budgetary cuts that arise are consistent with economic policies and resources that are available as well as the forecasted investments.

The same study that we have elaborated on the basis of surveys with questions to more than four hundred people to analyze what information and topics should be treated in a law of transparency and access to information to be implemented in Spain, have been reached following conclusions†:

---

* 2012 Economic Report of the President http://www.whitehouse.gov/administration/eop/cea/economic-report-of-the-President

† MINISTERIO DE LA PRESIDENCIA. Gobierno de España. Anteproyecto de ley de transparencia y acceso de los ciudadanos a la información pública. http://www.access-info.org/documents/Access_Docs/Advancing/Spain/Espana_Anteproyecto_Ley_Transparencia.pdf

Access to information by citizens as a right of the person.

That this right could be applied to any kind of public entity, the powers of the State, and those entities that are private and which perform public functions.

That this right was wide enough to cover any information developed and owned by public enterprises regardless of how we can access to it (digital format, web page, diary of session, etc.).

Requests for this information by citizens must be in a simple, fast and free way.

The duty and obligation to help people who work in public institutions (officials) to those who request this information.

Criminal sanctions against offenders acting on behalf of public administrations.

The refusals to this information must be limited and covered by a law.

Persons requesting such information should have the right to appeal if refused in cases that the law does not prohibit

Institutions and public, semi-public and private entities with public capital should on its own initiative provide this basic information without its being necessary to make an application

There must be an independent body that guarantees the right of access to this information

The application and implementation of these laws on transparency of information allows countries to implement social policies more transparent and so they could benefit from a direct way to the ecosystem and the environment.*

---

* El Consejo de Ministros aprobará un anteproyecto de Ley de Transparencia "régimen sancionador administrativo y penal
EUROPAPRESS 20/03/2012
http://www.europapress.es/nacional/noticia-consejo-ministros-aprobara-anteproyecto-ley-transparencia-20120319185915.html

PART 2:
MANAGEMENT

CUSTOMER RETENTION IN NON-CONTRACTUAL RELATIONSHIPS: THE FUZZY-DELPHI METHOD AND THE COUNTER-EXPERTISE THROUGH UNCERTAIN VALUES

ANNA M. GIL-LAFUENTE
Faculty of Economics, University of Barcelona, Avda. Diagonal 690
Barcelona, Spain 08034

MAURICIO ORTIGOSA HERNANDEZ
Faculty of Economics, University of Barcelona, Avda. Diagonal 690
Barcelona, Spain 08034

Mª LUISA SOLÉ MORO
Faculty of Economics, University of Barcelona, Avda. Diagonal 690
Barcelona, Spain 08034

In marketing customer retention in the company has been studied in order to calculate the customer lifetime value (CLV). The research performed is based on deterministic or random models. However, when it is not possible to apply these schemes, customer retention in the company remains uncertain. Therefore, the present project develops a methodological proposal that allows the estimation of customer retention in the company utilizing uncertain theoretical tools.

1. Introduction

In Marketing, the customer retention or working life in a company has been studied from different angles. For example, Grayson and Ambler (1999), supported by previous studies by Moorman, Zaltman, and Deshpandé (1992), argue that within the marketing of services the long-term relationships between customers and companies have a "dark side" that can cause a reduction in the intensity in the confidence in mentioned relationships.

On the other hand, Moorman, Zaltman and Deshpandé (1992) explain their mentioned results, stating dynamic factors in long-term relationships exist. For example, they argue that in lasting relations each side acquires experience, which can provoke a loss in objectivity. Furthermore, they justify that the very prolonged relationships can transform the perception of each one of the opposites as very similar which can reduce the added value of the relationship.

Another argument that is mentioned is if the relationship of service between the client and the company is maintained long-term, this can cause a greater service expectancy that comes with a greater possibility of dissatisfaction. The authors mention that the clients may believe the service provided to them in a long-term relationship can be taken as a sign of trust between one of the parties and act opportunistically. As we see, these arguments go against the basic principles of relationship marketing.

In opposition of that indicated in the previous paragraph, the study of trust in relationship marketing has resulted in the theory called "Commitment-Trust" developed by Morgan and Hunt (1994) placing said element as a key for the success of long-term relationships. It is important to understand that the established ties between the clients and the company will have characteristics qualitatively different between the relationships of greater time and those of lesser time, adapting the best dynamics in each case.

Another approach in the study of client duration is one that has to do with the benefits it brings. This line was developed by Reichheld and Sasser (1990), Reichheld (1993), (1994), (2002), and several other supporters. They explain that consumers who are loyal to increasing the retention rate, that is the customer retention, generate four additional benefits to the benefit base, these are: profits from higher sales, price premium, lower operating costs, and from referrals. Nevertheless, Reinzartz and Kumar (2000) have developed one of the most rigorous investigations in order to show the weakness of the findings established by the line of Reichheld and his followers under a non-contractual context because in this situation the client can stop buying at any moment with the absence of a document that commits the client to the company at least until a certain date.

With these different perspectives that we have shown in studying the client's life-cycle we see that time plays an important role if it's related with other variables such as: added value, confidence, and the benefits among others.

In the current study, we are going to make our main focus the time of client retention in non-contractual relationships because it is essential to calculate the customer lifetime (economic) value (CLV). Making the clarification on our part that in previous publications made by Gil Lafuente, Ortigosa, and Merigó (2007), and Gil Lafuente and Ortigosa (2009) they showed the first models on the customer value under uncertainty in contractual relationships where the variable of time is taken as given in the certainty of being an established relationship under contract or agreement. In these cases the uncertainty in relation to the validity of the client as an active or "living" client is relatively null and void. We know that companies often use so-called exit barriers in order to try and keep the client until the end of the contract. However, in many real-life scenarios such contracts do not exist or there are types of agreements whose deadline is not specified. Therefore, we are going to work on the problem where the client can become inactive in any moment of time, in this way the uncertainty becomes present with greater force.

To respond to the treatment of customer retention under uncertainty a methodology is proposed using the Fuzzy-Delphi method developed by the professors Kaufmann and Gil Aluja (1986) requesting information through trapezoidal fuzzy numbers and improving obtained information on that stage with a technique called "counter-expertise".

2. Preliminary considerations with the proposed method: chance and uncertainty

The words chance and uncertainty are terms frequently used as synonyms. As an example only, authors such as Pfeifer and Carraway (2000), in their models of customer value, mention that they face uncertainty through the use of the Markov Chain. Other authors such as Calciu (2009) develop stochastic models of customer value assuming that said models follow certain laws of probability putting other variables of marketing to the side that can influence the dynamic behavior of the consumer. Other authors such as Kumar, et al. (2008) have developed proposals to calculate the customer value adopting the model developed by Dwyer (1997) where a client can purchase or not in each period, without leaving the relationship completely, these clients are called "always-a-share" where it is assumed that a client never belongs to only one company, but rather shares their purchases even if they are the same product from various companies. In the case of the CLV model developed by Kumar, et al. (2008), three predictions are required to be made: the quantity of customer-oriented marketing contacts, the probability of a client purchasing in each period and the economic contribution that each client generates in their purchase. With this sample of references we want to make clear that many authors could face uncertainty through probabilistic, stochastic, or chance schemes.

In order to avoid confusion in the presented document, we consider it important to stress that the term uncertainty, has a very different meaning in our research. In fact, uncertainty and chance do not correspond to the same level of information.

When we say that a phenomenon has a random nature, we mean that it is governed by the laws stated in the time of Kolmogorov (1956). Chance is linked to the concept of probability, which is a measure of repeated observations in time and space and carried out in the same conditions; therefore, chance is a measure of observed facts in the past, completely objective. Conversely, uncertainty does not possess laws, it is poorly structured and when it tries to be explained it's done subjectively. The authors Kaufmann and Gil Aluja (1990) state that an uncertain event has a chance of fulfillment that can't be placed in time and space, it makes reference to the future, and the past does not contribute much, if anything at all, to predict events.

Gil Aluja (2002) mentions that when he talks about chance, meaning probabilities and how we are not capable of justifying objectively or even vaguely these probabilities, we are deceiving ourselves.

In revised literature, we discover tools for predicting behavioral patterns of future consumer purchases, which allow us to have another element as an input in the calculation of the customer lifetime value. This facilitates estimating time or the remaining life of a customer in a company under probabilistic models. The Pareto/NBD model developed by Schmittlein, Morrison and Colombo (1987) is proof of this. This model was used by Reinartz and Kumar (2000) in order to determine among other things, the probability that a client is active/living in a future period. Although it is a good model because of its complexity in estimating certain parameters, its application is not easy in everyday situations. For this reason, an alternative model has to be used. The BG/NBD model developed by Fader (2005) and it gives very similar results and is easier to apply.

The sample of previous models reveals that the treatment of uncertainty rules under chance schemes, once again confirming that in our research the term uncertainty has a different meaning.

The new perspectives from the recent decades in the field of uncertainty have given way to a new approach to mainstream science. Studies are emerging whose base is found in the theory of the fuzzy subsets, which in other fields of business management have allowed a positive advance in formal developments. For the above reasons, we will propose an alternative solution to solve the problem of estimating retention or customer lifetime of a non-contractual customer scenario, supported by the theory of fuzzy subsets. The original contribution of this aspect lies in the fact that an alternative way has to be made when it is not possible to use the laws of chance or the reasoning that they are connected to, meaning the probabilistic models. In this way we are gapping the empty space in the body of knowledge when we only count subjective information.

3. Methodology Proposed for estimating the duration of the client under uncertainty

Kaufmann and Gil Aluja (1992) established a clear difference between probability and possibility. They mention that when a measure of probability is established, it is accepted as objective and therefore accepted by everybody. The notion is that probability is found to be linked to chance, governed by its own laws. So, when we use the term probable we associate it to the notion of measurement. Whereas the term possibility, defined by professor Lofti A. Zadeh, introducer of the fuzzy idea in 1965, is one of the many valuations in the theory of the fuzzy subsets. A valuation is a subjective piece of information provided by one or several persons each one of them immersed in their circumstances. Therefore, when we use the term possible we associate it with subjectivity in the absence of an objective measurement.

Keeping this in mind, we analyze the customer retention in the company in the field of uncertainty in situations where the probabilistic models cannot be used for various reasons. Among these reasons we have the lack of objective information, poorly structured information, incomplete information, and many others. For this purpose we are going to use the traditional Delphi method, under methods conducted by Kaufmann and Gil Aluja (1986) called the Fuzzy-Delphi. Additionally, as a result of the above method and with the aim of reducing even further the degree of uncertainty, we propose the use of counter-expertise with the intention of corroborating with other experts (other than those who participated in the Fuzzy-Delphi method) with observations made by the first ones. To do this, we briefly describe the conceptual elements and joined by a numerical example we show the methodology that we propose.

4. Trapezoidal fuzzy numbers (TrFN) and information within the Fuzzy-Delphi method

We know that the Delphi method came from the research group Rand Corporation of Santa Monica in the United States from the mid-sixties where they asked a group of experts for future dates of major scientific and technical projects. The professors Kaufmann and Gil Aluja (1986) propose a modification to said method requesting information through fuzzy numbers in their different modalities; in our case we will do it through the trapezoidal fuzzy numbers (TrFN). Using this methodology, we are going to solve the problem of calculating the customer retention (or time) in the company when a contractual relationship does not exist that obligates you to stay with the company until a determined date, and further when we do not have adequate information that allows utilizing conventional methods specific to the field of chance (probabilistic/statistical).

We begin by recalling that a trapezoidal fuzzy number (TrFN) contains the valuation of three values, where the maximum assumption level is a confidence interval, so, if $\tilde{A}$ = (a1; [a2; a3] ; a4) it is a TrFN, then the values will not fall under a1, or over a4; the maximum assumption value is not a real figure as with triangular fuzzy numbers (TFN), it is a confidence interval [a2; a3] and under the assumed proportionality between this interval and the extremes, we have the shape of a trapezoid, hence the name attributed to the fuzzy number (see figure 1).

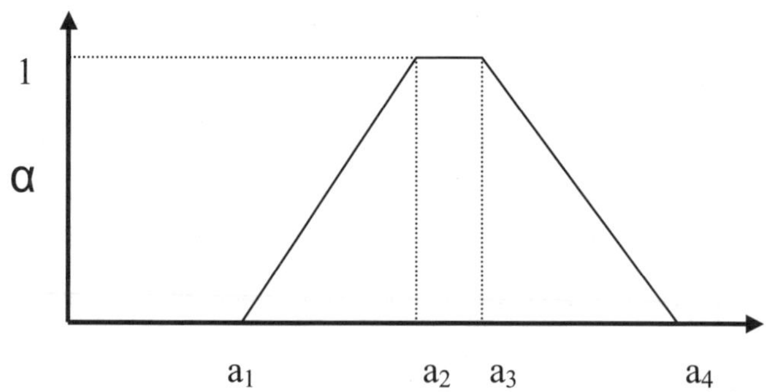

Figure 1. Graphic representation of a trapezoidal fuzzy number (TrFN).

It is possible and often happens in reality that other assumptions other than the extremes of the two dimensions are unknown and cannot be calculated (lower extremity a1 and upper extremity a4). Having an assumption level of zero (α =0), it is not known absolutely what can happen and as an estimate of the maximum assumption (α =1) it is given the liberty, in this case, of expressing itself in the form of a confidence interval [a2 ; a3].

With this brief introduction into the TrFN, we will solve the problem of estimating the duration of the client in the company when a contractual relationship does not exist and we cannot apply a scheme in the framework of probability.

The example that we illustrate below will allow us to show the utility of the Fuzzy-Delphi method (phase 1) and the use of counter-expertise with the m-expertons (phase 2) to reach a consensus on further information provided by the first experts. It should be made clear, as mentioned by the same authors Kaufmann and Gil Aluja (1993), that experts in the context of the present study are understood as qualified persons, sometimes specialists, and sometimes persons that possess some knowledge in several fields. The same authors mention that an expert opinion might be directed at anything, concrete or abstract, an image, an object, a calculation, a theory, an idea, and a behavior among other things.

Example. Phase 1 of the proposed methodology is to use the Delphi method. To do this, let's assume that we are able to gather a group of five experts to take into account their opinions about the nearest moment (not before) for a client to withdraw or leave a company definitively, the furthest moment (not after) for a client to withdraw definitively from the company; and as it was mentioned in previous paragraphs, the TrFN. We are going to request an interval of confidence from this group of experts that represents the two moments considered to be the greatest possibilities of the client withdrawing (the maximum assumption).

We will talk in general terms of periods (or moments) of time in order to avoid specific dates. In this way, said periods (or moments) can be: days, weeks, months, years, etc. according to the specific situation.

In this case the questions about the issue being discussed appear to be:

- Can the nearest (not before) period (or moment) that a client leaves a company definitively be estimated?
- Can an interval of periods (or two moments) of greater possibility that a client leaves a company definitively be estimated?
- Can the furthest (not after) period (or moment) that a client leaves a company definitively be estimated?

The following provides the results in our numerical example, considering that all of the experts received the same requested information (see table 1):

Table 1. Periods of moments (years, months, weeks, days, etc.).

Experts	Nearest period	Interval of greater assumption	Furthest period
1	3	[5; 7]	9
2	2	[4; 9]	12
3	3	[5; 6]	10
4	4	[6; 10]	13
5	3	[7; 9]	14

Once this information is obtained from the experts that participated in the Delphi method, we proceed to calculate the average trapezoidal fuzzy number:

$$\underset{\sim}{E}_{\text{TrFN}} = [15/5; [27/5; 41/5]; 58/5] = [3; [5.4; 8.2]; 11.6]$$

In order to find the value that best represents the previous average TrFN, we take said number to the scope of determinism, drop the entropy, calculate the arithmetic mean given, as normal, double the maximum importance of assumption, which in turn is an interval, and this reduces the scope of determinism to its midpoint.

Development:

[5.4 ; 8.2] reduced in the determinism is 6.8

[3; 6.8; 11.6] reduced in the determinism is:

$$\mathbf{E}_{TrFN} = \frac{3+6.8+6.8+11.6}{4} = 7.05$$

Once the first information is obtained, we go on to calculate the absolute deviations of the opinion from each expert in relation to the average trapezoidal fuzzy number. With this, we have the following result (see table 2).

Table 2. Absolute Deviations

Experts	Deviations in left value $3 - \tilde{E}$ NBTpi	Deviations in left value with the interval of maximum assumption $5.4 - \tilde{E}$ NBTpi	Deviations in right value with the interval of maximum assumption $8.2 - \tilde{E}$ NBTpi	Deviations in right value $11.6 - \tilde{E}$ NBTpi
1	0	0.4	1.2	2.6
2	1	1.4	-0.8	-0.4
3	0	0.4	2.2	1.6
4	-1	-0.6	-1.8	-1.4
5	0	-1.6	-0.8	-2.4

With a quick inspection of table 2 we can observe that no real significant differences exist. Maybe there is a slight deviation in the right value of the maximum assumption of expert 3 and in the deviations in the right values of expert 1 and 5, however if we consider the information from the table as a whole, such deviations are not important. As the traditional Delphi method indicates, it is recommended to show such deviations individually to each expert with the purpose of examining any possible change in any of them to calculate the deviations again with the new information. For the purposes of our example, we assume that all of the experts confirm their opinions knowing the average trapezoidal fuzzy number. Which means that we have finished gathering the information from the opinions of the five experts in relation to the duration of the client to the company, giving the result of retention of 7.05 periods.

Now we move on to phase 2 of our numerical exercise using the counter-expertise and the m-expertons. This method is useful when you want to show subjective information from various experts to a different group of experts keeping in mind the liberty the second experts have in confirming the original information or having the ability to modify it if necessary.

5. The counter-expertise and the m-expertons

As a result from the previous section we have the opinion of the 5 experts that yields the average trapezoidal fuzzy number:

$$\underset{\sim}{E}\,\text{TrFN} = [3;\ [5.4;\ 8.2];\ 11.6]$$

With the purpose of arriving at a more convincing result, we will use the "counter-expertise." Since the intention is to corroborate the observations made by the firsts with other experts and thereby reduce the degree of uncertainty "compressing" the intervals that describe the previous average TrFN.

As in the current example, the estimations were expressed in triplets where the value of the center is itself another confidence interval (the highest assumption). To take advantage of this information, we ask the counter-experts for their valuation in triplet form of confidence in relation to the two extremes of the TrFN and the position relative to the maximum assumption, using the same endecadarian scale. In this way, we "compress" the extreme values on both sides; compare the interval of maximum assumption obtained by the counter-experts and the original interval of high assumption obtained by the first experts, in order to obtain the period interval of greatest possibilities in the withdrawal of the client.

Requesting the information from the counter-experts in the form of triplets of confidence, we can construct the so called m-expertons. Kaufmann and Gil Aluja (1992) define an m-experton as an experton in which the intervals of confidence are composed of confidence triplets, where the maximum assumption can be an interval or a valuation.

For each level of assumption α we have :

$$[a_1(\alpha);\ [a_2(\alpha);\ a_3(\alpha)];\ a_4(\alpha)]$$

With: $0 \leq a_1(\alpha) \leq a_2(\alpha) \leq a_3(\alpha) \leq a_4(\alpha) \leq 1$, $\alpha \in \{0; 0.1; 0.2; \ldots 0.9; 1\}$

$a1(\alpha)$: is the smallest value that is accepted
$a4(\alpha)$: is the biggest value that is accepted
$[a2(\alpha); a3(\alpha)]$: is the interval of confidence that corresponds to the maximum assumption.

There may be variations where the confidence triplet is expressed with a single maximum assumption:

$$[a_1(\alpha);\ [a_2(\alpha) = a_3(\alpha)];\ a_4(\alpha)] = [a_1(\alpha);\ a_3(\alpha);\ a_4(\alpha)]$$

Or as a single interval:

$$[a_1(\alpha) = a_2(\alpha);\ a_3(\alpha) = a_4(\alpha)] = [a_1(\alpha);\ a_4(\alpha)]$$

Or as a single valuation:

$$[a_1(\alpha) = a_2(\alpha) = a_3(\alpha) = a_4(\alpha)] = a_1(\alpha)$$

The previous authors mention that the m-expertons allow expressing knowledge with a greater sensitivity. The algebra of the m-expertons coincide with that of the expertons, at the same time that they constitute a generalization for the assessment of the expertons when necessary. In our case, because we want to take advantage of the information from the first experts of the confidence interval of maximum assumption, we consider that this justifies the utilization of m-expertons.

If an interval that is looked up does not give an adequate result by being too small for one or several counter-experts, they can propose new values and create a new interval formed by the smallest value between those proposed and the largest value between those proposed: this ensures that all liberty of opinion is given to the experts. We suppose that in our example, the extreme values of the average trapezoidal fuzzy numbers are readily accepted. $\underset{\sim}{E}$ TrFN = [3; [5.4; 8.2]; 11.6]

In order to confirm the made observations by the first experts and, if possible, reduce the amplitude of the intervals without losing information, we are going to ask 5 counter-experts, different from the previous ones, a valuation of the withdrawal of a client using the following endecadaria scale and the interval over which the consultation is formed by the extremes of the average trapezoidal fuzzy number $\underset{\sim}{E}$ TrFN, : [3; 11.6].

0: the withdrawal of the client takes place in 3 periods
0.1: the withdrawal of the client takes place in practically 3 períods
0.2: the withdrawal of the client takes place in almost 3 periods
0.3: the withdrawal of the client takes place close to 3 periods
0.4 : the withdrawal of the client takes place closer to 3 than of 11.6 periods
0.5 : the withdrawal of the client takes place as close to 3 as that of 11.6 periods
0.6 : the withdrawal of the client takes place closer to 11.6 than of 3 periods
0.7: the withdrawal of the client takes place close to 11.6 periods
0.8: the withdrawal of the client takes place in almost 11.6 periods
0.9: the withdrawal of the client takes place in practically 11.6 periods
1: the withdrawal of the client takes place in 11.6 periods

Once the semantics used are understood, they are given to the counter-experts with the greatest liberty possible to express their opinions about the interval, through confidence triplets which can be reduced to intervals of confidence and to even valuations.

In this way, each counter-expert provides a confidence triplet in [0,1], meaning:

[a1i; [a2i; a3i]; a4i]

With: $0 \leq a1i \leq a2i \leq a3i \leq a4i \leq 1$ to conserve the horizontal monotony, and where a1i and a4i represent the opinions of the extreme values and, [a2i; a3i] the relative position to the confidence interval of the maximum assumption.

Just as an example, if the counter-expert issues its valuation with the triplet [0.3; 0.6; 0.9], it means that the counter-expert thinks "the withdrawal of the client takes place close to 3 periods" in the worst case; "the withdrawal of the client takes place in practically 11.6 periods" in the best case; but you have to be suspicious to think that the maximum is possible when "the withdrawal of the client takes place closer to 11.6 than 3 periods. It is possible that several experts reduce their opinions to an interval or to a single valuation; however, the idea is to try and recover the information that can come from the opinion of the maximum assumption under the form of triplets.

To continue our numerical example, suppose that the results of the 5 counter-experts are the following:

Counter-expert 1: [0.3; [0.5; 0.6]; 0.8]
Counter-expert 2: [0.3; 0.6]
Counter-expert 3: 0.5
Counter-expert 4: [0.4 ; 0.7 ; 0.9]
Counter-expert 5: [0.2; 0.5]

From this information we construct the m-experton. To do this we follow the same procedure as when we when dealing with the experton, meaning, performing the following three steps:

Statistics or absolute frequencies
Realative or normalized frequencies
Complementary cumulative frequencies

The three previous phases illustrate for us the tables shown below:

To help us interpret the m-experton with greater ease, we will obtain the mathematical expectancy expressed in the bottom of the m-experton in the following way:

[1 + 1+ 0.8 + 0.4 + 0.2 + 0 + 0 + 0 + 0 + 0] 1/10 = [3.4]1/10 = 0.34
[1 + 1+ 0.8 + 0.6 + 0.6 + 0.2 + 0.2 + 0 + 0 + 0]1/10 = [4.4]1/10 = 0.44
[1 + 1+ 1 + 1 + 1 + 0.6 + 0.2 + 0 + 0 + 0]1/10 = [5.8]1/10 = 0.58
[1 + 1+ 1 + 1 + 1 + 0.6 + 0.4 + 0.4 + 0.2 + 0]1/10 = [6.6]1/10 = 0.66

We can notice in the confidence triplet, which summarizes the information contained in the m-experton, that the opinions are very well balanced around the value 0.5. Therefore, we can expect as much reduction in the extreme values as well as in the confidence interval of maximum assumption that form the original average TrFN thanks to the opinion of the counter-experts.

To check what was mentioned in the previous paragraph, it is time to transform the valuations in [0, 1] carried out by the counter-experts, into periods (or moments) of time, we referred to so-called R+-m-expertons.

Relative Frequencies				
0				
0.1				
0.2	0.2	0.2		
0.3	0.4	0.2		
0.4	0.2			
0.5	0.2	0.4	0.4	0.4
0.6			0.4	0.2
0.7		0.2	0.2	
0.8				0.2
0.9				0.2
1				

Statistics			
0			
0.1			
0.2	1	1	
0.3	2	1	
0.4	1		
0.5	1	2	2
0.6		2	1
0.7		1	
0.8			1
0.9			1
1			

m-expertón =

Relative cumulated frequencies				
0	1	1	1	1
0.1	1	1	1	1
0.2	1	1	1	1
0.3	0.8	0.8	1	1
0.4	0.4	0.6	1	1
0.5	0.2	0.6	1	1
0.6	0	0.2	0.2	0.4
0.7	0	0.2	0.2	0.4
0.8	0	0	0	0.4
0.9	0	0	0	0.2
1	0	0	0	0

[0.34; [0.44; 0.58] ; 0.66]

Kaufmann and Gil Aluja (1993) mention that if an expert chooses an interval [α 1 ; α 2] for a valuation in the interval [A* ; A*] , similar to that of our problem, then it will correspond by linear transformation.

$$[A_1 ; A_2] = A_* (+) ((A^* - A_*) (\bullet) [\alpha_1 ; \alpha_2])$$

Applying the previous expression to n experts, the formula is extended to the m-expertons to form the so-called R+-m-expertons. Therefore, Kaufmann and Gil Aluja (1992) mention that a R+-m-experton is obtained using the following formula:

$$R^+\text{-m-experton} = A_* (+) ((A^* - A_*) (\bullet) \text{m-experton})$$

Where (A*, A*) is the interval considered in the valuations. In a more explicit way at an individual level we have:

$$[a_{i1} ; [a_{i2} ; a_{i3}]; a_{i4}] = A_* (+) ((A^* - A_*) (\bullet) [\alpha_{i1} ; [\alpha_{i2} ; \alpha_{i3}]; \alpha_{i4}])$$

Where α i1, α i2, α i3, α i4 are the valuations are issued by the counter-expert i and ai1, ai2 , ai3, ai4 are time periods resulted from such valuations. Appying the formula above to our problem with the interval: [3; 11.6] and with the obtained m-experton we have:

R+-m-experton = 3 (+) ((11.6 – 3) (•) m-experton)

Substituting we have:

R^+-m-experton = 3 (+) (8.6) (•)

m-experton				
0	1	1	1	1
0.1	1	1	1	1
0.2	1	1	1	1
0.3	0.8	0.8	1	1
0.4	0.4	0.6	1	1
0.5	0.2	0.6	1	1
0.6	0	0.2	0.6	0.6
0.7	0	0.2	0.2	0.4
0.8	0	0	0	0.4
0.9	0	0	0	0.2
1	0	0	0	0

[0.34; [0.44; 0.58] ; 0.66]

R^{+}-m-expertón =

R+-m-expertón				
0	11.6	11.6	11.6	11.6
0.1	11.6	11.6	11.6	11.6
0.2	11.6	11.6	11.6	11.6
0.3	9.9	9.9	11.6	11.6
0.4	6.4	8.2	11.6	11.6
0.5	4.7	8.2	11.6	11.6
0.6	3.0	4.7	8.16	8.2
0.7	3.0	4.7	4.7	6.4
0.8	3.0	3.0	3.0	6.4
0.9	3.0	3.0	3.0	4.7
1	3.0	3.0	3.0	3.0

[5.9; [6.8; 8.0] ; 8.7]

As expected, we observe in the bottom part of the R+-m-experton a considerable reduction in the values compared with the average TrFN obtained through the fuzzy-delphi method.

$$\underset{\sim}{E}_{\text{TrFN}} = [3;\ [5.4; 8.2];\ 11.6]$$

On the extremes, we have obtained a reduction from [3; 11.6] to [5.9; 8.7]. Regarding the maximum assumption intervals, we propose the following general criteria to obtain a definite interval.

If [b1; b2] is the revisi assumption interval obtained by average trapezoidal fuzzy number by the first experts and [cb1; cb2] is the maximum interval of assumption obtained as a result of the valuation in [0, 1] from the counter-experts, then:

Case 1. If [b1; b2] $\cap$ [cb1; cb2] = φ Review the opinion of the two groups due to the big differences in the intervals of maximum assumption. We consider this case as atypical, but because of the liberty of opinion the experts have, it can occur.

Case 2. If [b1; b2] $\cap$ [cb1; cb2] $\neq$ ϕ Then the approach proposed is to consider the intersection of the magnitudes or periods present in both confidence intervals in order to stay with the uncertainty period of maximum assumption covered by the two groups of experts and counter-experts.

In our numerical example we have:

[5.4 ; 8.2] $\cap$ [6.8 ; 8.0] = [6.8 ; 8.0]

Therefore, in this particular case no alternation is undergone, the counter-expertise remains the confidence triplet defined as:

[5.9 ; [6.8 ; 8.0]; 8.7]

The above triplet, under the assumption of proportionality between the maximum assumption and the extreme values, it gives us a graphic representation of the trapezoidal fuzzy number reducing the uncertainty of the first experts, with the support of counter-expertise. We see graphically what has been obtained (See Figure 2):

Figure 2.Reduction of uncertainty by counter-expertise performed.

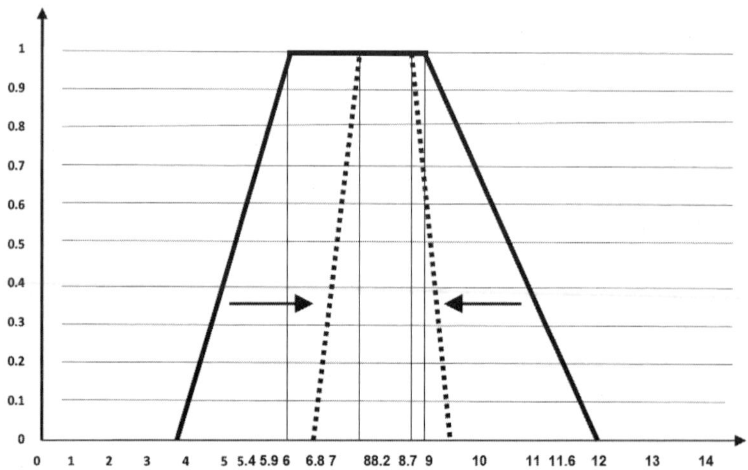

As recommended by our teachers, we drop the entropy at the end in order to conserve to the maximum all of the information from our problem. In this case, to have a more precise idea, it becomes the average confidence triplet in a single figure, recalling that the maximum assumption is taken into account twice. Performing the operations we have:

From the interval of larger assumption [6.8 ; 8.0] the midpoint is 7.4

Therefore, the average is: $\dfrac{5.9+7.4+7.4+8.7}{4}=7.35$

Because the opinions of the experts and counter-experts do not differ considerably, we can observe that this result is very similar to the average of the TrFN in the determinism whose result was 7.05. Thus, we find the possible length of time for a client to withdraw from a company can be placed in just over 7 periods.

6. Conclusions and reflections of interest

An immediate conclusion with the presented example is that just by requesting a valuation from experts on customer-retention with the company, under the form of a trapezoidal fuzzy number (TrFN), it is possible to say that the client will leave the company in a little over 7 periods. This number is a satisfactory outcome, if there is no prior information from the client or historical data that can permit utilizing traditional schemes in the field of chance (probabilistic). It is important to highlight that the information only comes from a subjective assessment, but we insist, it is very valuable coming from the so-called experts.

A very natural extension to this problem is to think that the application of the information on customer-retention in the company can be performed through the so-called random fuzzy subsets, which is a generalization of the concept of fuzzy subsets. In figure 3 you can see the transit of the TrFN to the random fuzzy subsets when requesting information from the experts on customer-retention in a company (see figure 3).

Figure 3.Generalization in the requesting of information from the experts.

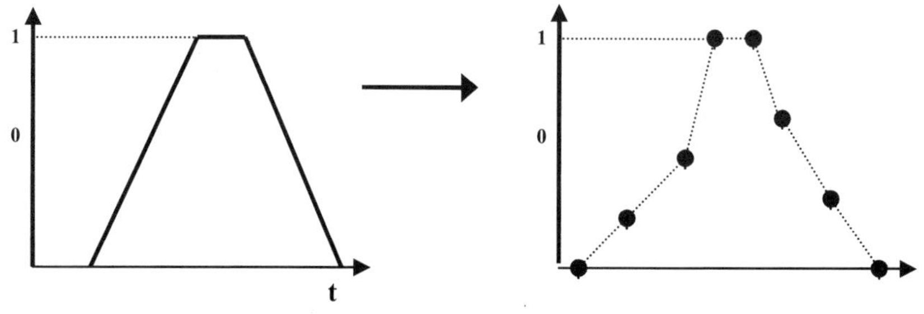

Finally, we mention that when little or incomplete information exists, it is enough to prevent the correct use of the already known schemes in the field of certainty or chance.

References

1. S. Borle, S.S. Singh and D.C. Jain, "Customer Lifetime Value Measurement". *Management Science*, 54(1), 100-112 (2008).
2. M. Calciu, "Deterministic and stochastic Customer Lifetime Value models. Evaluating the impact of ignored heterogeneity in non-contractual contexts". *Journal of Targeting, Measurement, and Analysis for Marketing*. 17(4), 257-271 (2009).
3. R.F. Dwyer, "Customer Lifetime Valuation to Support Marketing Decision Making". *Journal of Direct Marketing*, 11(4), 6-13 (1997).
4. P. S. Fader, B.G.S Hardie and K. L. Lee, "Counting your Customer" the Easy Way: An Alternative to the Pareto/NBD Model". *Marketing Science*, 24(2), 275-284 (2005).
5. J. Gil Aluja, Introducción de la Teoría de la incertidumbre en la gestión de empresas. Vigo: Editorial Milladoiro (2002).
6. A.M. Gil Lafuente, M. Ortigosa and J.M. Merigó, Teoría de la incertidumbre aplicada al valor del cliente en situaciones contractuales con intervalos de confianza (2007). Disponible en: URL: http://www.upo.es/RevMetCuant/art15.pdf
7. A.M. Gil Lafuente and M. Ortigosa, "El valor del cliente en relaciones contractuales con estimaciones inciertas". *Revista de Administración, Finanzas y Economía*, 3(2), 91-110 (2009).
8. K. Grayson, and T. Ambler, "The dark Side of Long-Term Relationships in Marketing Services". *Journal of Marketing Research*, 36(1), 132-141 (1999).
9. A. Kaufmann and J. Gil Aluja, Introducción de la teoría de los subconjuntos borrosos a la gestión de las empresas. Santiago de Compostela: Editorial Milladoiro (1986).
10. A. Kaufmann and J. Gil Aluja, Las revision 1 del azar y de la incertidumbre: Elementos básicos para su aplicación en economía. Madrid: Editorial Centro de Estudios Ramon Areces (1990).
11. A. Kaufmann and J. Gil Aluja, Técnicas de gestión de empresa: Previsiones, Decisiones y Estrategias. Madrid: Ediciones Pirámide (1992).
12. A. Kaufmann and J. Gil Aluja, Técnicas especiales para la gestión de expertos. Vigo: Editorial Milladoiro (1990)..
13. A.N. Kolmogorov, Fundations of the theory of Probability. New York: Chelsea Publishing Company (1956).

14. V. Kumar, R. Venkatesan, T. Bohling and D. Beckmann, "The Power of CLV: Managing Customer Lifetime Value at IBM". *Marketing Science*, 27(4), 585-589 (2008).
15. C. Moorman, G. Zaltman and R. Deshpandé, "Relationships Between Providers and Users of Market Research: The Dynamics of Trust Within and Between Organizations". *Journal of Marketing Research*, 29(3), 314-328 (1992).
16. R.M. Morgan and S.D. Hunt, "The Commitment-Trust Theory of Relationship Marketing". *Journal of Marketing*, 58(3), 20-38 (1994).
17. P.E. Pfeifer and R.L. Carraway, "Modeling Customer Relationships as Markov Chains". *Journal of Interactive Marketing*, 14(2), 43-55 (2000).
18. F.F. Reichheld and W.E. Sasser, "Zero Defections: Quality Comes to Services". *Harvard Business Review*, 68(5), 105-111 (1990).
19. F.F. Reichheld, "Loyalty Based Management". *Harvard Business Review*, 71(2), 64-73 (1993).
20. F.F. Reichheld, "Loyalty and The Renaissance of Marketing". *Marketing Management*. 2(4), 10- 21 (1994).
21. F.F. Reichheld, El efecto lealtad: Crecimiento, Beneficios y Valor último. Barcelona: Editorial Ariel (2002).
22. W.J. Reinartz and V. Kumar, "On the Profitability of Long-Life Customers in a Noncontractual Setting: An Empirical Investigation and Implications for Marketing". *Journal of Marketing*, 64(4), 17-35 (2000).
23. D.C. Schmittlein, D.G. Morrison and R. Colombo, "Counting your customers: Who are they and What will they do next?". *Management Science*, 33(1), 1-24 (1987).

A NEW APPROACH FOR IMPROVING BUSINESS PERFORMANCE USING ARTIFICIAL INTELLIGENCE AND CASE-BASED REASONING

ALEKSANDAR VUJOVIC
Associated Professor at Faculty of Mechanical Engineering, University of Montenegro, Cetinjski put bb, Podgorica 81000, Montenegro

ZDRAVKO KRIVOKAPIC
Associated Professor at Faculty of Mechanical Engineering, University of Montenegro, Cetinjski put bb, Podgorica 81000, Montenegro

MIRKO SOKOVIC
Full Professor at Faculty of Mechanical Engineering, University of Ljubljana, Kongresni trg 12, Ljubljana 1000, Slovenia

SLAVKO ARSOVSKI
Full Professor at Faculty of Mechanical Engineering, University of Kragujevac, Sestre Janjica 13, Kragujevac, 34000, Serbia

MARC ARTHUR DIAYE
Associated revision l Ecole Nationale de la Statistique et de l'Analyse de l'Information, Rennes Area, Bruz/Paris 35172, France

JELENA JOVANOVIC
Associated Professor at Faculty of Mechanical Engineering, University of Montenegro, Cetinjski put bb, Podgorica 81000, Montenegro

This paper represents a main part of doctoral dissertation which was presented at Faculty of Mechanical Engineering in Montenegro and represent an original research. That thesis has bees developing in cooperation with colleagues from Faculty of Mechanical Engineering in Kragujevac – Serbia, colleagues from University of Slovenia and ENSAI Economics Department in Paris. The main aims of this paper are: to find (regardless of size or type of organization) area in organization which have priority from the standpoint of improvement, to establish new concept of Degree of Readiness and Coefficient of Significance and to develop and testing in real condition an expert system for improvement business process performances even those of financial character base on analogy with human body function. Two unique data base where made. Data were identified in over than 380 organization. This data is significant, and in huge percent represent a real condition and original bases for research. Many approaches were conducted such as: case base reasoning-CBR, object oriented programming, artificial intelligence tools, Analytic Hierarchy Process-AHP, expert choice, testing in real condition and other. We are also introducing a new approach based on new concept of Degree of Readiness and Coefficient of Significance for achieving business excellence. This new concept show intensity of action which should be provide in sense of achieving best results. We are finding a priority area in any organization from the standpoint of improvement and achievement business excellence. One expert system was build, tested in real condition in one organization which will be involved in competition for European quality award competition for business excellence. We found that this systems has to be effective and efficient.

1. Introduction

This informational environment has been recognized in the world and because of there are significant rising in the use of artificial intelligence tools. It is necessary that organizations use information technology as a tool for developing a sense of learning, acquire and use knowledge. Information tools should not be use like tools for automation of existing processes. There should be another aspect or already obsolete category. With this aspects, thinking and attitudes, it can be said that we living in the century of knowledge and that we have already overcome period of information technology which should be, simply, implemented like support in the way for achieving knowledge.

There is evidence that is a great number of eligible to use and easily available software for needs of the development of such as systems in the field of artificial intelligence. Also, in [1] states that investment and implementation of artificial intelligence show significant results, particularly in attempt of to get higher profit. Specified conditions, particularly from the standpoint of the necessities of knowledge, and also the fact that in area of research topic for the purposes of quality management systems, there are evident gap [2, 3,4,5,6, 7, 8, 9, 10, 11], justifying the author's striving to be in this research and accept to use artificial intelligence tools for developing systems oriented to knowledge. These views and attitudes were in agreement: that there is no correct programming software that has a strong base of knowledge that could assist in identification of a problem, that has not developed a single expert system that deals with the measurement, evaluation, corrective and preventive action to improve organizational performance and the like [12, 13, 14, 15, 16, 10]. It is also an incentive to be based on such analogies create a foundation set up and entered the field of artificial intelligence in order to obtain knowledge as one of the most important factors for creating competitiveness in the market [17, 18, 19, 20].

The aim is to develop a system in the field of artificial intelligence that would be based on the analysis in the quality management system and that has given recommendations for achieving business excellence and improve the financial performance of the organization.

2. The main targets, methods and paper contribution

Based on the introduction and results of researching literature source and practice, we are deciding to set up main targets of this paper and that are:

- to find (regardless of size or type of organization) area in organization which have priority from the standpoint of improvement,
- to establish new concept of Degree of Readiness and Coefficient of Significance which can show intensity and type of action which should be provide in direction of achieving business excellence and
- to develop and testing in real condition an expert system for making decision and improvement business process performances even those of financial character base on analogy with human body function.

In this sense, we are using science method for inductive and deductive way of deciding and concluding. First one, we are using for collecting, estimating and analyzing of experimental data, or to making general knowledge by using specific knowledge and particular facts. The second one we are using for applying and checking specific conclusion in real condition. Also, like science approaches were used: analogy method, expert decision and "ex post facto" or previous case and facts.

Beside that, many other methods and tools were conducted like: knowledge discovery in data base, data mining, case base reasoning-CBR, object oriented programming, artificial intelligence tools, Analytic Hierarchy Process-AHP, expert choice, testing in real condition, Visual Basic and Select Query Language.

Through a detailed analysis of literature sources and software, it was found evident gap in applying artificial intelligence tools for improvement business process performances based on Quality Management System-QMS and especially in experience of other and case reasoning. In this paper, analogy between human body function and process oriented organization were established, and areas in organization which is prior from the standpoint of improvement were identified. Two unique data bases and significant number of company and data, make original experimental value and bases for research. Also, new concept of Degree of Readiness and Coefficient of Significance for achieving business excellence stay in the basis of new expert system for achieving business excellence. By applying this expert system, especially on prior area, employees should drive they process performances to excellent condition, even those of financial character. Also, many actions for improvement with appropriate coefficients which show theirs intensity where found. This action should be understood also like preventive action for strengthening organizational condition to avoid some failure in the system. This expert system was tested in real conditions in one very successful organization which will be participant in competition for European Award for business excellence. This test and verification showed that the system could be useful and also the efficient and effective.

3. Experimental research, areas for research and reasons for developing expert systems

The basic facts of this paper are attempted to define two levels of experimental data. The first level of the data is related to quality management systems and nonconformities that have emerged. This is a basic level of data which reflects the situation in the quality management systems and identify critical places that are subject to improvement. The base of these data is unique and consists of the **1009** nonconformities (cases), identified in over than **350** organizations. If we know that in our area in the field of competent certification body has, approximately 500 certificates, then the number of 350 is about **70%** of the total number. That fact points out to the significance of sample for analysis.

The term nonconformities refer to any non-conformance of requirements of ISO 9001, nonconformity non-fulfilment of a requirement [21]. During the external audits of quality management system, competent and trained auditors can identify several types of nonconformities (Figure 1). We are using most significant data from highest level of pyramid at which were collected at the level of many country like external estimation and evaluation of they performance and condition.

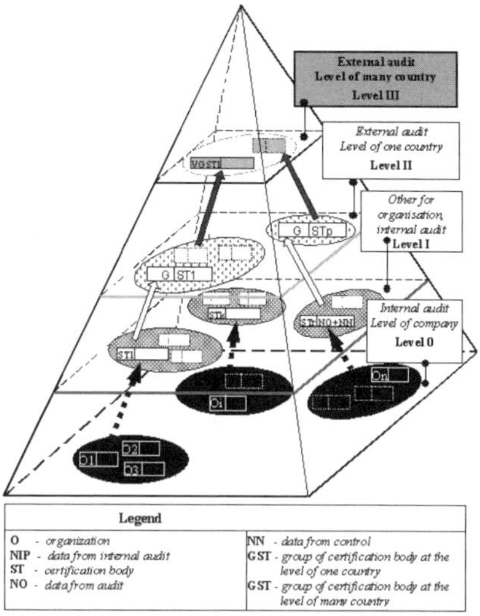

Figure 1. Data source (highest level of data significance)

Data base of nonconformities which is under consideration in this paper contains only nonconformities that represent a great deviation from the essential requirements, and that giving greater importance to this research and gives greater significance results.

Non-conformances are identified in accordance with the structure requirements defined in the ISO 9001 standard as follows:

- Quality management systems: 4.1 general requirements, 4.2 documentation requirements,
- Management responsibility (module 5): 5.1 management commitment, 5.2 customer focus, 5.3 quality policy, 5.4 planning, 5.5 responsibility, authority and communication, 5.6 management review,
- Resource management (module 6): 6.1 provision of resource, 6.2 human resources, 6.3 infrastructure, 6.4 work environment,
- Product realization (module 7): 7.1 Planning of product realization, 7.2 customer related processes, 7.3 design and development, 7.4 purchasing, 7.5 production and service provision, 7.6 control of monitoring and measuring devices,
- Measurement, analysis and improvement (module 8): 8.1 general, 8.2.1 customer satisfaction, 8.2.2 internal audit, 8.2.3 monitoring and measurement of processes, 8.2.4 monitoring and measurements of product,

8.3 control of nonconforming product, 8.4 analysis of data, 8.5 improvement.

Accordingly, for example in the field of 8.2.1 from the standpoint of the appearance of non-conformances organizations have a significant and frequent or large deviations in the sense that it does not follow the information about the observations of users, it did not define the methods for obtaining this information, they do not have strong communication with customers and similar.

This data will be used like the basis of CBR approach or approach where it is possible to make significant conclusion in the sense of main target of this paper. This approach is shown in Figure 2.

The second level of data consist data from evaluation organizations that participated in the competition for the quality award based on European Quality Award criteria. This database is unique, as well as in the previous case. Data were transferred in encoded form in order to secure the identity of the organization. Data were collected in **100%** extent (**34 organizations**) and thus are significant and give a real picture of the situation in our organizations. These data are used for comparison with previous, basic level data. That is way for making improvement or exalt from basic level on the level of business excellence and way for making knowledge which reproduce expert system on his output. That is also comply with literature more existent attitude, and natural way that organization should first implement Quality Management System and after that system which is based on Total Quality Management concept [22, 23, 24, 25, 26, 27].

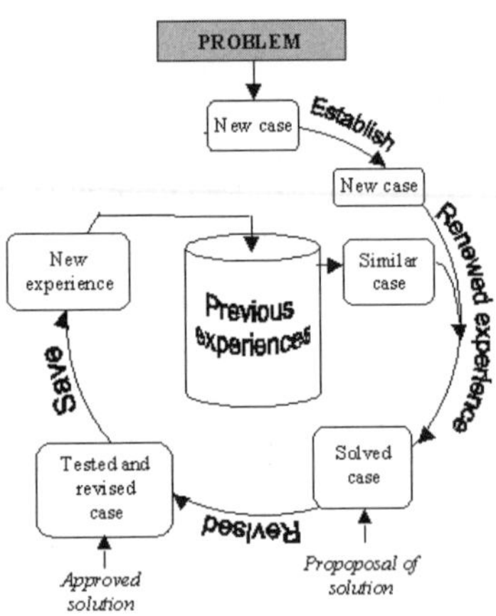

Figure 2. Case based approach

In order to show the current directions and trends in the field of development of software for quality, and to select under researched areas in the field of software quality, it was conducted a detailed review and analysis of a total of 143 software. All necessities information for that analysis are available in site (http://www.qualitymag.com-last accesed 09. 12. 2010) where are publish updated software items which are related to quality. The results of the analysis are shown in the Figure 3.

On the x axis diagrams are shown the software ability and orientation. Obviously is that the software in the field of quality is usually oriented to the control of documentation, statistical control and analysis, six sigma model, concept of total quality management, FMEA and QFD methodology, corrective action, flowchart and process mapping. However, there are specific tools for automation: the implementation of the quality management system documentation, description of information flow, implementation methods and techniques of quality, and more. Therefore, it can be concluded that there is no software that is based on the application of artificial intelligence tools in the sense of the definition of preventive actions for the purpose of improving the process. The greatest number of software is related to the application of statistical methods in the process of monitoring and improving quality. It is obviously that a large number of software is based on total quality management systems concept. The facts point out present approach which we develop in this paper and also justify further research in this area. It is interesting that a large number of software are base on the corrective actions and on the other hand there is not any registered software that has application for output preventive action what is, of course, main recommendation of ISO 9000 series. This fact also gives stimulus in terms of development of software that emphasis to the prevention. That approach is unique in the field of software for quality and makes this paper more significant.

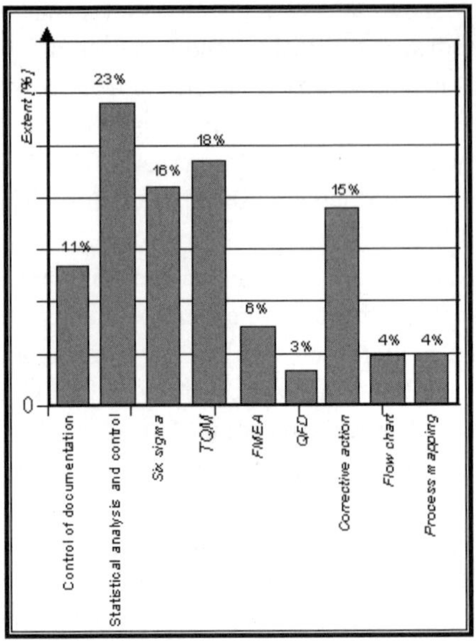

Figure 3. Results of analysis of existent software for quality

Beside this analysis, in this paper were analyzed huge amounts of available books in order to point out the justification of applying expert system. Expert systems are different from other artificial intelligence systems in that, they attempt to explicitly and unequivocally embody expertise and knowledge with the software [28]. Expert systems are also identified as one of the most commercial branches and in most number of projects used artificial intelligence tools [29, 30]. For example, it is estimated that in the first half of 21st century, even 75% of all legal documents be written with the assistance of expert systems [31]. Also expert systems will be of vital importance for measuring the quality of products and services [32, 33, 34]. Expert systems are an area of special importance with rise trends in modern business conditions [35, 36, 37, 38]. They have special significance in a highly developed countries where is actual knowledge based economy. This research highlight trends, significance and justification of developing and implementing expert systems.

Main idea and approach for developing expert system come from analogy between human body functions and process in some organization which was organized based on process modelling from ISO 9000 respect. This approach is present on Figure 4.

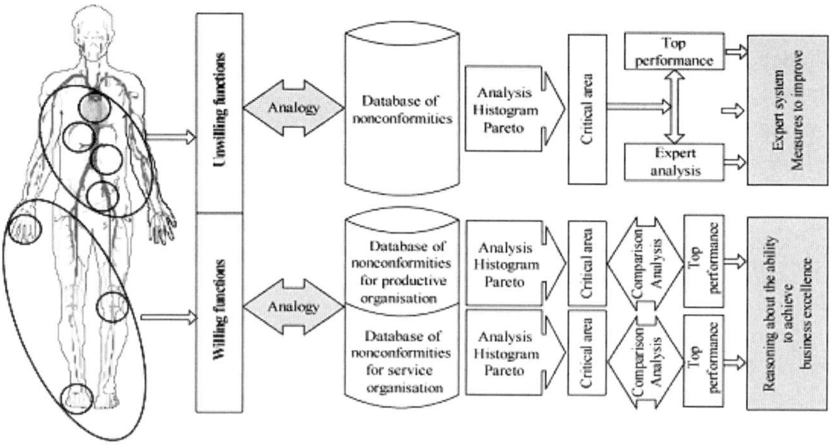

Figure 4. Analogy with the human organism in order to improve organizational performance

This paper tries to deal with perfection of functioning of the human body compare with a process modelling structures of the implemented quality management system. The challenge made in this way, tried to create a system that is universal for all sizes of organization, which incorporates a large number of gathered data, in fact a large number of experiences, in order to get a better image of the system status. This should be added to the primary goal which is to develop a model for improvement of management system, oriented to achieve BE according to show off how to maintain and improve the performance of the human body. However, the goal is also, to develop a system for measuring performance and capacity of each activity in the QMS, in order to obtain a true picture of the systems and capabilities in order to define the areas where improvements should be made, with clearly defined intensity of improvement. On the basis, thus established the analogy is made to compare elements of implemented QMS to the systems that have applied for Quality award for BE as a system with high performance.

To establish the analogy between the process modulated organizational structure and the human organism, so as to create the system that is independent from organizational functions and based only on the process model, following division of man functions was made [39, 40]:

- willing and
- unwilling functions.

Willing functions (term "functions" is used in medical terminology, although it is equally correct, to use a term "activities" in view of ISO 9000 standard terminology. For reasons of consistent referencing and use of theories from the field of medicine, the author has chosen to use the term functions.) are those dependent on man's profession and performed by man's will. They are variable and dictated by a central control of the organism. For example, when a worker at the construction site lifts his hand, it is not the same as when a referee at the game lifts his hand and etc. Willing functions refer to functions of external motoric organs.

Second category is made of unwilling or automated functions and their use is given by their existence. There are functions that are same in all professions and all people (considering that they exist, i.e. that human body is in good health) and do not depend on the man will but are simply executed. For example, those are functions of secreting enzymes, hormones, heartbeats, and similar, like ordinary body functions, and functions that cannot be controlled [41, 42].

With such a ratio of functions in the human body, we can establish the analogy of the system with implemented quality management system. Analogy in term of willing function goes in direction to developed all data in to two category, production and service organization and make some analyses, which is not subject of this paper.

In order to meet requirements of this paper, only analogy in terms of unwilling functions has been considered. The idea is to use all nonconformities (undependable of organization type or size) and base on case base reasoning approach, make conclusion about readiness of systems to making some top form.

4. Approach and expert system developing

Today are developed specialized tools for creating expert systems which allow a high degree of automation in process of developing expert systems. There are called expert system shells. From the standpoint of this work it was carried out choice of expert system shell from the aspect of next four criteria [43, 44, 45, Personal communication with group for consulting from London South Bank University, Business, Computing & Information Management, 2011]:

- programmability,
- comprehensiveness,
- universality,
- price.

During the election, it was revisio 58 shells. All information about shells are available on the Internet [2], and classified in a group of commercial shell. Detailed analyses were conducted separately for each tool through revision belonging site. For evaluation on the basis of the criteria it was adopted the scale of 1 to 5 where 1 is unsatisfactory grade. According to defined criteria as a most distinguished tool for the needs of the research was adopted ACQUIRE shell. Also, as sources of knowledge were used following:

- experience from eleven prestigious organizations in the world of field of quality management systems, business excellence and organizational performance [46],
- guidelines from standards for improving organizational performance [47],
- best practices from auditing of ISO 9001 oriented system [48],
- experience and practice of organizations that participated in the competition for the Oscar of quality award [49],
- theory and principles of TQM [50],
- experiences that are listed in [51] and indicate the path to business excellence.

The expert systems are included and knowledge gained through many concrete practical projects of quality management systems implementation, and many training on that topic. That knowledge is next:

- knowledge that are specific to certain companies,
- knowledge derived from specific experiences and on specific way of solving problem,
- knowledge of those that are best for certain jobs and are passed special training,
- knowledge of those that is proven in practice for the specific job and similar.

For the purposes of this paper, expert system was develop for modules 5 (management responsibility) and module 8 (measurement, analyses and improvement) of ISO 9001 standard. The reason for that is that these areas have the greatest importance in achieving business excellence [1] and therefore they should be considerate from the standpoint of improvement. Also, another reason is that module 8 has requirements that are oriented to the improvement and that is essence and priority.

The idea of this paper is to make the integration of decision support systems (DSS) which is operate on first level of experimental data, and expert system. That is modern approach of integration a number of tools with the aim of acquiring a larger volume of better knowledge [52] and make system with higher level of intelligence. Today trends are integration expert systems and traditional decision support systems which as output give data and information [53].

Integration of expert systems and decision support system can be achieved in two ways [54]. The purpose of this paper is to use model which is present on Figure 5. Based on the collection and analysis of data obtained at the output of the decision support system and it provide important information like one of inputs for expert system and its knowledge base. This is the model which is completely compatible with previous remarked analogy with human body. This two approach stay in base of this analogy integrative model for improvement business process performance.

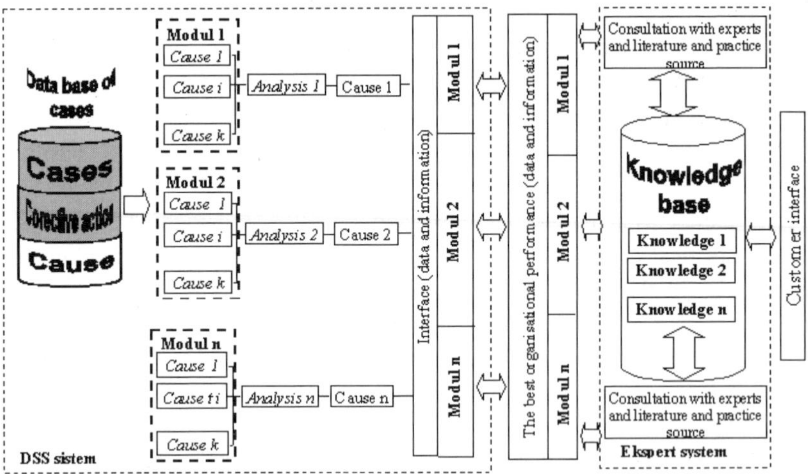

Figure 5. Integrative approach for merging expert system like separate part of DSS components

For the purposes of this paper, we developed a decision support system in the MS Access, Select Query Language and Visual Basic environment. This system is base on the first level of experimental data, and like one of outputs it gives results which are present on figure 6 (for module 8).

Applying Pareto method and rules of 70/30 it can be identified area which is crucial from the standpoint of improvement. Also, this system like support for making decision provides written presentation of nonconformities which can be shown as experience of other companies. That could be use like important data for the definition of knowledge in expert system. In addition, this system provides, and comparative analysis with the period of the four years before, which also has significance for the definition of knowledge in the expert system.

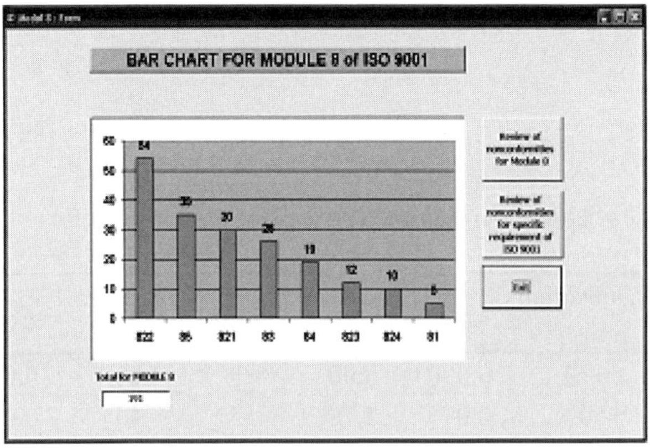

Figure 6. Results of DSS systems for module 8-measurement, analysis and improvement

Connection between data from the first and data from the second level was achieved through the introduction of the concept of "Degree of readiness (Si)" in achieving business excellence, in accordance with the following expression:

$$S_i = N_z[\%] * K_z, \quad i=1,2,\ldots,26 \qquad (1)$$

where:

Si	-	Degree of readiness for all type of organizations for all requests of ISO 9001
Nz	-	Power of a standard clause in terms of percentage. Nz=f(number of nonconformities from experimental database)
Kz	-	Coefficient of significance for achieving business excellence

That degree is applies to every single request of ISO 9001 and showing the willingness or the ability of organizations (both manufacturing and service sector) to attain business excellence in some areas. To find this degree, we are using method Analytic Hierarchy Process (AHP) and corresponding software Expert Choice. Results are shown in Table 1.

It is important to emphasize this because it was used and it is very important during definition of preventive measures in terms of defining their priorities and "power". Also, "power" of prevention was related with number of nonconformities in particular area. That means, larger number of nonconformities, or larger number of experience, make possibilities for defining more effective and efficient preventive action like output of expert system.

Through application of Pareto method, based on coefficient of significance following requests were identified as the most significant for achieving business excellence:

requests - 821, 823, 85, 84, 54, 824, 56, 53, 71, 41, 51, 72, 55

Table 1. Review of the degree of readiness for all type organization in relation to every request of the standard

Requests	Organization (power)	K_z	S_i	Req.	Organiz. (power)	K_z	S_i
821	66.67	0.090	**6.00**	83	50	0.036	1.8
823	50	0.075	**3.75**	52	40	0.035	1.4
85	37.14	0.072	**2.674**	81	60	0.033	1.98
84	57.9	0.066	**3.821**	822	46.3	0.032	1.481
54	48.72	0.064	**3.118**	73	76.19	0.026	1.981
824	40	0.064	**2.56**	61	100	0.022	2.2
56	44	0.059	**2.596**	75	37.5	0.022	0.825
53	70	0.054	**3.78**	64	63.64	0.019	1.21
71	56.52	0.04	**2.26**	76	44.68	0.018	0.804
41	65.22	0.038	**2.478**	62	62.07	0.008	0.496
51	72.73	0.038	**2.763**	74	52.94	0.008	0.423
72	56.76	0.038	**2.157**	63	50	0.005	0.25
55	66.67	0.037	**2.467**	42	49.26	0.005	0.246

At the same time, this is important areas, and have high level of priority for improvement from the standpoint of achieving business excellence and it is very important for defining preventive action of expert system and intensity of that action. If we take a look at the list of "Coefficients of significance" for business excellence achieving, especially the most important ones and perform comparison with the list of variables and their significance in terms of: Business Process Reengineering (BPR), manufacturing strategy, benchmarking and performance measurement, being the result of the appreciated research [55] and [56] it may be found significant intercompatibility.

This research was conduct from the standpoint of occurrence of nonconformities in all type of organisation regardless of they size or type (both for manufacturing and service organisation). Parallel the Pareto method (70/30) was carried out in that direction and based on that, it was identified next areas:

requests - 56, 75, 62, 822, 74, 76, 54, 72, 85, 821, 55, 63

Now we are search for common requests (area) that are most important and where **should be oriented focus and where should be provide extensively action in terms of achieving business excellence regardless of type or size of organization**. And they are:

- 821 – customer satisfaction,
- 72 – customer related processes,
- 54 – planning,
- 85 – continual improvement,
- 56 – management review and
- 55 – responsibility, authority and communication.

This area is most important for defining output of expert system and for defining intensity of action for improvement.

Objects were defined during the process of expert system development that depended of the problem which should be solved. They were based on ISO 9001 oriented check list and based on experience which can be found on DSS output. The expert system produces user's report, as the one presented on Figure 7.

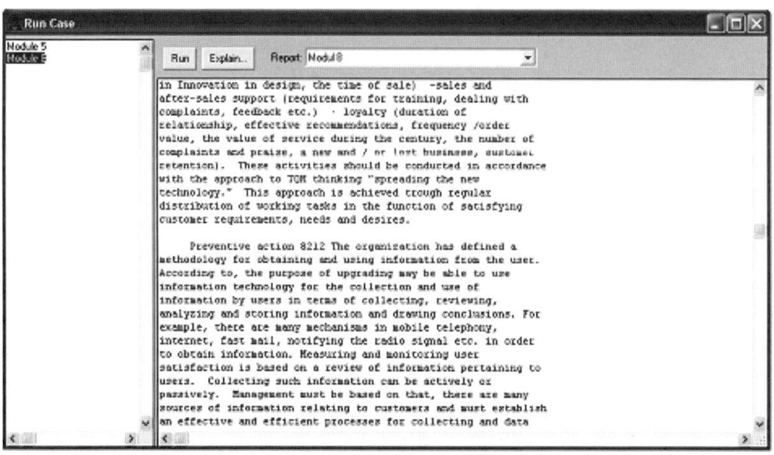

Figure 7. User's report

Data obtained from this report, user can use and implement knowledge that an expert system produces. However, users can improve performance of an organization in the field where such as performance are on lower level. Also, it can be improvement performances of other, non critical, area and can be reach level of business excellence. This expert system was developed in three iterative steps. Each of them resulted of the improvement, for example improvement of the definition of objects, set the input data, the relation between objects depending on the priorities of execution and more.

The expert system was implemented and tested in practical, real conditions in the organization that has a clear commitment to participate in the competition for the European Award for Business Excellence, also providing important measures in that direction. Evaluation was done on the basis of technical and ergonomic characteristics based on guidelines in standards ISO/IEC 9126/1:2001 for evaluation quality of software. The results are shown in Table 2.

Figures showed significant high mark by categories, and thus the total amount. Software was evaluated positive in terms of technical characteristics and in terms of ergonomic. In this sense, product has small time of response, it is compatible with most used operating system, it has an excellent user's oriented interface, and it has easy data entry and a good view of the output, installation is simple and the software is very competitive.

Table 2. Results of expert system evaluation

<table>
<tr><th></th><th>Category</th><th>Awerage mark</th><th>Awerage mark</th><th>Total awerage mark</th></tr>
<tr><td rowspan="3">Technical characteristic</td><td>Fault of presented software</td><td>8.2</td><td rowspan="3">8.7</td><td rowspan="5">9.2</td></tr>
<tr><td>Benefit of new software</td><td>8.7</td></tr>
<tr><td>Influence on job organisation</td><td>9.2</td></tr>
<tr><td rowspan="2">Ergonomic characteristic</td><td>General ergonomic characteristic</td><td>9.8.</td><td rowspan="2">9.7</td></tr>
<tr><td>System adaptability</td><td>9.6</td></tr>
</table>

Also, in this sense, within the organization, it was carried out the reorganization of the priority areas from the viewpoint of improvement, implemented preventive measures for the potentially unstable areas and also applied the measures for the improvement (offered by this system) leading to business excellence achieving.

5. Final considerations

Nowadays, very small number (a few per cent) of the scientific research activities in area of quality management systems are based on topic of the collection and analysis of information with aim to improvement business results. That fact justify author's effort to make preventive actions for improvement business performances through establishing synergy between area of quality management and artificial intelligence like area which is strictly oriented on producing knowledge. Also, through analysis of the available software for quality management, it can be concluded that there are no any software from field of artificial intelligence that was developed for quality management systems improvement. That means that each further step in this direction brings positive scientific research results. The paper point out necessity of making connection between more software solutions and tools in order to make the system with a higher level of intelligence. For this purpose, it is best to apply the integration of decision support systems and expert system. That is best world experience. With this approach it can be make system that producing knowledge and that is greatest resource which can make organization more competitive and can ensure improvement of organizations performances. Based on those facts in this research we developed unique analogy integrative approach which stays in the basis of model for improvement business process performance in the direction for achieving best organizational performances.

As the most important requests for achieving business excellences were identified requests which are mostly related to: measurement, analysis and improvement (module 8 – ISO 9001) and management responsibility (module 5-ISO 9001). The next area is most important for excellence organizational condition and at the same time area where should make very intensive action for improvement and strengthening: 821 – customer satisfaction, 72 – customer related processes, 54 – planning, 85 – continual improvement, 56 – management review and 55 – responsibility, authority and communication. It is interesting to highlight, that all activities and process which is related with customer and achieving his satisfaction and anticipation his needs, are in the focus and that should be direction and guidelines for all employees.

Also, it is shown that the strengthening, especially in these areas is used to lead to the significant progress in terms of: business process reengineering, manufacturing strategy, performance measurement and benchmarking, as very important aspects of market-oriented organization.

This paper present interesting and useful results which should be use for defining measurement for improvement business performance in way for achieving business excellence. Those results are related with term of Degree of readiness which show part (every request) of ISO 9001 certified model and they ability for achieving top business form. Also, interesting results are present through values of Coefficient of significance. This two indexes show direction about area and intensity of action which should be provide to make best organisational condition.

In organizations that have specific information through database and information systems, it is necessary to develop systems that will assist staff in decision making. These systems provide data and output information on the basis of which, in accordance with the principle of decision making base on fact, the employees make business decisions that certainly contribute to improve organizational performance. However, in the today complex business condition, organization must make stride from level of data and information to level of knowledge. That is way for ensuring prestigious position on the market. That could be achieving through development expert system base on expert knowledge and base on output of decision support system.

This approach could be related with one modern approach, which calls case base reasoning. This approach is base on experience of other companies, and that approach could be use for defining preventive action. In this sense, it can be use a system that was developed in this work. That system was testing in real condition and proved to be very useful and that showed great level of efficiency and effectiveness for real business conditions. According to process of testing and estimation, users of the system were put ratings that are present in table 2. They indicate that this system can: make financial benefits, provide better revision 1 of job, stimulate all employees to improving own process, synchronise function in revision 1, identify priority area for improvement, define intensity of action for improvement, stimulate preventive versus corrective action, encourage better involvement of new staff in to the activities, bring higher level of flexibility and other.

References

1. A. Vujovic, Improvement of business processes performances based on management systems by using artificial intelligence. PhD thesis, University of Montenegro, (2008).

2. K. S. Metaxios, J. Psarras and D. Askounis, Expert systems in production planning and scheduling: A state-of-the-art survey. Journal of Intelligent Manufacturing, Vol. 13, No. 4, pp. 253-260, (2001).
3. A. Smith, The role of tacit and explicit knowledge in the workplace. Journal of Knowledge Management, Vol. 5, No. 4, pp. 11-21, (2001).
4. C. Lang, Managerial concerns in knowledge management. Journal of Knowledge Management, Vol. 5, No. 1, pp. 43-59, (2001).
5. S. Bollinger and D, Smith, Managing organizational knowledge as a strategic asset. Journal of Knowledge Management, Vol. 5, No 1, pp. 8-18, (2001).
6. T. Clark and C. Rollo, Corporate initiatives in knowledge management. Education and Training, Vol. 43, No 4, pp. 206-14, (2001).
7. W. Coff, Human capital, shared expertise, and the likelihood of impasse in corporate acquisitions. Journal of Management, Vol. 28, No. 1, pp.107-128, (2002).
8. M. Jacob, Implementing formal design review. Industrial Quality Control, Vol. 23, No. 8, pp. 398-404, (2002).
9. A. Dommartin, ISO 9001:2000 and the EFQM excellence Model-The floor and the ceiling of the corporate house. ISO Management System, Vol. 3, No. 1, pp. 18-21, (2003).
10. S. Liao, Expert system methodologies and applications – a decade review from 1995 to 2004. Expert Systems with Applications, Vol. 28, No. 1, pp. 93-103, (2005).
11. N. Padhy, Artificial intelligence and Intelligent Systems. Oxford University Press: USA, (2005).
12. K. G. Kanji, An innovative approach to make ISO 9000 standards more effective. Total Quality Management, Vol. 9, No. 1, pp. 67 – 78, (1998).
13. M, Najmi and F. Kehoe, An integrated framework for post – ISO 9000 quality development. International Journal of Quality & Reliability Management, Vol. 17, No. 3, pp. 226 – 58, (2000).
14. R. Mohan and D. Miller, Expert systems applications for productivity analysis. Industrial Management & Data Systems, Vol. 104, No. 9, pp. 776-785, (2004).
15. D. Elmuti, World-class standards for global competitiveness: an overview of ISO 9000. Industrial Management, Vol. 38, No. 5, pp. 5-9, (2004).
16. A. Srdoc, A. Sluga and I. Bratko, A quality management model based on the deep quality concept. International Journal of Quality & Reliability Management, Vol. 22, No. 3, pp. 278-302, (2005).

17. M. Shin, T. Holden and A. Schmidt, From knowledge theory to management practice: towards an integrated approach. Information Processing and Management, Vol. 37, No. 2, pp. 335–355, (2001).
18. V. Kreng and C. Ming Tsai, The construct and application of knowledge diffusion model. Expert Systems with Applications, Vol. 25, No. 2, pp. 177-186, (2003).
19. M. Augier and T. Knudsen, The architecture and design of the knowledge organization. Journal of Knowledge Management, Vol. 8, No. 4, pp. 6-20, (2004).
20. J. Murray and M. Chao, A cross-team framework of international knowledge acquisition on new product development capabilities and new product market performance. Journal of International Marketing, Vol. 13, No. 3, pp. 54-78, (2005).
21. ISO 9000:2005, Quality management systems – Fundamentals and vocabulary" International organisation for standardization, Geneva, 2005, 30 p, (2005).
22. Z. Zhang, Developing a model of quality management methods and evaluating their effects on business performance. Total Quality Management, Vol.11, No.1, pp. 129 – 37, (2000).
23. H. Sun, Total quality management, ISO 9000 certification and performance improvement. International Journal of Quality & Reliability Management, Vol.17, No.2, pp.168 – 79, (2000).
24. C. Escanciano, E. Fernandez and C. Vazquez, Influence of ISO 9000 certifcation on the progress of Spanish industry towards TQM. International Journal of Quality & Reliability Management, Vol.18, No.5, pp.481 – 94, (2001).
25. D. Gotzamani and D. Tsiotras, The true motives behind ISO 9000 certification. Their effect on the overall certification benefits and their long term contribution towards TQM. International Journal of Quality & ReliabilityManagement, Vol.19, No.2, pp.151 – 69, (2002).
26. R. Tummala and L. Tang, Strategic quality management, Malcom Baldrige and European quality awards and ISO 9000 certification: core concepts and comparative analysis. International Journal of Quality & Reliability Management, Vol. 13, No. 4, pp. 8-38, (2003).
27. M. Casadesus and S. Karapetrovic, An Empirical Study of the Benefits and Costs of ISO 9001: 2000 Compared to ISO 9001/2/3: 1994. Total Quality Management, Vol. 16, No.1, pp.105–120, (2005).
28. B. Kosko, Neural networks and fuzzy systems: a dynamical systems approach to machine intelligence. Prentice Hall: New Jersey, (1992).

29. H. Bidgoli, Modern information system for managers. Department of Management, California State University: Bakersfield-California, (1997).
30. M. Welbank, A review of knowledge acquisition techniques for expert systems. Ipswich: Martlesham Consultancy Services, Martlesham, United Kingdom. 49 p., (1983).
31. L. Paquin, F. Blanchard and C. Thomasset, Loge–expert: from a legal expert system to an information system for non-lawyers. In Proceeding ICAIL '91 Proceedings of the 3rd international conference on Artificial intelligence and law in Oxford. St. Catherine's College: Oxford., (1991).
32. M. Eppinette and R.A, Inman, Expert systems and the implementation of quality customer service. Industrial Management &Data Systems, Vol. 97, No. 2, pp. 63–68, (1997).
33. M. Alavi and D.E. Leidner, Review: Knowledge Management and Knowledge Management Systems: Conceptual Foundations and Research Issues. MIS Quarterly, Vol. 25, No. 1, pp. 107-136, (2001).
34. K. Karhu, Expertise cycle – an advanced method for sharing expertise. Journal of Intellectual Capital, Vol. 3, No. 4, pp. 430-46, (2002).
35. G. Winn, B. Gopalakrishnan, M. Akladios and R. Premkumar, Expert systems – what SH&E managers need to know about software verification and validation. Professional Safety, Vol. 50, No. 8, pp. 45-52, (2005).
36. J. Comesana and J. Carlos, Creating an expert system for detailed scheduling. International Journal of Operations & Production Management, Vol. 22, No. 7, pp. 806-819, (2002).
37. J. Giarratano and R. Gary, Expert systems: Principles and Programming-4th edition. PWS Publishing Company: Boston, (2004).
38. D. Fleet, T. Peterson and E. Van Fleet, Closing the performance feedback gap with expert systems. Academy of Management Executive, Vol. 19, No. 3, pp. 23-35, (2005).
39. M. Relja and N. Klepac, From gene to therapy- huntingtonova korea. Biochemia medica, Vol. 12, No. 1-2, pp. 35-39, (2002).
40. L. Belak, N. Gacina and T. Radic, Food technology. In revision 1 material for students of High school for management in tourism in Sibenik: Sibenik, (2005).
41. K. Vilber, No limits-Popular psychology. Babun: Beograd, (2002).
42. I. Gilja, Prostate urinary incontinence. Medix, Vol. 11, No. 60/61, pp. 119-120, (2005).
43. L. Bielawski and R. Lewand, Expert systems development – Building PC based applications. John Wiley & Sons, Hoboken: New Jersey, (1988).

44. J. Elder and D. Abbott, A comparison of Leading Data Mining Tools. In Knowledge Discovery and Data Mining proceedings of the Fourth international Conference in New York, Elder Reasearch: New York, (1998).
45. M. Goebel and L. Gruenwald, A surveyof data mining and knowledge discovery software tools. SIGKDD Explorations, Vol. 1. No.1, pp. 20-33, (1999).
46. J. Oakland, Total Organizational Excellence – Achieving world class performance. Elsevier Butterworth – Heinemann: Oxford, (2001).
47. MEST ISO 9004:2009, Managing for the sustained success of an organization. A quality management approach, International Organization for Standardization, Geneva, 2009, p. 54, (2009).
48. R. Tricker, Best Practice – ISO 9001:2000 – The Quality Management Process. Van Haren Publishing: Zaltbommel-Netherlands, (2006).
49. FQCE, Course for auditors based on Oscar for quality award, Fond for Quality Culture Excellence, Beograd, 2004, p.217, (2004).
50. M. Perovic, Management – informatics – quality, Kragujevac. CIM Center-Faculty of Mechanical Engineering: Kragujevac, (2003).
51. R. Rakovic, Quality toward business excellence. Energoprojekt – Ingraf: Beograd, (2006).
52. A. Aamodt and E. Plaza, Case-Based Reasoning: Foundational Issues, Methodological Variations, and System. AI Communications – IOS Press, Vol. 7, No. 1, pp. 39 – 59, (2004).
53. W. Wen, W. Wang and C. Wang, A knowledge – based intelligent decision support system for national defense budget planning. Expert Systems with Applications, Vol. 28, No. 1, pp. 55–66, (2005).
54. E. Turban and H. Watson, Integrating expert systems and decision support systems. Management Information Systems Quarterly, Vol. 10, No. 2, pp. 121-136, (2008).
55. N. Vujica-Herzog, A. Polajnar and S. Tonchia, Development and validation of business process reengineering (BPR) variables: a survey research in Slovenian companies. International Journal of Production Research., Vol. 45, No. 24, pp. 5811-5834, (2007).
56. N. Vujica-Herzog, S. Tonchia and A. Polajnar, Linkages between manufacturing strategy, benchmarking, performance measurement and business process reengineering. Computers & Industrial Engineering, Vol. 57, No. 3, pp. 963-975, (2009).

IMPLEMENTATION OF A MANAGEMENT SYSTEM OF STORAGE FOR SERFELSA LABORATORIOS LTDA

EVER Á. FUENTES R.
Industrial Engineering Departament, Universidad Libre, Bogotá D .C, Cundinamarca

EDNA R. GONZALEZ P, MAGDA M. ROJAS O
Hotbed of research Saiop, Bogotá D.C, Cundinamarca

The development of this work, is the application of a mathematical model in a laboratory sector company, dedicated to the production and distribution of cosmetics in Funza Cundinamarca City, denominated "SERFELSA LABORATORIES LTDA.", directs its strategic focus on implementing a warehouse management system, as this allows the optimization of costs through planning and organization of functions that have a direct relation on the residence time in the store, and it solves the resource needs and locations according to the policies and objectives set by management. The warehouse management system allowed to maximize the product distribution strategies, the implementation of standards that increase the productivity, accurate inventory data, revision location of stocks and logistics efficiency, through a participating research and action, involving workers and suppliers for observation, analysis, development and conclusions with results that increase the level of customer satisfaction. In the process we examined the materials and stocks management as an important aspect of planning, control and logistics teams to improve products dedicated to these activities. To make the analysis of inventory model is performed to study the probabilistic demand by trend charts, this model is known as the method of multiple items with restricted space, decreasing costs in stocks investment, select products demand and optimize the available space to generate the stocks policy. Finally, through the simulation model was validated to ensure efficiency and compliance with the warehouse management system in Serfelsa LTDA Laboratory.

1. Introduction

To SERFELSA LABORATORIES LTD., A company specializing in production and distribution of beauty products, is vitally important to the implementation of warehouse management system to reduce costs and order fulfillment you do. It also is intended that each operation of process materials and supplies required at a specific point to be effective and easy to use. Within the process can be verified that the materials will be delivered in time and place and the right amount.

The development of an inventory model directs management to make decisions, so that changes the variables that generate higher costs in the process, therefore becomes an indispensable tool due to the optimum use of space, cost reduction and profit maximization.

2. Methodological Process

The methodological research aims to link each specific objective as its methodlogy, with a series of steps applying techniques for collecting and data ratio.

To identify the appropriate inventory model for the company uses various methodological tools that contribute to the collection of important and basic data of the project. You must to define the data collection techniques to allow the construction of instruments to get them from reality, a data collection instrument is any resource that uses the researcher to approach phenomena and extract information.

See Figure 1 which it shows the methodology that was undertaken for the development of the research:

Figure 1: Methodology

SPECIFIC OBJECTIVES	***METHODOLOGY***	***TECHNICAL DATA COLLECTION***
To diagnose the current situation of Serfelsa Laboratory LTDA. To identify the faults that presents within the warehouse	Through a questionnaire and interviews, analyze various aspects inside the organization as receiving and storage system, collection system, recruitment and dispatch, among others. Classification of the products according to their rotation in the warehouse.	Structured questionnaire. Visit to the company. Interview with the warehouse's manager structured observation. Inventory Classification through the ABC Method
To Develop a system for material handling and allocation of goods in the warehouse of Serfelsa LTDA Laboratory to increase productivity in the handling of goods in the warehouse.	Team will review the material handling with the transport, storage and cluster products. To make easy the administration of the media and materials that help people to accomplish their functions of storage receipt and shipping, the shelf warehouse will be analyzed. The necessary distances and operations will be evaluated from the reception to the	Through structured observation, analyzing the characteristics of the equipment that the warehouse has. Through observation we will check kind of the shelf and the existing coding in the warehouse. Interview with the warehouse's manager

	dispatch articles in order to reduce them according to the new location. Process diagrams in the warehouse. The internal transport systems will be analyzed An analysis of the shelf will be done.	
To choose a mathematical model for the process improvement in the warehouse of Serfelsa LTDA Laboratory.	We will check some mathematical models that adjust to the needs that the warehouse has, keeping in mind the different variables (demand, space per item, total space, total cost, unit cost, income, returns) is proposed inventory model with space restriction.	Researching Bibliographic queries
To Develop a simulation and a validation of a warehouse management system, to ensure efficiency and compliance of the system in Serfelsa LTDA Laboratory	To select, implemented and approved by the Warehouse Management System	Software

Source: The Authors. 2012

3. Model Development

EOQ Multiple item with storage limit [4] [7] [8]

This model works with n (> 1) items whose individual fluctuations of the stock, follow the same pattern of not allowing any missing. The difference is that the items are competing with a limited storage space.

IDENTIFY VARIABLES

Qj: The optimal quantity
K: Cost of the order
Dj: Demand
Cj: Storage Cost
T: Period to analyze

Y: Lagragiano
Vj: Space per item
V: Total space occupied
TC: Total Cost
CTj: Total cost per product
bj: Unit Cost
C1j: Unit cost of storage

Subject to + X = V

$$Qj = \sqrt{\frac{2 \bullet k \bullet Dj}{Cj \bullet T - Y \bullet Vj}} \tag{1}$$

$$V = \sum_{j=1}^{m} Vj \bullet Qj \tag{2}$$

$$CT = \sum_{j=1}^{m} CTj = \sum_{j=1}^{m} bj \bullet D + \sum_{j=1}^{m} \frac{1}{2} \bullet C1j \bullet Qij \bullet T + \sum_{j=1}^{m} Kj \bullet \frac{Dj}{Qj} \tag{3}$$

Sujeto a $\sum_{j=1}^{m} V_j \,.\, Q_{ij} \leq V \qquad \sum_{j=1}^{m} V_j \,.\, Q_{ij} + \text{X} = \text{V}$ **(4)**

Keeping in mind the information collected under the parameters of the research methodology and based on historical information such as product and demand, you can consolidate and adjust this information to analyze the model variables and to make the approach.

Once you have all the information necessary, you proceed to perform the simulation, which objective is to validate the system, where we analyze the different sceneries which will comply with all restrictions raised and in this way Laboratories Serfelsa make decisions that generate increased revenue, improved inventory and where the storage will be efficient internal processes. [5] [9]

4. Results

Through a questionnaire and interviews were analyzed several aspects inside the organization as: receiving and storage system, collection system, recruitment and dispatch, material handling equipment, physical organization and Lay-out, inventory management, indicators management, information and technologies systems, quality assurance system. The first results generated in the project are related to the ABC classification of products (Figure 1) as a fundamental source to continue the inventory model.

Chart 1: ABC Clasification to warehouse, 273 products references

TYPE	# REFERENCES	REPRESENT IN MONEY	% REFERENCES	% PROFIT
PRODUCT A	55	$ 748.120.991	20,15	48,24
PRODUCT B	82	$ 496.298.994	30,04	32,01
PRODUCT C	136	$ 306.316.622	49,82	19,75
TOTAL	**273**	**$ 1.550.736.607**	100	100

Source: The authors. 2012.

Chart 2: **Products ABC PROFIT**

	PRODUCTS	PROFIT
PRODUCT A	20,15	48,24
PRODUCT B	30,04	32,01
PRODUCT C	49,82	19,75

Source: The authors. 2012.

Figure 1: ABC Clasification and its profit

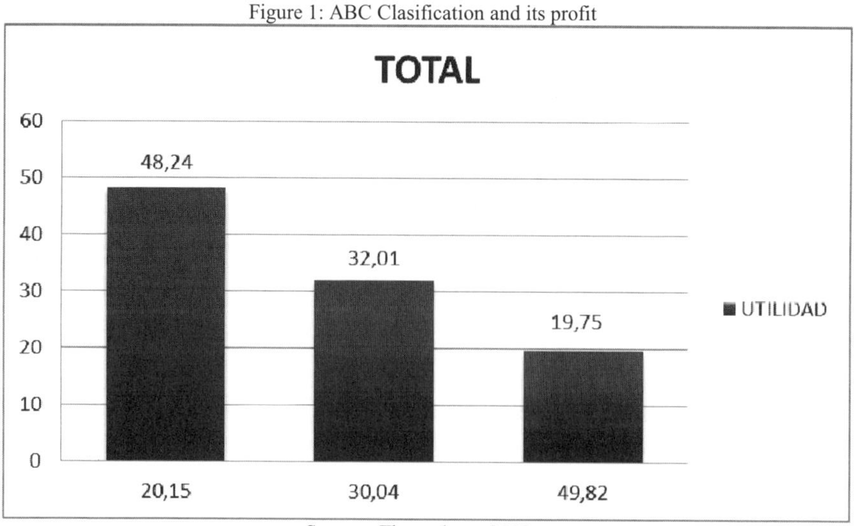

Source: The authors. 2012.

After the simulation, we can see an example of some results obtained that show the characteristics of space for storage of goods in the warehouse and several of the values obtained with the model, also an optimal order quantity that will be distributed in the warehouse of Serfelsa LTDA Laboratory.

Chart 3

Costo de pedido	Costo de almacenaje	Precio venta	Ingresos totales	Devoluciones	Ingreso neto	Cantidad óptima
$ 201.849,07	$ 1.170.942,79	8.688	$ 58.702.946	$ 587.029	$ 15.651.062	1140
$ 152.430,56	$ 904.546,24	6.414	$ 44.330.760	$ 443.308	$ 11.798.944	2157
$ 136.750,16	$ 775.506,18	6.021	$ 39.770.494	$ 397.705	$ 10.621.187	1068
$ 357.071,67	$ 1.595.626,08	19.951	$ 103.845.702	$ 1.038.457	$ 28.162.556	621
$ 6.042,31	$ 25.351,29	360	$ 1.757.259	$ 17.573	$ 478.212	1814

Source: The authors. 2012.

Now we use the formula of the optimal order quantity and trial and error with the numbers of LaGrange. Can approach the amount and the space required to supply the warehouse and complete the customer orders.

Chart 4

y	-0,2	y	-0,3	y	-0,4	y	-0,1	y	-0,05
Cantidad Optima	Espacio	Cantidad Optima	Espacio	Cantidad Optima	Espacio	Cantidad Optima	Espacio	ntidad Optir	Espacio
22670,5	8,6	21781,2	8,3	20988,8	8	23679	9	24236	9
132284,1	1,5	127094,5	1,4	122471,3	1	138166	2	141418	2
31249,2	6,2	30023,2	6,0	28931,1	6	32639	7	33407	7
67080,3	2,9	64448,7	2,8	62104,3	3	70063	3	71712	3
25405,8	7,7	24409,1	7,4	23521,2	7	26536	8	27160	8
15706,6	12,4	15090,4	11,9	14541,5	12	16405	13	16791	13
124996,7	1,6	120093,0	1,5	115724,5	1	130555	2	133627	2
176772,1	1,1	169837,1	1,1	163659,2	1	184632	1	188977	1
27204,7	7,2	26137,4	6,9	25186,6	7	28414	7	29083	8
69875,3	2,8	67134,0	2,7	64692,0	3	72982	3	74700	3
111800,5	1,7	107414,4	1,7	103507,1	2	116772	2	119520	2
24834,3	7,9	23860,1	7,6	22992,1	7	25939	8	26549	8
72166,9	2,7	69335,7	2,6	66813,6	3	75376	3	77150	3
12166,3	16,1	11689,0	15,4	11263,8	15	12707	17	13006	17
117833,3	1,7	113210,6	1,6	109092,5	2	123073	2	125969	2
61235,6	3,2	58833,3	3,1	56693,2	3	63959	3	65464	3
90208,6	2,2	86669,6	2,1	83517,0	2	94220	2	96437	2
11106,3	17,6	10670,5	16,9	10282,4	16	11600	18	11873	19
11106,3	17,6	10670,5	16,9	10282,4	16	8304	13	11873	19
1205703,5	**122,6**	**1158402,5**	**117,8**	**1116264,6**	**113,5**	**1256020,3**	**122,8**	**1288951,3**	**131,0**

Source: The authors. 2012.

In addition to the inventory model of multiple items with limited storage, alternately develops critical part is the management and handling of products and inventory, and the same coding for product placement.

To make easier the administration of the media and materials that help people to accomplish their functions of storage and shipping receipt, is analyzed using the shelf warehouse. With the method of considering material handling numerical data to solve the problem with the help of records and statistics to analyze the behavior of the factors that directly affect inventories.

Internal material handling

Storage of Serfelsa Laboratories Ltd., is divided into three sections [1]
Part 1: Products Czech
Part 2: Products Ghem
Part 3: "sub-warehouse" combination of the two types of products, for this reason the products have different locations.

Shelves: For storage handles three types of metal shelves, each of five levels, are differentiated by the type of product, dimensions and color. For the proper functioning of the shelves is necessary to consider height as the bearing capacity of floor to ceiling height available, the capacity of handling equipment available. The heavy and bulky materials should be stored at the bottom.

Figure 2. Area of storage

1 estanteria	alto	3,50	estibas	1,2
	ancho	2,24		1,2
	largo	2,70		1,2
	total	21,17	total	1,728
10 estanteria	total	211,68		10,368
	total area de almacenamiento	222,048	mt3	

Source: The authors. 2012.

Packaging: The packaging of the products is: Glass and plastic. The glass products are stored on shelves fixed to the wall to prevent accidents in cardboard boxes. Glazes are packaged in cardboard boxes as reference.

Internal organization of the warehouse [3]: Inside the warehouse, where are analyzed the use of spaces and special areas where storage was keeping in mind:

Hallways: The hallways are organized in a straight line leading directly to the outlets are not located where there is more light and visibility. The pedestrian corridor peripheral is 70 cm. to 90 cm., and the materials stored and the walls of the store, not provide inspections, fire prevention. The aisles are not marked and they are constantly hampered by boxes and pallets containing finished product.

Encryption: To facilitate the location of the products stored in the warehouse and provide greater agility tasks receipt and delivery of materials and to facilitate the internal organization and reduce the number of errors, we designed a system identification codes through the shelves and aisles.

Shelf: Each shelf has associated a corresponding coding in the same way that in each one of them, their blocks are also identified with numbered, as well as the heights of the shelves, starting level.

For Hall [2]: In this case, the corridors are those identified with consecutive numbers. In this case are two shelves each coding their blocks, since the relation is a corridor for every two shelves. The depth of the shelves is encoded bottom-up, assigning even numbers and odd right to left, starting with the opposite end into the next hallway.

Figure 3. **Parameters of codification and location**

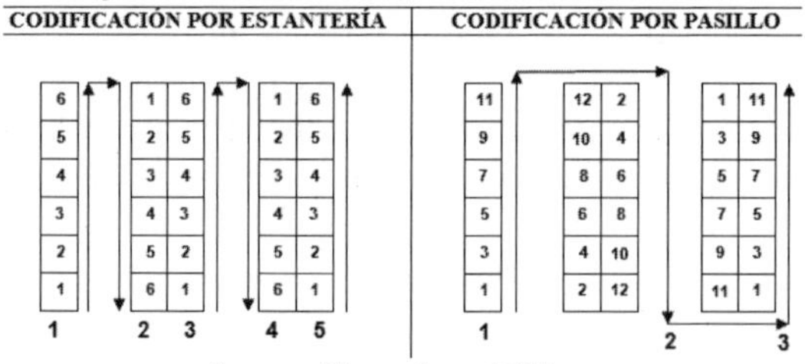

Source: The authors. 2012.

To make easy the location for the operators and wholesalers, from each reference standard for a product if A, B, or C, each code is identified by colored labels rates (Table 3) for easy viewing in each compartment of the rack.

Chart 5: Codification

Clasificación de producto	Color
A	**VERDE**
B	**AZUL**
C	**ROJO**

Source: The authors. 2012.

5. Conclusions

1. The ABC classification of goods inside the warehouse to determine the decision criteria for the handling of the goods, their orders and how they will be stored in the cellar.
2. The model complies with the restrictions of space not only to determine the optimal amount but makes appropriate use of space, thus contributing to making wise decisions regarding products should be required for higher profits, taking into account the efficient use of resources to avoid incurring costs unnecessarily large inventories.

3. Were 273 references with a high degree of stock, which was performed with the simulation model, keeping in mind the use of the numbers of LaGrange, cost, demands, space and amounts were determined and thus the optimum amounts of order and its storage space.
4. The inventory model with restricted space allows cost optimization through planning and organization of functions that are directly related to the period spent in the store, likewise providing solutions to the needs of accommodations according to the policies and objectives of the company ·

References

1. Anaya, Julio Juan (2000). *Almacenes, Análisis, diseño y organización*: Editorial Gestión.
2. Fred E, Meyers y Matthew P, Stephens (2006). *Diseño de instalaciones de manufactura y manejo de materiales:* Prentice Hall.
3. Frazelle, Edward H. Norma (2007). *Logística De Almacenamiento Y Manejo De Materiales De Clase Mundial*: Ediciones gestión
4. García C, Alfonso (2004). *Enfoque Prácticos para Planeación y Control de Inventarios*: Editorial Trillas.
5. Heizer, Jay y Render, B. (1987). *Dirección de la Producción*, Cuarta edición: Prentice Hall.
6. Hillier y Lieberman (2002). *Investigación de Operaciones*. Mc Graw Hill.
7. Mauleon, Mikel (2008). *Gestión de stock*. Ediciones Díaz de Santos.
8. Roll, Allen (1999). *Dirección y Control de Almacenes*, Capítulo 4: Editorial Reverte S. A.
9. Roux, Michel (1997). *Manual de logística para la gestión de almacenes*. Barcelona: Ediciones gestión

PROJECT PLANNING AND CONTROL WITH PERT-CPM

SAMIR ZAKI MOHAMED MEHREZ

Address: 19 Omar Ibn El Khattab St., Ismailia Square, Heliopolis, Cairo, Egypt

The successful management of large-scale projects requires careful planning, scheduling, and coordinating of numerous interrelated activities. To aid in these tasks, formal procedures based on the use of networks and network techniques which were developed by using PERT and CPM which will be dealt with in this paper that illustrates the differences between these two procedures. Nowadays the two approaches have been merged in what is usually referred to as PERT-type system.

1. Introduction

PERT (Program evaluation and review technique) and CPM (Critical – path method) are basically time-oriented methods in the sense that they both lead to the determination of a time schedule. Although the two methods were developed independently, they are strikingly similar. Perhaps the most important difference is that originally the time estimates for the activities were assumed deterministic in CPM and probabilistic in PERT. To day, PERT and CPM actually comprise one technique and the differences, if any, are only historical. Consequently, both techniques will be referred to as "Project scheduling" techniques.
Project scheduling by PERT-CPM consists of three basic phases: planning, scheduling, and controlling.

2. Planning and scheduling networks

The prerequisites for using PERT and CPM techniques include separating the project to be scheduled into independent jobs, or activities, and determining an order of precedence for these jobs. That is, we must see which jobs have to be completed before others can be started. The next step is drawing a picture, or graph, which portrays each of these jobs and the predecessor and successor relations among them.

2.1. Terminology

Activity: A specific task or set of tasks that are required by the project, use up resources, and take time to complete.

Event: The result of completing one or more activities. An identifiable end state occurring at a particular time.

Network: The combination of all activities (usually drawn as arcs) and events (usually drawn as nodes at the beginning and end of each arc) define the project and the activity precedence relationships.

Networks are usually drawn starting on the left and proceeding to the right. Arrowheads placed on the arcs are used to indicate the direction of flow – that is, to show the proper precedence. Before an event can be realized-that is achieved-all activities that immediately precede it must be completed. These are called its predecessors. Thus, an event represents an instant in time when each and every predecessor activity has been finished. Events themselves have no time duration and use no resources.

Path: The series of connected activities (or intermediate events) between any two events in a network.

Dummy Job: A dummy job that does not exist in reality in the project. The dummy job is necessary so as to avoid ambiguity in the job sequence. The completion time of the dummy job is always zero, and it is added in the project network whenever we want to avoid an arc (i, j) representing more than one job in the project.

2.2. Constructing the network

Analysis by PERT/CPM techniques uses the network formulation to represent the project activities and their ordering relations. Construction of project network is done as follows:

Arcs in the network represent individual jobs in the project.

Nodes represent specific points in time which mark the completion of one or more jobs in the project.

Direction on the arc is used to represent job sequence. It is assumed that any job directed toward a node must be completed before any job directed away from that node can begin.

2.3. Simplified Project Management Problem

The analysis of a simplified project management problem is useful to both PERT and CPM. In the simplified problem the completion times of all the project activities and their technological sequence are known. The management wants to determine the minimum time in which the project can be completed, and to identify the crucial jobs whose delay can delay the entire project.

2.4. Solution by Network Analysis

Earliest time: The earliest time of node j, denoted by Uj, is the earliest time at which event j can occur. We know that event j can occur as soon as all the jobs (arcs) directed towards node j are completed. The general formula for calculating Uj is

$$U_j = \max_i (u_i + t_{ij}) \tag{1}$$

Where the index i ranges over all nodes for which arc (i, j) exists, and tij is the completion time of the job represented by arc (i, j). Note that the earliest time of the last event in the project network gives the earliest time of completing the project.

Latest time: The latest time of node i, denoted by Vi, is the latest time at which event i can occur without delaying the completion of the project beyond its earliest time.

The general formula to calculate Vi becomes

$$V_i = \min_j (V_j + t_{ij}) \tag{2}$$

Where the index j ranges over all nodes for which arc (i,j) exists.

Slack Time: The difference between the latest time and the earliest time of an event is called the slack time of that event. The slack time denotes how much delay can be tolerated in reaching that event without delaying the project completion date.

Critical path: The critical path for a project is a path through the project network such that the jobs on this path have zero slack times. The critical jobs are the arcs (jobs) in the critical path.

To prepare a project schedule in terms of the activities, it is essential to have the starting time and the ending time of all jobs. From the event times it is possible to get the following information on each one of the activities in the project:

1. The earliest starting time
2. The latest starting time
3. The earliest finishing time.
4. The latest finishing time
5. The slack time.

3. Critical Path Method (CPM)

A critical path for a project is a path through the network such that all the activities on this path have zero slack. The basic assumption in CPM is that the activity times are proportional to the level of resources allocated to them. By assigning additional resources (capital, people, materials, and machines) to an activity, its duration can be reduced to a certain extent. Shortening the duration of an activity is known as crashing in the CPM terminology. The additional cost incurred in reducing the activity time is called the crashing cost.

3.1. Properties of critical paths

1) A project network always has a critical path, and sometimes, there is more than one.

2) All activities having zero slack must lie on a critical path, whereas no activities having slack greater than zero can lie on a critical path.

3) All events having zero slack must lie on a critical path, whereas no events having slack greater than zero can lie on a critical path.

4) A path through the network such that the events on this path have zero slack need not be a critical path because one or more activities on the path can have slack greater than zero.

4. Case study:

Fig. 1 shows the initial project network for building a house. This network indicates that the excavation must be done before the foundation is laid, and then the foundation must be completed before the rough wall is put up. Once the rough wall is up, three tasks (rough electrical work, rough exterior plumbing, and putting up the roof) can be done in parallel. Tracing through the network further then spells out the ordering of subsequent tasks. After the network for a project has been developed, the next step is to estimate the time required for each of the activities. These estimates for the house construction of Fig. 1 are shown by the darker numbers (in units of work days) next to the arcs in Fig. 2. These times are used to calculate two basic quantities for each event, namely, its earliest time and its latest time.

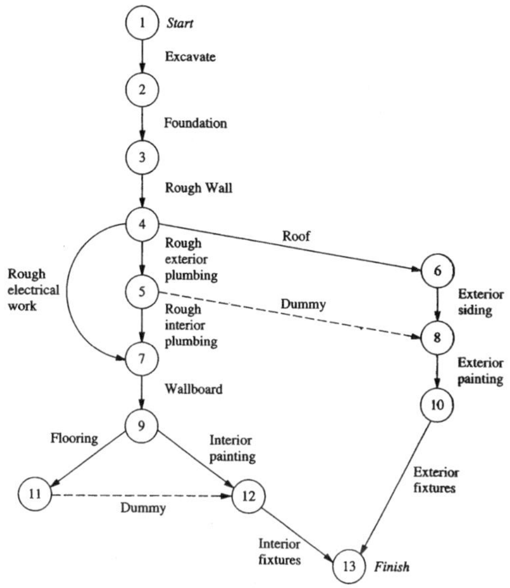

Figure 1: Initial project network for construction a house

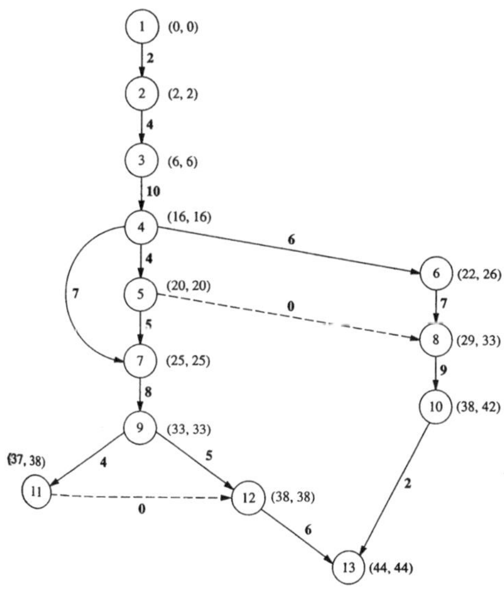

Figure 2: Project network for construction a house after recording the estimated activity times (shown in boldface) as well as the earliest time and latest time for each event (shown in parentheses)

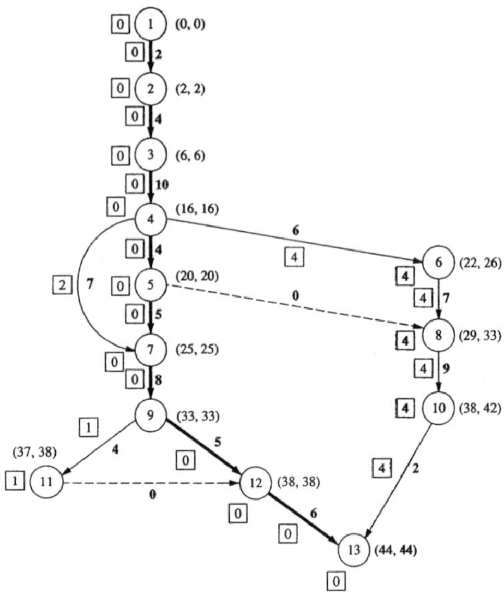

Figure 3: Final project network for constructing a house after recording the slacks (shown inside a box) for each event and activity. The dark arrows show the resulting critical path.

Figure 3. illustrates all the properties of critical paths mentioned previously. In this case, 1 → 2 →3 →4 →5 →7 →9 →12 →13 is the only critical path. The activities having zero slack are (1, 2), (2, 3), (3, 4), (4, 5), (5, 7), (7, 9), (9, 12) and (12, 13), and they all lie on this critical path. None of the activities having slack greater than zero lie on the critical path. (if any did, this would violate the definition of critical path) The events having zero slack are 1, 2, 3, 4, 5, 7, 9, 12, 13, and all lie on the critical path, whereas none of the other events do. To illustrate the fourth property, look at the path 1 → 2 → 3 → 4 → 7 → 9 → 12 → 13, which deviates from the critical path by including activity (4, 7) instead of activities (4, 5) and (5, 7). Every event on this path has zero slack, but the path is not a critical path because activity (4, 7) has slack greater than zero. The reason this activity has slack greater than zero is that its estimated time is less than the sum of the estimated times for activities (4, 5) and (5, 7).

To illustrate a project network that has more than critical path, suppose that the estimated time for activity (4, 6) in Fig. 3 is increased from 6 to 10. This decreases the slack from 4 to zero for activities (6, 8), (8, 10), and (10, 13), as well as for events 6, 8 and 10. Therefore, the path 1 → 2 → 3 → 4 → 6 → 8 → 10 → 13 now is a second critical path.

5. The PERT Three-Estimate Approach

Thus far we have implicitly assumed that reasonable accurate estimates can be made of the time required for each activity of the project. In actuality, there frequently is considerable uncertainty about what the time will be; it really is a random variable having some probability distribution. The original version of PERT took this uncertainty into account by using three different types of estimates of the activity time to obtain basic information about its probability distribution. This information for all the activity times is then used to estimate the probability of completing the project by the scheduled date.

The three time estimates used by PRET for each activity are a most likely estimate, an optimistic estimate, and a pessimistic estimate. The most likely estimate, denoted by m, is intended to be the most realistic estimate of the mode (the highest point) of the probability distribution for the activity time. The optimistic estimate, denoted by a, is intended to be the unlikely but possible time if everything goes well. Statistically speaking, it is an estimate of essentially the lower bound of the probability distribution. The pessimistic estimate, denoted by b, is intended to be the unlikely but possible time if everything goes badly. Statistically speaking, it is an estimate of essentially the upper bound of the probability distribution. The intended location of these three estimates with respect to the probability distribution is shown in Fig. 4.

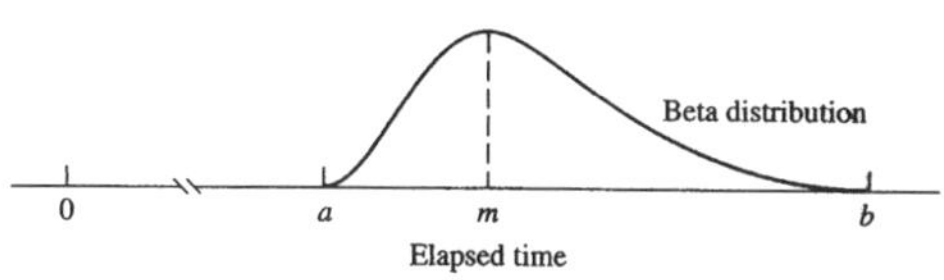

Figure 4: Model of the probability distribution of activity times for the PERT three-estimate approach : m = most likely estimate, a = optimistic estimate, and b = pessimistic estimate

Two assumptions are made to convert m, a and b to estimates of the expected value t_e and variance σ^2 of the elapsed time required by the activity.

Assumption 1: The spread between a (the optimistic estimate) and b (the pessimistic estimate) is 6 standard deviation. Consequently, the variance of an activity time is.

$$\sigma^2 = \left[\frac{1}{6}(b-a)\right]^2 \tag{3}$$

To obtain the estimated expected value t_e we also need an assumption about the form of the probability distribution.

Assumption 2: The probability distribution of each activity time is (at least approximately) a beta distribution.

Beta distribution have the form shown in Fig. 4 with a single mode (m) and two endpoints (a and b), where we assume that $0 \leq a \leq b$. Thus, it fits our definitions of the three time estimates well, and it gives a reasonable shape for a distribution of activity times.

Under these assumptions, the expected value of the activity time is approximately

$$t_e = \frac{1}{3}[2m + \frac{1}{2}(a+b)] \quad (4)$$

Where t_e is the weighted arithmetic mean of the mode and the midrange, with the mode carrying two – thirds of the entire weight.

Table 1: Expected value and Variance of Each Activity Time for the House Construction Example

Activity	Optimistic Estimate α	Most Likely Estimate m	Pessimistic Estimate b	Expected Value t_e	Variance σ^2
(1, 2)	1	2	3	2	$\frac{1}{9}$
(2, 3)	2	$3\frac{1}{2}$	8	4	1
(3, 4)	6	9	18	10	4
(4, 5)	1	$4\frac{1}{2}$	5	4	$\frac{4}{9}$
(4, 6)	4	$5\frac{1}{2}$	10	6	1
(4, 7)	3	$7\frac{1}{2}$	9	7	1
(5, 7)	4	4	10	5	1
(6, 8)	5	$6\frac{1}{2}$	11	7	1
(7, 9)	3	9	9	8	1
(8, 10)	5	8	17	9	4
(9, 11)	4	4	4	4	0
(9, 12)	1	$5\frac{1}{2}$	7	5	1
(10, 13)	1	2	3	2	$\frac{1}{9}$
(12, 13)	5	$5\frac{1}{2}$	9	6	$\frac{4}{9}$

For example, suppose that the three-estimate approach has been applied to the house construction example shown in Fig. 1, where the three estimates for each activity are given in table 1. Plugging these estimates into the expressions for t_e and σ^2 then gives the expected value and variance of each activity time, as shown in the last two columns of table 1 are the same as the times used in Fig. 2 and 3. Therefore, the critical path based on expected times still is the one shown in Fig. 3, and the times on this path still add to 44.

However, the actual time required on this critical path now can be different from 44. For example, suppose that every activity time turned out to equal its pessimistic estimate. Then the times on this critical path would add up to 69 days. Furthermore, another path ($1 \rightarrow 2 \rightarrow 3 \rightarrow 4 \rightarrow 6 \rightarrow 8 \rightarrow 10 \rightarrow 13$) would require even more time, namely, 70 days. Thus, the critical path based on expected times can turn out to require less time than another path.

Suppose now that the deadline for completing the house construction project is in 47 workdays. How can the information in table 1 be used to determine the probability of meeting this schedule?

Having used the first two assumptions to obtain the last two columns of table 1, we now need three additional assumptions (or approximations) to enable us to calculate the probability of completing the project on schedule.

Assumption 3: The activity times are statistically independent random variables.

Assumption 4: As an approximation, assume that the critical path based on expected times always requires a longer total elapsed time than any other path.

Assumption 5: The probability distribution of project time is at least approximately an normal distribution.

We find the answer of the previous question by calculating Z, where

$$Z = (D - \mu)/\sqrt{\sigma_\mu^2} \tag{5}$$

and

D = The desired project completion time

μ = The critical time of the project, the sum of the total estimate times for activities on the critical path.

σ_μ^2 = The variance of the critical path, the sum of the variances of activities on the critical path.

Z = The number of standard deviations of a normal distribution (the standard normal deviate)

Z as calculated above can be used to find the probability of completing the project on time.

Using the numbers in our case study D = 47, $\mu = 44$ and $\sigma_{\mu}^{2} = 9$

$$Z = \frac{47 - 44}{3} = 1 \text{ standard deviation}$$

Thus, the scheduled completion time of 47 is 1.0 standard deviation above the mean. Using $K_{\alpha} = 1.0$ in table 2 Areas under the normal curve from K_{α} to ∞ then gives an approximate probability of 1-0.1587 $\approx$ 0.84 that this schedule will be met.

Table 2: Area under the normal curve from K_{α} to ∞

$$P\{\text{normal} > K\alpha\} = \int_{K\alpha}^{\infty} \frac{1}{\sqrt{2\pi}} e^{-x^2/2} dx = \alpha$$

Kα	.00	.01	.02	.03	.04	.05	.06	.07	.08	.09
0.0	.5000	.4960	.4920	.4880	.4840	.4801	.4761	.4721	.4681	.4641
0.1	.4602	.4562	.4522	.4483	.4443	.4404	.4364	.4325	.4286	.4247
0.2	.4207	.4168	.4129	.4090	.4052	.4013	.3974	.3936	.3897	.3859
0.3	.3821	.3783	.3745	.3707	.3669	.3632	.3594	.3557	.3520	.3483
0.4	.3446	.3409	.3372	.3336	.3300	.3264	.3228	.3192	.3156	.3121
0.5	.3085	.3050	.3015	.2981	.2946	.2912	.2877	.2843	.2810	.2776
0.6	.2743	.2709	.2676	.2643	.2611	.2578	.2546	.2514	.2483	.2451
0.7	.2420	.2389	.2358	.2327	.2296	.2266	.2236	.2206	.2177	.2148
0.8	.2119	.2090	.2061	.2033	.2005	.1977	.1949	.1922	.1894	.1867
0.9	.1841	.1814	.1788	.1762	.1736	.1711	.1685	.1660	.1635	.1611
1.0	.1587	.1562	.1539	.1515	.1492	.1469	.1446	.1423	.1401	.1379
1.1	.1357	.1335	.1314	.1292	.1271	.1251	.1230	.1210	.1190	.1170
1.2	.1151	.1131	.1112	.1093	.1075	.1056	.1038	.1020	.1003	.0985
1.3	.0968	.0951	.0934	.0918	.0901	.0885	.0869	.0853	.0838	.0823
1.4	.0808	.0793	.0778	.0764	.0749	.0735	.0721	.0708	.0694	.0681
1.5	.0668	.0655	.0643	.0630	.0618	.0606	.0594	.0582	.0571	.0559

6. Conclusion

Management of big projects that consist of a large number of activities pose complex problems in planning, scheduling and control, especially when the project activities have to be performed in a specified technological sequence. With the help of PERT (Program Evaluation and Review Technique), and CPM (Critical Path Method), the project manager can: First, plan the project ahead of time and foresee possible sources of troubles and delays in completion. Second, schedule the project activities at the appropriate times to conform with proper job sequence so that the project is completed as soon as possible. And third, coordinate and control the project activities so as to stay on schedule in completing the project.

Thus both PERT and CPM are aids to efficient project management. They differ in their approach to the problem and the solution technique. The nature of the project generally dictates the proper techniques to be used.

References

1. Hamdy A. Taha Operations Research An Introduction third edition 1976
2. Frederick S. Hiller, Gerald J. Lieberman Introduction to Operations Research Sixth Edition 1995
3. Jack R. Meredith, Samuel J. Mantel. JR. Project Management Third Edition 1995.
4. Dennis Lock Project Management Seventh Edition 2000.
5. A. Ravindran, Don T. Phillips, James J. Solberg Operations Research Principles and Practice Second Edition 2006.

STRATEGIC ANALYSIS UNDER UNCERTAINTY: FINDING THE EXTERNAL FACTORS OVER BUSINESS

ANNA MARIA GIL-LAFUENTE
Department of Business Administration, Faculty of Economics, University of Barcelona, Avda Diagonal, 690, 08034 Barcelona, Spain

EMILI VIZUETE-LUCIANO
Department of Business Administration, Faculty of Economics, University of Barcelona, Avda Diagonal, 690, 08034 Barcelona, Spain

SEFA BORIA-REVERTER
Department of Business Administration, Faculty of Economics, University of Barcelona, Avda Diagonal, 690, 08034 Barcelona, Spain

The objective of this paper is to present a technical procedure to determine the impact of the external factors over the economic and financial structure of the business, considering that the size and sector are important in this analysis and fundamental in the decision making for the governments in each country. The fuzzy logic through the forgotten effects emerge as a powerful tool to analyze the enterprises and consider those factors that nowadays have been overlook; to consolidate this theory a business simulation with the purpose of evaluating this theory is shown, describing all outcomes and conclusions generated by the analysis.

1. Introduction

The globalization phenomena has brought important developments inside the business boundary, nowadays any business has a chance to open to the overseas market, however this phenomena also forces every business man to create strategies that allow them to continue to grow and to be competitive in every market target.

The financial analysis of any kind of project establishes the mathematical, financial and analytical techniques that may bring about benefits or losses arising from investments or some other movements. This tool also supports the decision making on the investment activities. The traditional financial analysis has been focused on numbers, however, nowadays this is not sufficient to realize a success analysis due we have to consider strategic and economical tendencies that the business manager must know to achieve viability on the long term; this kind of analysis is called strategic analysis in which we will focus on the impact of environmental factors, being aware of either as an opportunity of making business and projects or dangers that might affect them [2,16].

The macroeconomic effect has a sensitive impact principality in the small and medium enterprises (SME's), by its special and limited characteristics e.g. do not have protection about of the change of currency, do not have reserves economics in case of financial crisis, their patrimony is guaranty of the banker credit; but is important to considerate than the effect is different for each economical sector e.g. if the economic problem is increase in the oil price, the principal sector affected is industrial, but tourism sector is affected indirectly way by the increase in the transport but there are more opportunities by protect; with those simples examples it is possible to conclude that the incidence of the changes in the phenomenon's of the economy is different in each sector or size of business.

It is a big deal to have all the information that allows us:

- Fulfilling strategic analysis that point out required actions for the business survival and up-date.
- Evaluating incidences of certain elements of the environment, about the main indicators of the business financial health.
- Evaluating competitiveness and make the best economic decisions.

The section 2 shows the object of the analysis and the relation of external factors in the analysis financial. Section 3 shows the analysis through "The forgotten Effects Theory" and the results in matrix shape and finally Section 4 provides the conclusions followed by the Bibliography.

2. Determination of the Objective

The external factors are all those economic, politic and social factors that affect in either directly or indirectly way the financial situation of a business and we cannot modify them, it could become impossible to establish a list of factors for all the businesses in each country, however we do this first approach taking into consideration those factors that always affect companies no matter which country we could mention.

In the Figure 1 we can see the relation between the elements in the financial structure and the financial evaluation; the Figure 2 shows the relation of the external factors over the financial and economic structure.

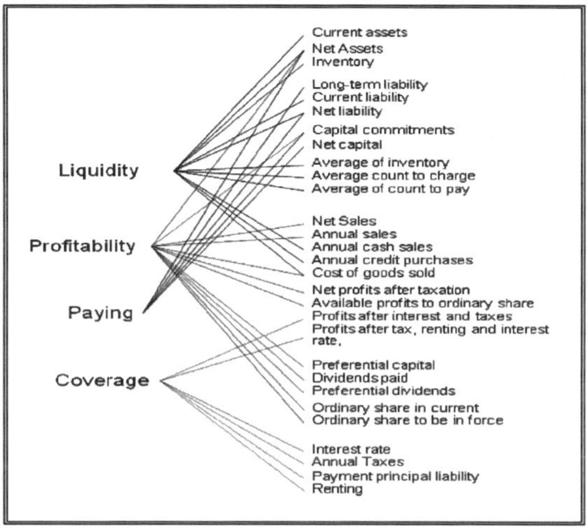

Figure 1. Relation between the elements in the financial structure and the financial evaluation.

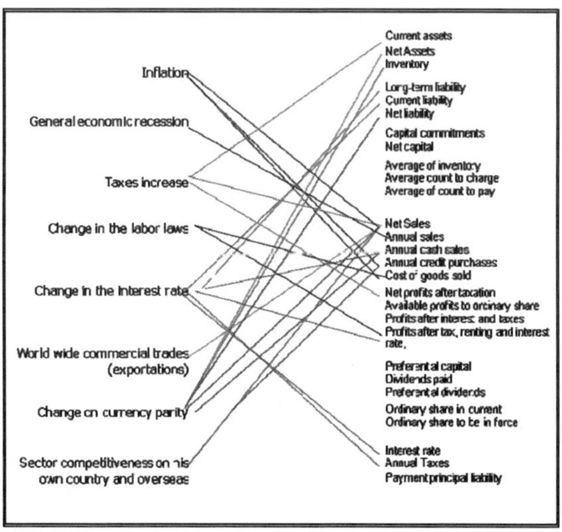

Figure 2. Relation of the External Factors over the financial and economic structure.

In this moment, the question is: What will happen in the evaluation financial of the business if are there changes in some element of the external factors? We can see in the Figure 3, that when there are variations of the elements in the financial structure generate by external factors, the financial evaluation is affected directly e.g. if there are some parity changes, the direct affectation will be on the passive elements as well as on the sales and purchases and in consequence the status of liquidity, paying and profitability seem to be agitated and with these all the financial movements of the business (Figure 3).

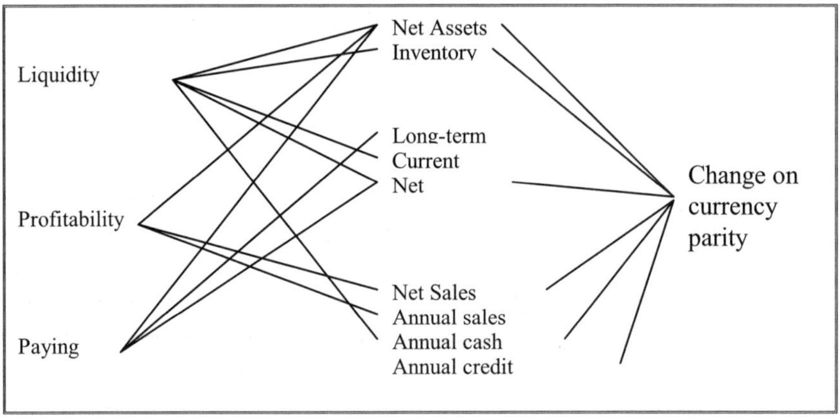

Figure 3. Effect in the financial ratios when there are changes on currency parity.

The modifications on the interest rates will affect liquid funds, paying and coverage of the business, so we can continue to mention implications without any more study than the reasoning and the experience of the analyst, who evaluates all the financial information of the business, so it will be easy establish the incidence of each external factor to the business economical-financial structure (Figure 4).

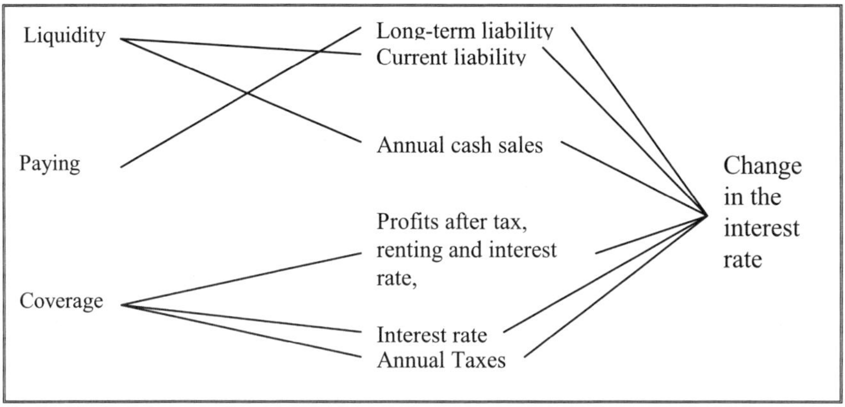

Figure 4. Effect in the financial ratios when there are changes on the interest rate.

At first sight and with the analyst experience, it will be easy to make that evaluation and would be enough that an expert expresses his opinion about implications that each factor could carry out however all the relationship possibilities of the external factors itself could not be considered in a precision way.

The Fuzzy-Logic theory applied into the science since 1965 and introduced by Lofty A. Zadeh has evolved worldwide in different knowledge fields, including the economical-financial [4,7,11], giving scientific models which analyze deeply the incidence topic, the forgotten effects theory, relating the effect idea over an element group over other element or over itself.

3. Analysis through "The Forgotten Effects Theory"

The forgotten effects theory provides tools* that allow us through the called qualitative incidence matrix [14, 21], research cause-effect mechanisms, that it is not possible to find out through intuition or experience, which is the reason that motivate the study and application of this methodology, evaluating in this way the incidence of the external factors over the economical-financial structure of the business.

The analysis of several problems of different areas using incidence matrix, shows us that in the cases in which experts are aware of possible intermediate incidence, the matrix result with higher coherency in relation with the base of

* Composition of max-min, incidence qualitative matrices of first, second and consecutive order, application of reliable intervals and triplets, and development of expertons.

recovering process of intermediate effects, in which it is considered as a valid hypothesis the transitivity in all orders, out coming a consequence of a few forgotten effects [7]. This study includes the incidence of the external factors and the financial economic structure itself to reduce those forgotten effects. The models used in this study were formulated and proposed by Kaufman and Gil Aluja and the first approach to this topic was done by Gil Lafuente [9].

All organization whit the objective of analyze and evaluate the development of the SME's could be to use this model for to observer the effects of the economic and financial changes in countries and establish development of the politics in this business sector; for to present the compression easy of this tool , we show the application in one business considering than the results by each business will be accumulate whit other fuzzy logics tools *, in this paper is not presenting because need a profound study.

Due to each business has different characteristics, according to the branch that they belong, geographic situation, size, sales destination as well as their purchase base, we simulate a manufacture medium size branch business, that is purchasing on his own country (America), and his sales are assigned 80% local and 20% overseas; according to the opinion of several experts who have evaluated the economical-financial situation and the external factors incidence on the financial-economic structure, getting the next matrix. At first, we specify the input required for our study [1]:

External Factors: Fulfilling an evaluation of main factors exposed by the science community during the last 10 years†, Gil Lafuente analysis and the most representative factor on those develop economies [3,5,10,17,18,19,20].

A_1	Inflation	A_5	Change in the interest rate
A_2	General economic recession	A_6	Worldwide commercial trades (exportations)
A_3	Taxes increase	A_7	Change on currency parity
A_4	Change in the labor laws	A_8	Sector competitiveness on his own country and overseas.

Elements of the economical-financial structure: The financial statement elements have been listed in Figure 1 and we have considered that the origin of the financial evaluation can be represented in a general way through the next

* Expertons, reliable intervals and triplets.

† 519 paper was analyzed in the dates base Isi Web, whit the keywords relative at external factors in the business field and results of the personal study making in México, Chile and Argentina.

titles (They are the elements of the economic and financial structure and represent the origin of the financial ratios):

B_1	Current assets	B_7	Annual credit purchases	B_{13}	Foreign sales
B_2	Fixed asset	B_8	Cost of goods sold	B_{14}	Operating expenses
B_3	Current liability	B_9	Interest	B_{15}	Taxes
B_4	Long-term liability	B_{10}	Leasing	B_{16}	Net profit
B_5	Capital Commitments	B_{11}	Annual cash sales		
B_6	Annual cash purchases	B_{12}	Annual credit sales		

The objective of this study is not to set items of strict nature but to establish a methodology that can be clear with the objective of being a tool that allows finding the effect of external factors in the financial-economic structure.

We will start the process of analysis through next steps:

a)The object of study is the incidence of external factors in the financial situation, that is why an evaluation has been made, where the opinion of experts has been collected, who consider that the conditions of the business have been taken from the next incidence matrix R (Figure 5). Boxes that have 0 (zero) incidence mean that in this case, has been not consider a relation of causation between this elements.

$\underset{\sim}{R}$	Current assets	Fixed asset	Current liability	Long term liability	Capital Employed	Annual cash purchases	Annual credit purchases	Cost of goods sold	Interest	Leasing	Annual cash sales	Annual credit sales	Foreign sales	Operating expenses	Taxes	Net profit
Inflation	0,9	1	0,7	0,7	1	0	0	1	1	0	0	0	0	0,8	0	0,7
General Economic recession	0	0	0	0	0	0,8	0,8	0	0,6	0,6	0,9	0,9	0,3	0,5	0	0,9
Taxes increase	0,4	0	0,3	0	0	0	0	0	0	0	0	0	0	0,2	1	0,3
Change in the labor laws	0	0,4	0,4	0,5	0	0	0	0,2	0	0,1	0	0	0	0	0,4	0,3
Change in the interest rate	0,6	0,4	0,5	0,3	0	0	0,7	0	1	0	0	0,4	0	0	0	0,1
World wide commercial trades (exportations)	0	0	0	0	0	0,1	0,2	0,5	0	0	0,3	0,7	1	0	0,5	0,4
Change on currency parity	0,3	0,2	0,2	0,1	0	0	0,1	0	0	0	0,3	0,7	1	0,2	0	0,2
Sector competitiveness on his own country and overseas	0,4	0,5	0,4	0,3	0,4	0	0	0,5	0	0	0	0	0,8	0,9	0	0,8

Figure 5. Matrix R, external factors incidence over the Economical-financial structure of the business.

b)With the purpose of avoiding that there are forgotten effects in the analysis, and continue with the Kauffman and Gil Aluja's models [14,8], has been requested to experts that give their opinion about the incidence that have the financial structure elements over themselves (Figure 6) and appraisal of the external factors over themselves (Figure 7).

$\underset{\sim}{F}$	Inflation	General Economic recession	Taxes increase	Change in the labor laws	Change in the interest rate	World wide commercial trades (exportations)	Change on currency parity	Sector competitiveness on his own country and overseas
Inflation	1	1	0,5	0,4	0,8	0,6	0,9	0,7
General Economic recession	1	1	0	0	0,7	0,8	0,3	0,9
Taxes increase	0	0,9	1	0	0,4	0,6	0	0,8
Change in the labor laws	0,3	0,5	0,7	1	0	0	0	0,8
Change in the interest rate	0,9	0,8	0,3	0	1	0,4	0,2	0,6
World wide commercial trades (exportations)	0,2	0	0,1	0,4	0,2	1	0	0,6
Change on currency parity	0,8	0,5	0	0	0,2	0,7	1	0,8
Sector competitiveness on his own country and overseas	0	0	0	0	0	0,7	0	1

Figure 6. Matrix F, incidence of external factors over themselves.

It is very important outline that to get the matrix E the International Accounting Standard Board rules [12] have been considered and later on the appraisal of the numbers from business that is been evaluated.

$\underset{\sim}{E}$	Current assets	Fixed asset	Current liability	Long term liability	Capital Employed	Annual cash purchases	Annual credit purchases	Cost of goods sold	Interest	Leasing	Annual cash sales	Annual credit sales	Foreign sales	Operating expenses	Tases	Net profit
Current assets	1	0,1	0,2	0	0,1	0	0	0,3	0,3	0,1	0	0	0	0,4	0,2	0,4
Fixed asset	0	1	0	0	0	0	0	0,1	0,3	0	0	0	0	0,5	0	0
Current liability	0,1	0	1	0	0,4	0	0,9	0	0,2	0	0	0	0	0,3	0	0
Long term liability	0	0	0	1	0,1	0	0,4	0	0,1	0	0	0	0	0,1	0	0
Capital Employed	0,2	0	0	0	1	0	0	0	0	0	0	0	0	0,2	0	0
Annual cash purchases	0,2	0	0	0	0	1	0	0,2	0	0	0	0	0	0	0,3	0,2
Annual credit purchases	0,1	0	0,5	0,3	0	0	1	0,2	0	0	0	0	0	0,3	0,4	0,2
Cost of goods sold	0,3	0	0	0	0	0	0	1	0	0	0,4	0,4	0,4	0	0,3	0,3
Interest	0,3	0,4	0,7	0,8	0,5	0	0,4	0	1	0,4	0	0,5	0,2	0,4	0	0,3
Leasing	0,1	0,2	0,1	0	0	0	0	0	0,3	1	0	0	0	0,2	0	0,1
Annual cash sales	0,2	0	0	0	0,1	0	0	0	0	0	1	0	0	0	0,3	0,3
Annual credit sales	0,3	0	0	0	0,1	0	0	0	0	0	0	1	0	0,1	0,3	0,5
Foreign sales	0,2	0	0	0	0,1	0	0	0	0	0	0	0	1	0,3	0,3	0,7
Operating expenses	0	0	0	0	0	0	0	0	0	0	0	0	0	1	0,6	0,6
Tases	0,2	0	0,4	0	0	0	0	0	0	0	0	0	0	0	1	0,3
Net profit	0	0	0	0	0,5	0	0	0	0	0	0	0	0	0	0	1

Figure 7. Matrix E, incidence of financial structure elements over themselves

c)The matrix method is more comfortable and the use of correlation max-min, avoid the possible mistakes that can be done when math are done directly over a chart [7]. Without trying to do some huge the development of the analysis and using the technique of composition of max-min [15], we realize the composition (the usual symbol is "o") between matrix F and R, and the incidence matrix give us the outcomes shown in Figure 8.

FoR	Current assets	Fixed asset	Current liability	Long term liability	Capital Employed	Annual cash purchases	Annual credit purchases	Cost of goods sold	Interest	Leasing	Annual cash sales	Annual credit sales	Foreign sales	Operating expenses	Taxes	Net profit
Inflation	0,9	1	0,7	0,7	1	0,8	0,8	1	1	0,6	0,9	0,9	0,9	0,8	0,5	0,9
General Economic recession	0,9	1	0,7	0,7	1	0,8	0,8	1	1	0,6	0,9	0,9	0,8	0,9	0,5	0,9
Taxes increase	0,4	0,5	0,4	0,3	0,4	0,8	0,8	0,5	0,6	0,6	0,9	0,9	0,8	0,8	1	0,9
Change in the labor laws	0,4	0,5	0,4	0,5	0,4	0,5	0,5	0,5	0,5	0,5	0,5	0,5	0,8	0,8	0,7	0,8
Change in the interest rate	0,9	0,9	0,7	0,7	0,9	0,8	0,8	0,9	1	0,6	0,8	0,8	0,6	0,8	0,4	0,8
World wide commercial trades (expoitations)	0,4	0,5	0,4	0,4	0,4	0,1	0,2	0,5	0,2	0,1	0,3	0,7	1	0,6	0,5	0,6
Change on currency party	0,8	0,8	0,7	0,7	0,8	0,5	0,5	0,8	0,8	0,5	0,5	0,7	1	0,8	0,5	0,8
Sector competitiveness on his own country and overseas	0,4	0,5	0,4	0,3	0,4	0,1	0,2	0,5	0	0	0,3	0,7	0,8	0,9	0,5	0,8

Figure 8. Matrix of composition of F or R matrixes.

With this procedure we have interrelated the matrix R with the incidence the external factors have in a reflexive matrix that allow to decrease the forgotten effects or establish a matrix with accumulated effects.

Since this moment, is possible to watch that the main changes are created where expression effects to fix: asset, employed capital, cost of sales, current asset; incidences that in original matrix were no considers with the experts opinion.

d)Continue with our analysis, first stage has been covered, lets back to do the correlation between this second degree matrix (FoR) and matrix E that represent the incidence of elements of financial structure with themselves. The matrix's outcomes (Figure 9) have the full incidences, because it has, not only the causation's relationship of external factors over the elements of economical-financial structure, but the incidence's relationship of those factors and elements with themselves.

Due to the accumulation of the effects of second generation, is necessary to remove the effects of first degree from effects of first and second degree to avoid that we are seeing ratings with a high intensity*.

FoRoE	Current assets	Fixed asset	Current liability	Long term liability	Capital Employed	Annual cash purchases	Annual credit purchases	Cost of goods sold	Interest	Leasing	Annual cash sales	Annual credit sales	Foreign sales	Operating expenses	Tases	Net profit
Inflation	0,9	1	0,7	0,8	1	0,8	0,8	1	1	0,6	0,9	0,9	0,9	0,8	0,6	0,9
General Economic recession	0,9	1	0,7	0,8	1	0,8	0,8	1	1	0,6	0,9	0,9	0,8	0,9	0,6	0,9
Taxes increase	0,4	0,5	0,6	0,6	0,5	0,8	0,8	0,5	0,6	0,6	0,9	0,9	0,8	0,8	1	0,9
Change in the labor laws	0,4	0,5	0,5	0,5	0,5	0,5	0,5	0,5	0,5	0,5	0,5	0,5	0,8	0,8	0,7	0,8
Change in the interest rate	0,9	0,9	0,7	0,8	0,9	0,8	0,8	0,9	1	0,6	0,8	0,8	0,6	0,8	0,6	0,8
World wide commercial trades (exportations)	0,4	0,5	0,4	0,4	0,5	0,1	0,4	0,5	0,3	0,2	0,4	0,7	1	0,6	0,6	0,7
Change on currency parity	0,8	0,8	0,7	0,8	0,8	0,5	0,7	0,8	0,8	0,5	0,5	0,7	1	0,8	0,6	0,8
Sector competitiveness on his own country and overseas	0,4	0,5	0,4	0,3	0,5	0,1	0,4	0,5	0,3	0,1	0,4	0,7	0,8	0,9	0,6	0,8

Figure 9.- Matrix of results from the composition of F, R y E matrixes.

However is important point that 0 (zeros) that we get from next matrix (Figure 10) are identical evaluations with the original matrix (R) and it allows to us identifying which the forgotten effects were not considered in the first approach. $\tilde{F} \circ \tilde{R} \circ \tilde{E} - \tilde{R}$

FoRoE - R	Current assets	Fixed asset	Current liability	Long term liability	Capital Employed	Annual cash purchases	Annual credit purchases	Cost of goods sold	Interest	Leasing	Annual cash sales	Annual credit sales	Foreign sales	Operating expenses	Tases	Net profit
Inflation	0	0	0	0,1	0	0,8	0,8	0	0	0,6	0,9	0,9	0,9	0	0,6	0,2
General Economic recession	0,9	1	0,7	0,8	1	0	0	1	0,4	0	0	0	0,5	0,4	0,6	0
Taxes increase	0	0,5	0,3	0,6	0,5	0,8	0,8	0,5	0,6	0,6	0,9	0,9	0,8	0,6	0	0,6
Change in the labor laws	0,4	0,1	0,1	0	0,5	0,5	0,5	0,3	0,5	0,4	0,5	0,5	0,8	0,8	0,3	0,5
Change in the interest rate	0,3	0,5	0,2	0,5	0,9	0,8	0,1	0,9	0	0,6	0,8	0,4	0,6	0,8	0,6	0,7
World wide commercial trades (exportations)	0,4	0,5	0,4	0,4	0,5	0	0,2	0	0,3	0,2	0,1	0	0	0,6	0,1	0,3
Change on currency parity	0,5	0,6	0,5	0,7	0,8	0,5	0,6	0,8	0,8	0,5	0,2	0	0	0,6	0,6	0,6
Sector competitiveness on his own country and overseas	0	0	0	0	0,1	0,1	0,4	0	0,3	0,1	0,4	0,7	0	0	0,6	0

Figure 10. Matrix of composition of F or R or E matrixes, less the original matrix (R).

* Kauffman and Gil Aluja 1989, pages 35- 40

The next is looking for the intermediate incidences through the forgotten effect [8] were made. Taking matrix R (Figure 5) and compare the input row and the output column to find the biggest minimal from next forgotten effects, consider the most outstanding to have a huge appraisal and a null relation considered by the experts at the moment to do the incidence matrix R (Figure 10). Now is possible to see that at the beginning no value had been given to the effect that a general economic recession has over the fixed asset, equity, cost of goods sold and current assets because it was no consider a direct incidence, however through the results of this model those effects have to be considered.

In the same way, inflation and increase of taxes, is considered that at the beginning, they produce direct affectation in the accounts of the statement of financial condition, without important modifications on the accounts of income statement, but the model reflects high incidence in sales accounts. The same happens with the relationship between changes in the bank interest with equity and cost of goods sold. Let see which are the intermediate relationships that make this appraisal in order to define such important variation that will help us of take decisions when the financial statements are evaluated. Let's consider the nomenclature used at the beginning of this document, to make easy the introduce of this analysis.

General economic recession → Current assets

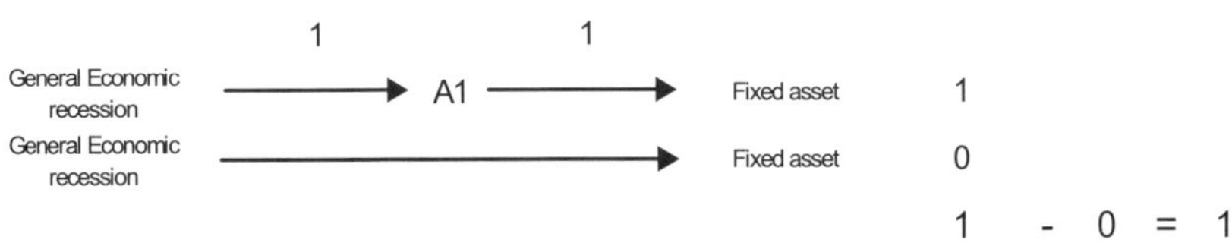

In this way is possible to identify that the first appraisal of 1 is created in the matrix of max-min composition F or R due to the relationship that exists the inflation itself (A1,A1) as showed in Figure 11

v (A2 , B2) =

(A1 , A1)	= (	1,0	∧	1,0	) =	1
(A2 , A2)	= (	1,0	∧	-	) =	0
(A3 , A3)	= (	-	∧	-	) =	0
(A4 , A4)	= (	-	∧	0,4	) =	0
(A5 , A5)	= (	0,7	∧	0,4	) =	0
(A6 , A6)	= (	0,8	∧	-	) =	0
(A7 , A7)	= (	0,3	∧	0,2	) =	0
(A8 , A8)	= (	0,9	∧	0,5	) =	1

Figure 11. Determination of value from the incidence of (A2,B2) Through Max-min composition method for F o R. matrixes.

It means that it is a factor did not consider at the beginning through this subjective analysis. Using the same procedure the intermediate relationships are obtained to other forgotten factors (Figure 12).

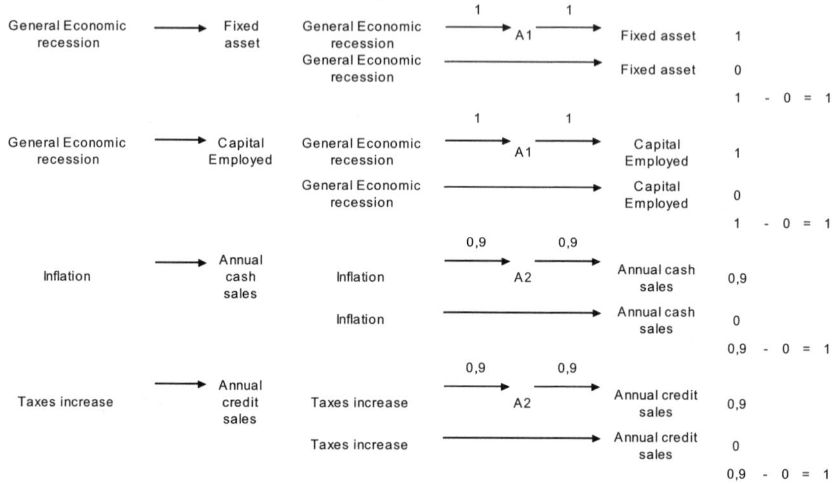

Figure 12. Relationship of forgotten set factors.

The chart that is introduced next (Figure 13) shows in a visual way what was described through process of correlation max-min of blurred matrix. It represents the "connection that expert's mind should done to link a cause with an effect" [10], however, do this assessment in a intuitive way would be complex and extremely difficult with chances of make mistakes, the procedures described by Kauffman and Gil Aluja have been used in many projects and showed to fulfill the properties to back up the outcomes.

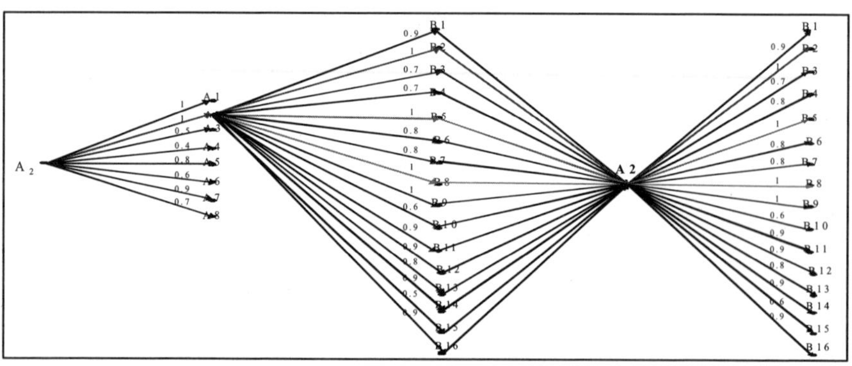

Figure 13. To get of forgotten effects through of charts, unknown because for the General Economic recession in the current liability, capital commitments and cost of goods sold.

With the support of the Expertons [13] (tools of the fuzzy logic) is possible to integrate the results of the groups or economic sectors how the SME's whit this results is possible to analyze the comportment and affectation by the external factors in their situation economic and financial structure and take the best decision in the politics for their development. The objective of that procedure is to accumulate the results and offered general dates about of the two or many groups.

4. Conclusions

The intuition in the analysis financial, leads us to consider some incidences, but it is not until those ideas are captured and assessed through the mathematical procedures, what let us set that by drawing lines in a subjective way will bring itself omissions that Fuzzy Logic theory has rescued through procedures.

If an element of financial-economic structure is not properly assessment or showed for a better decision taking, without considering those external factors that have an incidence over the numbers that reflect, we can take decisions that in the future will be affected.

Nowadays in Latin America's countries there are procedures that allow reflecting the affectation of the inflation as a big external factor for these economies, however, the indirect repercussions can be assessed through the model told before, because as we saw in some examples, inflation still affects in an indirect way the assessment of others concepts.

The application of this model at institutional level, offered results of importance for the investigation of the sensitive sectors (SME's) to the economic – political and social changes of a country, in this case, it is possible to evaluate the impact that produces these alterations and giving sufficient information to establish measurements of action on this matter.

References

1.Anselin Avila, E., "*The effects of the Incidence of External Factors in the Economical and Financial Structure of the Business: Application of the Fuzzy Logic",* International Conference on Modelling and Simulation, at the Universidad Michoacana de San Nicolas de Hidalgo, Morelia, Michoacán, México, April 27-29, 2005.

2.Arrarte Mera, R., "*Importancia del Análisis Estratégico de los Estados Financieros Empresariales*" Asociación Interamericana de Contabilidad, Lima Perú, Free Press (Web) 2003.

3.Bala Subrahmanya, M.H., "*Pattern of technological innovations in small enterprises: a comparative perspective of Bangalore (India) and Northeast England (UK)*", Technovation, Vol. 25 Issue 3, p269, 12p; DOI: 10.1016/S0166-4972(03)00094-4; 2005.
4.Bosca, J.E.; Escriba, J.; Murgui, M.J., "*Total Factor Productivity Growth in Spanish Regions: Effects of Quasi-Fixed and External Factors and Varying Capacity Utilization*" Regional Studies, v. 38, iss. 6, pp. 587-601, August 2004.
5.Capello, R.; Faggian, A., "*Collective Learning and Relational Capital in Local Innovation Processes*", Regional Studies, Vol. 39 Issue 1, p75, 13p; 2005.
6.Dholakia, R.R; Kshetri, N., "*Factors Impacting the Adoption of the Internet among SMEs*"; Small Business Economics, v. 23, iss. 4, pp. 311-22, November 2004.
7.Gento, A.; Lazzari, L.; Machado E., "*Reflexiones acerca de las matrices de incidencia y la Recuperación de efectos olvidados*" VI Congreso de SIGEF, Morelia, Michoacán, México, Trabajo desarrollado en el marco del Proyecto UBACyT TE22, noviembre de 1999.
8.Gil Lafuente, A.M.; Anselin Avila, E., "*Comportamiento de los elementos en la Teoría de los Efectos Olvidados*" XII Congress of International Association for Fuzzy-Set Management end Economy, Bahía Blanca – Argentina, October 26-28, 2005.
9.Gil Lafuente, A.M., "*Fundamentos de Análisis Financiero*" Ariel, S.A., Córcega, 270, Barcelona, España. 1993.
10.Gil Lafuente, A.M., "*Determination of the possible strategies for the reduction of the indebtedness of the company*" Fuzzy Economic Review No. 1 Vol. I, pp.59-82, Mayo 1996.
11.Gollier, C; Treich, N. "*Decision-making under scientific uncertainty: The economics of the precautionary principle*" Journal of Risk and Uncertainty 27 (1): 77-103 AUG 2003.
12.International Accounting Standard Board (IASB), International Accounting Standards Committee Foundation, 2004.
13.Kaufmann, A.; Gil Aluja J., "*Técnicas Especiales para la gestión de expertos*" Ed. Milladoiro, Santiago de Compostela, 1993.
14.Kaufmann, A.; Gil Aluja J., "*Modelos para la investigación de efectos olvidados*" Santiago de Compostela, Milladoiro, 1989.
15.Kaufmann, A.; Gil Aluja J., "*Técnicas Operativas de Gestión para el tratamiento de la incertidumbre*" Santiago de Compostela, Milladoiro, 1989.
16.Melville, N.; Kraemer, K.; Gurbaxani, V., "*Information technology and organizational performance: an integrative model of it business value*" MIS Quarterly, Vol. 28 Issue 2, p283, 40p, 2 charts, 1 diagram., Junio 2004.
17.Méndez Morales, J.S., "*Fundamentos de Economía*", McGraw-Hill, México, 1994.

18.Mundaca, G., "*Optimal bailout during currency and financial crises: A sequential game analysis*", Memorandum 27/2002, Oslo University, Department of Economics, 2003.

19.Raynauld, A., "*The Impact of External Shocks on the Current Account*" Atlantic Economic Journal, 0197-4254, Vol. 18, Issue 1, March 1, 1990.

20.Reyes Guzmán, G.; Muñoz Santiago, B.; Moslares García, C. "*El tipo de cambio flexible y la política monetaria en México: 1995-2003; Problemas del Desarrollo*", v. 35, iss. 136, pp. 49-63.

21.Vizuete Luciano, E.; Merigó J.M.; Gil Lafuente, A.M.; Boria Reverté, S.; "OWA Operators in the Assignment Process: The Case of the Hungarian Algorithm" Modeling and Simulation in Engineering, Economics and Management: 2012; vol. 115, pp. 166-177.

OPTIMIZATION OF DISTRIBUTION PROCESSES SERFELSA LABORATORIES S.A.

EVER Á. FUENTES

Industrial Engineering Departament, Universidad Libre, Bogotá D .C, Cundinamarca

JULIANA M. CASTELLANOS

Research Saiop, Bogotá D.C, Cundinamarca

Serfelsa Laboratories SA is a company specialized in making products for the personal care of the women. The company has a plant of production based in the municipality of Funza, Colombia. The product is taken from the factory to different places in the center, north, and south of the country. The company has no control on the timing and the costs generated after the deliveries; sometimes, the vehicles in charge of the deliveries are immobilized in repeated occasions, which generate breach in the delivery, clients unsatisfied, returns of the merchandise and extra costs. Considering this situation, we propose design an efficient mobility system applying three different mathematical models, based on the information, tests in real time and sources that contribute to set optimum solutions; having a comparison between the models, the company will be able to improve the decision making, response on time, costs and quality of the service with the objective of generating high efficiency in its operation.

1. Introduction

The improvement in logistics processes in a company is of great importance. Well as the new markets and the competitive require not only more efficient production processes, but accurate tools in logistics and distribution processes. Where the objective is to study and analyze the issue under different conditions. Let's get a basic overview and comparison of the processes that may arise, analyzing the impact of each of the factors or variables involved, making their behavior and predict when subjected to a given situation.

Serfelsa Laboratories SA is a company responsible for developing personal care products specially targeted to the female, has a production plant located in the municipality of Funza, Colombia. From this it takes the product to different parts of the country, south central and north.

The company has no control over the timing and costs incurred after delivery, is generated defaults, merchandise returns, dissatisfied customers and high costs. Thus, we performed a routing system through the application of three different mathematical models developed through information management, real-time testing and sources of information that allowed the generation of optimal solutions, was compared and approved the decision-making, obtaining improvements in the time, cost and quality of service. Allowing the company more competitive potential.

By developing a routing system in the company, this distribution processes allowed to run continuously, and now it is certain that the application of the model used is useful in companies with similar characteristics. This allows the optimum deployment of resources from them.

2. Objectives

General: Optimizing routing system through the application and validation of mathematical models to problems in the processes of distribution Serfelsa Laboratories SA

Specific:

- Perform diagnostic distribution processes Serfelsa SA Laboratories
- Comparing routing models that fit the problems seen in Serfelsa Laboratories SA
- Select the routing models that fit the needs of Laboratories SA Serfelsa
- Develop a routing model Serfelsa Laboratories SA
- Validate the selected routing model.

3. Description of the Problem

The distribution of the goods is one of the most critical logistical problems, framed in the supply chain management. To fulfill the purchase orders were presented difficulties because there is no control to transport goods from one place to another, leading to delays in delivery times and disagreements on the part of customers. The following diagram is related in a cause and effect, the problem identified in the company for the distribution of goods from the place of origin to different destinations

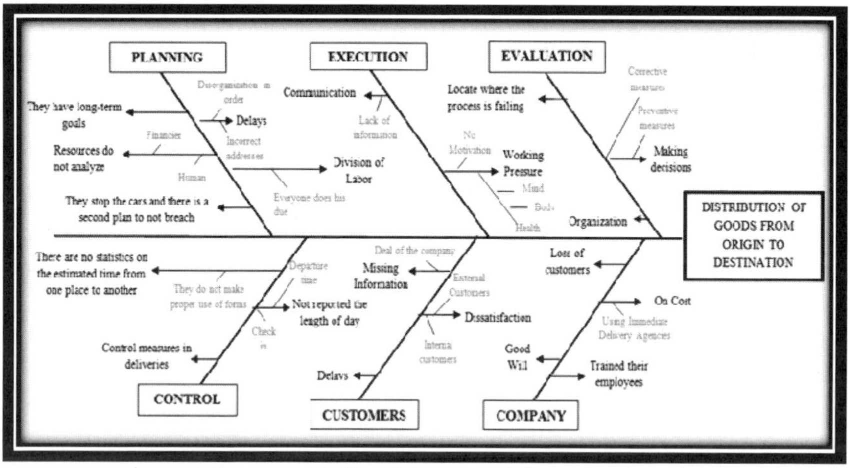

Figure 1 Cause and Effect Diagram of the research problem.

4. Methodology

In the project developed was applied a type of experimental research, since it is an exploratory study which seeks to formulate a problem setting a more precise investigation which brought solutions to the identified problem situation, which had not been implemented corrective measures.

Through the data collection a technique appropriate meets and summarizes the experiences reported by people involved directly with the problem identified, it is not written but is collected as a reference for research. This diagnosis was made SerfelsaLaboratorios SA, which identified the areas where problems were occurring in the different processes of operation. Now should be having a maximum control variable. [1, 2, 3]

The company's vision is to consolidate within a select group of the top 10 cosmetics companies in Colombia on a plane for 5 years and become a supplier to occupy a predominant position in NAFTA exports. Currently provides safety and welfare in relation to the environment by offering the best alternative in cosmeticsand strengthening the beauty dream, based on production systems and sustainable technology in a timely and efficient service. Forming true partnerships with strategic suppliers to implement highly cost competitive in the cosmetics market. All this through the formation of a team with high ethical values, with a commitment to quality, motivation and commitment to customers. In addition to the excellent results obtained from the use of appropriate decision tools, which gave way to analysis and subsequent decision making.

For the development of routing system was considered the city of Bogotá and its surroundings. Progress was made in a time of 18 months using Serfelsa Laboratories SA as the main study which evaluated the different logistics processes in the distribution of goods. This was taken as the reference product units shipped since this determines the cost for the transport of the same.

For proper implementation of the mathematical models developed data collection techniques appropriate for meeting the objectives; to make the diagnosis for the distribution processes of the company as elemental tool uses observation, this was the first step locate problems. Once these proceeded to implement three different models metaheuristics such as Ant Colony, Tabu Search and the problem of traveling VRA, after the development of each model the optimal solution was obtained which allowed the development of the expected routing system.

5. Ant Colony

Ants are social insects that live in colonies and that, because of their mutual cooperation, are able to display complex behaviors and difficult tasks from the point of view of an individual ant. An interesting aspect of the behavior of many species of ants is their ability to find the shortest road between their nest and food sources. This is especially interesting when you consider that many species of ants are almost blind, which avoids the use of visual clues.

While moving between the nest and food source, some species of ants deposit a chemical substance called pheromone (a substance that can "smell"). If there is no trace of pheromone, the ants move in a basically random, but when there pheromone deposited, are more likely to follow the trail. In fact, experiments by biologists have shown that ants probabilistically prefer the roads marked with a higher concentration of pheromone [5, 6].

In practice, the choice between different paths takes place when several paths cross. Then, the ants choose the way forward with a probabilistic decision biased by the amount of pheromone: the stronger the pheromone trail, the more likely to choose it. Since the ants deposit pheromone on the road to follow, this behavior leads to a self-reinforcing process that concludes with the formation of traces marked by a high concentration of pheromone. This behavior also allows the ants find the shortest roads between their nest and food source [5].

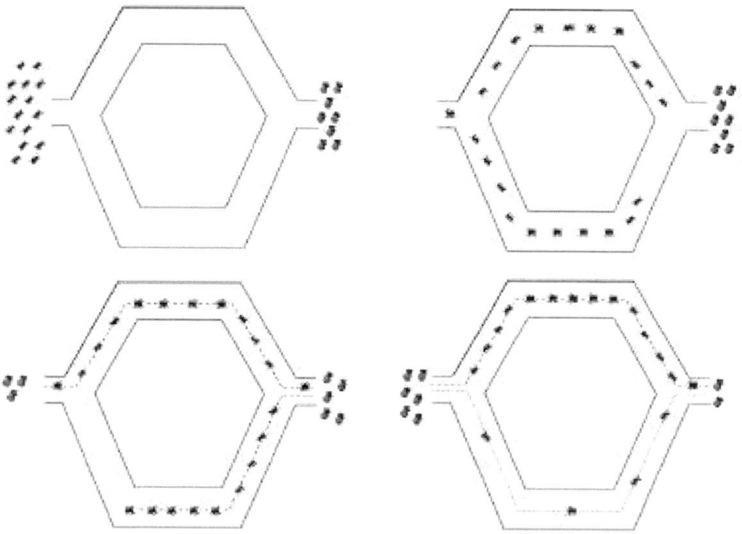

Figure 2. The behavior of the colony ends up getting the shortest path between two points. Based on a figure of [7]

Ant System [8], developed by Dorigo, Maniezzo and Colorni in 1991, was the first ACO algorithm. Initially, there were 3 different variants: SH-density, quantity and SH-SH-cycle that differ in the way that an update of the pheromone trails. In the first two, the ants deposit pheromone while building their solutions (ie, applied online update step pheromone), except that the amount of pheromone deposited on the SH-density is constant, while that the amount deposited in SH-depended directly on the desirability of the transition heuristic hrs. Finally, SH-cycle, pheromone deposition takes place once the solution is complete (post online update of pheromone). The latter option was the one who got better results and is therefore known as the SH in the literature.

The solutions in the SH are constructed as follows. At each construction step, an ant k chooses to go to the next node with a probability that is calculated as:

$$p_{rs}^{k} = \begin{cases} \dfrac{[\tau_{rs}]^{\alpha} \cdot [\eta_{rs}]^{\beta}}{\sum_{u \in N_r^k} [\tau_{rs}]^{\alpha} \cdot [\eta_{rs}]^{\beta}}, & si \quad s \in N_k(r) \\ 0, & en \quad otro \quad caso \end{cases}$$

Where Nk (r) is the neighborhood achievable by the ant k when it is in the node r, and a, b Î Â are two parameters that weight the relative importance of pheromone trails and heuristic information. Each ant k stores the sequence that has continued until now and his memory Lk, as explained above, is used to determine Nk (r) at each construction step.

Returning to the parameters a and b, its function is as follows: if a = 0, those nodes with a better heuristic preference are more likely to be chosen, making the algorithm very similar to a classical probabilistic greedy algorithm (with multiple starting points if the ants are located on different nodes at the beginning of each iteration). However, if b = 0, only takes into account the pheromone trails to guide the construction process, which can cause a rapid stagnation, ie a situation in which the pheromone trails are associated with a slightly higher resolution the rest, thereby causing the ants always build the same solutions, usually local optima [8].

6. Tabu Search

The tabu search uses a local search procedure or neighborhoods to move iteratively from a solution x to a solution x 'in the vicinity of x, to satisfy some stopping criterion. To explore regions of the search space that would be set aside by the procedure of local search, tabu search modifies the structure of neighbors for each solution as the search progresses. The solutions admitted to N * (x), the new neighborhood, are determined by using memory structures. The search then progresses iteratively moving from a solution x to a solution x 'in N * (x). [10, 11].

Formula used to consider the value of delay in completing the tasks that depend on the task considered, wj. The function to minimize is expressed as:

$$F = \sum_{j=1}^{n} w_j [C_j - d_j]^+,$$

Where Cj is the completion time of task j [Cj – dj] + = Max [0, Cj – dj]. The time of completion of a task j, Cj is equal to the processing time of task j plus the sum of processing times of all tasks that are performed before j.

The problem is to determine the order of sequencing of the tasks that minimizes the objective function value F. A sequence of tasks that fully defines a solution.

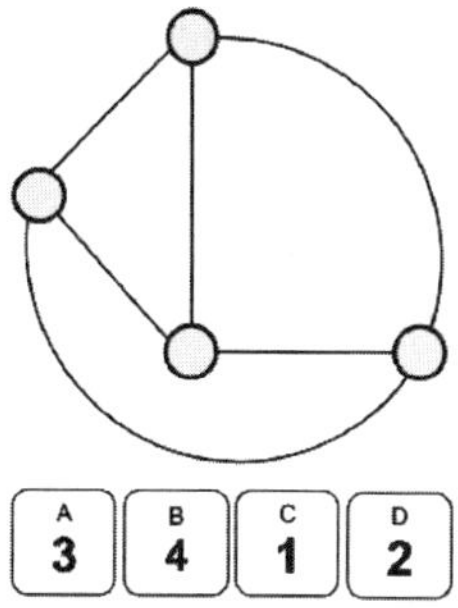

Figure 3. The behavior of the allocation of tasks.

The algorithm of AI takes the concept of memory and implemented using simple structures in order to direct the search taking into account the history of it, ie, the procedure is to extract information about what happened and act accordingly. In this sense we can say that there is some learning and the search is smart. In this way allows you to move to a solution but not as good as the present, so that they can escape from local optima and continue the search for solutions strategically even better (Figure 4).

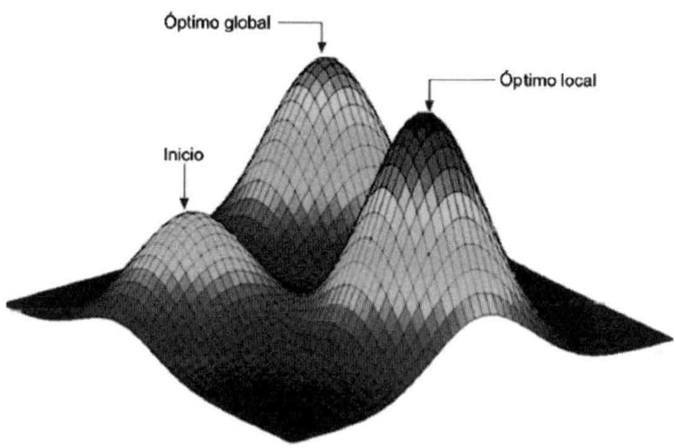

Figure 4. The behavior of the allocation of tasks from local optima

The tabu list that keeps the solutions by iterations which can generate more diverse neighborhoods with neighborhoods to avoid pre-built solutions [13, 14].

7. Traveller's Problem

Be N cities of a country. The goal is to find a route, beginning and ending in a specific city, go once for each of the cities and minimize the distance traveled by the salesman. That is, find a permutation $P = \{c0,\ c1,...,cN - 1\}$ such that is minimal.

$$d_P = \sum_{i=0}^{N-1} d[c_i, c_{i+1 mod(N)}]$$

The distance between each city is given by the matrix D: NxN, where d [x, y] represents the distance between city X and city Y. Is a linear problem with multiple solutions as shown in Figure 5.

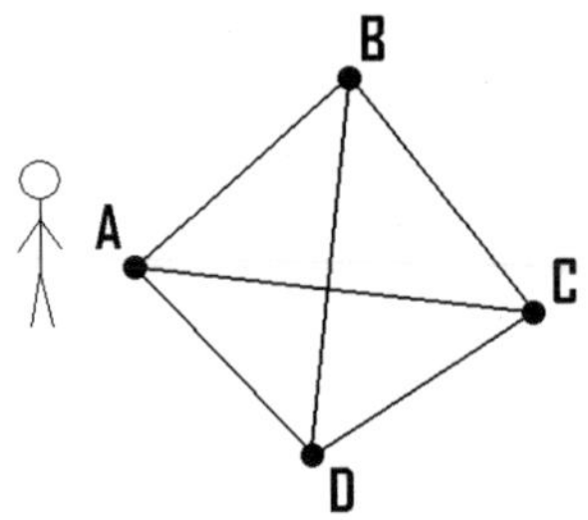

Figure 5. Linear behavior of the Traveling Salesman Problem.

8. Flow of Activities

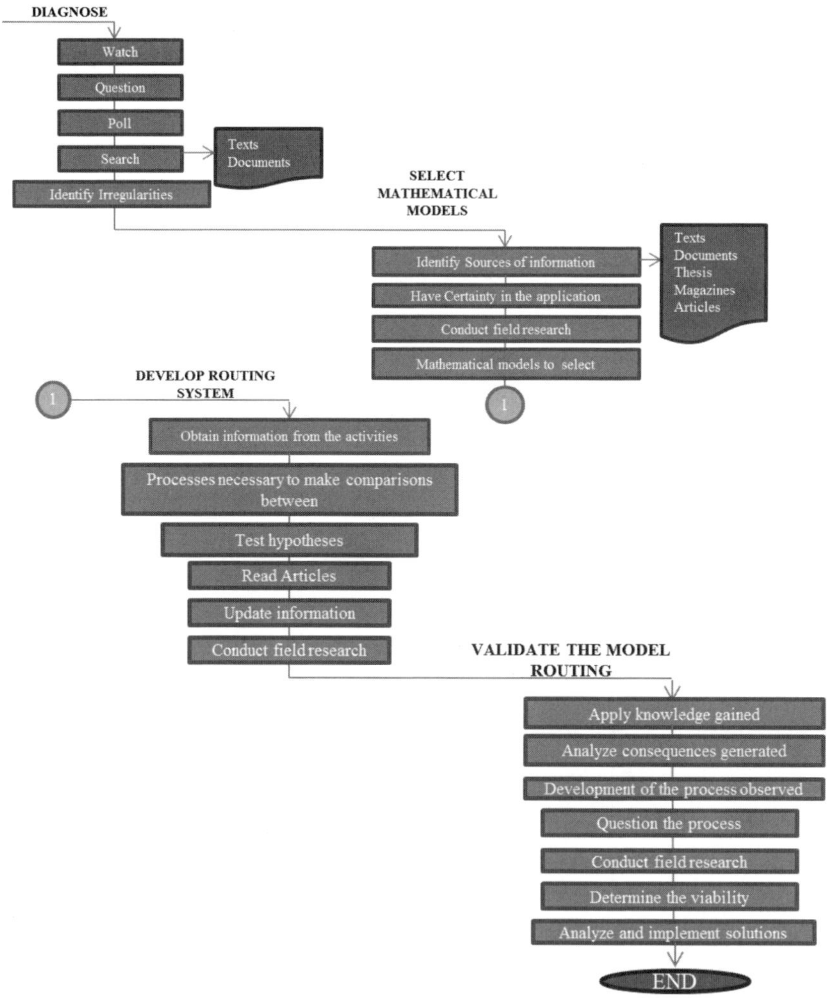

Figure 6. Flow of Activities

9. Analysis of Results

By using appropriate decision tools, companies are able to analyze and optimize their processes, and thus support their decisions. Following the implementation of three different mathematical models as they were: the ant colony, Tabu Search and VRA traveling salesman problem. It was concluded that it is sufficient to apply a single tool that supports decision making and you do not have a baseline to identify if this is optimal or not. Thus, the development of a routing system, together with the provision of information by the company allowed the application of metaheuristics to the area of distribution of goods. Where were different solutions to the same problem, under the same conditions, analyze and select the optimal solution.

ROUTE	ORIGINAL	ANT COLONY	VRP	TABÚ SEARCH	≠
1.Prado-Bachue	5.2	5	5.1	**4.8**	0.4
2.Siberia-Quirigua	3.3	3.2	2.9	**3**	0.3
3.Ciudadela-Fontibón	7.9	6.5	7.8	**6.2**	1.7
4.Ciudad Jardín-Altamar	5.4	5.1	5.3	**4.7**	0.7
5.Mosquera-Cota	10	8.3	7.2	**7.9**	2.1
6.Siberia-Patio Bonito	8.2	6.7	7.9	**7.5**	0.7
7.Chapinero-Ciudad Jardín	6.7	6.1	6.3	**5.5**	1.2
8.Restrepo-Kennedy	11.4	8.6	8.4	**8.3**	3.1
9.Soacha-Venecia	7.6	7.1	6.8	**5.5**	2.1
10.San Cristóbal-Bosa	3.8	3.5	3.6	**2.9**	0.9
11.Centro-Soacha	9.1	7.3	8.5	**7.8**	1.3

Table 1. Results obtained, evaluated in Km

According to the results obtained, the mathematical model that generated an optimal solution to the problem of logistics and distribution company is identified in the Tabu Search. Despite these variations existing variables were controlled.

By the nature of the coupling model allowed metaheuristics at different points within the route where you must deliver the goods, gaining control of distances, minimizing lead times and costs. Without neglecting the traffic that substantially affects the mobility of the country. Then the map which is related distribution activities are generated continuously and is the area in which research is conducted.

Figure 7. Coverage Area

10. Conclusions

After application of the metaheuristic has been shown to serve as an effective tool to improve logistics and distribution problems in companies. The process was identified variables such as weather, traffic, traffic lights which were considered for the analysis of information obtained; this analysis was conducted on a recurring basis and especially to get the results of applying mathematical models: the ant colony, Tabu Search and the problem of traveling VRA. Without diverting the company's goal to implement the results obtained allowed the routing system through the development of the model that generated the Tabu Search optimal solution to the research question posed.

During the development of routing system using the various tools and selecting the optimum between optimal paths are decreased by the equivalent of X km by road which benefits the company in reducing time, costs, generating an added value, generating security when competing offering the best service to be assured of quality. This was made possible by the result obtained in the mathematical model that generated Tabu search results.

References

1. Anonymous. IIE Annual Conference. Proceedings (2002): 1-33. PROQUEST
2. Bernal Torres Cesar Augusto. Metodología de la investigación para administración, economía, humanidades y ciencias sociales. Edición 2, México D.F, Pearson Prentice Hall, 2006. Pág. 146 a 156, 164 a 167, 174 a 178, 181 a 183,
3. Hernández Sampieri Roberto, Fernández Collado Carlos, Baptista Lucio Pilar. Fundamentos de metodología de la investigación. Edición 4, México D.F, McGraw Hill, 2007. Pág. 155 a 175
4. Méndez Álvarez Carlos Eduardo. Metodología Diseño y desarrollo del proceso de investigación con énfasis en ciencias empresariales. Edición 4, México D.F, Limusa Grupo noriega editores, 2010. Pág. 165 a 166, 228 a 250, 265 a 304.
5. S. Goss, S. Aron, J. L. Deneubourg, y J. M. Pasteels. Self-organized shortcuts in the Argentine ant. Naturwissenschaften, 76, páginas 579-581, 1989.
6. J. M. Pasteels, J.-L. Deneubourg, y S. Goss. Self-organization mechanisms in ant societies (I): Trail recruitment to newly discovered food sources. ExperientiaSupplementum, 54, páginas 155-175, 1987.
7. E. Bonabeau, M. Dorigo, y G. Theraulaz. Swarm Intelligence: From Natural to Artificial Systems. Oxford University Press, New York, NY, 1999.
8. M. Dorigo, V. Maniezzo, y A. Colorni. The Ant System: Optimization by a colony ofcooperating agents. IEEE Transactions on Systems, Man, and Cybernetics – Part B, 26: 1,páginas 29-41, 1996.
9. Glover, F. and M. Laguna. (1997). Tabu Search. Kluwer, Norwell, MA.

10. Glover, F. "Tabu Search — Part I", ORSA Journal on Computing 1989 1: 3, 190-206.
11. Glover, F. "Tabu Search — Part II", ORSA Journal on Computing 1990 2: 1, 4-32.
12. Cvijovic, D.; Klinowski, J. "Taboo search – an approach to the multiple minima problem". Science 1995 267, 664-666.
13. E. Talbi, J. Boisson, J. Humeau, T. Legrand,A. Liefooghe, L. Jourdan, N. Melab, A. Tantar,M. Fatene, T. Luong y A. Khanafer. INRIAParadisEO. http://paradiseo.gforge.inria.fr.
14. A. Díaz, F. Glover, H. M. Ghaziri, J. L. González, M. Laguna, P. Moscato y F. T. Tseng.Optimización Heurística y Redes Neuronales.Paraninfo, Madrid, España, 1996.

THE IMPORTANCE OF SALES PROMOTION

FRANCISCO JAVIER MAQUEDA LAFUENTE
Facultad Ciencias Económicas y Empresariales, Departamento Economía Financiera II, Universidad del País Vasco/Euskal Herriko Unibertsitatea. Avda. Lehendakari Agirre 83, 48015 Bilbao

JAIME GIL LAFUENTE
Facultad de Ciencias Económicas y Empresariales. Departamento de Economía y Administración de Empresas. Universidad de Barcelona / Universitat de Barcelona, Diagonal, 690, 08034 Barcelona

JOSÉ ROBERTO VILA OBLITAS
Facultad de Ciencias Económicas y Empresariales. Dpto. de Economía y Administración de Empresas. Universidad de Málaga, Campus de El Ejido. 29071 Málaga

In today's world, companies struggle to promote their products and services. The wide variety of promotions observed in the market has led to the emergence of many types of classifications in the literature. Furthermore, the development of new promotions, such as those related to loyalty club membership and the use of distributor's payment cards as well as social promotions developed by both manufacturers and retailers, has further increased the diversity of promotional activities. In this paper, we present ratings that consumers assign to sales promotions and present a proposal for a new classification of the promotional techniques aimed at consumers.

1. Introduction

In recent years, sales promotion has become one of the most powerful weapons for marketing strategy for many companies in many markets. Among the evidence that confirms its power and, as a result, its increased utilization, we can highlight the following:

Investment in sales promotion represents a significant percentage of the average annual marketing budget in general and of the communication budget in particular, reaching above 50% of the latter.

Due to the increasing investment in promotional activities, starting in 2000, the Infoadex report has included the following three promotional techniques within the category of unconventional means: "promotional games and contests," "loyalty cards" and "animation at the point of sale." As a result, there has been a revival and consolidation of the Spanish Association of Promotional Marketing (Asociación Española de Marketing Promocional, AEMP), whose member companies are experiencing a significant increase in sales year after year. The strength of this association demonstrates the existence of a significant number of companies involved in the planning and execution of promotional campaigns.

- Finally, sales promotion has an increasing presence in sales. For example, a third of the food product sales made in Spain are accompanied by a promotion, 36% of sales by volume and 34% by value (Yustas, 2000). On the other hand, 26.4% of distributor sales are promotional sales, reaching as high as 38% in the case of sales in hypermarkets (Orduña 2000).

The wide variety of promotions observed in the market has led to the emergence of a wide variety of classifications in the literature. Additionally, the development of new promotions, such as those related to loyalty club membership and the use of distributor's payment cards as well as the social promotions developed by both manufacturers and retailers, has further increased the diversity of promotional activities.

Given this scenario, the primary objective of this paper is to offer a new classification of the advertising techniques directed at consumers that includes these new promotional techniques.

2. The concept of sales promotion

Numerous definitions have been proposed for the promotion of sales (Biolley and Cohen, 1991; Brown, 1995; Fraiz and Varela, 1990; Ortega, 1990, Maqueda, 2011; Ulanof, 1992, Wilmshurst, 1993). All coincide in their description of the elements of a promotion that the target audience perceives, that is, the offer of a promotional incentive for a period of time. From the business management point of view, however, undertaking a sales promotion requires a structure to support and coordinate it. In this sense, a promotion implies the involvement of the entire company's business organization. Thus, taking into account that the same product is offered with an added promotional advantage, generating a new special offer, the company has to configure the offer (product policy), determine the compensation and sacrifices to be made by recipients to obtain the offer (pricing policy), make the product available (distribution policy) and above all, advertise the offer's occurrence (communication policy).

As in the case of any product offered by a company, the application of marketing research techniques allows the conditions of each promotion to be adjusted to the motivations and preferences of the specific target audience for which the product is destined (Ortega, 1991).

Additionally, other activities outside of the commercial aspects of the enterprise may be affected by the implementation of a sales promotion. For example, in the specific case of manufacturers, the production department is affected because any promotion that affects the product's shape, size or presentation requires the collaboration of this department to provide the necessary information for proper planning of the promotion, including the following factors:

- Limitations to in-pack and on-pack incentives, promotional brochures, etc.
- Limitations to the production of promotional packages, such as an increased amount for the same price, reusable containers, etc.
- Maximum production capacity.

The collaboration of the production department in the planning and development of the promotion implies, among other activities, the customization or adjustment of campaigns supported by *flexible production* and *flexible printing* so that it is easy to print different packages and containers without increasing costs to the point of erasing profitability (Martínez-Ribes, 2000). This collaboration between promotion and production is closely related to what the literature calls "advance purchase" or "forward buying" (Lee, Padmanabhan and Whang, 1997; Arcelus, ShanH and Srinivasan, 2001) when describing the behavior of distributors that increase the volume of purchases during promotional periods to obtain better prices and reduce their purchases in non-promotional periods. This behavior causes the "bullwhip effect" or speculative whip effect, consisting of sudden increases and decreases in inventory, increases in orders and stock ruptures.

Therefore, in our opinion, a promotion is not an activity that involves only the marketing department of a company, as may occur with other communication activities. Promotions may also affect other departments, which then have to assume different roles depending on the phase that the promotion is in. Examples include procurement activities and the funding of promotional incentives as well as compliance with current legislation.

In short, this is an activity that requires a high degree of coordination between different areas of the organization for successful development. Thus, taking into account the internal repercussions for a company when holding a sales promotion, we propose the following, more complete definition, which incorporates this aspect along with those normally presented in the existing literature: a set of activities undertaken by a company as a result of offering an incentive for a set period of time that involves the coordination of different functional areas of the company to achieve certain business objectives.

3. Exploratory study and empirical study

To achieve our goal, we began conducting an exploratory study using consumer focus groups, with the purpose, among others, of learning the expressions that consumers use when referring to the various sales promotions.

After this exploratory stage was finished and the information obtained was analyzed, we conducted a quantitative study consisting of personal interviews with consumers at the point of sale. The technical details of the study are presented in the following table:

Table 1. Technical details of the study

Environment	General population
Geographic location	Autonomous community of the Basque country
Method of collecting information	Personal survey given to departing buyers
Information collection facility	Hypermarkets: 3 in Bizkaia, 2 in Gipuzkoa and 1 in Araba
Sample size	776 valid surveys
Sample error	+/- 3.52% for a 95% confidence interval, under the hypothesis that p=q=0.5
Sampling method	Proportional on the basis of the population of each region of interest and systematic at the point of sale
Date of field work	16-21 February 2012.

The data were analyzed using the statistical packages SPSS and DYANE, which allowed us to conduct univariate, bivariate and multivariate analyses.

4. Results of the sales promotions

Sixteen promotions were evaluated; we chose them based on their degree of appearance in the group dynamics. We selected those that were most frequently mentioned. We also tried to adapt the descriptions of the promotions to the lexicon of consumers, identifying the promotions by the incentives they offer as well as by how to obtain the incentive in each program.

The statements about each promotion and the rating* each obtained are presented in the following table:

Table 2. Analyzed sales promotions

Description of the promotion	Score
Q1: Gift of a sample product with the purchase of another product.	3.83
Q2: Discount on the product price.	4.19
Q3: Part of the price paid for the product will go to a charity.	4.17
Q4: More product quantity for the same price.	3.98
Q5: Sending in the product label of the purchased product to participate in a raffle or contest.	2.44
Q6: Offers for two for one, two for three, etc.	3.71
Q7: Discounts on the prices of certain products by using the payment card of the establishment.	3.67
Q8: Free sample of a product that offers a gift for your purchase.	3.47
Q9: Free sample of a product that offers a discount for your purchase.	3.56
Q10: Direct gift for the purchase of a product.	3.87
Q11: Discount coupons for future purchases.	3.18
Q12: Gift to the first n recipients or until supplies last.	2.27
Q13: Sending gift tags to obtain a gift for a certain product.	2.65
Q14: Rebate after sending proof of purchase.	3.09
Q15: The package containing the product has utility for later use.	3.66
Q16: By purchasing the product, we receive points for a loyalty program.	3.63

We divided the promotions that involved obtaining gifts into those that limit the promotion to the first *n* recipients or until supplies last and those for which receipt of the gift is ensured by meeting the promotional requirements. This allows us to contrast the influence that such limitations may have on the consumer evaluation of these promotions. With the rest of the incentives, we did not distinguish among the initiators of the promotional activity† because our

* The following scale was used: 1- Very bad, 2- Bad, 3- Normal, 4-Good, 5- Very good.

† In this sense, it should be noted that due to the objectives of other studies cited in our work, we have considered the following promotions for evaluation: exhibitions and staging the point of sale, coupons redeemable at other facilities, decoration and animation in the store, etc., which are promotions exclusive to the retailer.

objective is to analyze sales promotion in general and how it is perceived and valued by the consumer. The most valued promotions are those that offer a discount on the price of the product, participation in a social action, more quantity for the same price or direct gifts for purchasing the advertised product. The least valued are those that offer a gift for the first *n* recipients received or until supplies last, the opportunity to participate in a raffle or contest, a guaranteed gift or a rebate for the product. The latter three are subject to the submission of a proof of purchase to the promoting business.

We should emphasize that for the four most valued promotions, a high percentage of consumers considers them good or very good promotions. This percentage varies from 75%, achieved by promotions that offer a direct gift, to 86.6%, obtained by offering a reduction in the price of the product. As for the least valued, those that limit obtaining the incentive to the first *n* requests or until supplies last were the least favorably viewed by the consumer, with 64.8% considering them poor or very poor promotions. Although it provides an economic incentive, rebates after sending in a proof of purchase are valued by 38.2% of consumers as poor or very poor promotions.

Conditions such as "gifts to the first *n* letter writers" or "while supplies last" have a negative and significant influence in consumer valuation compared to promotions that do not include those conditions.

These results affirm that although restrictive conditions reduce the randomness of the cost of a very important part of the promotion, such as the acquisition of incentives, they harm its rating by consumers, influencing consumer[*] behavior and therefore the profitability of the promotion.

We consider it interesting to highlight the deferred nature[†] of the least-valued promotions compared to the immediacy of the most-valued promotions, with the exception of social promotions. The explanation that we find for the high frequency of "bad" and "very bad" scores for the lowest-ranked promotions

---

[*] In this regard, we refer to the study conducted by Delphi Consultores Internationales, which analyzes consumer reaction to these restrictions. The results were that given the condition "while supplies last", 13.6% buy quickly, 62.1% buy at a leisurely pace, and 24.1% rejected the purchase of the product being promoted. The consumer behavior manifested by the condition "gift to the first n people to send a letter with proof of purchase" was that only 9.6% buy faster, 48.1% buy at a leisurely pace and 42.3% reject the purchase. See: ORTEGA, E. (1996), "Sales promotions and customer loyalty." Campaña. No. 489, May, p. 33 to 39.

[†] Deferred promotions are understood as those for which obtaining the incentive does not occur at the same time as the purchase, in comparison with those promotions whose incentive is obtained at the same time of purchase

is the mistrust of the consumer in obtaining the incentive. This suspicion may have been caused by negative experiences, both their own and those of others, with these types of promotions. Therefore, we consider it fundamental to plan and manage these promotions to meet the commitment to the consumer as well as to conduct advertising campaigns for the promotion, especially at the end of the promotion, with the aim of increasing the promotion's credibility.

An essential aspect of any communication action and of a sales promotion in particular is the definition of the target audience. Therefore, we analyzed a series of descriptive criteria* to identify those that can influence the assessment of sales promotions. The criteria for which we found significant differences in mean scores between the categories that compose them are presented below.

Women more positively valued the promotions analyzed, with an average score (3.53) that was higher than that obtained for men (3.32). An individual analysis of each of the promotions indicated that the scores for women exceeded those for men, although the differences were only significant for the promotions shown in the figure below:

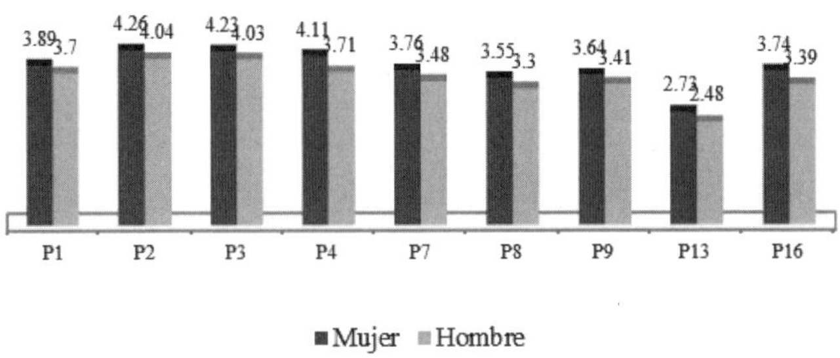

Figure 1. Average scores with significant differences.

We also found significant differences when assessing the promotions based on owning or not owning a loyalty card and found that consumers who have these cards value all† promotions more positively than those who do not possess them, with an average score of 3.49 versus 3.31.

* Specifically, the following descriptive variables were analyzed: gender, possession of a payment card, membership in a loyalty club, the presence of children under fourteen years of age in the household, use of a shopping list, employment status, age, income level, education level and number of working heads of the family. For dichotomous variables, we used the t test for independent samples with a confidence level of 99%. For variables with more than two categories, we performed an analysis of variance for one factor, also using the confidence level to reject or accept the null hypothesis of equal means.

† With the exception of the promotion that "the package containing the product has utility for later use", in which the average score for the holders of these cards was 3.66 compared to 3.67 obtained for those without such cards.

Only two of the promotions received higher scores individually than the comparison made as a function of these two groups. Logically, one of these is to offer points for loyalty club membership (Q16), whereas the second promotion (Q7) is based on a discount provided for the possession of a payment card from the establishment.

Therefore, we can say that individuals who have loyalty cards have a more favorable opinion regarding promotion techniques in general, so we believe that this group has a greater receptivity to promotional activities. This fact is considered particularly important for companies that sponsor these types of clubs.

With respect to age, significant differences exist in the general assessment of the promotions. Promotions obtained higher scores from the oldest segment of the simple population followed by the youngest segment. The lowest scores were obtained for the age groups in between these two.

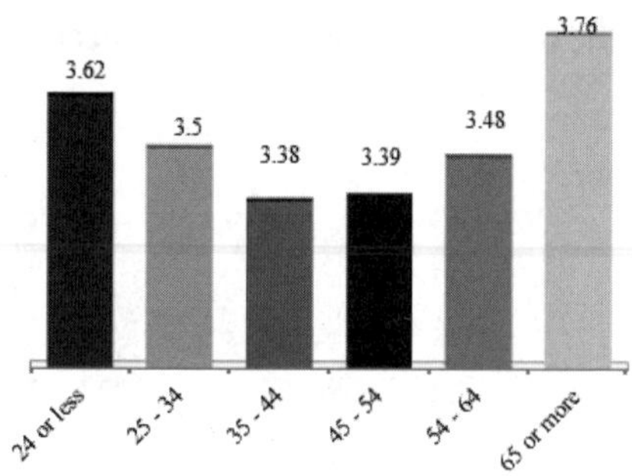

Figure 2. Average rating based on age.

The statistical tests of *post hoc*[*] analysis of variance or *a posteriori* analysis enabled the identification of two groups within the age criteria with different ratings. These are consumers between the ages of 35 and 54, who exhibit significantly lower ratings compared to other consumers.

Alongside the age criteria, income level and educational level also influence the evaluation of promotions. In both cases, there is an inverse relationship between income and education level and the evaluation of promotions (Figures 3 and 4).

[*] Specifically, we used the Bonferroni, Tukey and Scheffé tests.

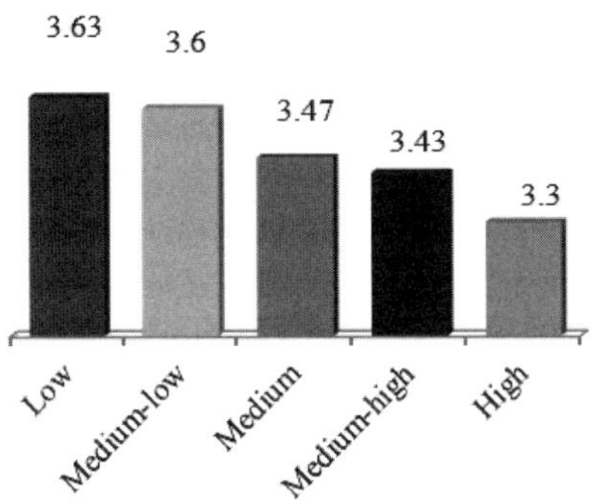

Figure 3. Mean ratings based on income.

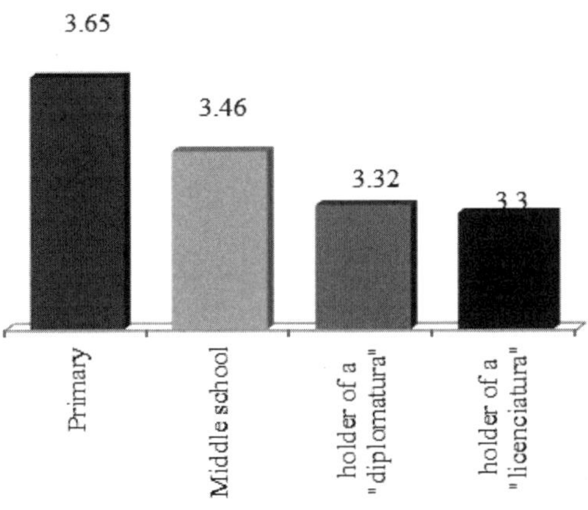

Figure 4. Mean ratings based on education level

In both cases, three groups were identified as the generators of the differences. In order of decreasing ratings, in terms of income level, we identified the low and middle, medium to medium high, and high segments of the population. With regard to educational level, we observed the segments of the population having completed primary, secondary and higher education.

Finally, the presence of children younger than fourteen years of age in the household negatively influences the assessment of the promotions. These households were associated with a lower score (3.39) and were significantly different than households with no children (3.49).

5. Consumer ratings and classification

Regarding the methodology used to obtain this classification, we performed a Principal Component Analysis (PCA). With this analysis, we tried to reduce the initial amount of information (sixteen promotions) into a set of factors or groups of promotions that would allow us to provide a classification based on the ratings that the consumer gives the promotions.

Before offering the final results, we briefly describe the procedure followed and the partial results obtained. Initial variables: we used the ratings given by respondents in each of the sixteen promotions described previously.

Verification of the technique's relevance: to assess the relevance of the selected method, we conducted KMO contrasts and Bartlett's test of sphericity on the correlation matrix with the following results [*]:

Table 3. Verification of the technique's relevance

KAISER – MEYER – OLKIN MEASURE OF SAMPLING ADEQUACY		0.869
Bartlett's test squared of sphericity	Chi –	3638
	d.f.	120
	Sig.	.000

Extraction and selection of factors: the absence of an exact quantitative basis for deciding how many factors to extract has led to the existence of different empirical criteria to aid in selection. In our case, we selected a number of factors, specifically six, that would allow us to represent an acceptable accumulated percentage of the total variance (67.1%) and allow the initial variables to obtain a commonality, after their extraction, of greater than 0.5.

Rotation of factors: to facilitate the interpretation of the selected factors, we performed a rotation of the initially obtained factors using the Varimax method.

The explained variance and its distribution among the six factors, obtained before and after rotation, are presented in the following table:

[*] These results allow us to reject the null hypothesis of linear noncorrelation of the variables, highlighting how good the KMO coefficient is. Along with these differences and individually for each variable, as to the extent of sufficient sampling (MSA), values ranging between 0.735 and 0.928 are reached, so that none of the variables initially included were rejected.

Table 4. Total explained variance

Component	Sums of the squared saturations of the extraction			Sums of the squared saturations of the rotation		
	Total	% of variance	% accumulated	Total	% of variance	% accumulated
1	4,987	31.171	31.171	3.132	19.573	19.573
2	1.770	11.064	42.235	2.278	14.236	33.809
3	1.141	7.128	49.363	1.730	10.812	44.621
4	1.114	6.964	56.327	1.494	9.336	56.957
5	.919	5.741	62.068	1.053	6.581	60.539
6	.802	5.012	67.080	1.047	6.541	67.080

Finally, after the described steps, we obtained the following factors:

Table 5. Factors obtained

Factor 1 (Mean value = 2,73)	Factorial weight
Gift for the first letters received or until supplies last.	.827
Sending a gift tag to obtain a guaranteed gift.	.796
Sending a ticket to enter a raffle or contest.	.772
Rebate after sending proof of purchase.	.667
Discount coupons for future purchases.	.625
Factor 2 (Mean value = 3.68)	**Factorial weight**
Free trial of a product that offers a gift for your purchase.	.836
Free trial of a product that offers a discount for your purchase.	.797
Direct gift for purchasing the product.	.622
Gift of a product sample with purchase of another product.	.492
Factor 3 (Mean value = 3.96)	**Factorial weight**

Greater quantity of a product for the same price.	.798
Discount on the price of the product.	.765
Offers of two for one, two for three, etc.	.496
Factor 4 (Mean value = 3.65)	Factorial weight
Discount on the price of certain products for using the payment card of the establishment.	.818
Receiving points for the loyalty program for purchasing the product.	.681
Factor 5 (Mean value = 4.17)	Factorial weight
A portion of the price paid for the product will go to a charity.	.878
Factor 6 (Mean value = 3.66)	Factorial weight
The package containing the product has utility for later use.	.912

Based on the results of our analysis, we can identify six types of promotions related to the promotional incentive offered to the consumer and the promotional mechanisms used. We identify the six types of promotions in the following way:

(F1) Deferred promotions: promotions in which the incentive is not obtained immediately, i.e., at the time of purchase, regardless of the randomness that can surround obtaining the incentive as well as the economic aspect. These promotions are not highly valued by consumers, primarily because of the mistrust they generate and the effort required by the consumer to obtain the incentive.

(F2) Immediate promotions: the fundamental difference between these and the aforementioned promotions is the immediacy of obtaining the incentive. Some of them, along with the promotional incentive, offer the best information a consumer can obtain: product testing, either through a demonstration, through tasting or by the delivery of a sample at the point of sale.

(F3) Economical promotions: promotions that directly affect the quantity/price relationship. The consumer obtains, in an objective manner, an economic incentive for the punctual alteration of this ratio.

(F4) Card promotions: we can define these types of promotions as those developed in the framework of a formal permanent relationship embodied primarily through the possession of a card, which gives the holder a number of benefits, including promotional incentives. Furthermore, the use of such cards by the consumer when making purchases offers sponsors a large quantity of useful information, for example, for planning sales promotions.

(F5) Social promotions: we consider promotions to be social when a third party (usually NGOs) also benefits from the fulfillment of the promotional conditions. These are promotions that obtain a high rating by the consumer, surpassed only by direct discounts in the product price.

(F6) Packaging for later use: as its name indicates, this category refers to promotions whose promotional incentive is the actual product package that the consumer purchases during the promotion, featuring a different aspect from the usual container to encourage the purchase or repeated purchases of it.

Later utility can be directly related to the use of the product itself, making it easier to use or store. Otherwise, the promotional packaging can also be used for other uses and may become a permanent advertising object for the brand.

6. Final conclusions

Sales promotion is an activity whose development affects not only the marketing department but other departments of the company that will assume different tasks depending on the phase in which the promotion is in. It is, therefore, an activity that requires a high degree of coordination between different areas of the organization for successful development.

Differences exist in the consumer's evaluation of promotional activities. The consumer feels more attracted to those activities that involve obtaining the incentive immediately, without active collaboration, whereas those in which active participation is required to achieve a deferred incentive are less valued.

The overall assessment that sales promotions receive from consumers depends on a series of descriptive criteria such as gender, the possession of loyalty cards, age, income level, educational level and the presence of children (under age 14) at home.

From the consumer's perspective and according to the average score obtained by each of the factors identified, we can find six groups of promotions, ordered in consumer-assigned value from highest to lowest: social promotions, economic promotions, immediate promotions, packaging promotions, card promotions and deferred promotions.

References

1. Y. Yustas, *Promociones de ventas en mercados españoles de alimentación*. Madrid, Idelco (2000).
2. I. Orduña, Recomendaciones AECOC sobre promociones eficientes, *Código 84*, 40-43 (2000).
3. G. Biolley and M. Cohen, *Tratado de promoción de ventas*, Barcelona, Hispano – Europea, (1991).
4. C. Brown, *The sales promotion handbook*. London, Kogan Page, (1995).
5. J.A. Fraiz and J.A. Varela, *La promoción de ventas*. Santiago, Tórculo (1990).
6. E. Ortega, *Nuevo diccionario de marketing*. Madrid, Expansión (1990).
7. F.J. Maqueda Lafuente, *Marketing, innovación y nuevos negocios*, Madrid, ESIC (2011).
8. S. Ulanoff , *Handbook of sales promotion*. New York, McGraw-Hill (1992).
9. J. Wilmshurst, *Below the line*. Oxford, Butterword-Heinemann (1993).
10. E. Ortega, La promoción de ventas y el pretest promocional, *Campaña* 391, 62-66 (1991)
11. L. Martínez-Ribes, Promociones ¿hacia donde van?, *Código 84*. Mayo/junio, 54 – 60 (2000).
12. H. Lee, V. Padmanbhan and S. Whang, The bullwhip effect in supply chains, *Sloan Management Review*. 38, 93 – 102 (1997).
13. F. Arcelus, N. Shah and G. Srinivasan, Retailer's response to special sales: price discount vs. Trade credit, *Omega,* 29, 417 – 428 (2001).

HUNGARIAN ALGORITHM AS AN EFFECTIVE MATHEMATICAL SUPPORT IN HUMAN RESOURCE MANAGEMENT UNDER CONDITIONS OF UNCERTAINTY

ANA M. GIL-LAFUENTE*, ANNA KLIMOVA, JOSE M. MERIGO-LINDAHL

Economics and Business Department, University of Barcelona, Av. Diagonal 690, Barcelona, 08028, Spain

This article is a study on the treatment of the assignment problem in the human resource management at a modern company. The Spanish enterprise that works in the energy sector of the country was considered. The assignment of potential employees to a limited number of job positions was studied. Hungarian algorithm was used. It was demonstrated its obvious efficiency for this type of problems in conditions of instability.

1. Introduction

The selection process of adequate staff is one of the most important objectives of a modern company. The key task consists on creating a team that is flexible and adaptable to changeable conditions of a global market.

There are two main factors that have influenced on changing the human resource management policy. The first one is the globalization process. This has led to the opening the markets of the most countries of the world providing the accessibility of a large number of people to the recruitment processes of the foreign companies. The second factor is an economic crisis that changed the preferences of business. The selection of adequate staff capable to adapt to a new situation became a very complex task. Classical techniques for the staff assignment problem, employee promotion from within a company, etc. are not so efficient as they were 20 years ago. The models that better adapt to so instable situation are based on multivalent logic and mathematics of uncertainty.

This article is a study on the treatment of the assignment problem in the human resource management. The Spanish company that performs in the energy sector of the country was considered. The assignment of potential candidates to a

* Work partially supported by grant 2-4570.5 of the Swiss National Science Foundation.

limited number of job positions was studied. The Hungarian algorithm was used. It was demonstrated its obvious efficiency for this type of problems.

The following aspects were considered: transition from traditional company organizational structures to flexible structures, an impact of this process on human resource management, new techniques in human resources management, assignment methods, theoretical aspects of Hungarian algorithm and study case.

2. From traditional organizational structures to flexible organization

Organizational structures that traditionally established the way of company's performance represent the result of different approaches that have been interlacing from the beginning of the last century in order to meet the increasing complexity of a business environment.

The first approach starts from the combination of the scientific structure presented by Taylor F.W., based on labor specialization and task specification, together with the organizations' restructuring into specialized functional units presented by Fayol [1].

Then, a new conception of Max Weber was added. It represented a bureaucratic structure based on hierarchical relationships, standards, established policies and technical competence for the tasks and promotion.

Later, new approaches based on human relationships have been introduced by Rorthlisberger and Dickson and by Argyris in the 60's, as a consequence of inability that the "mechanical bureaucracies" had in achieving a productivity growth without costs increase [1].

The 80's were characterized by continuous changes. In 90's the evolution and globalization made impossible the existence of old business structures and management systems [2,3]. Therefore, new systems were used. They allowed the integration between functions and new technologies, businesses and markets. These systems have led to a new organizational structure that focuses on achieving the flexibility and capacity of responsiveness to the market changes.

3. Impact on human recourse management

As a final synthesis, it was demonstrated that the organizations based on the work teams are moving to the traditional organizational structures and nowadays they are based on people's professionalism and their integration into a business project.

All modern organizational structures have a common basis. They are built on the employees' skills that lead to the development of human resources policies related to the evolution of organizational structure [1].

The function of human resources consists on both its mission and operational capacity. The employees are responsible not only for the company's performance in the situation of a market stability but also for implementing any business strategy. They are integrated into a strategic vertex structure as an agent of changes, with an internal advisory role, based on its overall management vision, production process knowledge and company's organizational structure comprehension [4].

The responsibility of the human resources is evolving into performance the functions that enable and encourage a support of the company's responsiveness onto the market's changes and also into a close relation with the areas of design and development of the organizational structure and management systems [4,5].

4. New mathematical techniques in human recourse management

The world of a small, medium or large company is extremely combinatorial. The task of assignment of more adequate job to each employee is very complex.

Let's describe some aspects of the human resource management where the modern techniques of mathematics of uncertainty are used successfully [6].

Candidate selection. Staff selection consists on choosing a person for a job with a specific profile determined through measures or assessments which are compared with the qualities of a candidate. The necessity of gradation of each task make possible the use of the fuzzy subsets theory.

Job selection. In this problem each candidate is represented by a Φ-fuzzy subset of qualities or skills; each job is represented by a Φ_1-fuzzy subset and studied in order to determine a better "index of compatibility" that will be more advisable for the candidate. The notion of distance is used.

Candidate selection by means of adequacy coefficient. The idea of "it is bed to not achieve a required level of qualification as well as to surpass it" is used.

Selection on the basis of expertons. A polyvalency concept is considered. It allows to do substitutions represented as a specialization or "adaptive skill". A fuzzy relation of normalized Hamming distances is provided. Pichat algorithm and Kaufmann and Gil Aluja algorithm are used.

The work in homogeneous groups. In this context the theory of affinities is used. Galois lattices provide the best associations of people and jobs.

Staff assignment problem. The idea is the following: there is a limited number of jobs and a large number of candidates willing to cover them. It is necessary to "assign", by the best possible way, each person to each job. Hungarian algorithm or "branch and bound" algorithm are used [6].

5. Development of the assignment methods. Hungarian algorithm in the human resource area of the company

The expression "assignment problem" (AP) has first appeared in 1952 in the paper of Votaw and Orden [7], but as the beginning of the wide development of practical solution methods and the variations on the classic assignment problem was the publication of Kuhn's article on the Hungarian method for its solution in 1955 [8,9]. The Kuhn's Hungarian method has become the starting point of a fast developing area such as Combinatorial Optimization.

AP is looking for an optimal matching of the elements of two or more sets, where the dimension of the problem refers to the number of sets of elements to be matched.

AP problems are categorized into linear, quadratic, multidimensional, bottleneck, etc. The AP can also be represented in a large number of forms such as mathematical programming, combinatorial, or graph-theoretic formulations, and constitute one of the most important objects in computer science, operations research, and discrete mathematics [10]. There are numerous applications of the AP in other disciplines of science and engineering such as chemistry, physics, electrical engineering, etc. [11-14].

A significant contribution in solving the assignment problems in the area of human resource management was made by J. Gil-Aluja [6]. The objective is to find the optimal assignment of candidates to different jobs The author highlights the Hungarian algorithm as a more adequate tool in solving this problem. A.M. Gil Lafuente made a great contribution in the financial area [15,16].

6. Theoretical aspects of Hungarian algorithm

The objective consists on looking for the process of optimization basing on two sets of elements that are related between themselves through the known matrix.

We start from the matrix of distances, $\left[\underset{\sim}{P}'\right]$. This matrix is converted into matrix $\left[\overline{\underset{\sim}{P}'}\right]$. There are the following steps [6,15,16]:

1. We take the first column (P_1) and subtract the smallest element from each element of the same. In each box we have:

$$P_{ij}^{(1)} = P_{ij} - \min_i P_{ij} \tag{1}$$

This process is repeated for each of the remaining column so that one zero at least appears in each one of them.

Then we do the same operations for each one of the rows so that once again at least one zero appears in each one. We then have:

$$P_{ij}^{(1)} = P_{ij} - \min_{j} P_{ij} \quad (2)$$

2. Once we have arrived at matrix $\left[\underset{\sim}{B}\right]$ we check to see if it is possible to make an assignment in which the values $P_{ij}^{(1)}$ of the solution are all zeros. If this is so then we have arrived at the optimum. On the contrary the process is continued by means of the following steps:
   a) The rows containing the least zeros are taken one by one.
   b) One of the zeros of the considered row is framed and the remaining zeros that are members of the same are crossed out, as well as the zeros in the column of which the framed zero is a member.
   c) This process is repeated for each row until there are no zeros to frame.
3. Obtain the least number of rows and columns that contain all the zeros; we must proceed with the following steps:
   a) All the rows in which there are not framed zeros are signaled with an arrow.
   b) The columns in which a crossed out zero does exist in a row with an arrow are signaled.
   c) The columns in which a squared zero does exist in a column signaled with an arrow are likewise signaled. This process is repeated until no further rows or columns can be signaled.
   d) Finally a line is drawn through the rows that are not signaled by arrows and through the columns that are signaled with arrows. These rows and columns constitute the least number that possess framed or crossed out zeros.

The rows and columns through which a line has been drawn constitute the so-called "minimum support" of matrix $\left[\underset{\sim}{B}\right]$.

4. The lowest value is taken from among the elements of the matrix that have not been lined. The figure that is taken is subtracted from the elements of the columns that are not lined and this is added to the rows that are lined.
5. With this new matrix the process is restarted at point 2, by continuing on with the same operations used for the previous matrix. In the event of arriving at an optimum solution the process is stopped; to the contrary continue the process from points 3 and 4.

7. Study case. Optimal solution using Hungarian algorithm

7.1. Definition of the problem

The Spanish company that performs in the energy sector supposes to optimize the assignment of potential candidates to the work positions. 11 jobs are considered. There are 12 qualities required for these positions. 14 candidates take part in the assignment process.

In order to get an optimal assignment of candidates to each job the Hungarian algorithm is used. Let's start from the information given below.

7.2. Definition of the input data

Work positions are represented by the set S:

$$S=\{S_1,S_2,S_3,S_4,S_5,S_6,S_7,S_8,S_9,S_{10},S_{11}\}$$

where S_1 – electrical support engineer; S_2 – administrative assistant; S_3 – suppliers management section chief; S_4 – configuration technician; S_5 – mechanical design engineer; S_6 – mechanical support drawing engineer; S_7 – mechanical section chief; S_8 – financial technician; S_9 – marketing manager; S_{10} – maintenance material list responsible; S_{11} – blade technical worker.

These work positions have the following characteristics:

$$C=\{C_1,C_2,C_3,C_4,C_5,C_6,C_7,C_8,C_9,C_{10},C_{11},C_{12}\}$$

where C_1 – promote the improvement of environmental performance, health and safety prevention; C_2 – have a wide knowledge of the company's business lines; C_3 – revisi the threats (opportunities) and strengths (weaknesses) of the company; C_4 – achieve the goals, optimizing human, financial and material resources; C_5 – establish and maintain good relationships with internal (external) customers and meet their expectations; C_6 – act as a manager in supporting and encouraging the changes; C_7 – provide innovative ideas about products, processes or organization structure; C_8 – do a monitoring of the plans anticipating all possible risks; C_9 – do a coherent delegation of the tasks; C_{10} – take advantage of the relationships with external agents to enhance the company's image; C_{11} – demonstrate good teamwork skills creating a good working environment; C_{12} – do negotiations successfully providing objectives' achievement.

14 are potential candidates. They are represented by the set P:

$$P=\{P_1,P_2,P_3,P_4,P_5,P_6,P_7,P_8,P_9,P_{10},P_{11},P_{12},P_{13},P_{14}\}$$

Regarding the qualities and in order to establish the relationship between the work positions and candidates, the endecadaria scale is defined semantically. The scale is generalized for 12 qualities. It has the following representation [17]:

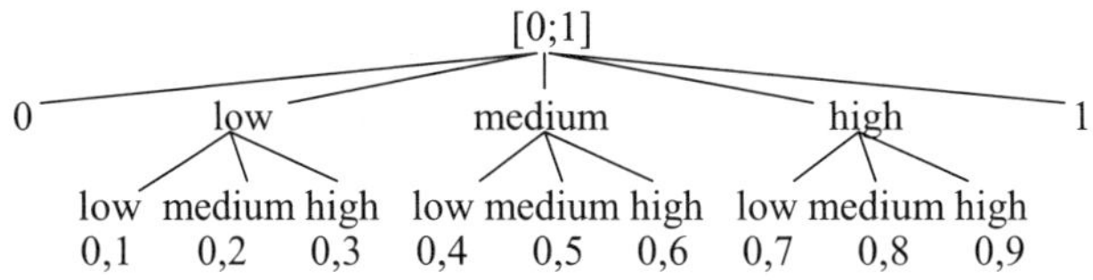

We have the following relationship between the jobs *S* and skills *C*.

	C_1	C_2	C_3	C_4	C_5	C_6	C_7	C_8	C_9	C_{10}	C_{11}	C_{12}
S_1	0,7	0,6	0,4	0,6	0,6	0,3	0,6	0,7	0,4	0,5	0,8	0,7
S_2	0,6	0,5	0,3	0,5	0,4	0,1	0,3	0,6	0,1	0,6	0,7	0,5
S_3	0,9	0,8	0,7	0,9	0,9	0,8	0,8	0,9	0,8	0,9	0,9	0,9
S_4	0,7	0,5	0,3	0,7	0,4	0,2	0,4	0,4	0,1	0,3	0,7	0,2
S_5	0,9	0,8	0,5	0,8	0,6	0,5	0,9	0,7	0,5	0,6	0,8	0,7
S_6	0,7	0,6	0,3	0,7	0,5	0,2	0,3	0,5	0,2	0,3	0,7	0,2
S_7	0,9	0,7	0,7	0,8	0,7	0,8	0,8	0,9	0,8	0,7	0,8	0,8
S_8	0,7	0,6	0,4	0,6	0,5	0,1	0,3	0,4	0,1	0,5	0,7	0,5
S_9	0,7	0,9	0,9	0,8	0,9	0,8	0,7	0,9	0,8	1	0,8	1
S_{10}	0,8	0,7	0,5	0,7	0,7	0,3	0,4	0,7	0,4	0,7	0,7	0,7
S_{11}	0,8	0,7	0,4	0,7	0,4	0,2	0,3	0,2	0,1	0,3	0,7	0,2

The experts have the relation that reflects the candidate's correspondence level with each quality. This relationship is introduced by the sets *P* and *C*.

	C_1	C_2	C_3	C_4	C_5	C_6	C_7	C_8	C_9	C_{10}	C_{11}	C_{12}
P_1	0,6	0,5	0,5	0,6	0,5	0,3	0,6	0,7	0,3	0,5	0,7	0,7
P_2	0,6	0,6	0,3	0,6	0,5	0,2	0,4	0,7	0,2	0,6	0,5	0,6
P_3	0,9	0,8	0,8	0,7	0,9	0,8	0,7	0,7	0,8	0,7	0,9	0,9
P_4	0,8	0,6	0,7	0,7	0,5	0,2	0,4	0,5	0,4	0,4	0,7	0,5
P_5	0,7	0,7	0,7	0,8	0,7	0,5	0,8	0,5	0,6	0,6	0,7	0,7
P_6	0,7	0,5	0,6	0,6	0,4	0,2	0,7	0,6	0,3	0,5	0,4	0,5
P_7	0,8	0,8	0,8	0,6	0,7	0,8	0,9	0,8	0,8	0,5	0,7	0,8
P_8	0,7	0,7	0,6	0,7	0,5	0,1	0,5	0,6	0,4	0,6	0,6	0,5
P_9	0,9	0,8	0,6	0,8	0,8	0,8	0,7	0,7	0,8	0,9	0,8	0,8
P_{10}	0,7	0,6	0,7	0,7	0,6	0,3	0,4	0,6	0,5	0,7	0,5	0,6
P_{11}	0,7	0,5	0,5	0,6	0,6	0,2	0,3	0,5	0,5	0,4	0,5	0,2
P_{12}	0,8	0,7	0,6	0,8	0,6	0,6	0,5	0,7	0,6	0,5	0,8	0,7
P_{13}	0,7	0,4	0,4	0,6	0,7	0,5	0,7	0,6	0,5	0,7	0,6	0,6
P_{14}	0,6	0,6	0,5	0,6	0,6	0,6	0,7	0,6	0,5	0,6	0,6	0,5

The valuations assigned to *S* and *P* represent the levels of maximum acceptance.

7.3. Obtaining the "qualification coefficient"

Let's obtain the "qualification coefficient". The process is based on progressive acceptance of those qualities that correspond to the candidates whose valuations remain on the threshold established by the job positions. If the skill overpasses the established level then this skill is penalized. There are:

$\mu_{C_b}(P_i) \in [0;1]$ - a membership function value related to the candidate P_i and quality C_i.

$\mu_{C_b}(S_j) \in [0;1]$ - a membership function value related to the job S_j and skill C_j.

We have:

1. If $\mu_{C_b}(P_i) \preccurlyeq \mu_{C_b}(S_j)$ then the skill is accepted with the valuation determined as $(1 - \mu_{C_b}(S_j))$.
2. If $\mu_{C_b}(P_i) \succ \mu_{C_b}(S_j)$ then the skill is accepted with the valuation as $\overline{1 \wedge (\mu_{C_b}(S_j) + \mu_{C_b}(P_i))}$.

Let's compare S_1 and P_1 in relation to each quality. We have:

C_1: $\mu_{C_1}(P_1) \preccurlyeq \mu_{C_1}(S_1)$ as 0,6≼0,7 then $(1 - \mu_{C_1}(S_1)) = (1 - 0,7) = 0,3 \ldots$

C_3: $\mu_{C_3}(P_1) \succ \mu_{C_3}(S_1)$ as 0,5≻0,4 then $\overline{1 \wedge (\mu_{C_3}(S_1) + \mu_{C_3}(P_1))}$

$\overline{1 \wedge (0,4 + 0,5)} = \overline{0,9} = 0,1 \ldots\ldots$

The weighted sum of the obtained valuations for each quality is as follows: $Q(P_1; S_1) = 0,383$

The qualification coefficients for the rest of the jobs are the following:

$Q(P_1; S_1) = 0,383$;.. $Q(P_1; S_{11}) = 0,242$; $Q(P_2; S_1) = 0,383$;.. $Q(P_2; S_{11}) = 0,333$;

$Q(P_3; S_1) = 0,025$;.. $Q(P_3; S_{11}) = 0,042$; $Q(P_4; S_1) = 0,317$;.. $Q(P_4; S_{11}) = 0,308$;

$Q(P_5; S_1) = 0,108$;.. $Q(P_5; S_{11}) = 0,158$; $Q(P_6; S_1) = 0,343$;... $Q(P_6; S_{11}) = 0,317$

;

...

$Q(P_{13}; S_1) = 0,233$;.. $Q(P_{14}; S_1) = 0,217$;... $Q(P_{14}; S_{11}) = 0,200$.

7.4. Assigning the valuations to the characteristics

In order to estimate the characteristics in relation to each job it is necessary to normalize the valuations established for the purpose to make a convex weight. Let's summarize the matrixes of the previous part into one matrix $[\underset{\sim}{P}]$.

	P_1	P_2	P_3	P_4	P_5	P_6	P_7	P_8	P_9	P_{10}	P_{11}	P_{12}	P_{13}	P_{14}
$\underset{\sim}{S}_1$	0,38	0,36	0,03	0,33	0,10	0,33	0,11	0,26	0,04	0,25	0,33	0,20	0,23	0,21
$\underset{\sim}{S}_2$	0,26	0,27	0,02	0,27	0,15	0,37	0,10	0,31	0,03	0,19	0,37	0,11	0,22	0,23
$\underset{\sim}{S}_3$	0,15	0,15	0,13	0,15	0,15	0,15	0,11	0,15	0,15	0,15	0,15	0,15	0,15	0,15
$\underset{\sim}{S}_4$	0,26	0,32	0,03	0,28	0,10	0,33	0,10	0,24	0,02	0,22	0,38	0,08	0,22	0,18
$\underset{\sim}{S}_5$	0,31	0,31	0,08	0,27	0,19	0,27	0,10	0,27	0,09	0,23	0,31	0,18	0,24	0,27
$\underset{\sim}{S}_6$	0,28	0,37	0,03	0,34	0,13	0,31	0,09	0,28	0,01	0,22	0,41	0,08	0,20	0,20
$\underset{\sim}{S}_7$	0,22	0,22	0,11	0,22	0,22	0,22	0,15	0,22	0,14	0,22	0,22	0,22	0,22	0,22
$\underset{\sim}{S}_8$	0,32	0,33	0,02	0,32	0,09	0,35	0,14	0,27	0,02	0,19	0,37	0,11	0,23	0,23
$\underset{\sim}{S}_9$	0,15	0,13	0,11	0,13	0,10	0,15	0,13	0,15	0,13	0,15	0,15	0,13	0,15	0,15
$\underset{\sim}{S}_{10}$	0,34	0,38	0,08	0,35	0,18	0,30	0,12	0,31	0,03	0,31	0,35	0,16	0,26	0,25
$\underset{\sim}{S}_{11}$	0,24	0,32	0,04	0,31	0,16	0,32	0,09	0,28	0,02	0,23	0,38	0,13	0,23	0,20

This matrix shows the adequacy of the candidates to the jobs. The closer the valuations are to 1 the greater is the level of similarity. The qualities have a different importance for the job. These weights in the interval [0;1] are established:

	C_1	C_2	C_3	C_4	C_5	C_6	C_7	C_8	C_9	C_{10}	C_{11}	C_{12}
$\underset{\sim}{S}_1$	0,7	0,5	0,4	0,6	0,6	0,4	0,7	0,7	0,3	0,4	0,9	0,8
$\underset{\sim}{S}_2$	0,7	0,5	0,3	0,4	0,4	0,3	0,4	0,3	0,2	0,7	0,8	0,6
$\underset{\sim}{S}_3$	0,8	0,8	0,7	0,9	0,9	0,7	0,8	0,8	0,7	0,7	0,8	0,9
$\underset{\sim}{S}_4$	0,7	0,6	0,5	0,8	0,5	0,4	0,4	0,5	0,3	0,4	0,9	0,4
$\underset{\sim}{S}_5$	0,8	0,9	0,6	0,8	0,7	0,6	0,9	0,7	0,5	0,7	0,9	0,8
$\underset{\sim}{S}_6$	0,7	0,7	0,5	0,8	0,5	0,3	0,4	0,7	0,3	0,5	0,8	0,4
$\underset{\sim}{S}_7$	0,9	0,8	0,7	0,8	0,6	0,7	0,8	0,9	0,9	0,8	0,9	0,8
$\underset{\sim}{S}_8$	0,7	0,7	0,5	0,6	0,6	0,3	0,5	0,6	0,3	0,7	0,8	0,7
$\underset{\sim}{S}_9$	0,8	0,9	0,9	0,7	0,8	0,7	0,6	0,9	0,7	0,9	0,7	0,9
$\underset{\sim}{S}_{10}$	0,7	0,7	0,6	0,8	0,7	0,5	0,5	0,8	0,4	0,8	0,9	0,8
$\underset{\sim}{S}_{11}$	0,6	0,8	0,5	0,7	0,4	0,3	0,4	0,3	0,3	0,5	0,8	0,4

Let's normalize the previous matrix. We have the following matrix $\left[\underset{\sim}{E}\right]$:

	C_1	C_2	C_3	C_4	C_5	C_6	C_7	C_8	C_9	C_{10}	C_{11}	C_{12}
$\underset{\sim}{S}_1$	0,10	0,07	0,06	0,09	0,09	0,06	0,10	0,10	0,04	0,06	0,13	0,11
$\underset{\sim}{S}_2$	0,13	0,09	0,05	0,07	0,07	0,05	0,07	0,05	0,04	0,13	0,14	0,11
$\underset{\sim}{S}_3$	0,08	0,08	0,07	0,09	0,09	0,07	0,08	0,08	0,07	0,07	0,08	0,09
$\underset{\sim}{S}_4$	0,11	0,09	0,08	0,13	0,08	0,06	0,06	0,08	0,05	0,06	0,14	0,06
$\underset{\sim}{S}_5$	0,09	0,10	0,07	0,09	0,08	0,07	0,10	0,08	0,06	0,08	0,10	0,09
$\underset{\sim}{S}_6$	0,11	0,11	0,08	0,12	0,08	0,05	0,06	0,11	0,05	0,08	0,12	0,06
$\underset{\sim}{S}_7$	0,09	0,08	0,07	0,08	0,06	0,07	0,08	0,09	0,09	0,08	0,09	0,08
$\underset{\sim}{S}_8$	0,10	0,10	0,07	0,09	0,09	0,04	0,07	0,09	0,04	0,10	0,11	0,10
$\underset{\sim}{S}_9$	0,08	0,09	0,09	0,07	0,08	0,07	0,06	0,09	0,07	0,09	0,07	0,09
$\underset{\sim}{S}_{10}$	0,09	0,09	0,07	0,10	0,09	0,06	0,06	0,10	0,05	0,10	0,11	0,10
$\underset{\sim}{S}_{11}$	0,10	0,13	0,08	0,12	0,07	0,05	0,07	0,05	0,05	0,08	0,13	0,07
$\underset{\sim}{S}_1$	0,10	0,07	0,06	0,09	0,09	0,06	0,10	0,10	0,04	0,06	0,13	0,11

Let's convert each matrix $\left[\underset{\sim}{P_i}\right]$ into vector. For this purpose the product $\left[\underset{\sim}{E}\right]\cdot\left[\underset{\sim}{P_i}\right]$ is found by taking one element of $\left[\underset{\sim}{E}\right]$ and multiplying it for one element of $\left[\underset{\sim}{P_i}\right]$. The products are summed to each row. By this manner the vector is obtained for each matrix $\left[\underset{\sim}{P_i}\right]$.

	P_1	P_2	P_3	P_4	P_5	P_6	P_7	P_8	P_9	P_{10}	P_{11}	P_{12}	P_{13}	P_{14}
$\underset{\sim}{S}_1$	0,357	0,357	0,030	0,287	0,131	0,311	0,089	0,260	0,056	0,267	0,336	0,199	0,233	0,233
$\underset{\sim}{S}_2$	0,266	0,271	0,009	0,252	0,146	0,320	0,102	0,261	0,014	0,132	0,325	0,096	0,161	0,259
$\underset{\sim}{S}_3$	0,146	0,146	0,124	0,146	0,146	0,146	0,107	0,146	0,146	0,146	0,146	0,146	0,146	0,146
$\underset{\sim}{S}_4$	0,261	0,314	0,042	0,244	0,128	0,323	0,097	0,233	0,013	0,213	0,358	0,059	0,233	0,184
$\underset{\sim}{S}_5$	0,287	0,287	0,081	0,253	0,193	0,253	0,109	0,253	0,101	0,221	0,287	0,191	0,224	0,253
$\underset{\sim}{S}_6$	0,273	0,348	0,036	0,320	0,158	0,285	0,088	0,242	0,008	0,214	0,379	0,059	0,209	0,211
$\underset{\sim}{S}_7$	0,211	0,211	0,110	0,211	0,211	0,211	0,148	0,211	0,143	0,211	0,211	0,211	0,211	0,211
$\underset{\sim}{S}_8$	0,297	0,306	0,009	0,299	0,103	0,337	0,127	0,231	0,009	0,169	0,351	0,090	0,216	0,226
$\underset{\sim}{S}_9$	0,140	0,140	0,100	0,115	0,121	0,140	0,096	0,140	0,115	0,140	0,140	0,115	0,140	0,140
$\underset{\sim}{S}_{10}$	0,327	0,363	0,088	0,327	0,201	0,290	0,134	0,296	0,029	0,302	0,339	0,168	0,272	0,266
$\underset{\sim}{S}_{11}$	0,240	0,313	0,045	0,287	0,160	0,292	0,117	0,258	0,010	0,223	0,343	0,127	0,243	0,212

This matrix is taken as a basis for the development of the assignment model.

7.5. Hungarian algorithm

Let's find the matrix $\left[\overline{\underset{\sim}{P}'}\right]$ that is complementary to $\left[\underset{\sim}{P}'\right]$.

	P_1	P_2	P_3	P_4	P_5	P_6	P_7	P_8	P_9	P_{10}	P_{11}	P_{12}	P_{13}	P_{14}
$\underset{\sim}{S}_1$	0,643	0,643	0,970	0,713	0,869	0,689	0,911	0,740	0,944	0,733	0,664	0,801	0,767	0,767
$\underset{\sim}{S}_2$	0,734	0,729	0,991	0,748	0,854	0,680	0,898	0,739	0,986	0,868	0,675	0,904	0,839	0,741
$\underset{\sim}{S}_3$	0,854	0,854	0,876	0,854	0,854	0,854	0,893	0,854	0,854	0,854	0,854	0,854	0,854	0,854
$\underset{\sim}{S}_4$	0,739	0,686	0,958	0,756	0,872	0,677	0,903	0,767	0,988	0,788	0,642	0,941	0,767	0,816
$\underset{\sim}{S}_5$	0,713	0,713	0,919	0,747	0,807	0,747	0,891	0,747	0,899	0,779	0,713	0,809	0,776	0,747
$\underset{\sim}{S}_6$	0,727	0,652	0,964	0,680	0,842	0,715	0,912	0,758	0,992	0,786	0,621	0,941	0,791	0,789
$\underset{\sim}{S}_7$	0,789	0,789	0,890	0,789	0,789	0,789	0,852	0,789	0,857	0,789	0,789	0,789	0,789	0,789
$\underset{\sim}{S}_8$	0,703	0,694	0,991	0,701	0,897	0,663	0,873	0,769	0,991	0,831	0,649	0,910	0,784	0,774
$\underset{\sim}{S}_9$	0,860	0,860	0,900	0,885	0,879	0,860	0,904	0,860	0,885	0,860	0,860	0,885	0,860	0,860
$\underset{\sim}{S}_{10}$	0,673	0,637	0,912	0,673	0,799	0,710	0,866	0,704	0,971	0,698	0,661	0,832	0,728	0,734
$\underset{\sim}{S}_{11}$	0,760	0,687	0,955	0,713	0,840	0,708	0,883	0,742	0,990	0,777	0,657	0,873	0,757	0,788
F_1	1	1	1	1	1	1	1	1	1	1	1	1	1	1
F_2	1	1	1	1	1	1	1	1	1	1	1	1	1	1
F_3	1	1	1	1	1	1	1	1	1	1	1	1	1	1

1. Following the process described in the part 6.1 we obtain the matrix $\left[\underset{\sim}{B}\right]$:

	P_1	P_2	P_3	P_4	P_5	P_6	P_7	P_8	P_9	P_{10}	P_{11}	P_{12}	P_{13}	P_{14}
$\underset{\sim}{S}_1$	0	0,006	0,094	0,040	0,080	0,026	0,059	0,036	0,091	0,035	0,043	0,013	0,039	0,033
$\underset{\sim}{S}_2$	0,084	0,085	0,108	0,068	0,058	0,010	0,039	0,029	0,125	0,163	0,047	0,108	0,104	0
$\underset{\sim}{S}_3$	0,211	0,217	0	0,181	0,065	0,191	0,041	0,150	0	0,156	0,232	0,065	0,126	0,120
$\underset{\sim}{S}_4$	0,082	0,035	0,068	0,069	0,069	0	0,037	0,050	0,120	0,076	0,007	0,138	0,025	0,067
$\underset{\sim}{S}_5$	0,058	0,064	0,030	0,061	0,005	0,071	0,026	0,031	0,032	0,068	0,079	0,007	0,035	0
$\underset{\sim}{S}_6$	0,084	0,015	0,088	0,007	0,054	0,052	0,060	0,054	0,139	0,089	0	0,152	0,063	0,055
$\underset{\sim}{S}_7$	0,146	0,152	0,014	0,115	0	0,126	0	0,085	0,004	0,091	0,167	0	0,060	0,054
$\underset{\sim}{S}_8$	0,060	0,058	0,116	0,028	0,109	0	0,021	0,065	0,138	0,134	0,027	0,121	0,056	0,040
$\underset{\sim}{S}_9$	0,193	0,199	0	0,188	0,066	0,173	0,028	0,132	0,008	0,138	0,215	0,073	0,108	0,102
$\underset{\sim}{S}_{10}$	0,030	0	0,036	0	0,010	0,047	0,014	0	0,117	0	0,040	0,043	0	0
$\underset{\sim}{S}_{11}$	0,088	0,021	0,050	0,011	0,022	0,016	0,002	0,009	0,107	0,050	0,006	0,056	0	0,025
F_1	0,233	0,239	0	0,203	0,087	0,213	0,024	0,172	0,022	0,178	0,255	0,087	0,148	0,142
F_2	0,233	0,239	0	0,203	0,087	0,213	0,024	0,172	0,022	0,178	0,255	0,087	0,148	0,142
F_3	0,233	0,239	0	0,203	0,087	0,213	0,024	0,172	0,022	0,178	0,255	0,087	0,148	0,142

2. Following the process described in the part 6.2 we have results:

	P_1	P_2	P_3	P_4	P_5	P_6	P_7	P_8	P_9	P_{10}	P_{11}	P_{12}	P_{13}	P_{14}
$\underset{\sim}{S}_1$	[0]	0,006	0,094	0,040	0,080	0,026	0,059	0,036	0,091	0,035	0,043	0,013	0,039	0,033
$\underset{\sim}{S}_2$	0,084	0,085	0,108	0,068	0,058	0,010	0,039	0,029	0,125	0,163	0,047	0,108	0,104	[0]
$\underset{\sim}{S}_3$	0,211	0,217	[0]	0,181	0,065	0,191	0,041	0,150	~~0~~	0,156	0,232	0,065	0,126	0,120
$\underset{\sim}{S}_4$	0,082	0,035	0,068	0,069	0,069	[0]	0,037	0,050	0,120	0,076	0,007	0,138	0,025	0,067
$\underset{\sim}{S}_5$	0,058	0,064	0,030	0,061	0,005	0,071	0,026	0,031	0,032	0,068	0,079	0,007	0,035	~~0~~
$\underset{\sim}{S}_6$	0,084	0,015	0,088	0,007	0,054	0,052	0,060	0,054	0,139	0,089	[0]	0,152	0,063	0,055
$\underset{\sim}{S}_7$	0,146	0,152	0,014	0,115	~~0~~	0,126	[0]	0,085	0,004	0,091	0,167	~~0~~	0,060	0,054
$\underset{\sim}{S}_8$	0,060	0,058	0,116	0,028	0,109	~~0~~	0,021	0,065	0,138	0,134	0,027	0,121	0,056	0,040
$\underset{\sim}{S}_9$	0,193	0,199	~~0~~	0,188	0,066	0,173	0,028	0,132	0,008	0,138	0,215	0,073	0,108	0,102
$\underset{\sim}{S}_{10}$	0,030	~~0~~	0,036	~~0~~	0,010	0,047	0,014	[0]	0,117	~~0~~	0,040	0,043	~~0~~	~~0~~
$\underset{\sim}{S}_{11}$	0,088	0,021	0,050	0,011	0,022	0,016	0,002	0,009	0,107	0,050	0,006	0,056	[0]	0,025
F_1	0,233	0,239	~~0~~	0,203	0,087	0,213	0,024	0,172	0,022	0,178	0,255	0,087	0,148	0,142
F_2	0,233	0,239	~~0~~	0,203	0,087	0,213	0,024	0,172	0,022	0,178	0,255	0,087	0,148	0,142
F_3	0,233	0,239	~~0~~	0,203	0,087	0,213	0,024	0,172	0,022	0,178	0,255	0,087	0,148	0,142

3. We follow the process described in the part 6.3. As a result we have:

	P_1	P_2	P_3	P_4	P_5	P_6	P_7	P_8	P_9	P_{10}	P_{11}	P_{12}	P_{13}	P_{14}	
$\underset{\sim}{S}_1$	[0]	0,006	0,094	0,040	0,080	0,026	0,059	0,036	0,091	0,035	0,043	0,013	0,039	0,033	
$\underset{\sim}{S}_2$	0,084	0,085	0,108	0,068	0,058	0,010	0,039	0,029	0,125	0,163	0,047	0,108	0,104	[0]	◄
$\underset{\sim}{S}_3$	0,211	0,217	[0]	0,181	0,065	0,11	0,041	0,150	⊗	0,156	0,232	0,065	0,126	0,120	◄
$\underset{\sim}{S}_4$	0,082	0,035	0,068	0,069	0,069	[0]	0,037	0,050	0,120	0,076	0,007	0,138	0,025	0,067	◄
$\underset{\sim}{S}_5$	0,058	0,064	0,030	0,061	0,005	0,071	0,026	0,031	0,032	0,068	0,079	0,007	0,035	⊗	◄
$\underset{\sim}{S}_6$	0,084	0,015	0,088	0,007	0,054	0,052	0,060	0,054	0,139	0,089	[0]	0,152	0,063	0,055	
$\underset{\sim}{S}_7$	0,146	0,152	0,014	0,115	⊗	0,126	[0]	0,085	0,004	0,091	0,167	⊗	0,060	0,054	
$\underset{\sim}{S}_8$	0,060	0,058	0,116	0,028	0,109	⊗	0,021	0,065	0,138	0,134	0,027	0,121	0,056	0,040	◄
$\underset{\sim}{S}_9$	0,193	0,199	⊗	0,188	0,066	0,173	0,028	0,132	0,008	0,138	0,215	0,073	0,108	0,102	◄
$\underset{\sim}{S}_{10}$	0,030	⊗	0,036	⊗	0,010	0,047	0,014	[0]	0,117	⊗	0,040	0,043	⊗	⊗	
$\underset{\sim}{S}_{11}$	0,088	0,021	0,050	0,011	0,022	0,016	0,002	0,009	0,107	0,050	0,006	0,056	[0]	0,025	
F_1	0,233	0,239	⊗	0,203	0,087	0,213	0,024	0,172	0,022	0,178	0,255	0,087	0,148	0,142	◄
F_2	0,233	0,239	⊗	0,203	0,087	0,213	0,024	0,172	0,022	0,178	0,255	0,087	0,148	0,142	◄
F_3	0,233	0,239	⊗	0,203	0,087	0,213	0,024	0,172	0,022	0,178	0,255	0,087	0,148	0,142	◄
			▲			▲			▲					▲	

The rows and columns crossed by the line represent a "minimum support" of the matrix $\left[\underset{\sim}{B}\right]$

4. We follow the steps described in the part 6.4. The smallest element of the matrix is 0,005. As a result we get an appropriate matrix.
5. The process of the parts 6.2, 6.3 and 6.4 are repeated to obtain an optimal solution.

   We obtained the optimal solution. The final matrix is shown below:

	P_1	P_2	P_3	P_4	P_5	P_6	P_7	P_8	P_9	P_{10}	P_{11}	P_{12}	P_{13}	P_{14}
$\underset{\sim}{S}_1$	[0]	0,010	0,246	0,052	0,145	0,059	0,187	0,050	0,221	0,039	0,062	0,078	0,062	0,076
$\underset{\sim}{S}_2$	0,041	0,046	0,217	0,037	0,080	⊗	0,124	[0]	0,212	0,124	0,023	0,130	0,084	⊗
$\underset{\sim}{S}_3$	0,081	0,091	0,022	0,063	⊗	0,094	0,039	0,034	⊗	0,030	0,121	[0]	0,019	0,033
$\underset{\sim}{S}_4$	0,056	0,013	0,194	0,055	0,108	0,007	0,139	0,038	0,224	0,054	[0]	0,177	0,022	0,084
$\underset{\sim}{S}_5$	0,015	0,025	0,139	0,030	0,027	0,061	0,111	0,002	0,119	0,029	0,055	0,029	0,015	[0]
$\underset{\sim}{S}_6$	0,065	[0]	0,221	⊗	0,081	0,154	0,064	0,235	0,093	0,074	⊗	0,198	0,067	0,079
$\underset{\sim}{S}_7$	0,081	0,091	0,101	0,062	[0]	0,094	0,063	0,034	0,069	0,030	0,121	⊗	0,018	0,032
$\underset{\sim}{S}_8$	0,027	0,029	0,235	0,007	0,141	[0]	0,116	0,046	0,235	0,105	0,013	0,153	0,046	0,050
$\underset{\sim}{S}_9$	0,062	0,072	0,021	0,069	⊗	0,075	0,025	0,015	0,007	0,011	0,103	0,007	[0]	0,014
$\underset{\sim}{S}_{10}$	0,026	⊗	0,184	0,008	0,071	0,076	0,138	0,010	0,243	[0]	0,055	0,104	0,019	0,039
$\underset{\sim}{S}_{11}$	0,065	0,002	0,179	[0]	0,064	0,026	0,107	⊗	0,214	0,031	0,002	0,098	⊗	0,045
F_1	0,081	0,091	⊗	0,063	⊗	0,094	[0]	0,034	⊗	0,030	0,122	⊗	0,019	0,033
F_2	0,081	0,091	⊗	0,063	⊗	0,094	⊗	0,034	[0]	0,030	0,122	⊗	0,019	0,033
F_3	0,081	0,091	[0]	0,063	⊗	0,094	⊗	0,034	⊗	0,030	0,122	⊗	0,019	0,033

We have the following results:

7. $P_1 \to S_1$; 2) $P_2 \to S_6$; 3) $P_3 \to F_3$; 4) $P_4 \to S_{11}$; 5) $P_5 \to S_7$; 6) $P_6 \to S_8$; 7) $P_7 \to F_1$; 8) $P_8 \to S_2$; 9) $P_9 \to F_2$; 10) $P_{10} \to S_{10}$; 11) $P_{11} \to S_4$; 12) $P_{12} \to S_3$; 13) $P_{13} \to S_9$; 14) $P_{14} \to S_5$

The candidates P_3, P_7 and P_9 are discarded because the job positions F_1, F_2, F_3 are fictitious.

8. Conclusions

The objective of this study was to demonstrate the importance of the assignment method in the human resource management nowadays.

In the first section, the evolution process of traditional organizational structures to the modern flexible structures was described.

The next section highlights the impact that the changes produced in the human resource management. Flexibility and immediate adaptability to the market changes are decisive characteristics for the management policies.

In this context, new mathematical techniques and models have to be used in order to guarantee a correct decision making process in the human resource management.

The Hungarian algorithm was considered as a more adequate mathematical tool for this type of problems. Moreover, this method is appropriate for nowadays-Spanish economy. This algorithm allows to optimize the assignment process between two groups of variables according to some common qualities.

We developed a study case basing on the real database. The Spanish company was considered. The obtained results demonstrate the best alternative of the assignment process, taking into account a relative importance that the described qualities have for each of the variables. A large number of input elements were used in order to demonstrate the efficiency of this model.

To resume, the Hungarian algorithm for the assignment of the employees is effective in an environment under uncertainty. The models based on the mathematics of uncertainty improves a decision making process of business.

References

1. M. Ordóñez Ordóñez, *La nueva gestión de los recursos humanos*, Barcelona, Gestión (2000).
2. G. Soros. *The new paradigm for financial markets: the credit crisis of 2008 and what it means*. Public Affairs. London (2008).
3. B. Yang, Financial Globalization, Economic Growth, and the Crisis of 2007-09, *Journal of Economic Issues* **45 (3)**, 736-738 (2011).
4. J. Ariza Montes, *Dirección y administración integrada de personas: fundamentos, procesos y técnicas en práctica*, Madrid, McGraw-Hill (2004).
5. Raymond A. Noe Human resource management: gaining a competitive advantage, Boston (Mass.), Mcgraw-Hill /Irwin (2008).

6. J. Gil-Aluja, *Interactive management of human resources in uncertainty*, Kluwer Academic Publishers, Dordrecht (1998).
7. D. Votaw, A. Orden, The personnel assignment problem, *Proceedings of the Symposium on Linear Inequalities and Programming*, SCOOP 10, US Air Force, 155-163 (1952).
8. D. König, Théorie der endlichen und unendlichen graphen (1916).
9. H. Kuhn, The Hungarian method for the assignment problem, *Naval Research Logistics Quarterly* **2 (1-2)**, 83-97 (1955).
10. P. Krokhmal and P. Pardalos, Random assignment problems, *European Journal of Operational Research* **194**, 1-17 (2009).
11. P. Pardalos and L. Pitsoulis, *Nonlinear assignment problems: algorithms and applications*, The Netherlands, Kluwer Academic Publishers (2000).
12. R. Burkard, Selected topics on assignment problems, *Discrete Applied Mathematics* **123 (1-3)**, 257-302 (2002).
13. D. Pentico, Assignment problems: A golden anniversary survey, *European Journal of Operational Research* **176 (2)**, 774-793 (2007).
14. S. Geetha and K. Nair, A variation of the assignment problem, *European Journal of Operational Research* **68 (3)**, 422-426 (1993).
15. A.M. Gil Lafuente, *Nuevas estratégicas para el análisis financiero en la empresa*, Barcelona, Ariel (2001).
16. A.M. Gil Lafuente, *Fuzzy logic in financial analysis*, Berlin, Heidelberg, New York, Springer (2005).
17. J. Bonet, S. Linares and X. Bertran, Cálculo mixto estadístico-fuzzy, por comparación, aplicado a la previsión de variables económicas. *Proceedings of the XVI International Congress of the SIGEF on Economical and Financial Systems in Emergent Economies*, Morelia Michoacán, Mexico (2010).

A PROPOSED MODEL BASED ON SEARCH ENGINE OPTIMIZATION TO ENHANCE COMPETITIVE ADVANTAGE OF SMALL AND MEDIUM BUSINESS ENTERPRISES

NEVINE M. LABIB

Chair of Computer and Information Systems, Faculty of Management, Sadat Academy for Management Sciences, Cairo, Egypt

NASHAAT EL-KHAMEESY

Dean & Head of Chair of Computer and Information Systems, Faculty of Management, Sadat Academy for Management Sciences, Cairo, Egypt

SAMIA M. GHAREIB

Tanta International Trade Point, Ministry of Industry & Foreign Trade, 75 Al Geish Street, Tanta, 31111, Egypt

Small and Medium Business Enterprises (SMEs) play a significant role in the world economy due to their remarkable effective contribution towards the problems of unemployment as well as to the overall economy. There has been a continuous interest in enhancing services and enabling success to SMEs and recently due to the suffering of the Egyptian economy after the 25th revolution it has become a must to support such SMEs projects. One challenging issue is how to enhance the competitive advantages of SME via different alternatives of search engine optimization. This paper presents a case study which highlights the current status and problems facing SMEs after the recent revolution. In this paper we present a prototype model adopting number of aspects of search engine optimization to enhance the hosting websites for SMEs as it's always a challenge how to promote and market their products. The implemented prototype provide a unified interface to display SMEs information and product catalogue, and it also facilitate navigation between these companies web sites by using URLs that can be stored in SMEs Database. The implemented prototype has proven successful use of Search Engine Optimization techniques to improve the SMEs web-based network ranking in search engine results. It also verified a cost effective marketing technique for the target SMES and its success were also proven via a number of reports and statistics about the web site traffic. These results can be further analyzed to enable selection and updating the keywords and the ranking factors.

1. Introduction

Although 25 January Egyptian Revolution has ousted the previous regime, local political events and disturbances affected the Egyptian economy negatively. Many sectors of the Economic activities have been affected like manufacturing, tourism, construction and investment [1]. The Egyptian Stock Exchange also suffered from dramatic losses since 25 January, 2011. Steel mills and textile factories are the most suffered from financial problems and their inability to get their needs of raw materials. The consequences of the disturbances after 25 January revolution had significant negative effects on the investment rates. The Sectors of communications and information technology, construction, services, and tourism were the most affected by low capital in the economic activities. Unemployment rate recorded 12.4% during the second quarter of FY 2011/2012 up from 8.9% during the correspondent period a year before to reach 3.3 million unemployed compared to 2.3 million in the same period a year before. This high percentage recorded in second quarter of 2011/2012 is sharply influenced by the political and economic instability witnessed after the revolution as a number of companies were negatively affected reducing the number of their employees to offset their losses. [2].Governments in most countries are giving special attention to the promotion of Small and Medium Business enterprises (SMEs), as they play an important role in economic growth, export promotion and employment creation. There is a strong rationale for supporting SME development: SMEs account for 75% of employment and around 80% of GDP, according to the UNDP 2008 Egypt Human Development Report [3]. This importance has been visible during the economic chaos of the world financial crisis. When many large firms and multinational companies were reducing their number of workers and production because of problems in the international market, SMEs sector, was stable. Accordingly SMEs can work in crisis period as impetus for the national economy. Characteristics of these sectors make it capable of facing the changing work environments and unfavorable economic circumstances. SMEs have many characteristics and advantages which make them suitable for many countries especially those with tangled economic activities. These characteristics can be summarized as follows:

1- The ability to create jobs because of their labor intensive nature.
2- Wide geographical spread, in all Egypt's governorates
3- The ability to use capital in relatively high productivity.
4- Highly specialized so that they are able to make major cut in production costs.

5- Utilization of locally available human & material resources.
6- Quick capital turnover.

2. Different Approaches of Search Engine Optimization

Search engine optimization (SEO) is the practice of optimizing a web site so that enhance its ranking on the search engine results pages. The Following factors affect the ranking of the web pages in the search result pages.

1. Domain Names:

Keyword-rich domain names are an important ranking factor, especially for small sites that are just starting out. Choosing domain names includes more than just deciding among .com, .net, and .org. [4]

2. Keywords in the <Meta> Description Tag:

The text in the <Meta> description tag is not visible on the page itself, but is often displayed in search results. This should be enough of an imperative to fully optimize this tag. [5]

3. Keywords in the Heading Tags:

Make proper use of your H1 heading tags. Webmasters have used multiple H1 tags in the belief that search engines give those tags priority. The problem with this and similar techniques is that search engines are not stupid and will adapt very quickly to counterattack less scrupulous techniques such as this. Use H1 tags where and when they are appropriate. [6].

4. Keywords in the Link Anchor Text

The link anchor text is all about keyword relevance. In general, all links should contain relevant keywords in the link anchor text.

5. Quality Outbound Links

It is about what your web visitors want. Can you provide them with great content on your site plus any relevant links where they can find related information?

6. Site Maps

Over the years, search engines realized the benefit of Sitemaps. Google jumped on this concept in 2005 with the creation of its own Google Sitemap Protocol.

Shortly after, Yahoo!, Microsoft, Ask, and IBM jumped on the bandwagon. During 2006, Google Sitemaps Protocol was renamed XML Sitemap Protocol, to acknowledge its "universal" acceptance. The work of these joint efforts is now under the auspices of Sitemaps.org. The premise of using XML Sitemap Protocol was that it would help search engines index content faster while providing ways to improve their existing crawling algorithms. Using XML Sitemap Protocol does not guarantee anything in terms of better page rankings. Furthermore, use of XML Sitemap Protocol is not mandatory for all sites. In other words, a website will not be penalized if it is not using XML Sitemaps [7].

7. Entry and Exit Pages

Entry and exit pages are the first and last pages that a user sees of your web site. It's important to understand that an entry page isn't necessarily the home page on your web site. It can be any other page where a user lands, either by clicking through search engine results, by clicking a link from another web site or a piece of marketing material, or by book marking or typing directly into the address bar of a browser .Entry pages are important in SEO, because they are the first page users see as they come onto the web site. The typical web site is actually several small connected sites. Your company web site might contain hubs, or central points, for several different topics. Say you're a pet store. Then you'll have hubs within your sites for dogs, cats, birds, fish, and maybe exotic animals. Each hub will have a main page, which will likely be your entry page for that section, and several additional pages leading from that central page to other pages containing relevant content, products, or information about specific topics [7].

3. Semantic Web and XML

Some of today's basic Web limitations include search, database support, interoperable applications, intelligent business logic, automation, security, and trust. Information revolution awaits the next break-through of semantic web. The Semantic Web is a web that is able to describe things in a way that computers can understand. Semantic web uses some tools like Extensible Markup Language (XML), Resource Describe Framework, Ontology, and Ontology Web language (OWL). XML is the synthetic foundation layer of the Semantic Web. All other technologies providing features for the Semantic Web will be built on top of XML. Requiring other Semantic Web Technologies, like the Resource Description Framework to be layered on top of XML Guarantees a base level of interoperability [8].

4. The Proposed Approach

This web-Based network allows access to Small and Medium Business Enterprises websites and make information about these companies and their products available to the visitors in both Arabic and English languages. This gives these companies the ability of being available online and increases their capability of competitiveness. It also allows access to Friendly web sites useful for the exporters and making these sites URL available in one place so that it makes it easy to reach them. We can move from one member's web site to another by URLs which is stored along with other information about each company like, contact details, products, and Product catalogue. So that visitors can access to a wide variety of Small and Medium Business enterprises information and web sites through a single web interface. After developing the interfaces, the web site is submitted to Google search engine. Optimization of the web pages is performed continuously to enhance ranks of the whole network in Search Engines result pages. After submitting the web site, Google analytical tool is used to analyze the web site rank. After getting these results, keyword structure and other rank factors should be reviewed and updated. Figure(1) below shows the main steps in the proposed optimization phase:

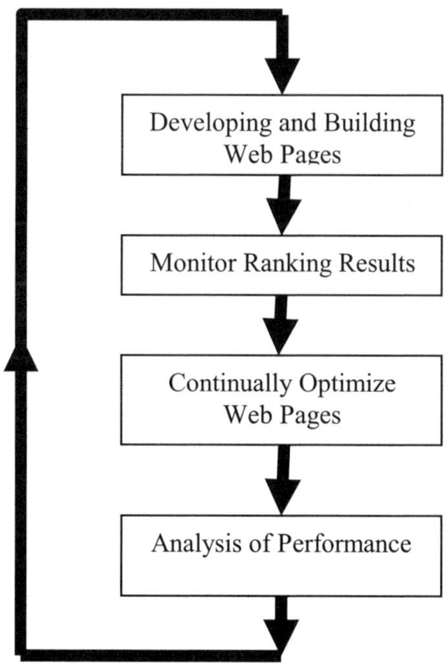

Figure 1. Optimization Phase by Steps

8. Optimize the Meta Description Tag:

We use The Meta tag element was used in the master page file which acts like a design template for the web pages. Meta tag lies in the <head></head> section of the page, as shown in Figure 2.

2- Optimize Keywords in the Heading Tags: Heading Tags was used instead of state of the art text, in order to help optimize the pages; this is illustrated in Figure 3.

3-Outbound Links: External links to other organization and governmental sectors that can be useful for the Network web site visitors was used. The network can benefit from these links and their traffic in optimizing ranks in the search engine result pages, especially if these sites have high traffic rates. Outbound links was used as shown in Figure 4.

4-Site Maps: 2 XML site maps were used for the SMEs web-based network, one for the Arabic version and the other is for the English version. Example of English XML site map was shown in Figure 5.

5-Entry and Exit Pages: Breadcrumbs was used for site navigation and as entry and exit pages. This is shown in Figure 6.

```
<%@ Master Language="C#" AutoEventWireup="true" CodeFile="EMasterPage.master.cs"
    Inherits="EMasterPage" %>
<!DOCTYPE html PUBLIC "-//W3C//DTD XHTML 1.0 Transitional//EN" "http://www.w3.org/TR/xhtml1/DTD/xhtml1-transitional.dtd">
<html xmlns="http://www.w3.org/1999/xhtml">
<head id="Head1" runat="server">
<meta name="decription" content="Small and medium Enterprises Exporters network for Egyptian exporters " />
<meta name="keywords" content="electronic catalogue,egyptian products,small and medium enterprises,export" />
<meta name="author" content="Egyptian International Trade Point " />
<meta http-equiv="content-type" content="text/html;charset=UTF-8" />
    <title>Small and Medium Enterprises Network </title>
    <link rel="stylesheet" type="text/css" href="App_Themes/Theme1/style2.css" />
</head>
```

Figure 2. Meta Tag Used in Site Web Pages

```
<%@ Page Language="C#" MasterPageFile="~/AMasterPage.master"
AutoEventWireup="true" CodeFile="cataloge.aspx.cs" Inherits="cataloge"
Title=" Electronic Catalogue For Small and Medium Enterprises " %>
<asp:Content ID="Content1" ContentPlaceHolderID="ContentPlaceHolder1"
Runat="Server">
    <table dir="rtl" style="width: 100%">
        <tr>
        <td colspan="2"><h3><strong> Electronic Catalogue </strong> </h3>
        </td>
        </tr>
```

Figure 3. Using of Heading Tags

Figure 4. Outbound Links

```
<?xml version="1.0" encoding="utf-8" ?>
<siteMap xmlns="http://schemas.microsoft.com/AspNet/SiteMap-File-1.0" >
  <siteMapNode url="enhome.aspx" title="Home">
     <siteMapNode url="eneitp.aspx" title="EITP" />
     <siteMapNode url="ensms.aspx" title="SMES Network"/>
     <siteMapNode url="encontact.aspx" title="Contact Us"/>
     <siteMapNode url="ensmap.aspx" title="Site Map"/>
     <siteMapNode url="encompany.aspx" title="Company of SMES Network" >
     <siteMapNode url="company_e_details.aspx" title="Company Details"
 </siteMapNode>
     <siteMapNode url="ecatalog.aspx" title="Product Catalogue">
       <siteMapNode url="eproduct_cat.aspx" title="Product Category />
       <siteMapNode url="eproduct_co.aspx" title="Company Products" />
     </siteMapNode>
 <siteMapNode url="news_e_details.aspx" title="News Details"  />
</siteMapNode>
</siteMap>
```

Figure 5. English XML Site Map

Figure 6. Entry and Exit Pages (Bread Crumbs) Used in Site Navigation

5. Conclusions and Future Work

As a result of analyzing the proposed model as well as evaluating its applicability we briefly highlight a number of conclusions as follows:

1. The Web-Based Network for SMEs efficiently provided a unified interface to display SMEs information and product catalogue.
2. Using URL that can be stored in SMEs Database improves and facilitates navigation between these companies' web sites.
3. Applying Search Engine Optimization techniques can improve the proposed SMEs web-based network ranking in search engine results. This provides a cost effective marketing technique to SMES for marketing their products locally and internationally.

4. The optimization process of the web pages is continuous. After submitting the web site in the search engines, reports should be analyzed to help update the optimization plan. Web analytics tools are used to measure the web traffic to the site like Google web Analytical Tool.
5. SMEs web-based network doesn't subscribe to all the properties of standard web-based network; it is a prototype that can be enhanced by more use and testing

In future work, it is hoped to explore the adequacy of the proposed models towards further improvements such as multi-language support, adding more capability based on BI analytics and also integrating the adopted ideas into mobile environment.

References

1. The Central Agency for Public Mobilization and Statistics – CAPMAS, Egypt Statistics, 2011.
2. Alexandria Bank, Egypt Country Report, Second Quarter of Fiscal Year 2011/2012, May 2012.
3. http://www.xing.com/net/ revi/business-forum-51093/smes-small-minded-enterprises-24401007/
4. Browsing date 11-6-2012 time 11 A.
5. John I. Jerkovic, "SEO Warrior", O'Reilly Media, Inc., 2010.
6. Eric Enge, Stephen Spencer, Rand Fishkin, and Jessie C. Stricchiola, "Art of SEO", O'reilly Media, Inc., 2010.
7. Dan Sisson, "Google SEO Secrets", Blue Moose Webworks, Inc., 2003
8. Cristian Darie, Karli Watson, "Beginning ASP.NET 2.0 E-Commerce in C# 2005: From Novice to Professional", Apress, Inc., 2005
9. Michael C. Daconta, Leo J. Obrst, Kevin T. Smith, "The Semantic Web, a Guide to the Future of XML, Web Services, and Knowledge Management", 2003.

THE STANDARD COST ESTIMATIONS BY FUZZY LOGIC ELEMENTS: METHODOLOGY, ORGANIZATION AND INTERPRETATION OF THE INFORMATION

ANNA M. GIL-LAFUENTE
Department of Economics and Business Organization,
University of Barcelona. Barcelona, Spain

ARAS KEROPYAN
Department of Economics and Business Organization,
University of Barcelona. Barcelona, Spain

VICENTE FERRER GRAU
Department of Accounting,
University of Barcelona. Barcelona, Spain

Abstract. The calculation of standard or pre-established costs is a widely used procedure in the operational development of the business world. It is essential to define standards correctly in order to have accurate and useful information. This paper is the first approach to the use of fuzzy logic elements as a methodology for fixing the standard costs. This methodology is not intending to substitute the other methods, but it can be used as a complementary to the existing methods. We believe that the insertion of fuzzy logic in standard cost estimations will allow us to obtain a well-arranged process that consists of developing a theoretical framework of definitions and concepts.

1. Introduction

Cost control is an essential tool for planning and well-functioning of operations of the companies. The cost estimation provides information for proper implementation and monitoring of inputs, whether labor or capital and enables to recognize the efficiency of the system. Similarly, the cost analysis answers the information needs for budget planning. Under these premises, it is necessary to find a standard reference which must define the standard cost.

The standard cost is a technical and economic forecast of the quantities and prices of the inputs and labor factors and capital needed to obtain the output. The advantages of defining the standard costs are:

-Having a contrast or measuring tool of the efficient productivity.

-Enabling to analyze the generated deviations between the standard costs and actual costs, thus obtaining information on the fulfillment of expectations, which also allows to define the responsibility centers.

-Reducing the paperwork and providing more information, by involvement of greater efficiency of accounting.

-Facilitating control and cost reduction.

-Providing a detailed analysis of the manufacturing process, which helps to rationalize the work; improving methods, time and motion study, and so on.

As it is shown above, it is essential to set the standard cost correctly in order to avoid deviations and distortions of business information product of heading error.

Usually two systems have been used by technicians and management to calculate the standard cost, the use of traditional quantitative techniques and the use of expert opinion.

Quantitative techniques can be classic and linear regression models or multivariate analysis, are used to determine the behavior of explanatory variables of the cost function with a static and predictable performance. These methods of forecasting methods should not be understood as incompatible with the expertise, but part of it. In certain variables that have a very static and steady behavior, the expert's opinion may well be based on quantitative methods cited. Therefore, the expertise reinforces the classical techniques, as in the more erratic behavior of certain factors, or in foreseeable situations but not estimable, it reduces the error of estimates.

Another way to determine the standard cost is through the expertise of a technician but not based on any standardized mathematical calculation, but based on subjective valuations and intuitive. In the business world, informed and reasoned opinion of an expert is considered a highly valuable asset. The application of fuzzy logic elements not only reduces the effectiveness of the expert opinion and reinforces it, as it involves a systematic approach and organized them.

At the same time, be considered the paradigm of utility business information, must be that relevant, reliable and timely. The proposed methodology is operational and agile both in their calculation as in its interpretation.

The characteristics that outline the application of fuzzy logic, make it particularly valuable as a method of estimating the standard cost in a business context.

2. Standard Costing

Definition 1: The standard cost is an estimate of the measurement and valuation of consumption of a productive resource. Therefore consists of two components, the technical standard (quantity) and the economic standard (prices).

The standard cost can be interpreted not only as an estimate of the cost, but can be defined more broadly. For example, you can designate a target to meet, either an objective of seeking growth or production efficiency.

The standard cost can be formulated in the following ways:

- Standard optimal: it involves achieving maximum production efficiency and therefore the minimum cost per unit. This forecast is very rigid, as it involves the calculation of costs ideals.
- Basic standard: is determined by the level of activity most likely long-term.
- Standard Normal: those that are calculated based on market circumstances and considering as basic assumption the optimal use of resources.
- Standard supply: is calculated based on the level of activity to be achieved, based on normal use of production potential.
- Standard range: its calculation is based solely on past experience. These are considered by the literature for future projections.
- Standard wide: in its calculation takes into account all contingencies and system failures that are reasonable in order to determine reliably the normal efficiency of the production process.

2.1. Determination of Standard Costs

The determination of the standard costs is a very important phase of the cost control process. The logical steps of determining the standard cost are:

a) Schedule of the activity.
b) Determination of the technical or physical standards (primary standards).
c) Determination of the economic standards.

From the list above it can be deduced the following scheme of work for the quantification of the standard cost:

1- Determination of the standard's goal: to reflect a minimum cost, normal, a goal

→ 2- Choosing the calculation method

→ 3- Calculation of the standard with the methodology chosen and for successive phases:
- Standard Activity
- Technical Standard
- Economic Standard

The aim of this study had any decisive impact in step 2 of the chart above, the choice of method of calculation.

Traditionally, the standard real business costs are determined in three key ways:

1- By applying basic quantitative techniques such as econometric models or traditional forecasting models.
2- To set a goal. This is valid, in the case of standard is not intended to reflect a forecast but rather to be a goal.
3- Using the professional experience of the entrepreneurs and managers and management.

The third method is one of the most effective ways to determine a correct standard cost, but is usually applied according to subjective criteria and not standardized. It is therefore an accurate approximation based on the good judgment of experts.

3. The model and hypothesis:

The application of fuzzy logic elements and techniques based on the systematization and expertise implies a sort of a basic method of proven effectiveness. We assume the following for the model: This paper is a theoretical approach to the application of fuzzy logic for costing standards. Therefore, you must enroll in specific conceptual framework determined by some fundamental assumptions.

The business reality is complex and changing, so this theoretical framework is simple and small. But at the same time, the underlying methodology is valid as long as they fit the working hypothesis to reality under study.

Hypothesis 1: It is conceived purely industrial company whose main production factors are:

- Inputs: materials, hereinafter mp
- Labor input: represented by the cost of labor process in future mod
- Factors of capital: they are the investment and resources consumption than those other two factors. For example; electricity consumption, depreciation of equipment, rentals, etc. It symbolizes ggf.

The enterprise's choice for searching for a model obeys the model that simplifies and shows clearly the underlying objectives of the work. This is not the limit of the scope thereof, it would be equally valid for other companies as the service can be provided that will define their corresponding factors.

Hypothesis 2: The cost of output is determined by the full cost model industry. This model attributed solely to the product manufacturing costs (mp, mod and ggf), other business costs (administration, advertising, distribution, ..) are considered as an expense.

Graphically:

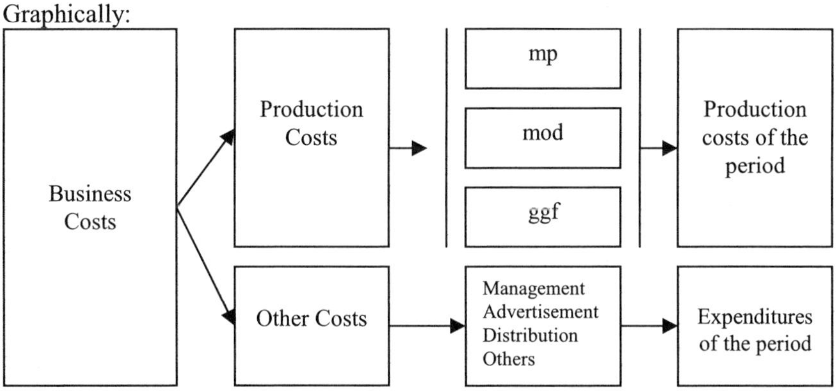

Hypothesis 3: It is considered that the production process is divided into n sections. The costs of each section are configured by the sum of the attributable factors (German model costs).
Graphically:

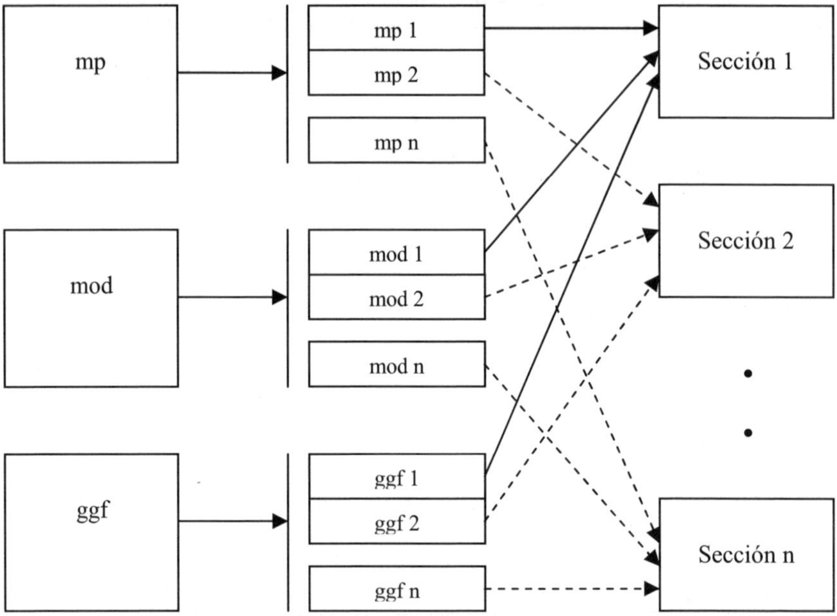

The combined application of scenarios 2 and 3 determines the cross-industry models and full cost of the German model. This combination means that the cost factor is previously charged to the product passing through the sections of production.

Thus, the standard costs are calculated by factor and by section, allowing perfectly delineate responsibility centers generated if deviations.

Regarding the structural costs are considered attributable to each section as part of manufacturing overheads. The cost allocation structural sections by seeking an allocation key objective, as can be the distribution function of the activity or use, size, etc.

3.1. Organization of Information

Following the suggested model, information is organized by cost matrix factors and organized in sections. Therefore, matrices coupled factors sections form a matrix that is

$$\begin{pmatrix} \text{mp 1} \\ \text{mp 2} \\ . \\ . \\ . \\ \text{mp n} \end{pmatrix} + \begin{pmatrix} \text{mod 1} \\ \text{mod 2} \\ . \\ . \\ . \\ \text{mod n} \end{pmatrix} + \begin{pmatrix} \text{ggf 1} \\ \text{ggf 2} \\ . \\ . \\ . \\ \text{ggf n} \end{pmatrix} = \begin{pmatrix} \text{s1} \\ \text{s2} \\ . \\ . \\ . \\ \text{sn} \end{pmatrix}$$

Fulfills the cost of the sum of the cost factors is equal to the sum of the sections:

$$\sum_{j=1}^{n} mp + \sum_{j=1}^{n} \text{mod} + \sum_{j=1}^{n} ggf = \sum_{j=1}^{n} s$$

The decisional matrix resulting from the process will be organized by factors and in sections:

$$\begin{array}{l} \\ \textbf{mp} \\ \textbf{mod} \\ \textbf{ggf} \end{array} \begin{array}{c} \begin{array}{cccc} \textbf{s1} & \textbf{s2} & \ldots & \textbf{sn} \end{array} \\ \begin{pmatrix} \text{mp1} & \text{mp 2} & \ldots & \text{mp n} \\ \text{mod 1} & \text{mod 2} & \ldots & \text{mod n} \\ \text{ggf 1} & \text{ggf 2} & \ldots & \text{ggf n} \end{pmatrix} \end{array}$$

The sum of the resultant matrix rows gives the cost of each factor:

$$cmp = \sum_{j=1}^{t} s_{1j} \;;\; \text{mod} = \sum_{j=1}^{t} s_{2j} \;;\; ggf = \sum_{j=1}^{t} s_{3j}$$

The sum of the resultant matrix columns gives the cost of each section:

$$cs_j = \sum_{j=1}^{n} mp_j + \sum_{j=1}^{n} \text{mod} \quad j + \sum_{j=1}^{n} ggf_j$$

This organization form of the standard costs enables to control precisely the arising deviations in the period. It also allows a dual level decisional factors control and control sections.

4. Conclusions

Fuzzy logic is proposed as a methodology for determining the standard cost estimation. At the same time, is compatible with other methodologies and can act as a reinforcement of the same flexibility and providing prospective information.

The proposed model systematizes and mandates the use of expert opinion to establish standard costs.

The resulting information model deviations are organized by sections, as technical and economic component factors. Thus, one can measure the efficiency of resource consumption of each factor in each section, noting if the price and quantity consumed are in accordance to the defined standard. The model allows to define responsibility centers with detailed information.

The calculation of deviations using fuzzy logic is equally feasible, and the organization of the resulting information is useful in an operational and business context that is characterized by instability and constant changes.

The use of expert opinions in a systematized context also involves a bridge between the standard calculation and decision making process. Indeed, the choice of a decision must be based on the objectives, but the decision ultimately will be taken by an expert or responsible managers. Fuzzy logic allows standardizing in operational decision making as a part of the expert opinion and it is focused on the same goal.

References

1. J. Gil-Aluja, Elementos para una teoría de la decisión en la incertidumbre, *Editorial Milladoiro, Spain* (1999).
2. J. Gil-Aluja, Introducción de la teoría de la incertidumbre en la gestión de empresas, *Editorial Milladoiro, Spain* (2002).
3. Zimmermann, H.J.: Fuzzy Set Theory and Its Application, Kluwer Academic Publishing, Boston (1991).
4. Zadeh, L.A.: Fuzzy sets. Information and Control. 8, 338-353 (1991)

5. Keropyan, A., Gil-Lafuente, A. M: A fuzzy-based decision model application on strategic management, African Journal of Business Management, Vol. 5(15), pp. 6586-6590 (2011).
6. Pap, E., Bosnjak, Z., Bosnjak, S.: Application of fuzzy sets with different t-norms in the interpretation of portfolio matrices in strategic management, Fuzzy Sets and Systems. 114, 123-131 (2000)
7. Bellman, R.E., Zadeh, L.A.: Decision-making in a fuzzy environment. Management Science. 17, 141-164 (1970)
8. Merigó, J. M., Gil Lafuente, A. M., Gil-Aluja, J.: Decision Making with the Induced Generalized Adequacy Coefficient. Applied and Computational Mathematics. 10 (2), 321-339 (2011)
9. Colin, D.: Standard Costing. Chartered Institute of Management Accountants Academic Press, London and San Diego (1992)
10. Curran, R., Kundu, A. K., Raghunathan, S. and Eakin, D.: Costing Tools for Decision Making within Integrated Aerospace Design. Concurrent Engineering, vol. 9 (4), 327-338 (2001).

PART 3:
FINANCE AND ECONOMICS

SEPARATING INDEPENDENT COMPONENTS UNDERLYING PARALLEL FOREIGN EXCHANGE RATES: RECONSTRUCTING AND FORECASTING STRATEGIES

VASILE GEORGESCU

Department of Statistics and Informatics, University of Craiova,
13 A.I.Cuza Craiova, 200858, Romania

DUMITRU CIOBANU

Department of Statistics and Informatics, University of Craiova,
13 A.I.Cuza Craiova, 200858, Romania

In this paper we assume each time series depends on several distinct underlying factors, being essentially a mixture of them. It is these factors or source signals that are of primary interest, but they are buried within a large set of measured signal mixtures. Separating a relatively small number of distinct time-varying causal factors becomes crucial in multivariate financial time series analysis, when attempting to explain past co-movements and to predict future evolutions. Actually, we use Independent Component Analysis for revealing fundamental factors behind several parallel series of foreign exchange rates. More accurate predictions can be performed via these independent components, after their separation, using different forecasting strategies and settings.

1. Revealing Fundamental Factors behind Financial Time Series

The inherent complexity of financial time series, which are typically noisy and non-stationary, appears to be rooted in some kind of fundamental processes that can not be directly observed or revealed, but are rather the latent source of some visible mixtures of effects. The same pattern applies to any type of data generation mechanisms. This means that almost every signal measured within a real-world system is actually a mixture of statistically independent source signals.

The intuition that financial markets are driven by a few latent common factors is reinforced by the parallel way in which many financial times series evolve, known as co-movement. Currency exchange rates or daily stock returns are good examples.

One key strategy for unmixing signals into their constituent components is to look for unrelated time-varying signals within these mixtures. The property of being unrelated is of fundamental importance and can be captured in terms of *statistical independence*. Due to their very nature as fundamental factors, these signals are assumed to be not only uncorrelated with each other, but also unconditionally independent. In addition, they are supposed to typically follow non Gaussian-distributions.

It is worth to mention that the nongaussianity is a common feature for a large number of financial time series, especially in case of high-frequency data generation processes. All these characteristics recommend financial data as a highly promising application field. Thus, accurately identifying independent factors behind financial data might reveal important driving mechanisms that otherwise remain hidden. For instance, if one could find the maximally independent mechanisms generating stock price movements, this might help in minimizing the risk in the investment strategy. As its name suggests, independent component analysis separates a set of *signal mixtures* into a corresponding set of statistically *independent component* (*source*) signals.

The source signals are generally assumed to have non-Gaussian distributions. By contrast, any mixture of source signals tends to have a distribution that is more Gaussian than that of any of its constituent source signals, whatever their distribution is. Then extracting independent signals, with non-Gaussian distributions and low complexity structure from a set of signal mixtures should recover the original signals.

2. Data Preprocessing: Centering and Whitening

Let us consider a random vector $x = (x_1 \dots x_N)^T$ with N elements. There is available a sample $x(1), \dots, x(T)$ from this random vector. The most basic and necessary preprocessing is to center the observed vector $x = (x_1 \dots x_N)^T$, i.e., substract its mean vector $m_x = E\{x\}$ so as to transform x into a zero mean vector y.

After centering, another useful preprocessing strategy is to perform a pre-whitening of the data. This means that the already centered vector y is linearly transformed into a new vector z, which is white (spherical), i.e., its covariance matrix equals the identity matrix: $\Sigma_z = E\{z\, z^T\} = I$.

Whitening uses the eigenvalue decomposition (EVD) of the covariance matrix of y, which is computed from the available sample. Performing its EVD, we obtain $\Sigma_y = E\{y\, y^T\} = EDE^T$, where E is the orthogonal matrix of eigenvectors, and D is the diagonal matrix of its eigenvalues. Whitening can now be done by $z = D^{-1/2} E^T y$.

3. Approaches to Extracting Independent Factors from Signal Mixtures

3.1. Nongaussianity-oriented versus independence-oriented approaches

While we focus on linear mixtures, the already centered and whitened vector $z_t \in \Re^N$ can be expressed as:

$$z_t = A s_t, \quad t = 1, 2, \ldots, T \tag{1}$$

where $s_t \in \Re^M$ is the unknown source vector, with $M \leq N$, and $A \in \Re^{N \times M}$ the unknown *mixing* matrix. The objective is to recover the source vector realizations $\{ s_t \}$ from the corresponding realizations of the observed vector $\{ z_t \}$. This means to find a matrix W that makes the components of z_t statistically independent. We call such a matrix a *separating* matrix. The process involves, explicitly or implicitly, the inversion of matrix A, which is thus assumed to be full column rank. The separator output is computed as $\hat{s}_t = W z_t$, where $W \in \Re^{M \times N}$ is the separating matrix. A perfect separating matrix is such that the global filter $G = W A$ can be written as the product of a non-singular diagonal matrix D and a permutation matrix P, i.e., $G = PD$. The diagonal elements of matrix D account for the unknown scales of the separated sources, whereas the permutation matrix P reflects the fact that the sources can appear in any order at the separator output. Such source scale and permutation indeterminacies are typically admissible in ICA.

A solution to the problem of estimating a separating matrix W that will give us the independent components $\hat{s}_i$, can be found based on the optimization of a cost function, also called *contrast* function.

There are two alternative ways to define such contrast functions and thus to set the optimization problem: either to maximize a measure of nongaussianity, or to maximize a measure of independence. Actually, nongaussianity and independence are strongly related. According to the central limit theorem, the distribution of a sum of independent random variables tends toward a Gaussian distribution, under certain conditions. Loosely speaking, a sum (or linear combination) of several independent random variables usually has a distribution that is closer to Gaussian than any of the original random variables.

Thus, to estimate one of the independent components, we can consider a linear combination of the z_i. Let us denote this by $\hat{s}_j = w^T z = \sum_i w_i z_i$, where

w is a vector to be determined, denoting one of the rows of the matrix $W = A^{-1}$. Note that we also have $\hat{s}_j = w^T A s = q^T s = \sum_i q_i s_i$. Thus, $\hat{s}_j$ is a certain linear combination of the s_i, with coefficients given by $q^T = w^T A$.

In practice, we do not know the values of q, but because $q^T s = w^T z$ we can just let w vary and look at the distribution of $w^T z$. Therefore, we could take as w a vector that maximizes the nongaussianity of $w^T z$.

However, instead of maximizing a nongaussianity measure, one can use a general-purpose measure of the dependence of the components of a random vector. Using such a measure, one could define ICA as a linear decomposition that minimizes that dependence measure. Such an approach can be developed using mutual information, which is a well-motivated information-theoretic measure of statistical dependence. In order to find source signals that are independent we need a measure that will let us know how close the extracted signals are to being independent. This permits us to iteratively change the unmixing matrix so as to increase the degree of independence of the extracted signals. A quantity which is related in a useful way to independence is *entropy*. Finding independent signals by maximizing entropy is one common interpretation of ICA, known as *infomax* ([2]).

Another common interpretation of ICA (different from infomax) is as a *maximum likelihood* (ML) method for estimating the optimal unmixing matrix W that provide the best fit of the extracted signals $\hat{s}$ to a given model (e.g., the assumed joint pdf p_s of source signals).

3.2. The FastICA Algorithm

FastICA is a computationally efficient algorithm for performing ICA estimations by optimizing orthogonal contrast functions of the form

$$\Upsilon_G(W) = \sum_{i=1}^{N} E\left\{G_i\left(w_i^T z\right)\right\} \tag{2}$$

where the data z are prewhitened and matrix W is constrained to be orthogonal. The functions $G_i(\cdot)$ can fundamentally be chosen in two ways:

In a maximum likelihood framework, $G_i(\hat{s}_i) = \log p_{s_i}(\hat{s}_i)$ where p_{s_i} is the pdf of the *i*-th independent component. The functions $G_i(\cdot)$ can be fixed based on prior information of the independent components, or they can be estimated from the current estimates $\hat{s}_i$. In many applications, the independent components are known to be super-Gaussian (sparse), in which case all the functions $G_i(\cdot)$ are often set a priori as

$$G_i(\hat{s}) = -\log\cosh\hat{s} \tag{3}$$

This corresponds to a symmetric super-Gaussian pdf and has the great benefit of being very smooth; a non-smooth $G_i(\cdot)$ can pose problems for any optimization method. Maximum likelihood estimation is equivalent, under some assumptions, to information-theoretic approaches such as minimum mutual information and minimum marginal entropy.

A second framework consists in using cumulants. Consider the simple case of maximizing the kurtosis $kurt(\hat{s}) = E\{\hat{x}^4\} - 3(E\{\hat{s}^2\})^2$ of the estimated signals $\hat{s}$. Because we assume that the estimated signals have unit variance, due to prewhitening and the orthogonality of w, this reduces to maximizing the fourth moment $E\{\hat{s}^4\}$, thus $G_i(\hat{s}) = \hat{s}^4$. This means that the contrast is essentially the sum of kurtosis. If we know a priori that the independent components are super-Gaussian, the maximization of this contrast function is a valid estimation method. If the sources are all sub-Gaussian, we switch the sign and choose $G_i(\hat{s}) = -\hat{s}^4$, which becomes again a valid contrast.

Function $G_i(\cdot)$ is implicitly expressed in the algorithm via its derivative, a nonlinearity $g_i(\cdot)$; that corresponding to $G_i(\hat{s}) = -\log\cosh\hat{s}$ is the hyperbolic tangent function (tanh).

FastICA is an efficient fixed point based algorithm. For a given sample of the prewhitened vectors z, an iteration is defined as follows:

1. Take a random initial vector w_0 of norm 1. Let $k = 1$.
2. Let $w_k = E\{z(w_{k-1}^T z)^3\} - 3w_{k-1}$. The expectation can be calculated using a sample of z vectors.
3. Divide w_k by its norm, i.e. $w_k = w_k / \|w_k\|$.
4. If $\|w_k - w_{k-1}\|$ is not small enough, let $k = k+1$ and go back to step 2. Otherwise, output the vector w_k.

The final vector w_k given by the algorithm separates one of the underlying factors in the sense that $w_k^T x'(t)$, $t = 1, 2, \ldots$ equals one of the factors. To separate m independent factors, we run this algorithm m times. To ensure that we separate each time a different factor, we use the deflation algorithm that adds a simple projection inside the loop. Recalling that the rows of the separating matrix W are orthonormal because of the prewhitening (sphering), we can separate the factors one-by-one by projecting the current estimate w_k on the space orthogonal to the rows of the separating matrix W previously found.

4. Experiments with Separating Independent Factors Underlying Foreign Exchange Rates

In our experiments, 8 parallel series of foreign exchange rates w.r.t. Romanian currency are used. We start by supposing that there are some independent components, closely tied to the evolution of the currencies that affect their co-movement, such as macroeconomic fundamentals, extraneous influences, interest rates, psychological factors, and so on. The ICA transformation tends to produce component signals that are more structured and regular. We actually use FastICA, a computationally efficient fixed point based algorithm for performing ICA estimations. Figure 1 shows 8 original foreign exchange series (mixtures, before preprocessing). As we easily can see, the time series are clearly non-stationary and present some trends.

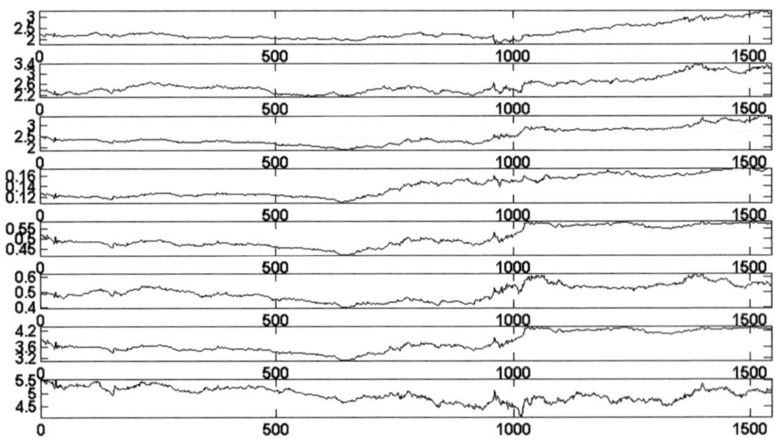

Figure 1. Original foreign exchange series (mixtures).

Figure 2 shows the 8 series, after centering and whitening. Clearly, after preprocessing, the time series become stationary. Whitening uses the eigenvalue decomposition (EVD) of the covariance matrix of centered data. Figure 3 shows the 8 eigenvalues. The contribution in percents of the first 3 eigenvalues is: λ_1 : 70.181%; λ_2 : 13.004%; λ_3: 7.0641. Their cumulate contribution is 90.25%.

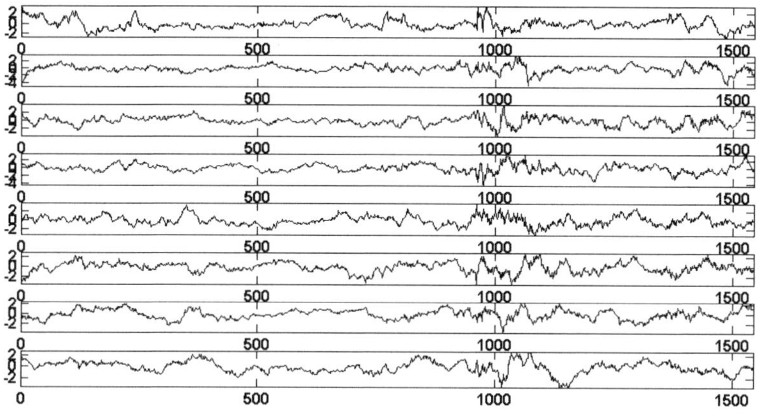

Figure 2. Foreign exchange series after centering and whitening.

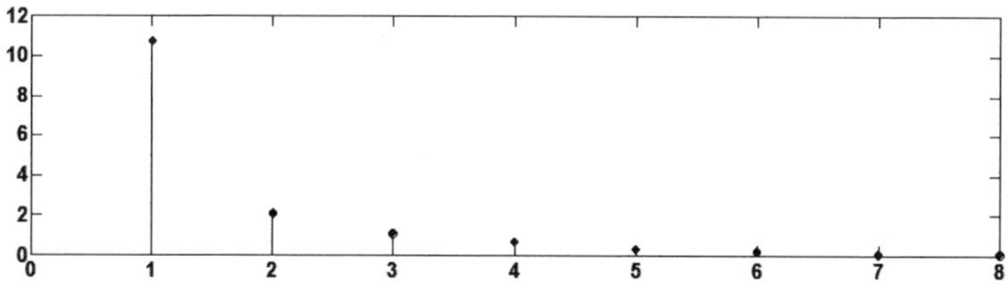

Figure 3. Eigenvalues of the covariance matrix of centered data.

The first 8 independent components are shown in Fig. 4. As one can see, they have very distinct shapes. By contrast with the original time series, which display similar shapes, due to common influences affecting their co-movement, one can see that the independent components have very distinctive shapes, corresponding to mutually different factors.

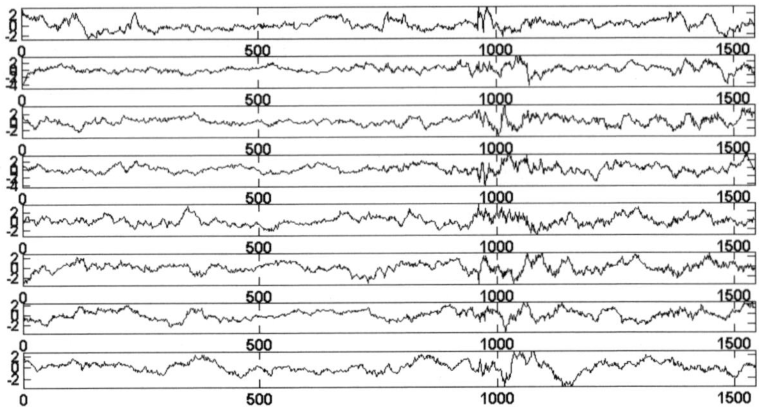

Figure 4. Independent components.

Now, let us reconstruct the original mixtures starting from the independent component estimates $\hat{s}$ and using the mixing matrix A, i.e., $\hat{z} = A\hat{s}$. Aditionally, we can apply to $\hat{z}$ the de-whitening matrix $E\,D^{1/2}$ in order to reconstruct the centered data, i.e., $\hat{y} = E\,D^{1/2}\,\hat{z}$, and finally to add the mean, i.e. $\hat{x} = \hat{y} + m_x$. Our experiments show that the reconstruction is absolutely exact for all these time series, i.e., $\hat{z} = z$, $\hat{y} = z$ and finally $\hat{x} = x$.

The independent components we have separated are really more structured and regular, representing distinctive influence sources.

However, they are still somewhat noisy.

There are many alternative techniques for denoising time series. For instance, performing a wavelet decomposition through wavelet shrinkage and thresholding method, developed by David Donoho, is probably the most popular option.

Denoising can be also carried out by a powerful method called Singular-Spectrum Analysis. Singular Spectrum Analysis (SSA) is a nonparametric method for time series structure recognition and identification. The SSA algorithm has two basic stages: decomposition and reconstruction. Basically, it first builds the trajectory matrix associated to a time series, whose columns are formed by a sequence o lagged vectors extracted from the time series with a sliding window. Afterward, the *singular value decomposition* is applied to the trajectory matrix. For the reconstruction of the denoised part of the time series the most dominant eigenvalues are considered, whereas the rest of eigenvalues are used to compute the residuals.

Figure 5 shows the denoised representation and the corresponding residuals for the first independent component.

The ultimate goal in using ICA is to predict financial time series observed as some mixture signals by first going to the ICA space (spanned by the independent components), doing the prediction there, and then transforming back to the original time series. The prediction can be done separately and with a different method for each independent component, depending on its time structure.

There are two ways to forecast with ICA.

In the first approach, the idea is to compute the *h-step ahead* forecast of x_t regression on s_t and some lagged factors.

$$x_{t+h} = \alpha_h + \sum_{j=1}^{N} \beta_{j,h} \hat{s}_{t+h-j} + e_{t+h}, \quad t = 1,\ldots,T-h \tag{4}$$

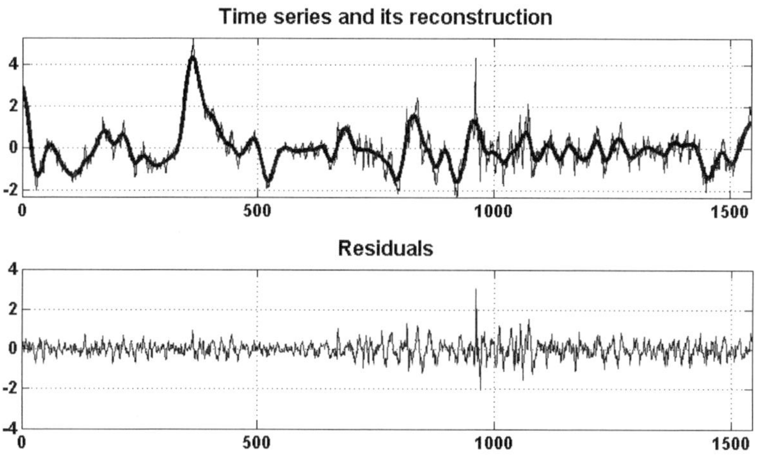

Figure 5. Denoised independent component and its residuals.

We estimate the fundamental factors by ICA, using the historical data.

The factors and their lags are used to forecast x_t by the following linear regression model:

$$\hat{x}_{t+h|T} = \hat{\alpha}_h + \sum_{j=1}^{N} \hat{\beta}_{j,h} \hat{s}_{t+h-j|T} + e_{t+h} \tag{5}$$

where h is the forecast time horizon, and the regression coefficients, $\{\alpha_h, \beta_{j,h}\}$ are estimated by OLS.

In the second approach, the idea is to forecast in the space of the latent factors (using an auto-projective technique) and then transform back to the original data. The three steps of the procedure are the following:

We estimate the common factors, by ICA, of x_t, and simultaneously we find the coefficient of the mixing matrix, A.

We fit an ARIMA model to each component and we compute, separately, the *h-step-ahead* forecast of each factor,

$$\left\{\hat{s}_{j,T+h|T}\right\}_{j=1}^{T} \tag{6}$$

We obtain the forecasts for the observed data multiplying the forecasts for each component by the corresponding weights:

$$\hat{x}_{T+h|T} = \hat{A}\,\hat{s}_{T+h|T} \tag{7}$$

Further experimental results are equally interesting, but need more room for details. In order to present them, an extended version of this paper is intended.

5. Conclusion

Financial time series can be viewed as mixtures of several distinct underlying factors. This paper uses Independent Components Analysis for revealing fundamental factors behind several parallel series of foreign exchange rates, in an attempt to produce more structured and regular representations and more accurate predictions.

References

1. A.D. Back and A.S. Weigend, A first application of independent component analysis to extracting structure from stock returns. *International journal of neural systems*, 8(4) , 473–484 (1997).
2. A.J. Bell, and T.J. Sejnowski, An information-maximization approach to blind separation and blind deconvolution. *Neural computation*, 7, 1129–1159 (1995).
3. A. Cichocki, and S. Amari, *Adaptive blind signal and image processing – learning algorithms and applications*. London, John Wiley & Sons (2002).
4. N. Goljadina, V. Nekrutkin, A. Zhigljavky, *Analysis of Time Series Structure: SSA and related techniques*, London: Chapman and Holl (2001).

5. A. Hyvärinen, J. Karhunen and E. Oja, *Independent component analysis*. New York, John Wiley & Sons (2001).
6. S. G. Mallat, G. Peyré, *A Wavelet Tour of Signal Processing: The Sparse Way*, Academic Press, 3rd Edition (2009).

METHODOLOGICAL STRUCTURE FOR THE AGGREGATION OF MUNICIPALITIES UNDER UNCERTAINTY CONDITIONS: THE CASE OF MICHIOACAN, MEXICO

VICTOR G. ALFARO – GARCÍA

Department of Business Administration, University of Barcelona, Av. Diagonal 690, Barcelona, 08034, Spain.

ANNA M. GIL – LAFUENTE

Department of Business Administration, University of Barcelona, Av. Diagonal 690, Barcelona, 08034, Spain.

GERARDO G. ALFARO – CALDERÓN

Facultad de Contaduría y Ciencias Administrativas, Universidad Michoacana de San Nicolas de Hidalgo, Av. Francisco J. Mujica S/N Edificio AII Col. Felicitas del Rio, Morelia, 58030, México.

Through the last years, there has been an increasing interest for accelerating the economic, social and environmental development of cities through associations, organization and creation of synergies. Our investigation pretends to apply administration models for the analysis and treatment of variables, combinatory processes and affinity models, which could find the most similar municipalities of one region. The results obtained by this study pretend to support projects in order to increase the regional development of the Latin-American State of Michoacán, México. Through the model, process and results we look forward to offer a strategic proposal for associations between similar municipalities, by doing this action, we try to fill the gap that is found in the field of analysing the present frames of associations, which are mainly driven by empirical decisions. In order to achieve this task we will use tools for the treatment of fuzzy sets theory, evaluating related elements and finding similarities between municipalities under the Pichat algorithm.

1. Introduction

The investigation about the regional development of the State of Michoacán de Ocampo grows from the profound changes that the emergent economies have suffered in present years. It is in this complex reality, where different factors such as globalization, open markets, creative economies, and innovation play different roles in the development of cities and regions; therefore the adoption of decisions under uncertainty has gained special relevance. These kinds of studies and research have been increasing since the last century, and have proven efficacy while dealing with complex phenomena.

In relation to the theory of decision under uncertainty, the investigation initializes with the theory of Fuzzy Sets (Zadeh, 1965), with the appearance of the article "Fuzzy sets. Information and Control", made by the professor Lofti Zadeh, instructor at the university of Berkeley. The theory of Fuzzy Sets has been applied in the field of the formal sciences, but in the past 43 years, researchers from all around the world have been publishing many research studies with applications in diverse fields of knowledge.

The intention of this work is to classify and group, with a certain level of significance, different municipalities of the State of Michoacán de Ocampo, which could by the association, organization and creation of synergies, increase their competitiveness as a whole. The method to classify and group these municipalities will have as a basis the known Pichat Algorithm (Pichat, 1970), and the theory of fuzzy sets. These approximations allow us to create a generalized model adapted to the conditions of expectancy and instability.

2. Preliminaries

This section tries to engage the reader in the general aspects of this study. In order to do so, we introduce some aspects of the origins of the theories that support our investigation, basic description of the region in which our investigation is oriented, municipalities in which we will focus attention and the methodology that we will follow through our research.

2.1. Origins

The origins of this study rely on the importance and relevance that emerging economies thus, emergent cities are exhibiting. Moreover the positive impact which studies in Regions and Mega Regions present, in which finding the connections, relations, and similarities that exist between some cities could generate synergies and raise the level of competitiveness of the cities. These efforts in organization and synergy should exert benefits in the economical, social and environmental realm by producing greater effects than the sum of the individual efforts of the cities.

In the publication "The Creative Cities" Florida (2008) the concept of region and mega – region is described as a "new natural economical unit: it is not an artifact of political frontiers, such as the concept of State – Nation or their provinces, but the product of the concentration of innovation centers, production and consumer markets." He also explains the technical considerations of the mega – region, which has to be an area of contiguous light with more than one city or important metropolitan region and produce more than 100,000 million of dollars in terms of LRP (Light Regional Production).

In the article "Cities and Competitiveness" (Begg, 1999) the concept of competitiveness and its relationship with the city is analyzed. As the author describes, there are different definitions related to the concept, but what is a fact is that "the capacity of a city to compete is made by the connections between attributes of localization, strengths and weaknesses of the enterprises that reside in it". This idea leads us to understand the link that unifies the competitiveness of a city and starts the discussion of knowing and finding the differentials that cause the diverse capacity of growth, which has been shown, varies among cities.

In this investigation we maintain an approach to these theories, which will lead us to obtain the variables that will be used to formulate the model and sustain our results, we now proceed to present the studied region.

2.2. Studied Region

A total of 32 States integrate the United Mexican States, 31 of them are free and sovereign entities, which have the right of having an own constitution and legislative powers. The last State is the federal District territory under the share dominance of the Mexican Federation and the local government entities.

The State of Michoacán de Ocampo occupies the 3.0% of the National territory with a surface of 58,599 km2, it has a total population of 4,351,037 habitants from which 2,248928 are women, and 2,102,109 are men. The State presents a distribution of 69% of urban locations and 31% of rural locations. In terms of schooling it is observed that from every 100 people: 10.7 do not have access to education, 61.8 have the primary education, 0.4 have a technical or commercial primary school, 4.8 have finalized the high school, 11.8 have concluded university, 0.5 is not specified. In the State 92% of the population is considered catholic, less than 3% of the population speaks a native language. In 2010 there were 1,066,061 private homes, from which: 87.7%, have access to potable water, 88.6%, have access to drainage 98.0% counts with electricity. The main economic indicators present that the State provides 2.5 % to the GDP being the activity of commerce the most relevant one, the primary sector provides 11.27% of the State GDP, the secondary activities provide the 19.97% to the State GDP and the third sector of economic activities provide 68.76% to the State GDP.

2.3. Municipalities

In this study we will take 12 of the whole 113 municipalities that the studied region concentrate, we chose these municipalities due to the level of economical importance and the amount of people that reside in them. Almost 50% of the total population of the State lives in these 12 municipalities; therefore the importance of these localities and the interest in focus our attention on them. It is important to mention that this study can be expanded and could in further research add more cities to advance in the knowledge of synergies that could be applied in the whole region.

The municipalities chosen to be analyzed in our methodology are: Morelia, Uruapan, Zamora, Lázaro Cárdenas, Zitácuaro, Apatzingán, Hidalgo, La Piedad, Pátzcuaro, Maravatío, Tarímbaro and Zacapu.

Each of the municipalities chosen present different attributes, culture, population, economical drivers, education levels, etc. Those attributes are precisely what we need to analyze in order to obtain the most affine cities, and the possible connections that could raise the competitiveness of them.

2.4. Methodology

Due to the complexity of the nature that we are trying to analyze, the use of the fuzzy sets theory and the theory of affinities are approaches that in general terms will lead our investigation. The methodology that will be employed in order to obtain the affinity between the municipalities chosen will be:

2.4.1. Acquisition of Variables

In general terms is the proposition of variables that are relevant to each municipality; these variables concentrate economical, social, cultural, political and environmental data which gives a general overview of the city and its main drivers. The variables chosen are presented in section 3 of this study.

2.4.2. Measurement of the municipalities regarding the variables found

Each municipality due to its inherent characteristics will be evaluated through a linguistic tag between 0 and 1 in which:

1,0: Excellent performance
0,9: Great performance
0,8: Really good performance
0,7: Good performance

0,6: Rather a better tan a poor performance
0,5: Nor a good or poor performance
0,4: Rather a poor tan a good performance
0,3: Poor performance
0,2: Really poor performance
0,1: Worst performance
0,0: Disastrous performance

2.4.3. Finding distances between municipalities

In this analysis we will use a whether known concept: Hamming's relative distance. In order to obtain Hamming's relative distance between two sets of fuzzy sets, the general procedure is to subtract the existent levels in each criteria, add those differences in absolute values and divide the sum by the number of criteria chosen, so the final result would be numbers between 0 and 1.

$$\delta(\tilde{A},\tilde{B}) = \sum_{i=1}^{n} |\mu_{A}(x_i) - \mu_{B}(x_i)| \qquad (1)$$

$donde\ x_i \in X, \forall i = 1,\dots,n\ y\ 0 \leq d(\tilde{A},\tilde{B}) \leq n$

2.4.4. Matrix of distances

With the results obtained by the Hamming's relative distance, we now proceed to create a matrix in which the symmetrical and anti-reflexive relationship between the elements is stated.

2.4.5. Matrix of similarities

In this step we create another matrix known as the similarity relationship, in which we just state the complementarity to the unit of the matrix of differences.

2.4.6. Maximum similarity associations: Pichat Algorythm

In order to get the maximum similarity associations we will use the Pichat Algorythm (Pichat, 1970). The main products of the Pichat Algorythm are sub-matrixes, which allow us to identify the main groups of entities that reveal the greater similarities. These are the main steps to follow:

1. The starting point comes from the existence or creation of a Boolean relation of similarity.
2. From that relation (matrix) we consider only the part above the main diagonal.
3. From the matrix we only take into account the zeros in each line, multiplying the elements from those columns in which zeros are presented. Then we proceed to make a Boolean addition of the element from the line with the last product.
4. The additions have to follow the next rules: the process excludes the lines without zeros. During the process of addition, whether in the sum appears an element in two terms and one of those is isolated, the addition is substituted by the element.

   Therefore: $a + abc = a \; (because \; a + abc = a(1 + bc) = a \cdot 1 = a)$

5. Finally we get an addition of elements. For each one it is necessary to obtain the complementary element in relation to the reference of elements. Each of those complementary elements is the maximum sub-matrixes of similarity.

2.4.7.Aggregation and Results

The final step in our methodology is the process of making groups out of the similar municipalities and obtaining results, these results have to be explained.

3. Preliminaries

In this section we state the variables that will be used in our methodology, all of the variables were chosen to create a basis in which they reflected the reality in different aspects of the municipality. As we stated in the methodology they were evaluated from 0 to 1, and it is necessary to mention that the evaluation was supported by data collected form the National Database of Statistics and Regional Plans of development from the municipalities. It is important to mention that these variables are not exhaustive and they have been treated with the same level of importance, we are presently working on further investigation, in which the nature of the variables and the importance of them affect, and apply certain weights in the model.

3.1. Introduced variables

3.1.1 Integration of the Population: The level in which the population of the city is merged. Whether the integration is higher, the better evaluation gets. This index comprehends elements like: Native population, Level of immigrants, Number of religions professed, and Digital centers of integration.

3.1.2 Infrastructures of the city: The level in which the infrastructure of the city provides support to the communities. This index comprehends elements like: Number of schools, hospitals, health centers, sport units, airports, highways, post offices, railroads, ports, toll free roads, and telecommunication centers.

3.1.3 Public Services: The level in which the municipalities offer public services, the major coverage of the services, the higher index level it gets. This index comprehends elements like: percentage of coverage of electricity, water and drainage.

3.1.4 Tourism: The level in which the city attracts and provides services for tourists. This index comprehends elements like: Touristic centers, tourists attracted, crafts, and local festivities.

3.1.5 Recreation: the level in which the city provides special zones for the people to make sports, recreational activities and creative zones. This index comprehends elements like: Number of stadiums, sport clubs, cultural houses, museums, parks.

3.1.6 Political alternation: the level in which the Political party is changed from period to period in the last 5 periods. The major changes give a higher index.

3.1.7 Education. The level in which the city enhances education policies. This index comprehends elements like: percentage of the population with a bachelors degree, percentage of the population with a postgraduate degree, level of literacy, number of teachers and amount of schools and universities in the location.

3.1.8 Active population: The level in which the population is inserted in economical activities, as a percentage of the whole working force of the location.

3.1.9 Minimum wage: Percentage of the population that aspires for more than 2 minimum wages per day of labor.

3.1.10 Marginality: Level in which the community is catalogued as a marginal zone or not.

3.1.11 Economy of the zone: Level in which the economical drivers of the city relies on the first, second or third economic units.

3.1.12 Technology: Level in which the community utilizes and develops technology. This index comprehends elements like: Number of high technology industries, number of patents registered.

3.1.13 Human development index: The level in which the UNCTAD catalogues the HDI for each municipality.

3.1.14 Security: The level in which the security is perceived in the locality. This index comprehends elements like: number of offenses presented in the municipality, rate of people with a condemnatory sentence.

3.2. Evaluation matrix

In this section we present the evaluation matrix, in which we assigned levels between 0 and 1 to the different municipalities and for the different variables that we stated before. This process is explained in step 2.4.2 of our methodology. The results we obtained are the following:

Table 1: Evaluation Matrix (Source: National Institute of Statistics and Geography 2012, Enciclopedia de los Municipios de México 2011)

	Integration	Infraestructure	Public Services	Tourism	Recreation	Political Alternance	Education	Active Population
Morelia	0.8	0.9	0.8	1	1	0.8	0.9	1
Uruapan	0.8	0.7	0.6	0.8	0.4	0.3	0.8	0.8
Zamora	0.4	0.4	0.7	0.4	0.1	0.3	0.5	0.8
Lázaro Cárdenas	0.7	0.6	0.4	0.5	0.3	0.3	0.6	0.8
Zitácuaro	0.8	0.4	0.2	0.2	0.1	1	0.6	0.3
Apatzingán	0.4	0.3	0.8	0.3	0.3	0.3	0.2	0.8
Hidalgo	0.4	0.3	0.3	0.4	0.1	0.3	0.3	0.3
La Piedad	0.3	0.3	0.9	0.4	0.1	0.1	0.4	0.8
Pátzcuaro	0.4	0.3	0.3	0.8	0.1	0.3	0.4	0.3
Maravatío	0.3	0.3	0.2	0.3	0.1	0.3	0.2	0.1
Tarímbaro	0.1	0.3	0.8	0.1	0.1	1	0.2	0.3
Zacapu	0.4	0.3	0.8	0.4	0.1	1	0.3	0.3

	Minimum Wage	Marginality	Primary Sector	Secondary Sector	Third Sector	Technology	HDI	Security
Morelia	0.8	1	0.1	0.3	1	0.8	1	0.6
Uruapan	0.8	1	0.3	0.3	0.8	0.3	0.7	0.7
Zamora	0.8	0.8	0.8	0.3	0.8	0.1	0.7	0.7
Lázaro Cárdenas	1	0.8	0.3	0.8	0.8	0.9	0.8	0.8
Zitácuaro	0.3	0.1	0.8	0.3	0.3	0.8	0.3	0.8
Apatzingán	0.8	0.3	0.8	0.1	0.8	0.1	0.3	0.7
Hidalgo	0.3	0.1	0.3	1	0.3	0.1	0.3	0.6
La Piedad	0.8	0.8	0.3	0.8	0.8	0.8	0.8	0.6
Pátzcuaro	0.3	0.3	0.3	0.8	0.8	0.3	0.3	0.6
Maravatío	0	0.1	1	0.3	0.3	0.3	0.2	0.8
Tarímbaro	0.3	0.1	0.8	0.3	0.1	0.1	0.3	0.7
Zacapu	0.8	0.8	0.3	0.8	0.8	0.8	0.8	0.7

4. Procedure

In this section we introduce the procedure and main matrixes we obtained following the steps mentioned in the methodology in order to identify the affinities between the municipalities we chose. All of the next are results from working the evaluation matrix.

4.1. Distance matrix

Applying the Hamming relative distance stated in step 2.4.3 of our methodology, we obtain:

	Morelia	Uruapan	Zamora	Lázaro Cárdenas	Zitácuaro	Apatzingán	Hidalgo	La Piedad	Pátzcuaro	Maravatío	Tarímbaro	Zacapu
Morelia	0.00	0.21	0.36	0.30	0.48	0.44	0.58	0.34	0.48	0.64	0.58	0.34
Uruapan	0.21	0.00	0.17	0.17	0.40	0.26	0.38	0.24	0.28	0.43	0.46	0.29
Zamora	0.36	0.17	0.00	0.21	0.33	0.12	0.29	0.16	0.26	0.30	0.29	0.21
Lázaro Cárdenas	0.30	0.17	0.21	0.00	0.36	0.31	0.34	0.15	0.28	0.44	0.50	0.20
Zitácuaro	0.48	0.40	0.33	0.36	0.00	0.33	0.24	0.41	0.28	0.19	0.18	0.31
Apatzingán	0.44	0.26	0.12	0.31	0.33	0.00	0.26	0.24	0.24	0.24	0.22	0.28
Hidalgo	0.58	0.38	0.29	0.34	0.24	0.26	0.00	0.29	0.10	0.18	0.21	0.28
La Piedad	0.34	0.24	0.16	0.15	0.41	0.24	0.29	0.00	0.24	0.40	0.40	0.11
Pátzcuaro	0.48	0.28	0.26	0.28	0.28	0.24	0.10	0.24	0.00	0.23	0.29	0.24
Maravatío	0.64	0.43	0.39	0.44	0.19	0.24	0.18	0.40	0.23	0.00	0.19	0.39
Tarímbaro	0.58	0.46	0.29	0.50	0.18	0.22	0.21	0.40	0.29	0.19	0.00	0.30
Zacapu	0.34	0.29	0.21	0.20	0.31	0.28	0.28	0.11	0.24	0.39	0.30	0.00

4.2. Similarities matrix

Applying the methodology stated in step 4.2.4 of our methodology, we obtain:

	Morelia	Uruapan	Zamora	Lázaro Cárdenas	Zitácuaro	Apatzingán	Hidalgo	La Piedad	Pátzcuaro	Maravatío	Tarímbaro	Zacapu
Morelia	1.00	0.79	0.64	0.70	0.52	0.56	0.43	0.66	0.53	0.36	0.43	0.66
Uruapan	0.79	1.00	0.83	0.83	0.60	0.74	0.62	0.76	0.72	0.57	0.54	0.71
Zamora	0.64	0.83	1.00	0.79	0.67	0.88	0.71	0.84	0.74	0.70	0.71	0.79
Lázaro Cárdenas	0.70	0.83	0.79	1.00	0.64	0.69	0.66	0.85	0.73	0.56	0.50	0.80
Zitácuaro	0.52	0.60	0.67	0.64	1.00	0.68	0.76	0.59	0.72	0.81	0.82	0.69
Apatzingán	0.56	0.74	0.88	0.69	0.68	1.00	0.74	0.76	0.76	0.76	0.78	0.72
Hidalgo	0.43	0.62	0.71	0.66	0.76	0.74	1.00	0.71	0.90	0.83	0.79	0.73
La Piedad	0.66	0.76	0.84	0.85	0.59	0.76	0.71	1.00	0.76	0.60	0.60	0.89
Pátzcuaro	0.53	0.72	0.74	0.73	0.72	0.76	0.90	0.76	1.00	0.78	0.71	0.76
Maravatío	0.36	0.57	0.61	0.56	0.81	0.76	0.83	0.60	0.78	1.00	0.81	0.61
Tarímbaro	0.43	0.54	0.71	0.50	0.82	0.78	0.79	0.60	0.71	0.81	1.00	0.70
Zacapu	0.66	0.71	0.79	0.80	0.69	0.72	0.73	0.89	0.76	0.61	0.70	1.00

4.3. Maximum similarity associations: Pichat's Algorithm

Continuing with our methodology we now proceed to generate the Algorithm using a significance level of $\alpha = 0.70$, this means we will take as part of the procedure only those elements in the similarity matrix, which exceed the 0.70. We then obtain the next binary matrix:

	a	b	c	d	e	f	g	h	i	j	k	l
a	1.00	1.00	0.00	0.00	0.00	0.00	0.00	0.00	0.00	0.00	0.00	0.00
b		1.00	1.00	1.00	0.00	1.00	0.00	1.00	1.00	0.00	0.00	1.00
c			1.00	1.00	0.00	1.00	1.00	1.00	1.00	0.00	1.00	1.00
d				1.00	0.00	0.00	0.00	1.00	1.00	0.00	0.00	1.00
e					1.00	0.00	1.00	0.00	1.00	1.00	1.00	0.00
f						1.00	1.00	1.00	1.00	1.00	1.00	1.00
g							1.00	1.00	1.00	1.00	1.00	1.00
h								1.00	1.00	0.00	0.00	1.00
i									1.00	1.00	1.00	1.00
j										1.00	1.00	0.00
k											1.00	0.00
l												1.00

We proceed to develop the algorithm and the next equation as we stated in the methodology.

$$S=(a+\dot{b}cdefghijkl)\bullet(b+\dot{e}gjk)\bullet(c+\dot{e}j)\bullet \\ (d+\dot{e}fgjk)\bullet(e+\dot{f}hl)\bullet(h+\dot{j}k)\_(j+\dot{l})\bullet(k+\dot{l}) \tag{2}$$

We obtain the next aggrupation:

$$S' = fgi+\dot{a}b+\dot{e}gi+\dot{c}fghi+\dot{b}cfhi+\dot{c}fgik+\dot{f}gijk+\dot{e}gijk \tag{3}$$

As a way to ascertain the results obtained before, we now present the sub – matrixes of each association, in which is easy to observe that all the elements inside are above the level of significance of $\propto = 0.70$.

	f	g	i
f	1.00	0.74	0.76
g		1.00	0.90
i			1.00

	a	b
b	1.00	0.79
b		1.00

	e	g	i
e	1.00	0.76	0.72
g		1.00	0.90
i			1.00

	c	f	g	h	i
c	1.00	0.88	0.71	0.84	0.74
f		1.00	0.74	0.76	0.76
g			1.00	0.71	0.90
h				1.00	0.76
i					1.00

	b	c	f	h	i
b	1.00	0.83	0.74	0.76	0.72
c		1.00	0.88	0.84	0.74
f			1.00	0.76	0.76
h				1.00	0.76
i					1.00

	b	c	d	h	i
b	1.00	0.83	0.83	0.76	0.72
c		1.00	0.79	0.84	0.74
d			1.00	0.85	0.73
h				1.00	0.76
i					1.00

	c	f	g	i	k
c	1.00	0.88	0.71	0.74	0.71
f		1.00	0.74	0.76	0.78
g			1.00	0.90	0.79
i				1.00	0.71
k					1.00

	f	g	i	j	k
f	1.00	0.74	0.76	0.76	0.78
g		1.00	0.90	0.83	0.79
i			1.00	0.78	0.71
j				1.00	0.81
k					1.00

	e	g	i	j	k
e	1.00	0.76	0.72	0.81	0.82
g		1.00	0.90	0.83	0.79
i			1.00	0.78	0.71
j				1.00	0.81
k					1.00

4.4. Aggregation and results

Consequently to the results of the Pichat algorithm, the most similar municipalities in the State of Michoacán, México are aggregated as follows:

1)(f, g, i): Apatzingán, Hidalgo, Pátzcuaro.
2)(a, b): Morelia, Uruapan.
3)(e, g, i): Zitácuaro, Hidalgo, Pátzcuaro.
4)(c, f, g, h, i): Zamora, Apatzingán, Hidalgo, La Piedad, Pátzcuaro.
5)(b, c, f, h i): Uruapan, Zamora, Apatzingán La Piedad, Pátzcuaro.
6)(b, c, d, h, i): Uruapan, Zamora, Lázaro Cárdenas La Piedad, Pátzcuaro.
7)(c, f, g, i, k): Zamora, Apatzingán, Hidalgo, Maravatío, Tarímbaro.
8)(f, g, i, j, k): Apatzingán, Hidalgo, Pátzcuaro, Maravatio, Tarímbaro.
9)(e, g, i, j, k): Zitácuaro, Hidalgo, Pátzcuaro, Maravatío, Tarímbaro.

These municipalities have shown high affinity under the variables proposed. We can assure with a high level of statistical certainty that they share common aspects which could be used in order to create synergies between them, although further research is been developing in the creation of different scenarios in which their affinities could be linked and aid the growth of economical, social and environmental sectors, therefore this research pretends to be leverage for further analyses.

5. Conclusion

Through the process and methodology stated in this study, we have obtained the most similar municipalities that share common factors, by associating, organizing and creating synergies between these municipalities the State of Michoacán de Ocampo, could increase the probability of success in major plans that associate different relative elements. By knowing the most affine municipalities, the State should be able to target specific resources to promote positive social and economical development to the region. This analysis contributes to the improvement of emergent city's economies and could be replicated in similar regions to associate different municipalities and increase the benefits of programs, plans and projects of the State.

References

1.J. Allen, The cultural economies of cities. International Journal of Urban and Regional Research, 21, pp. 323–339. Doi: 10.1111/1468-2427.00075 (1997).

2.I. Begg, Cities and competitiveness. Urban Studies, 36, pp. 795-809 (1999).

3.M. Castells, Globalisation, Networking, Urbanisation: Reflections on the Spatial Dynamics of the Information Age. Urban Studies, 47, pp. 2737-2745 (2010).

4.P. Costa, Magalhães M, Vasconcelos B, Sugahara G, On 'creative cities' governance models: a comparative approach, The Service Industries Journal, 28:3, pp. 393-413 (2008).

5.R. Florida, The rise of the creative class. Basic Books, USA (2002).

6.R. Florida, Mellander C, Stolarick K, Inside the black box of regional development – human capital, the creative class and tolerance. Journal of economical geography, 8, pp. 615-649 (2008).

7.R. Florida, Who's your city?, Basic Books, USA (2008).

8.Gobierno del Estado de Michoacán. Enciclopedia de los Municipios (2011).

9.J. Gil-Aluja, Elements for a theory of decision under uncertainty, Kluwer Academic Publishers, Dordrecht (1999).

10.A.M. Gil-Lafuente, Fuzzy logic in financial analysis, Springer, Berlin (2005).

11.A.M. Gil-Lafuente, and J.M. Merigó, Acquisition of financial products that adapt to different environments, Lectures on Modelling and Simulation, 7, pp. 42-48 (2006).

12.J. Gil-Lafuente, The index of maximum and minimum level in the selection of players in sport management (in Spanish), In: Proceedings of the 10th International Conference of the European Academy of Management and Business Economics (AEDEM), Reggio Calabria, Italy, pp. 439-443 (2001).

13. J. Gil-Lafuente, Algorithms for revision . Keys for being revision in sport management (in Spanish), Ed. Milladoiro, Vigo. (2002).
14. E. Graeme, Creative cities, creative spaces and urban policy. Urban Studies, 46, pp. 5-6 (2009).
15. P. Hall, Creative cities and economic development. Urban Studies, 4, pp. 639-649 (2000).
16. A. Kaufmann and J. Gil Aluja, Modelos para la Investigación de efectos olvidados. Milladoiro. Santiago de Compostela, España (1988).
17. C. Landry and F. Bianchini, The creative city. Demos, London (1995).
18. A. Pratt, Creative cities: the cultural industries and the creative class. Geografiska Annaler: Series B, Human Geography, 90, pp. 107–117 (2008).
19. Programa de las Naciones Unidas para el Desarrollo. Informe sobre el desarrollo humano Michoacán. Producción Creativa. 2008.
20. A. Scott, Creative cities: conceptual issues and policy questions. Journal of Urban Affairs, 28, pp. 1-17 (2006).
21. A. Klimova, Agrupaciones económicas de las regiones de la Federación Rusa mediante métodos matemáticos en condiciones de incertidumbre. Universidad de Barcelona (2009).

NEW PRODUCT DEVELOPMENT RISK MANAGEMENT AND DECISION-MAKING: THE USE OF REAL OPTIONS

HENRIQUE MARTINS ROCHA

FER, Associação Educacional Dom Bosco – AEDB & Universidade do Estado do Rio de Janeiro – UERJ, Av. Darci Ribeiro no. 2535
Resende, RJ, 27523-000, Brazil

MAURÍCIO CÉSAR DELAMARO

FEG, Universidade Estadual Paulista, Av. Ariberto Pereira da Cunha, 333
Guaratinguetá, SP, 12.516-410, Brazil

LIGIA MARIA FONSECA AFFONSO

Master's Student, Centro Universitário Volta Redonda, Av. Gal. Affonseca, 1026/104
Resende, RJ, 27520-173, Brazil

Companies must continuously develop new products to achieve and sustain a strategic position in a fierce market. But developing new products involves a lot of risk and uncertainty on profit and losses. In the present article, the concept of real options theory is prospected and a model to use the real options in new product development (NPD) is proposed, so that financial aspects can be properly considered at each project phase of the product development. The real option valuation method is often presented as an alternative to the conventional net present value (NPV) approach. It is based on the same principals of financial options: the right to buy or sell financial values at a predetermined price, with no obligation to do so. In NPD, a multi-period approach that takes into account the flexibility of, for instance, being able to postpone prototyping and design decisions, waiting for more information about technologies, customer acceptance, funding, etc., is considered. Conclusion is that such model can provide more robustness to the decisions processes within NPD.

1. Introduction and Problem Definition

In the nowadays-competitive environment, companies must continuously develop new products to achieve and sustain a strategic position in a fierce market [3]. Competitiveness is based on developing and offering products and services that are recognized by customers as value-added possibilities. Therefore, new product development (NPD) decisions must be wisely made, no longer based on trial and error, because the changes occur more quickly than the lessons can be learned [32] [33].

Product development is the process of transforming market information into information required to the production of finished goods for commercial purposes [6]. Customer requirements, as well as other stakeholders' needs, such as financial, legal, environmental, operation management, etc., shall be managed by the NPD team in a complex balance analysis, in line with corporate strategy. Prior to developing a project, one must establish cost-objectives and perform value-engineering analysis, so that a combination of quality, functionality, and price desired by the customers can be incorporated to evaluate the profit feasibility [27]: there must be a compromise between the factors that add value to the product and those that cause cost increase [3].

Relevance

Companies need to introduce new products continuously, to prevent competitors from getting part of their market share. But, out of ten ideas about new products, three will be developed, 1.3 will be launched, and only one will be profitable [3] [44]. Research performed in the 90's showed that only 45% of companies were able to keep production costs within the budget and only 49% launched their products on schedule: on average, products cost 13% above the budget and are released six months late [3].

Therefore, it is critical to identify the connection between concepts of return and risk in NPD processes decision-making with better practices and models to help management to maximize the expected value of the investments in product development [33].

The present article purported to study NPD methodologies related to return and risk management, with the intent to maximize the expected return value of the investments in product development. Krishnan and Bhattacharya [22] approached to such proposal, suggesting a model to evaluate the optimal point to freeze technology through stochastic formulas.

Several methods have been proposed to financially evaluate projects, such as payback method, internal return rate (IRR), net present value (NPV), decision trees, etc. But the appropriate risk-adjusted discount rate is still virtually indeterminate. The real option valuation method is often presented as an alternative to the conventional net present value (NPV) approach. It is based on the same principals of financial options: the right to buy or sell stocks at a predetermined price, with no obligation to do so. Options associated with non-financial investment opportunities are called "real options", i.e., the right, but not the obligation, to take an action at a pre-determined cost, for a pre-determined period of time. In NPD, it might represent a multi-period approach that takes into account the flexibility of, for instance, being able to postpone prototyping and design decisions, waiting for more information about technologies, customer acceptance feedbacks, funding availability, etc.

2. Theoretical Foundations

The following theoretical references are briefly described ahead, in order to provide the necessary background to discuss the NPD decision process: project lifecycle, product lifecycle, and real options theory.

a. Project Lifecycle

Projects, defined as temporary efforts undertaken to create a product or service, have a certain degree of uncertainty. Therefore, organizations have better management control by dividing the project in stages (or phases), so that each stage is set by the conclusion of activities, in a tangible and verifiable form. The stages are linked, composing a logical sequence, called project lifecycle. The end of the lifecycle is reached when the project objectives are achieved [30].

NPD, which are ultimately projects, are usually broken into sequential phases, so that requirements can be checked against plans to evaluate the process alignment and trends towards the objectives. Checkpoints between phases involve "go/no go" decisions, leading the process towards later management decisions or terminating projects that do not offer good chances of revenue/profits to the company.

b. Product Lifecycle

Product lifecycles start after NPD (projects) are concluded. Many authors studied the product lifecycle [3] [18] [21] [31] [42]. Kotler [21] divides it in five periods: development, introduction, growth, maturity, and decline. According to author, during the development period of a new product, the company accumulates investments costs i.e., there is a cumulative negative cashflow, which are expected to be paid back along the next periods: The period of introduction is characterized by the launch of the product in the market, followed by an increase in sales and revenue (growth). After that, the product goes in a period of stability (maturity), and from this point on, sales and profits decline.

c. Real Options

In the corporate finance literature, the value of a risky project is calculated by the net present value (NPV) of its cashflows, discounted at a discount rate that reflects the project risk: such method is not able to capture the management flexibility along the decision-making process. The decision-making along the NPD requires that the existing options can be evaluated based on expected values earnings and involved risks.

This concept can be calculated by the Capital Asset Pricing Model (CAPM) [10] [15] [34]. The calculation establishes a discounting factor to be used in the analysis of an investment by its net present value (NPV): the discount tax is increased to compensate the existing risk. However, in the NPD, the risk variation has no linear relation with the expected returns: at phases transition, the project evaluation will drive to a decision whether the project goes on (if favourable conditions occur), requires changes (due to consumer needs changes, competition, technological change or a composition of diverse factors), or even be cancelled.

In markets characterized for competitive change, uncertainty and interactions, management has the flexibility to change operation strategy to capitalize favourable future chances or to minimize losses [39]. The probability of success in a project usually increases with the reduction of the inherent risk along the time [30]. Therefore, the deducted cashflow understates projects, because it ignores the main strategic questions in its analyses, which is: management does not have to accept a NPV calculation, positive or negative, unless an explanation to it exists [24]. Therefore, the CAPM becomes inadequate: some models are used to measure the return and risk in the process of decision making, mainly the Black & Scholes formulae and the binomial model, used in the financial market. However, these methodologies assume a passive managerial involvement and action [9], as shown in Fig. (1).

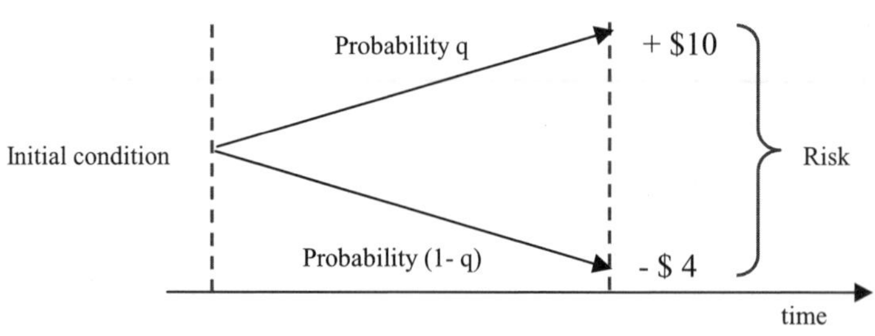

Fig. 1. Binomial model

Assuming an event along the NPD is to occur and result is unknown – a positive result (such as customer acceptance) will drive to a profit of \$10, while a negative result would drive to a loss of (\$4). The expected event value would be:

$$E(v) = 10.q + (-4).(1-q)$$

However, in the real world, the project manager would just abandon the project if the outcome of the event became unfavourable. Therefore, the loss would never happen, so, the expected event value would not have his negative portion, due to such managerial flexibility.

The real options fill this gap: based in contracts of options in the financial market, it becomes a powerful ally in the management process in risk conditions, since management flexibility is a possibility, but not obligation to modify a project in different stages of its operational life [26]. The decision on future investments is function of the expected profit when management action is taken and the cost to continue the project [37]. Copeland and Antikarov [7] describe the steps to use real options into project evaluation: 1) Calculate NPV; 2) Model uncertainty variables; 3) Incorporate decision flexibility – management decisions based in new incoming information; and 4) Recalculate NPV with flexibilities.

Management flexibility can be applied in many different situations, such as [9]:

- Option to wait: postpone an investment, benefiting by value favourable movements in the project (as increase on product prices), and preventing losses if unfavourable scenarios occur;
- Option to abandon (sell): abandonment of a project when future losses are foreseen and/or selling the project (for example, to another company);
- Option to expand: expand the operation scale of a project previously defined, if foreseen conditions are more favourable than initially revisio;
- Option to contract: opposite of the expansion option;
- Option to move: changes in conditions (for example, to restart operations), or changes of a product or technology; and
- Composed option: combination of any of the previous ones (called rainbow options).

Several applications of real options have been developed, such as digital cartographic bases (used for geo-marketing, urban zoning, environmental licensing, etc.) project evaluation [29]; reservoirs' decisions based on management flexibility [36]; project portfolio management [12] [13]; organizational restructure in merges and acquisitions [40]; forest projects [4]; and leasing contracts [25]. Many authors studied the use of real options to evaluate R&D prior to production investments [1] [2] [5] [8] [11] [14] [16] [19] [20] [23] [28] [35] [38] [39] [41] [43], while Keizer and Vos [17] describe a method to identify, measure and manage the risks in product development, however the decision-making process has not been revisio by the authors.

3. Proposed model for decision-making in NPD using real options

A complete NPD can be represented by its cashflow, based on expected investments and expenditures along the project phase and operational costs along the product lifecycle, as well as expected revenue during the product lifecycle. Those figures can be used to calculate the product NPV (i.e., the first step defined by Copeland and Antikarov [7], with no management flexibility).

Also, based on the budget and phases information, an event-tree is created, with all key decision-points along the NPD, as shown in Fig. (2).

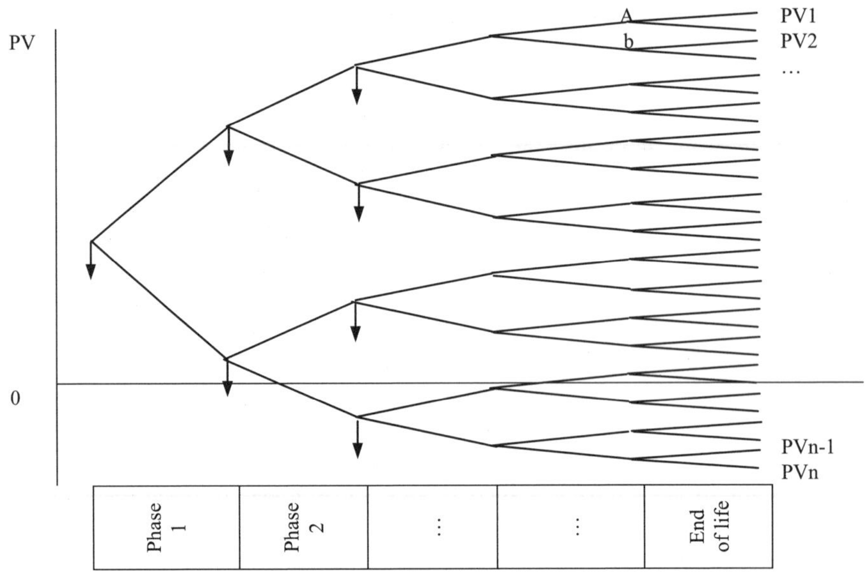

Figure 2. NPV event tree.

Then, management flexibility is incorporated in the event tree, transforming it in a decision-tree [7], by overruling alternatives were NPV would be reduced, due to negative values, to zero, so that the adjusted project NPV (adding flexibility benefits) would be calculated. A new calculated value goes back as an input to the previous event, i.e., to the next felt-side event along the tree and the calculation goes on until the very first decision point.

Decisions are made along the time, from "left to right", but calculation goes backwards. The calculation – "from right to the left" – in the whole decision-tree would mathematically represent the flexibility and management action since the very first NPD steps, as part of the decision-making process.

4. Final Considerations

The article proposes the use of real options for project phase assessment, as a tool to deal with uncertainty and to support management decision-making. Santiago and Bifano [37] described the use of the real options in the development of a laser ophthalmoscope, showing as the project can be managed by the estimate of its value and determining the management actions to be taken at each phase revision. However, the authors had only used of the options of continue, improve technology, and abandon the project at the last project phases, while the proposal of the present article is to use real options to evaluate all phases and explore all known potential type of options [9].

Therefore, a gap in real options application is identified, since uncertainty is present along the whole project and product lifecycles: it is recommended that companies developing new products to use real options at each NPD phase and along the whole product lifecycle.

References

1. J. Aken and A. Nagel, *Organizing and Managing the Fuzzy Front End of New Product Development*. Eindhoven Centre for Innovation Studies, The Netherlands, Working Paper 04.12, Department of Technology Management (2004).
2. G. Alesii, Rules of Thumb in Real Options Analysis, *Proceedings of Real Options: Theory Meets Practice*, 8th Annual International Conference, Montreal, Jun 17-19 (2004).
3. M. Baxter, *Product Design*: Practical methods for the systematic development of new products, Chapman and Hall, London, UK (1995).
4. W. Brobouski, Teoria das Opçoes Reais Aplicada a um Contrato de Parceria Florestal com Preço Minimo. *Proceedings of the XXVI SBPO*, Sao Joao del-Rei, Brazil (2004).
5. M. Chen and M, Iyigun, Generating Market Power via Strategic Product Development Delays, *Proceedings of the Econometrics Society Summer Meeting*, Providence, USA (2004).
6. K. Clark and T. Fujimoto, *Product Development Performance: Strategy, Organization, and Management in the World Auto Industry*, Boston: Harvard Business School Press (1991).

7. T. Copeland and V. Antikarov, *Opçoes Reais – Um Novo Paradigma para Reinventar a Avaliacao de Investimentos*, Campus, Rio de Janeiro, Brazil (2002).
8. T. Davila, *Performance and Design of Economics Incentives in New Product Development*, Research paper no. 1647, Graduate School of Business, Stanford University, USA (2000).
9. L. Figueiredo Neto, J. Manfrinato, and A. Crepaldi, Teoria das Opcoes reais: de que se esta falando? *Proceedings of the X SIMPEP*, Bauru, Brazil (2003).
10. L. Gitman and J. Madura, *Administracao Financeira – Uma Abordagem Gerencial*, Pearson, Sao Paulo, Brazil (2003).
11. S. Grenadier, *Investment under Uncertainty and Time-Inconsistent Preferences*, Research paper no. 1899, Graduate School of Business, Stanford University, USA (2005).
12. J. Gustafsson, *Portfolio Optimization Models for Project Valuation*, Ph.D. thesis – Department of Engineering Physics and Mathematics, Helsinki University of Technology, Helsinki, Finland (2005).
13. J. Gustafsson and A. Salo, *O.R.*, **53**, 946-956 (2005).
14. A. Heirman and B. Clarysse, *Do Intangible Assets and Pre-founding R&D Efforts Matter for Innovation Speed Start-ups?* Vlerick Leuven Gent Management School, Working Paper 2004/04, Ghent University, The Netherlands (2004).
15. M. Hoji, *Administracao Financeira: Uma Abordagem Pratica: Matematica Financeira Aplicada, Estrategias Financeiras, Analise, Planejamento e Controle Financeiro*, Atlas, Sao Paulo, Brazil (2004).
16. B. Kamrad and K. Ord, Market and Process Risks in Production Opportunities: Demand and Yield Uncertainty, *Proceedings of Real Options: Theory Meets Practice*, 7th Annual International Conference, Montreal, Canada (2003).
17. J. Keizer and J. Vos, *Diagnosing Risks in New Product Development*, Eindhoven Centre for Innovation Studies, The Netherlands, Working Paper 03.11, Department of Technology Management (2003).
18. S. Keppler, *Entry, Exit, Growth and Innovation over the Product Life Cycle*, Department of Social and Decision Sciences, Carnegie Mellon University, USA (1996).
19. R. Kok, B. Hillebrand, and W. Biemans, *Market-Oriented Product Development as an Organizational Learning Capability: Findings from Two Cases*, SOM Research School, University of Groning, The Netherlands (2002).
20. P. Kort, P. Murto, and G. Pawlina, The Value of Flexibility in Sequencing Growth Investment, *Proceedings of the Real Options: Theory Meets Practice*, 8th Annual International Conference, Montreal, Canada (2004).

21. P. Kotler, *Administracao de Marketing – Analise, Planejamento, Implementacao e Controle*, Atlas, Sao Paulo, Brazil (1996).
22. V. Krishnam and S. Bhattacharya, *Man. Sci.*, **48**, 313 (2002).
23. B. Lin and A. Herbst, *Valuation of a Startup Business with Pending Patent using Real Options*, Startup Junkies Organization (2003).
24. M. Macedo, Avaliacao de Projetos: Uma Visao da Utilizacao da Teoria das Opçoes, *Proceedings of the XVIII ENEGEP*, Niteroi, Brazil (1998).
25. A. Martinez, *RAE* **38**, 36 (1998).
26. A. Minardi, *Teoria de Opçoes Aplicada a Projetos de Investimento*, Atlas, Sao Paulo, Brazil (2004).
27. D. Norton and R. Kaplan, *Estrategia em Acao: Balanced Scorecard*, Campus, Rio de Janeiro, Brazil (1997).
28. M. Ostrovsky and M. Schwarz, *Synchronization under Uncertainty*, Research paper no. 1923, Graduate School of Business, Stanford University, USA (2005).
29. C. Pinto and R. Montezano, *Gestao.Org*, **3**, 3 (2005).
30. PMI, *A Guide to the Project Management Body of Knowledge (PMBOK)*, Project Management Institute, Newton Square, USA (2008).
31. M. Porter, *Vantagem Competitiva: Criando e Sustentando o Desempenho Superior*, Campus, Sao Paulo, Brazil (1986).
32. H. L. M. M. Quintella, H. M. Rocha, and M. F. Alves, *Prod.* **15**, No.3, 334 (2005).
33. H. M. Rocha and M.C, Delamaro, M. C., *Product Development Process: using real options for assessment and to support the decision-making at decision gates*, in Loureiro, G. and Curran, R. (Orgs.), Complex Systems Concurrent Engineering – collaboration, technology innovation and sustainability, Springer-Verlag, London, UK, pp. 96-103 (2007).
34. S. Ross, R. Westerfield, and B. Jordan, *Principios de Administracao Financeira*, Atlas, Sao Paulo, Brazil (2000).
35. J. Sadowsky, *The Value of Learning in the Product Development Stage: A Real Options Approach*, Working Paper, Stanford University, Department of Management Science and Engineering, USA (2005).
36. R. Saito, D. Schiozer, and G. Castro, *RAE* **40**, 64 (2000).
37. L. Santiago and T. Bifano, *IEEE-TEM*, **52**, 269 (2005).
38. E. Santos, *Um Estudo sobre a Teoria de Opçoes Reais Aplicadas a Analise de Investimentos em Projetos de Pesquisa e Desenvolvimento (P&D)*, M.Sc. thesis. Escola Federal de Itajuba, Brazil (2001).
39. E. Santos and E. Pamplona, *RAUSP* **40**, 235 (2005).
40. D. Santos, *A Teoria das Opçoes Reais como Instrumento de Avaliacao na Analise de um Processo de Fusao/Incorporacao de Empresas*, M.Sc. thesis. Universidade Federal Fluminense, Niteroi, Brazil (2004).

41. W. Silva, Uma Aplicacao da Teoria das Opçoes Reais a Analise de Investimentos para Internet em Tecnologia ASP, *Proceedings of the XXVI SBPO*, Sao Joao Del-Rei, Brazil (2004).
42. N. Slack, S. Chambers, and R. Johnston, *Administracao da Producao*, Atlas, Sao Paulo, Brazil (2002).
43. J. Wesseler, The Option Value of Scientific Uncertainty on Pest-Resistance Development of Transgenic Crops, *Proceedings of the 2nd World Congress of Environmental and Resource Economists*, Monterey, USA (2002).
44. D. C. Duber-Smith and G. Black, *GCI – Beauty Business, Brand Impact*, Apr 2012 (2012).

THE NECESSITY OF IMPLEMENTATION MONITORING FRAMEWORK USING OPEN SOURCE TECHNOLOGIES IN ROMANIAN INFORMATION SYSTEMS MARKET

EMILIA CORINA CORBU

Mathematics and Computer Science Department, University of Petroşani, Petroşani, Romania

EDUARD EDELHAUSER

Management Department, University of Petroşani, Petroşani, Romania

MONICA LEBA

Computer Engineering and System Control Department, University of Petroşani, Petroşani, Romania

In last decade, enterprises began to feel the necessity to have better access to information for decision making, through visibility at all times into activities at all levels of business. For this scope, emerged the discipline Business Intelligence (BI) which nowadays covers areas like data warehousing, data integration technologies, query, reporting, and analysis tools for fulfilling the requirements of better and controlled access to business information and processes. The Business Activity Monitoring(BAM) technologies can provide real-time business analysis and alerts on information from sources like Web services, message queues, etc. The present interest of this paper consists in identification of elements required for implementing a solution for help in their activity, small and medium Romanian enterprises.

1. Introduction in Business Activity Monitoring

In the early 1990s, emerged the discipline Business Intelligence (BI) to fulfill the necessity of enterprises to have better access to information for decision making, through visibility at all times into activities at all levels of business. Nowadays, the Business Intelligence (BI) which covers areas like data warehousing, data integration technologies, query, reporting, and analysis tools

Today, time and information are competitive advantage and due to that fact, managers of event-driven enterprises are becoming increasingly stressed as time necessary to process data is increasing and simultaneously the information amount becomes unbearable. For this reason many software heavyweights, such as Microsoft, IBM and Oracle, have joined the struggle for a piece of the BI expanding market.

Staying ahead of the competition requires the ability to predict and respond to trends in the market in real-time. BI products work with historical data gathered from data warehouses, therefore the latency introduced by moving data into a data warehouse is too high to be able to respond in real-time. To be able to catch business activities issues before or right after they occur companies can't rely only on traditional BI systems.

Emerged in July 2001 by Gartner enterprise, the Business Activity Monitoring (BAM) concept, an event-driven extension of BI defines providing real-time access to critical business performance indicators to improve the speed and effectiveness of business operations. These technologies can provide real-time business analysis and alerts on information from sources like Web services, message queues therefore are solutions becoming more sophisticated.

2. Existing software for Business Activity Monitoring and Platforms required

During the 2010, another concepts like business dashboards emerged, which made BAM solutions a viable scenario in enterprise business management because processing event streams requires robust and quick solutions.

Today vendors have some interesting dashboard tools. Some have also tried for a complete set of tools to build BAM solutions like: Progress Software's Apama [10], Coral8 (merged with Aleri)[1], Oracle[12] and SL – real time visibility[16]. As an open source CEP solution, there are only few available like Esper and Pion, nevertheless Esper Tech is widely referred as "the only open source option"[8].

Today's Complex Event Processing CEP platforms in the market are mainly divided into three Event Pattern Language (EPL) different approaches [13]: SQL-like (e.g. Coral8, Esper, Oracle, StreamBase); Rule-based (e.g. AmiT from IBM or Reaction RuleML from RuleML); Abstract user interface and java-like code generation (e.g. Tibco, AptSoft).

Performance dashboards meet the user's requirements when speaking of enterprise business intelligence by reporting and analysis capabilities within an intuitive dashboard interface. Performance dashboards aim to deliver access to the right data to the right people at the right time. In the market, there are some dashboard builders like Progress Software and Coral8. But they are not open source solutions.

BAM solution provides three main features to the user: near real-time business key performance indicators monitoring (using the charts to display the information in order to ease its reading by the user) called the dashboard component of a BAM solution. The alarmist component alerts to notify target users about important previously defined business behaviors. The third component is report generation with system behavior important information.

3. Platforms required

We have researched which are requires that an Order Management System (OMS) is a software system for order processing within an organizational business process. This system has to empower the coordination and execution of an order, given the priorities, error handling and data transformation, measuring the results and informing the interested systems.

As a result of research, such a system can uses Jboss Business Process Management, Jboss Enterprise Service Bus, Jboss Messaging technologies and Oracle DBMS.

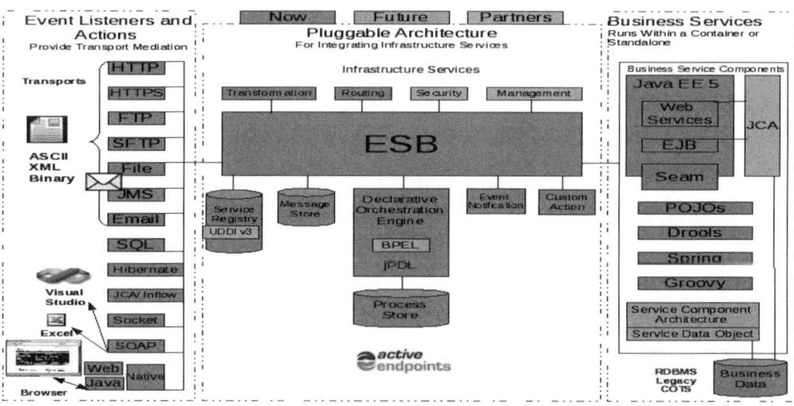

Figure 1. Jboss ESB architecture Source: Jboss at http://www.jboss.org/jbossesb/Jboss ESB uses a flexible architecture based on Service Oriented Architecture

Jboss Business Process Management is a extensible and flexible framework which through Jboss Process Definition Language (jPDL) expresses business processes graphically in terms of task.

Jboss Application Server (Jboss AS), free software/open-source Java EE-based application server is a platform for developing enterprise Java applications, Web applications, and Portals. Jboss AS supports the addition of some Modules/Enterprise Applications with integration purposes, including clustering, caching, and persistence. [17] Beings a part of a Service Oriented Infrastructure (SOI), Jboss Enterprise Service Bus (Jboss ESB) can be used like standalone or application server.

Jboss Messaging, composed of several services work together to provide Java Message Service (JMS) API level services to client applications. Jboss Messaging is Jboss's JMS implementation and therefore is a Message-Oriented-Middleware (MOM) [11].

Oracle Database Management System (DBMS) is a database management system produced and marketed by Oracle Corporation.

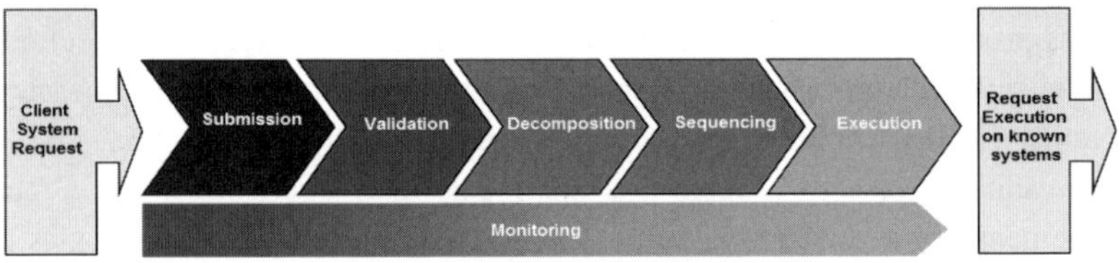

Figure 2. High level perspective of an Order Management System. Source: Xpand-IT documentation

For structuring the BAM solution, the essential requirements that the developed technologies have to fulfill are: the manner to establish connection points for event gathering and processing and the estimated event flow for defining CEP engine. In Xpand-IT documentation their OMS architecture can support an event flow by 10.000 events per day.

Esper, an Event Stream Processing (ESP) and correlation engine Complex Event Processing (CEP) is open-source software and available for Java. Esper enable the development of applications that process very large volume of incoming messages or events and also contain Event Stream Intelligence Figure 3. Being able to use containers, and XML document management [3].

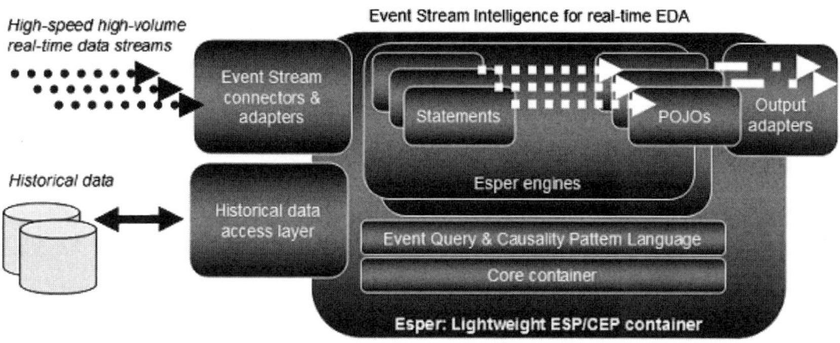

Figure 3. Esper's event stream intelligence; Source: http://www.espertech.com/products/esper.php

For managing event data storage we have thought that is need to find a fast way for storing data. Now, we are researching the possibilities of using an Oracle Berkeley DB, a family of open-source databases.

In what's regarded the development of classes, as result of our research we can say that Hibernate allows working with inheritance, polymorphism, association, composition on Java collections framework [3].

4. The Actual Stage of Romanian Information Systems Market in Small and Medium Romanian Enterprises

For identify the actual stage or Romanian information market in small and medium enterprise we have begun a research began between 16 May and 25 June 2010, totalized 22 questions and it had a number of 440 respondents [2]. The investigated organizations were in proportion by 93% enterprises with less than 150 employees remaining 7% enterprises with over 250 employees.

Response	Total	% of responses	%
1. under 50%	11		7%
2. between 50% and 80%	30		19%
3. over	56		36%
4. using all	57		37%

Figure 4.The level of using of soft resources in Small and Medium Romanian Enterprises

The investigated enterprises have used in that period the software of the following Software producer: Total Soft, Wizrom Software,Senior Software, EBS, WinMentoror Alfa Software. These types of software are designed especially for Small and Medium Enterprises, that stage of research revealed some very important results.

Response	Total	% of responses	%
1. aplications for processing documents and spreadsheets (eg. Word, Excel)	82		19% 40%
2. software applications for commercial activities	176		37%
3. software applications integrated in a informatic system	105		24%
4. integrated system for decision support (eg. ERP CRM)	77		18%

Figure 5. The level of using of ERP and BI module

We can say that although 36% uses soft resources, only 15% of enterprises are using module of Business Intelligence in their organization.

Response	Total	% of responses	%
1. not are necessary all modules	19		50%
2. the module isn't 100% appropriate with the business	21		55%
3. the personnel isn't accommodate with the system's require	11		29%
4. the partners are using other systems (incompatibility's problems)	6		16%
5. clients are using other systems (incompatibility' problems)	6		16%
6. lack of qualifications of the employees	9		24%
7. Other problems	2		5%

Figure 6. Causes of inefficient use of an Integrated Information System

From the perspective of very serious effect, a critical analysis induced flaws that show system and causes major damage especially hard and a low involvement of the implementer (possible service contracts, warranty and post warranty concluded against the beneficiary).

Perhaps the most important question of the questionnaire which focused on integrated systems deployment in Romanian Small and Medium Romanian Enterprises (SME) proved if proof were needed that organizations try to gain competitive advantage in the market and advanced management methods are an essential element of these strategies.

Response	Total	% of responses	%
1. operating errors mades by employees	73		52%
2. lack of employees adaptation of system's requires	37		26%
3. system's inflexibility to correct errors	45		32%
4. interruptions caused by system errors	36		26%
5. fluctation of employees	20		14%
6. lack of training of the employees	28		20%
7. interruption in networks connection	39		28%
8. bad colaboration with IT' supplier	18		13%
9. other problems	14		10%

Figure 7. Problems encountered in using IIS

Another conclusion was that the most important obstacle to the use of advanced management methods in an economy that we face an increased poverty is certainly lack of money, and less acceptance of the new.

Response	Total	% of responses	%
1. current problemesof the enterprises	43		20%
2. the price of the informatic systems	114		52%
3. the lack of the qualified employees	50		23%
4. bad response to changing applications	90		41%
5. other	19		9%

Figure 8. Obstaclesarisingin the implementation of IBS

Market applications for Business Intelligence (BI) increased by 13.4% worldwide in 2010 compared to 2009, according to a recent study by U.S. consulting and IT research Gartner. According to Gartner, reflecting increased customer interest for solutions to streamline business and to obtain competitive advantage in economic crisis.

Moreover, BI applications have increased in 2009 compared to 2008, even if worldwide software spending with business applications fell. BI market is controlled in proportion of 59% of major vendors: SAP, IBM, Oracle and Microsoft.[Gartner Source].

Trying to develop solutions of Business Activity Monitoring on open-source framework can represent a real solution for small and medium enterprises to accomplish the process of making decision.

5. Conclusions

Under current conditions in the private sector in Romania is trying to survive, and the lack of money is more acute, we're trying to come to support SMEs with solutions to help them in decision-making process. The research show clearly BI modules and need to open their presence in daily activities. We believe that Business Activity Monitoring development solutions built on open source would solve the problems facing small and medium Romanian enterprises.

References

1. Aleri, *Coral8 engine*, Retrieved November 25, available at http://www.aleri.com/products/aleri-cep/coral8-engine, (2009).
2. Cătinean and D. Cândea, The Adoption and Use of Information Systems in Romanian SMEs, *Proceedings of the 1st Management Conference: Twenty*

Years After, How Management Theory Works, Technical University of ClujNapoca, Todesco Publishing House, pp. 43-54 (2010).

3.E.C. Corbu and M. Leba, Dezvoltarea aplicatiilor informatice pe revisio .NET, *Universitas Publishing House*, Petrosani, (2010).

4.E.C. Corbu and S. Riurean, Notiuni introductive in Internet si comert electronic, *Universitas Publishing House*, Petrosani, (2009).

5.W.W. Eckerson, Performance Dashboards, Measuring, Monitoring and Managing your Business, *John Wiley & Sons*, Inc, New Jersey, USA, (2006).

6.E. Edelhauser, Sisteme informatice în managementul resurselor umane, *Universitas Publishing House*, Petroşani, (2011).

7.S. Graham, S. Simeonov and T. Boubez, Servicii Web cu Java. XML, SOAP, WDSL si UDDI, *Teora Publishing House*, Bucuresti, (2003).

8.M. Gualtieri and J. R. Rymer, The forrester wave: Complex event processing (cep) platforms, Forrester, Retrieved December 1, (2009).

9.D. McCoy, R. Schulte, F. Buytendijk, N. Rayner, and A. Tiedrich, Business activity monitoring: The promise and reality, Gartner, July (2001).

10.P. Software, Apama, Retrieved November 25, 2009, available at http://web.progress.com/en/apama/index.html, (2009).

11.R. Hat, Jboss messaging, Retrieved December 21, 2009, available at http://www.redhat.com/docs/manuals/jboss/jboss- 4.3/doc/messaging/ J. Boss, Messaging_User_Guide, /html/index.html, (2009).

12.Oracle, Oracle Berkeley db, Retrieved March 5, 2010, available at http://www.oracle.com/us/products/database/ revisio-db/index.html, (2010).

13.F.S. Rainer von Ammon, C. Emmersberger and C. Wolff, Event-driven business process management and its practical application taking the example of dhl, October 2008. Retrieved October 28, available at http://icep-fis08.fzi.de/papers/iCEP08_8.pdf.(2008).

14.S. Rîurean and E.C. Corbu, *Internet şi eBusiness*, Universitas Publishing House, Petroşani, (2010).

15.Spring Source Tool Suite Version: 2.8.1.RELEASE, Build Id: 201111221000 Copyright (c) Spring Source, a division of Vmware, Inc. All rights reserved. http://springsource.com/products/sts. This product includes software developed by the Apache Software Foundation http://www.apache.org (2007 – 2011).

16.S. R. T. Visibility, Business activity monitoring (bam) solution, retrieved November 25, 2009, available at http://www.sl.com/solutions/busactivity.shtml, (2009).

17.J. Community, Hibernate, Retrieved September 27, 2010, available at http://www.hibernate.org/, (2010).

A COMPARATIVE RELEASE PATTERN: SEASONALITY, REVENUE AND SURVIVAL OF MOTION PICTURES AT THE SPANISH BOX OFFICE

VANESA F. GUZMAN PARRA

Facultad de Ciencias Económicas y Empresariales. Departamento de Economía y Administración de Empresas. Universidad de Málaga, Campus de El Ejido. 29071 Málaga

FRANCISCO JAVIER MAQUEDA LAFUENTE

Facultad Ciencias Económicas y Empresariales, Departamento Economía Financiera II, Universidad del País Vasco/Euskal Herriko Unibertsitatea. Avda. Lehendakari Agirre 83, 48015 Bilbao

JAIME GIL LAFUENTE

Facultad de Ciencias Económicas y Empresariales. Departamento de Economía y Administración de Empresas. Universidad de Barcelona / Universitat de Barcelona, Diagonal, 690, 08034 Barcelona

This study examines the market for motion pictures in Spain by analyzing data from 2002–2011. The paper aims to enhance comprehension of the Spanish film industry by analyzing seasonality and lifetime in theaters and by performing a clustering analysis to add to our knowledge of this particular industry. The results allow us to make comparisons between Spanish and foreign films exhibited in Spain. The empirical analysis shows that Spanish films have different peak-season periods from foreign films and a shorter lifetime in theaters and that they have different levels in variables such as gross and rank. Conclusions and implications for the sector are discussed.

1. Introduction

The importance of the release date is magnified in movies with higher expected revenue because the first week accounts for an average of almost forty percent of the total domestic box office revenue (Einav, 2007). Many researchers find that release date plays a significant role in the revenue of a film (De Vany and Walls, 1997; Terry, Buttler and De´Armond, 2003; Ainslie Drèze and Zufryden, 2005; McKenzie, 2012).

Einav (2007) notes that there are three types of release: wide release, platform release, and limited release. Wide releases are the most common with the main distributors. Screening of the movie begins in a large number of theaters, typically several thousand, accompanied by an extensive national advertising campaign.

The application of duration analysis to box office demand has previously received attention from De Vany and Walls (1997), Walls (1998), Nelson, Donihue, Waldman and Wheaton (2001), Deuchert, Adjamah and Pauly (2005), Chisholm and Norman (2006), McKenzie (2009), and Walls (2009).

As Smith and Smith (1986) note, "Given the interesting characteristics of movies as ideal examples of differentiated products and of the institutional arrangements governing their production and distribution, such increased data availability would make this an exceptionally attractive area for applied micro economic research."

The number of viewers who can see a movie is limited by the number of theaters booked in its release (De Vany and Walls, 1997).

The American movie industry has long dominated world markets (Jedidi, Krider and Weinberg, 1998; Waterman and Jayakar, 2000; Augros, 2000; Terry, Butler and De´Armond, 2003; Marvasti and Canterbery, 2005 and Miller, 2005), and many researchers have carried out comparative studies of American and local industries to confirm this domination. (Sunada, 2010; Vang and Chaminade, 2007; Bagella, and Becchetti, 1999; Waterman y Jayakar (2000; Jansen, 2005; Cucco, 2010 and Vila, Guzmán and Quintana 2012).

As Scott (2004) notes, the American majors maintain extensive distribution and marketing networks not only in North America but also in other countries. These majors directly control distribution systems in all their principal foreign markets, and this control includes the Spanish market.

This paper is organized as follows: the next section describes the methodology. Section 3 provides results about seasonality and a clustering analysis as well as documents the survival of motion pictures at the Spanish box office. Section 5 provides concluding remarks.

2. Methodology

To study a film's release pattern in Spain, we have performed two types of analysis and compiled two different databases. The first data set registers the audience every month from January 1, 2002 to December 31, 2011 for both Spanish films and foreign films exhibited in Spanish theaters. These data have been extracted from Ministerio de Cultura of Spain and have allowed us to analyze seasonal variations affecting the audience for Spanish and foreign films from 2002-2011 and observe differences between the two series.

In addition, we have studied all films exhibited in 2011 and compiled variables such us release date, gross, rank and lifetime in theaters. The film-level data have allowed us to perform a clustering and survival analysis and compare the patterns for Spanish films and foreign films. These data were obtained from Mojo Box Office for the 475 films that were exhibited in Spain that year.

3. Results

3.1. Seasonality in the film industry

Einav (2007) shows that one of the main strategic decisions made by distributors is the release date of a movie. In the USA, the demand for movies has strong seasonal effects. Vila, Guzman and Quintana (2012) demonstrate that the Spanish movie market also has high seasonality.

Figure 1 shows the first approximation before the seasonal breakdown. It presents the audience evolution by film nationality, including the monthly results, from which we can make two observations. Taking into account the current economic recession, we shall analyze the series' trends to clearly detect the level of seasonal variation and determine whether this is a sustained decline.

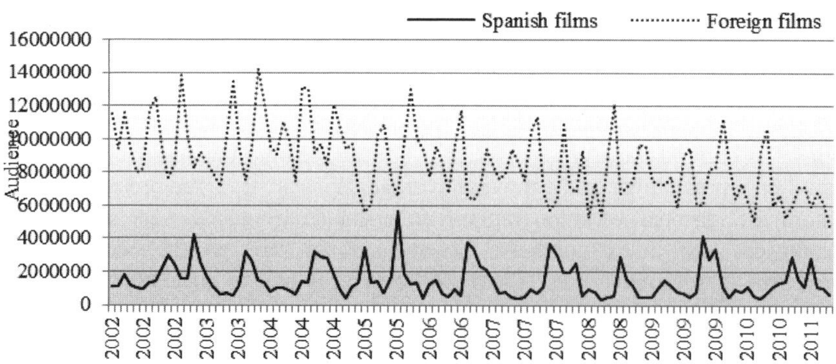

Figure 1. Evolution of movie audience.

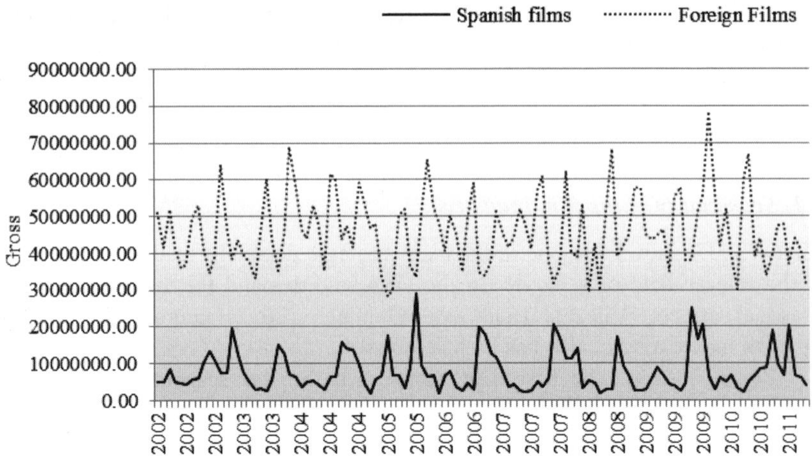

Figure 2. Gross evolution, 2002-2011.

Figure 2 presents an overview of gross evolution from 2002-2011, which is similar to the viewers' evolution.

We can observe the high seasonal variation existing in both variables, and we also note fewer number of theaters for Spanish films compared to foreign films. To correctly analyze the series, we must separate the seasonal variations based on a breakdown of the moving average. We start from the premise that the pattern of seasonal variation remains constant from year to year and can be quantified with index numbers. Several authors refer to the behavior and treatment of seasonal series (Einav, 2007; Vila, Guzmán and Quintana 2012). Box and Jenkins (1970) indicates that the seasonal series (Yt) of the number of audience, with t=1,..,T, can equally be expressed as:

$$Yt = f(Tt, Ct, Et, It) \text{ o } Yt = TCt*St*It, t=1,\ldots,n$$

where:

-Tendency or Tt: the regular movement in the long term. It represents the long-term trend of the series.

-Cyclical factor or Ct: the oscillatory movement. In practice, it is difficult to separate Tt from Ct. Hence, both components are usually represented as one, known as the trend-cycle component TCt, which reflects the changes in level (height of the sequence graph) throughout the development of the series.

-Seasonal variation or seasonal component St: oscillations of the series within the same year.

-Irregular movement It: variations of the series not included in the above. In the case of the seasonal series of the size of the audience, the model can be applied because the variables should not contain lost incrusted data and there is a component of periodic date.

In general, the typical deviation for each year increases as the mean value increases, which indicates that the aggregation pattern of the components of this series is multiplicative.

Figure 3 shows the cycle of audience trends in which we no longer see the marked peaks, which is a consequence of the seasonal variation, thus enabling us to easily note the trend. Particularly in foreign films, we can identify a decline in the number of the audience.

The diagnosis of the seasonal factor, summarized in Table 1, illustrates that when the value is greater than 1 in a specific period, the variable value will be higher than the average for this period, while when it is lower than 1, the opposite occurs.

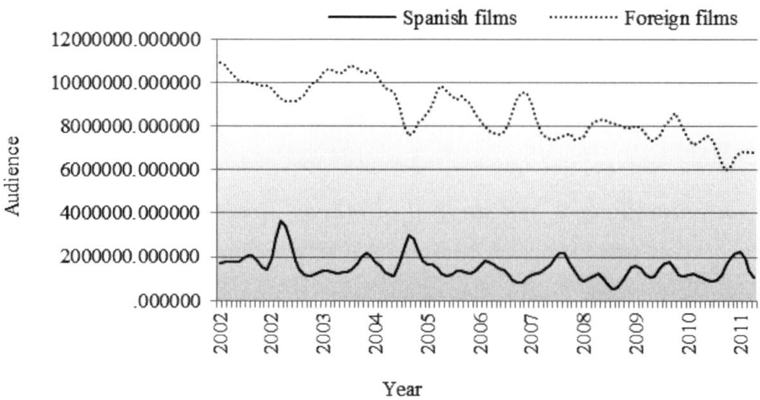

Figure 3. Series' trend.

Examining the seasonal variation provided in Table 1, we can observe that during the months of the low season, the seasonal variation component has lower values, while in high season, this component has higher values. The two series have different seasonal behavior. Examining the seasonal variation for Spanish films, we can observe that this component has lower values in the months of autumn, while in July, August and September, this component has higher values. Foreign films' audience shows peaks in the holiday periods, such as Christmas and summer, as shown in table 1.

Table 1. Seasonal factor.

Period	Spanish Films audience Seasonal Factor (%)	Foreing Films audience Seasonal Factor (%)
January	92,6	110,9
February	66,4	95,3
March	76,7	94,5
April	78,2	94,6
May	73,3	91,4
June	45,5	72,4
July	63,4	119,4
August	54,1	134,9
September	135,5	86,4
October	222,7	82,0
November	160,9	90,7
December	130,7	127,4

6. Clustering analysis and survival of motion pictures at Spanish box office

We have performed two types of analyses – clustering and survival analysis – to better comprehend the Spanish motion picture market. In this paper, we attempt to account for the dynamic patterns in the data. In addition, we have analyzed the distribution of cumulative revenue across films, which is consistent with the winner-take-all nature of an elimination tournament (Walls, 2009). The weekly Spanish box office revenue is highly convex in rank (de Vany and Walls, 1997). Next, we detail the results obtained from clustering and survival analysis.

a. Clustering analysis

Patterns for gross and lifetime in theaters were analyzed statistically using Two Step Cluster analysis to describe the different case subgroups and the variation within them. This approach provides an opportunity to explore structures existing in data prior to attempting to explain why they exist. In particular, with the two-step cluster method, mixed-type attributes can be managed, and the number of clusters can be automatically determined.

Our analysis indicated that four clusters provide the best segmentation of our sample. Table 2 provides a statistical comparison of the clusters. Cluster Four is characterized by higher gross and longer lifetime than the other clusters. Clusters 1 and 2 include a huge number of films that have a lower gross level and a shorter lifetime than Cluster 4. Cluster 3 is characterized by low-medium lifetime and a low gross level. Spanish films are mainly included in this cluster except for two films that are assigned to Cluster 4.

Table 2. Custer profiles.

Cluster profiles		Cluster 1	Cluster 2	Cluster 3	Cluster 4	Total
Gross	Mean	487612.24	2571171.86	764520.37	16092735.14	2089133.92
	Std. Deviation	824647.025	2433282.700	1540488.806	6608326.630	4065520.180
Weeks	Mean	4.50	10.92	5.32	15.57	7.53
	Std. Deviation	1.967	3.834	3.938	6.831	4.924
Foreign	Frequency	152	145	0	19	316
	Percent	48.1%	45.9%	.0%	6.0%	100.0%
Spanish	Frequency	0	0	91	2	93
	Percent	.0%	.0%	97.8%	2.2%	100.0%

In Figure 4, box plots are displayed to represent gross and lifetime intervals for means in each cluster.

We are able to note different levels for the variables that characterize each cluster.

b. Survival analysis

McKenzie (2009) shows that supply is frequently adjusted to demand by changing the length of a film's theatrical run because the admission price is previously decided at each cinema location and the number of prints is fixed ex-ante prior to the release date. Therefore, the analysis of duration is relevant in the motion picture industry because increasing or shortening the length of the run is the most common way to adjust supply to demand (McKenzie, 2009; de Vany and Walls, 1997). In each movie theater, moviegoers pay the same price for each movie at all times, with the exceptions of matinee rates and other discounts (Orbach and Einav, 2007).

The number of weeks that a film remains on the charts may provide useful information in relation to film performance (McKenzie, 2009).

Films live and die in the box office tournament as they are challenged during their run by a randomly evolving cast of new competitors (de Vany and Walls, 1997).

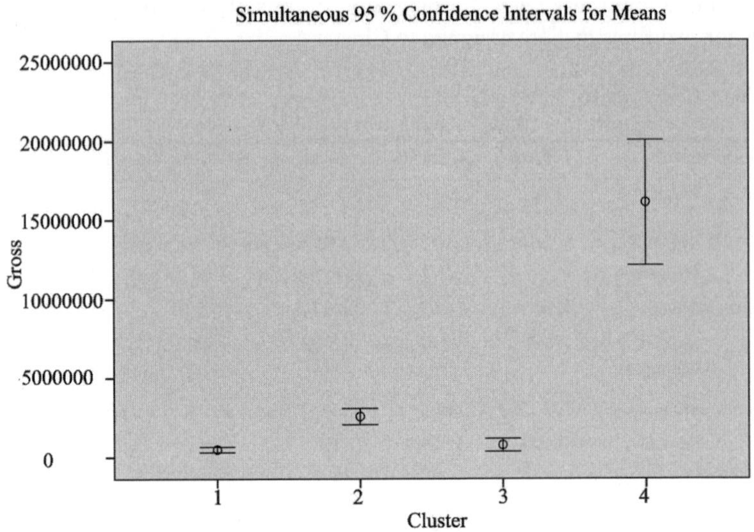

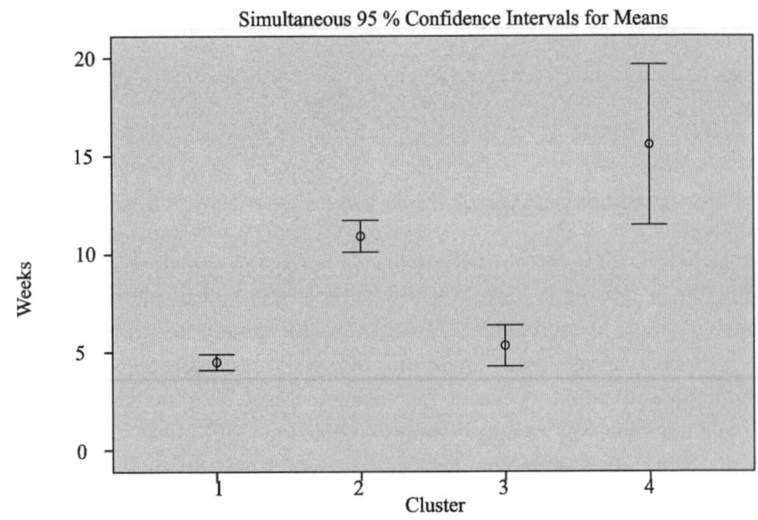

Figure 4. Gross and life-time intervals form means in each cluster.

This study proposes a duration analysis to consider the life-length of films that went into wide release in Spain in 2011 by examining the number of weeks spent in the motion picture distributors' weekly charts during the calendar year 2011. The analyzed films were a total of 475 films.

The objective of using survival and hazard functions is to better understand the life-length pattern on Spanish-exhibited films and to examine whether national movies have a different theatrical life cycle from foreign films.

Table 3 describes and summarizes the sample survival times by measuring the number of weeks that the films were shown in theaters.

Table 3. Survival times.

Nationality	Total number of movies		Less than 10 weeks		10 or more weeks		15 or more weeks		20 or more weeks	
Foreing films	369	78%	256	70%	113	30%	29	8%	10	3%
Spanish Films	105	22%	85	81%	20	19%	6	6%	1	1%

The Kaplan-Meier survival estimator is an important tool for analyzing these types of data. A plot of the Kaplan-Meier estimate of the survival function, as Figure 5 shows, results in a series of horizontal steps of declining magnitude that approaches the true survival function for that population when a large enough sample is taken. Small vertical tick-marks indicate losses, where a film's survival time has been right-censored

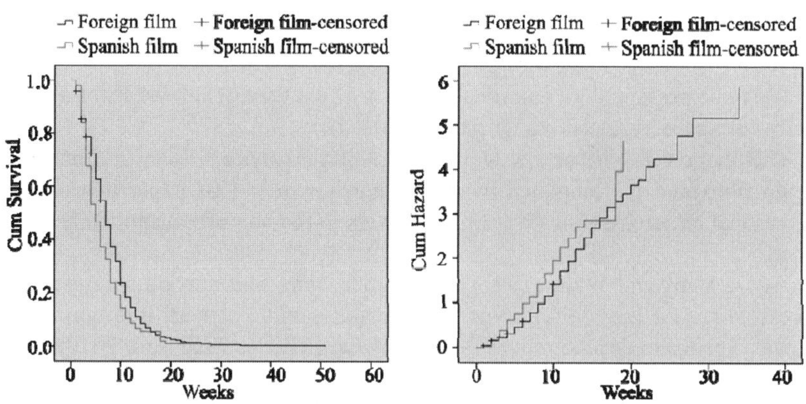

Figure 5. Survival Functions and Hazart Function.

To compare the two different Kaplan-Meier curves, table 4 shows the test of equality of survival distributions for the two groups.

The log-rank test compares estimates of the hazard function of the two groups at each observed event time.

It is constructed by computing the observed and expected number of events in one of the groups at each observed event time and then adding these to obtain an overall summary across all time points where there is an event (a film is out of theaters).

Table 4. Test of equality of survival distributions.

	Chi-Square	df	Sig.
Log Rank (Mantel-Cox)	6,940	1	,008
Breslow (Generalized Wilcoxon)	9,345	1	,002
Tarone-Ware	9,089	1	,003

The results allow us to conclude that foreign films have a longer lifetime in Spanish theaters than national films. The hazard function of foreign films surpasses 20 weeks unlike Spanish films, as shown in Figure 5. Table 3 highlights the results obtained from the test of equality of the survival distributions.

As table 4 shows, the two hazard functions are significantly different. Because the significance values are less than 0.05, we conclude that survival curves are different across the groups.

4. Conclusions

We have presented an empirical analysis of the theatrical market for motion pictures in Spain by analyzing data from 2002–2011.

The market is characterized by competition between Spanish films and foreign films and is dominated by Hollywood imports. This paper investigates the seasonal pattern, the survival of the movies in the box office and the revenue earned.

As De Vany and Walls (1997) demonstrate, long film runs do not guarantee success. Many of the longest-lived films in our sample earned little box office revenue. For example, the movie *Inside the Job* (Charles Ferguson, 2010), with 34 weeks of life, earned $862,111 gross and was ranked 162 out of the 475 films exhibited in 2011. On the other hand, number one ranked *Torrente 4* (Santiago Segura, 2011) had a screening time of only 11 weeks in theaters and earned $29,031,125 gross. The results show that revenue is highly convex in rank because the movie markets (as Walls (2009) shows) have the winner-take-all nature of an elimination tournament.

Our paper uses empirical evidence from Spanish and foreign films exhibited in Spain and demonstrates the differences between them. For example, Spanish film audiences have a strong seasonal pattern, a different peak season, a lower gross level and audience level and a shorter lifetime in theaters than foreign films.

The results of this study are particularly interesting for the strategic management of movie theaters. Distributors should be aware of the study of optimal choice in variables such as release date or time in theaters. Movie theaters adjust supply to demand by changing the length of a film's theatrical run.

The findings have important implications for the film sector in Spain. For example, our results show that the differences in seasonality patterns between Spanish and foreign films could stimulate investigation of changing the release dates of Spanish films to other seasons.

Finally, our findings, although descriptive, provide a view of motion pictures at the Spanish box office and have demonstrated the differences between Spanish and foreign films in variables such us gross, release dates, audience, seasonality and lifetime in theaters. The detected differences provide a direction to improve the competitive strategies of Spanish national cinema.

Further research is particularly recommended for exploring survival in the box office in different international markets and/or with longer periods of study.

An interesting area for future research would be to examine seasonality patterns across countries and to determine whether groups of countries emerge with similar patterns. Future work could examine film attributes and distribution characteristics of American films and their effect on the competitiveness of those films' at the box office.

References

1. Einav, L. (2007). Seasonality in the U.S. motion picture industry, *RAND Journal of Economics, 38 (1),* 127-145.
2. De Vany, A., Walls, W.D. (1997). The Market for motion Pictures: Rank, Revenue, and Survival. Economic Inquiry, 35, 783-797.
3. Terry, N., Butler, M., De´Armond (2003). Determinants of the Box Office performance of Motion Pictures, *Proceedings of the Academy of Marketing Studies, 8 (2),* 23-27.
4. Ainslie, A., Drèze, X., Zufryden, F. (2005). Modeling Movie Life Cycles and Market Share, *Marketing Science, 24 (3),* 508-517.
5. McKenzie, J. (2012). The economics of movies: a literature Survey, *Journal of Economic Surveys,26* (1), 42-70
6. Walls, D. (1998). Product survival at the cinema: Evidence from Hong Kong. Applied Economics Letters, 5, 215–219.
7. Nelson, R., Donihue, M., Waldman, D., & Wheaton, C. (2001). What's an Oscar worth? Economic Enquiry, 39(1), 1–16.
8. Deuchert, E., Adjamah, K., & Pauly, F. (2005). For Oscar glory or Oscar money? Journal of Cultural Economics, 29, 159–176.

9. Chisholm, D., & Norman, G. (2006). When to exit a product: Evidence from the US motion picture industry. The American Economic Review, 96(2), 57–61.
10. McKenzie, J. (2009). Revealed word-of-mouth demand and adaptive supply: survival of motion pictures at the Australian box office. *Journal of Cultural Economics, 33,* 279-299.
11. Walls, W.D.(2009). The Market for Motion Pictures in Thailand: Rank, Revenue, and Survival at the Box Office, *International Journal of Business and Economics*, 8 (2), 115-131.
12. Smith, S. P., and V. K. Smith. (1986). Successful Movies: A Preliminary Empirical Analysis. *Applied Economics,* 18(5), 501-507.
13. Jedidi, K., Krider, R.E., Weinberg, C.B. (1998). Clustering at the Movies, *Marketing Letters 9 (4)*, 393–405.
14. Waterman, D., Jayakar, K.P. (2000). The Competitive Balance of the Italian and American Film Industries, *European Journal of Communication, 15 (4),* 501-528.
15. Augros, J. (2000): *El dinero de Hollywood.* Financiación, producción, distribución y nuevos mercados. Paidós Ibérica, Barcelona.
16. Marvasti, A., Canterbery, R. (2005). Cultural and other barriers to motion Pictures trade, *Economic Inquiry, 43 (1),* 39-54.
17. Miller, T.; Govil, N.; McMurria, J.; Maxwell, R. (2005): *El Nuevo Hollywood. Del imperialismo cultural a las leyes del marketing.* Paidós, Barcelona.
18. Sunada, M. (2010). Vertical Integration in the Japanese Movie Industry, *Journal of Industry, Competition and Trade, 10*, 135–150.
19. Vang, J., and Chaminade, C. (2007). Cultural Clusters, Global–Local Linkages and Spillovers: Theoretical and Empirical Insights from an Exploratory Study of Toronto's Film Cluster, Industry and Innovation, 14 (4), 401-420.
20. Bagella, M., and Becchetti, L. (1999). The Determinants of Motion Picture Box Office Performance: Evidence from Movies produced in Italy, Journal of Cultural Economics, 23 (4), 237-256.
21. Jansen, C., (2005). The Performance of German Motion Pictures, Profits and Subsidies: Some Empirical Evidence, Journal of Cultural Economics, 29, 191–212
22. Cucco, M. (2010). The borders of the domestic market and their importance for the economy of the film industry: The Swiss case study, *European Journal of Communication, 25 (2),* 153-167.
23. Vila Oblitas J.R., Guzmán Parra, V.F., Quintana García, C. (2012). Análisis de la estacionalidad en el sector cinematográfico: estudio comparativo entre la industria extranjera y española. *Investigaciones Europeas de Economía de la Empresa, 18 (2), 177-182.*

24. Scott, A. (2004). Hollywood and the world: the geography of motion-picture distribution and marketing, *Review of International Political Economy, 11 (1),* 33-61.
25. Box, G.E.P., Jenkins, G.M. (1970). Time Series Analysis Forecasting and Control. San Francisco: Holden-Day
26. Orbach, B.Y., Einav, L. (2007). Uniform prices for differentiated goods: The case of the movie-theater industry, *International Review of Law and Economics, 27,* 129–153.

INDICATIONS OF CHAOTIC BEHAVIOR IN BUCHAREST STOCK EXCHANGE BET INDEX

VASILE GEORGESCU

Department of Statistics and Informatics, University of Craiova, 13 A.I.Cuza, Craiova, 200858, Romania

In this paper, several tests are undertaken in an attempt to detect the presence of chaos in a time series taken from an emerging stock market: Bucharest Stock Exchange. Any nonlinear scalar time series is assumed to be the output (by an observation function) of a deterministic, nonlinear (and eventually chaotic) dynamical system. Time series embedding and reconstruction is a method for detecting strange attractors in the multidimensional phase space of the underlying dynamical system, which would be an indication of chaotic behavior. Various different tests for chaos, related to the embedding methodology, have been proposed in literature. Some of the most important have been included in our experimental design, in order to increase the reliability of our results and to eventually avoid misleading conclusions.

1. Testing for Chaotic Dynamics in Time Series

Chaotic attractors display symmetric structures with self-similarity at different scales. These attractors have certain unique characteristics that make their empirical detection possible. For instance, they exhibit a non-integer fractal dimension and sensitive dependence on initial conditions; the latter can be checked by measuring the Lyapunov exponents (at least one Lyapunov exponent should be positive). In recent years, many statistical tests on the existence of deterministic chaos in time series have proliferated. We present some of them.

1.1. Phase space reconstruction and embedding dimension

One of the indications of chaotic behavior is the existence of strange attractors, which can be easily observed by means of the phase space reconstruction and phase space plot. The phase space reconstruction is the basis of the other methodologies such as BDS test and correlation dimension estimation.

A univariate time series $\{x_t\}$, can be viewed as a projection of the signal generator source, represented by an unknown but underlying d – dimensional dynamic state vector $\{x_t^d\}$. The multidimensional dynamic state vector is composed of d variables, represented through its dimension d. Takens' theorem (1981) represents a technique to reconstruct an approximation of the unknown dynamic state vector $\{x_t^d\}$ in $d-$dimensional state space by lagging and embedding the observed time series $\{x_t\}$. The procedure consists of four steps:

1. Suppose that a time series of N observations is available as follow:

$$\{ x_1, x_2, \ldots, x_{N\text{-}1}, x_N \} \tag{1}$$

2. Determine an appropriate time delay τ;
3. Determine the embeddind dimension d;
4. Embedd the series of observations into an $d-$dimensional space by forming d-length vectors of the following form:

$$x_t^d = \left(x_t, x_{t+\tau}, \ldots, x_{t+\tau(d-1)}\right), \qquad t = 1, \ldots, N - \tau \cdot (d-1) \tag{2}$$

This reconstructed approximation is the state vector, composed of time-delayed samples of $\{x_t\}$, where τ is the time delay and d is the embedding dimension of the system. The accurate calculation of d and τ guarantees through the Embedding theorem, that the sequential order of the reconstructed state vector $x_t^d \to x_{t+1}^d$ is topologically equivalent to the generator state vector $x_t \to x_{t+1}$, allowing x_t^d to represent without ambiguity the actual source of the observed time series $\{x_t\}$.

1.1.1. Determining a Reasonable Time Delay: Mutual Information

The time delay τ can be determined by the *mutual information function*, first proposed by A. M. Fraser and H. L. Swinney (1986). The criterion which was suggested is that the delay should be set at the *first local minimum of mutual information between the coordinates*. For two discrete variables X and Y whose joint probability distribution is $P_{XY}(x,y)$, the mutual information between two coordinates of $\{x_t^d\}$, e.g. x_t^d and $x_{t+\tau}^d$, is measured in bits by

$$MI(\tau) = \log_2 \frac{P\left(x_t^d, x_{t+\tau}^d\right)}{P\left(x_t^d\right) P\left(x_t^d\right)} \tag{3}$$

where $P\left(x_t^d, x_{t+\tau}^d\right)$ is the joint probability density function of x_t^d and $x_{t+\tau}^d$. The average mutual information of all coordinates is calculated by:

$$AMI(\tau) = \sum_{x_t^d, x_{t+\tau}^d} P\left(x_t^d, x_{t+\tau}^d\right) \log_2 \frac{P\left(x_t^d, x_{t+\tau}^d\right)}{P\left(x_t^d\right) P\left(x_t^d\right)} \tag{4}$$

A good choice for the time delay is that, given the state of the system x_t^d, provides maximum information at $x_{t+\tau}^d$. Actually, the best value of time delay τ

is *the smallest* τ *for which* $AMI(\tau)$ *is a local minimum* (i.e., *the first minimum of the AMI function*), and assures the independence between the coordinates of the multidimensional vector $\{x_t^d\}$. This value of time delay may be used for the phase space plots. Thus $AMI(\tau)$ must be calculated from joint densities $P\left(x_t^d, x_{t+\tau}^d\right)$ for many values of τ. Mutual information can detect nonlinear correlations. Thus while plots of $AMI(\tau)$ vs. τ are reminiscent of simple autocorrelation plots, they are sensitive to dependencies of any kind.

1.1.2. Determining the Embedding Dimension: the Cao's method

The signal reconstruction in state space requires a dimension that will guarantee no overlap of the orbits of the dynamical system. To understand how to select a good embedding dimension, *d*, it is helpful to understand what is happening geometrically. As *d* increases in the reconstruction of a data series, the chaotic attractor "unfolds". When completely unfolded, a sequential path from one dimensional point to the next will never cross itself. If *d* is too small, various paths of the projected attractor will cross.

The method of false nearest-neighbors (for example, see Arbanel (1996)) recognizes that, where the attractor's paths appear to cross, two neighboring points actually will be far away in the sequential order of the true embedded data series. Using this idea, Cao (1997) proposed a method for determining a good embedding dimension. Let

$$E_1(d) = \frac{E(d+1)}{E(d)} \tag{5}$$

with

$$E(d) = \frac{1}{N - d\tau} \sum_{t=1}^{N-d\tau} \frac{\left\| x_t^{d+1} - x_t^{d+1,\,NN} \right\|}{\left\| x_t^d - x_t^{d,\,NN} \right\|} \tag{6}$$

where *N* is the length of the original data series, the *d* refers to the embedding dimension, and the superscript *NN* means the nearest neighbor to the other vector as defined by the metric in the last equation. As *d* gets large enough, $E_1(d)$ will tend to one. The appropriate embedding dimension is given by the value of *d* where $E_1(d)$ stops changing. Practically, this means choosing the *d* where $E_1(d)$ begins to "level out", near unity.

Cao (1997) also proposed a related method for determining whether or not the original data series is random. Using a different metric,

$$E_2(d) = \frac{E^*(d+1)}{E^*(d)} \tag{7}$$

where

$$E^*(d) = \frac{1}{N - d\tau} \sum_{t=1}^{N-d\tau} \left| x_{t+m\tau} - x_{t+m\tau}^{NN} \right| \tag{8}$$

then a random signal will have an $E_2(d)$ that is close to unity for *all* values of d, whereas a chaotic signal will have an $E_2(d)$ that is less than one for small values of d.

$$MI(\tau) = \log_2 \frac{P\left(x_t^d, x_{t+\tau}^d\right)}{P\left(x_t^d\right) P\left(x_t^d\right)} \tag{9}$$

1.2. The BDS Test

BDS test was suggested by Brock, Dechert & Scheinkman (1987). BDS test cannot test chaos directly, but only non-linearity, provided that any linear dependence has been removed from the data. Nevertheless, since a *nonlinear* process is the first indication of chaos, we may use the BDS test to detect such indication.

The BDS test is derived from the correlation integral, which is a measure of spatial correlation of scattered points in the m-dimensional space. In a time-series context, $\{x_t\}$ is embedded in the m-space by forming m-histories $x_t^m = \left(x_t, x_{t-1}, \ldots, x_{t-m+1}\right)$. The correlation integral reads

$$C(\varepsilon, m) = \int_u \int_v I\left(u, v, \varepsilon\right) dF_m(u)\, dF_m(v)) \tag{10}$$

where the indicator kernel function $I(\cdot)$ is one when $\|u - v\| < \varepsilon$, zero otherwise, and $F_m(\cdot)$ is the distribution function of x_t^m. Hence, it indicates the concentration of the joint distribution of m-consecutive observations.

To estimate the probability that two m-length vectors are within ε, define the generalized U-statistic

$$C_{m,N}(\varepsilon) = \frac{2}{(N-m)(N-m+1)} \sum_{t<s} I(x_t^m, x_s^m, \varepsilon) \tag{11}$$

where N is the sample size, m is the so-called *embedding dimension* and

$$I(x_t^m, x_s^m, \varepsilon) = \begin{cases} 1 & \left\| x_t^m - x_s^m \right\| < \varepsilon \\ 0 & otherwise \end{cases} \tag{12}$$

Brock et al. (1987) have shown that $C_{m,N}(\varepsilon)$ is a consistent estimator of $C(\varepsilon, m)$ provided that $\{x_t\}$ is an absolutely regular and strictly stationary stochastic process. Under the null hypothesys of independence and identical distribution (iid) of the process $\{x_t\}$, one must have $F_m(x_t^m) = \prod_{i=0}^{m-1} F_1(x_{t-i})$ and $E(C_{m,N}(\varepsilon)) = (E(C_{1,N}(\varepsilon)))^m$.

Brock et al. (1987) use this relation to construct the following BDS test statistic for detecting deviations from the iid property

$$W_{m,N}(\varepsilon) = \sqrt{n-m+1}\frac{C_{m,N}(\varepsilon) - C_{1,N-m+1}^m(\varepsilon)}{\sigma_{m,N}(\varepsilon)} \tag{13}$$

where $C_{m,N}(\varepsilon)$ is a nontrivial function of the correlation integral, and $W_{m,N}(\varepsilon)$ asymptotically distributes $N(0,1)$. The test is two-sided, therefore the null of independence and identical distribution is rejected at the 5% significance level if $|w_{m,N}(\varepsilon)| > 1.96$.

1.3. Fractal Dimension

Fractal dimension, also called *capacity* dimension, or *Hausdorff dimension*, is a dimension in which nonintegral values are permitted. Objects whose *Hausdorff* dimension is different from their Lebesgue covering dimension are called fractals. The *Hausdorff* dimension of a compact metric space X is a real number $d_{fractal}$ such that if $n(\varepsilon)$ denotes the minimum number of open sets of diameter less than or equal to ε, then $n(\varepsilon)$ is proportional to ε^{-D} as $\varepsilon \to 0$:

$$d_{fractal} \equiv \lim_{\varepsilon \to 0^+} \frac{\ln N}{\ln \varepsilon} \tag{14}$$

where N is the number of elements forming a finite cover of the relevant metric space and ε is a bound on the diameter of the sets involved (informally, ε is the size of each element used to cover the set, which is taken to approach 0).

There are many types of fractal dimensions, but the most useful is the so called *correlation dimension*. The correlation dimension assumes that as r approaches zero, the rate at which $C(r)$ changes is given by the relation:

$$C(r) = \lim_{r \to 0} k r^{D_C}. \tag{15}$$

or, solving for D_C:

$$D_C = \lim_{r \to 0} \frac{\log C(r)}{\log r}. \tag{16}$$

Since the data set will not be continuous, r cannot get too close to zero (there will be no points in the sphere). To handle this situation, one plots $\log C(r)$ versus $\log r$ and selects the apparently linear portion of the graph. The slope of this portion will approximate D_C. If D_C is noninteger, then the attractor is "strange" and the system exhibits chaos.

1.4. The Largest Lyapunov Exponent

One of the most common technique to determine the presence of chaotic behavior is the largest Lyapunov exponent, which measures the divergence of nearby trajectories. As the system evolves, the sum of a series of attractor point values (in each dimension) will converge or diverge. Lyapunov exponents measure the rate of convergence/divergence in each dimension, and a chaotic system will exhibit trajectory divergence in at least one dimension. Thus, if the largest Lyapunov exponent exceeds zero, then the system is chaotic. To determine the largest Lyapunov exponent, the following function is used:

$$\lambda_{\max} = \frac{1}{N\Delta t} \sum_{t=0}^{N-1} \ln\left(\frac{|s(t+\Delta t) - s'(t+\Delta t)|}{|s(t) - s'(t)|} \right). \tag{17}$$

where the primed and unprimed data points are distinct but close. As Δt increases, the value of the exponent will, theoretically, converge to its true value. In practice, however, due to a finite data sets and noise, the exponent can only be determined within a range of values.

1.5. Prediction

As discussed previously, though chaos is fundamentally deterministic, it is unpredictable beyond short intervals. This section covers how short this interval will theoretically be and how accurate predictions can be made within that period. The (approximate) period limit on accurate predictions of a chaotic system is a function of the largest Lyapunov exponent (Abarbanel 1997):

$$\Delta t_{\max} = \frac{1}{\lambda_{\max}}. \tag{18}$$

To be chaotic, the largest Lyapunov exponent must exceed zero. If it exceeds one, the maximum length of an accurate prediction is less than the data series sampling frequency. Thus, only for systems with Lyapunov exponents between zero and one are chaotic predictions of any practical use. If the exponent is much less than one, long, accurate predictions are possible.

For prediction, one starts with the unfolded attractor in d-dimensional space and time lag τ . Given an initial vector $\mathbf{y}(t_0)$, one selects the k nearest trajectories (not points) on the attractor, and then the k nearest points to $\mathbf{y}(t_0)$, one on each trajectory. An average of these trajectories is used to find the next point on the predicted trajectory, $\mathbf{y}(t_0 + d\tau)$. The predicted point is then set as the new starting vector and the process is repeated. Only short term predictions can be made.

2. Determining the Presence of Chaos in a Financial Time Series: the Bucharest Stock Exchange BET Index Daily Values

The tests presented above are now used to detect chaos in a financial time series, namely the Bucharest Stock Exchange BET Index. Figure 1 shows this time series. Actually, we shall consider for analysis only the last 3000 observations.

Figure 1. Bucharest Stock Exchange BET Index daily values.

To facilitate computation of time delay, Figure 2 shows the mutual information function. The first minimum of this function occurs at a time delay of $\tau = 17$.

Cao's methods for determining the embedding dimension d and for determining whether or not the time series is random are plotted in Figure 3.

The plot of $E_1(d)$ seems to level out at around $d = 5$, so this is selected as the data set's embedding dimension. $E_2(d)$ is less than one for small d, suggesting that the series is not random.

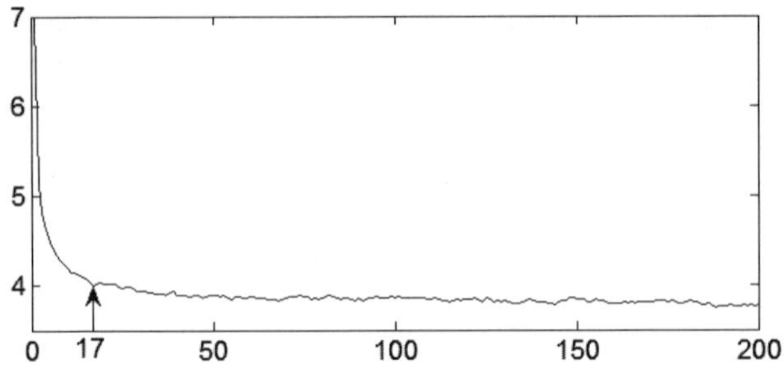

Figure 2. Mutual information function.

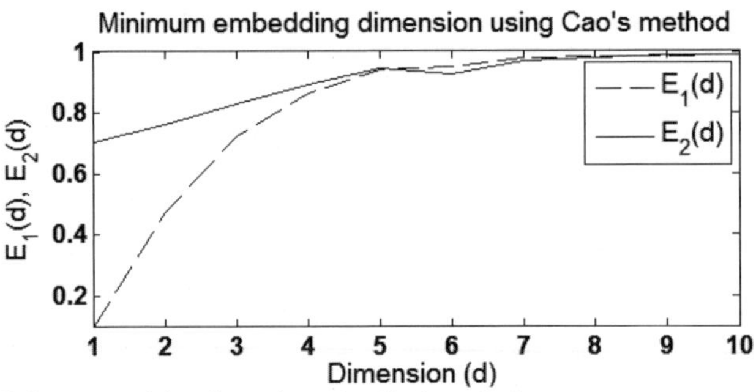

Figure 3. Minimum revision dimension using Cao's method.

The projection of the time series embedded in a 5-dimensional phase space into a 3-dimensional phase space is shown in figure 4. This representation is consistent with Hick's statement that time series exhibiting chaotic behavior does not fill up the entire phase space, such as randomly generated data.

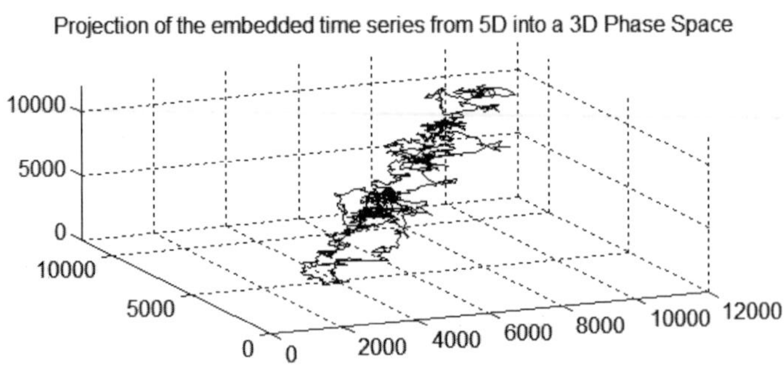

Figure 4. The projection of the time series embedded in a 5-dimensional phase space into a 3-dimensional phase space.

The BDS test has been applied to the Bucharest Stock Exchange BET Index Daily Values time series.

The maximum embedding dimension was set to 15. The measure of dimensional distance, EPSILON, was chosen such that the first-order correlation integral estimate (C1) lies around 0.7. The results of the *BDS test* on the original time series are summarized in Table 1. The null hypothesis is rejected for all dimensions. Thus the series is not independently and identically distributed.

Table 1. BDS Test Output.

Dimension	BDS statistics W for each dimension	Correlation integral estimates C	P-value
2	240.987388558403	0.6942843522891	0
3	260.140217617108	0.689897814202907	0
4	284.083660402517	0.686335200353892	0
5	318.183684990338	0.683215461461136	0
6	364.503454118967	0.680326038833371	0
7	425.643039907732	0.677548213701041	0
8	505.302336072799	0.674883328479465	0
9	608.658213063886	0.672463245351026	0
10	742.549903395569	0.670262515528749	0
11	916.043651781902	0.668200346644497	0
12	1141.20925347242	0.666215212136603	0
13	1434.18820791507	0.664301217816249	0
14	1816.47271747031	0.662446399232575	0
15	2316.70787471998	0.660632701350019	0

The correlation (fractal) dimension has been computed for the Bucharest Stock Exchange BET Index Daily Values time series. The correlation sum is shown in figure 6, where $\log C(r)$ versus $\log r$ is ploted. The linear part of the plot has a noninteger slope of approximately 0.85, indicating the presence of chaos.

Figure 7 plots the prediction error with respect to the number of steps ahead. It shows the increase of the prediction error versus the prediction time.

3. Conclusion

We conclude that most common tests for chaos give some convincing indications of chaotic behavior in case of Bucharest Stock Exchange BET Index, confirming that financial markets are multi-fractal in nature and exhibit erratic dynamics and strange attractors, which make them hard to predict, even in short run.

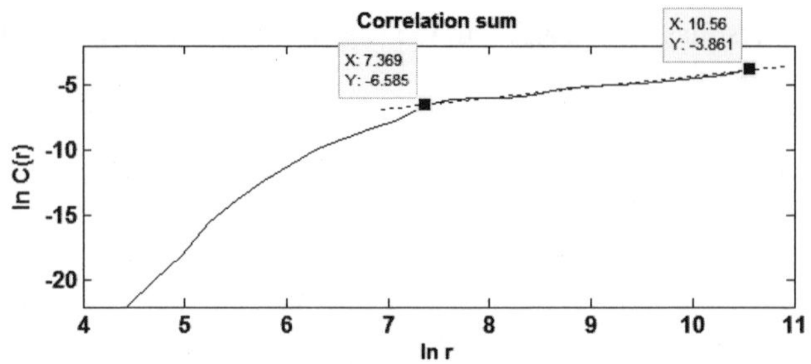

Figure 6. Correlation dimension for BSE BET Index daily values.

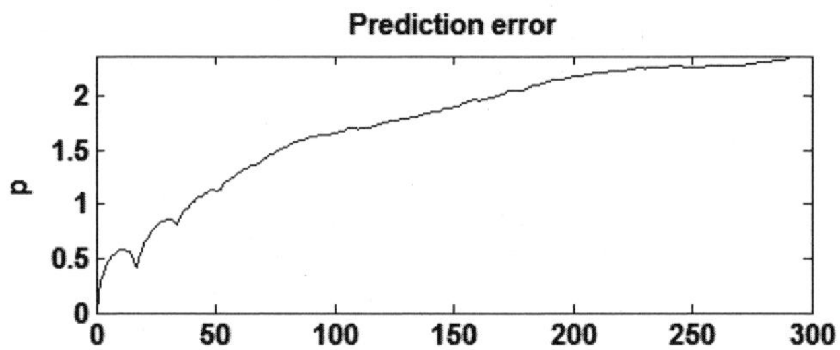

Figure 7. The prediction error versus the prediction time.

References

1. H. D. I. Abarbanel, *Analysis of observed chaotic data*, Springer (1996).
2. W. A. Brock, W. Dechert and J. Scheinkman, *A test for independence based on the correlation dimension*. Working paper (1987).
3. L. Cao, Practical method for determining the minimum embedding dimension of a scalar time series, *Physica D: Nonlinear Phenomena* (1997).
4. M. Fraser and H. L. Swinney, Independent coordinates for strange. Attractors from mutual information, *Phys. Rev.* A 33: 1134-1140 (1986).
5. Hsieh, David. Chaos and Nonlinear Dynamics: Applications to Financial Markets, *Journal of Finance* 46, N5, 1839-1877 (1991).
6. F. Takens, Detecting strange attractors in turbulence, *Lecture notes in mathematics*, vol. 898, 366-381, Springer (1981).

A JELS PROBABILISTIC INVENTORY MODEL FOR ONE VENDOR MULTI-CUSTOMERS SITUATION WITH RANDOM DEMANDS HAVING TRUNCATED NORMAL DISTRIBUTIONS

D.A. KHAN

Department of Computer Applications, National Institute of Technology, Jamshedpur, 831014, India

In a single vendor and multi customer probabilistic inventory situation the relations between them in terms of optimum demands, optimum costs, the effect of vendor's ELS on the customer and the effect of customers ELS on the vendors have been discussed. Then a probabilistic JELS (Joint Economic Lot Size) model has been developed when the random and stock level of the customer are independent and identically random variables having truncated normal distribution. It has been proved that the adoption of joint optimum lot size under certain conditions is more beneficial to both vendor and customer than individual optimal lot size.

1. Introduction

As we know that in case of single vendor-single customer situation, it is easy (under certain conditions) for both the parties to come to a point of compromise at their common JELS associated with certain amount of unit price adjustments such that each of them will derive a benefit out of this of negotiation. But in case of single vendor-multi customer situation, the matter becomes different. The conditions mentioned above may be fulfilled in case of some of the customers while they may not be fulfilled in case of others, as a result some of the parties may be at an advantageous position and the rest will have to face certain amount of penalty. Obviously these advantages and penalties of the parties will very much depend upon their individual cost ratios. Assuming the set of all the negotiators in the process (including the vendor) as a universal set U, if the sum of the Absolute Cost Advantages of a subset S (denoted by ACA_s) be more than the sum of the Absolute Cost Penalties of its complement S' (denoted by $ACP_{s'}$) then the difference between the two values being positive can be called the Joint Absolute Cost Advantage of the entire universal set and be denoted by $JACA_u$ which can be shared reasonably among all the members of the universal set U. On the other hand, if the sum of Absolute Cost Advantages of the subset S (i.e.

ACA_s) is less than the sum of Absolute Cost Penalties of its complement (i.e. $ACP_{s'}$), then such a sharing is not possible. In that case the difference between the two values (i.e. $ACP_{s'} - ACA_s$) will be the Joint Absolute Cost Penalty of the universal set which can be denoted by $JACP_u$. This amount can be compensated by the vendor through a unit price discount out of his own unit price profit fixed by him earlier. It is obvious that this unit price profit fixed by the vendor earlier must be sufficiently high to meet such eventualities. Of course by the process mentioned above vendor's estimated profit will be reduced, but he is liable to gain the goodwill of the customers in general, which is very important in inventory control system.

One thing more is to be noted. The vendor while negotiating with n different customers who approach him at a time has to fix up the same unit price discount for all the customers, as he cannot make any discrimination between one customer and the other. In the process of offering uniform unit price discount to all, he must be prepared to sacrifice certain additional part of his net gain, because his sacrifice will ultimately lead to his net gain in the form of goodwill and reputation in the market attracting the customers in large numbers with higher demands and more frequent orders, which will ultimately benefit him.

In this model, the vendor carries on negotiations with different customers individually and persuades each one of them to compromise at his individual JELS (z_i^*) offering a common unit price discount to all. After the negotiations are over in the light of present discussion, all the n-customers place their orders and the vendor immediately satisfies their demands (with lead time zero), because the horizon of his lot size (i.e. inventory level) is indefinitely large.

2. Development of the Model

2.1. Assumption

The following assumptions are used in developing the model.

1) X_i (i = 1, 2, 3, ...n) and Y are identically distributed independent random variables belonging to truncated standard Normal law defined by the conditional distribution function P $\{X_i \le x \mid X_i \in [0, \infty)\}$ and a common truncated density function h (x) where

$$h(x) = \begin{cases} \dfrac{f(x)}{\int_o^\infty f(y)dy}, & x \in [0,\infty) \\ 0, & x < 0 \end{cases}$$

f(x) being the standard Normal probability density function (pdf).

As we know

$$h(x) = \begin{cases} \frac{2}{\sqrt{2\pi}} \exp[-x^2/2], & \text{for } x \geq 0 \\ 0, & \text{for } x < 0 \end{cases}$$

2) Initially n customers come to a vendor together and place orders to the vendor for a particular item of goods of which the vendor is the sole supplier.

3) There is a perfect understanding between the vendor and all the customers to part with the cost information and agree upon a common price adjustment (like unit price discount offered by the vendor).

4) On receiving the cost information from the purchasers, the vendor calculates his own Economic Lot Size (ELS), as well as the ELS of each customer C_i ($i = 1, 2, 3, \ldots\ldots..n$)

5) On the basis of cost information received from the vendor, each customer computes his own ELS and the ELS of the vendor independently.

6) After proper negotiation between the vendor and individual customers, the vendor finds his optimum cost, production inventory plan and computes a reasonable price support he may offer to the customers.

7) While fixing the unit price discount, the vendor has to estimate the joint benefit of optimization between himself and individual customer C_i by dividing the total joint benefit by the expected demand of C_i with a view to satisfy the customer.

8) There is no set-up cost

9) Shortages are allowed for each party (i.e. each customer C_i and the vendor).

10) Lead time is zero

2.2. Notations

The following notations are used in developing the model

i = an integer such that $1 \leq i \leq n$

C_i = represents the ith customer.

$X_i =$ Random demand (lot size) of the customer C_i (i = 1, 2 ….n) with a common truncated density function h_i (x)

such that $h_i(x) = \begin{cases} \dfrac{f(x)}{\int_o^\infty f(y)dy}, x \in [0,\infty) \\ 0 \qquad , \text{otherwise} \end{cases}$

f(x), being the standard normal density function

Y = Random inventory stock level (lot size) of the vendor with density function h (x) such that

$$h(x) = \begin{cases} \dfrac{f(x)}{\int_o^\infty f(y)dy}, (0 \le x < \infty) \\ 0 \qquad , \text{otherwise} \end{cases}$$

f(x), being the standard normal density function

t = Scheduling period which is a prescribed constant and over which the carrying costs and shortage costs per unit item as well as the random lot sizes of the customers and the vendor are calculated.

$C_{v1} =$ Carrying (holding) cost of the vendor per unit item per t time units.

$C_{v2} =$ Shortage cost (penalty) of the vendor per unit item per t time units.

$C_{p1}^{(i)} =$ Carrying cost of the customer C_i per unit item per t time units.

$C_{p2}^{(i)} =$ Shortage cost of the customer C_i per unit item per t time units.

Z = Variable lot size which is assumed to be the same for the vendor and the individual customer during negotiation.

$z_p^{(i)*} =$ Optimum order level of the customer C_i

$z_v^* =$ Optimum lot size of the vendor

$z^{(i)*} =$ Optimum common lot size when the vendor and the customer C_i adopt the Joint Economic Lot Size (JELS).

$\alpha^{(i)} = C_{p2}^{(i)} / C_{v2}$

$\beta^{(i)} = (C_{p1}^{(i)} + C_{p2}^{(i)})/(C_{v1} + C_{v2})$

$C_p^{(i)}\left(z_p^{(i)*}\right) =$ Optimum (i.e. minimum) total relevant cost TRC of the customer C_i

$C_v\left(z_v^*\right) =$ Optimum (i.e. minimum) TRC of the vendor

$C_p^{(i)}\left(z_v^*\right) =$ Total relevant cost of the customer C_i if he adopts the optimum lot size z_v^* of the vendor.

$C_v\left(z_p^{(i)*}\right) =$ Total relevant cost of the vendor if he adopts the optimum lot size $z_p^{(i)*}$ of the Customer C_i.

$C_p^{(i)}\left(z^{(i)*}\right) =$ The total relevant cost of the customer C_i if he adopts $z^{(i)*}$.

$C_v\left(z^{(i)*}\right) =$ The total relevant cost of the vendor if he adopts the $z^{(i)*}$.

$$I_i = C_v\left(z_p^{(i)*}\right) - C_v\left(z^{(i)*}\right)$$

$$J_i = C_p^i\left(z^{(i)*}\right) - C_p^{(i)}\left(z_p^{(i)*}\right)$$

$ACA_\theta\,(z' \rightarrow z'') =$ Absolute Cost Advantage of the party 0 when the party θ changes from the lot size z' to the lot size z'' at any point of time.
The party θ may be the vendor or any individual customer C_i.

$ACP_\theta\,(z' \rightarrow z'') =$ Absolute Cost Penalty of the party θ when the party θ changes from the lot size z' to the lot size z'' at any point of time.

The party θ may be the vendor or any individual customer C_i.

$JACA_{(v,c_i)}\left(z_p^{(i)*} \to z^{(i)*}\right)$ = Joint Absolute Cost Advantage during negotiation between the vendor and the customer C = $ACA_v\left(z_p^{(i)*} \to z^{(i)*}\right)$ - $ACP_p\left(z_p^{(i)*} \to z^{(i)*}\right)$

E (X_i) = Expectation of the random demand of the customer C_i

E (Y) = Expectation of the random stock level of the vendor

2.3. The Model with n Customers

X_i (i = 1, 2, 3, ……..n) and Y are independent and identically distributed random variables belonging to truncated Normal law defined by the conditional distributions P $\{X_i \le x \mid X_i \in [0, \infty)\}$, and P $\{Y \le x \mid Y \in [0, \infty)\}$ and a common truncated probability density function h (x) where

$$h(x) = \begin{cases} \dfrac{f(x)}{\int_o^\infty f(y)dy}, & x \in [0,\infty) \\ 0, & x < 0 \end{cases} \qquad (2.3.1)$$

f(x) being the standard normal density function

Therefore we have,

$$h(x) = \frac{\frac{1}{\sqrt{2\pi}} \exp[-x^2/2]}{\frac{1}{\sqrt{2\pi}} \int_o^\infty \exp[-y^2/2]dy}$$

$$= \frac{\frac{1}{\sqrt{2\pi}} \exp[-x^2/2]}{\frac{1}{2}}$$

[$\because \frac{1}{\sqrt{2\pi}} \int_{-\infty}^\infty \exp[-y^2/2]dy = 1$ and exp $[-y^2/2]$ is an even function of y]

$$= \frac{2}{\sqrt{2\pi}} \exp[-x^2/2] \quad \text{for } x \geq 0 \qquad = 0 \quad \text{for } x < 0 \tag{2.3.2}$$

The vendor negotiates with an individual customer say C_i, and a compromise is arrived at, to adopt individual JELS, $z^{(i)*}$ with a price adjustment in the form of discount according to single vendor-single customer situation. This will be generalized to all values of i (i = 1, 2, …n). Then a common strategy for price adjustment has to be designed by the vendor.

i) under certain conditions, the vendor offers unit price discount to the customer to persuade him to adopt JELS while

3. Under some other conditions, the customer offers unit price increase to the vendor, to

persuade him to adopt JELS. In the model which we are going to develop, we shall concentrate on the possibility (i) only and shall ignore possibility (ii), because according to Banerji A. [1, pp 309] this is "contrary to current practice in most traditional bargaining processes".

2.4. The following results can be obtained corresponding to different results of Khan, Ray and Panda [13]:

$$z_p^{(i)*} = \phi^{-1}\left(\sqrt{\frac{\pi}{2}}\frac{C_{p2}^{(i)}}{C_{p1}^{(i)} + C_{p2}^{(i)}}\right) \tag{2.4.1}$$

$$z_v^* = \phi^{-1}\left(\sqrt{\frac{\pi}{2}}\frac{C_{v2}}{C_{v1} + C_{v2}}\right) \tag{2.4.2}$$

$$C_p^{(i)}\left(z_p^{(i)*}\right) = 2\left[\frac{\beta^{(i)}(C_{v1} + C_{v2})}{\sqrt{2\pi}} e^{-\left(z_p^{(i)*}\right)^2/2} - \frac{C_{p1}^{(i)}}{\sqrt{2\pi}}\right] \tag{2.4.3}$$

$$C_v\left(z_v^*\right) = 2\left[\frac{C_{v1}+C_{v2}}{\sqrt{2\pi}}e^{-z_v^{*2}/2} - \frac{C_{v1}}{\sqrt{2\pi}}\right] \tag{2.4.4}$$

$$C_p^{(i)}\left(z_v^*\right) = 2\left[\frac{z_v^*}{2}C_{v2}(\beta^{(i)}-\alpha^{(i)}) + \frac{\beta^{(i)}(C_{v1}+C_{v2})}{\sqrt{2\pi}}e^{-z_v^{*2}/2} - \frac{C_{p1}^{(i)}}{\sqrt{2\pi}}\right] \tag{2.4.5}$$

$$C_v\left(z_p^{(i)*}\right) = 2\left[C_{v2}\frac{(\alpha^{(i)}-\beta^{(i)})}{2\beta^{(i)}}z_p^{(i)*} + \frac{C_{v1}+C_{v2}}{\sqrt{2\pi}}\exp\left\{-\left(z_p^{(i)*}\right)^2/2\right\} - \frac{C_{v1}}{\sqrt{2\pi}}\right] \tag{2.4.6}$$

$$z^{(i)*} = \phi^{-1}\left(\sqrt{\frac{\pi}{2}}\,\frac{C_{p2}^{(i)}+C_{v2}}{C_{p1}^{(i)}+C_{p2}^{(i)}+C_{v1}+C_{v2}}\right) \tag{2.4.7}$$

$$C_p^{(i)}\left(z^{(i)*}\right) = 2\left[\frac{z^{(i)*}}{2}C_{v2}\frac{\beta^{(i)}-\alpha^{(i)}}{\beta^{(i)}+1} + \frac{\beta^{(i)}(C_{v1}+C_{v2})}{\sqrt{2\pi}}\exp\left\{-\left(z^{(i)*}\right)^2/2\right\} - \frac{C_{p1}^{(i)}}{\sqrt{2\pi}}\right] \tag{2.4.8}$$

$$C_v\left(z^{(i)*}\right) = 2\left[\frac{z^{(i)*}}{2}C_{v2}\frac{\alpha^{(i)}-\beta^{(i)}}{1+\beta^{(i)}} + \frac{C_{v1}+C_{v2}}{\sqrt{2\pi}}\exp\left\{-\left(z^{(i)*}\right)^2/2\right\} - \frac{C_{v1}}{\sqrt{2\pi}}\right] \tag{2.4.9}$$

Lemma : 2.1 Khan, Ray, Panda [14]

$$\alpha^{(i)} < \beta^{(i)} \Rightarrow z_p^{(i)*} < z^{(i)*} < z_v^* \tag{2.4.10}$$

$$\alpha^{(i)} > \beta^{(i)} \Rightarrow z_v^* < z^{(i)*} < z_p^{(i)*} \tag{2.4.11}$$

$$\alpha^{(i)} = \beta^{(i)} \Rightarrow z_p^{(i)*} = z^{(i)*} = z_v^* \tag{2.4.12}$$

The negotiation between the vendor and the individual customer C_i will be exactly the same as Khan, Ray, Panda [14]. If the ELS of the vendor be in effect and all the customers change over to respective JELS, then this will give rise to a situation in which customers will suggest the vendor for a unit price increase (of course, fulfilling certain conditions). We ignore this because such type of bargaining is against the current practice. Hence ignoring such a possibility, we concentrate upon the ELS of the individual purchaser C_i in effect trying to switch over to the individual JELS ($z^{(i)*}$).

2.5. ELS of Purchasers in Effect

Here, $I_i = C_v\,(z_p^{(i)*}) - C_v\,(z^{(i)*})$

$$= 2\left[\begin{array}{l} \dfrac{z_p^{(i)*}}{2} C_{v2} \dfrac{\alpha^{(i)} - \beta^{(i)}}{\beta^{(i)}} + \dfrac{C_{v1} + C_{v2}}{\sqrt{2\pi}} \left\{ \begin{array}{l} \exp\left(- \left(z_p^{(i)*}\right)^2 / 2 \right) - \\ \exp\left(- \left(z^{(i)*}\right)^2 / 2 \right) \end{array} \right\} - \\ - \dfrac{z^{(i)*}}{2} C_{v2} \dfrac{\alpha^{(i)} - \beta^{(i)}}{1 + \beta^{(i)}} \end{array}\right] \tag{2.5.1}$$

$$= 2\left[\begin{array}{l} - \dfrac{z_p^{(i)*}}{2} C_{v2} \dfrac{\beta^{(i)} - \alpha^{(i)}}{\beta^{(i)}} + \dfrac{C_{v1} + C_{v2}}{\sqrt{2\pi}} \left\{ \begin{array}{l} \exp\left(- (z_p^{(i)*})^2 / 2 \right) - \\ - \exp\left(- \left(z^{(i)*}\right)^2 / 2 \right) \end{array} \right\} + \\ + \dfrac{z^{(i)*}}{2} C_{v2} \dfrac{\beta^{(i)} - \alpha^{(i)}}{1 + \beta^{(i)}} \end{array}\right] \tag{2.5.2}$$

and, $J_i = C_p^{(i)}\,(z^{(i)*}) - C_p^{(i)}\,(z_p^{(i)*})$

$$= 2\left[\frac{z^{(i)*}}{2} C_{v2} \frac{\beta^{(i)} - \alpha^{(i)}}{\beta^{(i)} + 1} - \frac{\beta^{(i)}(C_{v1} + C_{v2})}{\sqrt{2\pi}} \left\{ \begin{array}{l} \exp\left(-\left(z_p^{(i)*}\right)^2 / 2\right) - \\ - \exp\left(-\left(z^{(i)*}\right)^2 / 2\right) \end{array} \right\}\right] \quad (2.5.3)$$

$$\therefore I_i - J_i = 2\left[-\frac{z_p^{(i)*}}{2} C_{v2} \frac{\beta^{(i)} - \alpha^{(i)}}{\beta^{(i)}} + \frac{C_{v1} + C_{v2}}{\sqrt{2\pi}} \left\{\exp\left(-\left(z_p^{(i)*}\right)^2 / 2\right) - \exp\left(-\left(z^{(i)*}\right)^2 / 2\right)\right\}\left(1 + \beta^{(i)}\right)\right]$$

(2.5.4)

Moreover, $E(X_i) = \sqrt{\dfrac{2}{\pi}}$ for i = 1, 2, ... n (2.5.5)

If $\alpha^{(i)} < \beta^{(i)}$,

$$\mu^{(i)} = \sqrt{\frac{2}{\pi}} \frac{C_{v1} + C_{v2}}{C_{v2}} \frac{\beta^{(i)}(1 + \beta^{(i)})}{\beta^{(i)} - \alpha^{(i)}} \left\{\exp\left(-\left(z_p^{(i)*}\right)^2 / 2\right) - \exp\left(-\left(z^{(i)*}\right)^2 / 2\right)\right\} \quad (2.5.6)$$

And, under the condition

$$z_p^{(i)*} < \mu^{(i)} < z^{(i)*} \quad (2.5.7)$$

we have $I_i > 0$, $J_i > 0$ and $I_i - J_i > 0$
which also means

$$I_i = ACA_v\left(z_p^{(i)*} \to z^{(i)*}\right) \quad (2.5.8)$$

$$J_i = ACP_{Ci}\left(z_p^{(i)*} \to z^{(i)*}\right) \quad (2.5.9)$$

and $I_i - J_i = JACA_{(v,c_i)}\left(z_p^{(i)*} \to z^{(i)*}\right)$ (2.5.10)

If $\alpha^{(i)} > \beta^{(i)}$,

$$\lambda^{(i)} = \sqrt{\frac{2}{\pi}} \frac{\beta^{(i)}(1 + \beta^{(i)})}{\alpha^{(i)} - \beta^{(i)}} \left(\frac{C_{v1} + C_{v2}}{C_{v2}}\right) \left[\exp\left\{-\left(z^{(i)*}\right)^2 / 2\right\} - \exp\left\{-\left(z_p^{(i)*}\right)^2 / 2\right\}\right]$$

(2.5.11)

And, under the condition

$$z^{(i)*} < \lambda^{(i)} < z_p^{(i)*} \tag{2.5.12}$$

As $I_i > 0$, $J_i > 0$ and $I_i - J_i > 0$ which also means

$$I_i = ACA_v\left(z_p^{(i)*} \to z^{(i)*}\right) \tag{2.5.13}$$

$$J_i = ACP_{Ci}\left(z_p^{(i)*} \to z^{(i)*}\right) \tag{2.5.14}$$

and $I_i - J_i = JACA_{(v,c_i)}\left(z_p^{(i)*} \to z^{(i)*}\right)$ (2.5.15)

The optimum value of the unit price discount given by the vendor to the individual customer C_i should be

$$\frac{1}{2}\frac{JACA_{(v,c_i)}\left(z_p^{(i)*} \to z^{(i)*}\right)}{\sqrt{\frac{2}{\pi}}}$$

$$= \sqrt{\frac{\pi}{2}}\left[ACA_v\left(z_p^{(i)*} \to z^{(i)*}\right) - ACP_{C_i}\left(z_p^{(i)*} \to z^{(i)*}\right)\right] \tag{2.5.16}$$

2.6. Before finalizing our strategy for a unified (common) unit-price discount by the vendor, let us concentrate on the following discussions.

From (2.3.14)

$\alpha^{(i)} = \beta^{(i)} \Rightarrow z_p{}^{(i)*} = z^{(i)*} = z_v{}^{(i)*}$ (i = 1, 2, ……. M)

which means that the individual ELS of all these m customers and the vendor coincide with their individual JELS i.e. $z^{(i)*}$ (= z_v^{*}) and hence there will be no difficulty in their mutual compromise at $z^{(i)*}$ (i = 1, 2, ……. M).
Since $\alpha^{(i)} = \beta^{(i)}$, therefore from 2.5.8 and 2.5.9 we have $I_i = 0 = J_i$ (i = 1,2,…..m).

Hence from (2.5.10)

$JACA_{(v,ci)}\,(z_p^{(i)*} \rightarrow z^{(i)*}) = I_i - J_i = 0$

and there is no necessity of giving any unit price discount to these m customers; that means all these m-customers will be satisfied even if no unit-price discount is given to them. But in practice such a situation will not arise and these m customers also get the same unit price discount as others.

Let $\alpha^{(i)} < \beta^{(i)}$ for $i = m + 1, m + 2, \ldots\ldots. M + r$

Combining (2.4.10) and (2.5.9) together we have

$$z_p^{(i)*} < \mu^{(i)} < z^{(i)*} < z_v^{*} \qquad (2.6.1)$$

$$(i = m + 1, m + 2, \ldots\ldots., m + r)$$

Suppose $\{z_p^{(i)*}\}$ $(i = m + 1, m + 2, \ldots\ldots., m + r)$ has been arranged in an ascending order, so that

$$z_p^{(m+1)*} < z_p^{(m+2)*} < z_p^{(m+3)*} \ldots\ldots < z_p^{(m+r)*} < z_v^{*} \qquad (2.6.2)$$

and,

$$\left.\begin{array}{l} z_p^{(m+1)*} < \mu^{(m+1)} < z^{(m+1)*} < z_v^{*} \\ z_p^{(m+2)*} < \mu^{(m+2)} < z^{(m+2)*} < z_v^{*} \\ \ldots\ldots\ldots\ldots\ldots\ldots\ldots\ldots\ldots\ldots\ldots\ldots \\ z_p^{(m+r)*} < \mu^{(m+r)} < z^{(m+r)*} < z_v^{*} \end{array}\right\} \qquad (2.6.3)$$

Let $\mu' = M_{in}\,(\mu^{(m+1)}, \mu^{(m+2)}, \ldots\ldots\ldots \mu^{(m+r)})$ (2.6.4)

If $z_p^{(m+r)*} < \mu' < z^{(m+r)*}$ (2.6.5)

Consider $G_i = z^{(i)*} / z^{(i+1)*}$ then corresponding to $G_i > 1$, all the inequalities given in (2.6.3) will be satisfied, as will be clear from the graphical representation given below:

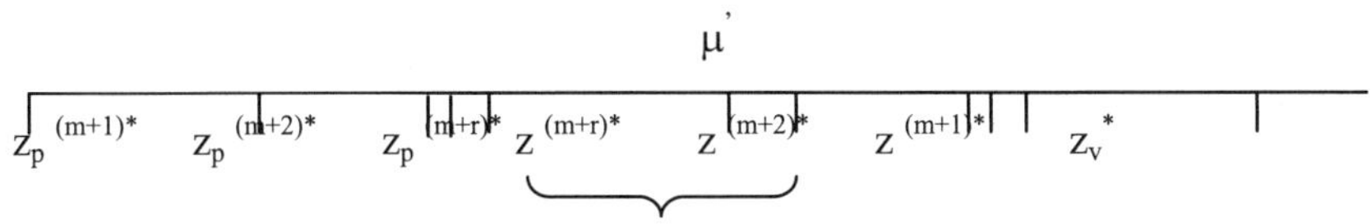

(Case $\alpha^{(i)} < \beta^{(i)}$, $G_i > 1$, $i = m+1, m+2, \ldots, m+r$)

Corresponding $G_i < 1$, we shall get

$$z^{(m+1)*} < z^{(m+2)*} < \ldots.. < z^{(m+r)*} \tag{2.6.6}$$

In that case if $z_p^{(m+r)*} < \mu' < z^{(m+1)*}$ (2.6.7)

then all the inequalities in (2.6.3) will be satisfied as will be evident from the graphical representation given below:

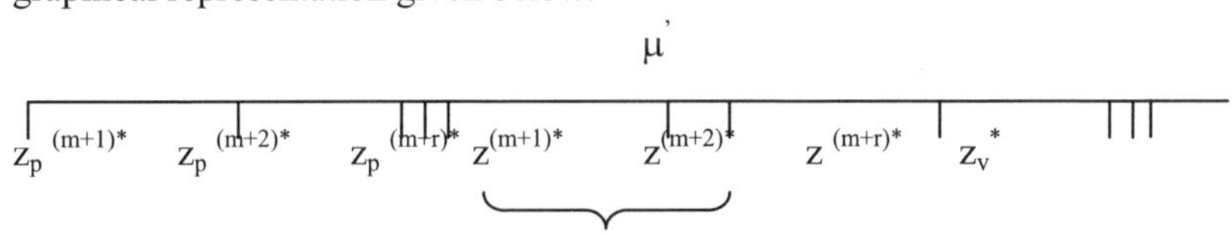

(Case $\alpha^{(i)} < \beta^{(i)}$, $G_i < 1$, $i = m+1, m+2, \ldots, m+r$)

Combining the conditions given in (2.6.5) and (2.6.7) , we can claim that irrespective of whether
$G_i > 1$ or $G_i < 1$, if the following condition is fulfilled namely,

$$z_p^{(m+r)*} < \mu' < \text{Min}\left(z^{(m+1)*}, z^{(m+r)*}\right) \tag{2.6.8}$$

then the vendor will be in a position to give total discounts to the customers $C_{m+1}, C_{m+2}, \ldots, C_{m+r}$ respectively as follows:

$$\frac{JACA_{v,c_{m+1}}\left(z_p^{(m+1)*} \to z^{(m+1)*}\right)}{2}, \quad \frac{JACA_{v,c_{m+2}}\left(z_p^{(m+2)*} \to z^{(m+2)*}\right)}{2}$$

$$\frac{JACA_{v,c_{m+r}}\left(z_p^{(m+r)*} \to z^{(m+r)*}\right)}{2} \tag{2.6.9}$$

Hence unit price discounts acceptable to the purchasers will be respectively

$$\frac{JACA_{v,c_{m+1}}\left(z_p^{(m+1)*} \to z^{(m+1)*}\right)}{2\,E(X_{m+1})}, \ldots\ldots, \frac{JACA_{v,c_{m+r}}\left(z_p^{(m+r)*} \to z^{(m+r)*}\right)}{2\,E(X_{m+r})}$$

(2.6.10)

i.e.

$$\frac{1}{2}\sqrt{\frac{\pi}{2}}JACA_{v,c_{m+1}}\left(z_p^{(m+1)*} \to z^{(m+1)*}\right), \ldots, \frac{1}{2}\sqrt{\frac{\pi}{2}}JACA_{v,c_{m+r}}\left(z_p^{(m+r)*} \to z^{(m+r)*}\right)$$

(2.6.11)

Let $\delta = Max\frac{1}{2}\sqrt{\frac{\pi}{2}}JACA_{v,c_{m+k}}\left(z_p^{(m+k)*} \to z^{(m+k)*}\right)$ for $1 \le k \le r$

(2.6.12)

Since δ is the maximum of the unit price discounts mentioned in (2.6.12) therefore the vendor can satisfy all the customers $C_{m+1}, C_{m+2}, \ldots, C_{m+r}$ with this discount and persuade them to adopt individual JELS.

Let $\alpha^{(i)} > \beta^{(i)}$ for i = (m+r) + 1, (m+r) + 2, ……., (m+r) + s
Combining 2.5.12 with 2.4.11, we have

$$z_v^* < z^{(i)*} < \lambda^{(i)} < z_p^{(i)*} \qquad (2.6.13)$$

for i = (m+r) + 1, (m+r) + 2, ……., (m+r) + s.
i.e. for i = N +1, N + 2,……….., N + s where N = m + r (2.6.14)

In case $G_i > 1$,

$z^{(N+1)*} > z^{(N+2)*} > \ldots\ldots > z^{(N+s)*}$

Suppose $\{z_p^i\}$ (i = N +1, N + 2,……….., N + s) has been arranged in an ascending order, so that

$$z_v^* < z_p^{(N+1)*} < z_p^{(N+2)*} < z_p^{(N+3)*} \ldots\ldots < z_p^{(N+s)*} \qquad (2.6.15)$$

and

$$\left.\begin{array}{l} z_v^* < z^{(N+1)*} < \lambda^{(N+1)} < z_p^{(N+1)*} \\ z_v^* < z^{(N+2)*} < \lambda^{(N+2)} < z_p^{(N+2)*} \\ \cdots\cdots\cdots\cdots\cdots\cdots \\ z_v^* < z^{(N+s)*} < \lambda^{(N+s)} < z_p^{(N+s)*} \\ \text{Let } \lambda' = \text{Min}\,(\lambda^{(N+1)}, \lambda^{(N+2)}, \ldots\ldots\, \lambda^{(N+s)}) \end{array}\right\} \qquad (2.6.16)$$

The graphical representation will be as follows :

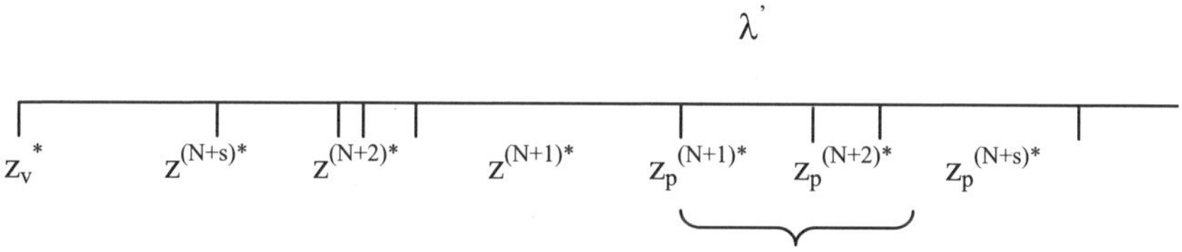

(Case $\alpha^{(i)} > \beta^{(i)}$, $G_i > 1$, $i = N+1, N+2, \ldots. N+s$)

In this case, if $z^{(N+1)*} < \lambda' < z_p^{(N+1)*}, \ldots\ldots$ (2.6.17)

all the inequalities mentioned in 2.6.16 will be satisfied.
In case $G_i < 1$,

$$z^{(N+1)*} < z^{(N+2)*} < \ldots\ldots < z^{(N+s)*} \qquad (2.6.18)$$

As $\{z_p^{\,i}\}$ $(i = N+1, N+2, \ldots., N+s)$

has been arranged in ascending order, therefore 2.6.16 will remain unchanged. Hence the graphical representation will be as follows:

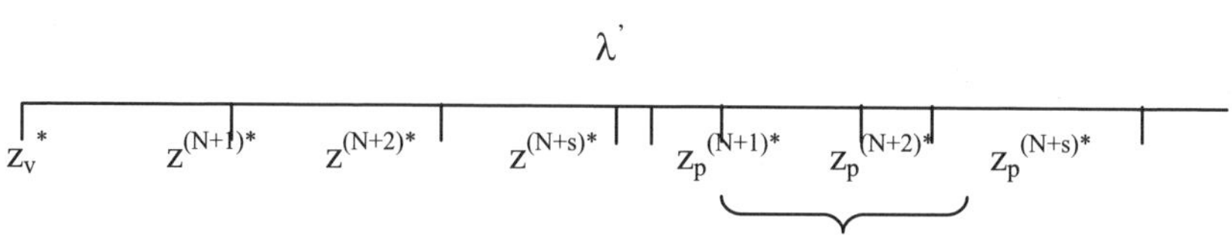

In this case if $z^{(N+s)*} < \lambda' < z_p^{(N+1)*}$ (2.6.19)

then all the inequalities mentioned in 2.6.16 will be satisfied.

Combining 2.6.17 with 2.6.19, we can conclude that whether $G_i > 1$ or $G_i < 1$, if the following condition is fulfilled:

$$\text{Max}\left(z^{(N+1)^*}, z^{(N+s)^*}\right) < \lambda' < z_p^{(N+1)^*} \tag{2.6.20}$$

then all the inequalities mentioned in 2.6.16 will be satisfied.

Hence in that case the vendor will be in a position to give discounts to the customers $C_{N+1}, C_{n+2}, \ldots C_{N+s}$ respectively as follows:

$$\frac{JACA_{v,c_{N+1}}\left(z_p^{(N+1)^*} \rightarrow z^{(N+1)^*}\right)}{2}, \ldots\ldots\ldots, \frac{JACA_{v,c_{N+s}}\left(z_p^{(N+s)^*} \rightarrow z^{(N+s)^*}\right)}{2}$$

(2.6.21)

Hence unit price discounts acceptable to the customers will be respectively

$$\frac{JACA_{v,c_{N+s}}\left(z_p^{(N+1)^*} \rightarrow z^{(N+1)^*}\right)}{2\,E(X_{N+1})}, \ldots\ldots\ldots, \frac{JACA_{v,c_{N+s}}\left(z_p^{(N+s)^*} \rightarrow z^{(N+s)^*}\right)}{2\,E(X_{N+s})}$$

(2.6.22)

i.e. $\frac{1}{2}\sqrt{\frac{\pi}{2}} JACA_{v,c_{N+1}}\left(z_p^{(N+1)^*} \rightarrow z^{(N+1)^*}\right)$,.......,

$\frac{1}{2}\sqrt{\frac{\pi}{2}} JACA_{v,c_{N+s}}\left(z_p^{(N+s)^*} \rightarrow z^{(N+s)^*}\right)$

Let $\bar{\delta} = Max \frac{1}{2}\sqrt{\frac{\pi}{2}} JACA_{v,c_{N+k}}\left(z_p^{(N+k)^*} \rightarrow z^{(N+k)^*}\right)$ for $1 \le k \le s$ (2.6.23)

This $\bar{\delta}$ is the maximum unit price discount which will satisfy all the customers

$C_{N+1}, C_{N+2}, \ldots\ldots C_{N+s}$

Let $\Delta = \text{Max}\,(\delta,\ \bar{\delta})$ (2.6.24)

Obviously this unit price discount Δ will satisfy all the m customers C_1, C_2,…. C_m who have $\alpha^{(i)} = \beta^{(i)}$, all the r customers C_{m+1}, C_{m+2},… C_{m+r} who have $\alpha^{(i)} < \beta^{(i)}$ satisfying condition 2.6.1 and all s customers $C_{(m+r)+1}$, $C_{(m+r)+2}$, … $C_{(m+r)+s}$, customers having $\alpha^{(i)} > \beta^{(i)}$ and fulfilling the condition 2.6.13. It is to be noted that the conditions mentioned in 2.6.8 and 2.6.17 are only of theoretical interest. For practical purpose, after arranging $\{z_p^{\,i}\}$ (i = m+1, m+2, …) in ascending order, r and s have to be found out satisfying 2.6.16 and 2.6.3 and unit price discount Δ as mentioned in 2.6.24 has to be given to satisfy m+r+s customers.

However, some more number of customers (say M) may be left out in the process whose $\alpha^{(i)} < \beta^{(i)}$ but the condition 2.6.1 is not fulfilled and whose $\alpha^{(i)} > \beta^{(i)}$, but the condition 2.6.13 is not fulfilled. In such cases, individual JELS model will not work. For these customers, the vendor may insist to adopt vendor's ELS (z_v^*) associated by unit price discountΔ. As the vendor is the sole supplier of the item, these customers will be compelled to accept the proposal given by the vendor.

In that case the total lot size (i.e. order level of all the n-customers) will be equal to $\left(\sum_{i=1}^{n-M} z^{(i)*} + M.z_v^*\right)$, with lead time zero, as the inventory level of the vendor is sufficiently high.

3. Conclusion

Although many scholars like Lu Lu [11] etc, have tried to develop some new models in search of an alternative approach to Banerji's [1], [2] JELS model with a view to eliminate the possibility of making open the different types of costs involved in deciding the individual inventory pricing policies under similar condition as though of Banerji'e [1], The Model is developed to make more realistic in nature, when different customers approach a vendor with different individual inventory policies. The vendor negotiates with each individual customer and compromises at the individual JELS. The inventory levels (lot size) of the vendor are revision 1 to meet all the demands. The optimum demands of all cutomers can revision of the available stocks of the vendor immediately (i.e., with lead time 0) and no replenishment is necessary. The model deals to derive are revision 1 unified condtions and to formulate unit price discount to suit all the n customers to make the JELS model a success.

References

[1] Benerji , "A Joint Economic – Lot Size Model for Purchaser and Vendor," Decision Sciences 17, 292-311, 1986a

[2] A. Banerji, "On A Quantity Discount Pricing Model to Increase Vendor Profits," Management Science 32, 1513-1517, 1986b.

[3] S. K. Goyal, "On improving the single-vendor single buyer integrated production inventory model with a generalized policy, European Journal of Operation Research," 125, 429-430, 2000.

[4] S. K. Goyal, "An Integrated Inventory Model for a single Supplier – Single Customer Problem," Int. Journal of Prod. Res., 15, No.1, 107-111, 1976.

[5] A. Kosadat, "Joint Economic Lot-Size Model with back-ordering policy," Thesis, Department of Industrial Engg.. Texas Tech University, Lubbock, Texas, 2000.

[6] V. Ongsakul, "Joint Economic Lot Size problem with pipeline inventory cost," Thesis, Department of Industrial engg., Texas Tech. University, Lubbock, Texas, 1998.

[7] S. Viswanathan, "Optimal Strategy for the integrated vendor-buyer inventory model," European Journal of Operation Research, Vol. 105, issue 1, 38-42, 1998.

[8] S. K. Goyal and Y.P. Gupta, "Integrated Inventory Models: the Buyer – Vendor co-ordination," European Journal of Operation Research, 41, 261-269, 1989.

[9] Eric Sucky, "A single buyer – single supplier bargaining problem with asymmetric information- Theoretical approach and software implementation," Geothe – University, p-80a, HICSS '03, Track 3, 2003.

[10] H. L. Lee and M.J. Rosenblatt," A Generalized Quantity Discount pricing Model to Increase supplier's Profits," Management science 32, 1177-1185, 1986.

[11] Lu Lu, "Theory and Methodology a One-vendor Multi Buyer Integrated Inventory Model," European Journal of Operation Research 81, 312-323, 1995.

[12] D. A. Khan, U.C. Ray and G. Panda, "A JELS models under different demand rates in different cycles," AMSE Modeling Measurement & Control, Vol. 22, No. 3,4, 47-56, 2001.

[13] D. A. Khan, U.C. Ray and G. Panda, "A JELS probabilistic Inventory model with random demand having uniform distribution in a one vendor-one customer situation", AMSE Modeling Measurement & Control, , Vol. 27 no. 1, 19-34, 2006.

[14] D. A. Khan, U.C. Ray and G. Panda, "A JELS probabilistic Inventory model with random demand having truncated normal distribution in a one vendor- one customer situation", AMSE Modeling Measurement & Control, Vol. 28 no. 1-2, issue 1, 2007.

[15] D. A. Khan, "A JELS probabilistic Inventory model with random demand having uniform distribution in a one vendor and multi customer situation", AMSE Modeling Measurement & Control, Vol. 30, Issue 1, 2009.

[16] D. Saraswati, A. Cakravastia, B. P. Iskandar & A. H. Halim, "Joint Economic Lot Size Model with Quality Improvement for A Single Supplier and A Single Buyer Cooperative Collaboration", IEEE IEEM, 1956-1960, 2009.

[17] M. R. Akbari Jokar and M. Sheikh Sajadieh, "Optimizing a Joint Economic Lot Sizing Problem with Price-Sensitive Demand", Scientia Iranica, Vol. 16, No. 2, pp. 159-164, 2009.

ALEATORY AND EPISTEMIC MODELING OF UNCERTAINTY FOR QUANTITATIVE SIMULATIONS

HANS SCHJÆR-JACOBSEN
Copenhagen University College of Engineering, 15 Lautrupvang, 2750 Ballerup, Denmark

Two alternative approaches to quantitative modeling of uncertainty are available today and have been applied to a number of real world uncertainty problems, such as investment analyses and budgeting of large infra structure projects. This paper further contributes to the understanding of similarities and differences of the two approaches. The probability approach offers a good framework for representation of randomness and variability whereas the possibility approach is particular well suited for representation of uncertainty of a non-statistical nature due to lack of knowledge and requires less information than the probability approach. Based on the kind of uncertainty and knowledge present, these aspects are discussed in the case of rectangular representation of uncertainty by the uniform probability distribution and the interval, respectively. Also triangular representations are dealt with and compared.

1. Introduction

This paper is concerned with exploration and comparison of the propagation of uncertainty in non-monotonic models when uncertainty is quantified by probability and possibility. Representation of uncertain numbers by probability distributions is used when the situation is characterized by *aleatory uncertainty*. This means that the uncertainty at hand is a result of randomness and statistical variances. This kind of uncertainty is practically irreducible because it is inherently a consequence of processes and phenomena that are beyond control. As an example consider the influence of weather conditions on the building cost of a construction project: Conditions can be described based on statistical meteorological data and incorporated in the risk budget of the project and the resulting cost is basically best described by a probability distribution. On the other hand we have *epistemic uncertainty* where the source of uncertainty is ignorance or lack of knowledge. This kind of uncertainty is best described by possibility distributions like intervals and, more generally, fuzzy numbers. As an example, consider the uncertainty connected with implementation of a project partly based on technology not yet available in a form sufficiently mature to allow determining the cost to be incurred. However, this kind of uncertainty can be reduced by further research and investigations into the technology: If the uncertainty is represented by an interval, the values at the end points of the interval can be further qualified and the width of the interval, i.e. the uncertainty, can be reduced.

Earlier work by the author on the problems addressed in this paper includes [1] – [6]. The results presented in the following have been developed partly as a response to numerous questions from practitioners to the author concerning the computational similarities and differences between the alternative approaches to representation of uncertainty. Whereas representation by probabilities is widely used in the risk and uncertainty business, often in connection with Monte Carlo simulation, the possibility representation is hardly applied or even known.

2. Basic calculations with rectangular distributions

By a rectangular distribution we refer to a distribution of the form shown in Figure 1. It is defined by the numbers a and b and may be interpreted as a uniform probability distribution with mean value μ and standard deviation σ as well as an interval [a; b], which is special form of a fuzzy number.

There is currently a heated discussion both involving researchers and practitioners whether it is relevant to distinguish between a rectangular distribution being interpreted as a probability distribution or a possibility distribution. One thread of discussion was triggered by [7] resulting in a number of responses [8] – [11] as well as a response from the original author [12]. Basically, the discussion can be summarized this way. If all that is known, is than an uncertain variable lies between a and b, some people argue, like in [7], that it should be readily represented by a uniform probability distribution. However, the problem is that by choosing this representation extra information is added to the initial knowledge without justification, namely knowledge about the uncertainty at hand, i.e. the uncertainty is due to phenomena of an aleatory (random) character. Against this it is argued that a better representation is the interval [a; b] which is a precise representation of the knowledge available, namely that the uncertain variable lies between a and b and that is all we know. Thus we arrive at the representation of epistemic uncertainty by possibility distributions. Another way of putting this is to say that the possibility representation is characterized by requiring less information than does the corresponding probability distribution. Or the other way round: Probability representation is not suitably applied in cases where there is scarce information about the probability distribution.

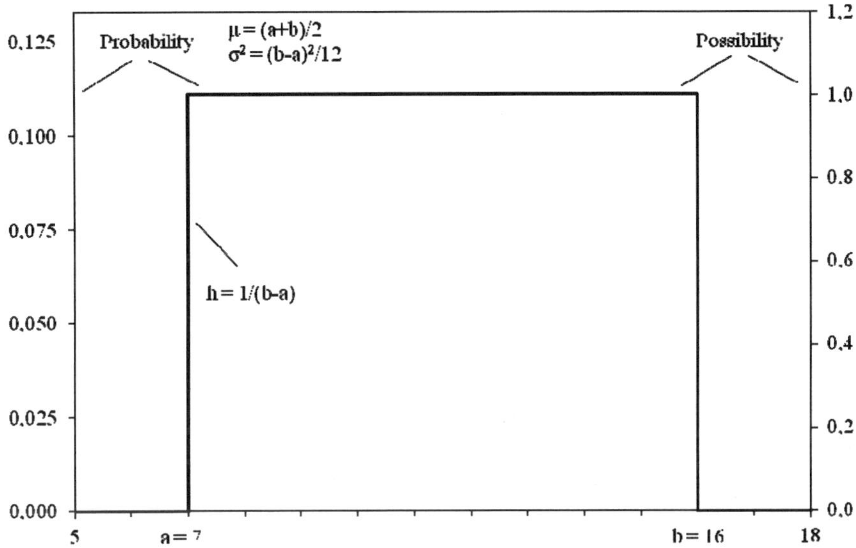

Figure 1. Alternative interpretations of a rectangular distribution.

Firstly, the two alternative representations reflect the two situations we have depending on the kind of knowledge, or lack of knowledge, we possess about the actual uncertainty at hand. Secondly, the two alternative representations call for quite different ways of calculations needed in order to propagate the uncertainty. To calculate the uncertain function of uncertain variables in this paper we make use of Monte Carlo simulation [13] in the probability case and global optimization in the possibility case [14]. Whereas Monte Carlo simulation is widely used by practitioners in the risk and uncertainty business, possibility calculations are not so commonly used. In order to do basic calculations with intervals in this Section we make use of interval arithmetic [15]. Due to page limitations addition and subtraction are omitted.

Figure 2 shows the multiplication of two identical variables like the one in Figure 1. The possibility product maintains the same possibility for any outcome of the product between 49 and 256. The probability distributions depend heavily on the degree of correlation where a 100% positive correlation gives a result quite close to that of the possibility distribution.

Finally, Figure 3 reveals the outcome of dividing the same two variables. The interval result is between 0,44 and 2,29 with equal possibility. By using a 100% negative correlation the shape of the probability distribution is graphically close to that of Figure 2.

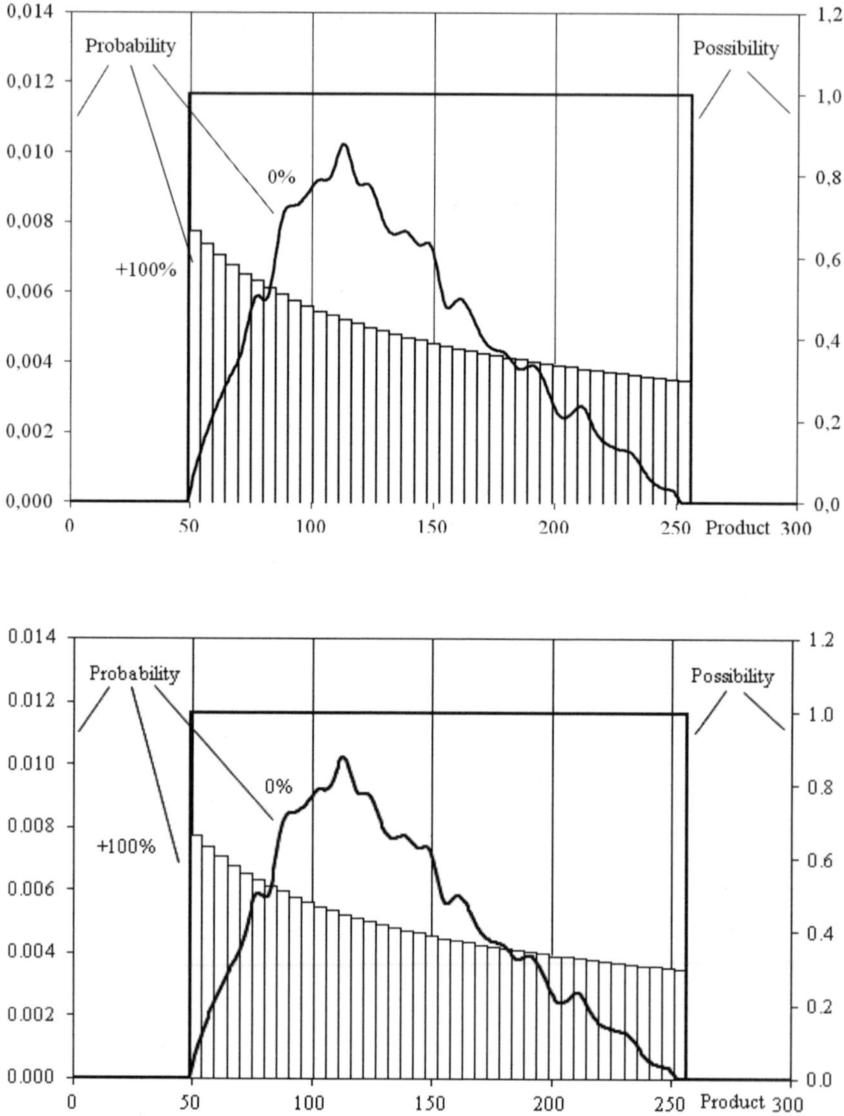

Figure 2. Multiplication of two rectangular distributions, correlation in per cent.

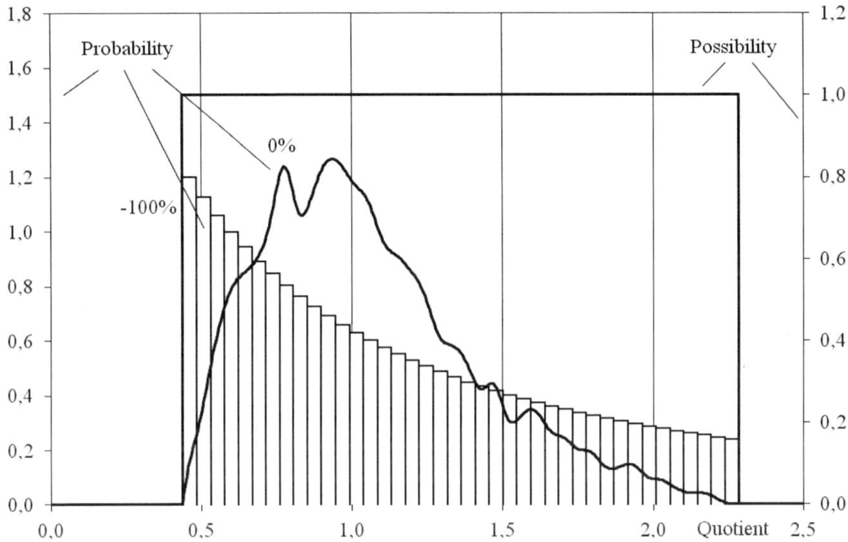

Figure 3. Division of two rectangular distributions, correlation in per cent.

Note that the probability distributions of uncorrelated variables in Figures 2 and 3 tend to roll off to zero at the ends of the finite support internals. Generally, it is one of the pitfalls when using probability representation that the less correlated the input variables are, the less uncertainty (i.e. standard deviation) is observed in the output variables. On the contrary, when the input variables are fully correlated (positively or negatively) the output variables are more uncertain. This becomes even clearer from the following examples.

3. Basic calculations with triangular distributions

The triangular distribution is often applied in practical risk and uncertainty management. Here we consider the triangular distribution in Figure 4, alternatively interpreted as a probability distribution with mean value μ and standard deviation σ and a possibility distribution. In order to calculate the resulting membership function we use interval arithmetic [15] on a series of α-cuts, $\alpha = 0(0{,}05)1$. In other words, we arrive at the resulting membership function by calculation on a series of nested intervals. In contrast to the rectangular possibility distribution the triangular distribution contains degrees of possibilities. For example, the possibility of c is equal to unity and the possibility of 8,5 and 13 is equal to 0,5.

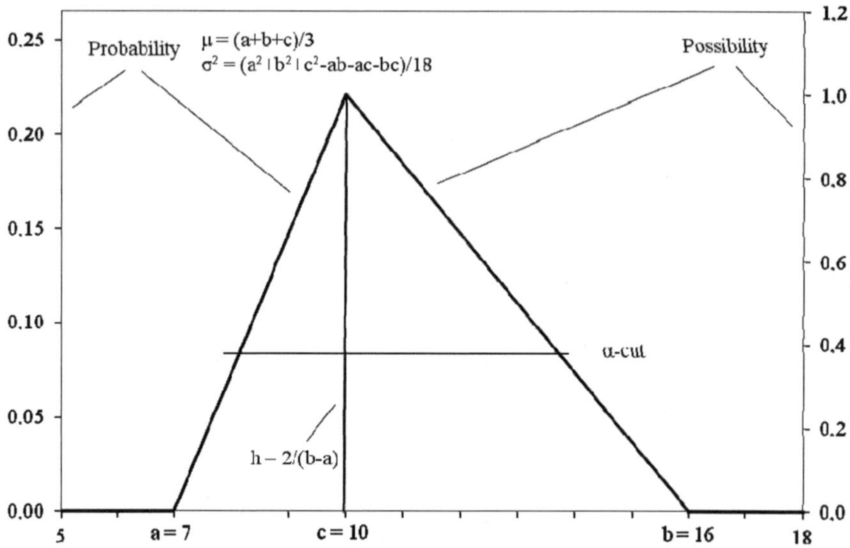

Figure 4. Alternative interpretations of a triangular distribution.

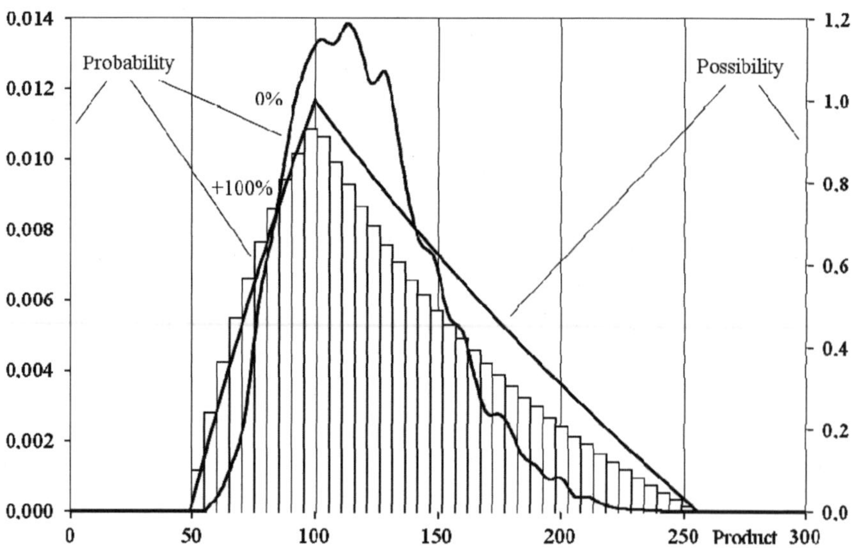

Figure 5. Multiplication of two triangular distributions, correlation in per cent.

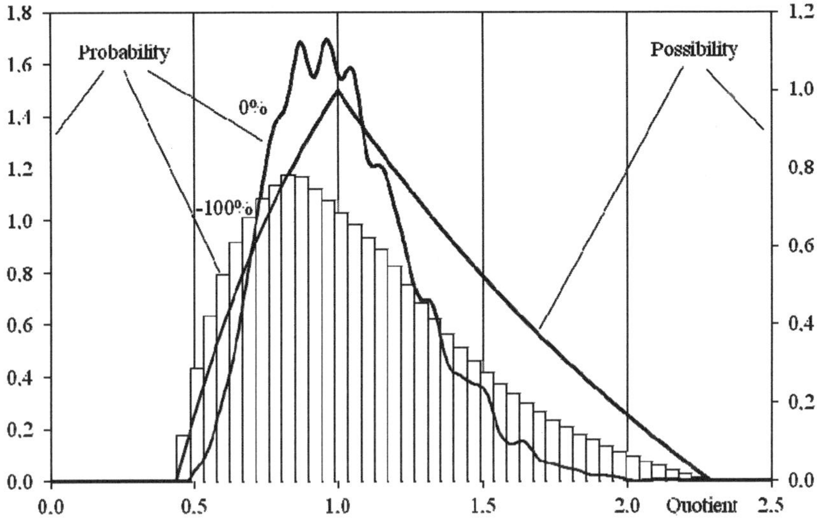

Figure 6. Division of two triangular distributions, correlation in per cent.

Figure 5 shows the product of two distributions and the quotient is shown in Figure 6. Note that the most possible values in both cases are attained by performing multiplication and division directly on the value of c = 10. Further note from Figure 6, that in case of division with 100% negative correlation the modus of the probability distribution and the highest possibility are attained at different values.

4. Simulation with non-monotonic functions

When a non-monotonic function of fuzzy arguments is calculated we can no longer use interval arithmetic. This is because the minimum and maximum of the function is no longer attained at the interval end-points but rather at some interior points. Consequently, we use global optimization to calculate correct intervals, [14]. In [6] an extensive analysis of calculation of a non-monotonic economic case was presented. To compare with the probabilistic representation we use here a simple non-monotonic function $f(x) = x(1-x)$. Obviously, when calculated on the interval [0; 1], the minimum 0 is attained at x = 0 and 1, and the maximum 0,25 is attained at x = 0,5. Straight forward application of interval arithmetic would yield the maximum equal to 1 which obviously is wrong. In cases when calculating functions where a variable appears more than once may also yield wrong results. A detailed discussion can be found in [6].

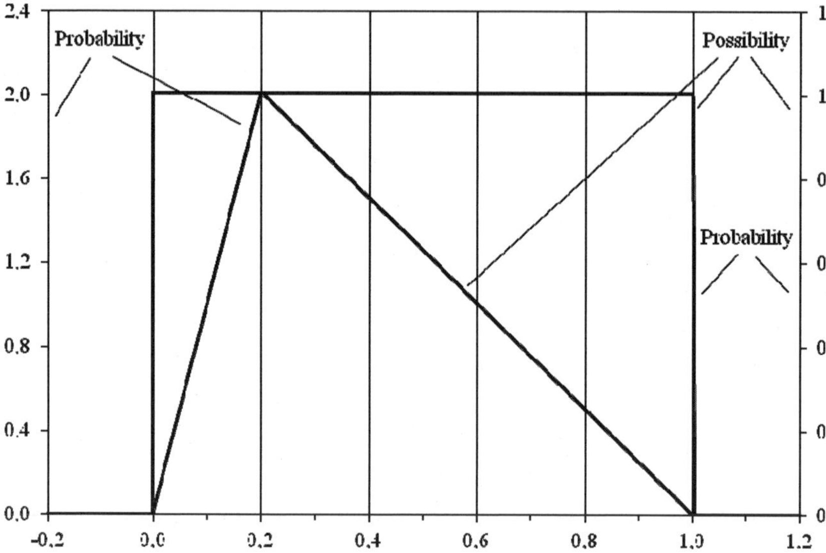

Figure 7. Rectangular and triangular arguments of x(1-x).

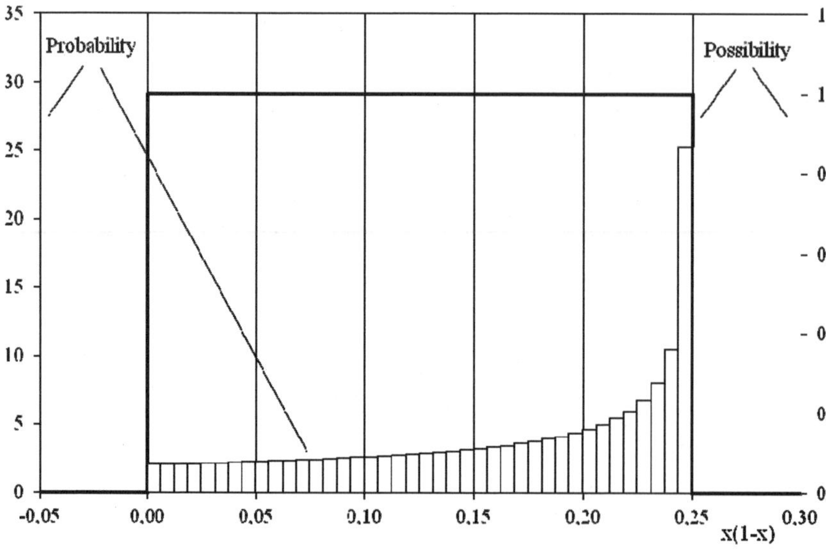

Figure 8. Function x(1-x) with rectangular argument.

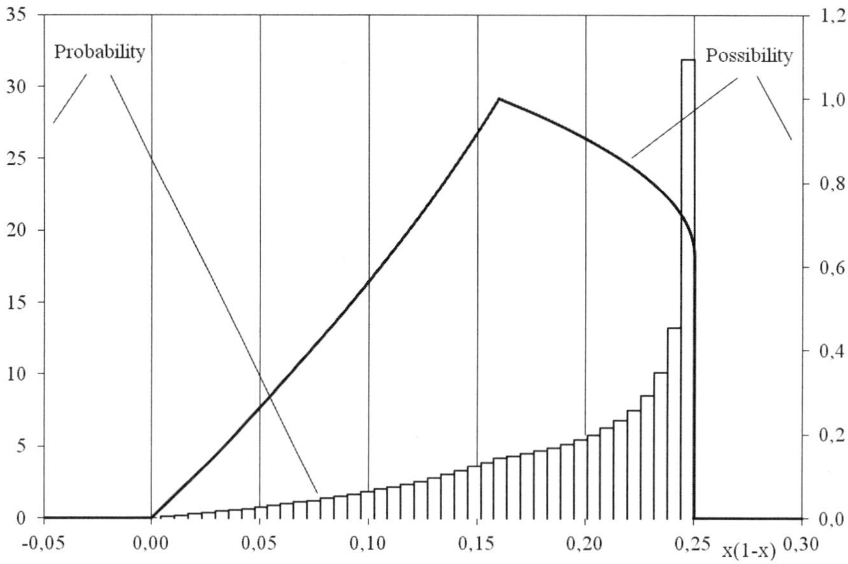

Figure 9. Function x(1-x) with triangular argument.

In Figure 8 the function is calculated with the rectangular arguments from Figure 7. The resulting possibility distribution is correctly bounded between 0 and 0,25 and so is the probability distribution obtained by Monte Carlo simulation. However, there is a noticeable graphical difference between the two distributions emphasizing the fact that the probability model contains more information than the possibility model.

Similar results but with triangular arguments from Figure 7 are shown in Figure 9. From the shape of the resulting membership functions the effect of the ncstcdncss of thc intcrnals corrcsponding to thc diffcrcnt α-cuts bccomcs clcar. For $\alpha > 0{,}7$ the α-cut does not contain the maximum of x(1-x) and consequently the right hand side of the membership function changes its form from vertical. The graphical forms of the two resulting distributions are in general remarkably different. Whereas the modus of the probability function is attained at 0,25 the maximum possibility (equal to unity) is attained at 0,16.

5. Conclusions

By means of quantitative numerical calculations some features of probability and possibility representation of uncertainty modeling have been demonstrated. By performing the basic calculations addition, subtraction, multiplication, and division similarities and differences between probability and possibility representation of uncertain variables have been established on the basis of numerically identical input variables. Rectangular and triangular uncertainty distributions with finite support have been considered and applied in a systematic manner. Standard Monte Carlo simulation has been applied to do calculations on probability representations with and without correlated variables. Further, calculations of a non-monotonic function x(1-x) have been made in order to demonstrate the necessity of applying global optimization if correct values without excessive uncertainty have to be obtained by possibility calculations whereas straight forward application of internal arithmetic yields incorrect (i.e. too wide) results.

Upcoming research into risk and uncertainty management is directed towards developing a better understanding of the similarities and differences in applying probability and possibility representations by further developing the classical risk matrix concept to include uncertain impacts with uncertain likelihoods.

References

1. H. Schjær-Jacobsen, "A new method for evaluating worst- and best-case economic consequences of technological development", *Int. J. of Production Economics,* **46-47**, 241-250 (1996).
2. H. Schjær-Jacobsen, "Representation and calculation of economic uncertainties: Intervals, fuzzy numbers, and probabilities", *Int. J. of Production Economics*, **78**, 91-98 (2002).
3. H. Schjær-Jacobsen, "Modeling of economic uncertainty", *Fuzzy Economic Review*, **9**, 49-73 (2004).
4. H. Schjær-Jacobsen, "Possibility and probability in revisio of economic uncertainty", in: G. Savoiu (Ed.), *Exploratory Domains of Econophysics*, 89-109, Editura Universitaria, Bucharest, Romania (2009).
5. H. Schjær-Jacobsen, "Modelling of economic risk and uncertainty in large infrastructure projects", in: A. M. Gil-Lafuente and J. M. Merigó (Eds.), *Computational Intelligence in Business and Economics*, 473-480, World Scientific (2010).
6. H. Schjær-Jacobsen, "Numerical calculation of economic uncertainty by internal and fuzzy numbers", *J. of Uncertain Systems*, 4, 47-58 (2010).
7. T. Aven, "On the need for restricting the probability analysis in risk assessment to variability", *Risk Analysis*, **30**, 354-360 (2010).
8. D. Dubois, "Representation, propagation, and decision issues in risk analysis under incomplete probabilistic information", *Risk Analysis*, **30**, 361-368 (2010).

9. B. J. Garrick, "Interval analysis versus probabilistic analysis", *Risk Analysis*, **30**, 369-370 (2010).
10. W. A. Huber, "Ignorance is not probability", *Risk Analysis*, **30**, 371-376 (2010).
11. D. W. North, "Probability theory and consistent reasoning", *Risk Analysis*, **30**, 377-380 (2010).
12. T. Aven, "Reply to discussants ...", *Risk Analysis*, **30**, 381-384 (2010).
13. Palisade Corporation, "@Risk 5.5, Monte Carlo simulation add-in module for MS Excel", www.palisade.com/risk (2008).
14. E. Hyvönen and S. De Pascale, "Interval Solver 2000 for Microsoft Excel. User's guide", Version 4.0, Delisoft LtD, Helsinki, Finland (2000).
15. R. E. Moore, "Interval arithmetic and automatic error analysis in digital computing", Ph.D. dissertation, Stanford University, USA (1962).

MANAGEMENT DECISION AND INFORMATION TECHNOLOGY IN ROMANIAN ORGANIZATIONS

EDUARD EDELHAUSER

Head of the Management Department, University of Petroşani, Petroşani, Romania

EMILIA CORINA CORBU

Mathematics and Computer Science Department, University of Petroşani, Petroşani, Romania

ANDREEA IONICĂ

Management Department, University of Petroşani, Petroşani, Romania

The present interest of this paper consists in the powerful impact IT&C technologies have upon the development of nowadays organizations as well as upon the daily life of each individual; nevertheless, one should not ignore the special condition Romanian economy and especially Romanian society as a whole is confronted with during the current period. The motivation of the approach is supported by the fact that IT&C industry has had an explosive development during the last 20 years in Romania. Accordingly, this industry represents 10% of Romania's gross domestic product, a quite high percent in case one notices that not long ago it represented only 3%. The connections between management decision and information technology are validated throughout research hypotheses, and the paper represent an explanatory investigation of the Romanian management information systems market, in 2004 and 2010.

1. Management Information Systems in the last 20 years in the Romanian Organizations

The evolution of the MIS in Romania during the last 20 years, is connected with the evolution of database software, from simple and non complex applications, designed by small software companies in Database Development Systems (DDS) such as FoxPro, to applications made in Relational Database Management Systems (RDMS) for Servers by huge software companies such as Oracle, IBM (International Business Machine) and Microsoft in Ms SQL (Structure Query Language) Server, and are reflected in a optimistic manner in the MIS software implemented for business function in Romanian companies.

Information systems are the means by which organizations and people, utilizing information technologies, gather, process, store, use and disseminate information. The domain of information systems requires a multi-disciplinary approach to studying the range of socio-technical phenomena which determine their development, use and effects in organizations and society. (UK Academy for Information Systems) We consider that the most relevant Information Systems for the Romanian organizations are the Management Information Systems. Also for historical reasons, many of the different types of Information Systems found in commercial organizations are referred to as “Management Information Systems”. However, within a pyramid model, Management Information Systems are management-level systems that are used by middle managers to help ensure the smooth running of the organization in the short to medium term. The highly structured information provided by these systems allows managers to evaluate an organization’s performance by comparing current with previous outputs [1].

In the last 20 years the classical and ordinary database software used in small applications and developed through DDS like FoxPro (1990-1995) are declining in front of new server oriented RDMS, led by Oracle, IBM (using data server DB2) and Microsoft (using Ms SQL Server). This is happening because the servers have become integrant part in a company. These database servers support ERP and BI software. In 1998-1999 because of the governmental requirements a move into another stage has been made, a stage that was considered as visionary, for that moment, and this was outsourcing. In fact, the externalization of IT services for the coal producer took place, by means of the detachment of that activity and the establishment of an independent company. The new economic conditions, from the last 20 years, corroborated with the technological progress made it possible for the number of PC to increase and then for them to develop into computer networks, easing the work not only of the software developers but also of the end users. Servers such AS400 had been used until 2001, but only as an archiving system. Software instruments have been permanently developed so that in 2003 DOS application coexisted with the newer Windows applications. So, reports with many graphical elements, became much more accessible. This conditions predicted the development of integrated solutions, fact that was confirmed by the future reality.

In order to demonstrate this 2004 market perspective, we have investigated in the first study the main national resource companies (most important one in coal, metal and salt – natural resources) [3].

CNH	National Bituminous Coal Company	15,800 employees
CNLO	National Brown Coal Company	16,500 employees
MINVEST	National Copper, Gold and Iron Company	4,700 employees

SALROM National Salt Company 1,550 employees
REMIN National Precious Metal and Non-Ferrous 5,200 employees

We made a managerial research, through a variety of business functions such as manufacturing, supply chain management, financials, human resources and customer relationship management. In every business function we focus on 4, 5 or 6 important and usually applications.

The research has finally revealed the global IT and specific ERP implementing level in the Romanian natural resource companies as well as some problems that are country-wide valid. As we have supposed the financial business function through using ERP is almost 100% implemented in every company, the new concepts of CRM and SCM have a very poor implementation (under 30%), the payroll of HRM is almost 100% implemented, but in the HRM only the most usual applications are implemented, and we found a relationship between computers and database software as a basis for the ERP software [3].

The year of 2005 meant a growth of the institutional needs as far as information providing concern. In Romania had already been implemented the tax records system which forced large agencies to migrate to integrated solutions. The availability of ERP solution implementation in the coal companies was low because of the organizational structure and of the aging technique. Another element that leads to that was the permanent perspective of the closing of coalmines and of the reorganization of activity, details that virtually blocked all the investment of the kind. However even in those given conditions the software instruments, following the natural course of development, was modernized and they have been developed into integrated system (human resources, financial, manufacturing, maintenance), the perspective being that of a dedicated ERP integration for the mining activity.

Subsequent in 2010 we have made a second study that set sights on newer IT&C Applications with a modern information technology architecture. Classes as Dashboard, Query and Reporting, Data Mining, Score Cards, ERP, CRM, SCM, HRIS, SFA, Data Warehouse, Data Marts, Master Data, and others, are investigated in our 2010 study.

We have analyzed the level of implementing of ERP applications in the functions of the enterprise through SIVECO Applications (SA), and that the implementation of analytical and managerial decision tools through SIVECO Business Analyzer (SBA) [4].

The research performed in 2010 aimed at investigating the Romanian society from the large size organizations and small and medium size enterprises point of view. We identified the fact that the management methods used differ but converge towards a single objective, namely increasing productivity. In this context the approach of large organizations was performed on the base of implementing informational systems “made in Romania”, of the SIVECO company (a 100% Romanian software company), and SME and micro-enterprises were analyzed by means of a mixed approach of the local solution implementations and international solutions. Comparatively analyzing the management methods, we observed which are the foreground methods used by Romanian organizations [4].

2. An explanatory investigation of the Romanian Management Information Systems market

2.1. Organizations

In the virtue of the questionnaire we achieved the results and we were able to formulate and validate hypothesis. Thus we formulated a hypothesis that decision is highly influenced through the IT&C methods and we have reached the conclusion that providing with excessive hardware is not necessarily a useful thing to do, if that hardware is not correlated with the software applications. Another objective of this study was to test die impacts of contingency factors, including size, on die one hand, and ERP systems success, on the other. We demonstrate that there would be a relationship between firm size and ERP success; the relationship between firm size and ERP success will be moderated by IT assets, such diat success will be higher in larger firms and that the relationship between firm size and ERP success will be moderated by IT resources, such that success will be higher in larger firms. We have concentrated on public organizations because we believe that the adoption of ERP systems might be higher there than in private sector organizations. We have analyzed the data using SPSS 17.0, and the respective response rates, excluding the unusable questionnaires received, was 7 organizations.

2.2. Methodology

2.2.1. Questionnaire, the research instrument

The study set sights on Romanian organizations which implemented a SIVECO ERP and BI software, and were collected in 2010 year. The instruments used for collecting data were a quantitative questionnaire, an qualitative one and an interview. The research based on the quantitative questionnaire was structured on 27 questions focused on hardware and software endowment (8 questions), implementation of the ERP business software for five business function such as manufacturing, SCM, financial, HRM and CRM (6 questions), other 6 questions were dedicated only to Human Resource Management function and the last 7 questions were dedicated to BI management methods such as Dashboard, Query and Reporting, Data Mining, Score Cards, Data Warehouse, Data Marts, Master Data.

2.2.2. Respondents

Even data were collected only from 7 organizations, these are representative for the 2010 Romanian economy, because in this economical moment Romania has only 5,000 companies that need an ERP and a BI software instrument as a advanced management method. So we have only 2,000 big companies having more than 250 employees which can afford to implement a SAP, Oracle or SIVECO ERP software. But these 2,000 companies generate incomes two times higher than the other 10,000 SMB, and equal those of the 500,000 small Romanian companies, that have under 50 employees. From these 2,000 big organizations most of them are branches from transnational companies, and have mostly implemented ERP existing in their main organization, usually SAP or Oracle. So, are likely to be investigated public organizations and private Romanian capital organizations. These two categories have a hundred percent Romanian management, and had to optimize it.

The regression analysis using the method of least squares requires a dataset of n pairs (xi,yi), where yi are the dependent variables and xi are the independent ones. There were analyzed over 500 Romanian enterprises, that implement a SIVECO ERP and were identified 7 distinct groups without any significant deviations among the enterprises forming each group. In order to apply this method there were chosen 7 companies that were included in the present study. Each of these 7 companies is representative for the enterprises group, having similar trend. This simplified version of the method is suitable for our problem because this way there were obtained very clear results.

3. Effects induced by the implementing of MIS in the Romanian organizations. Validation of scientific research hypotheses

The goal of paper was the validation of the research hypotheses formulated regarding the existing connections among management decision, advanced management methods, and information technology. The validation of these hypotheses regarding the existing connections among management decision, the advanced management methods, and information technology, allowed us to show the importance that information technology has upon an organization at informational, decisional, and methodological levels [7].

Hypothesis 1. Implementation of ERP and BI applications in all functions of an organization increases the influence of the advanced management methods in the decision making processes of the organization. Hypothesis 1 will be tested in particular from the perspective that BI applications influence the organization's performance management processes and less in terms of ERP applications.

Table 1. Variables used in proving the hypothesis 1

	organizatia	ERP_Mediu	Proprietate	CA_efect	PN_efect	BI_Mediu	BI_ERP_Mediu
1	Aeropotul Timisoara	0,50	0	1,15	0,52	0,25	0,71
2	ANIF Dunare Olt	0,50	0	1,13	0,42	0,75	0,14
3	Hidroserv Hateg	0,83	0	1,07	0,70	1,00	1,00
4	Apa Serv Valea Jiului	0,83	0	0,98	0,84	0,25	0,86
5	Aerostar Bacau	1,00	1	1,37	1,98	0,25	0,43
6	Meva Severin	1,00	1	1,71	2,65	0,75	0,29
7	Romvag Caracal	1,00	1	2,14	3,13	0,75	0,57

Table 2. Linear regression analysis between BI implementation and effect on profit growth for private organizations (proprietate=1)

Model Summary

Model	R Proprietate = 1 (Selected)	R Square	Adjusted R Square	Std. Error of the Estimate
1	,908[a]	,825	,650	,34347

a. Predictors: (Constant), BI_Mediu

ANOVA[b,c]

Model		Sum of Squares	df	Mean Square	F	Sig.
1	Regression	,556	1	,556	4,717	,275[a]
	Residual	,118	1	,118		
	Total	,674	2			

a. Predictors: (Constant), BI_Mediu

b. Dependent Variable: PN_efect

c. Selecting only cases for which Proprietate = 1

We have conducted a regression analysis to determine the link between the degree of implementation of BI applications such specific BI tools and profit growth effect induced by these organizations, and noticed that it is a very good (with a significance of correlation R = 0.908> 0.63 for only two degrees of freedom). Due to the low number of degrees of freedom F ratio is small and value Sig. is greater than 0.05 (0.275), and although the linear relationship between two variables which is very good (R = 0.908) is not necessarily explained by the influence of variable change on the dependent variable PN_efect and independent variable BI_Mediu for private organizations [5]. (Table 2)

We have conducted a regression analysis to determine the link between the degree of implementation of the mix type BI and ERP applications and profit growth effect induced by these organizations, and noticed that it is a very good correlation with a significance of R = 0.800 > 0.63 for only two degrees of freedom). Due to the low number of degrees of freedom, F ratio is small and value Sig. is greater than 0.05 (0.2), linear relationship between two variables that is good (R = 0.8), so this is not necessarily explained by the influence of variation in the independent variable on the dependent variable PN_efect BI_ERP_Mediu for public organizations.(Table 3)

Table 3. Linear regression analysis between ERP & BI implementation and the effect on profit growth in public organizations (proprietate=0)

Model Summary

Model	R Proprietate = 0 (Selected)	R Square	Adjusted R Square	Std. Error of the Estimate
1	,800[a]	,641	,461	,13682

a. Predictors: (Constant), BI_ERP_Mediu

ANOVA[b,c]

Model		Sum of Squares	df	Mean Square	F	Sig.
1	Regression	,067	1	,067	3,567	,200[a]
	Residual	,037	2	,019		
	Total	,104	3			

a. Predictors: (Constant), BI_ERP_Mediu

b. Dependent Variable: PN_efect

c. Selecting only cases for which Proprietate = 0

Hypothesis 2 The number of employees in an organization influences the role of the ERP applications within the respective organizations. The organization dimension is directly connected with the role of the ERP applications within the respective organization.

For this hypothesis we used regression analysis, as a statistical method to evaluate the relation between one independent variable (personal – size of organization) and another continuous dependent variable (ERP_BI given to the ERP and BI level of implementation). We have performed a linear regression analysis using the method of the least square in order to plot a line by a set of observations. Thus we have perform the analysis of the dependence and we have appreciated the extent to which the independent variable influence the dependent. With linear regression we output the regression coefficients necessary to predict one variable ERP_BI from the other personal. The model has been confirmed to be valid because the F test value were 49,35, with significant sig. smaller than 0,05 (0,02) [5]. (Table 4)

Table 4. Linear regression analysis between an independent variable called personal and a dependent variable called ERP_BI for private cases (proprietate=1)

Model Summary

Model	R proprietate = 1 (Selected)	R Square	Adjusted R Square	Std. Error of the Estimate
1	,980[a]	,961	,942	,05897

a. Predictors: (Constant), personal

ANOVA[b,c]

Model		Sum of Squares	df	Mean Square	F	Sig.
1	Regression	,172	1	,172	49,352	,020[a]
	Residual	,007	2	,003		
	Total	,179	3			

a. Predictors: (Constant), personal
b. Dependent Variable: ERP_BI
c. Selecting only cases for which proprietate = 1

The regression coefficient R=0,980 shows a very strong link between the variable ERP_BI given to the ERP and BI level of implementation and the independent variable personal showing the size of the organization, for the private sector. The model explains 96,1% from the total variation of the variable personal (R^2= 0,961). The rest of 3,9% is influenced by other residual factors not included in the model. (Table 4). In conclusion hypothesis has been confirmed. But in BI methods we found a weak link, so for the private sector we found R=0593 smaller than 063. This regression coefficient R=0,593 shows an intermediate link in these case. (Table 5)

Table 5. Linear regression analysis between an independent variable called personal and a dependent variable called BI for private cases (proprietate=1)

Model Summary

Model	R proprietate = 1 (Selected)	R Square	Adjusted R Square	Std. Error of the Estimate
1	,593[a]	,352	,028	,36973

a. Predictors: (Constant), personal

ANOVA[b,c]

Model		Sum of Squares	df	Mean Square	F	Sig.
1	Regression	,148	1	,148	1,086	,407[a]
	Residual	,273	2	,137		
	Total	,422	3			

a. Predictors: (Constant), personal
b. Dependent Variable: BI
c. Selecting only cases for which proprietate = 1

In the case of Hypothesis 1 because of the low number of degrees of freedom (responses on the issue of BI result from 6 organizations, 3 public and 3 private), and although because the linear relationship between variables that quantify the implementation of BI type applications, and the effect induced in profit organization, this relationship is not necessarily explained by the influence of variation in the independent variable. So the Hypothesis 1 is not confirmed. As a general conclusion we would say that public organizations successfully implement ERP applications and the private one are already focused on the implementation of BI applications. For Hypothesis 2 we have found out that only the dimension off the organization and the number of installed computers are of equal average according to the type of property; There is also a good link between the above mentioned characteristics. One the other hand concerning the role played by the ERP applications, in the private sector, considered by us more performing, their isn't a strong link between dimension and the role of the ERP applications, although the correlate coefficient is good. When using advanced methods, of BI type, and analyzing their effect on organizations management the situation is discouraging as there is no good connection even in the private sector, but on the other hand there is an strong link between dimension and the implementation of the ERP an BI mix in private organizations. Therefore the hypothesis is only partial confirmed.

The whole analysis we performed on seven main advanced decision management methods, found that reports and queries that are not really traditional managerial decision tools are considered by our respondents decision tools, and the real advanced management methods such as dashboards, key performance indicators against targets related (BSC Balanced Score Card) and OLAP technology have a less usage. Related to Balanced Score Card is possible that managers continue to perceive it incorrectly Even this is in fact the essence of management decision, allowing managers to select the appropriate measures for each objective, the translation strategy of the organization goals and objectives and assist organizations in implementing processes that support strategy management. Reports and queries are still mainly perceived as the basic methods in the decision, but surprisingly Excel is not very efficient used.

4. Conclusions

As a general conclusion we would say that public organizations successfully implement ERP applications and the private one are already focused on the implementation of BI applications. In this context the basic concepts of computer system provides the technical and behavioral foundation that helps applications such as ERP and decision-making process for building a company's strategic advantage over competitors. IT systems is reflected by the structure and IT hardware equipment and base software. Using the IT systems and their applications in operational management, can develop a competitive advantage for the organization at local, national and up to forms of electronic commerce and information exchange level.

We have chosen this research topic due to the fact that under the present social and economic circumstances the conceptualization and use of certain advanced management methods represent one of the main coordinates owing to which management asserts itself as a fundamental element of organizational culture. The period we face places organizations in an unpredictable and instable environment; the solution of coping with such circumstances can only be provided by a performing management. Meanwhile, IT&C definitely influences the existing organizations, and management methods become decisive for the organization's evolution. Consequently, we consider as necessary a radiography of Romanian society regarding the implementation of the advanced management methods based upon information technology capable of offering both an overall view of the implementation level of these methods within Romanian organizations and a prefigure of what it is going to be done in Romanian society at the level of modernizing the organizations' management.

References

1. T.H. Davenport, Putting the enterprise into the enterprise system, *Harvard Business Review*, no 4, pp. 121 (1998).
2. P.F. Drucker, The practice of Management, *Harper Paperbacks, New York*, (2006).
3. E. Edelhauser, Information System for Human Resources Management in a Company, *PhD Thesis*, Petrosani, (2004).
4. E. Edelhauser, A. Ionică, L. Lupu Dima, A Business Intelligence Software Made in Romania, a Solution for Romanian Companies During the Economic Crisis, *Proceedings of the MS'10 International Conference, Computational Intelligence in Business and Economics*, July 15-17, Barcelona, pp. 247-254, BVB65, (2010).
5. E. Edelhauser, IT&C Impact on the Romanian Business and Organizations. The Enterprise Resource Planning and Business Intelligence Methods Influence on Manager's Decision: A Case Study, *Informatica Economica Journal, Vol. 1, 5 No. 2/2011*, pp. 16-28, (2011).
6. J. Emblemsvag, B. Bras, Process Thinking – A New Paradigm for Science and Engineering, *Futures, Vol. 32, No. 7,* pp. 635 – 654, (2000).
7. R.R.K. Sharma, A. Sharma, ERP implementation in defenders and its influence on manager's job: a case study.(Enterprise resource planning), *International Journal of Business Research*, March 1, (2007).

AN ANALYSIS OF THE MOTION PICTURE INDUSTRY AT THE FRENCH BOX OFFICE

FRANCISCO JAVIER MAQUEDA LAFUENTE

Facultad Ciencias Económicas y Empresariales, Departamento Economía Financiera II, Universidad del País Vasco/Euskal Herriko Unibertsitatea. Avda. Lehendakari Agirre 83, 48015 Bilbao

VANESA F. GUZMAN PARRA

Facultad de Ciencias Económicas y Empresariales. Departamento de Economía y Administración de Empresas. Universidad de Málaga, Campus de El Ejido. 29071 Málaga

JOSÉ ROBERTO VILA OBLITAS

Facultad de Ciencias Económicas y Empresariales. Dpto. de Economía y Administración de Empresas. Universidad de Málaga, Campus de El Ejido. 29071 Málaga

This study examines the theatrical market for motion pictures in France by analyzing data from 1980–2010. In particular, this paper seeks to provide a greater understanding of the French film industry by assessing the seasonality and the release dates of the most successful movies in France during the examined period. The conclusions and implications of this analysis for the French film industry are subsequently discussed.

1. Introduction

The importance of a movie's release date is magnified for movies with higher expected revenues because the first week following a film's release accounts for an average of nearly forty percent of the movie's total domestic box office revenue (Einav, 2007). Many researchers find that a film's release date has a significant influence on its revenues (De Vany and Walls, 1997; Terry, Buttler and De´Armond, 2003; Ainslie Drèze and Zufryden, 2005; McKenzie, 2009).

Einav (2007) observes that there are three different types of releases for films, namely wide releases, platform releases, and limited releases. Wide releases are the most common type of release for major film distribution companies; in these releases, the screening of the movie begins in a large number of theaters (typically several thousand) and is accompanied by an extensive national advertising campaign.

Einav (2007) also indicates that one of the most important strategic decisions for film distributors is the release date of a movie. The demand for movies is highly seasonal in the USA (Einav 2007), the UK (Hand and Judge 2010) and Spain (Vila, Guzmán and Quintana 2012).

This paper is organized as follows. The next section describes relevant details of the French movie industry. Section 3 describes the methodology of the study. Section 4 documents the results regarding the seasonality of motion pictures at the French box office. Section 5 provides the conclusions.

2. The French movie industry

The movie industry is composed of three sectors: production, distribution, and exhibition (Dadek, 1962). The agents of the production, distribution, and exhibition sectors are producers, distributors and exhibitors, respectively. The producers make movies, the distributors distribute movies into the exhibition market, and the exhibitors own the theaters in which movies are shown to audiences (Gil, 2010).

The cinema industry in France is also influenced by the protection that it receives from the French government (Dubet, 1999; Siroën, 2000; Demil and Leca, 2003; Cocq, Dantec and Lèvy-Hartman, 2006). Cartier and Liarte (2010) demonstrate that a combination of factors cause the clustering of film release dates.

The French market with respect to movies is characterized by competition between French and American films (Siroën, 2003; Cocq, Dantec and Lèvy-Hartman, 2006; Cartier and Liarte, 2010).

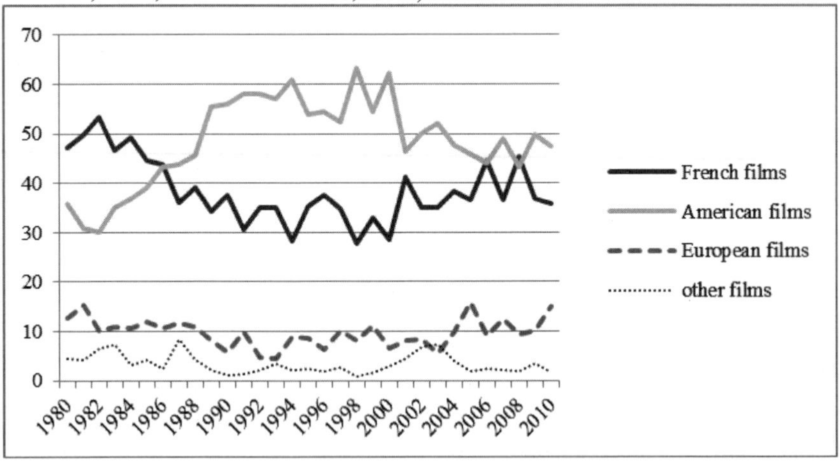

Figure. 1. Market shares in terms of receipts (%)

Figure 1 depicts the market shares of films from various countries in terms of receipts; this figure emphasizes the competition between French and American film industries at the French box office during the 1980-2010 period.

Throughout much of the 1980s, the French films dominated the French market; however, for the 1987-2006 period, American films possessed the greatest share of this market. In recent years, the market shares of French and American films have remained at similar levels.

3. Methodology

To examine the seasonality of the French box office, we have utilized a data set that includes monthly audience data from January 1, 1980 to December 31, 2010 for the films that were exhibited in French theaters. These data have been extracted from the CNC (Centre national du cinema et de l´image animèe) and have allowed us to assess the seasonal variations that affect the audience sizes for these films during the period in question.

In addition, to analyze the release data for the most successful movies, we have studied the top 10 movies that were exhibited from 2002-2010. These data were obtained from Mojo Box Office.

4. Results

Figure 2 presents an initial approximation of movie admissions trends prior to any attempts to conduct a seasonal analysis.

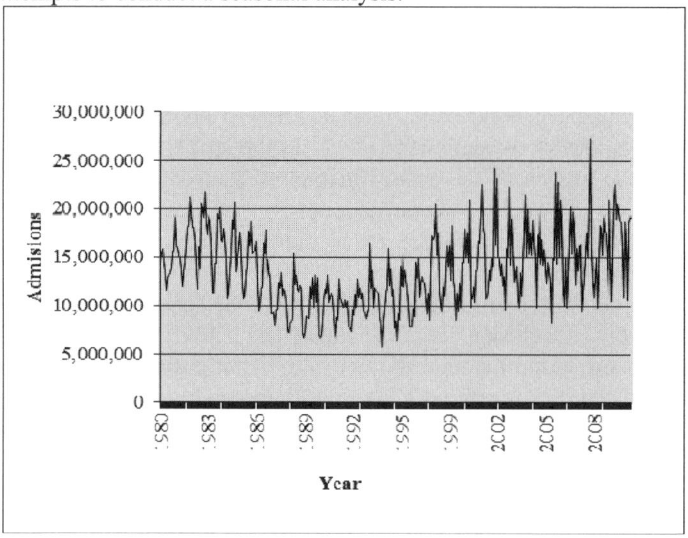

Figure 2. The evolution of movie admissions.

To appropriately assess the seasonal series for movie admissions, we must analyze the moving average of these admissions in a manner that allows us to extract the seasonal variations from the available data.

Several authors discuss the behavior and treatment of seasonal series (Einav, 2007; Vila, Guzmán and Quintana 2012). The seasonal decomposition procedure decomposes a seasonal series into a seasonal component, a combined trend and cycle component, and an "error" component (Makridakis, Wheelwright, & McGee, 1983). Decomposition models are typically additive or multiplicative. In many time series, the amplitude of both the seasonal and irregular variations increase as the level of the trend changes. In this situation, a multiplicative model is usually appropriate.

In the multiplicative model, the original time series is expressed as the product of trend, seasonal and irregular components. Box and Jenkins (1970) indicate that the seasonal series (Yt) of the number of audience, with t=1,..,T, can be expressed in the following form:

Yt=TCt*St*It, t=1,…,n

- The tendency, Tt, indicates the regular movement of the data over the long term. This component represents the long-term trend of the series.
- The cyclical factor, Ct, indicates the oscillatory movement. In practice, it is difficult to separate Tt from Ct. Therefore, these two components are usually represented as a single combined factor, the trend-cycle component TCt, which reflects the changes in level (the height of the sequence graph) throughout the development of the series.
- The seasonal variation, St, indicates the seasonal component oscillations of the series within the same year.
- The irregular movement, It, indicates the variations of the series that are not included in the aforementioned factors. In the case of the seasonal series of the size of the audience, the model that is presented above may be applied because the model variables should appropriately represent the periodic nature of the data without being forced to account for persistent and inexplicable features of these data.

Figure 3 shows the autocorrelations of the time serie in order to provide a more quantitative conclusion about the underlying periodicity.

The autocorrelation function shows a significant peak at a lag of 1 as Figure 3 shows. The significant peak at a lag of 12 suggests the presence of an annual seasonal component in the time serie.

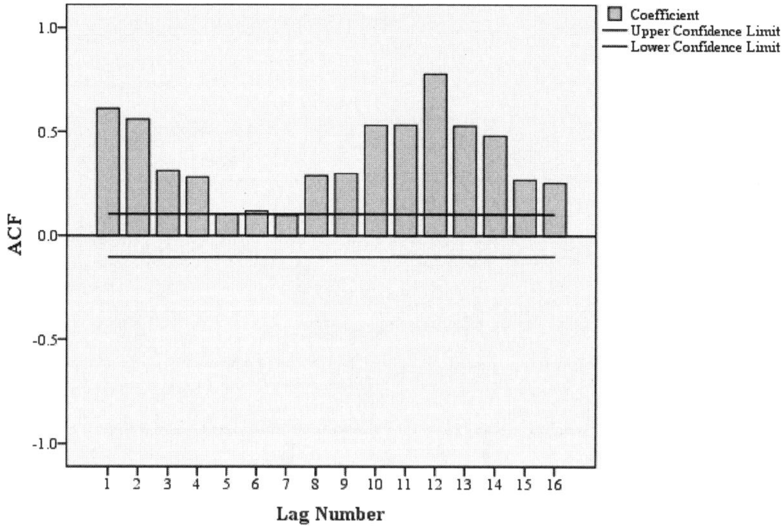

Figure 3. The autocorrelation function for movie admissions

Figure 4 examines the partial autocorrelation function and provides a more definitive conclusion. The significant peak at a lag of 12 in the partial autocorrelation function confirms the presence of an annual seasonal component in the admissions data.

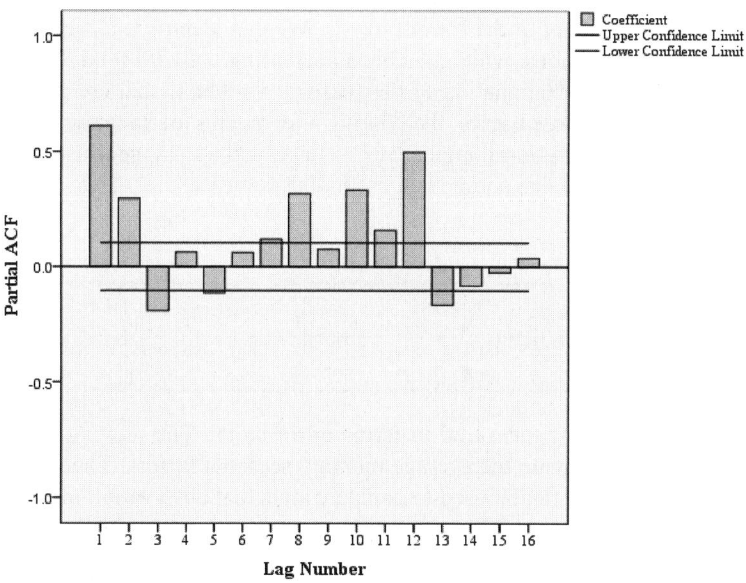

Figure 4. The partial autocorrelation function for movie admissions

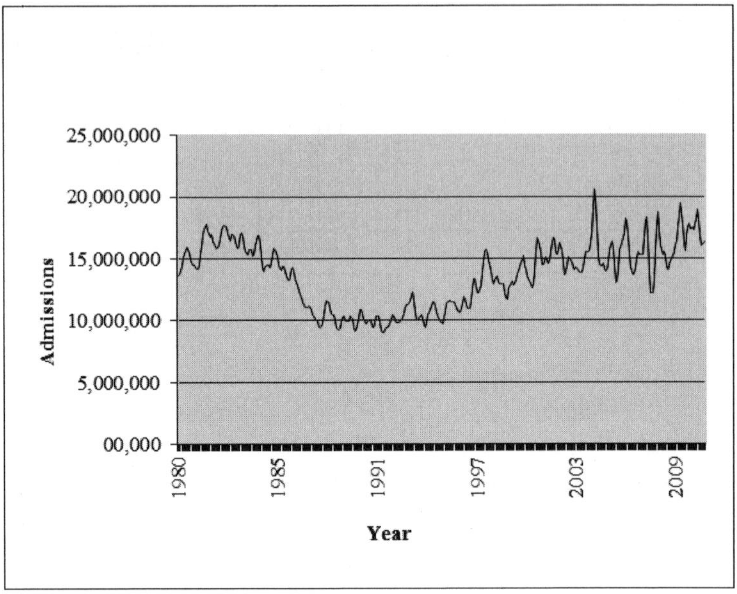

Figure 5. Serie's trend

Figure 5 presents a pattern of movie admissions in which we no longer observe marked peaks, which are a consequence of seasonal variations, thus enabling us to easily identify the overall trends. We can identify a change in the overall trend for admissions, which had been decreasing until 1990 but began to increase thereafter. An examination of the seasonal variations that are provided in Table 1 allows us to observe that during the months of the low-demand season, the seasonal variation component has lower values; by contrast, during the high-demand season, this component has higher values.

Table 1: Seasonal factors

Period (Month)	1	2	3	4	5	6	7	8	9	10	11	12
Seasonal Factor (%)	103.3	120.9	107.7	107.5	85.7	75.9	77.8	88.9	80.3	112.1	109.4	130.4

Seasonal variation is measured in terms of an index. The moving average approach is used to estimate the average monthly seasonal factors. The seasonal index is an average that can be used to compare an actual observation relative to what it would be if there were no seasonal variation. An examination of the factors of the seasonal variation allows us to observe that during the months of the low-demand season, the seasonal variation component displays lower values (see January, February, November and December); by contrast, in July, August and September, this component has higher values.

Table 2: The release dates of the top 10 movies in France for each year during the 2002-2010 period.

Month	1	2	3	4	5	6	7	8	9	10	11	12
French films	5	5	3	0	0	2	2	0	1	2	1	0
American films	9	4	4	4	9	10	12	6	3	3	7	8

Table 2 indicates that the release dates of the top ten movies in France differ depending on the nationality of the films in question. In particular, the peak times for the release of American films are near the summer and Christmas holiday seasons, whereas top-grossing French films are primarily released during the first two months of the year (January and February). This decision contrast with admissions pattern, which peaks in December, as results have shown.

Table 3: Attendance by day

Admissions (%)	Monday	Tuesday	Wednesday	Thursday	Friday	Saturday	Sunday	Total
1980	5,5	11,2	11,4	9,7	17,9	25,0	19,3	100,0
1985	19,0	7,8	11,4	8,6	13,8	25,2	14,2	100,0
1986	16,3	10,0	12,5	10,2	12,5	24,3	14,2	100,0
1987	15,7	7,7	11,3	9,2	14,9	23,2	18,0	100,0
1988	13,6	8,6	13,6	10,0	13,7	26,5	14,0	100,0
1989	15,2	9,1	13,0	9,3	11,8	27,0	14,6	100,0
1990	16,5	8,3	10,8	10,0	14,7	23,7	16,0	100,0
1991	14,7	9,3	11,3	9,4	15,7	23,9	15,7	100,0
1992	14,4	8,7	12,6	10,7	14,9	24,4	14,3	100,0
1993	10,1	11,2	14,5	9,5	13,3	23,2	18,2	100,0
1994	9,5	11,8	13,5	9,1	14,0	25,6	16,5	100,0
1995	9,0	11,6	14,2	11,7	13,1	24,4	16,1	100,0
1996	12,0	11,0	13,3	11,3	12,9	23,3	16,2	100,0
1997	9,8	11,7	12,5	9,0	15,2	25,8	16,0	100,0
1998	12,7	10,2	13,0	12,1	15,0	20,1	16,9	100,0

1999	11,7	10,6	12,4	9,5	14,2	22,3	19,3	100,0
2000	10,8	9,8	15,5	10,5	12,8	23,3	17,3	100,0
2001	8,9	9,6	13,3	11,4	15,8	24,6	16,4	100,0
2002	9,2	11,2	13,9	10,3	14,6	20,5	20,3	100,0
2003	10,3	9,8	14,3	8,9	14,2	23,3	19,2	100,0
2004	9,8	9,3	14,3	10,3	12,3	22,6	21,4	100,0
2005	11,8	9,8	12,5	8,4	9,9	28,4	19,2	100,0
2006	10,7	9,5	12,2	11,4	13,3	21,2	21,7	100,0
2007	9,7	12,1	14,0	7,6	15,4	22,2	19,0	100,0
2008	11,1	9,3	12,8	10,1	11,8	27,9	17,0	100,0
2009	10,4	10,4	14,7	9,8	16,9	19,9	17,9	100,0
2010	8,9	8,1	17,3	8,3	14,6	21,0	21,7	100,0

Table 3 shows that some days are particularly popular for movie-going. Saturdays usually accounts more than 20% of weekly admissions and more than 50% of admissions were between Friday and Sunday. The weekend outing is still a common element of movie-goers′ revisio.

5. Conclusions

We have presented an empirical analysis of the theatrical market for motion pictures in France by analyzing data from 1980–2010. The dominance of the Hollywood major studios in the global film market is a well-known fact (Barthel-Bouchier, 2012). The market is characterized by competition between French films and foreign films and is dominated by Hollywood imports. The French market with respect to movies is characterized by competition between French and American films (Siroën, 2003; Cocq, Dantec and Lèvy-Hartman, 2006; Cartier and Liarte, 2010).

Although our findings are merely descriptive, they provide a view of motion pictures at the French box office and demonstrate the differences between French and USA films with respect to release dates. The detected differences indicate a direction for improving the competitive strategies of French national cinema.

The data analysis illustrates the existence of a generally growing trend in French movie admissions since 1990 and a very pronounced seasonal pattern: the maximum annual value is systematically observed in the month of December, at the same time, in the months of May, June, July and August we see systematically the lowest minimum values.

The release dates of the top ten movies in France differ depending on the nationality of the films in question. In particular, the peak times for the release of American films are near the summer and Christmas holiday seasons (similar to admissions peak times), whereas top-grossing French films are primarily released during the first two months of the year (January and February).

Results of daily admission evolution show that the highest admission levels are observed on weekend days. Saturdays usually accounts more than 20% of weekly admissions and more than 50% of admissions were between Friday and Sunday.

The results of this study are particularly interesting for the strategic management of French movie theaters. Distributors should be aware of the study of optimal choice in variables such as release date or time in theaters.

Further research is particularly recommended for exploring the box office in different international markets and/or with longer periods of study.

An interesting area for future research would be to examine seasonality patterns across countries and to determine whether groups of countries emerge with similar patterns. Future work could examine release dates strategies, film attributes and distribution characteristics of American films and their effect on the competitiveness of those films' at the box office. Analyzing the differences in the seasonality patterns of French and American movies at the French box office or studying market response to seasonality across industries may be interesting directions for future research.

References

1. L. Einav, Seasonality in the U.S. motion picture industry, *RAND Journal of Economics, 38 (1),* 127-145 (2007).
2. A. De Vany and W.D. Walls, The Market for motion Pictures: Rank, Revenue, and Survival. Economic Inquiry, 35, 783-797 (1997).
3. N. Terry, M. Butler, M. De´Armond, Determinants of the Box Office performance of Motion Pictures, *Proceedings of the Academy of Marketing Studies*, 8 (2), 23-27 (2003).
4. A. Ainslie, X. Drèze and F. Zufryden, Modeling Movie Life Cycles and Market Share, *Marketing Science,* 24 (3), 508-517 (2005).
5. J. McKenzie, Revealed word-of-mouth demand and adaptive supply: survival of motion pictures at the Australian box office. *Journal of Cultural Economics*, 33, 279-299. (2009).

6.C. Hand and G. Judge, How stable is the seasonal pattern in cinema admissions? Evidence from the UK, *Applied Economics Letters*, 18 (1), 81-85 (2010).
7.J.R.Vila Oblitas, V.F. Guzmán Parra, and C. Quintana García, Análisis de la estacionalidad en el sector cinematográfico: estudio comparativo entre la industria extranjera y española. *Investigaciones Europeas de Economía de la Empresa,* 18 (2), 177-182 (2012).
8.W. Dadek, *Economía cinematográfica,* Madrid, Rialp (1962).
9.R. Gil, An empirical investigation of the Paramount antitrust case, *Applied Economics*, 42 (2), 171-183 (2010).
10.E. Dubet, Les fondements de l'intervention publique dans l'industrie cinématographique européenne. *Quaderni.* 39, 11-28 (1999).
11.J. Siroën, Le cinéma, une industrie ancienne de la nouvelle économie. *Revue d'économie industrielle*, 91, 93-118 (2000).
12.B. Demil and B. Leca Architecture de marché et régulation dans l'exploitation cinématographique francaise. *Revue française de gestion*, 142(1), 229-252 (2003).
13.E. Cocq, A. Dantec and F. Lèvy-Hartman, Combien tu m'aimes ? Pour une analyse économique de la politique cinématographique française, *Revue de l'OFCE*, 97(2), 273-328 (2006).
14.M. Cartier and S. Liarte, Timing d'entrée, incertitude et agglo mération temporelle : le cas de l'industrie cinématographique hollywoodienne. *M@n@gement,* 13(2), 70-98 (2010).
15.S. Makridakis, S. C. Wheelwright, and V.E. McGee, *Forecasting: Methods and applications,* New York, John Wiley & Sons (1983).
16.G.E.P. Box and G.M. Jenkins, *Time Series Analysis Forecasting and Control,* San Francisco, Holden-Day (1970).
17.D. Barthel-Bouchier, Exportability of Films in a Globalizing Market: The Intersection of Nation and Genre, *Cultural Sociology*, 6(1) 75–91 (2012).

PART 4:
APPLICATION IN OTHER FIELDS

APPLICATION OF THE FORGOTTEN EFFECTS MODEL TO THE EARLY DIAGNOSIS OF HEREDITARY HEMOCHROMATOSIS

ALEXANDRA BALVEY, ANNA MARIA GIL LAFUENTE, JOSÉ M. MERIGÓ
University of Barcelona
Av. Diagonal 690, 08034 Barcelona, Spain

XAVIER GARRIGA
School Pare Manyanet,
Les Corts, Barcelona, Spain

This research work pretends to get to know all the linked symptomatologies which can be showed in hereditary Hemochromatosis through mathematic models. This will allow us to know the disease in all its phases and start the treatment as soon as possible. This genetic and uncommon disease rises up in the late parts of the patient's life, has quite ineffective treatments and its research hasn't been well financed. On the other hand, the problems at diagnosing it are caused by the similar symptoms between this and other diseases. We tackle a mathematic model which can solve the early diagnosis, applied to the hereditary Hemochromatosis. It is based in a searching process which links different symptoms caused by different diseases with a common origin. The calculations obtained allow us to distinguish groups of symptoms which, raised together, allow us to detect a specific disease and reject other diseases which could cause confusion while diagnosing. In short, the mathematic models are useful to make an early and correct diagnostic without the need to make any genetic test or waiting for the late symptoms to appear.

1. Introduction

The hereditary Hemochromatosis is a disease which affects the iron metabolism, causing an excessive load of this metal in the organs and systems, injuring them. This disease is caused by a genetic mistake which blocks the iron absorption in the intestines, and increases a lot the quantity of iron in the blood.

The genetic mutation is placed in the HFE gene, which codifies the HFE protein, which regulates the iron absorption. It consists in two kind of mutation, where two pairs of complementary bases from the DNA swap.

The C282Y mutation consists in a guanine replacement instead of an adenine. The new base is an adenine, and this causes creation of a tyrosine aminoacid instead of a revisio. Between the 85 and 100% of the patients suffer from this mutation.

The H63D mutation consists in a guanine replacement instead of a cytosine. This causes the creation of a aspartic acid instead of an histidine aminoacid. This mutation is not frequent.

These genes are recessive, and they are placed in the X chromosome. This fact causes that most of the patients are males and not females.

The hereditary Hemochromatosis is a disease which is usually detected through blood tests or biopsies. The treatment is more effective the earlier you detect the disease, but it can happen to be completely ineffective if it's too late. It consists in reducing the iron levels in blood with periodical subtractions. Once the iron levels lower to normal, a special diet is taken by the patient, a poor iron and C vitamin diet. Some patients may have suffered liver damages, so they must avoid alcohol and sea food as well.

In physiological amounts, iron is vital for our body, thanks to its capacity to exchange electrons with other elements. But in big amounts, it loses this function and generates free radicals, cause of the disease's damage. When the iron interacts with the oxygen and generates free radicals, the metal oxidizes very quickly and reacts to generate oxygen reactive species which increase the oxidative stress of the metabolism. This causes an imbalance because the body can't detoxify all intermediate reagents and fix the damage caused by the oxygen reactive species.

Another element which must be taken into account is C vitamin. This vitamin helps the iron intestinal absorption, which benefits the body from suffering iron deficiency anemia. But if the patient already suffers from an iron excess, the C vitamin loses its beneficial character and becomes even dangerous. In normal and heterozygotic patients, the C vitamin in vivo is an antioxidant. But in recessive homozygotic patients, it causes imbalances in the iron absorption. Plus, several experiments have showed that the C vitamin in vitro behaves like a preoxidant, overall while being surrounded by transition metals (such as iron). This means that it helps to produce more iron oxide.

The normal iron amount in the body oscillates between 4 and 5 grams, spread in the hemoglobin (65%), endothelial reticle system and liver (25-30%), myoglobin (4%) and other enzymatic systems. Every day the body loses around 1mg of iron, and it's necessary to replace this excreted amount by providing iron with our diet. The Hemochromatosis alters this balance. There are two mechanisms which can explain how the homeostatic disorder occurs: the intestinal crypts and hepcidine.

On one hand, the iron is absorbed by the enterocytes placed in the small intestine crypts thanks to a protein named Ferroportin 1. The normal HFE qualifies the enterocytes to detect the amount of iron in the blood, allowing it to enter them. When the HFE suffers from a mutation, the iron amount cannot be detected, and it isn't absorbed by the enterocytes, causing an increase in the iron intestinal absorption.

On the other hand, the transferrin associates to the cell membranes to place the iron transported in the blood. The HFE is associated to the cell membranes with the transferrin receiver, decreasing its affinity with the transferrin. In this way, it avoids the iron deposit in the liver. Yet, the mutant HFE loses this inhibiting capacity on the receptor complex – transferrin union, and the iron is placed in the organs. While the C282Y mutation avoids its arrival at the cell, the H63D mutation interferes in the right function once the iron has arrived to the cell membrane. The result is in both cases an iron overdose in the liver.

The hepcidine is the other explanation. It is a hepatic peptide which works on the enterocytes, liver and macrophages, regulating the iron release in blood. In normal conditions, the iron increase stimulates the hepcidine secretion, which inhibits the metal transport from the enterocyte (through its interaction with the ferroportin), liver or endothelial reticle system, in the blood. This system doesn't work in patients with Hemochromatosis. The patients with a mutation in the HFE gene don't produce hepcidine, a fact which explains the iron overdose in the body. There are also patients with a mutation in the ferroportin gene, giving them a resistance to hepcidine. The result is the same as well.

2. Description and formulation of the model

We suggest a methodology managed to know the cause-effect relations that remain hidden when doing a causality study between different elements [6-7]. We'll start our approach with an uncertain cause-effect matrix defined by two groups of elements:

$A \quad a_i / i \quad 1,2,\ldots,n$, which act as causes

$B \quad b_j / j \quad 1,2,\ldots,m$, which act as effects

And a causality relation [M] defined by the matrix:

$M \quad {}_{a_i b_j} \quad 0,\ 1 / i \quad 1,2,\ldots,n; j \quad 1,2,\ldots,m$ being ${}_{a_i b_j}$ the characteristic pertinence relations from every single element of the matrix [M] (formed by the rows corresponding to the elements from de group A –causes- and the columns corresponding to the elements from the group B –effects-). We could say, then,

that the matrix [M] is composed by the estimations formed around all the effects where the elements from the group A exercise over the elements from the group B. The more meaningful this incidence relation is, the higher the value of each of the elements of the matrix will be. In this case, as we have departed from the fact that the characteristic pertinence relation had to take part in the interval [0, 1], we understand that the higher the incidence relation is, the nearer to 1 the assigned value will result. We must emphasize the fact that this initial matrix [M] is elaborated departing from the direct cause-effect relations, in other words, from the first generation. Our aim is based on obtaining a new incidence matrix, but reflecting not only the direct causalities, but the ones which, even though not being evident, still exist and are sometimes vital to appreciate certain facts. For this reason, it's necessary to build two additional incidence relations, which will pick up the possible effects which will come from deriving causes between causes (ion one hand) and effects between effects (on the other hand).
These two auxiliary matrixes are defined as:

$$A \quad _{a_i a_j} \quad 0,\ 1 / i, j \quad 1,2,\ldots,n$$

$$B \quad _{b_i b_j} \quad 0,\ 1 / i, j \quad 1,2,\ldots,m$$

The matrix [A] picks up the incidence relations which can be produced between each of the elements which act as causes, and the matrix [B] does the same with the elements which act as effects. Both [A] and [B] match up the fact that both of them are reflexive matrixes, in another way:

$$_{a_i a_j} \quad 1 / i, j \quad 1,2,\ldots,n$$

$$_{b_i b_j} \quad 1 / i, j \quad 1,2,\ldots,m$$

And they are translated in the fact that one element, cause or effect, has a bearing on itself at the maximum presumption.
In contrast none of [A] or [B] are symmetric matrixes, that is:

$$_{a_i a_j} \qquad _{a_j a_i} \ i, j \quad 1,2,\ldots,n$$

$$_{b_i b_j} \qquad _{b_j b_i} \ i, j \quad 1,2,\ldots,m$$

For obvious reasons.
Once built the matrixes [M], [A] and [B] the establishment of all possible incidence (direct or indirect) combinations must be proceeded. To achieve it, we'll realize the max-min composition of the three matrixes:

$$A \circ M \circ B \quad M^{*}$$

The obtained result will be a new matrix [M*] which picks up the incidences between causes and effects in second generation, in other words, the initial causal relations affected by the possible interposed incidence from a cause or effect.

$$\underset{A}{\begin{array}{c|cccc} & a_1 & a_2 & \cdots & a_n \\ \hline a_1 & 1 & a_1a_2 & \cdots & a_1a_n \\ a_2 & a_2a_1 & 1 & \cdots & a_2a_n \\ \vdots & \vdots & \vdots & & \vdots \\ a_n & a_na_1 & a_na_2 & \cdots & 1 \end{array}} \circ \underset{M}{\begin{array}{c|cccc} & b_1 & b_2 & \cdots & b_m \\ \hline a_1 & 1 & a_1b_2 & \cdots & a_1b_m \\ a_2 & a_2b_1 & 1 & \cdots & a_2b_m \\ \vdots & \vdots & \vdots & & \vdots \\ a_n & a_nb_1 & a_nb_2 & \cdots & 1 \end{array}} \circ \underset{B}{\begin{array}{c|cccc} & b_1 & b_2 & \cdots & b_m \\ \hline b_1 & 1 & b_1b_2 & \cdots & b_1b_m \\ b_2 & b_2b_1 & 1 & \cdots & b_2b_m \\ \vdots & \vdots & \vdots & & \vdots \\ b_m & b_mb_1 & b_mb_2 & \cdots & 1 \end{array}} =$$

$$= \underset{M^*}{\begin{array}{c|cccc} & b_1 & b_2 & \cdots & b_m \\ \hline a_1 & \overset{*}{a_1b_1} & \overset{*}{a_1b_2} & \cdots & \overset{*}{a_1b_m} \\ a_2 & \overset{*}{a_2b_1} & \overset{*}{a_2b_2} & \cdots & \overset{*}{a_2b_m} \\ \vdots & \vdots & \vdots & \vdots & \vdots \\ a_n & \overset{*}{a_nb_1} & \overset{*}{a_nb_2} & \cdots & \overset{*}{a_nb_m} \end{array}}$$

Therefore, the difference between the second generation effects matrix and the direct incidence matrix will allow us to know the level in which some causality relations have been forgotten:

$$O \quad M^{*} (\ ) M$$

$$O = \begin{array}{c|cccc} & b_1 & b_2 & \cdots & b_m \\ \hline a_1 & \overset{*}{a_1b_1} \quad a_1b_1 & \overset{*}{a_1b_2} \quad a_1b_2 & \cdots & \overset{*}{a_1b_m} \quad a_1b_m \\ a_2 & \overset{*}{a_2b_1} \quad a_2b_1 & \overset{*}{a_2b_2} \quad a_2b_2 & \cdots & \overset{*}{a_2b_m} \quad a_2b_m \\ \vdots & \vdots & \vdots & \vdots & \vdots \\ a_n & \overset{*}{a_nb_1} \quad a_nb_1 & \overset{*}{a_nb_2} \quad a_nb_2 & \cdots & \overset{*}{a_nb_m} \quad a_nb_m \end{array}$$

We must say, finally, that the higher the pertinence characteristic function value of the matrix [O] is, the higher is the forgotten level produced in the initial incidence relation. This is translated in the fact that the implications derived from some incidences not considered or taken into account in its fair intensity, can lead to mistaken decisions or not well estimated.

3. Variables and information

In the medical professional field, we often found ourselves in front of different diseases with common symptoms [1-5,8-12]. Sometimes, the symptoms are so similar that we can even mistake the diseases. When a patient comes to a surgery, he/she describes several nuisances he/she suffers, which can be initial signs from different diseases, sometimes distant diseases with very different prognostics. In this context, trying to establish links between symptoms and diseases with classical models based in probability isn't an infallible guarantee in the diagnosis. Every symptom is subjective in every patient, and so is his/her perception and feeling of pain and the way they describe it to the doctor. That's why objective tests (such as blood analysis or radiographies) and subjective estimations (being able to explain a certain level of pain, pills effect or possible allergies) are used. Only this way it's possible to obtain the whole incidence relations and the relation level.

We'll start the Forgotten Effects Model application statement showing two groups of elements, which will act as causes and effects. We'll call causes several diseases which could be suffered by a patient, and we'll call effects the different symptoms which can be cause by the diseases. The main aim is the possibility of detecting a disease by a single symptom or group of different symptoms from the usual ones, simply because a symptom can happen to be at the same time, symptom of another symptom. We'll show the mechanisms which can bring the hidden processes recuperation and we'll study the incidence level in which can be produced.

Causes (diseases which could cause confusion):

a_1 = Hereditary Hemochromatosis (100%)
a_2 = Arthritis (30-40%)
a_3 = Cirrhosis (60%)
a_4 = Diabetes (50-60%)
a_5 = Fibrosis (60%)

Effects (symptoms caused):

b_1 = Ferrous accumulation in the pituitary glands (15-35%)
b_2 = Testicular atrophy (15-35%)
b_3 = Weakness and tiredness (70-80%)
b_4 = Thyroid dysfunction (15-35%)
b_5 = Stomachache (60%)
b_6 = Hiperresonance to percussion (10%)
b_7 = General darkening of the skin (70%)
b_8 = Heart failure, arrhythmia and angina pectoris (20-30%)

b_9 = Pancreas failure (50-60%)
b_{10} = Liver failure (80%)
b_{11} = Rare noises in the respiratory tract (40%)
b_{12} = Increase of the bacterial infection risks (80%)
b_{13} = Suprarenal gland damage (15-35%)
b_{14} = Diarrhea (10%)
b_{15} = Sexual desire loss (15-35%)
b_{16} = Body hair loss (70%)
b_{17} = Weight loss (50%)
b_{18} = Increase of the thorax diameter (20%)
b_{19} = Fever (40%)
b_{20} = Malignant tumor development in the liver (5%)
b_{21} = Rash and pimples (60%)
b_{22} = Pain, inflammation and stiffness in the joints (30-40%)
b_{23} = Nasal polyps (20%)
b_{24} = Purulent nasal secretions (30%)
b_{25} = Warmness in the joints (30-40%)
b_{26} = Jaundice (70%)
b_{27} = Increase of the liver volume (50-60%)
b_{28} = Ascites (60%)
b_{29} = Digestive hemorrhage (40%)
b_{30} = Encephalopathy (conscience alterations, sleep disorders, confusion, mood changes) (85%)
b_{31} = Impotence (15-35%)
b_{32} = Menstruation disorder and/or early menopause (15-35%)
b_{33} = Varicose veins appearance (70%)
b_{34} = Increase of the parotid glands' size (15-35%)
b_{35} = Polydipsia, polyphagia and polyuria (15-35%)
b_{36} = Steatorrhea (70%)
b_{37} = Sickness and vomiting (45%)
b_{38} = Hypersensitivity in the paranasal womb (15%)
b_{39} = Blurry vision (40%)
b_{40} = Long cicatrization of the wounds (50-60%)
b_{41} = Numbness and frequent tingling on hands and feet (50-60%)
b_{42} = Dry skin (70%)
b_{43} = Frequent hemoptysis (40%)
b_{44} = Intestinal obstruction (70%)

4. Results

Incidence table between the different effects [B]

	E1	E2	E3	E4	E5	E6	E7	E8	E9	E10	E11	E12	E13	E14	E15	E16	E17	E18	E19	E20	E21	E22	E23	E24	E25	E26	E27	E28	E29	E30	E31	E32	E33	E34	E35	E36	E37	E38	E39	E40	E41	E42	E43	E44
E1	1	0	0	0	0	0	0	0	0	0	0	0	0	0	1	0,8	0	0	0	0	0	0	0	0	0	0	0	0	0	0	1	0	0	0	0	0	0	0	0	0	0	0	0	0
E2	0	1	0	0	0	0	0	0	0	0	0	0	0	0	0	0	0	0	0,2	0	0	0	0	0	0	0	0	0	0	0	0	0	0	0	0	0,2	0	0	0	0	0	0	0	0
E3	0,8	1	1	0	0	0	0,8	0	0	0	0	0	0	0	0,8	0	0	0	0	0	0	1	0	0	0,9	0	0	0	0	1	0,8	1	0	0	0	0	0	0	0	0	1	0	0	0
E4	0	0	0	1	0	0	0	0	0	0	0	0	0	0	0	0	0	0	0	0	0	0	0	0	0	0	0	0	0	0,6	0	0	0	0	0	0	0	0	0	0	0	0	0	0
E5	0	0	0	0	1	0	0	0	0	0	0	0	0	0	0	0	0	0	0	0	0	0	0	0	0	0	0	0	0	0	0	0	0	0	0	0	0	0	0	0	0	0	0	0
E6	0	0	0	0	0	1	0	0	0	0	0	0	0	0	0	0	0	0	0	0	0	0	0	0	0	0	0	0	0	0	0	0	0	0	0	0	0	0	0	0	0	0	0	0
E7	0	1	0	0,4	0	0	1	0	0	0	0	0	0	0	0	0	0	0	0	0	0	0	0	0	0	0	0	1	0,5	0,5	0	0	0	0	0	0,5	0	0	0	0	0	0	0	0
E8	0	1	0	1	0	0	0	1	0	0	0	0	0	0	0	0	0	1	1	0	0	0	0	0	0	1	0	1	0,4	0	0	0	0	0	0	1	0	0	0	0	0	0	0	0
E9	0	1	0	1	0	0	0	0	1	0	0	0	0	0,7	0	0	0	0	0	0,8	1	0	0	0	0	1	0	1	0	1	0	0	0	0	0	1	0	0	0	0	0	0	0	0
E10	0	0	0	0	0	0	0	0	0	1	0	0	0	0	0	0	0	0	0	0	0	0	0	0	0	0	0	0	0	0	0	0	0	0	0	0	0	0	0	0	0	0,4	0	0
E11	0	1	0	1	0	0	0	0	0	0	1	0	0	1	0	0	0	0	1	0	0	1	0	0	0,9	0	0	0	0	1	0	0	0	0	0	1	0	0	0	0	0	0	0	0
E12	0,2	1	0,1	0,2	0,2	0,1	0,1	0,1	0,1	0,2	0,1	1	0	0,6	0	0	0,4	0	1	0,1	0,3	0,6	0,1	0,5	0,6	0,2	0,1	0,2	0,1	0,7	0,2	0,2	0,4	0	0,1	0,7	0,4	0	0	0	0,1	0,4	0,2	0
E13	0	0	0	0	0	0	0	0	0	0	0	0	1	0	0	0	0	0	0	0	0	0	0,8	1	0	0	0	0	0	0	0	0	0	0	0	0	1	0	0	0	0	0	0	0
E14	0	0	0	0	0	0	0	0	0	0	0	0	0	1	0	0	0	0	0	0	0	0	0	0	0	0	0	0	0	0	0	0	0	0	0	0	0	0	0	0	0	0	0	0
E15	0	0	0	0	0	0	0	0	0	0	0	0	0	0	1	0	0	0	0	0	0	0	0	0	0	0	0	0	0	0	1	0	0	0	0	0	0	0	0	0	0	0	0	0
E16	0	0	0	0	0	0	0	0	0	0	0	0	0	0	0	1	0	0	0	0	0	0	0	0	0	0	0	0	0	0	0	0	0	0	0	0	0	0	0	0	0	0	0	0
E17	0	0	0	0	0	0	0	0	0	0	0	0	0	0	0	0	1	0	0	0	0	0	0	0	0	0	0	0	0	0	0	0	0	0	0	0	0	0	0	0	0	0	0	0
E18	0	0	0	0	0	0	0	0	0	0	0	0	0	0	0	0	0	1	0	0	0	0	0	0	0	0	0	0	0	0	0	0	0	0	0	0	0	0	0	0	0	0	0	0
E19	0	1	0	0	0,5	0	0	0	0	0	0	0	0	0,5	0,8	0	0	0	1	0	0,5	0,4	0	0	0	0	0	0	0	0,8	0	0,2	0	0	0	0,4	0	0,3	0	0,1	0	0	0	0
E20	0	1	0	0	0	0	0	0	1	0	0	0	0	0,4	0	0	1	0	0,1	1	0,4	0	0	0	0	0,8	1	0	0	0	0	0	0	0	0	0	0	0	0	0	0,3	0	0	0
E21	0	0	0	0	0	0	0	0	0	0	0	0	0	0	0	0	0	0	0	0	1	0	0	0	0	0	0	0	0	0	0	0	0	0	0	0	0	0	0	0	0,4	0	0	0
E22	0	1	0	0	0	0	0	0	0	0	0	0	0	0	0	0	0	0	0	0	0	1	0	0	1	0	0	0	0	0	0	0	0	0	0	0	0	0	0	0	0	0	0	0
E23	0	0,1	0	0	0	0	0	0	0	0	0	1	0	0	0	0	0	0	0,2	0	0	0	1	1	0	0	0	0	0	1	0	0	0	0	0	0	1	0	0	0	0	0	0	0
E24	0	0	0	0	0	0	0	0	0	0	0	0	0	0	0	0	0	0	0	0	0	0	0,3	1	0	0	0	0	0	0	0	0	0	0	0	0	1	0	0	0	0	0	0	0
E25	0	1	0	0	0	0	0	0	0	0	0	0	0	0	0	0	0	0	0	0	0	1	0	0	1	0	0	0	0	0	0	0	0	0	0	0	0	0	0	0	0	0	0	0
E26	0	0	0	0	0	0	0	0	0	0	0	0	0	0	0	0	0	0	0	0	0	0	0	0	0	1	0	0	0	0	0	0	0	0	0	0	0	0	0	0	0	0	0	0
E27	0	0,5	0	0,8	0	0,1	0	0	0,8	0	0	0	0	0	0	0	0,5	0,9	0	0,3	0	0	0	0	0	0,5	1	0	0	0	0	0	0	0	0	0,5	0	0	0	0	0,1	0	0	0
E28	0	0,9	0	1	0	0	0	0	0	0	0,4	0,8	0	0	0,1	0	0	0	0	0	0	0	0	0	0	0	0	1	0	0	0	0	0	0	0	0	0	0	0	0	0	0	0,1	0
E29	0	1	0	1	0	0	0,4	0	0	0	0	0,8	0	0,7	0,6	0	0,3	0	1	0	0	0	0	0	0	0	0	0	1	0	0	0,2	0	0	0,4	1	0	0,2	0,5	0,5	0	0,4	0,7	0
E30	0	1	0	0	0,8	0	0	0	0	0	0	0	0	0	0,7	0	0,6	0	0,6	0	0	0	0	0	0	0	0	0	0	1	0	0,5	0	0	0	0,1	0	0,4	0	0	0	0	0	0
E31	0	0	0	0	0	0	0	0	0	0	0	0	0	0	1	0	0	0	0	0	0	0	0	0	0	0	0	0	0	0	1	0	0	0	0	0	0	0	0	0	0	0	0	0
E32	0	1	0	0	0	0	0,1	0	0	0	0	0	0	0	0,7	0,8	0,4	0	0	0	0,2	0,6	0	0	0,4	0	0	0	0	0,6	0	1	0	0	0	0,2	0	0	0	0	1	0	0	0,8
E33	0	0,7	0	0	0,6	0	0	0	0	0	0	0,9	0	0	0	0	0	0	1	0	0,1	0	0	0	0	0	0	0	0	0,4	0	0	1	0	0	0	0,6	0	0	0	0	0	0	0
E34	0	0,2	0	0	0	0	0	0	0	0	0	0	0	0,3	0	0	0	0	0	0	0,2	0	0	0	0	0	0	0	0	0	0	0	0	1	0	0	0	0	0	0	0	0	0,5	0
E35	0	0	0	0	0	0	0	0	0	0	0	0	0	0	0	0	0	0	0	0	0	0	0	0	0	0	0	0	0	0	0	0	0	0	1	0	0	0	0	0	0	0	0	0
E36	0	1	0	1	0,2	0	0,1	0	0	0	0	0	0	0,7	1	0	0,8	0	0,7	0	0,2	0	0	0	0	0	0	0	0	0,6	0	0	0	0	0	1	0	0	0	0	0	0	0	0
E37	0	0	0	0	0	0	0	0	0	0	0	0	0	0	0	0	0	0	0	0	0	0	0,4	0,4	0	0	0	0	0	0	0	0	0	0	0	0	1	0	0	0	0	0	0	0
E38	0	1	0	0	0	0	0	0	0	0	0	0	0	0	0	0	0	0	0	0	0	0	0	0	0	0	0	0	0	0,8	0	0	0	0	0	0	0	1	0	0	0	0	0	0
E39	0	0	0	0	0	0	0	0	0	0	0	1	0	0	0	0	0	0	0	0	0	0	0	0	0	0	0	0	0	0	0	0	0	0	0	0	0	0	1	0	0	0	0	0
E40	0	1	0	0	0	0	0	0	0	0	0	0	0	0	0	0	0	0	0	0	0	0	0	0	0	0	0	0	0	0	0	0	0	0	0	0	0	0	0	1	0	0	0	0
E41	0	0	0	0	0	0	0	0	0	0	0	1	0	0	0	0	0	0	0	0	0,7	0	0	0	0	0	0	0	0	0	0	0	0	0	0	0	0	0	0,6	0	1	0	0	0
E42	0	1	0	0,8	0	0	0	0	0	1	0	0,9	0	0	0,2	0	1	0	1	0	0	0	0	0	0	0	0	0	0	0,7	0	0	0	0	0	0,1	0	0	0	0	0	0	0	0
E43	0	1	0	1	0	0	0,4	0	0	0	0	0,6	0	0	0,7	0	0	0	0	0	0	0	0	0	0	0	0	0	0,2	0	0	0	0	0	0	1	0	0	0	0	0	0	1	0
E44	0	0	0	0	0	0	0	0	0	0	0	0	0	0	0	0	0	0	0	0	0	0	0	0	0	0	0	0	0	0	0	0	0	0	0	0	0	0	0	0	0	0	0	1

Matrix [B]

Estimated incidences table between causes and effects [M]

	E1	E2	E3	E4	E5	E6	E7	E8	E9	E10	E11	E12	E13	E14	E15	E16	E17	E18	E19	E20	E21	E22	E23	E24	E25	E26	E27	E28	E29	E30	E31	E32	E33	E34	E35	E36	E37	E38	E39	E40	E41	E42	E43	E44
C1	0,2	0,8	0,2	0,6	0,1	0,7	0,3	0,5	0,8	0,4	0,2	0,8	0,2	0,1	0,2	0,7	0,5	0,2	0,4	0,1	0,6	0,3	0,2	0,3	0,3	0,7	0,6	0,6	0,4	0,8	0,2	0,3	0,2	0,2	0,7	0,4	0,2	0,4	0,6	0,5	0,7	0,4	0,7	0,7
C2	0	1	0	0	0	0	0	0	0	0,8	0	0	0	0	0	0	0,8	0	0,8	0	0,8	1	0	0	1	0	0	0	0	0	0	0	0	0	0	0	0	0	0	0	0	0	0	0
C3	0	1	0	0,8	0	0	0	0	0	0	0	0	0	0	0	0,8	1	0	0	0	0	0	0	0	0	1	1	1	0,6	1	0,8	0,6	0,1	0	0	0,8	0	0	0	0	0,2	0	0	0,8
C4	0	1	0	0,7	0	0	0	0	0	0	0	0,8	0	0	0	0	1	0	0	0	0	0	0	0	0	0	0	0	0	0	0,8	0,8	0	1	0	1	0	0,8	1	0,9	0,8	0	0	0
C5	0	1	0	1	0,7	0	0	0	0	0,9	0	0	0	1	0	0	0,9	0,8	0	0	0	0	0,8	1	0	0	0	0	0	0	0	0	0	0	1	0	1	0	0	0	0	0,7	1	0

Matrix [M]

Incidence table between the different causes $[A]$

	C_1	C_2	C_3	C_4	C_5
C_1	1	0,3	0,6	0,5	0,6
C_2	0	1	0	0	0
C_3	0	0	1	0	0,7
C_4	0	0	0	1	0
C_5	0	0	0	0	1

Matrix [A]

Max-min convulation table between the matrixes $[A]\circ[M]$

	E_1	E_2	E_3	E_4	E_5	E_6	E_7	E_8	E_9	E_{10}	E_{11}	E_{12}	E_{13}	E_{14}	E_{15}	E_{16}	E_{17}	E_{18}	E_{19}	E_{20}	E_{21}	E_{22}
C_1	0,2	0,8	0,2	0,6	0,6	0,7	0,3	0,5	0,8	0,6	0,2	0,8	0,2	0,6	0,2	0,7	0,6	0,6	0,4	0,1	0,6	0,3
C_2	0	1	0	0	0	0	0	0	0	0,8	0	0	0	0	0	0	0,8	0	0,8	0	0,8	1
C_3	0	1	0	0,8	0,7	0	0	0	0	0,7	0	0	0	0,7	0	0,8	1	0,7	0	0	0	0
C_4	0	1	0	0,7	0	0	0	0	0	0	0	0,8	0	0	0	0	1	0	0	0	0	0
C_5	0	1	0	1	0,7	0	0	0	0	0,9	0	0	0	1	0	0	0,9	0,8	0	0	0	0

	E_{23}	E_{24}	E_{25}	E_{26}	E_{27}	E_{28}	E_{29}	E_{30}	E_{31}	E_{32}	E_{33}	E_{34}	E_{35}	E_{36}	E_{37}	E_{38}	E_{39}	E_{40}	E_{41}	E_{42}	E_{43}	E_{44}
C_1	0,6	0,6	0,3	0,7	0,6	0,6	0,6	0,8	0,6	0,6	0,2	0,5	0,7	0,6	0,6	0,5	0,6	0,5	0,7	0,6	0,7	0,7
C_2	0	0	1	0	0	0	0	0	0	0	0	0	0	0	0	0	0	0	0	0	0	0
C_3	0,7	0,7	0	1	1	1	0,6	1	0,8	0,6	0,1	0	0,7	0,8	0,7	0	0	0	0,2	0,7	0,7	0,8
C_4	0	0	0	0	0	0	0	0	0,8	0,8	0	1	0	1	0	0,8	1	0,9	0,8	0	0	0
C_5	0,8	1	0	0	0	0	0	0	0	0	0	0	1	0	1	0	0	0	0	0,7	1	0

Matrix [A]∘[M]

Max-min convulation table between the matrixes $[A]\circ[M]\circ[B]=[M^{*}]$

	E_1	E_2	E_3	E_4	E_5	E_6	E_7	E_8	E_9	E_{10}	E_{11}	E_{12}	E_{13}	E_{14}	E_{15}	E_{16}	E_{17}	E_{18}	E_{19}	E_{20}	E_{21}	E_{22}
C_1	0,2	0,8	0,2	0,8	0,8	0,7	0,4	0,5	0,8	0,6	0,4	0,8	0,2	0,7	0,7	0,7	0,6	0,6	0,8	0,8	0,8	0,6
C_2	0	1	0	0	0,5	0	0	0	0	0,8	0	0	0	0,5	0,8	0	0,8	0	0,8	0	0,8	1
C_3	0	1	0	1	0,8	0,1	0,4	0	0,8	0,7	0,4	0,8	0	0,7	0,8	0,8	1	0,9	0,7	0,3	0,2	0,6
C_4	0,2	1	0,1	1	0,2	0,1	0,1	0,1	0,1	0,2	0,1	1	0	0,7	1	0,8	1	0	0,8	0,1	0,7	0,6
C_5	0	1	0	1	0,7	0	0,4	0	0	0,9	0	0,8	0	1	0,7	0	0,9	0,8	0,7	0	0	0

	E_{23}	E_{24}	E_{25}	E_{26}	E_{27}	E_{28}	E_{29}	E_{30}	E_{31}	E_{32}	E_{33}	E_{34}	E_{35}	E_{36}	E_{37}	E_{38}	E_{39}	E_{40}	E_{41}	E_{42}	E_{43}	E_{44}
C_1	0,6	0,6	0,6	0,8	0,6	0,8	0,6	0,8	0,6	0,6	0,4	0,5	0,7	0,8	0,6	0,5	0,6	0,5	0,7	0,4	0,7	0,7
C_2	0	0	1	0	0	0	0	0,8	0	0,2	0	0	0	0,4	0	0,3	0	0,1	0,4	0,4	0	0
C_3	0,7	0,7	0,4	1	1	1	0,6	1	0,8	0,6	0,1	0	0,7	0,8	0,7	0,4	0,5	0,5	0,6	0,4	0,7	0,8
C_4	0,1	0,5	0,6	0,2	0,1	0,2	0,1	0,8	0,8	0,8	0,4	1	0,1	1	0,4	0,8	1	0,9	0,8	0,4	0,5	0,8
C_5	0,8	1	0	0	0	0	0,2	0,8	0	0	0	0	1	1	1	0	0	0	0	0,4	1	0

Matrix [M*]

Forgotten effects table $[O]=[M^{*}](-)[M]$

	E_1	E_2	E_3	E_4	E_5	E_6	E_7	E_8	E_9	E_{10}	E_{11}	E_{12}	E_{13}	E_{14}	E_{15}	E_{16}	E_{17}	E_{18}	E_{19}	E_{20}	E_{21}	E_{22}
C_1	0	0	0	0,2	0,7	0	0,1	0	0	0,2	0,2	0	0	0,6	0,5	0	0,1	0,4	0,4	0,7	0,2	0,3
C_2	0	0	0	0	0,5	0	0	0	0	0	0	0	0	0,5	0,8	0	0	0	0	0	0	0
C_3	0	0	0	0,2	0,8	0,1	0,4	0	0,8	0,7	0,4	0,8	0	0,7	0,8	0	0	0,9	0,7	0,3	0,2	0,6
C_4	0,2	0	0,1	0,3	0,2	0,1	0,1	0,1	0,1	0,2	0,1	0,2	0	0,7	1	0,8	0	0	0,8	0,1	0,7	0,6
C_5	0	0	0	0	0	0	0,4	0	0	0	0	0,8	0	0	0,7	0	0	0	0,7	0	0	0

	E_{23}	E_{24}	E_{25}	E_{26}	E_{27}	E_{28}	E_{29}	E_{30}	E_{31}	E_{32}	E_{33}	E_{34}	E_{35}	E_{36}	E_{37}	E_{38}	E_{39}	E_{40}	E_{41}	E_{42}	E_{43}	E_{44}
C_1	0,4	0,3	0,3	0,1	0	0,2	0,2	0	0,4	0,3	0,2	0,3	0	0,4	0,4	0,1	0	0	0	0	0	0
C_2	0	0	0	0	0	0	0	0,8	0	0,2	0	0	0	0,4	0	0,3	0	0,1	0,4	0,4	0	0
C_3	0,7	0,7	0,4	0	0	0	0	0	0	0	0	0	0,7	0	0,7	0,4	0,5	0,5	0,4	0,4	0,7	0
C_4	0,1	0,5	0,6	0,2	0,1	0,2	0,1	0,8	0	0	0,4	0	0,1	0	0,4	0	0	0	0	0,4	0,5	0,8
C_5	0	0	0	0	0	0	0,2	0,8	0	0	0	0	0	1	0	0	0	0	0	0,6	0	0

Matrix [O]

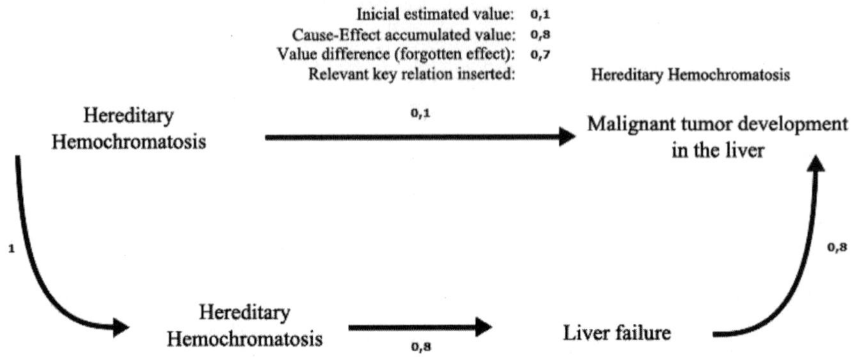

5. Discussion

Taking back all the information in the model, general talking, we obtain two kinds of very valuable information for our aim in this research work.

At first place, if we take a look to the information of the matrix [B], which is the one who links the symptoms with the diseases (effects linked to causes), it is showed that there are four symptoms (which are the increase of the bacterial infection risk, the digestive hemorrhage, menstruation disorder and/or early menopause and steatorrhea) which are the causes of a lot more symptoms directly linked with other diseases showed before. This can cause real problems in the medical diagnosis, due to the confusion the doctor makes when he doesn't know if they are primary symptoms or symptoms caused by other symptoms. In this research work we've made a process which makes it able to untie the primary symptoms form the secondary ones, and this is a great step for the diagnosing system.

If we continue the analysis from the followed process and we take a look on the matrix [M*], we can observe that this matrix procures the real relation between one of the five crossed diseases (named causes) and the crossed accumulated symptoms which are produced. These diseases are extremely linked because the hereditary Hemochromatosis causes Arthritis, Cirrhosis, Diabetes and Fibrosis. The interaction between these five diseases is showed in the matrix [A].

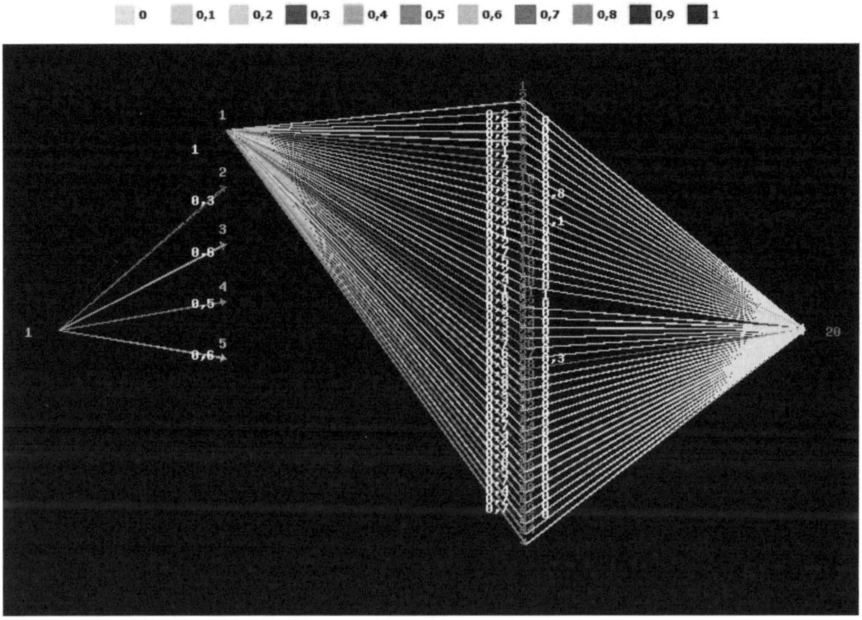

The matrix [M*] proposes a real effect measured between 0 and 1 from the analyzed diseases on the symptoms they cause, considering the crossed and accumulated effect of possible interactions between the variables which constitute the rows and columns. We could observe that the detection of an Hemochromatosis and the detection of a possible cirrhosis or possible diabetes through their symptoms would result basic for the early diagnosis of hereditary Hemochromatosis. This consideration comes from the high values which are observed in the matrix [M*].

This matrix acquires the highest relevance because it expresses the level with which a specific disease can cause different specific symptoms. This results are extremely important because they are the ones which the medical facultatives will use to establish necessary actuation protocols for the diagnosis and treatment of the hereditary Hemochromatosis. For example, a person goes to the doctor's surgery and suffers from symptoms such as: testicular atrophy, liver failure, sexual desire loss, weight loss, fever, rash and pimples, pain, inflammation, warmness and stiffness in the joints and encephalopathy, has a 87% possibilities to suffer from Arthritis and a 26% conditional possibility that this Arthritis is caused by a hereditary Hemochromatosis.

To arrive to this conclusion we've selected form the matrix [M*] the levels from the symptoms which are 0.8 or higher (80%) which show Arthritis (C_2

row). The reason why we've taken the higher levels it's because when a patient goes to the doctor, he/she normally tells about the most signifying symptoms suffered, forgetting the less important ones, in this way, the symptoms which can cause Arthritis and don't overpass the 50% of incidence haven't been considered.

The level of the considered symptoms has been submitted to a simple arithmetic mean. In this case, we've considered that all the symptoms have the same importance and weight. We could give one more step, and this would be a convex weighting in order to attribute to every symptom a specific weight according to the relative importance which they could have in the disease. We've opted to not complicate more this research work, even though it would be a more realistic position in the diagnosis framework.

The model used in this research work concludes obtaining the matrix [O], also called forgotten effects matrix. It is the one which gives us the information about the causality relations which are not considered at diagnosing. The information contained in this matrix is maybe the most important, because it reminds us about symptoms which are not taken into account normally. The values in the matrix [O] represent the forgotten level that we've incurred at making the initial causality relation. In other words; the more careful the symptom-disease valuation will be made, the lower the forgotten levels will be. On the other side, the more things we will forget in the first step, and the higher the forgotten levels will appear. To sum up, this matrix [O] shows the symptoms which have the risk to not being taken into account and not being linked to the disease.

To show how this method works, we've raised the interactions to one of the matrix [O] elements. This relation represents the followed process and shows that the brought element, which causes that an apparently insignificant incidence, could drag indirect and accumulated effects. So, we observe that, initially, there wasn't any symptomatologic relation between suffering hereditary Hemochromatosis and malignant tumor development in the liver. The model used shows that the relation is connected through the liver failure. That's because Hemochromatosis causes liver failure, and liver failure causes malignant tumors. Initially, the incidence of the tumors being caused by Hemochromatosis is only a 10%, but the forgotten effect rises up to an 80%.

This approach allows choosing symptoms which show significantly a specific disease. The results help to make an early detection of a hidden disease through indirect symptoms. It is clear that the individual causality relations can't solve the diagnosis problem, but analyzing them together, we could make an advanced analysis of diseases with a difficult detection, even diseases hidden by other diseases.

The most important symptoms we should take a look to diagnose the hereditary Hemochromatosis would be sickness and vomiting, fever, impotence, weight loss, encephalopathy, body hair loss, sexual desire loss, stomach ache, weakness and tiredness.

Some of these symptoms are usually considered by the doctors at making the first diagnostics, but we can find ourselves in the situation that, for example, sexual desire loss or weakness and tiredness are not specific symptoms directly linked to the hereditary Hemochromatosis, but if we add them to the rest of the symptomatology, they appear closely linked. This is why it's important for the doctors to have an actuation protocol starting from the elaboration of lists of common symptoms from different diseases hard to detect, in order to discover this kind of affections as soon as possible.

6. Conclusions

We obtained the following results: in first place, this new method earns resources to the medicals, because if the diagnosis is more precise from the beginning, this earns diagnostic tests, most of them difficult and expensive. The public health system gets benefits.

From the social point of view, the method earns suffering, queues, troubles, sick leaves and absences at the work to the patients. Finally, from the clinic point of view, it's important to add this new kind of tools because they optimize the interactions between the different medical disciplines. The medical protocols procedure becomes more efficient.

References

1. Basset, ML; Halliday, JW; Powell, LW (1986), Value of hepatic Iron measurements in early Hemochromatosis and determination of the critical iron level associated with Fibrosis, Hepatology Volume: 6, Issue: 1, Pages: 24-29.
2. Edwars, CQ; Griffen, LM; Goldgar, D, et al. (1988), blood-donors, New England Journal of Medicine, Volume: 318, Issue: 21, Pages: 1355-1362.
3. Feder, JN; Gnirke, A; Thomas, W, et al. (1996), A novel MHC class I-like gene is mutated in patients with hereditary Haemochromatosis, Naure Genetics, Volume: 13, Issue: 4, Pages: 399-408.
4. Feder, JN; Penny, DM; Irrinki, A, et al. (1998), The Hemochromatosis gene product complexes with the transferrin receptor and lowers its affinity for

ligand binding, Proceedings of the National Academy of sciences of the United States of America, Volume: 95, Issue: 4, Pages: 1472-1477.

5. Finch, SC; Finch, CA (1955), Idiopathic Hemochromatosis, an iron storage desease. A iron metabolism in Hemochromatosis, Medicine Volume: 34, Issue: 4, Pages: 381-430.
6. Gil Lafuente A. M.; Gil Aluja J. (2005), Nouvelles perspectives de la recherche scientifique en économie et de géstion, Editorial Reial Acadèmia de Doctors, Barcelona.
7. Kaufmann A.; Gil Aluja J. (1988), Modelos para la investigación de efectos olvidados, Editorial Milladoiro, Vigo.
8. McKie, AT; Marciani, P; Rolfs, A, et al. (2000), A novel duodenal iron-regulated transporter, IREG1, implicated in the basolateral transfer of iron to the circulation, Molecular Cell. Volume: 5, Pages: 299-309.
9. MerryweatherClarke, AT; Pointon, JJ; Shearman, JD, et al. (1997), Global prevalence of putative haemochromatosis mutations, Journal of Medical Genetics. Volume: 34, Issue: 4, Pages: 275-278.
10. Nemeth, E; Tuttle, MS; Powelson, J, et al. (2004), Hepcidin regulates cellular iron efflux by binding to ferroportin and inducing its internalization, Science, Volume: 306, Issue: 5704, Pages: 2090-2093.
11. Niederau, C; Fischer, R; Purschel, A, et al. (1996), Long-term survival in patients with hereditary hemochromatosis, Gastroenterology, Volume: 110, Issue: 4, Pages: 1107-1119.
12. Niedrau, C; Fischer, R; Sonneberg, A, et al. (1985), Survival and causes of death in cirrhotic and in noncirrhotic patients with primary Hemochromatosis, New England journal of Medicine. Volume: 313, Issue: 20, Pages: 1256-1262.

NEW PRODUCT DEVELOPMENT USING SET-BASED CONCURRENT ENGINEERING (SBCE)

HENRIQUE MARTINS ROCHA

FER, Associação Educacional Dom Bosco – AEDB & Universidade do Estado do Rio de Janeiro - UERJ, Av. Darci Ribeiro no. 2535 Resende, RJ 27523-000, Brazil

LIGIA MARIA FONSECA AFFONSO

MECSMA, Centro Universitário de Volta Redonda, Av. Gal. Affonseca, 1026/104 Resende, RJ 27520-173, Brazil

UÁLISON RÉBULA DE OLIVEIRA

ECHS, Universidade Federal Fluminense, R. Desembarg. Ellis Hermydio Figueira 783 Volta Redonda, RJ 27215-350, Brazil

This research purported to discuss the concept of Set-based Concurrent Engineering (SBCE) and its application in the automotive industry design. Based on the literature review about the subject and on a research performed at an automaker plant in southern Rio de Janeiro state, Brazil, it has been proved the efficiency of the company practice to develop three concepts (three ideas) for each mechanism or project detail, since such practice enables a substantial reduction in the likelihood of redesign through the development of multiple concepts and final concept decision postponement.

1. Introduction

Demands for sustainability are often related to product and company quality, flexibility, logistics performance, reduced costs, and technological innovation. In an environment of rapid change and fierce competitiveness [1] [2] [16] [32], the product development process (PDP) is a critical success factor for companies [30].

The present article discusses the principles of the Set-Based Concurrent Engineering (SBCE) as an enabler of a flexible, cost-effective, sustainable, and robust product development.

The research was performed at a Development Centre located in a commercial vehicle manufacturing plant installed in the southern Rio de Janeiro state, Brazil. With approximately 4,500 people and a production capacity of 300 units per day, the unit develops new models and new technology-embedded products. The choice of such unit for the research is justified by its relevance, as subject of study by several authors [8] [35], due to its Modular Consortium model, in which the partners interact directly on the final product assembly line, dividing physical space and responsibilities. Although such production system concept is quite relevant, it will not be discussed in this article.

2. Relevance and Objective

The design phase represents only 5% of the total costs of developing a product, but established 70% to 80% of its operating costs [22] [24]. However, mortality, since the basic idea until it becomes a profitable product, is as high as 95% [10]. Out of ten ideas about new products, three will be developed, 1.3 will be launched, and only one will be profitable [3]. Only 45% of companies are able to keep production costs within the budget and only 49% could launch their products on schedule: on average, products cost 13% above the budget and were released six months late [3].

Due to the relevance of such subject, this research purported to present the use of the SBCE to increase PDP flexibility, speed, and reliability, establishing the variables involved, expected development productivity gains, and its sensitivity to the variables, contributing to make project decisions more robust.

3. Related Literature

Based on Toyota's lean product development, Morgan and Liker [23] emphasise the front-loading effort, taking advantage of initial flexibility/freedom to change to fully exploit alternative solutions, having in mind that project conditions can change drastically along the development [5] [6]. SBCE foundations determine that acceptable design solutions are developed simultaneously, at the intersection of product capability, process and solution alternatives, postponing final concept decisions. As product launch deadline approaches, the set of alternatives will be gradually narrowed, eliminating weaker solutions: what appears infeasible and/or too inferior is discarded, while what remains acceptable continues to be studied, overlapping development activities [7] [9] [13] [23] [31] [34]. It contrasts to the traditional design practice, the "point-based design" [28], which "funnels" the decisions, closing possibilities as quick as possible, by determining the approximate design solution early in the project.

The multiple concept approach is not new: Krishnan and Bhattacharya [15] discussed product development in a technological uncertainty environment, deciding whether using a robust and proven technology or choosing a still uncertain technology capable to leverage competitive product. The authors developed stochastic models to establish the optimum technology innovation level, balancing risk involved with expected value generated. Stochastic models for PDP improvement have also been used by other authors [4] [14] [17].

Under certain circumstances, developing multiple design alternatives in parallel generates significant value, fully accounting for the increase in costs of doing so [36]. Inoue, Nahm, and Ishikawa [11] proposed a design approach that obtains a ranged set of feasible design solutions while incorporating the designer's preference for design parameters. Spahi and Hosni [38] have, also, determined the optimal degree of customisation from a product's structural design perspective, establishing an optimal solution to how far an organisation should customise a product to best satisfy its own organisational strategic goals.

The concept that seems counterintuitive, expensive, and inefficient [18] [39], purposes to prevent good ideas' premature abandonment, reducing development risks, reworks rates, and development time. The risk reduction on SBCE occurs due to redundancy, robustness, and knowledge absorption [12]. Since there must be a compromise between the factors that add value to the product and those that cause cost increase [3], a disadvantage of the SBCE would be the fact that it requires a lot of the people to develop the multiple solution areas [37]. However, Rocha, Delamaro, and Affonso [33] refute such idea based on a theoretical model of PDP gain through the use of multiple-concept, comparing the additional manpower required to develop more than one concept at the time versus the project reliability increment (thus design rework reduction). The authors assert that if the odds of developing a winner project concept were 90%, a product project requiring 50 new concepts would have a 0.5% "do-it-right-the-first-time" success rate ($0,9^{50}$ = 0.5145%), whereas, developing three concept simultaneously (for each concept area, i.e. each of the 50 product areas requiring the development of a new concept), the affected project area would fail only if the tree concepts fail, what would represent a 0.1% situation (0.1^{3} = 0.1%). Therefore, since the odds of each successful concept area would be, now, 99.9%, the overall expected success rate would be above 95% (0.999^{50} = 95.1206%).

Based on the additional resources required for multiple-design development, the authors deducted the gain provided by the use of multiple-concept (G) shown in Eq. (1).

$$G = 10 \log \frac{(1 - (1 - Ta)^{c})^{n}}{Ta^{n}\, c} \qquad (1)$$

where "Ta" is the Average concept (idea) success rate; "c" is the Quantity of different concepts for each design area; and "n" is the Quantity of design areas (areas requiring the development of new concepts)*.

4. Using the SBCE on PDP

The Concept Design Team at the studied company develops three concepts (three ideas) for each feature, mechanism or project subsystem. A new product being developed based on an existing 25 Ton 6 x 2 vehicle platform has been selected for the study. Initial figures estimated a total of twelve new concepts to be developed to customise the existing platform to the new product requirements, in areas such as powertrain and injection system, brake system, fuel tank, harness, chassis and suspension, etc.

Since the group had no historic data to establish its idea/concept success rate, Baxter [3] figures were used: 1.3 out of three ideas being launched, i.e., this study took the estimate of "Ta" equal to 43.3%. Calculating G (with Ta =0,433; "c" = 3; and "n" = 12), the gain of 28.34 confirms the advantage to use multiple concepts on automotive PDP.

A question that comes up is: why three concepts? Why not two, four, or one thousand? Since the quantity of ideas to be developed for a given project area is a managerial decision, it is important to identify an optimum number of concepts which would maximize the gain. Therefore, the objective function shall be Maximize G = f(c), i.e.:

$$\text{Maximize } G = 10 \log \frac{(1-(1-0.433)^{c})^{12}}{0.433^{12}\, c} \qquad (2)$$

"c" has been set as a non-negative, non-zero, and integer variable (positive integer). Using Excel Solver ©, the optimum solution found would be seven concepts (ideas), with G = 34.14. Such result must be analysed under a conservative prospect, since the common sense indicates that the task of developing seven different ideas for each concept area seems to be excessive. Variation of gain, based on concept quantity, shown in Fig. (1), provides a better understanding about this scenario. There is a strong gain grow as the quantity of

---

* In the proposed example, the gain, considering the additional resource usage, would be, based on Eq. (1), equal to 17.89, i.e., the gain is so high in terms of design reliability that it is expected that the development team will, in fact, work less when multiple concepts are developed, due to reduction on design loopings and reworks.

concepts increases to two and three, but the marginal growth decelerates very quickly after that.

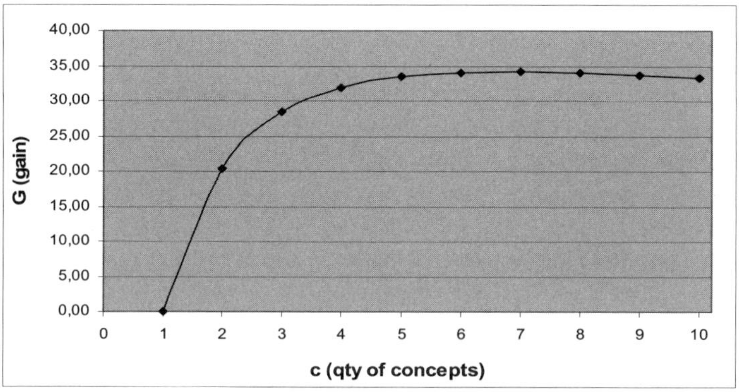

Figure 1. Gain variation as function of concept quantity

Such findings highlight the importance to perform the gain sensitivity analysis to the variables "Ta", "c", and "n". A 5,000-run simulation has been performed, adopting the following limits: "Ta" to be between 20% and 90%, since values out of those limits would be quite improbable; "c", between 2 and 10, justified by the fact that there must be at least two different concepts (ideas) for each area, while ten seem to be too much; and "n" to be between 2 and 30, based on the project complexity level ranges for automotive industry, i.e., 2 to 4: low complexity; 10 to 20, medium; and, 20 to 60, high [33].

As shown in Fig. (2), gain (G) is reduced as "Ta" increases*. Only one occurrence (out of 5,000 runs) of negative gain has been detected with "n" = 3 when "Ta" was below 50%, indicating, as a general rule, that developing three concepts increases significantly the odds of success†.

In Fig. (3), the analysis of "G" sensitivity to "c" shows results quite similar to the calculation shown in Fig. (1): as "c" increases, "G" initially increases quickly, slowing down beyond the range of 4-6 concepts. This finding indicates and reinforces the idea that development of three concepts is much better than

* A combination of low "c" and low "n" leads to a negative "G" (a loss) when "Ta" is above a 45-50% range. As "n" goes up, even with low "c", there is a tendency of "G" going up. Lower "Ta", by the other side, is usually related to high gains, except at the extreme situation of high "c" with low "n".

† The correlation coefficient between "Ta" and "G", calculated out of the 5.000-run was -0.66, reinforcing the inferred statement that the use of multiple-concept might not worthwhile when "Ta" is high.

two, although, going beyond three concepts might require further investigation, as it will be discussed latter[*†].

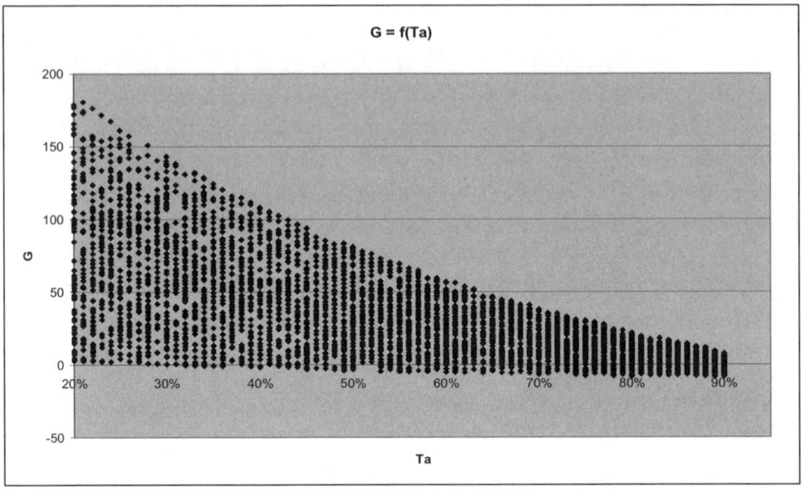

Figure 2 . Gain sensitivity to average concept success rate.

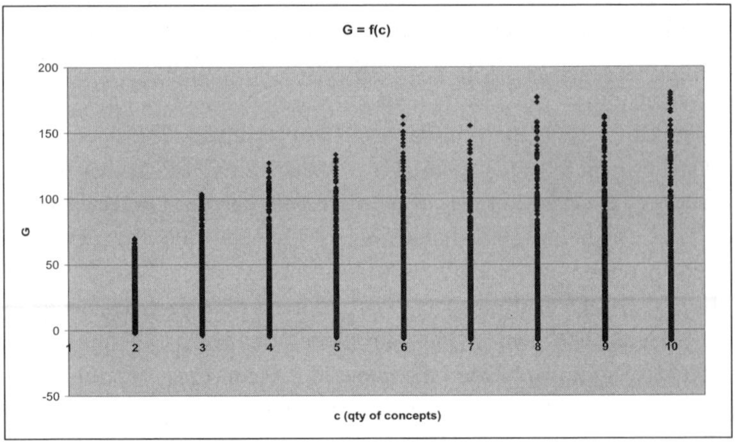

Figure 3 . Gain sensitivity to quantity of concepts.

[*] The correlation coefficient between "c" and "G", calculated out of the 5.000-run was +0.1, but due to discrete nature of "c", such result has no significance.

[†] The correlation coefficient between "n" and "G", calculated out of the 5.000-run was +0.64. The combination of "c" and "n" with low "Ta" on low/negative gains occurs basically with high "c" and low "n".

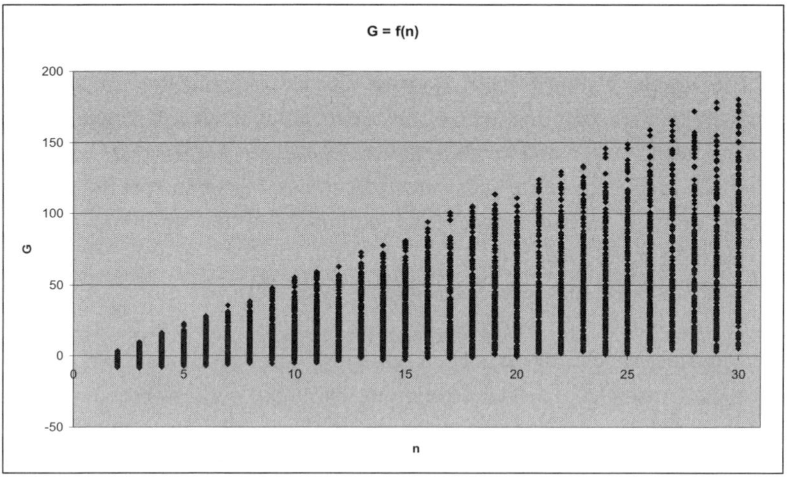

Figure 4 . Gain sensitivity to quantity of design areas.

5. Conclusions and Remarks

Unlike the PDP common practices, in which one seeks to establish the design concepts as early as possible, so that design can be frozen (usually being established as a project milestone), this paper asserts that the development of multiple concepts and decisions postponement might lead to considerable project development benefits, substantially increasing the chance of success, design reliability, and allowing time and cost reductions.

The decision about developing multiple concepts and the quantity of concept to be developed simultaneously affects the potential development benefits: if the development team usually achieves high rates of fail-free project concepts, benefits may fade away, because an elevated amount of workload to develop multiple concepts impacts negatively the overall development performance.

Based on a real project situation, the optimal concept quantity could be determined through the mathematical model presented, as long as the development success hit rate is known: for a commercial vehicle development, three to five concepts seem to be the most appropriated. Further simulations using the proposed model showed that the higher is the quantity of design areas requiring new concepts in a product project, the higher is the potential project gain by developing multiple-concepts. Therefore, simple follow-on products and/or well known concepts and proven technology would better use traditional one-hit design practice. SBCE provides great development advantages when used in mid to high complexity projects.

The article findings may be used by any organization that seeks to maximize returns on investments in new product development, fulfilling customer needs faster and more reliably. However, further research must be conducted, raising historical data rates of success / error in specific industries, enabling a more robust analysis and definition of the optimum amount of concepts to be developed.

Another subject to be studied/validated is the influence of the learning curve into the marginal design workload for each additional concept to be developed, since, in this article, it has been assumed that additional concepts were independent variables, i.e. that developing one more concept requires the some effort that has been required to develop the previous one.

References

1. A. Alvan and A. O. Aydin, The Effects of Mass Customisation on Productivity, *IJMassC*, Vol. 3, No. 1, 2009, pp.58–81.
2. D. Alford, P. Sackett, and G. Nelder, Mass Customisation: an automotive perspective, *IJPE*, Vol. 65, 2000, pp. 99-110.
3. M. Baxter, *Product Design*: Practical methods for the systematic development of new products, Chapman and Hall, London, UK, 1995.
4. N. Bhuiyam, D. Gerwin, and V. Thomson, Simulation of the New Product Development Process for Performance Improvement, *MS*, Vol.50, No.12, 2004, pp.1690-1703.
5. E. Bonabeau, N. Bodick, and R. W. Armstrong, A More Rational Approach to New-Product Development, *HBR*, Mar 01, 2008, pp.1-8.
6. R. Cooper, Managing Technology Development Projects, *IEEE Eng Manag Rev*, Vol. 35, No. 1, 2007, pp. 67-77.
7. R. Costa, and D. K. Sobek II, Iteration in Engineering Design: inherent and unavoidable or product of choices made?. *Proceedings of DETC'03*, ASME 2003, Chicago, USA.
8. D. Doran and A. Hill, A Review of Modular Strategies and Architecture within Manufacturing Operations, Proceedings of the Institution of Mechanical Engineers, Part D: *J. Automob. Eng.*, Vol.223, No.1, 2009, pp.65-75.
9. T. Eisto, V. Hölttä, K. Mahlamäki, J. Kollanus, and M. Nieminen, Early Supplier Involvement in New Product Development: a casting-network collaboration model, *WASET*, Vol. 62, 2010, pp. 856-866.
10. B. Hollins and S. Pugh, *Successful Product Design*: what to do and when, Butterworth & Co., London, UK, 1990.

11. M. Inoue, Y. Nahm, and H. Ishikawa, Application of Preference Set-Based Design Method to Multilayer Porous Materials for Sound Absorbency and Insulation, *IJCIM*, 2011, in press.
12. M. N. Kennedy, *Product Development for the Lean Enterprise*, The Oaklea Press, Richmond, Virginia, USA, 2003.
13. M. S. Khan, A. Al-Ashaab, E. Shehab, B. Haque, P. Ewers, M. Sorli, and A. Sopelana, Towards lean product and process development, IJCIM, 2011, in press.
14. A. V. Kleyner, *Determining Optimal Reliability Targets through Analysis of Product Validation Cost and Field Warranty Data*, Thesis (PhD Engineering). University of Maryland, College Park, USA, 2005.
15. V. Krishnan and S. Bhattacharya, Technology Selection and Commitment in New Product Development: the role of uncertainty and design flexibility, *MS*, Vol.48 i3, 2002, pp.313-349.
16. P. Lam and K. Chin, Identifying and prioritizing critical success factors for conflict management in collaborative new product development, *IMM*, Vol. 34, 2005, pp.761-772.
17. H. Lee and H. Suh, Estimating the Duration of Stochastic Workflow for Product Development Process, *IJPE*, Vol.111, i1, 2008, pp.105-117.
18. J. K. Liker and J. M. Morgan, The Toyota Way in Services: the case of lean product development, *AMP*, May 2006, pp.5-20.
19. B. MacCarthy and P. G. Brabazon, In the Business of Mass Customisation, *IEEE-ME*, Vol. 82, i.4, 2003, pp. 30-33.
20. A. MacCormack, R. Verganti, and M. Iansiti, Developing products on "Internet time": the anatomy of a flexible development process, *MS*, Vol.47, i1, 2001, p.133-152.
21. A. G. C. Machado and W. F. A. Moraes, W. F. A., Estratégias de Customização em Massa Implementadas por Empresas Brasileiras. *Prod.*, v.18, n.1, 2008, pp.170-183.
22. L. Miller, *Concurrent Engineering Design* – integrating the best practices for process improvement, SAE, Michigan, USA, 1993.
23. J. M. Morgan and J. K. Liker, *The Toyota Product Development System*: integrating people, process and technology, Productivity Press, London, UK, 2006.
24. J. Muniz Júnior, *Qualidade*, in: J. Muniz Junior (Org.), Administração de Produção, IESDE, Curitiba, Brazil, 2010, pp.143-160.
25. B. J. Pine, *Mass Customization*: the new frontier in business competition, Harvard Business Review Press, Boston, USA, 1992.
26. M. S. Pinto, R. H. Gutierrez, and H. L. M. M. Quintella, H. L. M. M., Competitive Factors of Mobile Operators' TV Services in Brazil: the mass customization option revisio, *IJMassC*, v. 3, 2010, pp. 273-287.

27. H. Qudrat-Ullah, B. S. Seong, and B. L. Mills, B. L., Improving High Variable-Low Volume Operations: an exploration into the lean product development, *IJTM*, Vol. 57, No. 1-3/2012, 2011, pp.49-70.
28. A. J. Qureshi, *Contributions à la Maîtrise de la Robustesse des Produits*: Formalisation par logique formelle, applications à la conception ensembliste et au tolérancement. Ph.D. Thesis (Génie Mécanique), l'École Nationale Supérieure d'Arts et Métiers, Paris, France, 2011.
29. H. L. M. M. Quintella and J. T. Oliveira, J. T., Mass Customisation and IT Influence on Brazilian Health Industries Competitiveness, *IJMassC*, Vol. 2, 2007, pp. 128-138.
30. H. L. M. M. Quintella, H. M. Rocha, and M. F. Alves, Automobile Project Management: critical success factors in product start-up, *Prod.*, Vol. 15, No. 3, 2005, pp. 334-346.
31. S. J. Rekuc, J. M. Aughenbaugh, M. Bruns, and C. J. J. Paredis, *Eliminating Design Alternatives based on Imprecise Information*, Georgia Institute of Technology, SAE International, 2006-01-0272.
32. H. M. Rocha and M.C, Delamaro, M. C., *Product Development Process*: using real options for assessment and to support the decision-making at decision gates, in Loureiro, G. and Curran, R. (Orgs.), Complex Systems Concurrent Engineering – collaboration, technology innovation and sustainability, Springer-Verlag, London, pp. 96-103.
33. H. M. Rocha, M. C. Delamaro, and L. M. F. Affonso, O uso da engenharia simultânea baseada em conjuntos de possíveis soluções (SBCE) no projeto de veículos automotivos. *Proceedings of the VIII SEGeT*, Resende, Brazil, 2011.
34. H. Rozenfeld, F. A. Forcellini, D. C. Amaral, J. C. Toledo, S. L. Silva, D. H. Alliprandini, and R. C. Scalice, R. C., *Gestão de Desenvolvimento de Produtos*: uma revision para a melhoria do revisi, Saraiva, São Paulo, Brazil, 2006.
35. M. S. Salerno, O. S. Camargo, and M. B. Lemos, Modularity Ten Years After: an evaluation of the Brazilian experience, *IJATM*, Vol. 8, n.4, 2008, pp. 373 – 381.
36. H. Schäfer and D. J. Sorensen, Creating Options while Designing Prototypes: value management in the automobile industry, *JMTM*, Vol. 21 Iss. 6, 2010, pp.721–742.
37. D. K. Sobek II, A. C. Ward, and J. K. Liker, Toyota's Principles Of Set-Based Concurrent Engineering, *SMR*, Vol. 40, No. 2, 1999, pp.67-83.
38. S. Spahi and Y. Hosni, Optimising the Degree of Customisation for Products in Mass Customisation Systems, *IJMassC*, Vol. 3, No.1, 2009, pp.82–114.
39. A. C. Ward, J. K. Liker, J.J. Cristiano, J.J., and D. K. Sobek II, The Second Toyota Paradox: how delaying decisions can make better cars faster, *SMR*, Vol.36, No.3, 1995, pp.43-61.

A PROPOSED APPROACH TO ENHANCE SECURITY OF CLOUD DATA STORAGE

NASHAAT ELKHAMEESY

Dean Research Centers& Head of Chair Computer and Information Systems, Sadat Academy for Management Sciences, Cairo, Egypt

HOSSAM ABDEL RAHMAN

Computer and Information Systems Chair, Sadat Academy for Management Sciences, Cairo, Egypt

Egyptian economic performance has been declined after the 25 January revolution. Although the country moved from authoritarianism, the economy is going through a critical period. 1,500 factories have been stalled due to financial and security reasons. Stalled factories have resulted in the rise of unemployment rate as more than 300,000 workers were unemployed. Small and Medium Business Enterprises (SMEs) play a significant role in the world economy, by contribution to economic and employment growth. This paper highlights the impact of post 25 January revolutions on the Egyptian Economy as many labor strikes, demonstrations, and protests affect the investment and production rates. Also the stalled factories dropped its dark shadows on the Egyptian Economy. The main aim of this work is to identify the advantages and characteristics of SMEs which enable them to adapt easily to the changing environment than large enterprises. So SMEs should be at the top of the government priorities in this phase to help reviving the national economy in this crucial phase. So, it would be necessary to work on a solution to help support SMEs in marketing their products. Developing Web-Based Network for Small and Medium Business Enterprises can provide a unified interface to display SMEs information and product catalogue, it also facilitate navigation between these companies web sites by using URLs that can be stored in SMEs Database. By applying Search Engine Optimization techniques to improve the SMEs web-based network ranking in search engine results , we can provide a Zero cost marketing techniques to SMES to market their products locally and internationally. Web analytical tools can be used to get reports and statistics about the web site traffic. These results can be analyzed to help build and update the keywords and the ranking factors.

1. Introduction

In cloud computing, moving data into the cloud offers great convenience to users since they don't have to worry about the complexities of direct hardware management [1]. Meanwhile, the emerging trend of outsourcing data storages at third parties (cloud storage) has recently attracted tremendous amount of attention from both research and industry communities [2]. Outsourced storage makes shared data and resources much more accessible as users can retrieve them anywhere from personal computers to smart phones, however the users will be at the mercy of their cloud service providers for the availability and integrity of their data. [3]. On the other hand, security remains the critical issue that concerns potential clients, especially for the banks and government sectors. A major challenge for any comprehensive access control solution for outsourced data is the ability to handle requests for resources according to the specified security policies to achieve congeniality, while also protecting the users' privacy [4]. Several solutions have been proposed in the past, but most of them didn't consider protecting privacy of the policies and users' access patterns which are essential aspect for users.

In this paper we address the main aspects related to security of cloud storage presenting and propose an effective flexible security policy and procedures explicit to enhance the security of cloud storage. Main aspects of such a proposed model are guided by a number of important aspects to be briefly surveyed in the following sections. Such aspects cover the major security challenges and problems, the common cloud deployment models and their design goals, methods for enhancing cloud data storage.

2. Threats and Attacks from Storage Perspectives:

While the benefits of storage networks have been widely acknowledged, consolidation of enterprise data on networked storage poses significant security risks. Following is brief listings of the major drivers to implement security for networked storage guided by the critical challenging threats and attacks:

- Perimeter defense strategies focus on the protection from external threats which makes such type of strategies insufficient turn to protect enterprise data, as it's possible that a single security breach can cripple a business [6].
- Number of internal attacks threatening NAS/SAN deployments which are part of the "trusted" corporate networks [7]. Reports such as the CSI/FBI's annual Computer Crime & Security Survey help quantify the significant threats caused by data theft
- Problems due to the incorrectness of data storage in the cloud as the data stored in the cloud may be updated by different users including insertion, deletion, modification, appending, reordering, etc [8].

- Problems due to integrity threats facing user's data as it's redundantly stored in multiple physical locations to further reduce the data integrity threats [9]. Moreover, risks due to compromised storage range from tangible loss such as business discontinuity in the form of information downtime, to intangibles such as the loss of stature as a secure business partner. With the number of reported security attacks on the rise, a firm understanding of networked storage solutions is a precursor to determining and mitigating security risksSemantic Web and XML.

Some of today's basic Web limitations include search, database support, interoperable applications, intelligent business logic, automation, security, and trust. Information revolution awaits the next break-through of semantic web. The Semantic Web is a web that is able to describe things in a way that computers can understand. Semantic web uses some tools like Extensible Markup Language (XML), Resource Describe Framework, Ontology, and Ontology Web language (OWL). XML is the synthetic foundation layer of the Semantic Web. All other technologies providing features for the Semantic Web will be built on top of XML. Requiring other Semantic Web Technologies, like the Resource Description Framework to be layered on top of XML Guarantees a base level of interoperability [8].

3. Cloud Deployment Models:

By large, there's quite agreement on three common cloud deployment models based on their features, approaches and considerations. Figure (1) below shows the main cloud deployment models including: (i) Public cloud, (ii) Private cloud and (iii) Hybrid cloud. Following is a brief review on the main features and aspects related to each cloud model in addition to other models such as the system model and the adversary one.

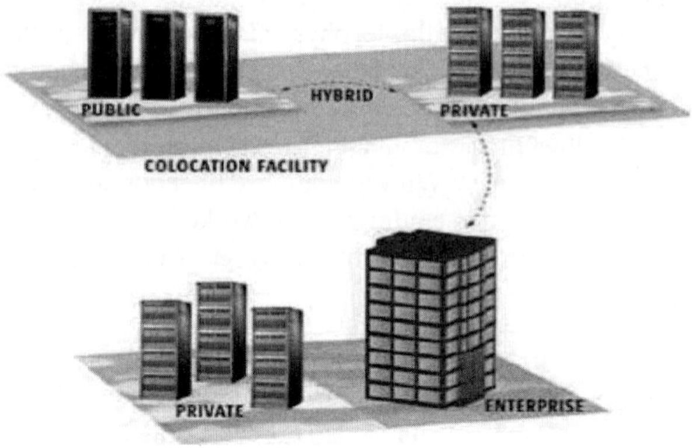

Fig (1) The Common Cloud Deployment Models

a. Public Cloud

A public cloud is one in which the services and infrastructure are provided off-site over the internet for general public users. These clouds offer the greatest level of efficiency in shared resources; however, they are also more vulnerable than private clouds. Public clouds are run by third parties, and applications from different customers are likely to be mixed together on the cloud's servers, storage systems, and networks.

b. Private Cloud

A private cloud is one in which the services and infrastructure are maintained on a private network. These clouds offer the greatest level of security and control, but they present significant cost investments as they require the company to still purchase and maintain all the software and infrastructure, which reduces one important gain from the concept of clouds, the cost savings. [10].

c. Hybrid Cloud

A hybrid cloud environment consist of multiple internal and/or external providers "will be typical for most enterprises". Integrating multiple cloud services enable users to ease the transition to public cloud services while avoiding issues such as PCI compliance. [11].

d. System Model

Cloud networking can be illustrated by three different network entities: Users, cloud Service provider (CSP) and Third Party Auditor (TPA). First, **Users refer to either** individual consumers or organizations and their data need to be stored in the cloud and also rely on the cloud for data processing and retrieval. Second, the **Cloud Service Provider (CSP) refer to a company which owns** and operates live Cloud Computing systems and **provides** significant resources and expertise in building and managing distributed cloud storage servers, Third, is the **Third Party Auditor (TPA) which** is trusted to assess and expose risk of cloud storage services on behalf of the users upon request based on his expertise and capabilities that users may not have.

e. Adversary Model:

There are two different sources for Security threats faced by cloud data storage.

1. CSP can be self-interested, un-trusted and possibly malicious. It may move data that is rarely accessed to a lower tier of storage for monetary reasons, but It may hide a data loss incident due to management errors and so on.
2. Economically motivated adversary, who has the capability to compromise a number of cloud data storage servers in different time intervals and subsequently is able to modify or delete users 'data while remaining undetected by CSPs for a certain period.[12]

There are two types of adversary: Weak adversary and strong adversary.

- Weak Adversary is mainly interested in corrupting the user's data files stored on individual servers. Once a server is comprised, an adversary can pollute the original data files by modifying or introducing its own fraudulent data to prevent the original data from being retrieved by the user.
- Strong Adversary, is the worst case scenario, in which we assume that the adversary can compromise all the storage servers so that he can intentionally modify the data files as long as they are internally consistent.

4. *Design Goals:*

To ensure the security and dependability for cloud data storage, we aim at designing efficient mechanisms for dynamic data verification and operation while also targeting the following goals:

- Storage correctness: to ensure the data are kept intact all the time in the cloud.
- Fast localization of data error: to effectively locate the malfunctioning server when data corruption has been detected
- Dynamic data support: to maintain the same level of storage correctness assurance even if users modify, delete or append their data files in the cloud.
- Dependability: to enhance data availability against Byzantine failures, malicious data modification and server colluding attacks.
- Lightweight: to enable users perform storage correctness checks with minimum overhead
- The Network Access Storage Data security system should explicitly separates the policy enforcement mechanism from the policy decision process and the file manager must be able to communicate policy decisions to the drives [13].
- The protocol should prevent unauthorized modification of client requests and capabilities along with protecting privacy of requests if dictated by the policies of clients or file managers.
- To minimize interaction with the file manager, the drive should be able to validate client operations without direct communication with the file manager.
- To allow for low memory drive implementations, there should be no long term state shared between drive and client. Overall state requirements of the drive should be kept at a minimum, but additional memory should enhance performance [14]. The security protocol should add as little overhead as possible in terms of computation and the number and size of messages.

5. The Proposed Approach to Improve Security of Cloud Data Storage:

The main ideas and solutions of the proposed approach are centered on a number of attributes including Access Control over the Data Storage which includes the necessary policies, processes and control activities for the delivery of each of the Data service offerings. The collective control Data Storage encompasses the users, processes, and technology necessary to maintain an environment that supports the effectiveness of specific controls and the control frameworks [15].The Security, correctness and availability of the data files being stored on the distributed cloud servers must be guaranteed by the following:

- Providing Security Policy & Procedure for Data **Storage**

- **Defense in Depth for Data Storage in cloud computing:** which is referred to as "DiD" is an excellent framework advocating a layered approach to defending against attacks, thereby mitigating risks.

❖ **Layer 1 – Devices on the Storage Network:**

In first layer, focus is given to securing devices on the storage network via considering the following risk-mitigation measures:

- Authentication schemes provided by the operating system should be evaluated. Schemes utilizing public- private key based authentication such as SSH or Kerberos, which also encrypt authentication communications on the network, should be used
- Authorization using Access Control Lists (ACL) to setup role-based access and appropriate permissions will enhance security
- Strong password schemes like minimum length passwords and periodic change of passwords should be enforced. The default username and passwords that are configured on the device should be changed in addition to constant monitoring of published OS-vulnerabilities using database, SANS Security Alert Consensus newsletter and the NAS vendor's support site, is a necessity to prepare for possible attacks
- Logging and auditing controls should be implemented to prevent unauthorized use, track usage and for incident response.[16]

Layer 2 – Network Connectivity:

NAS appliances face similar vulnerabilities as IP based network devices. Common techniques used to protect IP are also applicable to Storage Network along integrating the correctness and error localization challenge. Following are the main aspects proposed to enhance securing the network connectivity layer:

- Extending network perimeter defense strategies like using a Firewall and IDS device to filter traffic reaching the NAS appliance will increase protection
- Use VLANs for segregating traffic to the NAS appliances
- Separate and isolate management interface from data interfaces on the Storage Network, thus enforcing out- of-band management which is more secure
- Monitor traffic patterns on the data interfaces of the NAS devices for unusual activity

- Implement port binding on switches to prevent WWN spoofing. Port binding binds a WWN to a specific switch port allowing connections of that device only through the predefined port thereby preventing other devices to assume the WWN's identity
- Implement vendor specific security techniques. For example, Brocade's Secure Fabric OS provides for additional security by enforcing switch authentication
- Create a separate management network which is isolated from the data network, thus preventing insecure in-band management activities[17].

Layer 3 – Management access:

Management access is a significant source of attack which request identifying the main vulnerabilities, following guidelines are given towards improving the management access aspect:

- Disable the use of telnet and HTTP and enforce management access through SSH and HTTPS for encrypted communication[18]
- Create separate user accounts based on the management tasks assigned to the users
- Implement strong authentication mechanisms like two-factor authentication using tokens, biometrics, etc
- Strong password schemes like minimum length passwords and periodic change of passwords should be enforced
- Implement authorization using Access Control Lists to setup role based access and appropriate permissions
- Enforce logging and auditing to prevent unauthorized use, track usage and for incident response [19].
- Restrict the management of the storage network devices from specific hosts

6. Correctness Verification and Error Localization

Error localization is a key prerequisite for eliminating errors in storage systems. Response protocol

- The response values from servers for each challenge not only determine the correctness of the distributed storage, but also contain information to locate

Reliability of the Analysis Strategy of the Experiment

The reliability of secure data storage strategy depends on security procedure and the coefficients of the backup data [20]. When one or more nodes cannot be accessed, the secure strategy can ensure that the data will be restored as long as one of the k nodes can be accessed. However, traditional data storage methods require all the data in the k nodes to be retrieved. Thus, the more blocks the data are split into, the poorer the reliability of traditional data storage

7. Conclusions

This paper suggests a methodical application of defense in depth (DiD) security techniques that can help reduce security risks in networked storage. More importantly, a DiD based networked storage security policy provides a comprehensive framework to face future attacks as the current technologies are more clearly understood. The emerging standards in storage security in conjunction with "DiD" are claimed to make storage much more resistant to future threats. Highlights on the main aspects and problems facing data security in cloud data storage, which is essentially a distributed storage system as well as surveying some target measures considered to enhance security levels in the data storage networks. The presented approach is centered on a three layer measures along a guideline criteria to enhance the security of cloud data storage. We proposed an effective and flexible security policy and procedure with explicit data support, including block update, delete, and append. The proposed scheme achieves the integration of storage correctness insurance while maintaining data error localization. Additionally, following considerations are also concluded:

- Accountability for security and privacy in public clouds remains with the organization
- Federal agencies must ensure that any selected public cloud computing solution is configured, deployed, and managed to meet the security, privacy, and other requirements of the organization.
- Organizational data must be protected in a manner consistent with policies, whether in the organization's computing centre or the cloud.
- The organization must ensure that security and privacy ontrols are implemented correctly and operate as intended.

References

1. V. Krishna Reddy, B. Thirumal Rao, Dr L.S.S. Reddy, P. Sai Kiran
2. "Research Issues in Cloud Computing " Global Journal of Computer s and Technology, Volume 11,Issue 11, July 2011.
3. What is Cloud Computing? Retrieved April 6, 2011, available at: http://www.microsoft.com/business/engb/solutions/Pages/Cloud.aspx
4. What is Cloud Computing? Retrieved April 6, 2011, available at: http://www.ibm.com/developerworks/cloud/newto.html

5. What is Cloud? Retrieved April 6, 2011, available at: http://www.rackspace.co.uk/cloud-hosting/learn- more/what is cloud/
6. S. De Capitani di Vimercati, S. Foresti, S. Paraboschi, G. Pelosi, and P. Samarati. “Efficient and private access to outsourced data”. In Proc. Of the 31st International Conference on Distributed Computing Systems (ICDCS 2011), Minneapolis, Min- nesota, USA, June 2011.
7. R. Chow, P. Golle, M. Jakobsson, E. Shi, J. Staddon, R. Masuoka, and J. Molina. Controlling data in the cloud: Outsourcing computation without outsourcing control. In ACM Workshop on Cloud Computing Security, 2009
8. Subashini S, Kavitha V., “A survey on security issues in service delivery models of cloud computing,” Journal of Network and Computer Applications (2011) vol. 34 Issue 1, January 2011 pp. 1-11.
9. IT Cloud Services User Survey, pt.2: Top Benefits & Challenges. http://blogs.idc.com/ie/?p=210.
10. New IDC IT Cloud Services Survey: Top Benefits and Challenges. Retrieved April 8, 2011 from http://blogs.idc.com/ie/?p=730
11. Security guidance for Critical Areas of Focus in Cloud Computing. http://www.cloudsecurityalliance.org/guidance/csagui de.pdf.
12. An Information-Centric Approach to Information Security. http://virtualization.sys- con.com/node/171199.
13. End-User Privacy in Human–Computer Interaction. http://www.cs.cmu.edu/~jasonh/publications/fnt-end- user-privacy-in-human-computer-interaction-final.pdf.
14. Latest cloud storage hiccups prompts data security questions. http://www.computerworld.com/action/article.do?command=viewArticleBasic&articleId=9130682&sourc e=NLT_PM.
15. Catteddu, D. and Hogben, G. Cloud Computing: benefits, risks and recommendations for information security. Technical Report. European Network and Information Security Agency, 2009.
16. Danwei Chen, Yanjun He, Computer Technology, Nanjing University of Posts and Telecommunications, Journal of Convergence Information Technology Volume 5, Number 7- September 2010
17. Cong Wang, Qian Wang, and Kui Ren Department of ECE Illinois Institute of Technology, International Journal of Recent Technology and Engineering (IJRTE) , April ,12- 2011.

SUPPLY SYSTEM IN PAP POWER SAS

FANNY PATRICIA MUÑOZ ALVARADO
Industrial Engineering, Libre University, Avenue 70 Street 53-40 Bogota, DC, Cundinamarca, Colombia

EVER ANGEL FUENTES
Industrial Engineering, Libre University, Avenue 70 Street 53-40 Bogota, DC, Cundinamarca, Colombia

In general terms, any production system to ensure its operation needs to get since outside a range of inputs and materials from which they made the transformation processes. From this, in Pap power SAS supplying or procurement as logistic function focuses its main objective to plan and provide the material required to develop products to focus on cost reduction and customer satisfaction. Among its main activities are: 1.The calculation of needs, where logistics planning is involve for the determination of material amounts required for a given time. 2. The purchase or acquisition of materials function that has as main objectives: To maintain continuity of supply, pay fair prices, prevent damage, waste and duplication, seek sources of supply, alternatives, and identifying new products and materials. 3. Obtaining, aimed at contributing to the continuity of activities, avoiding delays and making the respective quality checks. 4. Storage, with specific objectives such as control of the accuracy of their stocks, conservation of materials; and timely replenishment. 5. Office or distribution function to ensure that customer requirements are addressed in a timely and appropriate manner. 6. Stocks control, where it must keep in mind the exact quantities to supply to meet the requirements of material without exceeding the storage capacity [9]. In order to comply with these activities is necessary to design management strategies and control for each, thereby taking Pap Power SAS a policy of purchasing, warehousing, inventory and plans to help to determinate the quantities of material to apply to according to the needs and requirements of the company bearing in mind the key success factor of an adequate supply, costs reduction.

1. Introduction

When it talks to supply it refers to a set of operations that meet the goal of placing at the disposal of the company all products and materials that are required for its operation taking into account the possible conditions of quantity, quality, price and time.

In Pap Power SAS (company dedicated to the production of footwear), supply raw materials properly, the right amounts and at the right time is one of the most important aspects where more control is made by the management department due to the impact that the costs have on the profitability of the company.

Supply of materials is included in the supply chain which includes an entire logistics process since the receipt of raw materials until the finished product is obtained [1].

A optimal management of supply of materials must to calculate the needs of the company, achieving a sufficient inventory in order to do not have missing raw materials and other supplies for the production, minimize inventory investment, from a good stock management can minimize the storage costs for loss or damage, establish an efficient information system to inform to all company departments the inventory and the dollar value of material stocks, to cooperate with the sales department for economical purchases maintaining an efficient transportation activities including dispatch and receipt of goods [4].

A product or service has little value if it is not available to customers when and where they require it [1]. In addition to this, customers are looking for quality in products offered. Based on this, Pap Power SAS has focused its objectives in order to not increase production costs through an excellent planning where are involve factors that influence it such as the selection of suitable suppliers, optimal inventory levels and quantity of materials required in a given time.

2. What is and how work the supply of materials process?

The supply process goes beyond the acquisition of raw materials because within a company should handle multiple operations with other departments ensuring the correct functioning of all production processes [3]. Below is the process of purchasing and logistics of Pap Power SAS:

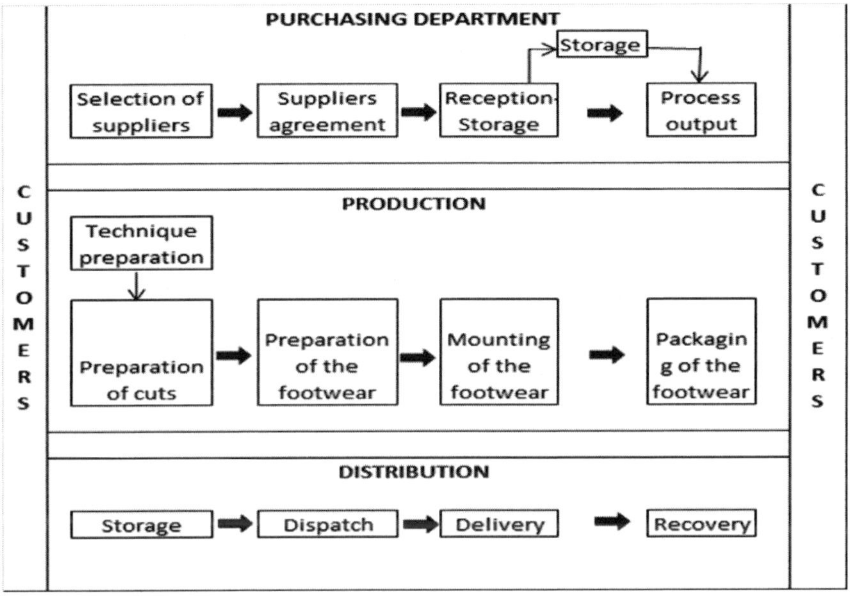

Figure 1. Logistic process in Pap Power SAS, 2011.

The act of buying part of the concept of supplying, the main objective is to ensure an effective supply to the company by ensuring a low cost. When you want to calculate the cost of the integral logistic, the point for start is the acquisition of raw materials to suppliers and it is here that is important to note that a purchases represent more than half the retail price of the finished product, in some cases, these costs represent up to 80% of the price (above costs in salaries, general and selling expenses). This means that over 50% of sales revenue is reinvested in the purchase of materials. Hence, the process of purchasing management is currently developing a major role in the company Pap Power SAS.

The market is constantly changing and every day is more demanding and increasingly less chance to recover from a failure [4], therefore, there are new factors that have influence in the supply process, some of these are:

- Constant change in product demand.
- Uncertainty in the forecasts
- Unstable supplies

- Instability in the price of raw materials
- Globalization

In the supply process, as mentioned above, the purchasing area occupies a key role and must be closely connected with a good inventory management and storage. Hence, in order to have a good inventory management some companies are based in a Material Requirements Plan (MRP) and Master Production Plan (MPP).

A production system that is well organized must to produce only what is necessary or demanded so as not to raise inventory costs [2].

The products and services must be delivered on time and on budget costs. In pursuing this objective, managers of operations conduct production planning as the following:

- Develop aggregate capacity plans, which usually cover 6 to 18 months. These medium-term plans should be given the necessary production capacity to meet customer demands for products and services.
- Establish systems for production planning to guide organizations in meeting delivery promises to customers, meeting the objectives of inventory and maintaining low production costs.
- Provide sufficient inventory of finished products to meet the dual goals of low operating cost and prompt delivery of products to customers.
- Schedule the production of products and services necessary to meet delivery promises to customers, so as to keep low production costs.
- Plan for acquisition, storage and shipment of materials, so that the correct materials are available in the right quantity and at the right time, to support production schedules [7].

The following table shows the demand forecast of PAP Power SAS, company dedicated to the production of footwear, the results were obtained from a Box and Jenkins method:

Table 1. Forecasts of demand for Pap Power SAS.

	Month										
Product	1	2	3	4	5	6	7	8	9	10	11
Shoes for men N- 40	10 0	10 0	10 0	10 0	12 5	10 0	15 0	10 0	12 5	15 0	10 0
Shoes for women N-37	10 0	15 0	12 5	12 5	12 5	10 0	12 5	10 0	12 5	15 0	12 5
Shoes for children N-28	10 0	10 0	12 5	12 5	12 5	10 0	10 0	10 0	12 5	15 0	10 0
Total	**30 0**	**35 0**	**35 0**	**35 0**	**37 5**	**30 0**	**37 5**	**30 0**	**37 5**	**45 0**	**32 5**

Then, It is important to do a Master Production Plan. The master production plan is a method used to plan the resources needed for production in one period to assess in particular.

According to table 1, the master production plan has been prepared following a strategy of persecution by seeking to react quickly to unanticipated changes in demand through changes in the workforce, hiring or laying off staff. Below are the Master Production Plan (MPP) results:

Table 2. Master Production Plan

	Month										
Product	1	2	3	4	5	6	7	8	9	10	11
Shoes for men N-40	150	150	150	150	150	150	150	150	150	150	150
Shoes for Women N-37	150	150	150	150	150	150	150	150	150	150	150
Shoes for women N-28	150	150	150	150	150	150	150	150	150	150	150
Total	**450**	**450**	**450**	**450**	**450**	**450**	**450**	**450**	**450**	**450**	**450**

Table 3. Inventory control

Product	Month										
	1	2	3	4	5	6	7	8	9	10	11
Shoes for men N-40	50	50	50	50	25	50	0	50	25	0	0
Shoes for women N-37	50	0	25	25	25	50	25	50	25	0	0
Shoes for children T-28	50	50	25	25	25	50	50	50	25	0	0
Total	**150**	**100**	**100**	**100**	**75**	**150**	**75**	**150**	**75**	**0**	**0**

According to Table 3. Are generate high inventory costs and therefore it is revision to adjust the Master Production Planning, taking into account the market to analyze the possibility of having a safety stock and likewise the plant capacity.

Table 4. Material Requirements Plan for the first three months

Product	Level MRP	Material	Month			Total Parts
			1	2	3	
	1	White Bullon	100	100	100	300
	1	Black Bullon	100	100	100	300
Shoes for men N-40	2	Heels	100	100	100	300
Shoes for women N-37	1	White Bullon	200	100	200	500
	2	Black Bullon	150	250	100	500
	2	Heels	150	150	200	500
Shoes for Children N-28	1	White Bullon	50	50	50	150
	1	Black Bullon	50	50	50	150
	2	Heels	50	50	50	150
TOTAL			**951**	**952**	**953**	**2850**

After defining the material requirements plan based on the Master Production plan establishing a matrix of costs, such as that shown below, in accordance with the requirements of the production plant of PAP Power SAS:

Table 4. Materials costs.

Product	Level MRP	Material	Cost by unit	Total Parts	Total Cost
Shoes for men N-40	1	White Bullon	$9,800	300	$ 2,940,000
	1	Black Bullon	$10,300	300	$ 3,090,000
	2	Heels	$14,300	300	$ 4,290,000
Cost by product			**$34,400**	**900**	**$ 10,320,000**
Shoes for women N-37	1	White Bullon	$9,800	500	$ 4,900,000
	1	Black Bullon	$10,300	500	$ 5,150,000
	2	Heels	$17,400	500	$ 8,700,000
Cost by product			**$37,500**	**1500**	**$ 18,750,000**
Shoes for children N-28	1	White Bullon	$9,800	150	$ 1,470,000
	1	Black Bullon	$10,300	150	$ 1,545,000
	2	Heels	$6,350	150	$ 952,500
Cost by product			**$26,450**	**450**	**$ 3,967,500**
TOTAL			**$98,350**	**2850**	**$ 33,037,500**

To these costs must be added indirect materials costs in order to obtain the total cost of production.

When making a supply of materials should include that there are some restrictions to be met, one of which is the space or storage capacity of the plant. It is essential to be clear about how many units are going to require, how many are in the process, how many are in stock so as not to generate cost overruns.

3. Quantitative methods to determine the supply of materials required at the right time.

In order to not only depend on the master production plan, it is necessary to compare with other methods like the following.

The main equation to determine the amounts to demand or supply needs, if you know the dates on which to make the supply of a product is as follows [2]:

$$Q\text{-} (F+C+P)\ K - (E+T-B) \quad (1)$$

Where is defined that:

Q = Number of units to order
F = Deadline for the delivery date (Time units)
C =Safety factor to ensure compliance with the requirements of the organization.
P = Delivery deadline
K = Average of number of units consumed (Predicted by Simple Moving Average)
E = Current stock in the warehouse
T = Orders in process
B = Amounts committed to hold if it is customary.

When you have a less complex logistics system equation can be transformed into a simpler one:

$$Q = K\text{-}E \quad (2)$$

In PAP power SAS calculating materials (black bullon) is performed using Equation 2 as follows:

$$Q = K\text{-}E$$

K = 400 (Amount consumed in the month, calculated by mobile simple average)
E = 150 (Quantity in inventory)
Q= 400-150 = 250.

The monthly amount to request of black bullon is 250 units.

Equation 1 and Equation 2 can also be useful in determining the economic cost of order, after evaluating the available inventory and the needs of the company.

4. Conclusions

The whole process of supply in Pap power SAS is done in coordination with the entire logistics system. The inventory, storage and marketing department are involved directly with supply process.

A proper production planning contributes not only to reduce costs, also contributes substantially to the effectiveness of the process when you have the necessary resources at the right time, this has been viewed on PAP Power SAS.

As noted throughout this article, the success of an organization that offers products in the market depends largely on who can reasonably combine the quantity, quality, timeliness and cost of goods or services produced.

The purchases department in Pap power SAS has an 80% interest in the supply process, it is this department that collects and analyzes information for all items and materials required and defines, classifies and maintains constant communication with the main source of supply: Providers.

This investigation aims to improve even more all the logistics processes of the company mentioned above and the techniques involved in Pap Power SAS not only apply to this sector and this type of company but can be implemented in any industry and company.

References

1. BALLOU, Ronald H. *Logística. Administración de la cadena de suministros,* Quinta edición, Pearson Prentice Hall. México. (2004).
2. CHAVES Vega, Eric, *Administración de materiales,* Editorial EUNED, (2005).
3. CHOPRA, Sunil, *Administración de la cadena de suministro: Estrategia, planeación y operación,* México; Pearson – Prentice Hall, (2008).
4. ESCUDERO Serrano, María Jose. *Gestión de aprovisionamiento,* Tercera edición. España (2009).
5. LAMBER, D.M, *Opinión – Estrategia empresarial último modelo;* http://search.proquest.com/docview/466181536?accountid=49777 , (2004)

6. MARTÍNEZ Moya, Emilio. *Negociación y estrategias de aprovisionamiento.* Cuarta Edición, España (2007).
7. NORMAN Gaither, Greg. *Administración de producción y operaciones.* Octava Edición, Thomson Editores, México. (2000).
8. SIPPER, D. y Bulfin, R. Planeación y control de la producción. México. (1998).
9. www.monografias.com/trabajos17/abastecimiento/abastecimiento.shtml.
10. industrial.frba.utn.edu.ar/MATERIAS/proyecto_final/archivos/compras_terlevich.pdf

ACQUISITION OF ACROBATS/ARTISTS WHO ARE ADAPTABLE TO THE DIFFERENT NEEDS OF A THEME PARK

JAIME GIL LAFUENTE

School of Economic and Business Sciences. Department of Economics and Business Administration. University of Barcelona / Universitat de Barcelona, Diagonal, 690, 08034 Barcelona

VANESA F. GUZMAN PARRA

School of Economic and Business Sciences. Department of Economics and Business Administration. University of Málaga, El Ejido Campus. 29071 Málaga

FRANCISCO JAVIER MAQUEDA LAFUENTE

School of Economic and Business Sciences, Department of Financial Economics II, University of the Basque Country/Euskal Herriko Unibertsitatea. Avda. Lehendakari Agirre 83, 48015 Bilbao

Over the past few decades, we have developed several models and algorithms that minimize the levels of uncertainty in selecting athletes for incorporation onto a specific team, specifically whether to fill a single position[*] or various positions interchangeably[†]. Currently, the latter alternative is increasingly more valued because of the economic crisis in almost all European countries. Spain is one such country, and its businesses seek to reduce costs by hiring workers who can perform different tasks, thus avoiding hiring specialists who perform only one task. This approach is being used by an important amusement park that requires actors, dancers and expert acrobats, and it has chosen to hire artists who can perform in several consecutive shows[‡] while considering certain

[*] Gil Lafuente, J.: "Les Universitats en el Centenari del Futbol Club Barcelona. Estudis en l'àmbit de l'esport", [The University in the Centenary of the Barcelona Football Club. Studies in the sports arena] (J. Gil Aluja Ed.): "L'optimització del fitxatge d'un esportista en l'ambit de l'esport", [Optimizing the signing of an athlete in the sports arena]. Publicaciones del F.C. Barcelona. Ed. Milladoiro, Santiago de Compostela, 1999, pages 3 to 55.

[†] Gil Lafuente, J.: "Management of an investment in a polyvalent player". Conference Proceedings: "International Conference on Artificial Intelligence ICAI'99". Durban (Sudáfrica), September 24, 25 and 26, 1999, pages 169 to 172.

[‡] Gil Lafuente, J.: "Algoritmos de la Excelencia. Claves para el Éxito en la Gestión Deportiva [Algorithms of Excellence. Keys for Success in Sports Management]". Ed. Milladoiro, Publicaciones del F.C. Barcelona, Vigo, 2002.

priorities and indispensable conditions. The proposed methodology will allow a company to hire workers near the "ideal" for various types of activities; thus, they can adapt to the three different types of shows with certain minimum requirements and priorities.

1. Introduction

Currently, companies in countries strongly impacted by the economic crisis are trying to reduce costs and have had to operate without certain workers. Whether this is the case or whether the decline in employees is from unforeseen circumstances (voluntary resignations and retirement, etc.), new staff members should adapt to other tasks in the company in addition to their primary specialty through playing the "wild card" or becoming the regular versatile employee who performs duties previously performed by several workers with greater pay.

A company that has requested to remain anonymous has chosen to hire two workers with the following considerations for both cases.

1. An acrobat/artist with the ability to perform the primary work of an expert-acrobat in a show with a comedic tone.
2. The minimum necessary skills include the acrobat/artist being able to dance and sing in front of an audience.
3. Acrobat/artist must have acting skills, which are necessary for both the acrobatics show and to connect with the audience before and after the dances.

On this basis, we will adapt a series of models and algorithms that provide the best chance for success in this decision-making process.

2. Basic elements of the proposed approach

To achieve this goal, it is important to consider the significance of each characteristic, quality or singularity that comprise the "perfect worker" (from the most important to the least significant) for performing such functions, which should be carefully and appropriately valued[*]. In fuzzy logic, these descriptions are assigned on an 11-point scale[†] by company experts or outside experts if necessary. If it is appropriate and necessary, they could also assign different weights to each description in accordance with the value.

---

[*] Kaufmann, A. and Gil Aluja, J.: "Introducción a la teoría de los subconjuntos borrosos a la gestión de las empresas [Introduction to the theory of fuzzy subsets in business management]". Ed. Milladoiro (3rd edition). Santiago de Compostela, 1993.

[†] From the Greek "Endekas" (eleven) and "-adas" (group): group of eleven; a scale composed of eleven decimal values between 0 (null) and 1 (the total).

The best way to proceed to determine when an employee is suitable for meeting certain obligations in a theme park can be described as follows.

a. Using the description of company experts, as well as fuzzy subsets, to determine the requirements for the three jobs.
b. Using human resource managers' decisions to determine the priority levels for each activity, considering that certain activities are more important.
c. Similarly, establishing minimum levels required for each activity to avoid offsets* (brilliance in one activity could offset poor performance in another).
d. Analyzing candidates for employment at the company and then describing them using fuzzy subsets and the criteria in point a.
e. Selecting the coefficient, distance or index choice that best measures the candidates' suitability in accordance with the required needs.
f. Using the resulting order, hire the candidates closest to the required ideals.

Next, we followed the above steps to select two workers with the assurance that their contributions will allow the company to reduce expenses while minimizing the possible impact on the service quality offered to visitors.

3. Description of the specific needs for each task

Technical specialists for the company's shows agreed on the required characteristics, qualities or singularities for each of the three jobs. After meeting, they ranked the following factors as follows.

$C^{(1)}$: Expert-Acrobat Position:

$C_1^{(1)}$: Ability to overcome obstacles at great heights
$C_2^{(1)}$: Jumping ability
$C_3^{(1)}$: Horse riding ability
$C_4^{(1)}$: Knowing how to fall

$C^{(2)}$: Actor Position:

$C_1^{(2)}$: Physical performance ability
$C_2^{(2)}$: Vocal performance ability

* Gil Lafuente, J.: "Nuevo instrumento de selección: el índice de descartes por superación-distancia [New selection tool: the elimination index by superseding-distance]". Cuadernos del Cimbage, Mayo, Buenos Aires (Argentina), 2005, p. 43-60.

$C_3^{(2)}$: Ability to improvise

$C^{(3)}$: Dancer and Singer Position:

$C_1^{(3)}$: Vocal ability
$C_2^{(3)}$: Rhythm
$C_3^{(3)}$: Coordination

Below is a general description for addressing the first step, which requires that we describe the three jobs.

Consistent with the methodology proposed in the International Conference on Artificial Intelligence (ICAI'99)*, we must establish an "ideal profile" for the worker, which comprises the profiles related to each task, such that only one ideal worker type would perfectly meet each requirement for the jobs.

This adaptive employee is described using a unique fuzzy subset, which is the result of combining fuzzy subsets for the different needs of each of the three activities that must be performed.

From a general perspective, the form for this fuzzy subset is as follows.

Let j = 1, 2,…, m candidates to fill a certain position(s) in the company, which require certain characteristics, qualities or singularities valued as C_i, i = 1, 2,…, n (a candidate can exceed the required ideal level without error).

Let h = 1, 2,…, z positions. From these data, we have z fuzzy subsets, which are descriptors for each hypothetical ideal worker to perfectly adapt to the theme park requirements.

$D_h =$

C_1	C_2	C_3		C_{n-1}	C_n
μ_{1h}	μ_{2h}	μ_{3h}	…	μ_{n-1h}	μ_{nh}

h = 1, 2,…, z

Grouping the descriptors into a single fuzzy subset takes the following form.

* Gil Lafuente, J.: "Management of an investment in a polyvalent player". Conference Proceedings: "International Conference on Artificial Intelligence ICAI'99". Durban (Sudáfrica), September 24, 25 and 26, 1999, pages 169 to 172.

$D_{1, 2, \ldots, z} =$

C_1	C_2		C_n	C_1	C_2		C_n	C_1	C_2	
μ_{11}	μ_{21}	$\cdots$	μ_{n1}	μ_{12}	μ_{22}	$\cdots$	μ_{n2}	μ_{13}	μ_{23}	$\cdots$

	C_n	C_1		C_n	C_1	C_2		C_n	C_1		C_n
$\cdots$	μ_{n3}	μ_{14}	$\cdots$	μ_{n4}	μ_{1z-1}	μ_{2z-1}	$\cdots$	μ_{nz-1}	μ_{1z}	$\cdots$	μ_{nz}

This fuzzy subset represents the ideal profile of a hypothetical worker who can perform each assigned task.

As noted above, if the number of candidates is j = 1, 2,…m, a fuzzy subset $P_j^{(h)}$ will be constructed for each, which is repeated z times if necessary with the same characteristics and the fuzzy subset P_j that describes such factors.

From the basic fuzzy subset,

$P_j =$

C_1	C_2		C_{n-1}	C_n
$\mu_1^{(1)}$	$\mu_2^{(j)}$	$\cdots$	$\mu_{n-1}^{(j)}$	$\mu_n^{(j)}$

fuzzy subsets will result, such as

$P_j^{(h)} =$

C_1	C_2		C_n	C_1	C_2		C_n		C_1	C_2		C_n
μ_1^j	μ_2^j	$\cdots$	μ_n^j	μ_1^j	μ_2^j	$\cdots$	μ_n^j	...	μ_1^j	μ_2^j	$\cdots$	μ_n^j

Position $C^{(1)}$ Position $P^{(2)}$ Position $P^{(z)}$

for all j $\in$ { 1, 2, …, m}.

Based on this premise, we proceeded with the process proposed to produce an ideal worker profile that perfectly adapts to the different demands based on the z fuzzy subsets that describe ideal workers for the different jobs as follows.

$D_1 =$

C_1	C_2		C_n
μ_{11}	μ_{21}	…	μ_{n1}

$D_2 =$

C_1	C_2		C_n
μ_{12}	μ_{22}	…	μ_{n2}

....

$D_z =$

C_1	C_2		C_n
μ_{1z}	μ_{2z}	…	μ_{nz}

The ideal profile for the "adaptable employee" is the following, as discussed above.

$D_{1, 2, \ldots, z} =$

C_1	C_2		C_n	C_1	C_2		C_n		C_1	C_2		C_n
μ_{11}	μ_{21}	…	μ_{n1}	μ_{12}	μ_{22}	…	μ_{n2}	…	μ_{1z}	μ_{2z}	…	μ_{nz}

m artist-acrobat candidates were at our disposal, which were described by the fuzzy subsets that are referenced with the same descriptors as above.

$P_1 =$

C_1	C_2		C_n
$\mu_1^{(1)}$	$\mu_2^{(1)}$	…	$\mu_n^{(1)}$

$P_2 =$

C_1	C_2		C_n
$\mu_1^{(2)}$	$\mu_2^{(2)}$	…	$\mu_n^{(2)}$

....

$P_m =$

C_1	C_2		C_n
$\mu_1^{(m)}$	$\mu_2^{(m)}$	…	$\mu_n^{(m)}$

Each candidate is described several times if necessary in accordance with the requested needs to approach the ideal worker.

	C_1	C_2	…	C_n	C_1	C_2	…	C_n	C_1	C_2	…	C_n
$P_1^{(h)} =$	$\mu_1^{(1)}$	$\mu_2^{(1)}$	…	$\mu_n^{(1)}$	$\mu_1^{(1)}$	$\mu_2^{(1)}$	…	$\mu_n^{(1)}$	$\mu_1^{(1)}$	$\mu_2^{(1)}$	…	$\mu_n^{(1)}$

	C_1	C_2	…	C_n	C_1	C_2	…	C_n	C_1	C_2	…	C_n
$P_2^{(h)} =$	$\mu_1^{(2)}$	$\mu_2^{(2)}$	…	$\mu_n^{(2)}$	$\mu_1^{(2)}$	$\mu_2^{(2)}$	…	$\mu_n^{(2)}$	$\mu_1^{(2)}$	$\mu_2^{(2)}$	…	$\mu_n^{(2)}$

……………………………………………………………………………………………………

	C_1	C_2	…	C_n	C_1	C_2	…	C_n	C_1	C_2	…	C_n
$P_j^{(m)} =$	$\mu_1^{(m)}$	$\mu_2^{(jm}$	…	$\mu_n^{(jm)}$	$\mu_1^{(m)}$	$\mu_2^{(m)}$	…	$\mu_n^{(m)}$	$\mu_1^{(m)}$	$\mu_2^{(m)}$	…	$\mu_n^{(m)}$

In practice, the positions are described as follows.

$C^{(1)}$: Acrobat Position:

	Obst. Heights	Jumping	Horse Riding	Falling
$C^{(1)} =$	.9	.7	.7	1

$C^{(2)}$: Actor Position:

	Phys. Perf.	Vocal Perf.	Improvisation
$C^{(2)} =$	.9	.6	.9

$C^{(3)}$: Dancer and Singer Position:

	Vocal	Rhythm	Coordination
$C^{(3)} =$	.9	.6	.8

The 8 candidates who passed the initial tests are as follows.

	Obst. Heights	Jumping	Horse Riding	Falling	Phys. Perf.	Vocal Perf.	Inprovisation	Vocal	Rhythm	Coordination
$P_1 =$	.3	.6	.9	.9	.2	.7	.6	.9	.8	.5
$P_2 =$	.5	6	.6	.4	.5	.6	.8	.6	.6	.6
$P_3 =$	1	.5	.5	.9	.7	.2	.6	.6	.7	.8
$P_4 =$	.6	.7	.5	.7	.9	1	.5	.7	.8	.7
$P_5 =$	.6	.8	.7	.7	.5	.9	.5	.7	.5	.9
$P_6 =$	.9	.6	1	.5	.8	.7	.8	.5	.9	.8
$P_7 =$	.2	.4	.2	.7	.9	.7	.3	.7	.5	.9
$P_8 =$	.5	.8	.9	.6	.6	.9	.6	.5	.6	.9

Notably, the company's show managers argue that for both workers, expert-acrobat performance is much more important than acting or singing-dancing given the time necessary to develop the skill, its importance for the public and security. Therefore, we weighted the skills as follows.

Expert-Acrobat: $\varpi_1 = .7$; Actor: $\varpi_2 = .2$; Singer-Dancer: $\varpi_3 = .1$

However, an acceptable minimum for each skill is required such that if the minimum is not met, the candidate would not be a suitable employee. The *sine qua non* conditions for each function are considered as follows.

Expert-Acrobat: $\Xi_1 \geq .8$; Actor: $\Xi_2 > .7$; Singer-Dancer: $\Xi_3 > .85$

Using these data, we find the similarity between the company preference and the candidates' skills.

4. Similarity between the candidates and ideals

The order that facilitates decision making with a low degree of uncertainty can be produced in different ways; we used one such method that likely adapts to the nature of the problem, but we recognize that the Hamming distance and Euclidean distance* approach as well as the maximum and minimum level index† approaches are interesting alternatives. We used the adequacy ratio‡ because expert informants from the company confirmed that if the candidates surpass the ideal levels, they would consider such a result the same as if the levels were met.

5. Generating the results

The adequacy ratio without convex weighting was performed as follows.

$$K(C \rightarrow P) = \frac{1}{n} \cdot \sum_{i=1}^{n} \left(1 \wedge \left(1 - \mu_{\mu_i}^{(C)} + \mu_{\mu_i}^{(P)}\right)\right)$$

i = C1, C2,..., Cn

D = P1, P2,..., Pm

This process provides degrees of "closeness" that are necessary for making an easy decision when choosing between the two suitable candidates.

$K(C^{(1)} \rightarrow P_1) = .8;$ $k(C^{(1)} \rightarrow P_2) = .7;$ $k(C^{(1)} \rightarrow P_3) = .87;$
$k(C^{(2)} \rightarrow P_1) = .66;$ $k(C^{(2)} \rightarrow P_2) = .83;$ $k(C^{(2)} \rightarrow P_3) = .7;$
$k(C^{(3)} \rightarrow P_1) = .9;$ $k(C^{(3)} \rightarrow P_2) = .83;$ $k(C^{(3)} \rightarrow P_3) = .9;$

$k(C^{(1)} \rightarrow P_4) = .8;$ $k(C^{(1)} \rightarrow P_5) = .9;$ $k(C^{(1)} \rightarrow P_6) = .85;$
$k(C^{(2)} \rightarrow P_4) = .86;$ $k(C^{(2)} \rightarrow P_5) = .73;$ $k(C^{(2)} \rightarrow P_6) = .93;$
$k(C^{(3)} \rightarrow P_4) = .9;$ $k(C^{(3)} \rightarrow P_5) = .9;$ $k(C^{(3)} \rightarrow P_6) = .86;$

---

* Gil Lafuente, J.: "The adquisition of having inmobilized inmaterial in the sports societies". Conference Proceedings: "Congreso Internacional MS'99 [International MS Conference '99]". Santiago de Compostela, May 17, 18 and 19, 1999, volume 1, pages 185 to 196.

† Gil Lafuente, J: "El 'Índice del Máximo y Mínimo Nivel' en la Optimización del Fichaje de un Deportista".[The 'Maximum and Minimum level Index' in the Optimization of the Trading of Athletes] Actas del Congreso: "X Congreso Internacional A.E.D.E.M.". Reggio Calabria (Italia), 4, 5 y 6 de Septiembre del 2001, páginas 439 a 443.

‡ Gil Lafuente, J: "Les Universitats en el Centenari del Futbol Club Barcelona: Estudis en l'Àmbit de l'Esport [The University in the Centenari of the Barcelona Football Club: Studies in the Sports Arena] (J. Gil Aluja (ed.))".

$k\,(C^{(1)} \rightarrow P_7) = .55;$ $k\,(C^{(1)} \rightarrow P_8) = .8;$
$k\,(C^{(2)} \rightarrow P_7) = .8;$ $k\,(C^{(2)} \rightarrow P_8) = .8;$
$k\,(C^{(3)} \rightarrow P_7) = .9;$ $k\,(C^{(3)} \rightarrow P_8) = .86$

Considering the necessary conditions for each function required by the human resource managers of the theme park, we will generate the results in the table below, wherein the candidates who meet the conditions *sine qua non* are clear.

	P_1	P_2	P_3	P_4	P_5	P_6	P_7	P_8
$\Xi_1 \geq .8$ for $C^{(1)}$	.8	.7	.87	.8	.9	.85	.55	.8
$\Xi_2 > .7$ for $C^{(2)}$	.66	.83	.7	.87	.73	.93	.8	.8
$\Xi_3 > .85$ for $C^{(3)}$	.9	.83	.9	.9	.9	.86	.9	.86

Clearly, only 4 candidates meet the non-compensatory conditions P_4, P_5, P_6 and P_8.

The weighted adequacy ratios for the position and each candidate's skills are as follows:

$$k\,(C \rightarrow P_1) = .7 \cdot .8 + .2 \cdot .66 + .1 \cdot .9 = .782;$$
$$k\,(C \rightarrow P_2) = .7 \cdot .7 + .2 \cdot .83 + .1 \cdot .83 = .739;$$
$$k\,(C \rightarrow P_3) = .7 \cdot .87 + .2 \cdot .7 + .1 \cdot .9 = .839;$$
$$k\,(C \rightarrow P_4) = .7 \cdot .8 + .2 \cdot .87 + .1 \cdot .9 = .824;$$
$$k\,(C \rightarrow P_5) = .7 \cdot .9 + .2 \cdot .73 + .1 \cdot .9 = .866;$$
$$k\,(C \rightarrow P_6) = .7 \cdot .85 + .2 \cdot .93 + .1 \cdot .86 = .867;$$
$$k\,(C \rightarrow P_7) = .7 \cdot .55 + .2 \cdot .8 + .1 \cdot .9 = .635;$$
$$k\,(C \rightarrow P_8) = .7 \cdot .8 + .2 \cdot .8 + .1 \cdot .86 = .806.$$

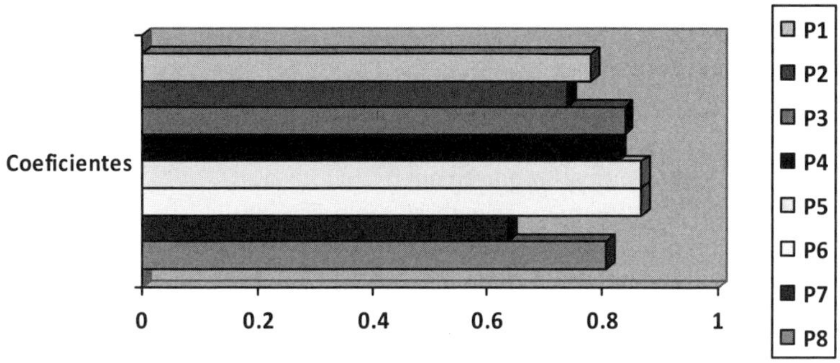

Therefore, using the typical non-compensatory method, the order of preference is as follows:

$$P_6 \succ P_5 \succ P_3 \succ P_4 \succ P_8 \succ P_1 \succ P_2 \succ P_7.$$

However, the company imposed certain minimum requirements that only 4 candidates met, as mentioned above. Thus, the priority order is as follows:

$$P_6 \succ P_5 \succ P_4 \succ P_8.$$

Interestingly, there is almost no difference in the coefficients between Candidate P_6 (.867) and Candidate P_5 (.866), which confirms that both are suitable employees for the park.

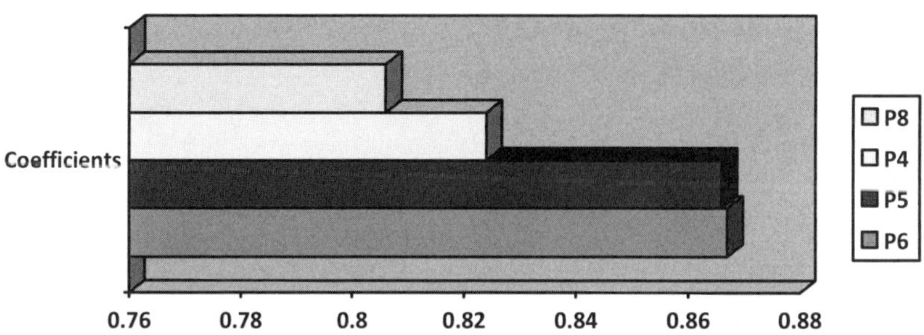

Where the company desired only one worker, this negligible difference could be analyzed using confidence intervals[*] or triplets[*].

[*] Gil Lafuente, J.: "Algoritmos de la Excelencia. Claves para el Éxito en la Gestión Deportiva [Algorithms of Excellence. Keys for Success in Sports Management]". Ed. Milladoiro, Publicaciones del F.C. Barcelona, Vigo, 2002.

In accordance with the particular interests, the overall ordering is as follows.

1. P_6 (meeting all requirements)
2. P_5 (meeting all requirements)
3. P_4 (meeting all requirements)
4. P_8 (meeting all requirements)
5. P_3 (meeting two of the three requirements)
6. P_1 (meeting two of the three requirements)
7. P_7 (meeting two of the three requirements)
8. P_2 (meeting just one of the three requirements)

As shown below, this ordering varies with the option of compensatory ordering.

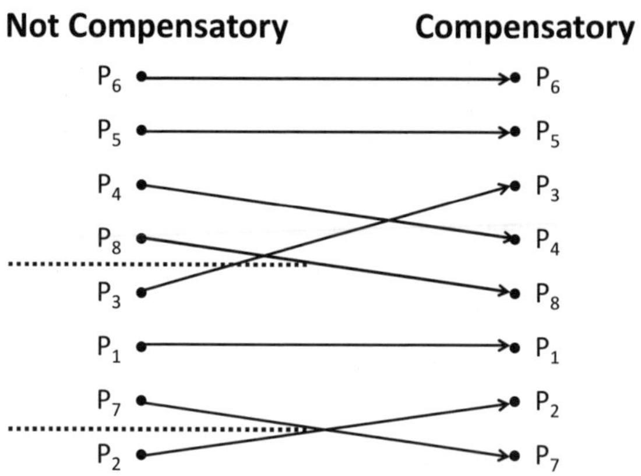

6. Conclusions

The practical method herein is based on research and was used to emphasize the advantages of a non-compensatory system for decision making based on ordering. The real needs that the problem posed led us to produce a specific adaptation by considering a weighted polyvalence to perform the functions necessary for this company.

* Gil Aluja, J.:"La gestión interactiva de los recursos humanos en la incertidumbre [Interactive management of human resources amidst uncertainty]". Ed. Centro de estudios Ramón Areces, S.A. Madrid, 1996.

We are one step closer to enhancing the process of providing company managers with ways to better operate in difficult moments such as under the current economic conditions.

In conclusion, we remind the audience that the entertainment field is a mainstay in Spain and that we depend on it for a slow but eventual end to the crisis*. If customers in a theme park are satisfied with its operation and more importantly with the personal treatment received, the resulting word-of-mouth advertising is an invaluable asset that accelerates the virtuous "product-customer" circle. Therefore, we believe in the importance of both hiring and training employees who embody the company image; furthermore, with minimal effort and using the tools at our disposal, it is possible, without excessive cost or complications, to limit the previously high levels of uncertainty in personnel selection.

References

De Luca, A. and Termini, S.: "A definition nonprobabilistic entropy in the setting fuzzy sets theory". Information and Control, 1972, 20, p. 301-312.

Gil Aluja, J.: "The interactive management of human resources in uncertainty". Kluwer Academic Publishers. Dortrech, 1989.

Gil Aluja, J.:"Elements for a theory of decision in uncertainty". Kluwer Academic Publishers. Dortrech, 1999.

Gil Aluja, J.:"La gestión interactiva de los recursos humanos en la incertidumbre [Interactive management of human resources amidst uncertainty]". Ed. Centro de estudios Ramón Areces, S.A. Madrid, 1996.

Gil Aluja, J.:"Selección de Personal. El problema de la polivalencia y el de la uniformida [Personnel Selection: The problems of versatility and uniformity]". Cuadernos CEURA. Madrid, 1987.

Gil Lafuente, J.: "Algoritmos de la Excelencia. Claves para el Éxito en la Gestión Deportiva [Algorithms of Excellence. Keys for Success in Sports Management]". Ed. Milladoiro, Publicaciones del F.C. Barcelona, Vigo, 2002.

Gil Lafuente, J.: "La asignación de deportistas a los puestos de un equipo [The assignment of athletes to team positions]". Conference Proceedings: "VI Congreso S.I.G.E.F [International Association for Fuzzy-Set Management and Economy Conference VI]". Morelia, Michoacán (México), November 15, 16 and 17, 1999, p. 284-299.

* Gil-Lafuente, J.: "Una esperanza para la recuperación económica del trabajo [A hope for the economic recovery of work]". Opening Speech at the Royal Academy of Doctors. Barcelona, July 5, 2011,

Gil Lafuente, J.: "Les Universitats en el Centenari del Futbol Club Barcelona. Estudis en l'àmbit de l'esport", [The University in the Centenary of the Barcelona Football Club. Studies in the sports arena] (J. Gil Aluja Ed.): "L'optimització del fitxatge d'un esportista en l'ambit de l'esport", [Optimizing the signing of an athlete in the sports arena]. Publicaciones del F.C. Barcelona. Ed. Milladoiro, Santiago de Compostela, 1999, p. 3-55.

Gil Lafuente, J.: "Management of an investment in a polyvalent player". Conference Proceedings: "International Conference on Artificial Intelligence ICAI'99". Durban (Sudáfrica), September 24, 25 and 26, 1999, p. 169-172.

Gil Lafuente, J.: "The adquisition of having inmobilized inmaterial in the sports societies". Conference Proceedings: "Congreso Internacional MS'99 [International MS Conference '99]". Santiago de Compostela, May 17, 18 and 19, 1999, p. 185-196.

Gil Lafuente, J: "El 'Índice del Máximo y Mínimo Nivel' en la Optimización del Fichaje de un Deportista [The 'Maximum and Minimum Level Index' in the Optimization of the Signing of an Athlete]". Conference Proceedings: "X Congreso Internacional A.E.D.E.M. [European Academy of Management and Business Economics Conference X]". Reggio Calabria (Italy), September 4, 5 and 6, 2001, p. 439 a 443.

Gil Lafuente, J: "Marketing para el nuevo milenio. Nuevas técnicas para la gestión comercial en la incertidumbre [Marketing for the new millennium. New techniques for business management amidst uncertainty]". Ed. Pirámide. Madrid, 1996.

Gil-Lafuente, J.: "Una esperanza para la recuperación económica del trabajo [A hope for the economic recovery of work]". Opening Speech at the Royal Academy of Doctors. Barcelona, July 5, 2011.

Kaufmann, A. and Gil Aluja, J.: "Introducción a la teoría de los subconjuntos borrosos a la gestión de las empresas [Introduction to the theory of fuzzy subsets in business management]". Ed. Milladoiro (3rd edition). Santiago de Compostela, 1993.

Kaufmann, A. and Gil Aluja, J.: "Técnicas especiales para la gestión de expertos [Special techniques for expert management]". Ed. Milladoiro. Santiago de Compostela, 1993.

Zadeh, L.: "Fuzzy Sets. Information and control". July 8, 1965, p. 338-353.

Zimmermann, H. J.: "Results of empirical studies in fuzzy sets theory". In Klir, G. J.: "Applied General Systems Research. Plenum. New York, 1978, p. 303-312.

SALVADOR IN 1551: A HISTORICAL SIMULATION OF A CITY

MARIA ANTONIA LIMA GOMES

Master's degree in Computation Modelling, Faculdade de Tecnologia SENAI CIMATEC, Avenida Pinto de Aguiar, s/n, CEP 40.000.00, Salvador – Bahia, Brazil

ALFREDO MATTA

Multi-institutional Multi-discipline Doctorade in Knowledge Diffusion, Master degree3 Program in Education and Contemporaneity, Universidade Estadual da Bahia, Rua Silveira Martins, 2555, Cabula, CEP 41150.000, Salvador – Bahia, Brazil

The research works on the development of a 3D revisio proposal for Salvador city – Brazil, at the time of its foundation. The study begins developing the discussion that supports the social-constructivism as basis for the interactivity revisio and pedagogic design of the computational model, based mainly on authors as Vigotsky and Bakhtin. It is through these bases and the "Historical Thinking" that the choice is made for the presentation strategies of the city environment simulation and its inhabitants in the middle of the XVI century, as well as it is created dialogue and interactivity principles among people of the XVI century and XXI century. The simulation is also evaluated in its usefulness as didactic material for education and its several modalities, as well as for other sides of studies that use digital support, because it makes possible new borders for the research in its several aspects.

1. Building 3D Didactic Material for the History

This work presents the first results of the pedagogic design use, which has as theoretical base the social-constructivist principles that, among other things, made possible the construction of a model / simulation in which the inhabitants of the XVI century, although supposed, dialogue with the ones of the current century, providing a room in which occur interactions and learnings in a type of computation revisio that is appropriate for environments or courses based on education and its several modalities, in other words, presential, on-line, semi-presential or other type of History learning that takes place starting from the support of digital environments. Thus, it is presented here the principles of this computation revisio to show the city of the XVI century, which is analyzed based on studies and testimonies about that time, for later to present some of the solutions of physical and human revisio of such city.

Finally, it is dedicated to present the model built in first version, the first reviews about its uses and usefulness for the teaching-learning of History and on the issue of the experimental study that is being realized..

2. Modelling through the intersection of the social-constructivist principles

The work of Vigotsky (2009) talks about the need of an individual to mediate his experience in a context that is concrete condition for his existence. It means that is through the process of collaboration that this individual builds his autonomy, and this autonomy is the starting point, or else, the most important, for the learning to be processed, consequently, the development of this individual. In his theoretical principles on thought and language, Vigotsky defends that the individual to build knowledge goes through three phases that would be ZDR (Real Development Zone – RDZ), ZDI (Immediate Development Zone – IDZ) and ZDP (Potential Development Zone – PDZ). Therefore, the individual apprehends through his process and historical construction. Being like this, the individual builds knowledge from the interaction with his context, from the mediated collaboration and from the interaction with the environmental and collective conditions of his existence.

It was in this way that we modeled the simulation of Salvador city of XVI century (1549-1551). As the individual-user has access and begins to interact with the simulation, he will be going to interact from his concrete social praxis, from his context and daily life. Each individual's praxis is always permeated of ZDR, element that comes from his life experiences. That will act mediated by the model of Salvador city, a simulation system prepared to collaborate with its users, equipped with its contexts, in other words, we projected the interactivity so that the simulation seeks the whole time, to engage the user and his social practices in the activities and in the experiences offered by the software. It is the individual's practical engagement in the mediation process of the simulation digital environment, that will make possible production of meaning and consequent knowledge construction, generating new approaches, improving the metacognitive reflections, mainly as it settles down the dialogue with the History.

Bakhtin (2003), in one of his principles, says that every human being emerges from the interaction with the other one. Being like this, the human being only has sense if he can depend on the contact with other one. In other words, we can only be through the collectivity. In this purpose, Bakhtin (2010) affirms that: 1) it is impossible to conceive / think the man outside his context; 2) that the other one provides me to see what myself alone I am unable of seeing;dialógica; 3) the other one is key-point in the dialogic reality; 4) that the sign refracts / reflects multiple voices; 5) the condition so that the sign (reflection of the multiple voices) constitutes semiotic and ideological reaction in and for the individual / other one, it imposes that it has a social value, in other words, be inside the reality of the group. Without the mentioned social value, this sign (although reflection of multiple voices, polyphonic individual) it might become isolated and empty of meaning for not reflecting the essence, the hermeneutic thinking that composes the society from which these individuals come from, what could bring this way, a break of the social consciousness / practice and possible breaks / fragmentation of and for a class conscience. This way, according to Bakhtin Apud Brait (2005), the man is product of the history; he cannot close himself in the past, because it is essentially dialogic.

This way, according to Vigotsky and Bakhtin thinking, were built the interactivity and conception of the History principles in the revisio. Bakhtin is present in the model, or software environment of Salvador city of the XVI century (1549-1551) with his dialogism idea: conception in which is considered that through the authors of an enunciated text, be it literary, historiographical, be it even mathematical, their existences, interactions and contacts pass and they can share existences with those that will be their readers and who will interpret, therefore living what was written, according to their own experiences.

"Historical thinking", according to Martineau (1997) in his studies, brings the concept of the problematisation in the history, because without problems there is no history, in other words, for the individual to develop the historical reasoning is necessary to look for questions in the present to answer to the past. For Martineau (1997), anybody can develop the historical reasoning since he presents these four operations: hypothesis formulation from question problems; to seek and to criticize sources of information; to interpret information and get conclusions and interpretative synthesis. Therefore, the insert of historical thinking gave us basis also for definitions of the knowledge construction, in other words, the whole process that engenders it, making possible to the individual means for freedom and transformation of the reality / context in that he lives.

Thus, starting from these dialogic and social-constructivist basis of education interpretation and interactivity, it is built the computation revisio proposal of this research work. In fact, the revisio exercise present is qualified as a project of construction of the social-constructivist revisio of Salvador city of the XVI century, interpreted from principles of the historical materialism. Therefore, this revisio of the complex social relationships involves the man and his daily praxis starting from the perspective of individuals of the present and of those who lived the colonial 'soteropolis' and their adventure in the new world.

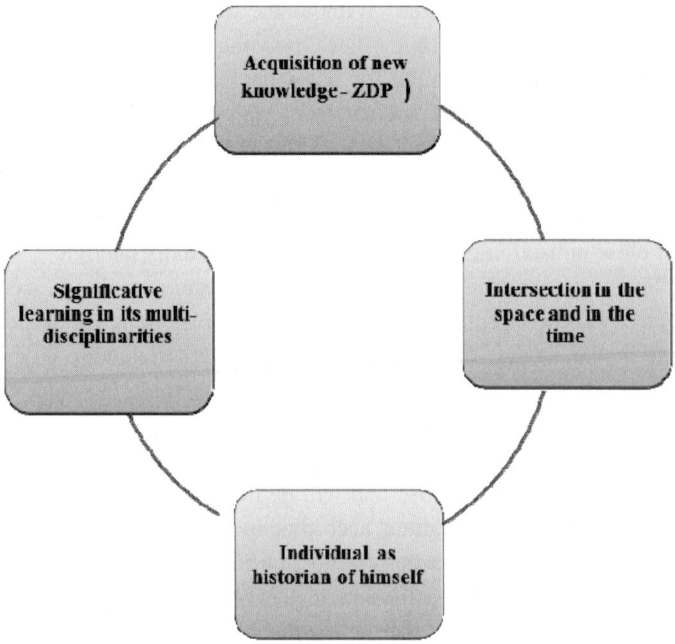

Illustration 1: Social-constructivist guiding principles present in the model . Source: Dissertação de mestrado em 20/09/2011: Maria Antonia Lima Gomes: Modelagem da Cidade do Salvador Século XVI (1549-1551) através de uma Abordagem Sócio-construtivista.

3. Space and time meet in revision

According to Machado (2001), "model is a formal abstraction", and "simulation is a symbolic experimentation of the model". Valente (1993) also affirms that the simulation allows the individual to explore situations that no more exist. To simulate in the Humanities is a recent border of the knowledge, with respect to its use in several areas, including the education, also it becomes more and more a path for the production of new forms of didactic material production, now mediatic and hypertextual.

The results are models that represent innovations in the form of engagement of the users-apprentices with the virtuality and with the digital environment. We think that History itself, which passes by, might be in a certain way experienced, at least in what refers to the dialogic feature of interaction, to contexts in the texts built by authors. This approach seems to present, in our opinion, true explorations of innovative fields of the culture and of the History studies.

And, dealing with a simulation on the History, the innovation of the revisio is larger, because the technique and methodologies belonging to the revisio and system engineering should be at the service of the pedagogic approach and the epistemological perspective, likewise as in accordance to the historical interpretation that are wanted in the model. Even the students of presential courses are obvious beneficiaries by the new constructions that are appearing. In addition it provided us parameters to deal with problems with respect to the teaching of History that is reported to us by the time so that we can live the historical events in a possible more real way.

4. Modelling physical and human aspects of Salvador city of the XVI century

At the end of a process of historical research and use of a dialectical approach of interpretation of the historical process, the result was also the construction of a 3D model with elements in 2D of Salvador city soon after its foundation, in the 1551 year.

The revisio was fully built according to social-constructivist principles and that involved paying attention to a model in which the interaction between the XVI century individuals and the XXI century ones, might produce immediate development zones (ZDIs) among them, doing that the centuries meet in the construction of the knowledge of the present time.

Illustration 2: Modelling (city's primitive nucleus panorama 1549-1551). Source: Dissertação de mestrado em 20/09/2011: Maria Antonia Lima Gomes: Modelagem da Cidade do Salvador Século XVI (1549-1551) através de uma Abordagem Sócio-construtivista.

5. Modelling process of XVI century's Salvador city

To give substance and form to this simulation of Salvador city's primitive nucleus, resources like Blender 3D, Adobe Photoshop, and Unity were used. The choice of such tools was due not only because of their great graphic resolution when used in revisio or animation, texturing, composition, rendering and their interactive applications in 3D and 2D, but also because it is free software (Blender 3D).

Those tools contributed so that the physical and historical model of Salvador city's primitive nucleus in 1551 was developed starting from the dialogical interpretation and historical research presuppositions, allowing that the individual / user, historian of himself, according to dialogical precepts, could build interaction with the simulation system, to create, to investigate, to raise hypothesis and this way, establishing an interaction relationship with the digital environment: which is physical and historical simulation of Salvador city between 1549 and 1551.

6. First beta version results of Salvador city software (1549-1551)

The first version, that we named beta, of the revisio of Salvador city in 1551, was ready on July 14, 2011, and it was introduced to the public by the WEB page of the 'Jornal A Tarde de Salvador, Bahia' newspaper, between July 15 and 23 of the referred year. It was in this implementation that we put into validation process, the social-constructivist presuppositions and its possibilities to generate system users' engagement, for then, to continue towards a coherent final version with the proposals of history revisio and education. In this meantime, 1.828 users' accesses were observed, and from that a total of 1.499 users interacted with the model in a way to confirm the presuppositions of interactivity, creative participation, engagement and reflection on the history of himself, starting from the dialogue with the interpretation of the history inside the model.

That amount of interactions, according to the criterion that we used, was considered intense because the exhibition to the public happened only 08 days. In this purpose, it was a result that showed how model dialogued well with the community and consequently with the user in subject because it made possible, among other meanings, the network collaboration, the intersection in the space and time, the historical rescue, the resolution of problem-situation as well as the significative learning. Thus, besides the local connection and the blog exhibition like the site www.ufrb.edu.br (Laboratório de Ensino de História do Recôncavo da Bahia), we also obtained propagation through the news of national revision 1 by the site www.tvcultura.com.br/educacaoemdia of TV Cultura de São Paulo (Fundação Padre Anchieta) entitled 'Imagens em dia'.

In the meantime while the model dialogued with the community, the criticisms were parameters to improve the model because it was built based in the social-constructivism, thus flexible and dynamic, what also contemplates for it to turn to an On-line Education environment (EAD), not isolated; however, dialogical and where the knowledge action is a continuous process, because according to Kenski (2003), an On-line Education environment (EAD), first of all, it has to have on-line interaction, cooperation and collaboration. In this context, result analysis of this model (On-line Education environment (EAD)) are being built in a discerning way in order to offer the community, be it presential, be it on-line, one more enriching way of independent knowledge construction of its cognition level.

7. Conclusion: Development and testing in museum or school environment

Therefore, considering the results of the experiment that we put into practice, in which internauts visited and used the 3D simulation of Salvador city in 1551, we can affirm that the revisio / simulation offers interactivity and dialogical relationship features with the users and visitors, inside the limits of the accomplished research. Models as this can provoke the sensation of sharing of time and different historical moments, which start to tangent each other dialogically. This way, through the revisio of the testimonies and simulations of the remainder of gone times, we provoke that the contemporary historical individuals dialogue with their history and conscience, what will enable them to dialogue with the legacy of individuals of the past, according to presupposed dialogical principles. When dialoguing with his historical past, using his own experiences and livings in this dialogue, the individual has good chance for building relationships between himself and his history, and it is this procedure that we understand to be that one of investigating himself. Those are different possibilities of other types of products and traditional didactic materials, especially useful to non-presential education, mostly on-line, because they make visible the concreteness of the historical relationship in each interaction, in each interpretation, analyzed as "contact" between temporalities.

The revisio showed also being capable to accomplish the history teaching-learning, in accordance with the principles of "Historical Thinking". The individual-apprentice exercises to build knowledge and not just to reproduce it, as evidenced by the experience. It was in this way that we observed it to be hypertextual contact with the historical source, with the Salvador city environment during the XVI century, with its potential inhabitants, capable to take the individual-apprentice of the current city to rebuild old social relationships that were established here in this period, beginning of the century (XVI), in the primitive Salvador city, what also ends up taking him to contemplate on the city today.

The idea is that the individuals / users / historians of themselves, through this revisio / simulation, obtain, in real time, a contribution for possible cognitive connections and, from the development of such connections, explore, interact, feel themselves subject of the process and, the most important, not only to establish relationships with the past and the present, but to rescue their historicity, to understand the complexity in that are involved the social overlaps that the reality presents; to elaborate and re-elaborate parallels, to create identity links, to become an individual being, although inside a collectivity; to rescue also, through this revisio, the dignity of the ethnic, of the person, of the revision l being they are.

In theoretical terms, at the current stage, the research satisfied other relevant aspect for the researchers because the social-constructivist didactic-pedagogic presuppositions and the own approaches for the on-line education (EAD) could be used as proposal of pedagogic-design applied to a prototype that can be presented in the form of 3D revisio produced by Blender 3D.

For everything presented, we come to the conclusion that the solution of historical simulation is really capable to conduct the learning and interactivity situations foreseen in the model. Presently it is possible to access the model / simulation of Salvador city during XVI century (1549-1551) through the site: http://www.matta.pro.br.

References

1. SMITH, Robert C. Arquitetura Civil do Período Colonial. Vol . 17, Rio de Janeiro. SPAN, (1969).
2. VALENTE, J. A. Computadores e conhecimento: repensando a educação, Unicampi : São Paulo, (1993).
3. MARTINEAU, R. *L'Echec de l'apprentissage de la pensée historique à l'eecole secondaire. Contribuition à l'elaboration de fondaments didatiques pour enseigner l'Historie.* Dissertação (Doutorado em Educação) – Université Laval , Quebec. (1997).
4. MACHADO, A. Máquina e imaginário: o desafio das poéticas tecnológicas. EDUSP: São Paulo, (2001)
5. BAKHTIN, M. M. Estética da Criação Verbal, São Paulo, Martins Fontes, (2003).
6. BAKHTIN, M. M.. Org. BRAIT, B.. Dialogismo e construção do sentido. São Paulo, Campinas, (2005).
7. MATTA, Alfredo Eurico Rodrigues. Tecnologias de aprendizagem em rede e ensino de história – utilizando comunidades de aprendizagens e hipercomposição . Brasília, Líber Livro Editora, (2006).
8. VIGOTSKY, L. S.. A construção do pensamento e da linguagem. Martins Fontes: São Paulo, (2009).
9. BAKHTIN, M. M. Marxismo e Filosofia da Linguagem: problemas fundamentais do método sociológico da linguagem. São Paulo: Haucitec, (2010).

PROPAGATION OF ERRORS IN NUMERICAL COMPUTATIONS

M. A. AKANBI
Department of Mathematics, Lagos State University,
P. M. B. 0001 LASU Post Office Lagos, Nigeria

The methods of Numerical Analysis are finite processes, and a Numerical result is an approximate value of the (unknown) exact result. This paper discusses the propagation of errors in numerical computations with a closer look at rounding errors, a small error made on almost every arithmetic operation done on a computer. The desire of a numerical analyst and the goal of this paper are to ensure that these small errors do not accumulate so badly as to invalidate the computation. There are examples to illustrate minimization of accumulated round–off errors.

1. Introduction

There are varieties of computers used for numerical computations. These range from (programmable or nonprogrammable) hand and desk calculators, microcomputers, minicomputers, and so on, to powerful and sometimes (specialized) large–scale computers.

Hand calculators may be useful in work involving not too much data and few operations, in quick spot checks of larger work or in gaining insight into a numerical method, by inspecting every detail of the computation. Perhaps the most important factor in scientific computing is that computers deal with a finite number of digits or characters, unlike the arithmetic within real number system accustomed to in pure mathematics.

A famous instance involved a new index set up by the Vancouver Stock Exchange in January 1982. It was initially set at 1000.000 (three decimal places of accuracy), and after 22 months had fallen to about 520 – whereas stock prices had generally increased in the period. The problem was caused by the index being recalculated thousands of times daily, and always being rounded down to 3 decimal places, in such a way that the rounding errors accumulated. Recalculating over the weekend of November 25–28, 1983 with better rounding gave an index value of 1098.892 at the end of the same period [1, 2].

Thus, a small error, called *rounding error* is made on almost every arithmetic operation done on a computer. The desire of a numerical analyst and the goal of this paper are to ensure that these small errors do not accumulate so badly as to invalidate the computation. There are examples to illustrate rounding–off rule with minimum error presented.

1. Error Propagation

In practice, because computers deal with finite word lengths, the value $\bar{y}_n$ obtained from a numerical computation will differ from the exact value y_n. If $\bar{y}_n$ is an approximate value of a quantity whose exact value is y_n, then the difference $\psi_n = \bar{y}_n - y_n$ is called the **error** of y_n.

The relative error

$$\psi_n^r = \frac{\psi_n}{y_n} = \frac{\bar{y}_n - y_n}{y_n} = \frac{Error}{Exact\,value}$$

Consequently, a quantity

$$\mu_n = y_n - \bar{y}_n = -\psi_n$$

is called the correction of y_n.

The Root Mean Square (RMS) error is given as

$$RMS = \sqrt{\frac{\sum_{i=1}^{n} (\bar{y}_i - y_i)^2}{n}} = \sqrt{\frac{\sum_{i=1}^{n} \psi_i^2}{n}}$$

Finally, y_n is bounded by a constant λ_n called the **error bound** [3–7], such that

$$|\bar{y}_n - y_n| \leq \lambda_n \quad \text{that is} \quad |\psi_n| \leq \lambda_n.$$

There are different sources of errors such as *programming errors, experimental errors, round–off errors, truncation errors* and so on. Truncation errors are errors caused by "truncating" (prematurely breaking off) a (finite or infinite) sequence of computational steps necessary for producing an exact result. These errors depend on the computational method used and must be dealt with individually for each method.

2. Rounding Errors

The arithmetic done by a computer is restricted to finitely many digits whereas the numerical representation of most real numbers requires infinitely many digits [8].

For example, such fundamental constants as π and e require an infinite number of digits for a numerical representation and can never be entered exactly in a computer. Moreover, even if numbers that have an exact numerical representation in the computer are started with, the processes of arithmetic require that certain errors be made eventually. These errors are called ***round–off errors.***

Rounding is the process of replacing a numerical value by another value that is approximately equal but most times the new value has a shorter, simpler, or more explicit representation. The essence of rounding is to obtain a value that is easier to write and handle than the original or to indicate the accuracy of a computed number.

Rounding is almost unavoidable in many computations, especially when dividing two numbers in integer or fixed-point arithmetic; when computing mathematical functions such as square roots, logarithms, and sines; or when using a floating point representation with a fixed number of significant digits [].

However, rounding introduces some round-off error in the result. In a sequence of calculations, these rounding errors generally accumulate, and in certain ill-conditioned cases they may make the result meaningless.

Accurate rounding of transcendental mathematical functions is difficult because the number of extra digits that need to be calculated to resolve whether to round up or down cannot be known in advance. This problem is known as "the table-maker's dilemma".

Rounding has many similarities to the quantization that occurs when physical quantities must be encoded by numbers or digital signals.

2.1. Round-Off Rule

In practice, rounding off a number to m decimals can take either of *"rounding up"* or *"rounding down"* depending on the $(m+1)$th and *subsequent* decimals. The rule for rounding off to n significant figures is the same, with *"decimal"* replaced by *"significant figure"*.

Rounding up: Discard the $(m+1)$th and all subsequent decimals. If the number thus discarded is greater than half a unit in the mth place, add one to the mth decimal.

Rounding down: Discard the $(m+1)$th and all subsequent decimals. If the number thus discarded is less than half a unit in the nth place, leave the mth decimal unchanged.

If the number to be discarded is exactly half a unit in the mth place, there is a dilemma. Traditionally, rounding up is the usual practice. However, this paper illustrates that rounding up in such a case would increase the accumulated errors in the computation.

In order to ensure that rounding up and rounding down happens about equally often, on the average, it is recommended to round off to the nearest *even* decimal [9, 10].

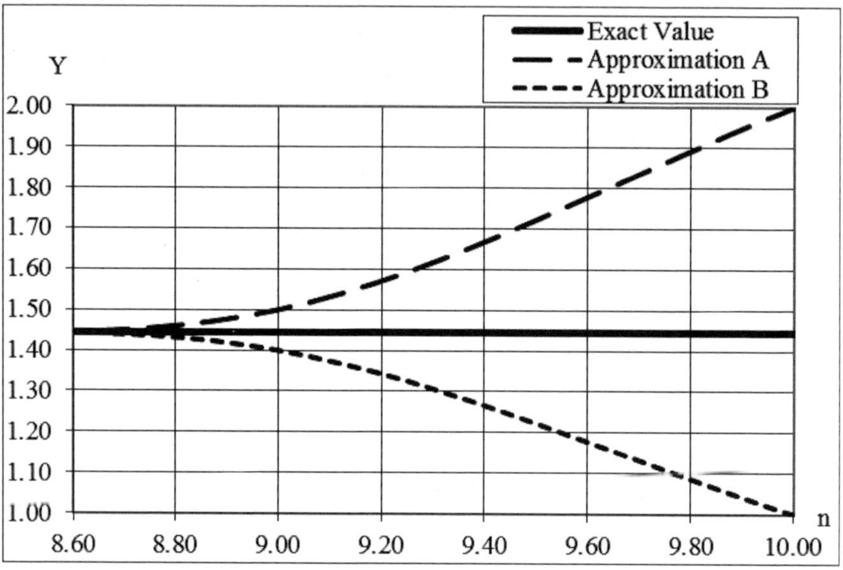

Figure 1. Exact Value Vs. Approximations A & B for Y = 1.444444445

Table 1: Comparison of Methods of Approximations A & B for Y = 1.444444445

n	Y			Error of Approx.		Relative Error of Approx.		Square of Error	
	Exact Value	Approx. A	Approx. B	A	B	A	B	A	B
1	1.444444445	1.444444445	1.444444445	0.00000E+00	0.00000E+00	0.00000E+00	0.00000E+00	0.00000E+00	0.00000E+00
2	1.444444445	1.444444450	1.444444440	5.00000E-09	5.00000E-09	3.46154E-09	3.46154E-09	2.50000E-17	2.50000E-17
3	1.444444445	1.444444500	1.444444400	5.50000E-08	4.50000E-08	3.80769E-08	3.11538E-08	3.02500E-15	2.02500E-15
4	1.444444445	1.444445000	1.444444000	5.55000E-07	4.45000E-07	3.84231E-07	3.08077E-07	3.08025E-13	1.98025E-13
5	1.444444445	1.444450000	1.444440000	5.55500E-06	4.44500E-06	3.84577E-06	3.07731E-06	3.08580E-11	1.97580E-11
6	1.444444445	1.444500000	1.444400000	5.55550E-05	4.44450E-05	3.84612E-05	3.07696E-05	3.08636E-09	1.97536E-09
7	1.444444445	1.445000000	1.444000000	5.55555E-04	4.44445E-04	3.84615E-04	3.07693E-04	3.08641E-07	1.97531E-07
8	1.444444445	1.450000000	1.440000000	5.55555E-03	4.44445E-03	3.84615E-03	3.07692E-03	3.08642E-05	1.97531E-05
9	1.444444445	1.500000000	1.400000000	5.55556E-02	4.44444E-02	3.84615E-02	3.07692E-02	3.08642E-03	1.97531E-03
10	1.444444445	2.000000000	1.000000000	5.55556E-01	4.44444E-01	3.84615E-01	3.07692E-01	3.08642E-01	1.97531E-01
							Root Mean Square Error =	1.76567E-01	1.41254E-01

Table 2: Comparison of Methods of Approximations A & B for Y = 1.4545454545

n	Y			Error of Approx.		Relative Error of Approx.		Square of Error	
	Exact Value	Approx. A	Approx. B	A	B	A	B	A	B
1	1.454545455	1.454545455	1.454545454	5.00000E-10	5.00000E-10	3.43750E-10	3.43750E-10	2.50000E-19	2.50000E-19
2	1.454545455	1.454545460	1.454545450	5.50000E-09	4.50000E-09	3.78125E-09	3.09375E-09	3.02500E-17	2.02500E-17
3	1.454545455	1.454545500	1.454545400	4.55000E-08	5.45000E-08	3.12812E-08	3.74688E-08	2.07025E-15	2.97025E-15
4	1.454545455	1.454546000	1.454545000	5.45500E-07	4.54500E-07	3.75031E-07	3.12469E-07	2.97570E-13	2.06570E-13
5	1.454545455	1.454550000	1.454540000	4.54550E-06	5.45450E-06	3.12503E-06	3.74997E-06	2.06616E-11	2.97516E-11
6	1.454545455	1.454600000	1.454500000	5.45455E-05	4.54545E-05	3.75000E-05	3.12500E-05	2.97521E-09	2.06611E-09
7	1.454545455	1.455000000	1.454000000	4.54546E-04	5.45455E-04	3.12500E-04	3.75000E-04	2.06612E-07	2.97521E-07
8	1.454545455	1.460000000	1.450000000	5.45455E-03	4.54545E-03	3.75000E-03	3.12500E-03	2.97521E-05	2.06612E-05
9	1.454545455	1.500000000	1.400000000	4.54545E-02	5.45455E-02	3.12500E-02	3.75000E-02	2.06612E-03	2.97521E-03
10	1.454545455	2.000000000	1.000000000	5.45455E-01	4.54545E-01	3.75000E-01	3.12500E-01	2.97521E-01	2.06612E-01
						Root Mean Square Error =		1.73094E-01	1.44778E-01

Table 3: Comparison of Methods of Approximations A & B for Y = 100.545454545

n	Y			Error of Approx.		Relative Error of Approx.		Square of Error	
	Exact Value	Approx. A	Approx. B	A	B	A	B	A	B
1	100.545454545	100.545454550	100.545454540	9.91010E+01	9.91010E+01	6.86084E+01	6.86084E+01	9.82101E+03	9.82101E+03
2	100.545454545	100.545454600	100.545454500	9.91010E+01	9.91010E+01	6.86084E+01	6.86084E+01	9.82101E+03	9.82101E+03
3	100.545454545	100.545455000	100.545454000	9.91010E+01	9.91010E+01	6.86084E+01	6.86084E+01	9.82101E+03	9.82101E+03
4	100.545454545	100.545460000	100.545450000	9.91010E+01	9.91010E+01	6.86084E+01	6.86084E+01	9.82101E+03	9.82101E+03
5	100.545454545	100.545500000	100.545400000	9.91011E+01	9.91010E+01	6.86084E+01	6.86084E+01	9.82102E+03	9.82100E+03
6	100.545454545	100.546000000	100.545000000	9.91016E+01	9.91006E+01	6.86088E+01	6.86081E+01	9.82112E+03	9.82092E+03
7	100.545454545	100.550000000	100.540000000	9.91056E+01	9.90956E+01	6.86115E+01	6.86046E+01	9.82191E+03	9.81993E+03
8	100.545454545	100.600000000	100.500000000	9.91556E+01	9.90556E+01	6.86462E+01	6.85769E+01	9.83182E+03	9.81200E+03
						Root Mean Square Error =		9.91085E+01	9.90946E+01

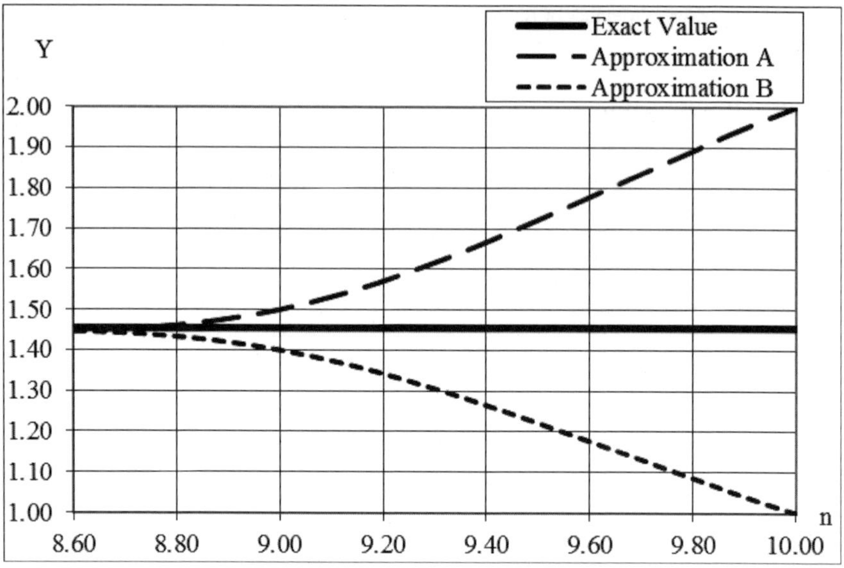

Figure 2. Exact Value Vs. Approximations A & B for Y = 1.4545454545

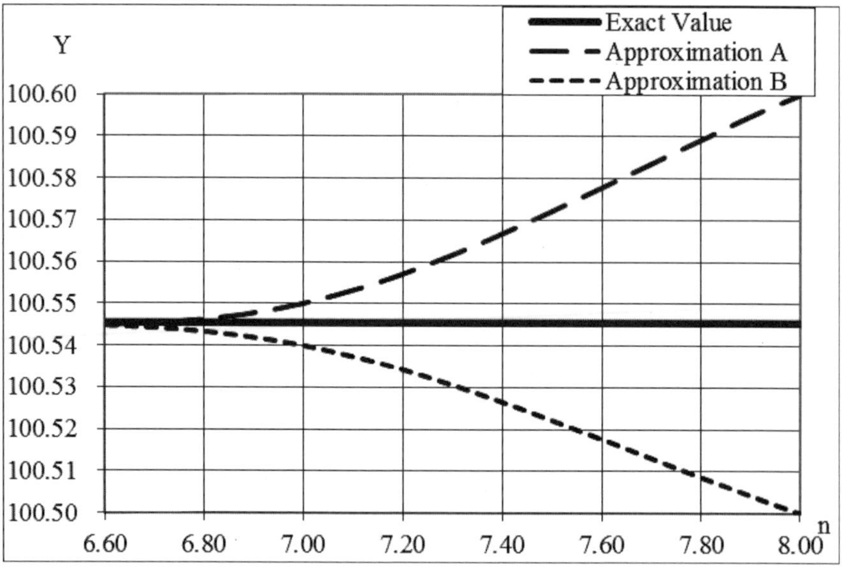

Figure 3. Exact Value Vs. Approximations A & B for Y = 100.545454545

3. Results and Discussion

Tables 1–3 and Figures 1–3 show the effect of ensuring that rounding up and rounding down happens about equally often, on the average (Approximation B), whenever the number to be discarded is exactly half a unit in the *m*th place, as supposed to rounding up every time (Approximation A).

The numbers used for the illustrations are "1.444444445", "1.4545454545", "100.545454545". These numbers were assumed to have been rounded off 8–10 times independently. Interestingly, the tables and the figures show that the errors of Approximation B for the first and third number are minimal compared with that of Approximation A.

Though, in case of the second number, the error fluctuates, however, the root mean square error show that the error of Approximation B is always minimal, whenever the number to be discarded is exactly half a unit in the *m*th place.

4. Conclusion

Though, round–off errors are small errors, but when accumulated they can influence the numerical computation greatly. Thus, the significance of (**Approximation B)** round–off rule cannot be overemphasized.

References

1. The Toronto Star, November 29, 1983.
2. The Wall Street Journal November 8, 1983, p.37
3. J. D. Lambert, *Numerical Methods for Ordinary Differential Systems: The Initial Value Problem.* John Wiley & Sons, England (1991).
4. P. Henrici, *Discrete Variable Methods in ODE,* John Wiley & Sons, New York (1968).
5. M. A. Akanbi, S. A. Okunuga and A. B. Sofoluwe, Error Bounds for 2–stage Multiderivative Explicit Runge–Kutta Methods, Adv. In Modelling & Analysis, A.M.S.E., Advances – A Vol. 45 No. 2, 57 – 69 (2008).
6. M. A. Akanbi, Propagation of Errors in Euler Methods, *Archives Of Applied Science Research, Vol. 2 Issue 2, 457 – 469* (2010).
7. M. A. Akanbi, S. A. Okunuga and A. B. Sofoluwe, Stepsize Bounds for a class of Multiderivative Explicit Runge–Kutta Methods. In: Engemann, Kurt J., Gil-Lafuente, Anna M., Merigó, José M. (Eds.) LNBIP 115, New York, Springer Berlin Heidelberg, 188-197 (2012).
8. J. M. Ortega and G. P. Jr. William, *An Introduction to Numerical Methods for Differential Equations.* Pitman Pub Ltd. USA (1981).

9. M. A. Akanbi and S. A. Okunuga, *Computational Mathematics–A first course.* WIM, Nigeria (2003).
10. E. Kreyzig, *Advanced Engineering Mathematics;* 7th Edition, Wiley, USA (2006).

SIMULATION OF A SERVICE POST FOR INTERMEDIATION OF MANPOWER: A CASE STUDY IN A NATIONAL EMPLOYMENT SYSTEM

FRANCISCO FIRMINO DA SILVA NETO
Universidade Federal Rural do Semi-Árido, Brazil

JÚLIA LORENA MARQUES GURGEL
Universidade Federal Rural do Semi-Árido, Brazil

DAVID CUSTÓDIO DE SENA
Universidade Federal Rural do Semi-Árido, Brazil

This article presents the application of computer simulation in an intermediation position of labor. In this public agency, the demand for their services is quite high, generally are formed long lines in which customers spend a considerable time to be served. Thus, this study aims to analyze the configuration of attending, looking for the best arrangement of resources in order to provide a satisfactory level of service to the community. For this study, will be used Simpy, a package of discrete event simulation based on process and written language called Python. The study will focus on attending services to register to compete for jobs and the unemployment insurance claim. Thus, with the scenarios simulation will be assessed the best alternative that meets the requirements and desired goals.

1. Introduction

In public services there are many difficulties and barriers to perform agile and quick service, more then another sector of the economy. All of this is due to scarce resources or legal bureaucracy needed to carry out processes and / or procedures critical to the implementation of activities. Thus, the formation of long queues and sometimes the absent of attending to candidates to public service is almost always perceptible by the population.

This study aims to analyze the configuration of tellers of an organ of public service, it is doing by searching the best arrangement of resources in order to provide a satisfactory level of service to the population. And so, to assess wheter the proposed improvements can generate better customer service.

The choice of this study was due to high demand of the population searching for this service, which usually leads to formation of queues in which customers spend a considerable time to be attended.

For this study, will be used *Simpy*, a simulation package for discrete event process-based writing and language called Python, which provides the modeler components of a simulation model including processes, for active components (clients, messages and vehicles), and resources for passive components that form limited capacity points of congestion (servers, checkout counters, and tunnels), monitors variables to obtain statistical data, and finally random module for random variables.

The study will be conducted in an attending post of National Employment System located in a city of west region of Rio Grande do Norte, Brazil. The study will focus on attending service of register to compete for jobs and the unemployment insurance claim.

2. Literature Review

2.1. Systems Simulation

A system is defined as an object or a group of objects whose properties have interest in parts of people to be study. (VELTEN, 2009) As a complement to this concept, the system is a collection of entities that act and interact together toward the accomplishment of some logical end. (SCHMIDT, 1970)

The simulation of a system is an operation of a system model. The represents the construction and operation of some system of interest, composed by the properties of behavioral of the real system, in other words, it must be an approximation to the real system and incorporates most of its salient characteristics. In the broadest sense, the simulation is a tool to assess the performance of a system existing or proposed, according to different configurations of interest and for long periods of real time. (MARIA, 1997)

For Pegden (2010) more formally, the simulation is a group of state variables and a mechanism for variation of these variables over the time.

Nowadays, the modeling of systems by simulation is the most used because it is an approach that gets a lot of gains, although the studies are expensive and time consuming to develop. According to Maria (1997), the benefits generated by the use of the simulation are: reducing the chances of failure in attending of the specifications, unforeseen removal of bottlenecks; avoids under or over-utilization of resources, and improves the system performance.

Still the same author in the case of a simulation study, are commonly used mathematical models which are developed with the help of simulation software. Such models are classified as static or dynamic, deterministic or stochastic.

A static simulation model is the representation of a system at a given time, or one that can be used to represent a system in which time simply do not performs any role, for example, simulations models are the ones of Monte Carlo. Moreover, a dynamic simulation model is system such as involving over the time as a transporter system in a factory.If a simulation model contains no probabilistic component is called deterministic. Many systems, however, must be shaped to have at least some random input components, and these give rise to stochastic simulation models, which in turn produces an output which is itself random, and must therefore be treated as only an estimate of the characteristics of the model. (LAW, 2000).

2.2. Process Simulation Modeling

To perform a simulation study, it is essential that you follow a few steps, as can be seen in the following figure:

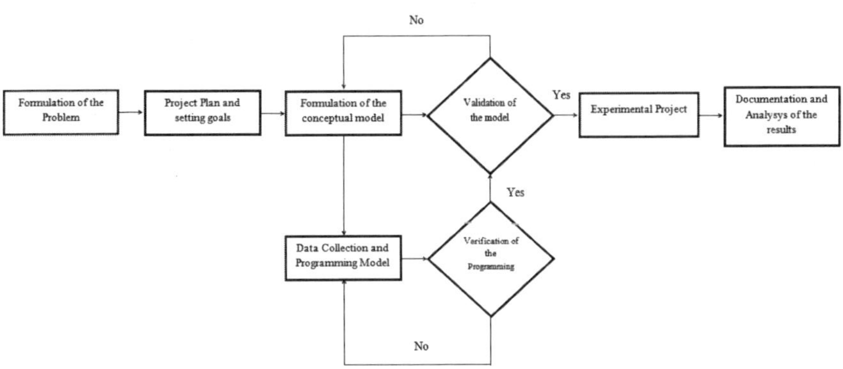

Figure 1. Process for modeling a simulation study.
Source: Sakurada and Miyake (2009)

Initially, the first stage of the study in the simulation is the definition of the problem to be studied. As such, it is essential to understand the reason for the study. (BANKS,1998) The objectives targeted by the study should also be established. In the same way the objectives pursued by the present study must be defined in that way that can be listed criteria for evaluating the system performance. (FILHO, 2008)

The purpose of project plan is to anticipate the need for resources to carry out the work and indicate the many scenarios to be investigated. For Banks (1998), in the step of building of the model term, the system under investigation in the real world is captured by a conceptual model, which is established in a series of mathematical and logical relationships of components and of the structure of the system.

"The data collected should represent well the real system behavior not only for the formulation of the model itself is well supported, but also because they are used in the later stage of validation." (Sakurada & Miyake, 2009)

For Filho (2008), the programming model relates to coding of the model in a form recognizable by the computer by means of a simulation language appropriate. According to Banks (1998) verification refers to the operational model, and its functionality. Thus, attests if the intent of the analyst is in agreement with the simulation model and the results are representative of the real system.

And the Validation is the determination that the conceptual model is an accurate representation of the real system. The greater the amount of approval validation tests, the higher the reliability of the model. (BONATE, 2011)

Finally, the documentation is required for various reasons, among which the simulation model will be used again for different analysts, it may be necessary to understand how the simulation model operates. (BANKS, 1998)

3. Model's Application

3.1. Problem Formulation

On visits in that organization, it was possible to visualize the formation of extensive queues, where customers spend a considerable time to be attended. It will be analyzed two types of service realized by SINE: register to compete for jobs and the unemployment insurance claim. The service of unemployment insurance requires a focus on the fulfillment of time limits, that can make the customer go away. With this, it is important that a bigger number of people be attended per day.

3.2. Definition of Objectives and General Planning

The aim of this study is decrease the waiting time in queue of customers. This way, in the planning phase of the study, was realized researches on the subject of study, after that, was collected materials about the sector and interviews with employees and the manager of the agency to understand the whole process of attending. As well as by observation of the environment work.

The data was collected from November the 15th to the 18th 2011, during the morning shift, in which there is a bigger search for the provided services.

Five alternatives, or scenarios, will be analyzed to identify which is the best option for achieving the desired objectives. And so, verify if the current model of the system is operating in accordance, or else the proposed alternatives will attend better the demand for services.

3.3. Model Conception

Through observation and perceptions of the attending system, it was possible to identify a model for a post of attending of the SINE-RN, as seen in the Figure 2 below.

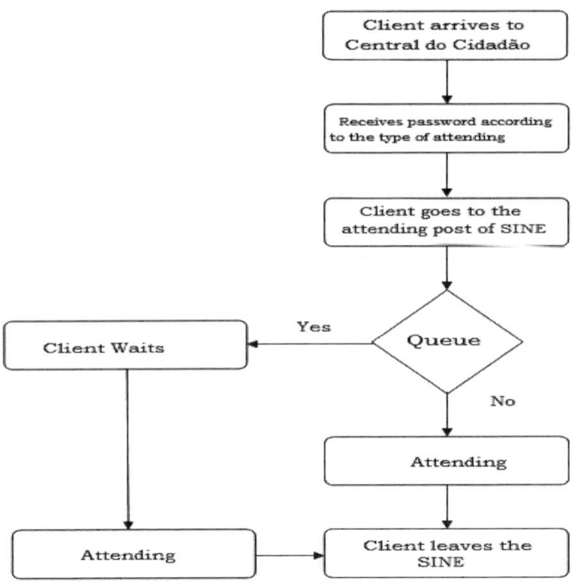

Figure 2: Flowchart of service process
Source: Authors

At the reception, the clients will receive a ticket according to the type of service required to SINE. In the attending room there are 03 booths, of which 02 (two) are for requirement of unemployment insurance and 01 (one) for the registration to compete for jobs. In a side room, there is an attendant to receive job offers that companies sign up and deal with the calls, and the manager of the agency to resolve any problems that aren´t standardized. Additionally, the tellers are multidisciplinary.

The period of service is from 7 to 19 o'clock in the days of Tuesday to Friday and from 7 to 15 o'clock in the Saturdays. The team is composed by 10 people, who are divided into two shifts.

After the model be formulated, it was questioned your validity by employees of the agency, which help in the conception of the same, confirmed the relationship with the real.

3.4. The Data Collection

Relating with the study objectives, was elaborated a spreadsheet to capture the data, such as time of arrival of the client, start and end of service, as well as the type of service performed.

3.5. Translation of Model

Once collected the data were entered into the Microsoft® Office® Excel® to determination of attending time (AT) and rhythm of clients (RC) arrival for both services, registration and insurance. Then, the founded times was be subject to an analysis of data distribution via the *Input Analyzer* software, which identifies the type of distribution will follow (Beta, Exponential, Gamma, Normal, Poisson, Triangular, and others). Defined the distributions, it was be modeled a program on *SimPy* software, that after its verification and validation, it was pass through simulations applicable to the real system. In summary, for better visualization of the input data, there is the following table:

Input Data			
Data – Time		Distribution	Expression
Service 1: Register for employment	Time Between Arrivals	Beta	-0.5 + 76 * BETA (0.793, 3.37)
	Service Time	Beta	3.5 + 12 * BETA (4.52, 2.88)
Service 2: Register to receive the benefit Unemployment	Time Between Arrivals	Exponential	-0.001 + EXPO (10.2)
	Service Time	Gamma	9.5 + GAMM (2.92, 3.92)

Table 1. Input Date
Source: Authors

According to Table 2, after analysis of the AT and RC in the Software Input Analyzer, it was found that the service registration, the program has a distribution curve for Beta both time and their equations, which contained the smallest error over the distribution of data. The same was held for insurance office, finding the explicit results in the table above.

3.6. Execution Model

With the configuration of the input data, it was modeled in the SymPy, which is a Python Module, program the main features in the system studied, trying to make a relationship between the conceptual model with the computational model proposed.

The output data that will be generated in this program are related to: number of attended clients; maximum, minimum and average time on the queue; maximum, minimum and average of attending; percentage of occupation of the clerks and number of dropouts. With respect to the objectives desired by the present study, the data of bigger interest will be: the number of clients served for each alternative and the average time clients spent in the queue.

3.7. Results

After obtaining the equations of the distributions for each type of service related to the interval of arrival and the service time, it was applied these equations in their respective codes in SympY. In each models, it was realized ten (10) replications with 10 different seeds, as it is possible to see in the table below:

Average Time in Queue – ATQ			
Service 1: Register for employment		**Service 2: Register to receive the benefit Unemployment**	
Replications		Replications	
Seed	Average	Seed	Average
1	28,56	1	171,81
2	10,73	2	195,22
3	7,59	3	183,22
4	10,93	4	195,37
5	39,94	5	181,69
6	7,47	6	196,16
7	29,89	7	177,05
8	12,90	8	184,88
9	12,99	9	187,28
10	6,96	10	190,72
Average	16,796	**Average**	186,34
Desvio Padrão	11,618145	**Desvio Padrão**	8,217928909
T Student (90%)	1,833	**T Student (99%)**	3,250
Standart Desviation	[10.7, 22.19]	**Standart Desviation**	[177.89, 194.78]
Real ATQ	18,8	**Real ATQ**	184,89
10,7 < **18,8** < 22,19		177,89 < **184,89** < 194,78	

Table 2. Validation of the model.
Source: Authors.

According to Table 3, it can be seen that the average time in the queue is inside of the confidence interval for the two types of services, using the Student's T of 90% for the cadaster service and 99% for the insurance service.

3.8. Verification and Validation of the Model

The verification and validation of the model were acceptable, in other words, the verification, the computer model is aligned to the conceptual model and, in turn, to validate the results obtained (output values) adhere to the real system.

3.9. Project of the Experiment

The suggested alternatives differ with respect to the number of servers, the efficiency of the service and what types of services the attendants carry, which are detailed in the table below, including the real scenario to perform the comparison between the simulated scenarios:

Alternatives					
Scenarios	Characteristics	Service type	Number of People Served		Average Time in Queue
Current	Current Condition of service	1	20	52	7,59
		2	32		171,81
A	Increase efficiency of the actual condition of service at 25%	1	23	66	6,42
		2	43		184,92
B	Increase a clerk in the service of the insurance with 25% efficiency	1	23	88	6,42
		2	65		183,16
C	All clerk do all the work	1 e 2	02	51	182,60
			49		
D	All clerk do all the work with 25% more efficiency	1 e 2	17	67	129,68
			50		
E	An attendant increase more, all performing various services with a 25% increase in efficiency of care.	1 e 2	21	86	123,72
			65		

Table 3. Results of the simulations and comparison with the actual condition.
Source: Authors

Some considerations must be made, as: in the scenario that there is a 25% increase in efficiency of attending, it is considered that the clerks have made a typing course and training to provide a greater efficiency of these services and that each one hour of service they have ten minutes of rest due to the typing activity require this pause in the service; and about the scenario number two, it was considered that the increase of a attendant was directed to the unemployment insurance service, considering the bigger search among the types of services offered.

4. Conclusions

With the scenarios simulation, it is possible to see that the alternative that better attends the desired objectives by the present work was the scenario B. However, it is known the difficulty to hire one more person for this sector. Thus, among the proposed alternatives the ones that considered the current resources in the system have the highest possibility of implementation. In this case is the first scenario A, because there was increases in both the services of attend people and to the cadaster service a decrease in the average time in queue, which does not occur in Scenario 4.

Therefore, among the proposed alternatives that they considered the current resources in the system have the highest possibility of deployment. This case is the first scenario, because there was an increase in both the services of people served and the service register a decrease in the average time in queue, which does not occur in Scenario 4.

Thus, the 25% improvement in efficiency would be given through courses and training in typing and attending service. Given that the attendants need to develop these skills better.

References

BANKS, Jerry. ***Handbook of simulation. Principles, methodology, Advances, Applications and Practice.*** Georgia Institute of technology. Atlanta, 1998.

BANKS, J.; CARSON II; J.S. & NELSON, B.L. ***Discrete Evet System Simulation***, 2nd Ed., Prentice Hall, Upper Saddle River, NJ, USA, 1996.

COSTA, Miguel Antonio Bueno Da. ***Simulação de Sistemas***. Universidade Federal de São Carlos, 2002.

Curso de simulação. Laboratório de simulação e controle de sistemas discretos EESC-USP.

DIAS, Fabio Klinkerfus. ***Estudo Comprobatório da Teoria das Filas pela Simulação de Eventos Discretos***. SEGET, 2008.

GORDON, G. **System simulation**. 2 ed. New Jersey: Prentice Hall, 1978.

LAW, A. M.; KELTON, W. D. **Simulation modeling and analysis**. 2 ed. New York: McGraw-Hill, 1991.

PINHEIRO, Ricardo Jurczyk. Software livre e Matemática: opções de Pesquisa e ensino. Universidade Federal do Rio de Janeiro, 2009.

PRADO, Darci Santos do. ***Teoria das Filas e Simulação.*** INDG Tecnologia e Serviços Ltda: Nova Lima –MG, 2006.

SAKURADA, Nelson; Miyake, Dario Ikuo. ***Aplicação de simuladores de eventos discretos no processo de modelagem de sistemas de operações de serviços.*** São Carlos-SP, 2009.

SHANNON, R. E. **Systems Simulation:** The Art and the Science. New Jersey: Prentice-Hall, 1975.

Sistema Nacional de Emprego – SINE. Disponível em: http://www.mte.gov.br/sine/oquee.asp. Acessado em: 20 de outubro de 2011.

Sistema Nacional de Emprego. Governo do RN. Disponível em: <http://www.sine.rn.gov.br/contentproducao/aplicacao/sine/principal/enviados/index.asp>. Acessado em: 19 de outubro de 2011.

SOUZA, Dércia Antunes de; GIL, Antônio Carlos. ***O Desempenho dos Postos de Atendimento ao Trabalhador na Perspectiva dos Empregadores da Região Bragantina (SP).*** Revista Contemporânea de Ec

MARIA, A. **Introduction To Modeling And Simulation.** State University Of New York, Binghamton, E.U.A. Proceedings of the 1997 Winter Simulation Conference.

PEGDEN, C. D. **Advanced Tutorial: Overview Of Simulation World Views.** Sewickley PA. Simulation Conference 2010.

LAW, A. M., KELTON, W. D. **Simulation Modeling and Analysis.** 3rd ed. Boston: Mc Graw Hill, 2000.

VELTEN, Kai. Mathematical modeling and simulation. Introduction for scientistis and engineers. WILEY-VCH, 2009.

SCHMIDT, J.W. TAYLOR, R.E. Simulation and analysis of industrial systems. HOMEWOOD, 1970.

BONATE, Peter L. Pharmacokinetic-Pharmacodynamic modelind and simulation. 2 ed. Springer, 2011.

FILHO, Paulo José de Freitas. **Introdução a modelagem e simulação de sistemas com aplicações em arena**. 2ed. São Paulo: Visual Books, 2008.

A MODEL FOR THE GENERALIZATION OF THE FORGOTTEN EFFECTS

SALVADOR LINARES MUSTARÓS
Department of Business Administration, University of Girona, Campus de Montilivi s/n, 71017 Girona, Spain

ANNA MARIA GIL LAFUENTE
Department of Business Administration, University of Barcelona Av. Diagonal 690, 08034 Barcelona, Spain

JOAN CARLES FERRER COMALAT
Department of Business Administration, University of Girona, Campus de Montilivi s/n, 71017 Girona, Spain

JOSÉ M. MERIGÓ
Department of Business Administration, University of Barcelona Av. Diagonal 690, 08034 Barcelona, Spain

This paper aims to show the current status of models used in the research of forgotten effects to present a control tool data errors valuation of the incidence matrices, which would improve the reliability of the work. It will provide a generalization of forgotten effects by proposing that the causes and effects variables are fuzzy variables, in the hope of attaining a method for impact.

1. Introduction

In mathematics, an incidence matrix is a matrix that shows the relationship between two classes of objects. If the first class is A = { ai / i=1, 2, …,n} and the second is B = { bj / j=1, 2, …,m}, the matrix has one row for each element of A and one column for each element of B. In Boolean logic, the entry in row i and column j is 1 if ai and bj are related and 0 if they are not. In fuzzy logic (Zadeh 1965, Zadeh article que existeix i que cal trobar de relacions), the entry in row i and column j is a value in [0,1].

The idea of using a composition of fuzzy incidences for possible causes that have no direct influence on a large effect is recognized in the economic literature by the name of Forgotten Effects (Kaufmann and Gil Aluja, 1988).

The aim of this study is to show the state of the art of the current model, a necessary step for a future generalization of the model that will allow the causes and effects to be fuzzy variables and the accumulation of a similar effect.

The methodology used in the study can be divided into five parts:

In the first part we show the classical method developed by researchers Arnold Kaufmann, a former professor of the Polytechnic Institute of Grenoble, and Jaime Gil Aluja, professor at the University of Barcelona, presented in 1988 in a book published by Milladoiro "Models for research into forgotten effects". In order to clarify the theoretical foundations and to illustrate its real potential application, concepts are accompanied by examples.

The second part aims to study the issue of bibliometric indicators of forgotten effects in order to facilitate a good understanding of their level of research activity and the speed at which research progresses in the topic.

The third part will analyze the forgotten effects literature in depth to detail different aspects of applicability of the model such as the number of cases, the amount of effects, the types of third sets of elements that are effects of causes or effects and the type of scales to measure the incidences.

The fourth part will discuss the possible inclusion of a new endecadary scale which can minimize errors allocation of inferences.

The last part will offers the possible generalization of the present model taking into account that causes or effects may be fuzzy variables.

The present paper is a joint proposal between two groups:

- the Risk in Insurance and Finance group of Ana María Gil Lafuente, professor at the University of Barcelona and researcher in the group formed by veteran researchers with practical experience in the field of implementation of models for the treatment of uncertainty; and

- the Mathematics for the Treatment of Uncertainty in Economics and Business group of Joan Carles Ferrer Comalat, professor at the University of Girona and principal investigator of the research group, composed by specialists in the creation and simulation of mathematical models for the treatment of uncertainty.

2. Presentation of the method of the forgotten effects

Equations should be centered and numbered consecutively, as in Eq. (1). An alternative method is given in Eq. (2) for long sets of equations where only one referencing equation number is wanted.

The idea of using a composition of incidents for possible causes that have no direct influence on a large effect is recognized in the literature by the name of Forgotten Effects.

For a better understanding of the following chapters we will present the nomenclature we use in this paper as we remember how the method works..

Imagine you have a set of elements $A = \{ a_i / i=1, 2, \ldots,n\}$, which we call causes, and a second set of elements $B = \{ b_j / j=1, 2, \ldots,m\}$, that could eventually be the same set A, which we call effects.

Imagine that each cause a_i affects each effect b_j with a value in the interval [0,1] and with this value denoted by the expression $v(a_i ,b_j)$.

The set of valued elements pairs defines the phenomenon called "direct incidence matrix", which shows the cause-effect relationships that occur with different degrees of the elements of set A (causes) and elements of the set B (effects). We will note that matrix by $[\underline{M}]$.

Now imagine a third set of elements $C = \{ c_k / k=1, 2, \ldots,p\}$ that act as effects of the set B (the case of acting as causes of this would be similarly set A).

Let $[\underline{N}]$, be the matrix that shows the cause-effect relationships that occur between elements of the set B (causes) and elements of the set C (effects).

The mathematical operator that allows for the effects of A on C is max-min composition of matrices represented by $[\underline{M}]o[\underline{N}]$ whose causal relationship of a_i on c_k is:

$$v(ai\,,ck) = \max_{b_j}\left(\min\left(v\left(a_i,b_j\right),v\left(b_{j,}c_k\right)\right)\right) \tag{1}$$

In the case of an incidence matrix $[\underline{M}]$ between elements of the set A (causes) and the elements of set B (effects), we note the incidence matrix of all causes-causes by $[\underline{A}]$ and the effects-effects by $[\underline{B}]$. The composition $[\underline{M}^*]$, for example $[\underline{A}]o[\underline{M}]o[\underline{B}]$, between these three types of matrices is aimed at obtaining a new matrix of incidences between the elements of set A (causes) and the elements of set B (effects) that reflect any non-direct causal relationships and can not be taken into account in strategic decision processes. To find possible effects that may have been overlooked, the Kaufmann and Gil algorithm proposes to study the values of the matrix $[\underline{M}^*] - [\underline{M}]$, since the obtained values are maximum values of indirect effects.

3. Bibliometric study of "Forgotten Effects"

The bibliometric study aims to provide us with an initial idea of the state of the art of Forgotten Effects.

For citation patterns in the book of forgotten effects we have used two primary sources. We have been monitoring all the articles indexed in the Scopus database with keyword "forgotten effects". Figure shows the results for this initial search: five articles. We want to show the importance of proper indexing of an article from its keywords and how an exhaustive listing of all items would perfectly track the influence of a scientific topic.

The second source consulted was a freely accessible web search engine "Google Scholar". Figure 2 shows that there are 39 citations of the Spanish book "Modelos para la investigación de efectos olvidados". Google Scholar references articles, thesis, research, communications, presentations or posters located on the Internet that mention a particular book or article. It's a great way to start stretching the thread of research to find non-English language articles.

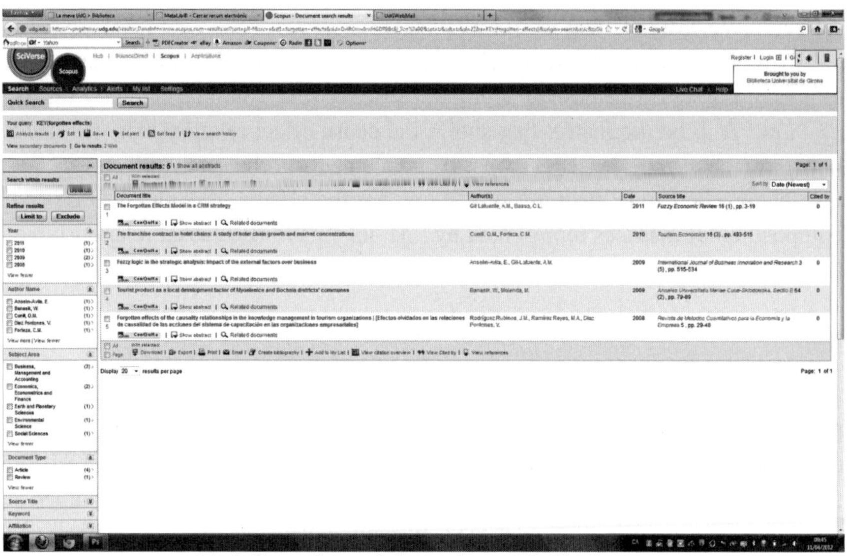

Fig 1. Screenshot with the results provided by Scopus

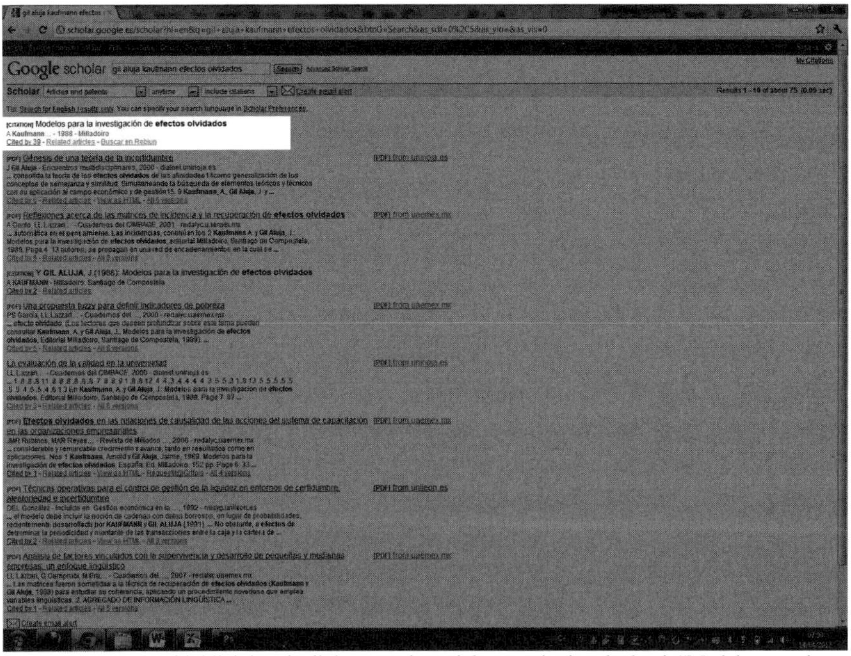

Fig 2. Screenshot highlighting the link to see the articles mentioning the book "Modelos para la investigación de efectos olvidados"

Based upon the communications and articles obtained by the two search tools, we get an initial representative set of papers related to the topic with which we can begin to get an idea of the level of research activity and the speed with which research on the topic is progressing.

Once we have discarded articles prior to communications, and communications or articles that even reference the book "Modelos para la investigación de efectos olvidados" but have not used a working model in the study, we are left with the fourteen works listed below:

Title	Year	Journals or Conferences	Authors
Una propuesta fuzzy para definir indicadores de pobreza	2000	Cuadernos de CIMBAGE, No.3, pp 11-26	P. S. García L. L. Lazarri E. A. M. Machado
La evaluación de la calidad en la Universidad	2000	Cuadernos de CIMBAGE, No.3, pp 81-97	P. S. García L. L. Lazarri

La asignación de recursos en acciones tendientes a mejorar la imagen de una PYME	2000	VI Congreso de la Pequeña y Mediana Empresa. Buenos Aires,	L. L. Lazzari
Aplicación de la metodología borrosa a la evaluación de la calidad de los posgrados	2001	Cuadernos de CIMBAGE, No.4, pp 99-132	A.M. García de Fanelli
Aplicación de herramientas borrosas al balance scorecard	2005	XXVIII congreso argentino de profesores universitarios de costos. Mendoza.	P. Eugenio Mallo M. A. Artola M. Javier Galante M. Enrique Pascual M. Morettini A. Raúl Busetto
Modelo Fuzzy de Influência entre Indicadores de Responsabilidade Social	2008	Simpósio de Excelência em Gestão e Tecnologia (SEGeT)	J. Domech More J.Carvalho Aguia
Efectos olvidados en las relaciones de causalidad de las acciones del sistema de capacitación en las organizaciones empresariales	2008	Revista de Métodos Cuantitativos para la Economía y la Empresa, Vol. 5, 29-48.	J.M. Rodríguez Rubinos M. A. Ramírez Reyes V. Díaz Pontones
Creación de estrategias de entrenamiento a partir del análisis de un procedimiento de ultrasonido mediante metodología borrosa	2008	Cuadernos de CIMBAGE, No.10, pp 75-101	Domech More Mamede Gonzalez Magalhâes Luiz
Fuzzy logic in the strategic analysis: impact of the external factors over business	2009	International Journal of Business Innovation and Research. Vol.3, No. 5, pp. 515-534	E. Anselin Ávila A.M. Gil Lafuente
Modelo para la determinación de variables que inciden en el consumo de productos financieros de ahorro	2009	XV SIGEF International Conference	A.M. Gil-Lafuente E. Vizuete Luciano O. Martorell Cunill
Herramientas con base en subconjuntos borrosos. Propuesta procedimental para aplicar expertizaje y recuperar efectos olvidados en la información contable	2010	Actualidad Contable FACES Vol.13, No.21 pp. 127-146	Rico F. Marco A. Tinto J.
The franchise contract in hotel chains: A study of hotel chain growth and market concentrations	2010	Tourism Economics Vol. 16, No.3, pp. 493-515	O. Martorell Cunill C. Mulet Forteza

Proceso de identificación de los atributos contemplados por los clientes en una estrategia CRM	2011	Cuadernos de CIMBAGE, No.13, pp 107-127	Gil Lafuente, A. M. Luis Bassa, C.
The Forgotten Effects Model in a CRM strategy	2011	Fuzzy Economic Review, Vol. 16, No. 1, pp. 3-19	A.M. Gil Lafuente C. Luis Bassa

The bibliometric indicators we used to measure changes in the topic of forgotten effects are: number of articles per year, number of researchers per year, and number of journals and conferences per year. We have specifically chosen these indicators of visibility and dissemination of their work so we could make a general idea of the research activity and the speed with which progress is made on the topic of forgotten effects.

	# papers	# authors	# journals and conferences
2000	3	3	2
2001	1	4	1
2005	1	6	1
2008	3	6	3
2009	2	4	2
2010	2	5	2
2011	2	2	5
	Total papers: 14	Total authors: 15	Total journals: 7 Total conferences: 4

From the information, we can see that the issue of forgotten effects has become part of the scientific literature and that its expansion becomes accentuated as of 2000.

4. Type of models and scales used in the work

First we will analyze the type of model to be followed at work.

Distinguish between types of models: $[\underline{M}][\underline{M}]$; $[\underline{A}][\underline{M}]$; $[\underline{M}][\underline{B}]$; and $[\underline{A}][\underline{M}][\underline{B}]$, the number of causes and the number of effects:

Title	Model type	# causes	# effects
Una propuesta fuzzy para definir indicadores de pobreza	$[\underline{M}]o[\underline{M}]$	6	6
La evaluación de la calidad en la Universidad	$[\underline{M}]o[\underline{M}]$	13	13
La asignación de recursos en acciones tendientes a mejorar la imagen de una PYME	$[\underline{A}]o[\underline{M}]o[\underline{B}]$	9	7
Aplicación de la metodología borrosa a la evaluación de la calidad de los posgrados	$[\underline{M}]o[\underline{M}]$	15	15
Aplicación de herramientas borrosas al balance scorecard	$[\underline{M}]o[\underline{M}]$	4	4
Modelo Fuzzy de Influência entre Indicadores de Responsabilidade Social	$[\underline{M}]o[\underline{M}]$	7	7
Efectos olvidados en las relaciones de causalidad de las acciones del sistema de capacitación en las organizaciones empresariales	$[\underline{A}]o[\underline{M}]$	10	6
Creación de estrategias de entrenamiento a partir del análisis de un procedimiento de ultrasonido mediante metodología borrosa	$[\underline{A}]o[\underline{M}]o[\underline{B}]$	7	19
Fuzzy logic in the strategic analysis: impact of the external factors over business	$[\underline{A}]o[\underline{M}]o[\underline{B}]$	8	16
Modelo para la determinación de variables que inciden en el consumo de productos financieros de ahorro	$[\underline{A}]o[\underline{M}]o[\underline{B}]$	10	11
Herramientas con base en subconjuntos borrosos. Propuesta procedimental para aplicar expertizaje y recuperar efectos olvidados en la información contable	$[\underline{M}]o[\underline{M}]$	5	5

The franchise contract in hotel chains: A study of hotel chain growth and market concentrations	$[\underline{A}]o[\underline{M}]o[\underline{B}]$	6	9
Proceso de identificación de los atributos contemplados por los clientes en una estrategia CRM	$[\underline{A}]o[\underline{M}]o[\underline{B}]$	15	12
The Forgotten Effects Model in a CRM strategy	$[\underline{A}]o[\underline{M}]o[\underline{B}]$	15	12
		$\overline{x} \approx 9$ $\sigma \approx 3{,}7$	$\overline{x} \approx 10$ $\sigma \approx 4{,}4$

Finally, we will determine the size and shape of the scale used in the work.

Will classify the semantic scale size depending on the type of scale used. The semantic scale types common used in fuzzy thematic work with a sample form for each are:

Title	Scale type	Scale form
Una propuesta fuzzy para definir indicadores de pobreza	Endecadary	0 : incidencia nula 0.1: incidencia prácticamente nula 0.2: incidencia casi nula 0.3: incidencia bastante cercana a nula 0.4: incidencia más cerca de nula que de plena 0.5: incidencia ni plena ni nula 0.6: incidencia más cerca de plena que de nula 0.7: incidencia bastante cercana a plena 0.8: incidencia casi plena 0.9: incidencia prácticamente plena 1 : incidencia plena
La evaluación de la calidad en la Universidad	Endecadary	0 : incidencia nula 0.1: incidencia prácticamente nula 0.2: incidencia casi nula 0.3: incidencia bastante cercana a nula 0.4: incidencia más cerca de nula que de plena 0.5: incidencia ni plena ni nula 0.6: incidencia más cerca de plena que de nula 0.7: incidencia bastante cercana a plena 0.8: incidencia casi plena 0.9: incidencia prácticamente plena 1 : incidencia plena

La asignación de recursos en acciones tendientes a mejorar la imagen de una PYME	Endecadary	0 : sin incidencia 0.1: prácticamente sin incidencia 0.2: casi sin incidencia 0.3: muy débil incidencia 0.4: débil incidencia 0.5: mediana incidencia 0.6: incidencia sensible 0.7: bastante incidencia 0.8: fuerte incidencia 0.9: muy fuerte incidencia 1 : la mayor incidencia
Aplicación de la metodología borrosa a la evaluación de la calidad de los posgrados	Endecadary	unspecified
Aplicación de herramientas borrosas al balance scorecard	Endecadary	0 : incidencia nula 0.1: incidencia prácticamente nula 0.2: incidencia casi nula 0.3: incidencia bastante cercana a nula 0.4: incidencia más cerca de nula que de plena 0.5: incidencia ni plena ni nula 0.6: incidencia más cerca de plena que de nula 0.7: incidencia bastante cercana a plena 0.8: incidencia casi plena 0.9: incidencia prácticamente plena 1 : incidencia plena
Efectos olvidados en las relaciones de causalidad de las acciones del sistema de capacitación en las organizaciones empresariales	Endecadary	0 : sin incidencia 0.1: prácticamente sin incidencia 0.2: casi sin incidencia 0.3: muy débil incidencia 0.4: débil incidencia 0.5: mediana incidencia 0.6: incidencia sensible 0.7: bastante incidencia 0.8: fuerte incidencia 0.9: muy fuerte incidencia 1 : la mayor incidencia
Creación de estrategias de entrenamiento a partir del análisis de un procedimiento de ultrasonido mediante metodología borrosa	Endecadary	0 : baja 0.1: prácticamente baja 0.2: casi baja 0.3: más baja que alta 0.4: ni baja ni alta 0.5: más alta que baja 0.6: más alta que baja 0.7: bastante alta 0.8: casi alta 0.9: prácticamente alta 1 : alta

Fuzzy logic in the strategic analysis: impact of the external factors over business	Endecadary	unspecified
Modelo para la determinación de variables que inciden en el consumo de productos financieros de ahorro	Endecadary	unspecified
Proceso de identificación de los atributos contemplados por los clientes en una estrategia CRM	Endecadary	0 : sin incidencia 0.1: prácticamente sin incidencia 0.2: casi sin incidencia 0.3: muy débil incidencia 0.4: débil incidencia 0.5: media incidencia 0.6: considerabla incidencia 0.7: bastante incidencia 0.8: fuerte incidencia 0.9: muy fuerte incidencia 1 : la mayor incidencia
The Forgotten Effects Model in a CRM strategy	Endecadary	0 : whitout incidence 0.1: Virtually without incidence 0.2: Almost without incidence 0.3: Very weak incidence 0.4: Weak incidence 0.5: Average incidence 0.6: Substantial incidence 0.7: Sufficient incidence 0.8: Strong incidence 0.9: Very strong incidence 1 : The highest incidence

Note that the endecadary semantic scale language created by Gil Aluja is chosen primarily to obtain input data from the incidence matrices. This seems to suggest that the authors of all the possible scale types usually use the scale that offers maximum nuance of the values of incidence.

Since only eleven semantic scales are found it seems reasonable to conclude that the endecadary scale is a maximum limit structure to subjectively valuate properties or characteristics of objects.

5. Proposal for the use of a new scale to minimize errors in the initial data

Given the importance of the exact values in the incidence matrices chosen by the experts, one idea to generalize the classical models of forgotten effect is to make possible to use a second endecadary scale that can help determine if the values assigned to the incidences are correct. The scale was presented by Professor Joan Bonet from the University of Girona at the XVI International Congress of SIGEF in October 2010 with the paper “Cálculo mixto estadístico-fuzzy, por comparación, aplicado a la revision de variables económicas” (Bonet, 2010). The main difference with respect to the classical scale is how to determine the level of subjective values. The determination process consists of a maximum of two phases with the ternary system of numeration after removing the extreme cases.

The idea of the new assignment is to specify an element of scale through two phases. The first phase of the assignment reflects the degree of truth of the statement, and a choice is made between the low (L), medium (M) and high (H) possibilities, once the completely false (zero N) and completely true (T total) possibilities have been discarded. In the case of giving us L, M or H, we then ask in a second phase comparing only with the elements of reference found in this group, if the item respect them is in the group L, M or H.

The final assignment is obtained from the following table of values:

N	L			M			H			A
	L	M	H	L	M	H	L	M	H	
0	0.1	0.2	0.3	0.4	0.5	0.6	0.7	0.8	0.9	1

For example, if we associate the incidence degree saying that better water treatment can have the effect of improving health, choose a first phase between low (L), medium (M) or high (H). Note that we discard the case of null cases (N) or absolute (H). Imagine that we have thought of high (H). Then, we enter a second phase considering in the set high, if it will be higher (H), low (L) or neither one nor the other (M).

6. Proposal for the generalization of forgotten effects models

Looking at the objectives of the papers we can conclude that the method of forgotten effects seems to be used to analyze possible future impacts which may produce changes in certain causes in the present. Along these lines appears the problem of not having developed the model for cases when causes or effects are fuzzy variables.

With this paper we announce the future study of this possibility to generalize the current model of forgotten effects. We hope that future communications will present a mathematical modeling in line with our expectations.

7. Conclusions

From the analysis of the work with existing forgotten effects in the current scientific literature we have seen how models for the investigation of forgotten effects have begun to be known by some of the scientific community dedicated to the problems of fuzzy logic. In order to make future work in this field more reliable we have shown a possible tool to control errors in the initial data of incidences estimated by valuation experts.

We have also shown a possible way to generalize forgotten effect models. The idea is based on thinking of cause and effect variables as fuzzy variables. We believe that this fact is fundamental to achieving impact assessment methodology based on finding the minimum initial actions that can produce maximum impact. The paper, therefore, can be considered a contribution in the theory of decision.

References

1. E. Anselin Ávila and A.M. Gil Lafuente, Fuzzy logic in the strategic analysis: impact of the external factors over business. *International Journal of Business Innovation and Research* **5(3)**, 515-534 (2009).
2. J. Bonet, S. Linares and X. Bertran, Cálculo mixto estadístico-fuzzy, por comparación, aplicado a la previsión de variables económicas. *Proceedings of the XVI International Congress of the SIGEF on Economical and Financial Systems in Emergent Economies*, Morelia Michoacán, Mexico (2010).
3. J. Domech More, J. Carvalho Aguia, Modelo Fuzzy de Influência entre Indicadores de Responsabilidade Social. *Simpósio de Excelência em Gestão e Tecnologia (SEGeT)*, Rio de Janeiro, Brasil (2008).
4. J. Domech More, L. Mamede Gonzalez Magalhâes Creación de estrategias de entrenamiento a partir del análisis de un procedimiento de ultrasonido mediante metodología borrosa. *Cuadernos de CIMBAGE*, **10**, 75-101 (2008).
5. P. Eugenio Mallo, M. Antonia Artola, M. Javier Galante, M. Enrique Pascual, M. Morettini y A. Raúl Busetto, Aplicación de herramientas

borrosas al balance scorecard. *XXVIII congreso argentino de profesores universitarios de costos*. Mendoza (2005).

6. P.S. García y L.L. Lazarri, E.A.M. Machado, Una propuesta fuzzy para definir indicadores de pobreza, *Cuadernos de CIMBAGE*, **3**, 11-26 (2000).
7. P.S. García y L.L. Lazarri, La evaluación de la calidad en la Universidad, *Cuadernos de CIMBAGE*, **3**, 81-97 (2000)
8. A.M. García de Fanelli, Aplicación de la metodología borrosa a la evaluación de la calidad de los posgrados. *Cuadernos de CIMBAGE*, **4**, 99-132 (2001).
9. A.M. Gil Lafuente, y C. Luis Bassa, Proceso de identificación de los atributos contemplados por los clientes en una estrategia CRM. *Cuadernos de CIMBAGE*, **13**, 107-127 (2011).
10. A.M. Gil Lafuente, E. Vizuete Luciano and O. Martorell Cunill Modelo para la determinación de variables que inciden en el consumo de productos financieros de ahorro. *XV SIGEF International Conference*, Lugo, Spain (2009).
11. A. Kaufmann and J. Gil Aluja, *Introducción de la Teoría de los Subconjuntos Borrosos a la Gestión de las Empresas*, Milladoiro, Santiago de Compostela (1988).
12. L.L. Lazzari, La asignación de recursos en acciones tendientes a mejorar la imagen de una PYME, *VI Congreso de la Pequeña y Mediana Empresa*. Buenos Aires (2000).
13. J.M. Rodríguez Rubinos, M. Armando Ramírez Reyes, V. Díaz Pontones Efectos olvidados en las relaciones de causalidad de las acciones del sistema de capacitación en las organizaciones empresariales. *Revista de Métodos Cuantitativos para la Economía y la Empresa*, **5**, 29-48 (2008).
14. F. Rico, A. Marco y A. Jaime Tinto Herramientas con base en subconjuntos borrosos. Propuesta procedimental para aplicar expertizaje y recuperar efectos olvidados en la información contable. *Actualidad Contable FACES* **13(21),** 127-146 (2010).
15. L. A. Zadeh, Fuzzy sets, Information and Control, **8** 338–353 (1965).

Author Index

Acknowledgement to Reviewers

Special thanks to all the referees for their support in the revision process of the papers submitted to the MS'12 Rio de Janeiro International Conference:

Luciano Barcellos
Christian Berger-Vachon
Messias Borges Silva
Josefa Boria
Antonio F. Branco Costa
Antonio C. de Azevedo Ritto
Aline de Castro Rezende
Mª Elvira Cassú
Kurt J. Engemann
Joan Carles Ferrer
Anna M. Gil Lafuente
Jaime Gil Lafuente
Wendy Haddad-Carraro
Aras Keropyan
Anna Klimova
Salvador Linares-Mustarós
Carolina Luis Bassa
José M. Merigó
Carles Mulet-Forteza
Fernando A. Silva-Marins
Emilio Vizuete

World Scientific Proceedings Series on Computer Engineering and Information Science

Series Founding Editor: Da Ruan

Series Editor: Jie Lu, University of Technology Sydney

Vol. 1: Computational Intelligence in Decision and Control
edited by Da Ruan, Javier Montero, Jie Lu, Luis Martínez, Pierre D'hondt and Etienne E. Kerre

Vol. 2: Intelligent Decision Making Systems
edited by Koen Vanhoof, Da Ruan, Tianrui Li and Geert Wets

Vol. 3 Computational Intelligence in Business and Economics
edited by Anna M. Gil-Lafuente and José M. Merigó

Vol. 4 Computational Intelligence: Foundations and Applications
edited by Da Ruan, Tianrui Li, Yang Xu, Guoqing Chen and Etienne E. Kerre

Vol. 5 Quantitative Logic and Soft Computing
edited by Guojun Wang, Bin Zhao and Yongming Li

Vol. 6 Methods for Decision Making in an Uncertain Environment
edited by Jaime Gil-Aluja and Antonio Terceño

Vol. 7 Uncertainty Modeling in Knowledge Engineering and Decision Making
edited by Cengiz Kahraman, Etienne E Kerre and Faik Tunc Bozbura

Vol. 8 Decision Making Systems in Business Administration
edited by Anna M. Gil Lafuente, Luciano Barcellos de Paula, José M. Merigó Lindahl, Fernando Augusto Silva-Marins and Antonio Carlos de Azevedo-Ritto